THE CATHOLIC TRADITION OF THE LAW OF NATIONS

By

JOHN EPPSTEIN

THE LAWBOOK EXCHANGE, LTD.
Clark, New Jersey

ISBN 9781584778226 (hardcover)
ISBN 9781616191030 (paperback)

Lawbook Exchange edition 2008, 2012

The quality of this reprint is equivalent to the quality of the original work.

THE LAWBOOK EXCHANGE, LTD.
33 Terminal Avenue
Clark, New Jersey 07066-1321

Please see our website for a selection of our other publications and fine facsimile reprints of classic works of legal history:
www.lawbookexchange.com

Library of Congress Cataloging-in-Publication Data

Eppstein, John, 1895-
The Catholic tradition of the law of nations / John Eppstein.
p. cm.
Originally published: London : Burns, Oates & Washbourne Ltd., 1935; reprinted from: Washington, D.C. : Published for the Carnegie Endowment for International Peace by the Catholic Association for International Peace, [1935].
Includes index.
ISBN-13: 978-1-58477-822-6 (cloth : alk. paper)
ISBN-10: 1-58477-822-9 (cloth : alk. paper)
1. International law--Religious aspects--Catholic Church. 2. Catholic Church--Foreign relations. 3. War--Religious aspects--Catholic Church. 4. Peace--Religious aspects--Catholic Church. 5. Nationalism--Religious aspects--Catholic Church. I. Title.
KB265.E67 2007
261.8'73088282--dc22 2006100182

Printed in the United States of America on acid-free paper

THE CATHOLIC TRADITION OF THE LAW OF NATIONS

By

JOHN EPPSTEIN

Published for the

CARNEGIE ENDOWMENT FOR INTERNATIONAL PEACE

by the

CATHOLIC ASSOCIATION FOR INTERNATIONAL PEACE

1312 Massachusetts Avenue, N.W.

WASHINGTON, D.C.

NIHIL OBSTAT:

Reginaldus G. Phillips, S.Th.L.
Censor deputatus.

IMPRIMATUR:

✠ Joseph Butt,
Vic. Gen.

Westmonasterii,
die 29a Augusti, 1935.

MADE AND PRINTED IN GREAT BRITAIN
FOR
BURNS OATES AND WASHBOURNE LTD

AD MAJOREM DEI GLORIAM

ET

IN PIAM MEMORIAM

BENEDICTI XV

PRINCIPIS PACIS VICARII DIGNISSIMI

CONTENTS

PART I

THE ORIGINS OF CHRISTIAN DOCTRINE UPON PEACE AND WAR

CHAPTER I

CHAPTER II

CHAPTER III

PART II

THE ETHICS OF WAR

CHAPTER IV

CHAPTER V

CHAPTER VI

PART III

THE PRESERVATION OF PEACE

CHAPTER VII

CHAPTER VIII

CHAPTER IX

PART IV

THE SOCIETY OF NATIONS

CHAPTER X

CHAPTER XI

CHAPTER XII

PART V

THE PLACE OF NATIONALITY IN THE LAW OF NATIONS

CHAPTER XIII

CHAPTER XIV

CHAPTER XV

DOCUMENTS APPENDED FOR REFERENCE

FOREWORD

UPON the foundation of the Carnegie Endowment for International Peace, Pope Pius X wrote in the following terms to Monsignor, afterwards Cardinal, Falconio, Apostolic Delegate to the United States :[1] 'To compose differences, to restrain the outbreak of hostilities, to prevent the dangers of war, to remove even the anxieties of so-called armed peace, is, indeed, most praiseworthy, and any effort in this cause, even though it may not immediately or wholly accomplish its purpose, manifests, nevertheless, a zeal which cannot but redound to the credit of its authors and be of benefit to the State. This is specially true at the present day. . . . Wherefore We most heartily commend the work already begun, which should be approved by all good men, and We most gladly lend the weight of Our authority to those who are striving to realize this most beneficent purpose.'

Under the Presidency of Dr. Nicholas Murray Butler the Carnegie Endowment has since then pursued a far-seeing policy, strengthening substantially and in an enduring manner the foundations of international understanding. Men like Dr. Butler and his colleagues, devoted to this cause, have naturally been impressed by the super-national character of the Catholic Church, discerning in it the strongest and most abiding influence in the world for International Peace. Their interest in Catholic scholarship has been shown more than once in the past. In 1927, for instance, a Commission headed by Mr. William Warner Bishop, the Librarian of the University of Michigan, was sent to Rome by the Endowment at the invitation of His Holiness, to report on recataloguing, according to modern methods, the books and manuscripts in the Vatican Library.

[1] Apostolic Letter, 'De Pace Tuenda,' June 11, 1911.

The recommendations of that Commission have, I believe, already resulted in making the collections more easily available to students. The Endowment has also promoted the study of international law, in the widest sense of the term, thus making better known the distinctive contributions of Catholic thought to the establishment of international justice. An admirable edition in Latin and English of the works of Franciscus de Vittoria, *De Indis et de Jure Belli Relectiones*, was published some years ago[1] and a course of lectures, replete with historical erudition, by M. Georges Goyau, *L'Eglise Catholique et le Droit des Gens*, is included in one of the volumes of the proceedings of the Academy of International Law at the Hague.[2] Again, in a recently published work—*The Catholic Conception of International Law*—Dr. James Brown Scott, Trustee and Secretary of the Carnegie Endowment, and President of the American Society of International Law, gives a masterly survey of the teaching and the historical significance of Franciscus de Vittoria and Franciscus Suarez. The present volume is an added recognition of Catholic scholarship. But it is more than that. It is a reminder to Catholics of their duty through organization to translate into action the principles of international justice laid down by successive Popes.

I remember very vividly one morning, March 22, 1927, in Paris, meeting Professor James T. Shotwell, Director of the Carnegie Endowment's Division of History and Economics. Before leaving he spoke of a memorandum he had in his pocket. That memorandum was to prove historical, for it was the outline of a plan which he was to put before M. Briand in the afternoon—a plan which has since become world famous under the title of the 'Pact of Paris.' Professor Shotwell, the originator of the Pact of Paris is also the originator of this volume. In 1930, during a conversation in New York, I mentioned how inspiring to me was the Church's unbroken tradition of international justice running through the ages. 'Would it not be a good thing,' he replied, 'if that tradition could

[1] In the series *Classics of International Law.*

[2] *Recueil des Cours*, VI, 1925.

be assembled in an historical work and published in English?'

So this book arose. There was no difficulty in choosing an author, for one man was pre-eminently fitted. Mr. Eppstein, with the advice of theologians and Church historians and the help of the Catholic Council for International Relations has produced a book which should have a wide influence. It is not my purpose, however, to discuss it here. Having been entrusted with the arrangements for its compilation and publication, my task is now finished. It remains only to express the gratitude of all future readers, both to the author and to the Carnegie Endowment for International Peace.

ROBERT WILBERFORCE.

Easter Sunday, 1935.

Brooks's Club,
St. James's Street,
London, W.

AUTHOR'S PREFACE

THE present work is an attempt to provide what until now has not been available in the English language—a compendium of the teaching and tradition of Catholic Christianity upon international morality. For 'Law' in the title of the book is to be understood to mean '*jus*' rather than '*lex*,' that is to say 'the sum of those rights and duties by which peoples and States are morally bound to one another.'[1] Few students have the means, or the knowledge of languages, to discover in the works of the Greek and Latin Fathers, the Bullaria or Acta of the Popes, the works of the Schoolmen and of the theologians of recent centuries, the principal passages which indicate the development of Catholic doctrine upon peace and war, military service, arbitration, the community of nations and all the rights and duties to which their mutual interdependence gives rise. It is even more difficult to follow the trend of thought concerning the contemporary problems of international law, politics and economics as expressed by authoritative Catholic theologians and publicists, whose works are published in French, German, Italian or Latin, but only too infrequently in English. Yet, to form a true or at least an adequate conception of the Catholic tradition upon so vast and varied a subject, it is necessary to trace the evolution of ideas through many centuries and to study the application in many lands and by many minds of the principles laid down from time to time by the Popes. This book is a modest endeavour to meet this need. It contains a number of papal utterances and passages from important works—such as the *Essay of Natural Law* of Taparelli d'Azeglio—which are not known to have been published before in the

[1] Plater, *Primer of Peace and War*, p. 10.

English language. I offer it to my fellow-students who are in communion with the Roman See, in the hope that it may help them to appreciate the wealth of their inheritance —ignored by too many Catholics—and incline them to a more vigorous participation in the Apostolate of Peace, to which Pius XI has summoned clergy and laity alike. I offer it with no less confidence to fair-minded men and women who do not share my spiritual allegiance, but who, as students of the development of ideas or of the moral forces which influence political and social life, wish to ascertain the actual position and teaching of the Catholic Church. Among them I venture to count the many friends and colleagues whose comradeship I have enjoyed for fourteen years in our common endeavour to maintain and strengthen the League of Nations.

The historical method has been, so far as possible, employed throughout this work. Both in the first two-thirds of the book, which are concerned with the main issues of peace and war, and within each of the subsequent chapters the evolution of doctrine and theory is followed from the earliest to the most recent authorities. The documents quoted in each chapter are, as a general rule, arranged in chronological order. But wherever it has seemed advantageous to argue a thesis from first principles this has been done and the conclusions set down. Documents which are desirable for reference but which would overweigh the several chapters will be found in the appendices at the end of the book.

The work is divided into five parts of three chapters each, varying in length, according not so much to the relative importance of the matters treated, as to the amount of elucidation which they require or have in fact received from the teaching Church. The first part deals with the origins of Christian doctrine upon Peace and War from the time of Christ Himself to the days of St. Ambrose. The second is devoted to the ethics of War, beginning with St. Augustine, the primary Catholic teacher on this subject, and ending with theologians and publicists of the present day. The third part examines the doctrine and practice of the Church with regard to the duty of preserving Peace, and seeks to show in what that Peace should consist. The fourth is concerned with the Community of Nations and the efforts to give it a positive form, culminating in the existing League of Nations. The fifth and last part deals with Nationality, the most dynamic force in the international life of the present age. It contains a chapter upon the rights of backward or uncivilized peoples. That is a special subject, which might well require a separate work as extensive as this volume—which is the reason for its length and the number of documents attached to it. But, since it is my duty to elucidate the contribution of an essentially missionary religion to the science of international ethics, I make no apology for the inclusion of it.

Biblical quotations are taken from the English version of the Holy Bible (Douay, A.D. 1609; Rheims, A.D. 1582) which is authorized and in general use among English-speaking Catholics. Unless otherwise stated, all passages quoted from Latin, French and German works have been specially translated from the originals.

JOHN EPPSTEIN.

Easter, 1935.

ACKNOWLEDGEMENTS

THE work has been prepared at the desire of the CARNEGIE ENDOWMENT FOR INTERNATIONAL PEACE, under the auspices of the CATHOLIC COUNCIL FOR INTERNATIONAL RELATIONS of Great Britain ; and I am exceedingly indebted to the officers and not a few members of the Council whose co-operation in the transcription and translation of texts has been invaluable. I owe a deep debt of gratitude to Mr. Robert Wilberforce, C.B.E., who, with Professor Shotwell, inspired this undertaking ; to Mr. V. L. P. Fowke, Hon. Secretary, and Miss Kathleen Fox, Assistant Secretary of the Council ; to Mr. V. Connolly, Mr. P. V. A. Reid, Mr. H. Norman, C.B., C.S.I., C.B.E., the Rev. Joseph Keating, S.J., editor of *The Month*, Mr. R. O'Sullivan, K.C., Dom Anthony Baron, O.S.B., the Rev. B. Schnitzler, Miss A. F. Wedd, Mr. G. Biddle, Mr. W. H. P. Boyd and Mr. B. Andrewes. The late Mr. F. F. Urquhart of Balliol College, Oxford, helped me greatly with books and advice ; so too have the Rev. J. F. Delos, O.P., of the University of Lille, and the Rev. Yves de la Brière, S.J., Editor of *Etudes*. I have had the great advantage of beng permitted to work in the libraries of Douai Abbey, Farnborough Abbey, Campion Hall, Oxford, and St. Mary's College, Oscott, and owe much to the kindness of the Librarians of the League of Nations at Geneva and of the League of Nations Union in London.

J. E.

PART I

THE ORIGINS OF CHRISTIAN DOCTRINE UPON PEACE AND WAR

CHAPTER I

THE GOSPEL OF PEACE

TO the Divine Founder of the Church are ultimately referred by Popes, Fathers, theologians and philosophers of the Christian age all the problems of Right and Wrong occurring in the dealings of men and of societies with one another. It is therefore in the recorded words of Christ and the writings of His Apostles that the seeds of Christian doctrine upon peace, war and the order of human society must first be sought.

Yet they will search in vain who hope to discover in the Gospels, the Acts of the Apostles or their Epistles any direct instruction upon international ethics. There was in the time of Christ no international problem in the proper sense : the *Pax Romana* held almost all the known world under a single sway. There was indeed a national problem very present to the minds of His first followers, to wit the longing of the Jews to recover from the Gentile Empire their national independence, and their conception of the promised Messiah as one who would 'restore the kingdom to Israel.'[1] Yet it is one of the marks of the Divinity of Jesus, that though the people were roused to fervour by His teaching, so that He was able to enter the capital in a popular triumph, He never by word or deed gave any justification for the belief that He was merely a nationalist leader. The conditions which would justify rebellion against tyranny were apparently present ; the pride of the Chosen People in their past and in their future mission was deep-rooted ; their disdain of foreigners traditional. The stage was set, according to human calculations, for a passionate if tragic uprising of the national spirit, with the young carpenter-prophet of

[1] Acts i : 6.

Nazareth as the Garibaldi of the scene. Yet the only political references to be found in the Gospels—and they are few—are counsels of restraint and obedience : 'Render to Cæsar the things that are Cæsar's.'[1] 'Love your enemies.'[2] The persons chosen for especial praise by the Messiah either in parable or in actual life included a Samaritan, a Roman officer, and an unpopular collector of the Roman taxes. And the hopes of 'self-determination' for Judæa were dashed with the sentence 'My kingdom is not of this world.'[3]

These considerations alone suffice to indicate the essentially supra-national character of the mission of Jesus Christ. 'Going, teach *all* nations'[4] was His last injunction. His every counsel or command is universal in application.

It is also, almost invariably, personal. No laws are directly laid down by Him to regulate the mutual relations of States ; to determine the right conditions of economic or industrial life ; to direct the operations of civil justice or international arbitration. To the conversion of the individual human soul the Christian doctrine was and is primarily directed, 'for what shall it profit a man, if he gain the whole world and suffer the loss of his soul ?'[5] As in every other sphere of morals, it was for the Living Church of the Apostles and their successors to develop the teaching of the Divine Master, to apply it to the changing social and political conditions of succeeding ages, and in particular to evolve from His doctrine of personal virtues a philosophy of collective ethics.

To the Catholic this constant interpretation of the mind of Christ by the Church and, in particular by the Papacy, implies no imperfection in the original Christian Revelation and calls for no apology. 'I have yet many things to say to you ; but you cannot bear them now.'[6] That is a motto of all sound education, whether the truths to be imparted are supernatural or natural. The Apostles, who were simple men, could not themselves understand forthwith the whole body of revealed truth with all its

[1] St. Matthew xxii : 21.
[2] St. Matthew v : 44.
[3] St. John xviii : 36.
[4] St. Matthew xxviii : 19.
[5] St. Mark viii : 36.
[6] St. John xvi : 12.

implications. Still less could they foresee all the contingencies which Christians would have to face, either as a persecuted minority within a pagan empire or (and this surely was hardly present to their minds) as being themselves responsible for the good government of kingdoms and empires. It is fundamental to the very conception of the Incarnation and the fulfilment of its purpose that the God Man, having sown the seed of revealed truth, should have appointed a visible body of men who, in age after age, should watch and tend it, themselves safeguarded from error by the Divine Spirit, so that without any change in the intrinsic nature of this living tradition, it might develop and evolve to meet the needs of all minds, all nations, all ages : 'But when he, the Spirit of truth, is come, he will teach you all truth.'[1] Christianity is not static but dynamic. It is by no parrot-like repetition of words uttered long ago that the student will expect to see the Church, or its visible head, whom Catholics revere as the Vicar of Christ, bring peace to the hearts of men, to human societies or to the world. It is rather by making actual in every changing century that which in the words of the Gospels is potential ; by bringing the infinite into contact with the finite ; by applying the spirit of the sacred writings to social or political conditions, utterly different from those which existed when the words were first spoken or written.

This warning is necessary since there has been in all ages a tendency, as there still is, for those who have some special cause to plead or point to prove, to pick this verse or that from the New Testament and to use its content indiscriminately, without reference to the context, to determine the merits or demerits of social, national, or international policies. Such interested quarrying in the Old Testament, now somewhat out of fashion, was not less ardently practised, particularly in regard to the justification of war, until a generation ago. That method is at once unscientific and, whether practised by Catholic or Protestant controversialists, equally repugnant to the spirit of Catholic Christianity. The true bearing of the teaching of Jesus Christ and His Apostles upon all the mutual dealings of States with one

[1] St. John xvi : 13.

another is not obvious: it requires careful and patient study.

It follows from what has been said that, since the whole subject matter of international ethics relates to the impact of eternal truth upon changing temporalities, there will in every age be much scope for honest differences of opinion among moral theologians concerning the application of Christian principles. Within a more limited sphere the voice of the Roman Pontiff or the conclusions of a General Council will intervene either to put an end to controversy, to elucidate a principle, or to declare, after generations of human discussion, the common mind of the Church. Thus, beginning with the New Testament and remotely but none the less really arising from the teaching contained in it, a minimum doctrine or tradition of international right has been evolved which cannot be questioned by Catholics; and of this the Holy See is the guardian. Beside it is a large body of opinions, some supported by a school of Christian philosophy so constant that they cannot be rejected without grave danger of error, others more speculative and uncertain because more closely entangled in topical events, though equally tenable by Catholics because based upon reason. Such are many of the conclusions which close the several parts of this book.

Christianity is not a social programme, and the establishment of external peace is not the direct object of the Christian revelation: rather is it the consequence of a Christian life. Political peace depends upon the observance of the Natural Law, which Christ came not to destroy but to fulfil. His revelation of supernatural religion presupposed it: it was not necessary, for the main part, to reassert it. Which is a reason both for the paucity of texts in the New Testament bearing upon our subject, and for the fact that only gradually and as the occasion arose did the Christian Church seek to elaborate a code of conduct for citizens and soldiers, for those in authority and for the mutual relation of princes. The spread of Christianity went far in the end to eradicate slavery; it diminished wars; it introduced civilizing influences with its missionaries in every country. But the extension of the Church as a supernatural community did not wait upon these social or political reforms. So deep and great was the spiritual fellowship between Christians that the distinction between bond and free, Gentile and Jew, was of comparatively little importance. Whenever an attempt has been made to treat Christianity as being mainly a pacifist or humanitarian system the desired effects have not followed. If ever the Church has been successful in inducing social reforms, in restricting conflicts, in promoting political unity, it has been through insistence upon the rights of God, the claims of the supernatural life, the primacy of the spiritual. 'Seek ye therefore first the Kingdom of God, and his justice, and all these things shall be added unto you.'[1]

While therefore we select in the following pages the passages which bear upon international ethics, it must not be supposed that they represent more than a small fragment of the teaching of the New Testament: the same is true of the selection of texts from the Fathers and theologians. They are part of the whole body of Christian tradition upon Faith and Morals, and should not be considered in isolation from it.

The texts which follow include those which have most frequently been quoted, either in exposition or controversy, as applicable to the relations between nations during the Christian ages. They are grouped in four divisions:

A. Peace as a consequence of the Incarnation and the mark of Christians.

B. Forgiveness, non-resistance and the use of force.

C. The Christian attitude toward civil authority.

D. The supra-national character of the Church.

A. PEACE AS A CONSEQUENCE OF THE INCARNATION

The prophecy of Zachary concerning his infant son: St. John Baptist:

And thou, child, shalt be called the prophet of the Highest: for thou shalt go before the face of the Lord to prepare his ways. To give knowledge of salvation to his people, unto the remission

[1] St. Matthew vi: 33.

of their sins. Through the bowels of the mercy of our God, in which the Orient, from on high, hath visited us. To enlighten them that sit in darkness and in the shadow of death : to direct our feet into the way of peace. (St. Luke i : 76–79.)

The angelic hymn at the Nativity of Christ :

And suddenly there was with the angel a multitude of the heavenly army, praising God, and saying : Glory to God in the highest : and on earth peace to men of good will. (St. Luke ii : 13–14.)

The Beatitudes :

And seeing the multitudes, he went up into a mountain, and when he was set down, his disciples came unto him. And opening his mouth he taught them, saying : Blessed are the poor in spirit : for theirs is the kingdom of heaven. Blessed are the meek : for they shall possess the land. Blessed are they that mourn : for they shall be comforted. Blessed are they that hunger and thirst after justice : for they shall have their fill. Blessed are the merciful : for they shall obtain mercy. Blessed are the clean of heart : for they shall see God. Blessed are the peacemakers : for they shall be called the children of God. Blessed are they that suffer persecution for justice sake : for theirs is the kingdom of heaven. Blessed are ye when they shall revile you, and persecute you, and speak all that is evil against you, untruly, for my sake ; Be glad and rejoice, for your reward is very great in heaven. For so they persecuted the prophets that were before you. (St. Matthew v : 1–12.)

Mutual love the mark of Christians :

A new commandment I give unto you : That ye love one another, as I have loved you, that you also love one another. By this shall all men know that you are my disciples, if you have love one for another. (St. John xiii : 34–35.)

The Peace of Christ :

Peace I leave with you, my peace I give unto you : not as the world giveth, do I give unto you. Let not your heart be troubled, nor let it be afraid. (St. John xiv : 27.)

Mystical union of Christians with Christ and with one another :

Abide in me : and I in you. As the branch cannot bear fruit of itself, unless it abide in the vine, so neither can you, unless you abide in me. I am the vine ; you the branches : he that abideth in me, and I in him, the same beareth much fruit : for without me you can do nothing. If anyone abide not in me : he shall be cast forth as a branch, and shall wither, and they shall gather him up, and cast him into the fire, and he burneth. If you abide in me, and my words abide in you, you shall ask whatever you will, and it shall be done unto you. In this is my Father glorified; that you bring forth very much fruit, and become my disciples. As the Father hath loved me, I also have loved you. Abide in my love. If you keep my commandments, you shall abide in my love; as I also have kept my Father's commandments and do abide in his love. These things I have spoken to you, that my joy may be in you, and your joy may be filled. This is my commandment, that you love one another, as I have loved you. (St. John xv: 4–12.)

Christ's last prayer for unity among his disciples:

And now I am not in the world, and these are in the world, and I come to thee. Holy Father, keep them in thy name, whom thou hast given me: that they may be one, as we also are. (St. John xvii: 11.)

And not for them only do I pray, but for them also who through their word shall believe in me: That they all may be one, as thou, Father, in me, and I in thee: that they also may be one in us: that the world may believe that thou hast sent me. And the glory which thou hast given me, I have given to them: that they may be one, as we also are one. I in them, and thou in me: that they may be made perfect in one; and the world may know that thou hast sent me, and hast loved them, as thou hast also loved me. (St. John xvii: 20–23.)

Pax Vobis:

Now when it was late that same day, the first of the week, and the doors were shut, where the disciples were gathered together for fear of the Jews, Jesus came and stood in the midst, and said to them: Peace be to you. And when he had said this, he shewed them his hands, and his side. The disciples therefore were glad, when they saw the Lord. He said therefore to them again: Peace be to you. As the Father hath sent me, I also send you. (St. John xx: 19–21.)

Love of God and of our neighbour:

Dearly beloved, let us love one another: for charity is of God. And every one that loveth is born of God, and knoweth God. He that loveth not, knoweth not God: for God is charity. By this hath the charity of God appeared towards us, because God hath sent his only begotten Son into the world, that we may live by him. In this is charity: not as though we had loved God, but because he hath first loved us, and sent his Son to be a propitiation for our sins. My dearest, if God hath so loved us, we also ought to love one another. (1st Epistle Catholic of St. John iv: 7–11.)

Fear is not in charity: but perfect charity casteth out fear, because fear hath pain. And he that feareth is not perfected in charity. Let us therefore love God, because God first hath loved us. If any man say, I love God, and hateth his brother; he is a liar. For he that loveth not his brother, whom he seeth, how can he love God, whom he seeth not? And this commandment we have from God, that he, who loveth God, love also his brother. (1st Epistle Catholic of St. John iv: 18–21.)

Charity to be preferred before all other gifts:

If I speak with the tongues of men and of angels, and have not charity, I am become as sounding brass, or a tinkling cymbal. And, if I should have prophecy and should know all mysteries and all knowledge, and if I should have all faith, so that I could remove mountains, and have not charity, I am nothing. And if I should distribute all my goods to feed the poor, and if I should deliver my body to be burned, and have not charity, it profiteth me nothing. Charity is patient, is kind: charity envieth not, dealeth not perversely, is not puffed up. Is not ambitious, seeketh not her own, is not provoked to anger, thinketh no evil: Rejoiceth not in iniquity, but rejoiceth with the truth. Beareth all things, believeth all things, hopeth all things, endureth all things. Charity never falleth away, whether prophecies shall be made void or tongues shall cease or knowledge shall be destroyed. For we know in part: and we prophesy in part. But when that which is perfect is come, that which is in part shall be done away. When I was a child, I spoke as a child, I understood as a child, I thought as a child. But, when I became a man, I put away the things of a child. We see now through a glass in a dark manner: but then face to face. Now I know in part: but then I shall know even as I am known. And now there remain faith, hope and charity, these three: but the greatest of these is charity. (1 Corinthians xiii: 1–13.)

Seek peace:

For the kingdom of God is not meat and drink: but justice and peace and joy in the Holy Ghost. For he that in this serveth Christ pleaseth God and is approved of men. Therefore, let us follow after the things that are of peace and keep the things that are of edification, one towards another. (Romans xiv: 17–19.)

The doctrine of the Mystical Body:

I therefore, a prisoner in the Lord, beseech you that you walk worthy of the vocation in which you are called; With all humility and mildness, with patience, supporting one another in charity. Careful to keep the unity of the Spirit in the bond of peace. One body and one Spirit: as you are called in one hope of your calling. One Lord, one faith, one baptism. One God and Father of all, who is above all, and through all, and in us all.

But to every one of us is given grace, according to the measure of the giving of Christ. Wherefore he saith: Ascending on high, he led captivity captive: he gave gifts to men. Now that he ascended, what is it, but because he also descended first into the lower parts of the earth? He that descended is the same also that ascended above all the heavens: that he might fill all things. And he gave some apostles, and some prophets and other some evangelists, and other some pastors and doctors: For the perfecting of the saints, for the work of the ministry, for the edifying of the body of Christ: Until we all meet into the unity of faith and of the knowledge of the Son of God, unto a perfect man, unto the measure of the age of the fulness of Christ. That henceforth we be no more children, tossed to and fro and carried about with every wind of doctrine, by the wickedness of men, by cunning craftiness by which they lie in wait to deceive. But doing the truth in charity, we may in all things grow up in him who is the head, even Christ: from whom the whole body, being compacted and fitly joined together, by what every joint supplieth, according to the operation in the measure of every part, maketh increase of the body, unto the edifying of itself in charity. (Ephesians iv: 1–16.)[1]

The gospel of peace:

Stand therefore, having your loins girt about with truth and having on the breastplate of justice: And your feet shod with the preparation of the gospel of peace. (Ephesians vi: 14–15.)

The God of peace:

And the peace of God, which surpasseth all understanding, keep your hearts and minds in Christ Jesus. For the rest, brethren, whatsoever things are true, whatsoever modest, whatsoever just, whatsoever holy, whatsoever lovely, whatsoever of good fame, if there be any virtue, if any praise of discipline: think on these things. The things which you have both learned and received and heard and seen in me, these do ye; and the God of peace shall be with you. (Philippians iv: 7–9.)

B. FORGIVENESS, NON-RESISTANCE AND THE USE OF FORCE

Reconciliation, forgiveness, love of enemies:

You have heard that it was said to them of old: Thou shalt not kill. And whosoever shall kill shall be in danger of the judgement. But I say to you that whosoever is angry with his

[1] See also 1 Corinthians xii: 12–27 for St. Paul's development of his doctrine of the Mystical Body.

brother shall be in danger of the judgement. And whosoever shall say to his brother, Raca, shall be in danger of the council. And whosoever shall say, Thou fool, shall be in danger of hell fire. If therefore thou offer thy gift at the altar and there thou remember that thy brother hath anything against thee ; leave there thy offering before the altar and go first to be reconciled to thy brother : And then coming thou shalt offer thy gift. (St. Matthew v : 21–24.)

You have heard that it hath been said : An eye for an eye and a tooth for a tooth. But I say to you not to resist evil : but if one strike thee on thy right cheek, turn to him also the other : and if a man will contend with thee in judgement and take away thy coat, let go thy cloak also unto him. And whosoever will force the one mile, go with him other two. Give to him that asketh of thee : and from him that would borrow of thee turn not away. You have heard that it hath been said : Thou shalt love thy neighbour and hate thy enemy. But I say to you : Love your enemies ; do good to them that hate you ; and pray for them that persecute and calumniate you : That you may be the children of your Father who is in heaven, who maketh his sun to rise upon the good and bad and raineth upon the just and unjust. For if you love them that love you, what reward shall you have ? Do not even the publicans this ? And if you salute your brethren only, what do you more ? Do not also the heathens this ? Be you therefore perfect, as also your heavenly Father is perfect. (St. Matthew v : 38–48.)[1]

St. Luke in his account of this teaching of Our Lord adds :

And as you would that men should do to you, do you also to them in like manner. (Luke vi : 31.)

Sicut et nos dimittimus . . . :

Thus therefore shall you pray : Our Father who art in heaven Hallowed be thy name. Thy kingdom come. Thy will be done on earth as it is in heaven. Give us this day our super-substantial bread. And forgive us our debts as we also forgive our debtors. And lead us not into temptation. But deliver us from evil. Amen. For if you will forgive men their offences your heavenly Father will forgive you also your offences. But if you will not forgive men neither will your Father forgive you your offences. (St. Matthew vi : 9–15.)

Then came Peter unto him and said : Lord, how often shall my brother offend against me, and I forgive him ? Till seven times ? Jesus saith to him : I say not to thee, till seven times, but till seventy times seven times. (St. Matthew xviii : 21–22.)

[1] Cf. St. Paul's instruction in the same spirit in Romans xii : 16–21.

Christ prays for his executioners:

And when they were come to the place which is called Calvary, they crucified him there: and the robbers, one on the right hand and the other on the left. And Jesus said: Father, forgive them, for they know not what they do. But they, dividing his garments, cast lots. (St. Luke xxiii: 33–34.)

Self-sacrifice for love of others:

But he willing to justify himself, said to Jesus: And who is my neighbour? And Jesus answering, said: A certain man went down from Jerusalem to Jericho and fell among robbers, who also stripped him and having wounded him went away leaving him half dead. And it chanced, that a certain priest went down the same way; and seeing him, passed by. In like manner also a Levite, when he was near that place and saw him, passed by. But a certain Samaritan, being on his journey came near him: and seeing him, was moved with compassion. And going up to him, bound up his wounds, pouring in oil and wine: and setting him upon his own beast, brought him to an inn and took care of him. And the next day he took out two pence and gave to the host and said: Take care of him; and whatsoever thou shalt spend over and above, I, at my return, will repay thee. Which of these three in thy opinion was neighbour to him that fell among the robbers? But he said: He that showed mercy to him. And Jesus said to him: Go, and do thou in like manner. (St. Luke x: 29–37.)

Greater love than this no man hath, that a man lay down his life for his friends. (St. John xv: 13.)

He that hath the substance of this world and shall see his brother in need and shall shut up his bowels from him: how doth the charity of God abide in him? My little children, let us not love in word nor in tongue, but in deed and in truth. (1st Epistle Catholic of St. John iii: 17–18.)

Peter reproved for using the sword:

And behold one of them that were with Jesus, stretching forth his hand, drew out his sword: and striking the servant of the High Priest, cut off his ear. Then Jesus saith to him: Put up again thy sword into its place: for all that take the sword shall perish with the sword. Thinkest thou that I cannot ask my Father, and he will give me presently more than twelve legions of angels? How then shall the scriptures be fulfilled, that so it must be done? (St. Matthew xxvi: 51–54.)

On the other hand there are words of Jesus Christ in the Gospels which seem to permit what is here forbidden, in particular His advice to His Apostles after the Last Supper :

When I sent you without purse and scrip and shoes, did you want anything? But they said : Nothing. Then said he unto them : But now he that hath a purse, let him take it, and likewise a scrip ; and he that hath not, let him sell his coat and buy a sword. For I say to you that this that is written must yet be fulfilled in me : And with the wicked was he reckoned. For the things concerning me have an end. But they said : Lord, behold here are two swords. And he said to them : It is enough. (St. Luke xxii : 35–38.)

On one occasion Our Lord Himself is recorded as having used *force in defence of the Rights of God :*

And he found in the temple them that sold oxen and sheep and doves, and the changers of money sitting. And when he had made, as it were, a scourge of little cords, he drove them all out of the temple, the sheep also and the oxen ; and the money of the changers he poured out, and the tables he overthrew. And to them that sold doves he said : Take these things hence, and make not the house of my Father a house of traffic. And his disciples remembered, that it was written : The zeal of thy house hath eaten me up. (St. John ii : 14–17. Also recorded by the other three Evangelists.)

That *military service was not sinful* in the eyes of Christ is adduced from the fact that He did not reprove, but rather praised the Centurion, whose boy He cured. No incident in the Gospels is perhaps more frequently called to mind by Christians, since the Centurion's words of humility and faith : '*Domine non sum dignus*' are still recited daily before priest or people receive Holy Communion throughout the Latin Church.

And when he had entered into Capharnaum, there came to him a Centurion, beseeching him, and saying : Lord my servant lieth at home sick of the palsy and is grievously tormented. And Jesus saith to him : I will come and heal him. And the centurion making answer said : Lord, I am not worthy that thou shouldst enter under my roof, but only say the word and my servant shall be healed. For I also am a man subject to authority, having under me soldiers. And I say to this, Go, and he goeth, and to another, Come, and he cometh, and to my servant, Do this, and he doeth it. And Jesus hearing this marvelled and said to them that followed him : Amen I say to you, I have not found so great faith in Israel. And I say to you that many shall come from the east and the west, and shall sit down with Abraham and Isaac and Jacob in the kingdom o heaven: But the children of the kingdom shall be cast out into the exterior darkness. There shall be weeping and gnashing of teeth. And Jesus said to the centurion: Go, and as thou hast believed so be it done to thee. And the servant was healed at the same hour. (St. Matthew viii: 5–13.)

When the missionary work of the Church began, the Apostles did not require soldiers to give up their profession before being baptized, of which the conversion of Cornelius (Acts x) is evidence. That, too, was an event of great moment in Christian history, for it was the occasion upon which the duty of baptizing Gentiles as well as Jews was, by a vision, revealed to the Prince of the Apostles. Cornelius, 'a centurion of that which is called the Italian band,' sent two of his servants and 'a soldier who feared the Lord' from Cæsarea to Joppe to fetch Peter. It is probable that among the 'many that were come together' in Cornelius' house were more soldiers 'of them that were under him': all were baptized after the Apostle had preached to them.

Military Service legitimate:

Frequent allusion will be made in the following pages to St. John Baptist's advice to the soldiers:

And the publicans also came to be baptized and said: Master what shall we do? But he said to them: Do nothing more than that which is appointed you. And the soldiers also asked him saying: And what shall we do? And he said to them: Do violence to no man, neither calumniate any man; and be content with your pay. (St. Luke iii: 12–14.)

Military Metaphors:

Military metaphors and similes are used by Christ as the medium of his doctrine: this would hardly be the case were war and military service utterly wrong in themselves. The most striking instance is the following:

Or, what king, about to go to make war against another king, doth not first sit down and think whether he be able with ten thousand to meet him that, with twenty thousand, cometh against him? Or else, while the other is yet afar off, sending an embassy, he desireth conditions of peace. (St. Luke xiv: 31–32.)

St. Paul in many places uses the terms proper to war and to the soldier's profession in order to describe the Christian's conflict with the forces of evil and never speaks with anything but respect of martial virtues. This might be regarded as nothing but conventional imagery; but his references to the wielding of the sword by those in authority shows his belief in the use of force for the sake of justice, as does his praise of the heroes of the Old Testament in the Epistle to the Hebrews xi: 32–34.[1]

These are not all the passages which relate directly or indirectly to war in the New Testament. There are others, the tone of which will frequently recur in later centuries, in which *war is regarded as a visitation of God*, a punishment for the wicked, a sore trial for the righteous. Mgr. Batiffol in the following passage treats of this conception of war and relates it to the principles and tendencies illustrated in the texts quoted above.

L'Eglise et le Droit de Guerre. (pp. 6–8.)

We must add that, as viewed in the Gospel, War is undoubtedly a scourge. To realize this, it is sufficient to read the passages in the Synoptic Gospels in which the ruin of Jerusalem and the end of the world are predicted. 'Fear ye not,' said Jesus, 'when you shall hear of wars and rumours of wars' (St. Mark xiii: 7; St. Matthew xxiv: 6), or 'wars and seditions' according to St. Luke (xxi: 9). The discourse of Jesus continues. 'For nation shall rise against nation, and kingdom against kingdom: and there shall be earthquakes in divers places and famines,' and 'terrors from heaven: and there shall be great signs.' War is a calamity comparable to plague and famine, a calamity like others by which the government of God is made manifest. It is a destructive force which God in his justice can allow to be unleashed. Jesus weeps over Jerusalem as he prophesies the war and the siege in which the city will perish. 'For the days shall come upon thee: and thy enemies shall cast a trench about thee and compass thee round and straiten thee on every side, and beat thee flat to the ground and thy children who are in thee. And they shall not leave in thee a stone upon a stone, because thou hast not known the time of thy visitation. (St. Luke xix: 43–44.) The enemies of Jerusalem are the executors of the most high works of God.

[1] For a striking instance of the use of military metaphors, see 2 Timothy ii: 3–4. Other instances are 1 Corinthians xiv: 8; Ephesians vi: 13–18; Colossians ii: 5.

In the Apocalypse of St. John the symbolic beings who carry out the Divine decrees appear in warlike guise to the Evangelist. One horseman mounted on a white horse 'went forth conquering that he might conquer.' (Apoc. vi : 2.) The other horseman who was mounted on a red horse had power given him 'that he should take peace from the earth,' that men should kill one another, 'and a great sword was given him' (vi : 4). Out of the sea arose a beast having seven heads—a symbol of the power of Rome—'and it was given unto him to make war with the saints and to overcome them' (xiii : 1, 7). At last appears the Word of God, sitting upon a white horse, 'and the armies that are in heaven followed him on white horses, clothed in fine linen, white and clean.' The battle is joined between the horsemen of heaven and the kings of the earth banded together to make war upon them. The kings are beaten, their army hacked to pieces, and the birds eat their flesh (xix : 11–21).

We need not consider this war waged upon the saints by the kings of the earth, for it is not a war in the proper sense of the word; it is a bloody persecution. We need only conclude from these apocalyptic visions that war is a scourge and that it can in certain cases be an act of God, a form of vengeance which God in His justice brings into operation: the warrior then is the soldier of God.

Thus three notions emerge from our study up to this point. First, the renunciation of self-defence and the prohibition to draw the sword: second, the esteem of the military profession: third, the conception of war as a scourge of God. These three ideas are not indeed contradictory, but they need to be coordinated: that was destined to be the task of the living tradition of the Church.

C. THE CHRISTIAN ATTITUDE TOWARDS CIVIL AUTHORITY

Temptation to earthly dominion rejected:

Again the devil took him into a very high mountain and showed him all the kingdoms of the world and the glory of them, and said to him: All these will I give thee if falling down thou wilt adore me. Then Jesus saith to him: Begone, Satan! For it is written: The Lord thy God shalt thou adore and him only shalt thou serve. (St. Matthew iv : 8–10.)

Duty to earthly rulers and duty to God:

Then the Pharisees going, consulted among themselves how to insnare him in his speech. And they sent to him their disciples with the Herodians, saying: Master, we know that thou art a true speaker and teachest the way of God in truth.

Neither carest thou for any man: for thou dost not regard the person of men. Tell us therefore what dost thou think? Is it lawful to give tribute to Cæsar or not? But Jesus, knowing their wickedness, said: Why do ye tempt me, ye hypocrites! Show me the coin of the tribute. And they offered him a penny. And Jesus saith to them: Whose image and inscription is this? They say to him Cæsar's. Then he saith to them: Render therefore to Cæsar the things that are Cæsar's; and to God the things that are God's. And hearing this they wondered and, leaving him, went their ways. (St. Matthew xxii: 15–22.)

Christ's kingdom not of this world: all power from God:

Pilate therefore went into the hall again and called Jesus and said to him: Art thou the king of the Jews? Jesus answered: Sayest thou this thing of thyself, or have others told it thee of me? Pilate answered: Am I a Jew? Thy own nation and the chief priests have delivered thee up to me. What hast thou done? Jesus answered: My kingdom is not of this world. If my kingdom were of this world, my servants would certainly strive that I should not be delivered to the Jews, but now my kingdom is not from hence. Pilate therefore said to him: Art thou a king then? Jesus answered: Thou sayest that I am a king. For this was I born and for this came I into the world; that I should give testimony to the truth. Everyone that is of the truth heareth my voice. Pilate saith to him: What is truth? And when he said this he went out again to the Jews and saith to them: I find no cause in him. (St. John xviii: 33–38.)

When the chief priests, therefore, and the servants had seen him they cried out, saying: Crucify him, crucify him. Pilate saith to them: Take him you, and crucify him: for I find no cause in him. The Jews answered him: We have a law; and according to the law he ought to die, because he made himself the Son of God. When Pilate therefore had heard this saying, he feared the more. And he entered into the hall again; and he said to Jesus: Whence art thou? But Jesus gave him no answer. Pilate therefore saith to him: Speakest thou not to me? Knowest thou not that I have power to crucify thee and I have power to release thee? Jesus answered: Thou shouldst not have any power against me, unless it were given thee from above. Therefore, he that hath delivered me to thee hath the greater sin. And from henceforth Pilate sought to release him. But the Jews cried out, saying: If thou release this man, thou art not Cæsar's friend. For whosoever maketh himself a king speaketh against Cæsar. Now when Pilate had heard these words, he brought Jesus forth and sat down in the judgement seat, in the place that is called Lithostrotos, and in Hebrew Gabbatha. And it was the parasceve of the pasch, about the sixth hour : and he saith to the Jews : Behold your king. But they cried out : Away with him : away with him : crucify him. Pilate saith to them : Shall I crucify your king ? The chief priests answered : We have no king but Cæsar. Then therefore he delivered him to them to be crucified. And they took Jesus and led him forth. (St. John xix : 6–16.)

Civic rights :

St. Paul showed on a number of occasions, chronicled in the Acts, his pride in his Roman citizenship. Arrested at Philippi and beaten uncondemned, he refused to go before extracting from the magistrates a recognition that they had outraged his civic rights :

And the keeper of the prison told these words to Paul. The magistrates have sent to let you go. Now therefore depart. And go in peace. But Paul said to them : They have beaten us publicly, uncondemned, men that are Romans, and have cast us into prison. And now do they thrust us out privately ? Not so : but let them come and let us out themselves. And the serjeants told these words to the magistrates. And they were afraid, hearing that they were Romans. And coming, they besought them : and bringing them out they desired them to depart out of the city. (Acts xvi : 36–39.)

At Jerusalem (Acts xxii) he escapes scourging by claiming the privilege of a Roman citizen.

But the Imperial patriotism of St. Paul in nowise conflicted with his local patriotism, his loyalty to the place of his birth. 'I am a Jew of Tarsus in Cilicia, a citizen of no mean city.' (Acts xxi : 39.)

Civic duties :

Both St. Peter and St. Paul teach the corresponding duties of citizenship, and inculcate obedience to the rulers of the state as holding their authority from God :

Be ye subject therefore to every human creature for God's sake : whether it be to the king as excelling, or to governors as sent by him for the punishment of evil-doers and for the praise of the good. For so is the will of God, that by doing well you may put to silence the ignorance of foolish men : as free and not as making liberty a cloak for malice, but as the servants of God. Honour all men, love the brotherhood, fear God, honour the king. (1 Peter ii : 13–17.)

It is noteworthy that this letter was written at a time when the Christian name was proscribed and Christians were liable to the death penalty. Even unjust persecution does not free the subject from 'rendering to Cæsar the things that are Cæsar's.' St. Paul is even more explicit in his injunctions :

Let every soul be subject to higher powers. For there is no power but from God : and those that are are ordained of God. Therefore, he that resisteth the power resisteth the ordinance of God. And they that resist purchase to themselves damnation. For princes are not a terror to the good work, but to the evil. Wilt thou then not be afraid of the power ? Do that which is good ; and thou shalt have praise from the same. For he is God's minister to thee for good. But if thou do that which is evil, fear : for he beareth not the sword in vain. For he is God's minister : an avenger to execute wrath upon him that doth evil. Wherefore be subject of necessity ; not only for wrath, but also for conscience' sake. For therefore also you pay tribute. For they are the ministers of God serving unto this purpose. Render, therefore, to all men their dues. Tribute, to whom tribute is due : custom, to whom custom : fear, to whom fear : honour, to whom honour. (Romans xiii : 1–7.)

Prayers for those in authority, which have filled so important a part in the Christian liturgies until this day, are enjoined by St. Paul in his first letter to Timothy :

I desire therefore, first of all, that supplications, prayers, intercessions and thanksgivings be made for all men : for kings and for all that are in high station : that we may lead a quiet and a peaceable life in all piety and chastity. For this is good and acceptable in the sight of God our Saviour, who will have all men to be saved and to come to the knowledge of the truth. (1 Timothy ii : 1–4.)

D. THE SUPRA-NATIONAL CHARACTER OF THE CHURCH

Christ the salvation of all peoples :

He [Simeon] also took him into his arms and blessed God and said : Now thou dost dismiss thy servant, O Lord, according to thy word in peace : because my eyes have seen thy salvation which thou hast prepared before the face of all peoples : a light to the revelation of the Gentiles and the glory of thy people Israel. (St. Luke ii : 28–32.)

The world-wide mission of the Apostles:

You are the salt of the earth. But if the salt lose its savour wherewith shall it be salted? It is good for nothing any more but to be cast out and to be trodden on by men. You are the light of the world. A city seated on a mountain cannot be hid. (St. Matthew v: 13–14.)

And this gospel of the kingdom shall be preached in the whole world for a testimony to all nations: and then shall the consummation come. (St. Matthew xxiv: 14.)

The commission to teach all nations:

And Jesus coming, spoke to them, saying: All power is given to me in heaven and on earth. Going, therefore, teach ye all nations: baptizing them in the name of the Father and of the Son and of the Holy Ghost. Teaching them to observe all things whatsoever I have commanded you. And behold I am with you all days even to the consummation of the world. (St. Matthew xxviii: 18–20.)

And he said to them: Go ye into the whole world and preach the gospel to every creature. He that believeth and is baptized shall be saved. But he that believeth not shall be condemned. And these signs shall follow them that believe: In my name they shall cast out devils. They shall speak with new tongues. They shall take up serpents: and if they shall drink any deadly thing, it shall not hurt them. They shall lay their hands upon the sick: and they shall recover. And the Lord Jesus, after he had spoken to them, was taken up into heaven and sitteth on the right hand of God. But they going forth preached everywhere: the Lord working withal, and confirming the word with signs that followed. (St. Mark xvi: 15–20.)

The authority and pastoral function of the Papacy:

And Jesus came into the quarters of Cæsarea Philippi: and he asked his disciples, saying: Whom do men say that the Son of man is? But they said: Some John the Baptist, and other some Elias, and others Jeremias or one of the prophets. Jesus saith to them: But whom do you say that I am? Simon Peter answered and said: Thou art Christ, the Son of the Living God. And Jesus answering, said to him: Blessed art thou, Simon Barjona, because flesh and blood hath not revealed it to thee but my Father who is in heaven. And I say to thee: That thou art Peter, and upon this rock I will build my church. And the gates of hell shall not prevail against it. And I will give to thee the keys of the kingdom of heaven. And whatsoever thou shalt bind upon earth, it shall be bound also in heaven: and whatsoever thou shalt loose on earth, it shall be loosed also in heaven. (St. Matthew xvi: 13–19.)

I am the good shepherd. The good shepherd giveth his life for his sheep. But the hireling and he that is not the shepherd, whose own the sheep are not, seeth the wolf coming and leaveth the sheep and flieth: and the wolf catcheth and scattereth the sheep. And the hireling flieth, because he is a hireling: and he hath no care for the sheep. I am the good shepherd and I know mine, and mine know me. As the Father knoweth me and I know the Father: and I lay down my life for my sheep. And other sheep I have that are not of this fold: them also I must bring. And they shall hear my voice: and there shall be one fold and one shepherd. (St. John x: 11–16.)

When therefore they had dined, Jesus saith to Simon Peter: Simon, son of John, lovest thou me more than these? He saith to him: Yea, Lord, thou knowest that I love thee. He saith to him: Feed my lambs. He saith to him again: Simon, son of John, lovest thou me? He saith to him: Yea, Lord, thou knowest that I love thee. He saith to him: Feed my lambs. He said to him the third time: Simon, son of John, lovest thou me? Peter was grieved, because he had said to him the third time: Lovest thou me? And he said to him: Lord, thou knowest all things; thou knowest that I love thee. He said to him: Feed my sheep. (St. John xxi: 15–17.)

The descent of the Holy Ghost:

And when the days of Pentecost were accomplished, they were all together in one place. And suddenly there came a sound from heaven as of a mighty wind coming: and it filled the whole house where they were sitting. And there appeared to them parted tongues, as it were, of fire. And it sat upon every one of them. And they were all filled with the Holy Ghost: and they began to speak with divers tongues, according as the Holy Ghost gave them to speak. Now there were dwelling at Jerusalem Jews, devout men, out of every nation under heaven. And when this was noised abroad, the multitude came together and were confounded in mind, because that every man heard them speak in his own tongue. And they were all amazed and wondered, saying: Behold, are not all these that speak Galileans? And how have we heard, every man our own tongue wherein we were born? Parthians and Medes and Elamites and inhabitants of Mesopotamia, Judea and Cappadocia, Pontus and Asia, Phrygia and Pamphylia, Egypt and the parts of Libya about Cyrene, and strangers of Rome, Jews also and proselytes, Cretes and Arabians: we have heard them speak in our own tongues the wonderful works of God. (Acts ii: 1–11.)

But Peter said to them: Do penance: and be baptized every one of you in the name of Jesus Christ, for the remission of your sins, and you shall receive the gift of the Holy Ghost.

For the promise is to you and to your children and to all that are far off whomsoever the Lord our God shall call. And with very many other words did he testify and exhort them, saying: Save yourselves from this perverse generation. They therefore that received his word were baptized, and there were added in that day about three thousand souls. And they were persevering in the doctrine of the Apostles and in the communication of the breaking of bread and in prayers. And fear came upon every soul. Many wonders also and signs were done by the Apostles in Jerusalem: and there was great fear in all. And all they that believed were together and had all things common. (Acts ii: 38–44.)

And the multitude of believers had but one heart and one soul. Neither did anyone say that aught of the things which he possessed was his own · but all things were common unto them. (Acts iv: 32.)

These then were the phenomena that marked the very birth of the Christian Church: first, that those who saw the miraculous descent of the Divine Spirit upon the Apostles were 'of every nation under heaven': second, that they were perfectly united in heart and in the comprehension of the Apostles' words without suppression of the native language of each one, for 'we heard every man our own tongue wherein we were born': third, that this international multitude of the first Christians felt so close a bond of affection for one another that they 'had all things in common.' Unity amid diversity of personal and national character; the obedience of all the parts to a divinely inspired authority at the centre; a sense of supernatural brotherhood transcending the distinctions of race, class, property, frontiers—such is the ideal of the peace of Christ in the reign of Christ which the Catholic Church does not cease to hold before men.

Jewish nationalism cedes to the universality of the Church:

And he (Peter) said to them: You know how abominable it is for a man that is a Jew to keep company or to come unto one of another nation: but God hath showed to me to call no man common or unclean. For which cause, making no doubt, I came when I was sent for. (Acts x: 28–29.)

And Peter opening his mouth, said: In very deed I perceive that God is not a respecter of persons. But in every nation, he that heareth him and worketh justice is acceptable to him. God sent the word to the children of Israel, preaching peace by Jesus Christ (he is Lord of all). (Acts x: 34–36.)

The divine origin and unity of mankind :

But Paul, standing in the midst of the Areopagus, said : Ye men of Athens, I perceive that in all things you are too superstitious. For passing by and seeing your idols I found an altar also, on which was written : To the Unknown God. What therefore you worship, without knowing it, that I preach to you. God, who made the world and all things therein, he being Lord of heaven and earth, dwelleth not in temples made with hands. Neither is he served with men's hands, as though he needed anything : seeing it is he who giveth to all life and breath and all things : and hath made of one, all mankind, to dwell upon the whole face of the earth,[1] determining appointed times and the limits of their habitation. That they should seek God, if haply they may feel after him or find him, although he be not far from every one of us. For in him we live and move and are ; as some also of your own poets said : For we are also his offspring. (Acts xvii : 22–28.)

Union of all nations in Christ :

For as the body is one and hath many members ; and all the members of the body, whereas they are many, yet are one body : so also is Christ. For in one Spirit were we all baptized into one body, whether Jews or Gentiles, whether bond or free : and in one Spirit we have all been made to drink. For the body also is not one member but many. If the foot should say : Because I am not the hand I am not of the body : Is it therefore not of the body ? And if the ear should say : Because I am not the eye, I am not of the body : Is it therefore not of the body ? If the whole body were the eye, where would be the hearing ? If the whole were hearing, where would be the smelling ? But now God hath set the members, every one of them, in the body as it hath pleased him. And if they all were one member, where would be the body ? But now there are many members indeed, yet one body. (1 Corinthians xii : 12–20.)

But our comely parts have no need : but God hath tempered the body together, giving to that which wanted the more abundant honour. That there might be no schism in the body ; but the members might be mutually careful one for another. And if one member suffer any thing, all the members suffer with it : or if one member glory, all the members rejoice with it. Now you are the body of Christ and members of member. (1 Corinthians xii : 24–27.)

For we are his workmanship, created in Christ Jesus in good works, which God hath prepared that we should walk in them. For which cause be mindful that you, being heretofore Gentiles

[1] Not ' self-determination.'

in the flesh, who are called uncircumcision by that which is called circumcision in the flesh, made by hands: that you were at that time without Christ, being aliens from the conversation of Israel and strangers to the testament, having no hope of the promise and without God in this world. But now in Christ Jesus, you who some time were afar off are made nigh by the blood of Christ. For he is our peace, who have made both one, and breaking down the middle wall of partition, the enmities in his flesh: making void the law of commandments contained in decrees: that he might make the two in himself into one new man, making peace. And might reconcile both to God in one body by the cross, killing the enmities in himself. And coming, he preached peace to you that were afar off: and peace to them that were nigh. For by him we have access both in one Spirit to the Father. Now therefore you are no more strangers and foreigners, but you are fellow citizens with the saints and the domestics[1] of God, built upon the foundation of the apostles and prophets, Jesus Christ himself being the chief corner stone: in whom all the building, being framed together, groweth up into an holy temple in the Lord. In whom you also are built together into an habitation of God in the Spirit. (Ephesians ii: 10–22.[2])

Giving thanks to God the Father, who hath made us worthy to be partakers of the lot of the saints in light: who hath delivered us from the power of darkness and hath translated us into the kingdom of the Son of his love: in whom we have redemption through his blood, the remission of sins; who is the image of the invisible God, the first-born of every creature. For in him were all things created in heaven and on earth, visible and invisible, whether thrones, or dominations, or principalities, or powers. All things were created by him and in him. And he is before all: and by him all things consist. And he is the head of the body, the church: who is the beginning, the first-born from the dead, that in all things he may hold the primacy. Because in him, it hath well pleased the Father that all fulness should dwell: and through him to reconcile all things unto himself, making peace through the blood of his cross, both as to the things that are on earth and the things that are in heaven. And you, whereas you were sometimes alienated and enemies in mind in evil works: yet now he hath reconciled in the body of his flesh through death to present you holy and unspotted and blameless before him. (Colossians i: 12–22.)

Now the God of patience and of comfort grant you to be of one mind, one towards another, according to Jesus Christ: that with one mind and with one mouth you may glorify God

[1] οἴκειοι (Members of God's household).

[2] Also Ephesians iv quoted above.

and the Father of our Lord Jesus Christ. Wherefore, receive one another, as Christ also hath received you, unto the honour of God. For I say that Christ Jesus was minister of the circumcision for the truth of God, to confirm the promises made unto the fathers, but that the Gentiles are to glorify God for his mercy, as it is written : Therefore will I confess to thee, O Lord, among the Gentiles and will sing to thy name. And again he saith : Rejoice, ye Gentiles, with his people. And again : Praise the Lord, all ye Gentiles : and magnify him, all ye people. And again, Isaias saith : There shall be a root of Jesse ; and he that shall rise up to rule the Gentiles, in him the Gentiles shall hope. Now the God of hope fill you with all joy and peace in believing : that you may abound in hope and in the power of the Holy Ghost. (Romans xv : 5–13.)

Conclusions

Subsequent chapters will show how the principles enunciated or implied in these recorded words of Christ and His Apostles have been interpreted and applied by the Fathers of the Church, by the Schoolmen and by modern Catholic authors ; how, too, amid conflicting opinions and various interpretations, the utterances of the Apostolic See have indicated the true mind of the Church concerning some of them. Here, therefore, only a few conclusions will be necessary.

(i) In the first place it is clear that the religion revealed by Jesus Christ and the Church which he founded were essentially and from the first supra-national. The jealous particularism of the Chosen Race which, through wars and persecution, had guarded the purity of faith in one Omnipotent God and the Decalogue, whose prophets had foretold the coming of the Messiah with an ever widening vision of His mission—this had now served its purpose. The truths revealed by Christ were to be taught to all peoples ; the Apostles in the earliest days broke down the barriers between circumcised and uncircumcised ; within a few years Christians were to be found among all the Mediterranean peoples and in countries as far distant as Spain and India. The idea of the Church being divided against itself by nationality, or of distinct National Churches, is wholly repugnant to primitive Christianity as shown in the Gospels, the Acts and the Epistles.

(ii) Love of one another was to be the mark of Christians: they were to be brothers: members of a single body: fed with the same divine bread: stones in the same building. Peace through Christ with one another was to be the characteristic of the Christians' life. Strife, contention and war between Christians would appear to be an utter violation of this conception.

(iii) Closely united as Christians were to be, and drawn from all nations, there is nothing to indicate that their unity would imply *uniformity*, or that the distinctive character and language of any nation would be suppressed by the Church. Rather would the Christian unity recognize diversity of gifts and of peoples, just as the individual soul was destined to supernatural union with God but never absorption by Him. United in Christ, the Jew did not cease to be a Jew, nor the Gentile a Gentile. It was in their several native languages that the crowd heard the Apostles preach at Pentecost. We have seen St. Paul's pride in the imperial citizenship of Rome, his local patriotism for his native town: a sentiment in which he did but reflect his Master's love for the capital of his native country, as he wept over its fate. Thus within the world-wide Christian Commonweal the continued existence of separate nations was to be envisaged.

(iv) Christians are not conceived as an elect people free from the jurisdiction of earthly rulers: rather is their political solidarity with the State of which they form part implied. Obedience to the king and to rulers is a Christian duty: they are encouraged by the example of the Apostles to exercise their civic rights. All authority, too, comes from God, and among the rights of that authority is the wielding of the sword—the use of force for justice's sake. Whence it follows that the same principles of justice and charity which guide Christians individually should govern the action of the State whereof they are citizens: and, secondly, that Christian citizens cannot logically dissociate themselves from the just use of force by the authority of the State when such is required. This consequence however was not immediately apparent.

(v) Christians are instructed in the strongest terms to

forgive injuries, to love their enemies, to refrain from retaliation, to suffer insults with meekness, not to return evil for evil. The counsel of non-resistance to evil is closely linked with the conception of charity as the predominant Christian virtue. Does it apply to the mutual dealings of societies as well as to those individuals? It took three centuries for the Church to find a sure answer. Suffice it to say here that the importance of emphasis cannot be overlooked. Whereas there is an abundance of positive teaching upon the duties of charity and upon forgiveness of injuries, the approval of military service and the permission of war are only adduced from the absence of disapproval in the Gospels.

(vi) The soldier's calling is spoken of with respect and soldiers are among the few persons chosen for ' honourable mention ' in the Gospels and the Acts.

Such are the conclusions which, in addition to the moral law and the Ten Commandments which the Christian revelation presupposed and confirmed, are offered by the New Testament, not indeed as the foundation for a complete philosophy of international life, but as indispensable guides to the living Church upon whom was laid the task of evolving that philosophy as the need arose.

CHAPTER II

MILITARY SERVICE

WE have deduced from the teaching of the New Testament that the solidarity of the Christian with his country and his loyalty to authority make it impossible for him to dissociate himself from the use of force by that authority in the cause of justice. But the conditions under which Christianity spread for the first three centuries were not such as to make this deduction evident. There was no question of a Christian state. Christians were a minority in a pagan state. They were intermittently subjected to savage persecution whenever their growing influence was feared. They were as a rule under no obligation to become soldiers. Should they or should they not choose the military profession when they could avoid it? It was a problem of private ethics. It was not at first seen that the solution of the problem depended upon the answer to a question of public ethics, namely whether the war made by the emperor or his generals, in which the Christian soldier might have to engage, was or was not a just war.

Certain elements had evidently to be taken into consideration by the Fathers who wrote on this subject in the post-Apostolic age. In the first place the emphasis upon non-resistance and forgiveness of enemies in the Gospels, on which we have dwelt, was vividly present to their minds. How could the disciples of a religion of love and forbearance wound and kill their fellow-men? There was in this a certain sense of sacrilege which, it will be seen, produced for a short space of time a school of rigorous pacifism. Its denunciation of all war has a simple and powerful appeal which troubles the consciences of the most sincere in different ages. In recent centuries it has been revived and consistently practised by the Society of Friends in Anglo-Saxon countries. To his advocacy of it Tolstoy owed not a little of his widespread influence. The reaction from the Great War of 1914–18 gave it a considerable impulsion, notably in the ranks of the Protestant ministry, among women's organizations and among the younger generation in the universities of several countries.

On the contrary, the spirit of loyalty to the imperial authority, so clearly taught by Christ and by St. Paul, was observed with heroic persistency by the leaders of the early Church. Proscribed, hunted, under sentence of death, they still taught obedience to the temporal power, loyal citizenship and support of the Roman rule for the maintenance of order. Was it consistent with this duty to induce Christians who were officers or officials of the Empire to leave their posts? Was it right to insist upon a course of conduct which if logically and generally followed would leave the Imperial authority without soldiers to quell civil riots or attacks by barbarians?

A third element, and one which made inevitable the controversy studied in this chapter, was the fact that soldiers had from the first been found among the converts to Christianity. Were Christians, simply because they were in the military service of the Empire, to be excluded from the Mysteries? Were they to be instructed to desert upon their conversion and face the certain penalty of death? Could they remain in the lower grades but not rise to the higher, in which were more serious responsibilities?

The whole of this question, until the eve of the conversion of the Empire, was complicated and confused by a fourth element, namely the obligation to sacrifice to the Emperor which was incumbent upon the higher grades, from that of centurion upward, from at least the middle of the second century. It was apparently extended, as a test, to all soldiers suspected of being Christian during the persecution of Diocletian. To offer this sacrifice was plainly an act of idolatry, and a great number of Christian officers and men suffered torture and death rather than be guilty of it.[1]

[1] See note on p 44

The knowledge that it would be required of those who took up the military career not unnaturally caused certain rigorist writers to conclude that military service was in itself sinful, and to subject it to a sweeping condemnation.

Faced with so difficult and often agonizing a choice, Christian thought for a time hovered in a half-way house, possible only in a non-Christian State of which Christians formed but a small part and for whose public conduct they seemed to have no responsibility. Christians were to refrain from enlisting in the army, so as to avoid incurring at once the guilt of bloodshed and the danger of idolatry, but should pray for the Emperor, helping his armies with their intercession. The conversion of the Empire put an end to this equivocal position.

The earliest Fathers continue the Pauline tradition of prayer for the state and for all in authority. The magnificent liturgical prayer for rulers and for peace from the Epistle of St. Clement of Rome (*c.* A.D. 95) to the Corinthians will be found on another page. Both he and St. Ignatius of Antioch use in their letters a military language which leaves no doubt of their admiration for the soldier's calling.

ST. CLEMENT. *Epist. I ad Corinthios, Cap. XXXVII :*

My brethren, let us serve as soldiers with all our strength under the irreproachable commands of God. Let us consider the soldiers who serve under our leaders, in what good order, how strenuously, how obediently they follow their orders. All are not prefects, or tribunes, or centurions or commanders of fifty men or the like ; but each in his proper rank carries out what he is bidden to do by the king and his commanding officers. The higher ranks cannot carry out their duty without the lower, nor the lower without the higher. All have a certain need one of another and are used to this state of things. Or take our body as example. The head is nothing without the feet, nor the feet without the head : but the least members of our body are necessary and useful to the whole body. All the members conspire together and employ a single hierarchy for the conservation of the whole body.

ST. IGNATIUS. *Ep. ad Polycarpum, VI,* 2 :

Work together one with another, fight in unison, run in unison, suffer together, sleep in unison, rise in unison as God's dispensers, assessors and ministers. Be pleasing to him whose soldiers you are and from whom you receive your pay. Let no deserter be found among you. Let your baptism remain as arms; faith be your helmet; charity your lance; patience your panoply. Let mortification be your (military) operations: that you may render worthily to God the things you have received. Be patient then one towards the other in mildness: and God will be so towards you.

If we except the speech of this bold and cheerful Bishop of Antioch to the Emperor Trajan before his condemnation to be devoured by the lions, the Apologia of St. Justin (A.D. 100–165) to the Emperor Antoninus Pius is apparently the first recorded address of Christians to the head of the State in which, among other matters, their political position is set forth. It is his theme that the faith of Christians, which he amply describes, and their refusal to use force is consistent with good citizenship.

St. Justin. *Apologia I pro Christianis.*

Chapter XI:

When you hear that we look for a kingdom you suppose, without making any inquiry, that we speak of a human kingdom: whereas we speak of that which is with God, as appears also from the confession of their faith made by those who are charged with being Christians, though they know that death is the punishment awarded to him who so confesses. For if we looked for a human kingdom, we should also deny our Christ, that we might not be slain: and we should strive to escape detection, that we might not obtain what we expect. But since our thoughts are not fixed on the present, we are not concerned when men cut us off: since also death is a debt which must at all events be paid.

Chapter XII:

More than all other men are we your helpers and allies in promoting peace, seeing that we hold this view, that it is alike impossible for the wicked, the covetous, the conspirator and for the virtuous to escape the notice of God, and that each man goes to everlasting punishment or salvation according to the value of his actions.

Chapter XVII:

It is our special care to be the first of all to pay our taxes and dues to those whom you have commissioned to receive them, as we have been instructed to do by Him (Christ).

St. Justin then retells the incident of the tribute money, and continues :

> Further, we adore God alone ; but in other matters we gladly serve you, we acknowledge you as kings and rulers of men, and we pray that you may be found to have health of mind together with the royal power.

Explaining Christ's counsel to turn the other cheek he says (Chapter XVI) :

> For it is not right to answer fighting with fighting (ἀντείρειν), nor does God wish us to imitate the wicked : but He has exhorted us to lead all men away from the shame and cupidity of the wicked by patience and gentleness.

And this doctrine of peace can already claim its victories ; it has lessened murders and wars ; it has induced among Christians a loyalty and a discipline comparable to that of the Imperial soldiery, whereby they willingly face martyrdom.

Chapter XXXIX :

> . . . For from Jerusalem there went out into the world, men, twelve in number, and these illiterate, of no ability in speaking : but by the power of God they proclaimed to every race of men that they were sent by Christ to teach to all the word of God ; and we who formerly used to murder one another do not only now refrain from making war on our enemies, but also, that we may not lie, nor deceive our examiners, willingly die confessing Christ, for that saying 'The tongue has sworn, but the mind is unsworn' might be imitated by us in this matter. But if the soldiers enrolled by you, and who have taken the military oath, prefer their allegiance to their own life, and parents and country, and all kindred, though you can offer them nothing incorruptible, it were verily ridiculous if we, who earnestly long for incorruption, should not endure all things, in order to obtain what we desire from Him who is able to grant it.

Upon the military service of Christians St. Justin is silent in the *Apologia* itself. But striking evidence of the strength of Christians in the army is contained in the letter of the Emperor Marcus Aurelius traditionally appended to the *Apologia*. It is addressed to the Senate and narrates the famous miracle of the '*Legio fulminata*' saved in A.D. 174 from perishing by thirst through the prayers of the Christians.

When therefore I had compared myself and the number of my men with the hoards of the barbarian enemy, I betook myself to pray to the Gods of my fathers. But, since they neglected me and I saw to what straits my forces were reduced, I called out of the ranks those whom we call Christians, and, having questioned them, I perceived what a great multitude of them there were and raged against them: which indeed I should not have done, because I afterward perceived their power. For they did not begin by the contemplation of spears or arms or trumpets (which is hateful to them because of the God which they keep in their conscience; for it seems as if these men, whom we suspect of being atheists, have a God residing of his own will in their conscience), but prostrating themselves upon the ground they prayed not for me only but also for the whole army, that they might slake our present hunger and thirst. For we had had no water for five days, because it was utterly lacking; and we were in the midst of Germany and in the enemy's country. But no sooner had they knelt upon the ground and invoked the God whom I know not, than a most cooling rain fell straight from heaven upon us, but upon the enemies of the Romans lightning and hail.

TERTULLIAN in his earlier writings shows the same attachment to the Empire, the same acceptance of the army as an institution. In describing the prayer of Christians for the state he includes among the objects of prayer the security of the Empire and the valour of its armies.

TERTULLIAN. *Apologeticus* 30:

For we offer prayer for the safety of our princes to the eternal, the true, the living God, whose favour, beyond all others, they must themselves desire. They know from whom they have obtained their power; they know, as they are men, from whom they have received life itself; they are convinced that He is God alone, on whose power alone they are entirely dependent, to whom they are second, after whom they occupy the highest places, before and above all the gods. Why not, since they are above all living men, and the living, as living, are superior to the dead? They reflect upon the extent of their power, and so they come to understand the highest; they acknowledge that they have all their might from Him against whom their might is nought. Let the emperor make war on heaven; let him lead heaven captive in his triumph; let him put guards on heaven; let him impose taxes on heaven! He cannot. Just because he is less than heaven, he is great. For he himself is his to whom heaven and every creature appertains. He gets his sceptre where he first got his humanity; his power where he got the breath of life. Thither we lift our eyes, with hands outstretched, because free from sin ; with head uncovered, for we have nothing whereof to be ashamed ; finally, without a monitor, because it is from the heart we supplicate. And, without ceasing, for all our emperors we offer prayer. We pray for life prolonged ; for security to the empire ; for protection to the imperial house ; for brave armies, a faithful senate, a virtuous people, the world at rest—whatever, as man or Cæsar, an emperor would wish.

A little later in the same work Tertullian seeks to show how rapidly Christianity has spread and how Christians play their part in every sphere of public life, the army included. They would be formidable did they not shrink from violence.

TERTULLIAN. *Apologeticus* 37 :

We are but of yesterday, and we have filled every place among you—cities, islands, fortresses, towns, market-places, the very camp, tribes, companies, palace, senate, forum—we have left nothing to you but the temples of your gods. For what wars should we not be fit, not eager, even with unequal forces, we who so willingly yield ourselves to the sword, if in our religion it were not counted better to be slain than to slay ?

Ibid., 42 :

We are your shipmates, your fellow soldiers ; with you we lead the life of the country and the life of trade ; indeed in all the arts we are intermingled.

Yet only twelve years later (*c.* A.D. 211) we find the powerful pen of Tertullian used to tell a very different story and to point another moral. He had joined the Montanists. This heresy of Montanus, the prophet of a Phrygian village, was shortlived. It consisted in an excessive Puritanism, an obsession with sin so great that the Church's power of forgiveness was denied, a prohibition of second marriages and a morbid seeking for martyrdom. Tertullian, while it lasted, was its most famous exponent. Inclined now to over-strictness in every doctrine, he leapt to the defence of a soldier who had been degraded and imprisoned for refusing to wear a chaplet on his head when receiving the gift made to the army by the Emperors Caracalla and Geta on their accession. Hence the title *De Corona* of the work which he wrote in defence of the man's attitude, since many Christians refused to regard him as a martyr.

TERTULLIAN. *De Corona*, 11:

To begin with the real ground of the military crown, I think we must first inquire whether warfare is proper at all for Christians. What sense is there in discussing the merely accidental, when that on which it rests is to be condemned? Do we believe it lawful for a human oath to be superadded to one divine, and for a man to come under promise to another master after Christ, and to abjure father and mother and all nearest kinsfolk, whom even the law has commanded us to honour and love next to God Himself, to whom the gospel, too, holding them only of less account than Christ, has in like manner rendered honour? Shall it be held lawful to make an occupation of the sword, when the Lord proclaims that he who uses the sword shall perish by the sword? And shall the son of peace take part in the battle when it does not become him even to sue at law? And shall he apply the chain, and the prison, and the torture, and the punishment, who is not the avenger even of his own wrongs? Shall he, forsooth, either keep watch-service for others more than for Christ, or shall he do it on the Lord's day, when he does not even do it for Christ Himself? And shall he keep guard before the temples which he has renounced? And shall he take a meal where the Apostle has forbidden him? And shall he diligently protect by night those whom in the day-time he has put to flight by his exorcisms, leaning and resting on the spear the while with which Christ's side was pierced? Shall he carry a flag, too, hostile to Christ? And shall he ask a watchword from the emperor who has already received one from God? Shall he be disturbed in death by the trumpet of the trumpeter, who expects to be roused by the angel's trump? And shall the Christian be burned according to the camp rule, when he was not permitted to burn incense to an idol, when to him Christ remitted the punishment of fire? Then how many other offences there are involved in the performance of camp offices, which we must hold to involve a transgression of God's law, you may see by a slight survey. The very carrying of the name over from the camp of light to the camp of darkness is a violation of it. Of course, if faith comes later, and finds any preoccupied with military service, their case is different, as in the instance of those whom John used to receive for baptism, and of those most faithful centurions, I mean the centurion whom Christ approves, and the centurion whom Peter instructs; yet at the same time, when a man has become a believer, and faith has been sealed, there must be either an immediate abandonment of it [military service], which has been the course with many; or all sorts of quibbling will have to be resorted to in order to avoid offending God, and that is not allowed even outside of military service; or, last of all, for God the fate must be endured which a citizen-faith has been no less ready to accept. For neither does military service hold out escape from punishment of sins, or exemption from martyrdom. Nowhere does the Christian change his character.

Desertion, then, or death is the only course open to the soldier convert.

This is believed to be the earliest instance of a Christian writer who condemns all military service on the authority of the Gospel. Less rhetorical but no less rigid is the same author's pacifism in his *De Idolatria* written in A.D. 211–212.

TERTULLIAN. *De Idolatria, Cap. XIX:*

But now inquiry is made about this point, whether a believer may turn himself unto military service, and whether the military may be admitted unto the faith, even the rank and file, or each inferior grade, to whom there is no necessity for taking part in sacrifices or capital punishments. There is no agreement between the divine and the human sacrament, the standard of Christ and the standard of the devil, the camp of light and the camp of darkness. One soul cannot be due to two [lords]—God and Cæsar. And yet Moses carried a rod, and Aaron wore a buckle, and John (Baptist) is girt with leather, and Joshua, the son of Nun, leads a line of march; and the people warred: if it pleases you to sport with the subject. But how will [a Christian man] war, nay, how will he serve even in peace, without a sword, which the Lord has taken away? For albeit soldiers had come unto John, and had received the formula of their rule; albeit, likewise, a centurion had believed; [still] the Lord afterwards, in disarming Peter, unbelted every soldier. No dress is lawful among us, if assigned to any unlawful action.

THE CANONS OF HIPPOLYTUS, traditionally attributed[1] to Hippolytus of Rome, denouncer of heresies, at one time anti-pope but reconciled to the Roman Church before his death in exile in 236, contain rules inspired by a similar hostility to military service. They suggest an uneasy compromise whereby the Christian may, if obliged, become a soldier provided he does not accomplish the acts for which soldiers are ultimately intended.

Canon 13: Soldiers may not kill, even if ordered to do so.

Canon 14: No Christian ought to volunteer for military

[1] Others believe them to be the work of the 5th or 6th century.

service nor become a soldier unless he is forced to by his ruler. Let him who bears the sword beware lest he shed blood. If he has shed blood let him be excluded from the mysteries (Holy Communion) until he be purified by making amends with tears and grief.

This notion that war was intrinsically evil and opposed to the will of God must have continued to dwell in the minds of certain Christian thinkers for about a century. It marked a stage in the evolution of moral theology important enough to make the whole Augustinian school of writers upon the morality of war, from St. Augustine himself to the Spanish neo-scholastics twelve hundred years afterwards, find it necessary to restate and refute the contention. Though in singular contrast to the increasing number of Christian soldiers in the Roman army it seems almost at one time to have penetrated the citadel of Orthodoxy. For Lactantius, despite his authority in other regards, and his belief that the fall of the Roman Empire would mean the end of the world, repeats at the beginning of the fourth century the prohibition of any act which directly or indirectly occasions the shedding of blood, deducing his doctrine, however, not like Tertullian from the sentence of Christ in the Garden of Gethsemane, but from the Decalogue. Observe the pathetic inconsistency of the two following passages—each instinct with sincere and profound conviction: they are both from the Divine Institutions.

LACTANTIUS. *De Divinis Institutionibus VII*, 20 :

When Rome, the head of the world, shall have fallen, who can doubt that the end is come of human things, aye, of the earth itself. She, she alone is the state by which all things are upheld even until now ; wherefore let us make prayers and supplications to the God of heaven if indeed His decrees and His purposes can be delayed, that that hateful tyrant come not sooner than we look for, he for whom are reserved fearful deeds, who shall pluck out that eye in whose extinction the world itself shall perish.

Ibid., *VI*, 20 :

. . . It is not therefore befitting that those who strive to keep to the path of justice should be companions and sharers in this public homicide. For when God forbids us to kill, He not only prohibits us from open violence, which is not even allowed by the public laws, but He warns us against the commission of those things which are esteemed lawful among men. Thus it will be neither lawful for a just man to engage in warfare, since his warfare is justice itself, nor to accuse anyone of a capital charge, because it makes no difference whether you put a man to death by word, or rather by the sword, since it is the act of putting to death itself which is prohibited. Therefore, with regard to this precept of God, there ought to be no exception at all; but that it is always unlawful to put to death a man, whom God willed to be a sacred animal.

The Roman Empire—the '*orbis romanus*'—which alone seemed to provide a stable framework to life—must, if God will, be saved. Yet Christians might not join in using the only means which, humanly speaking, could secure it from attack without and rebellion within, that is, military force. No wonder that the gap widened between the precept of the moralist and the practice of the citizen, a practice which the right mind of the Church was before long to sanctify and to rationalize.

Yet the quandary of Lactantius and, as will be seen below, of Origen, cannot be rightly judged without an appreciation of the circumstances of the times. More evidently repugnant then, than in later days, did the rule of force appear to the apologists of a religion of supernatural love and peace, driven as they were to a daily examination of the essential spirit of that religion by persecution, and by the need of replying to gibes, reproaches of disloyalty or the searching inquiry of acute Roman minds. The flogging and odious tortures which—as St. Augustine bears witness—were the normal accompaniment of the law courts; the harsh penalties of the military law, the wholesale brutalities of war, the ceaseless intrigues and conflicts of the rivals for the Imperial power, all these were in more flagrant contradiction to the whole tenor of the Gospels than were the systems of law and of war, based, at least formally, upon moral principles, of a later age. The enforced idolatry of the military officers, the cruel deaths meted out under the recent persecution of Diocletian to any soldiers who endeavoured to reconcile military duty to the Empire with their Christian conscience, was another fact which made the whole profession of arms seem a quite un-Christian thing.

And, if further reason is sought for the apparent lack of resolution in escaping from the dilemma which we have described, it can perhaps be found in a certain fatalism common to the moralists in this last century of the pagan Empire.[1] That the end of the world was at hand had been the belief of the Apostles. 'It is now the hour for us to rise from sleep. For now our salvation is nearer than when we believed' (Romans xiii : 11). There is no reason to doubt that the thought of the impending consummation of the world was equally present to the minds of the post-Apostolic Fathers. The crumbling of what they could not but regard as the very fabric of civilization was a sign of the terrors which, according to the prophecy of the Apocalypse, must precede the end. Rome 'urbs æterna' and the world were one. The impending collapse of both must be faced with resignation by Christians, who awaited the second coming of the Lord. Yet patriotism tugged at the heartstrings and prompted the prayer—so different from that of the aged St. John on Patmos : 'Surely, I come quickly. Amen. Come, Lord Jesus' (Apoc. xxii : 20)—that the advent of the Destroyer be, if possible, delayed.

It should, however, be added that other Fathers of the Church did not appear to have so scrupulous a horror of war. *St. Clement of Alexandria,* who died about A.D. 215, had treated the soldier's profession on a level with any other legitimate calling and sanctified it with a Christian motive.

> Art thou a countryman? Delve then thy land, but as thou dost delve confess thy God. Hast thou a taste for seafaring? Steer thy ship, but call upon the heavenly pilot. Or if the Christian faith has come upon thee in the profession of arms, obey the Captain who giveth just commands.[2]

Our study of this problem of war and military service in the non-Christian Empire can best be concluded by the relevant passages of the great Origen written in his old age in reply to Celsus (A.D. 245–250) a little while before the cruel torturing which ended in his death. Celsus had

[1] Bryce, *Holy Roman Empire,* pp. 20–21.

[2] Apud Batiffol, *L'Eglise et le Droit de Guerre,* pp. 17, 18.

levelled against Christian pacifism the old reproach of '*contemptissima inertia.*' Why would not Christians fight for their Emperor in time of need and help him with all their strength? Were they *sans patrie*? The Christian apologist replies:

ORIGEN. *Contra Celsum, V,* 33 (*Crombie*):

. . . And to those who inquire of us whence we come, or who is our founder, we reply that we are come, agreeably to the counsels of Jesus, to 'cut down our hostile and insolent "wordy" swords into ploughshares, and to convert into pruning-hooks the spears formerly employed in war.' For we no longer take up 'sword against nation,' nor do we 'learn war any more,' having become children of peace, for the sake of Jesus, who is our leader, instead of those whom our fathers followed, among whom we were 'strangers to the covenant,' and having received a law, for which we give thanks to Him that rescued us from the error [of our ways], saying: 'Our fathers honoured lying idols, and there is not among them one that causeth it to rain!' Our Superintendent, then, and Teacher, having come forth from the Jews, regulates the whole world by the word of His teaching.

What then of the Old Testament?—for Celsus has studied his subject. In it God commanded wars to be waged, culprits to be stoned, cities to be put to the sword. Origen's reply is of the utmost interest to our subject; for he contends that the nationalism of the Jewish dispensation has ceded to the universal, supra-national mission of Christianity. The legislation proper to the Jews as a chosen race passed away with the abolition of Jewish independence; and with the Old Law went the divine sanction of war.

ORIGEN. *Contra Celsum, VII,* 25–26:

Next Celsus brings forward this precept: 'To him who strikes thee once, thou shouldst offer thyself to be struck again,' though he does not quote from the Law the points which, in this respect, seem contrary to the words of the Gospel. We answer that we know that it was said to the ancients: 'An eye for an eye and a tooth for a tooth' (Exodus xxi: 24); but we have also read: 'But I say unto you, if a man strike thee on one cheek, turn to him also the other' (Matthew v: 39). Now inasmuch as Celsus has, I gather, formed his opinion from those who teach that there is one God of the Gospel and another God of the Law, the answer to him is that the notion of turning the other cheek was not unknown to the Old Scripture. For we read in the Lamentations of Jeremias: 'It is good for a man when he hath borne the yoke from his youth. He shall sit solitary and hold his peace, because he hath taken it upon himself. He shall put his mouth in the dust, if so there may be hope. He shall give his cheek to him that striketh him, he shall be filled with reproaches' (Lamentations iii: 27–30). So the God of the Gospel is not in conflict with the God of the Law, even about the striking of the cheek. Neither did Moses or Jesus belie one another, nor did the Father when He sent Jesus into the world forget that He had given commandments to Moses; He neither repented of His own laws and condemned them, nor sent He a messenger who would preach the contrary.

Now if a short explanation must be given of the difference between the laws of Moses which the Jews first followed and those which the Christians, taught by Jesus, now seek to follow, we will say this. The Mosaic law, understood in its obvious sense, was not accommodated to the nations called to the faith and subjected to the rule of the Romans, nor would it have been possible for the old Jews to preserve intact the constitution of their state had they been bound to follow the laws of the Gospel. For neither would the Christians have been able to kill their enemies, as the Mosaic law prescribes, and to burn or stone those who violated the law, according as they were condemned to one or other penalty. Why, even if the Jews wanted to do these things, as their law provides, nowadays they would not be allowed to. Again, had not permission been granted to the old Jews, who had their own particular laws and land, to attack their enemies, to wage war for their country, or to punish adulterers, murderers, and those guilty of similar crimes, nothing remained to prevent their sudden and complete extinction, the moment the enemy should fall upon them, as on a people who by their own law had been enfeebled and prevented from repelling attack. But that Providence, which once gave the Law but now has given the Gospel, did not wish the state of the Jews to last any longer, and destroyed their city, their temple, and the worship offered therein to God by sacrifices and other prescribed rites. And while God put an end to those things which He wanted to last no longer, so He caused the Christian religion to spread day by day, so that now it is freely preached, although six hundred obstacles were placed in the way of the dissemination of Christ's doctrine throughout the world. And because God desired the doctrine of Jesus Christ to benefit *all* nations, all the counsels of men against the Christians have been brought to nought; and the more emperors, rulers of nations and peoples persecuted them, the more has their number grown and their strength increased.

Yet in facing the direct challenge of Celsus to the loyalty of Christian moralists in refusing to sanction military service, Origen evidently feels the force of it; and for the first time we find in his words a distinction between righteous and unrighteous wars. 'Soldiers can fight in a just cause.' That cause is sanctified since Christians may and indeed ought to help them with their prayers. But war can also be waged unjustly: since Christians are to pray 'that whatever is opposed to those who act justly may be destroyed.' In the Fourth Book of the same work Origen draws a lesson from the bees which he says applies to 'just and regular wars, when such must needs be declared among men.'[1] To him a just war consists in 'battles for the defence of the fatherland.' The transition from praying for victory to striving physically for victory was bound to come: it came so soon as the conversion of the Empire first obliged the Christian Church to share responsibility for the public acts of the state.

ORIGEN. *Contra Celsum, VIII,* 73:

In the next place Celsus urges us 'to help the king with all our might, and to labour with him in the maintenance of justice, to fight for him: and, if he requires it, to fight under him, or lead an army along with him.' To this our answer is, that we do, when occasion requires, give help to kings, and that, so to say, a divine help, 'putting on the whole armour of God.' And this we do in obedience to the injunction of the Apostle: 'I exhort, therefore, that, first of all, supplications, prayers, intercessions and giving of thanks be made for all men, for kings, and for all that are in authority'; and the more anyone excels in piety, the more effective help does he render to kings, even more than is given by soldiers, who go forth to fight and slay as many of the enemy as they can. And to those enemies of our faith who require us to bear arms for the commonwealth and to slay men, we can reply: Do not those who are priests at certain shrines, and those who attend on certain gods, as you account them, keep their hands free from blood, that they may, with hands unstained and free from human blood, offer the appointed sacrifices to your gods; and even when war is upon you, you never enlist the priests in the army? If that, then, is a laudable custom, how much more so, while others are engaged in battle, these too should engage as the priests and ministers of God on behalf of those who are fighting in a righteous cause, and for

[1] *Contra Celsum*, IV, 82.

the king who reigns righteously, that whatever is opposed to those who act righteously may be destroyed! And as we by our prayers vanquish all demons who stir up war, and lead to the violation of oaths, and disturb the peace, we in this way are much more helpful to the kings than those who go into the field to fight for them. And we do take our part in public affairs, when along with righteous prayers, we join self-denying exercises and meditations which teach us to despise pleasures, and not to be led away by them. And none fight better for the king than we do. We do not indeed fight under him, although he require it; but we fight on his behalf, forming a special army—an army of piety—by offering our prayers to God.

Before passing to our conclusions we may do well to complete the picture of Christian practice concerning military service at the end of the third century by a brief note upon the military martyrs.

MGR. BATIFFOL. *L'Eglise et le Droit de Guerre, pp.* 23–25:

The Roman loyalty of the Christians continues to be affirmed with perfect consistency, in everything which does not do violence to their faith and their duties to God. They submit to the laws to the point of martyrdom, which itself is the most sublime form of that submission: they condemn civil war: they take their part in military service, so long as this service does not constrain them to acts of idolatry.

The critics agree that the case of the martyr Maximilian, put to death at Carthage, in the year 295, for having refused military service, to which as the son of a veteran he was liable, is exceptional for two reasons. In the first place, the proconsul of Africa who condemns him to death inflicts upon him a penalty which his refusal to join the army did not lawfully entail; in the second place—which is more important—this refusal is not a duty for Maximilian arising from his faith as a Christian. He was not justified in declaring: 'I am not allowed to be a soldier because I am a Christian.' And the proconsul knows it: for he reminds Maximilian that he will find in the army soldiers that are Christians. 'In the sacred guard of our lords Diocletian and Maximian, Constantius and Maximianus Galerius, there are Christian soldiers and they fight' (Acta S. Maximiliani, 1 and 2; Harnack, *Militia*, pp. 114–116).

In Egypt, at the time of the persecution of Decius, a letter of Denys, the bishop, speaks of four Christian soldiers who, being on guard for the prefect of Egypt while he is judging a Christian, themselves encourage the martyr to hold good.

Eusebius relates (*Hist. Eccles.*, VII, 15) that an officer called Marinus at Cæsarea in Palestine having attained the rank of centurion is denounced by one of his rivals as 'one who will not sacrifice to the Emperor.' The judge asks him to what doctrine he adheres. Marinus answers that he is a Christian. He is given three hours to change his mind, after which, since he refuses to renounce his faith, he is put to death. (Eusebius, *Hist. Eccles.*, VII, 15): The bishop Theotecnos comes to visit Marinus, during the three hours granted him for reflexion by his judge. He bids him choose between his sword and the book of the Holy Gospels. This marks a certain progress in military tolerance, for Marinus could have become a centurion, and could be a centurion without being obliged to offer sacrifices: he is denounced before being promoted. The evidence of this progress is greater in the case of the martyr Marcellus during the persecution of Diocletian, for Marcellus is actually a centurion. The incident takes place at Tangiers under Maximian Hercules. Marcellus, called upon to offer sacrifice, pulls off his soldier's belt and the vine, the sign of his rank, saying: 'I am a soldier of Jesus Christ the eternal King. . . . If this is the condition of men in military service, that they are compelled to sacrifice to gods and emperors, behold I throw away the vine and belt, I renounce the signs of my rank and I refuse to serve' (Harnack, *Militia*, p. 117). This shows that Marcellus has been able to reach the centurion's grade without his faith being troubled.

At this period—the beginning of the fourth century—Christians are more numerous than ever in the ranks of the Roman army, so much so that the persecution of Diocletian is primarily directed against 'the brethren who are in the service,' as Eusebius says (*H.E.*, VIII, 1, 2) without distinction of rank. The Emperor, he says, aims at 'those that are in the camps.' Then could be seen a great number of soldiers retiring into private life, 'that they might not deny the religion of the Creator of the Universe' (*H.E.*, VIII, 4, 2). And Lactantius writes (*De Mort. Persecut.*, 10): 'By written orders to the superintendents he ordered that even ordinary soldiers should be compelled to offer the wicked sacrifices, in order that those who did not obey should be removed from military service.' So even private soldiers were affected. Care has been taken to find, in the Acta Martyrum and in the Martyrologies, the names of the military martyrs: and their number is great.

The most memorable recorded case of Roman soldiers condemned to death because of their Christian faith is that of the Forty Martyrs, whose feast is kept in the Latin and in the Greek Church on March 10. These forty young soldiers, victims of the persecution of Licinius in A.D. 316, were condemned to die by lying naked throughout the night on a frozen pond at Sebaste in Armenia. All but one of them endured to the end, in spite of the warm bath which was kept ready for them, if they would renounce their religion. One of their guards, admiring their constancy and seeing a vision of angels bearing thirty-nine crowns, shouted out that he too would be a Christian, tore off his clothes and joined the other martyrs in their passion. A great devotion to these martyrs—almost the last to suffer before the general adoption of Christianity as the official religion of the Empire and the army—sprang up in the Church.[1]

Other military martyrs of this period who have exercised a powerful influence upon Christian devotion and art are St. George, patron of England, and St. Sebastian.

Conclusions

The three hundred years covered by this chapter were an age rather of problems than of solutions.

A. Yet one principle at least has been established : and it is of far more than historical interest.

It is that the non-Christian or even anti-Christian character of the state, or rather of the rulers who determine its action, does not absolve Christians from the full responsibilities of citizenship nor justify indifference on their part concerning the right or wrong of national acts. We say national acts ; for there is no intrinsic difference between the acts of a pagan emperor of the second century and those of the Government of the Lay State in the twentieth. To the civil authority, Christian or non-Christian, Christian citizens will ever owe an unmistakable debt of obedience—for all authority is from God : in it and in its actions they will ever have a proprietary interest : '*Noster est magis Cæsar, ut a Deo constitutus.*'

B. In the second place it is, in itself, permissible for

[1] (See the Lessons in the 2nd Nocturn of the Feast in editions of the Breviary prior to the last revision, and the magnificent commemorative sermons of St. Gregory of Nyssa on these martyrs in the *Patrologia Græca*, Vol. 46, Col. 749 *et seq.*, Col. 773 *et seq.*)

Christians to serve as soldiers. The blood of so many soldier-martyrs has established a doctrine more powerful than the purist theory of the pacifist philosopher. That doctrine is that the Christian fulfils a duty to God in the person of those who, in His name, wield authority over the state, by assuming physically and personally the responsibilities, hardships and dangers of resisting attacks, internal or external, upon the order of the state.

These two conclusions are of the first importance for the future of our study. For were Christians to be indifferent to the acts of non-Christian Governments, there could be no Christian contribution to the science of international ethics in a society of non-Christian or largely non-Christian states—as, for instance, to-day. Were war and consequently participation in war to be utterly condemned—as by Tertullian—Christian thought could contribute nothing to the task of limiting, circumscribing and directing physical force in the service of Moral Right; which is the greater part, if not the whole, of the modern international problem.

C. Military obedience—and the whole subservience to the public ends of the state which it exemplifies—can never be unconditional. Whenever there is collision between the two duties, rendering to God the things that are God's must take precedence over rendering to Cæsar his due. Only when Cæsar himself—Emperor or King, President or Cabinet—puts first his duty to God in all his public acts, will the danger of that collision pass. And in what did the deordination of loyalties consist, which in this first age the Christian soldier was bound at the cost of life itself to eschew? In the idolatry of the Emperor. For Emperor may we not read State, People, Nation? First lesson in the limits of sovereignty.

D. There remains, no wit lessened by the conclusion that Christians may be soldiers, an insuperable, fundamental Christian hatred of war. It is an evil (consequence, as later theologians will conclude, of the inevitable fact of Sin) which can only reluctantly be admitted as a necessary evil. In this very reluctance, in the very sadness with which the Christian is bound to admit its permissibility, lie the seeds of that future doctrine of war as the last resort, of the strict conditions with which its justification was hedged about, of the long endeavour—still far from achievement—to devise bloodless means for the vindication of national rights and the solution of international quarrels.

CHAPTER III

CIVIC DUTIES

THE official toleration of Christianity throughout the Empire was proclaimed by Constantine immediately after the victory of the Milvian Bridge in October, 312, and confirmed by him, jointly with the Tetrarch Licinius, in the famous Edict of Milan in 313. In those parts of the Roman world over which Constantine held effective sway, the tendency was now to regard soldiering not merely as something morally permissible, but as a sacred duty. Yet in the East the Christian soldier was still, as we have seen, to be the object of savage persecution from Licinius who, in breach of his word, defied Constantine and openly professed paganism. The Church for a time had to direct the consciences of the faithful under both régimes. This fact is the key to the solution of a curious dilemma presented by the apparently conflicting Canons of two Ecclesiastical Councils within eleven years of one another.

The Third Canon of the First Council of Arles in 314, at which, according to Hefele, 'all the provinces of the Empire of Constantine were represented,'[1] decreed '*ut qui in pace arma projicient excommunicentur.*' 'Those who throw down their arms in peace time are to be excommunicated.' Upon which has arisen a lively controversy. Some could not bring themselves to believe that the Church, who but a little time before had—through the eyes of venerated moralists—looked askance at all military service, could go so far as to exclude from the Mystical Body of Christ those who abandoned the military life in time of peace. To soften the condemnation of the Canon, '*in bello*' was coolly

[1] *Histoire des Conciles :* French Edition, edited by a Benedictine of Farnborough, p. 274.

substituted for '*in pace*' : .it is found in one manuscript of antiquity. But the weight of criticism is against this reading. Others, taking the text as it is, translated *projicere* to mean not 'throw away' but '*arma conjicere in alium*' ('throw spears at people'). But this is to twist the Latin out of all relation to the plain meaning. Others again, developing this idea, read the Canon to mean a condemnation of gladiatorial combats. It seems hard to evade the plain sense of the words, adopted by Migne and other authorities, that soldiers were forbidden to desert from their service in the army during periods of peace under pain of spiritual censures. Such an ordinance would seem natural enough from a consideration of the political circumstances. The Christian legionaries of Italy and the western provinces who had served under Constantine might feel that their work was done now that the Empire was Christian, now that the '*beata tranquillitas*,' which they found inscribed on the very coins with which they were paid, had been attained. Why should they any longer endure the discipline of the camp? The Emperor, however, and the Bishops, filled with devotion to him as they seem to have been, would know well that the needs of internal order, the danger of barbarian attack, and the threatened defection of the eastern provinces, all pointed to the necessity of preserving a loyal and efficient army.

In any case this positive reinforcement and sanctification of the military oath of obedience by ecclesiastical authority marks an important stage in the evolution of a Christian code of civic duties.

The Great Œcumenical Council of Niçæa in 325, opened by the Emperor Constantine in person—unbaptized as he still was—adopted a Canon which seems to express an utterly different spirit. It was after the main debates, in which the Arians were condemned and the famous Symbol drawn up, that the Bishops met again and proceeded to adopt 'twenty canons upon ecclesiastical discipline.' The Twelfth Canon reads as follows:

> They who, answering the call of grace, have first proclaimed their faith and abandoned the soldier's belt, but who afterwards, like dogs returning to their vomit, go so far as to give money

and presents to be readmitted into the army,—these must remain three years among the *audientes* (2nd degree of penance) and ten among the *substrati* (3rd degree of penance). But for these penitents, care must be taken to study their attitude and the quality of their contrition. Those of them who, in fear and tears, with patience and good works, show by their deeds a sincere desire to return to the fold, may, after accomplishing the time of their penance with the *audientes*, be admitted with those who pray (i.e. to assist at the whole of the liturgy) : and it is within the competence of the Bishop to treat them with even greater mercy, etc.

Read out of its historical context, this Canon of the first Great Council, in an Empire all but officially Christian, could only have one meaning—that military service was wholly incompatible with the Christian faith. But the 10th Canon mentions by name Licinius, enemy alike of Constantine and Christ, whom the Emperor had, only on the eve of the Council, defeated at Chrysopolis. All the canons relating to *lapsi* (lapsed Catholics) refer in the first instance to those who, under physical torture or moral pressure, had renounced Christianity in the territories or forces that had been controlled by Licinius.[1] We have given, in the incident of the Forty Martyrs, an instance of his drastic endeavours to free his army from Christians. It is clearly to that army, enrolment in which involved apostasy, that this disciplinary Canon refers. Either it incorporates, just after the danger had passed, a rule which had been in operation during the actual ascendancy of Licinius, or the actual date of the Canon's adoption must precede that of his condemnation and death which took place in the same year. The context of the Canon makes it clear that the penances proscribed relate to lapses which have taken place in the recent past. If it has any application to the future, it can only apply to acts of enrolment or re-engagement in an army under circumstances similar to those which obtained under Licinius, i.e. in such a way as to involve a denial of Christianity.

These precisions are necessary, for early Councils of the Church had a habit of clothing decisions which refer to

[1] A large proportion of the Bishops present came from those territories.

particular circumstances in the language of universality, and posterity an even more unfortunate habit of quoting such decisions uncritically. No less a person than Pope Innocent I, writing to Victorinus of Rouen, quotes, or rather misquotes, this Canon in such a way as to imply that it refers to military service in general, saying: 'The Synod of Nicæa decreed that if anyone, after the remission of his sins, should wear the belt of secular military service, he must on no account be admitted to be one of the clergy.'[1]

Yet, however confused and chequered was the progress from a condition of things in which the life of the army could with difficulty be dissociated from idolatry, to a condition in which it appeared as the service of true religion, it is certainly the case that the profession of arms came before very long to be honoured by the Church. St. Basil, indeed (A.D. 329–379), retains something of the old rigorous hatred of bloodshed which was destined to be lastingly enshrined in the Catholic tradition '*Ecclesia abhorret a sanguine*' and in the rule of the Canon Law forbidding priests to fight in however just a cause. He is hardly able to conciliate it with the doctrine, beginning to be elucidated, of Just War.

Documents and Commentary

St. Basil. *Epist. CLXXXVIII*, 13, (*P.G.*, *Col.* 682):

As to murders committed in war, our Fathers did not account them to be murders, pardoning, as I understand it, those who fight in the name of good sense and piety. But it is well to advise that those whose hands are not clean from blood, should abstain from Communion alone[2] for a space of three years.

St. John Chrysostom (A.D. 347–407) roundly condemns the sins of which soldiering is the occasion and of which he saw only too many instances.

St. John Chrysostom. *In Matt. Homil.*, *LXI* (*P.G.*, 58, *Col.* 590):

The Saint discourses upon Chapter XVIII, verses 21, 22, of St. Matthew's Gospel. ('Lord, how often shall my

[1] Mgr. Batiffol in his admirable study of this period, which has been closely followed by Goyau, Moncel and others, also quotes this Canon without any indication of its peculiar application.

[2] Not, that is, from assisting at the Mysteries.

brother sin against me and I forgive him? Until seven times? Jesus saith to him: I say unto you not until seven times, but unto seventy times seven.') He has enlarged upon the infinite goodness of God to men. But what return do men make to Him for His mercies?

Every day we violate His laws. Shall I begin with soldiers? Into how many sins do they plunge day by day? They insult, they abuse, they rave, they rejoice in the calamities of others, they are like wolves, they are never without crime any more than one could say that the sea is free from waves. What disease of the mind does not agitate them? With what plague is not their very soul obsessed? For they envy their equals, they seek after vainglory; they defraud avariciously those who are subject to them. . . . They are more harsh than wild beasts. They do nothing for Christ, but everything for their belly, for money, for vainglory. Can their misdeeds be counted in words?

And much more in the same strain.

This condemnation of the soldier's life can, however, hardly be read to mean that the Saint holds the extreme pacifist view of the Gospel precepts. In his homily upon the fifth chapter of St. Matthew he gives a noble exposition of the duty of forgiving, loving and praying for our enemies as the culmination of Christian duty. But he says that '*beati pacifici*' must be understood in the light of the next beatitude (v. 10): 'Blessed are they that suffer persecution for justice sake,' which, he says, Our Lord adds: 'lest you should think that peace is an absolute good.' This blessing is bestowed on those 'who suffer in the cause of virtue and the *protection of others* or of religion.'

To St. John Chrysostom, as we see from his homily (VII) on the First Epistle to Timothy, the only kind of war in the proper sense 'is the ordinary war when the soldiers on our side are attacked by the barbarians'; in which case there seems to be no doubt where the justice lies. The other two kinds of war are civil war and, what to the Saint is far more serious, the warfare of soul and body within man himself.

Now the central point of discussion is no longer the question whether a Christian can be a soldier, already settled in practice, though, as we shall see, to be re-examined and answered in theory at different stages of

Christian history. The public problem of just and unjust wars begins to appear: and the duties of the citizen begin to be examined in a philosophical manner upon the basis of reason. As to the judgement of which wars were, in the concrete, just and which unjust, no doubt seems to have been felt in the early days of the Christian Empire, even when Rome was no longer its political capital, that those wars by which the established order of the Roman World was defended against barbarians or pretenders to the Imperial dignity, were righteous wars. The great campaigns of Constantine against Licinius in Macedonia, the Bosphorus and Asia Minor, to which we have alluded, must have contributed powerfully to fix in the minds of the Church's leaders the notion that to take part in warfare might be a duty, a sacred act. For here was war on what was, for the times, a tremendous scale: and, less remarkable than the familiar duel for power between two rivals, which was politically the occasion of it, was the fact that, for the first time, a great army and a great fleet fought in order to save their fellow-Christians from unjust oppression and the violation of their religious rights.

'*Instinctu Divinitatis justis rempublicam ultus est armis*'—such is the inscription upon the triumphal arch of Constantine at Rome. 'By the inspiration of the Divinity, he avenged the state through the just use of arms.' It would do violence to history to represent this as a Christian inscription: like the non-committal religious pronouncements and official prayers of the greater part of Constantine's reign, and in particular the use of the impersonal terms '*deitas*' and '*divinitas*,' the formula could receive the assent alike of his pagan and of his Christian subjects. But of the fundamental justice of his cause, the latter had no doubt. The *Apostolic Constitutions*, the date of which the critics continue to dispute but which certainly represent what was believed in the middle of the fourth century to be the sense of the Apostles' doctrine, contain the first complete liturgy of the Eucharist, the most sacred part of which had for so long been kept secret through the '*disciplina arcani*.' This liturgy embodies the familiar prayer for the Emperor, on the lines of the passage from St. Paul's First Epistle to

Timothy, but intercession is also made 'ὑπερ παντὸς τοὺ στρατοπέδου,' for the whole army.

Constitutiones Apostolorum (*ed. Funk*), *VIII*, 12, 42 :

Almost immediately after the Consecration and commemoration of the Passion comes the prayer : 'We beseech Thee also, O Lord, for the King and for those in supreme authority and for the whole army, that our business may be blessed with peace, and we, living the whole space of our life in quiet and concord, may glorify Thee through Jesus Christ, our hope.' The army and peace were thus two complementary rather than contradictory ideas in the minds of the authors of the constitutions. Almost exactly the same petition recurs when, after the Bishop has completed the central part of the Canon and said to the people : 'The Peace of God be with you all,' the Deacon resumes his prayers for all sorts and conditions of men (13, 5). It seems that civil and international peace, in the Apostolic tradition, generally found its place next after the welfare and unity of the Church itself in solemn intercessions. Thus in the Gothic Missal (Migne, *Pat. Lat.*, 72, 314) the priest prays : 'Receive, O Lord, the service and honour which we offer Thee in Thy Name, for the peace of Thy Church, for the commemoration of all the Saints, for the purity of Thy priests and ministers and for a state of peace among kings . . .' (*Pro regum pacabilitate*). The same connection of ideas is retained in the Roman Missal between the Consecration and the Communion. 'Mercifully grant us peace in our days' comes in the prayer '*Libera nos*,' which is a continuation of the Lord's Prayer. This is followed by 'May the peace of the Lord be always with you,' recited by the priest as he makes the sign of the Cross with a particle of the sacred Host over the chalice ; 'Lamb of God, who takest away the sins of the world, grant us peace,' and next, the beautiful prayer for peace and unity in the Church which recalls the words of Christ to His Apostles : 'Peace I leave with you, My peace I give unto you.'

This same juxtaposition of ideas is again found in the Postcommunion prayer of the liturgy in the Apostolic Constitutions (15, 4) : 'Keep Thy priests without fault in Thy worship, preserve the kings in peace (τοὺς βασιλεῖς διατήρησον ἐν ἐιρήνη) and the magistrates in justice ; may the weather be calm, may fruits abound, may the whole world be kept in Thy almighty providence. Appease the warlike nations (τὰ ἔθνη τὰ πολεμικὰ πράϋνον) and convert those that stray from Thy way.' In another part of the Constitutions (xxxii, 10) dealing with the *admission of soldiers to Baptism*, St. Paul is quoted as giving the following instruction concerning the granting or refusal of Baptism to soldiers, repeating the words of St. John the Baptist.[1] 'If a soldier comes (to be baptized) let him be taught to do injury to no man, not to calumniate anyone, to be content with his pay. If he obeys these injunctions he is to be admitted, if he refuses he is to be rejected.'

A passage of a letter believed to be by St. Athanasius (A.D. 269–373), *Epistola ad Amunem Monachum*, though lacking in discrimination between the wars which do and those which do not deserve praise, sketches the main lines of what we shall afterwards see to be the all-important doctrine of *intention*, whereby an act, in itself indifferent, is good or bad according to the motive of the agent and the attending circumstances.

St. Athanasius. *Epist. ad Amunem Monachum* (*P.G.*, 26, *Col.* 1173) :

The writer has been treating of the union of the sexes, showing that the same act can be honourable when used, as intended by God, in lawful wedlock for the procreation of children, but otherwise sinful.

Also in other acts, which commonly take place in the course of this life, we find that certain distinctions must be made. Thus it is not permitted to kill : but to kill the enemy in battle is both lawful and worthy of praise. So those who have striven valiantly in war have great rewards presented to them, and monuments erected to celebrate their famous deeds. One and the same thing, then, is unlawful according to one aspect and at one time, but under another aspect and in its right time, is tolerated and allowed.

[1] In the previous and the following Canons, 9 and 11, Baptism is unconditionally forbidden to actors and actresses in theatres, gladiators or musical performers, all who take part in the games, magicians and the like.

The human intelligence cannot be at rest until it has found a rational explanation for conventions and rules of conduct, particularly when, as in the case before us, they are a matter of life and death. So far the texts of the Fathers which we have quoted have drawn their authority from two sources in the main—the Christian revelation to which the Gospels and the other writings of the Apostles bear witness, and the Jewish tradition. But Christianity had now begun to win to itself the best minds of the Empire, the leaders of Roman thought. They did not cease to be Roman in intellectual or in political tradition : all that was consistent with reason and natural law in their philosophy, and therefore consistent with Christianity, they retained so that it became interwoven with Christian thought. The Stoic philosophy which, in its practical consequences, had already led to a beginning of those reforms concerning the treatment of women, slaves and children, for which it is the habit to give Constantine credit, had developed an enlightened notion of private and public duties—and a hierarchy of virtues. The incorporation of these ideas into Christian ethics is an event of no mean importance to our subject. It is to be discerned in the treatise of St. Ambrose (A.D. 340–397), *Of Duties*, from which the following extracts are taken. Here we find not only the 'rationale' of self-preservation and the notion of what can justify war, but the principle of using 'the strength of all for the defence of each,' the merits of self-sacrifice, mutual help, forbearance and other duties arising from human solidarity, which can be said to form the basis of a Christian civic philosophy.

St. Ambrose. *De Officiis, Lib. I, Cap. XXVII,* § 126 *et seq.* :

§ 126. The first fount of duty is prudence. For what is so proper to the notion of duty as giving reverence and attention to the author of it ? And this fount leads to the other virtues : nor can there be justice without prudence, since to determine what is just and what unjust requires no little prudence : the highest error is in both (injustice and imprudence). For 'he who judges the just unjust, and the unjust just, is odious to God. How can acts of justice abound in the imprudent ?' says Solomon. Nor can there be prudence without justice : for dutifulness is the beginning of the knowledge of God. This we see to have been brought down by tradition rather than discovered by the wise : because a sense of duty (*pietas*) is the foundation of all the virtues.

§ 127. Dutifulness binding in justice is owed primarily to God, secondarily to one's country, thirdly to parents, then to all others : and this itself is the second duty of nature. For from the earliest age when reason begins to awake, we love life as a gift of God, then we love our country and parents, then our equals with whom we desire to associate. Hence is born charity which prefers others to itself, not seeking the things which belong to it ; and in this is the beginning of justice.

§ 128. In all living things is born the instinct first of self-preservation, of guarding against harmful things, desiring things which are advantageous such as pasture, and hiding-places where they may shelter from danger and from inclement weather—this is prudence. It follows that all living things are sociable, first with their own species and their like and then with the rest ; thus we see cattle in herds, horses in troops. Like most delights in associating with like—rooks with rooks and, most of all, men with men. What now shall I say of procreation and of offspring or of parental love, in which is to be found the principal kind of justice ?

§ 129. These, and other things, can be virtues in themselves. *For fortitude, which in war preserves the country from the barbarians, or helps the sick at home, or defends one's neighbours from robbers, is full of justice.*

Lib. I, Cap. XXVIII :

§ 135. Therefore by God's will and natural union we ought to help each other to carry on the struggle according to our rank and to pool, so to speak, all our forces : to use the words of scripture, we ought to give help one to another, in diligence, in doing our duty, in money, in works, in every way, that among us the strength of our society may be augmented. And let no one be intimidated in the discharge of duty by fear of danger : but let him command all things whether in adversity or in prosperity. For the holy Moses did not shrink from undertaking dangerous wars for the people of his land. He trembled not before the armies of a most powerful king, nor did he fear the ferocity of barbaric rage : but he put aside all consideration for his own safety that he might render his people their liberty.

De Officiis, I, XXXV :

§ 175. Now let us treat of fortitude which is more excellent than other virtues. It is of two kinds, the one proper to war, the other to civil life. But care for warlike things now seems alien to our duty because we are more intent upon the duty of the soul than of the body : nor is it to arms that the habit of our life is directed, but rather to the business of peace. Yet our fathers, such as Joshua, Hierobaal, Samson and David, won the greatest glory in warfare.

§ 176, 177. Courage is in a sense more excellent than the rest, but it is never a virtue that goes alone. For it cannot commission itself, and there are times when courage without justice is the source of injustice. For the stronger one is the more prompt to oppress the weaker. And I consider that, in the matter of war, care must be taken to see whether the wars are just or unjust. Never did David declare war unless he had first suffered injurious attack.

De Officiis I, XXXVI :

Therefore the glory of courage does not so much consist in the strength of muscles of the body but rather in spiritual virtue, nor is the law of virtue to be found in inflicting injury, but in repelling it from others. For he who does not ward off injury from his comrade, when he is able to, is just as guilty as he who does the injury. Thus holy Moses long since made trial of warlike courage. For when he saw a Hebrew being injured by an Egyptian he leapt to his defence, to such effect that he laid the Egyptian low and hid his body in the sand. And Solomon said also : 'Deliver them that are led to death.' (Proverbs xxiv : 11).[1]

The saying : '*Qui non repellit a socio injuriam, si potest, tam est in vitio quam ille qui facit,*' became an axiom of Christian morality as applicable to war. The thought is to be found in almost the same words in Gratian : it was at the root of the original conception of the Crusades. The duty of intervention to help others against unjust aggression was later defined as an obligation of the law of charity, if not of strict justice. The great Bishop of Milan goes on to declare :

§ 180. And in truth that is rightly called fortitude when anyone conquers his own self : contains his anger ; is weakened and turned from his course by no allurements ; is not perturbed by adversity nor puffed up with success, nor blown about, as by the wind, by the changes and variation of life. . . . This is

[1] The full quotation, a noble epitome of the duty of intervention, is 'Deliver them that are led to death, and those that are drawn to death forbear not to deliver. If thou say : "I have not strength enough," He that seeth into thy heart, He understandeth and nothing deceiveth the keeper of thy soul, and He shall render to a man according to his works.'

true courage which belongs to the athlete of Christ, who does not win the prize, save by a lawful struggle.

Lib. II, Cap. XXX:

§ 155. Let there be peace among you above every desire. Love one another. Nothing is more sweet than charity, nothing more pleasing than peace. And know also that I have loved and cherished you above the rest: as the children of one father you have been united in the love of kinship.

§ 156. Keep to the things that are good and the God of peace and love will be with you in the Lord Jesus: to whom be honour, glory, magnificence and power, with the Holy Ghost for ever and ever. Amen.

A scholarly note by Batiffol is here appended upon the affinities between Cicero and St. Ambrose, which are striking. It emphasizes an important aspect, but one only of the Christian moralist's great work; for instance, in appraising the dictates of Cicero and 'the philosophers' he clearly judges them by the Canon of the Hebrew and Christian scriptures, and in cases where the verdict is favourable he declares with more zeal, surely, than historic justice: 'Where Tully or Panætius or even Aristotle got this from is plain enough.' Actually St. Ambrose made a synthesis of all that was true and useful in the philosophy of his secular studies with the Christian tradition. His treatise must be read as a whole for its richness and the depth of its effect upon ideals of conduct to be appreciated.

Conclusions

To the conclusions which we have drawn in the previous chapters may now be added these:

1. The just use of force is fundamentally a social act. Both the duties of maintaining peace and of mutual assistance against aggression are necessary consequences of the essential sociability of human nature.
2. It is a Christian duty for the soldier to keep his oath of loyalty to the head of the State except he be required by his superior to commit an act against the laws of God.
3. It is just to go to war in defence of one's country.

4. It is a duty to intervene to defend others against injury and aggression, and this for a state is a just cause of war.
5. The obligation to strive for peace and to exercise forbearance and mercy is paramount.

Note on the Ciceronian Origin of St. Ambrose's Doctrine of Duties

Mgr. Batiffol. *L'Eglise et le Droit de Guerre, pp.* 35–37 :

St. Ambrose was a Roman—Roman by race, by culture and even, it must be added, by his career. Bishop and moralist as he was, his ethics were a form of Christianized stoic philosophy. When he wrote his *De Officiis*, the first attempt at a Christian treatise upon Duties, he borrowed from Cicero both the title and the matter of his treatise. Ambrose took from Cicero what he in turn had found in the περὶ καθή κοντος (What is seemly) of the Stoic Panætius, the Platonic classification of the four cardinal virtues. The Saint introduced this classification into Christian ethics, for which it was certainly an acquisition. Ambrose found in Cicero the distinction between the two forms of courage, the military and the civil, with the preference given to the latter.

'The opinion of most people that warlike qualities are to be more highly esteemed than the duties of citizenship ought to be reversed' (Cicero, *De Officiis*, I, 74). Ambrose, who was too much of a Roman to misjudge the soldier's valour, of which, moreover, he recalled the great instances which are to be found in the history of God's chosen people, set upon a higher plane that noble courage, which Cicero had never known, the courage of the martyrs. That was an ingenious or rather a profound thought which removed the old reproach of *inertia* which the Romans had levelled against the spirit of resignation taught in the Gospels.

The dominant virtue is Justice. Following in the steps of Cicero, Ambrose drew a distinction between the injustice which consists in the active perpetration of it and the injustice which consists in failing to defend someone else who is the victim of an injustice. 'There are two sorts of injustice,' we read in Cicero ; 'the one, of those who commit an injury ; the other, of those who do not avert the injury from those against whom it is committed, if they have the power to do so' (*De Officiis*, I, 23). We find this distinction reproduced literally in St. Ambrose. There is no such thing as lawful war without a just cause. Even in wars undertaken for conquest or for glory, Cicero required there to be a just cause. 'Even when empire is the object of the fighting and glory is sought by war, there can be no right ground for waging it except what I have set forth above as just causes of wars' (*de Officiis*, I, 38). Where Cicero has spoken of the enemy, Ambrose spoke of the barbarians ; for a Roman of the fourth century already knew only too well the need of protecting his fatherland against the barbarians.

In the conduct of war itself all the virtues have their part to play—prudence, moderation, temperance, magnanimity—those thoughts of Ambrose were inspired by Cicero, and the very names of the virtues which he employed belong to the vocabulary of the Roman Stoic.

Said Cicero : 'The foundation of Justice is good faith' (C. *de Officiis*, I, 23). Ambrose exactly repeated these words[1] (A. *de Officiis*, I, 29)—from which it will be seen how great was the Saint's dependence upon that philosopher. But Ambrose, like Cicero himself, was an eclectic : he borrowed, or rejected or corrected as he thought best. He knew that good faith (*fides*) was not always enough, but that it needed to be enlightened. So Ambrose completed the theory of justice with that new feature, which marked the emergence of an authority capable of completing with certitude the uncertainties of the Natural Law, and if need be of acting as the arbiter of conflicts. '*Ecclesia autem quædam forma justitiæ est*' (*de Officiis*, I, 29). The Church is, in a certain sense, the determinant of justice. . . .

What then has become of the gospel 'pacifism'? Ambrose would answer this with a distinction which he derived from the Stoic philosophy and which is therein called the distinction between perfect duties and ordinary duties (C. *de Officiis*, I, 8). It is what we call the difference between Precepts and Counsels. It is expressed by Ambrose in definite terms. 'If thou wouldst be perfect, go, sell what thou hast and give to the poor, and follow Me' (Matthew xix : 21). These words of the Divine Master revealed perfection without imposing it as a duty. And it is possible not to desire to be perfect. *A fortiori* one has no right to impose perfection on others. In the evangelic perfection there is a voluntary renunciation of a natural right. Founded, as it is, upon the Natural Law, the State as a state could not make that renunciation without betraying the common good which is the end for which it exists. Nor indeed was it to the State that the Saviour preached perfection, but to the individual. The more the Gospel penetrated the Roman social life and the Roman Empire, the more the necessary requirements of the Natural Law were perceived. In so far, therefore, as it constitutes justice, social and political necessity established itself side by side with the spirit of evangelical renunciation in Catholic doctrine, which is no Tolstoyan instinct but a work of Reason.

[1] But with a different meaning.

PART II

THE ETHICS OF WAR

CHAPTER IV

THE AUGUSTINIAN DOCTRINE OF WAR

ST. AUGUSTINE, Bishop of Hippo (A.D. 354–430), is the great co-ordinator of Christian doctrine upon peace and war. Later writers have codified his thoughts, have developed this point or that or have defined the application of his judgements. Others have treated of certain factors of human society which were unknown to him, or of the mutual rights and duties of men and nations to which new political conditions have given rise. But none, in the orthodox Christian tradition, have altered the main body of teaching which he elaborated.

Nor has any substantial point of his doctrine been set aside from the main tradition as it developed, save perhaps his insistence upon the direct intervention of God to ordain wars, upon which Monceaux's observation, reprinted in this chapter, deserves attention. Students of the Fathers will remark a far more categorical tone in St. Augustine's vindication of the theocracy of the Old Testament than is to be found for instance in Origen's *Contra Celsum.* A Christian empire and a Christian army defending the nucleus of the civilized world against heretics and vandals created an atmosphere more favourable to the conception of a holy war waged by a Chosen People than did a pagan empire persecuting a Christian minority. The famous pages of the *Contra Faustum,* which we cite and which contain the strongest statements upon the divine authorization of war, were written when the Bishop was a comparatively young man—they are indeed his first recorded essay upon the subject of war. They are a part of a vigorous controversial reply to a protagonist of the Manichæan sect (to which Augustine himself had once belonged) who had written a thesis attacking the truth and worth of the Old Testament. A very different spirit inspires the letter written by the Saint in his old age to Count Darius. A tendency to find an alternative justification for the wars of Moses and Joshua in the violation of natural right and the law of nations is already apparent in his commentary on the Book of Numbers contained in *Quæstiones in Heptateuchum* written about the year 419.

But this main belief has outlasted the controversies and vicissitudes of Papacy and Empire, the rise and fall of the crusading spirit, the disruption of Christendom and the political development of recent centuries—namely, that war and peace are in the hand of God, that in His grand design He may will or permit war as a scourge to correct the overweening pride of men and punish the violation of His laws. Who could not have emphasized this fact in the face of the great barbarian invasions and the sack of Rome by the Goths? Thus Benedict XV, in his first appeal to the Catholics of the whole world :

> We exhort and even implore . . . all the sons of the Church, especially those in Holy Orders, to persevere, earnestly vieing with one another, privately in humble prayer, publicly in the united petitions of crowded congregations to beg that God, mindful of His mercy, may lay aside this scourge of anger with which He inflicts on the people the penalty of their sins.[1]

The Old Testament conception of wars willed by God had a powerful effect upon the history of Europe. It is the conception of a holy war ; and it was applied to wars enjoined by God's Vice-Regent on earth for the defence of his faithful peoples against the infidels. A typical example of a papal call to arms against the encroaching Moslems in the early Middle Ages is appended to this chapter, together with an equally typical example of the appeals of the modern Papacy for a wholly spiritual crusade against the enemies of the Christian name. During the nine intervening centuries the conception of war as the instrument of religion has slowly but definitely disappeared from the Christian philosophy. But, in the interests of historical accuracy, it

[1] September 8, 1914.

is necessary to give its proper prominence to St. Augustine's doctrine of wars commanded by God and the powerful effects for good and ill of its ready use and abuse, in an age when the Emperor and, even more, the Pope claimed to be and were universally regarded as Ambassadors of God. It was a time when the threat to the *respublica Christiana* seemed no less terrible or tangible than the threat of the Philistines to the Chosen People of old. It is important to observe how far not only political events but Catholic experience have compelled a change, through many different stages, to a wholly spiritual conception of papal leadership and of the Church militant.

That change is itself a victory for St. Augustine. The seeming conflict of ideas is a conflict not of principles but of emphasis. And the true emphasis in the Saint's writings as a whole is far less upon righteous battles than upon peace and mercy, forbearance and long suffering. It is by his praise of efforts to compose wars by reason; his exposition of peace as the greatest good of this life, proper outcome of man's natural sociability; his definition of that peace as the tranquillity of order; his linking of human tranquillity as by a mystic ladder to the peace of the Heavenly City—it is by these contributions to the spiritual heritage of men that St. Augustine is now remembered. If his vindication of holy war had a potent influence upon the conduct of nations, still more had his grand conception of the City of God. Of Charles the Great we read: '*Delectabatur et libris sancti Augustini, præcipueque his que De Civitate Dei prætitulati sunt.*'[1] Here was the inspiration of that great unifying force which imprinted upon the European races a conviction that they were part of a single whole, a conviction so deep, so nearly akin to nature that they cannot abandon the endeavour, as often renewed as it has been disappointed, to achieve a united political society—*naturam furca expellas*, one might almost repeat of the ideal of a League of Nations, *simul usque redibit.* 'It is hardly too much to say that the Holy Empire was built upon the foundation of *The City of God.*'[2]

[1] Eginhard, *Vita Karoli*, Cap. XXIV.
[2] Lord Bryce, *The Holy Roman Empire*, p. 73.

The historical method has served its purpose as the means best suited to explain the development of doctrine upon peace and war in the first four Christian centuries. Our subject has now become too complex for that method. Those parts of *The City of God* which are primarily concerned with peace as an organic whole will be found in the chapter devoted to peacemaking. Here only, with other relevant passages, are the texts relating to the ethics of war with an appreciation of them by a great Augustinian scholar.

They are followed by the Canons from the *Decretal of Gratian* upon the same subject : the majority, it will be seen, are directly taken from St. Augustine. Next, St. Thomas's chapter on war from the *Summa Theologica* will show how the chief of the Schoolmen accepted and restated, with his customary precision, the doctrine of the same master. A large number of quotations from other mediæval scholastics could be added, from the works of *St. Raymund of Pennafort*, the great canonist by order of whom, as General of the Dominican Order, St. Thomas wrote his *Summa contra Gentiles*, up to those of *Carletti and Joannes Lupus* who mark the beginning of that different age to which our next chapter is devoted. We have not, however, found in these writers any new element nor any line of thought which is absent from the works of the Fathers and St. Thomas or which is not developed more clearly by the Neo-scholastics of the sixteenth and seventeenth centuries. A summary of the teaching of these theologians and canonists by a qualified modern author is added for the benefit of students of these rare books : it will be seen to contain the necessary references to those parts of each which treat of the conditions of just war.

I. THE WORKS OF ST. AUGUSTINE

St. Augustine. *Contra Faustum* (*Patrologia Latina*, *t.* 42), *Lib. XII*, *Cap. LXXIV* (*date* A.D. 398). *The wars of the Old Testament : what is to be blamed in war : war sometimes required by justice : military service justified : soldiers not murderers but ministers of law.*

Wherefore, if man at last in his hardness of heart and in the perversity and depravity of his will realizes that it is of importance, whether anything be attained by human cupidity or fear or whether by obedience to the commands of God, who knows what, when and whom He commands or permits, let him not be surprised or horrified by the wars made by Moses. For in these he followed the divine will, not in anger but in obedience. Nor did God rage when He commanded those wars: but He gave what was due to those that had earned it and put fear into them that deserved it. For what is blamed in war? Is it the death of those who must die sooner or later, but who give up their lives to bring peace by overcoming guilty men? To blame this is the cry of cowards, not of religious people. The desire for harming, the cruelty of avenging, an unruly and implacable animosity, the rage of rebellion, the lust of domination and the like—these are the things which are to be blamed in war: and often to punish these things justly wars are waged by the good against those who resist with violence, either by God's will or at some legitimate command when, in the order of human things, that order constrains men in justice to command such a thing or to obey. To the soldiers who came to him to be baptized, saying: 'What shall we do?' John might have replied: 'Lay down your arms, depart from that military service: strike no one, wound no one, throw down no one.' But knowing that because they did this in military service, they were not murderers but ministers of the law, not avengers of their own wrongs but defenders of the public safety, he said to them: 'Do violence to no man, neither calumniate any man and be content with your pay' (Luke iii: 14). But since the Manichæans are accustomed to blaspheme John, let them listen to the Lord, Jesus Christ Himself, ordering to be rendered to Cæsar this pay which John declares to be sufficient for the soldier: 'Render,' He says, 'to Cæsar the things which are Cæsar's; and to God the things which are God's' (Matthew xxii: 21). And taxes are levied for this purpose, that pay may be found for the necessary soldiers. He justly praised the faith of the centurion who said: 'I am a man constituted in command, having under me soldiers; and I say to this man, Go, and he goeth; and to another, Come, and he cometh; and to my servant, Do this, and he doeth it' (Matthew viii: 9, 10). He did not command that soldier to desert. But it would be long to discuss just and unjust wars and it is not necessary now.

Cap. LXXV. War to be just must be by God's command, or declared by competent authority: responsibility for the justice of war rests not on the soldier but the ruler.

It is important to know from what causes and by whose authority men take up war: the natural order of mortal things, ordained for peace, demands that the authority for making war and inflicting punishments should rest with the ruler. In obeying warlike commands soldiers should have an eye to peace and the common good. War begun at God's command is certainly waged justly in order to frighten or break down or subjugate human pride : it is not waged for human cupidity, it cannot be contrary to the incorruptible God or to His saints : who are also pleased by the exercise of patience, the humbling of the proud, the bearing of paternal discipline. Nor has anyone power over soldiers except him to whom power is given from above. There is no power except from the command or permission of God (Romans xiii : 1). A just man can fight justly for maintaining public peace at the command even of a sacrilegious man, when what is commanded him is either not contrary to God's precept or not certainly against it ; thus although the king may commit sin in giving the order, the soldier obeying the order to fight is innocent. How much more innocently therefore are wars waged when God commands, for He can command nothing evil as everyone who serves Him knows.

Cap. LXXVI. The author seeks to reconcile the wars of the Old Testament with the teaching of the New :

If it is thought that God cannot command wars to be waged because afterwards our Lord Jesus Christ says : 'I say to you not to resist evil : but if one strike thee on thy right cheek, turn to him also the other' (Matthew v : 39), it ought to be understood that this disposition is not in the body but in the heart. For in the soul is the holy dwelling of virtue, which dwelt also in our ancient and just fathers. But the order of their times necessitated such a dispensation and distribution of things, that earthly goods (which were held by human kingdoms and by victories over enemies, by whom the power of the wicked and the worship of idols were spread through the world) seemed only to belong to the power and judgement of the one true God. Hence the Old Testament kept the secret of the kingdom of heaven, which was to be made clear when the time came,[1] by terrestrial promises and, as it were, wrapped in a cloud. But when the fulness of time came in which the New Testament should be revealed, veiled in the figures of the old, it was to be shown that there was another life for which this life is to be spurned and another kingdom for which all the adversities of earthly kingdoms should be patiently borne. Hence God is pleased to be testified to by the confession, passion and death of the martyrs, or witnesses as they are called in Latin.

[1] This notion of the law of the Old Testament, as a stage which is past and has given place to fuller revelation, may be compared with the corresponding passage in Origen's *Contra Celsum* (pp. 41, 42).

ST. AUGUSTINE. *De Civitate Dei,*[1] *Lib. I, Cap. XXI* (A.D. 413–423). *'Thou shalt not kill' not applicable to those acting in obedience to lawful authority.*

However, there are some exceptions made by the divine authority to its own law, that men may not be put to death. These exceptions are of two kinds, being justified either by a general law, or by a special commission granted for a time to some individual. And in this latter case, he to whom authority is delegated, and who is but the sword in the hand of him who uses it, is not himself responsible for the death he deals. And, accordingly, they who have waged war in obedience to the divine command, or in conformity with His laws have represented in their persons the public justice or the wisdom of government, and in this capacity have put to death wicked men; such persons have by no means violated the commandment: 'Thou shalt not kill.'

Lib. III, Cap. XXVI. The horror of war: the devils alone are the gainers.

In the Punic wars, again, when victory hung so long in the balance between the two kingdoms, when two powerful nations were straining every nerve and using all their resources against one another, how many smaller kingdoms were crushed, how many large and flourishing cities were demolished, how many states were overwhelmed and ruined, how many districts and lands far and near were desolated! How often were the victors on either side vanquished! What multitudes of men, both of those actually in arms and of others, were destroyed! What huge navies, too, were crippled in engagements, or were sunk by every kind of marine disaster! Were we to attempt to recount or mention these calamities, we should become writers of history. At that period Rome was mightily perturbed, and resorted to vain and ludicrous expedients. On the authority of the Sybilline books, the secular games were reappointed, which had been inaugurated a century before, but had faded into oblivion in happier times. The games consecrated to the infernal gods were also renewed by the pontiffs; for they, too, had sunk into disuse in the better times. And no wonder; for when they were renewed, the great abundance of dying men made all hell rejoice at its riches, and give itself up to sport: for certainly the ferocious wars, and disastrous quarrels, and bloody victories—now on one side and now on the other—though most calamitous to men, afforded great sport and a rich banquet to the devils.

[1] Roberts and Donaldson's translation.

Lib. IV, Cap. IV. 'Kingdoms without justice, how like they are unto thievish purchases.' [1]

Set justice aside then, and what are kingdoms but fair thievish purchases? because what are thieves' purchases but little kingdoms? for in thefts, the hands of the underlings are directed by the commander, the confederacy of them is sworn together, and the pillage is shared by the law amongst them. And if those ragamuffins grow up to be able enough to keep forts, build habitations, possess cities and conquer adjoining nations, then their Government is no more called thievish, but graced with the eminent name of a kingdom, given and gotten, not because they have left their practices, but because that now they may use them without danger of law: for elegant and excellent was that pirate's answer to the great Macedonian Alexander who had taken him: the king asking him how he durst molest the seas, so he replied with a free spirit: 'How darest thou molest the whole world? But because I do it with a little ship only, I am called a thief: thou, doing it with a great navy, art called an emperor.'

Lib. IV, Cap. VI. Imperialism condemned: conquest for its own sake unjust: small states more natural than a great empire.

Justinus, who wrote Greek or rather foreign history in Latin, and briefly, like Trogus Pompeius whom he followed, begins his work thus: 'In the beginning of the affairs of peoples and nations the government was in the hands of kings, who were raised to the height of this majesty not by courting the people, but by the knowledge good men had of their moderation. The people were held bound by no laws; the decisions of the princes were instead of laws. It was the custom to guard rather than to extend the boundaries of the empire; and kingdoms were kept within the bounds of each ruler's native land. Ninus, King of the Assyrians, first of all, through new lust of empire, changed the old and, as it were, ancestral custom of nations. He first made war on his neighbours, and wholly subdued as far as to the frontiers of Libya the nations as yet untrained to resist.' But to make war on your neighbours, and thence to proceed to others, and through mere lust of dominion to crush and subdue people who do you no harm, what else is this to be called than robbery on the grand scale?

[1] The sedate translation of Roberts and Donaldson has been employed for the other quotations from the *City of God*. I cannot forbear to use for one passage the rollicking seventeenth-century English of Healey.

Lib. IV, Cap. XV. On the same theme.

Let them ask, then, whether it is quite fitting for good men to rejoice in extended empire. For the iniquity of those with whom just wars are carried on favours the growth of a kingdom, which would certainly have been small if the peace and justice of neighbours had not by any wrong provoked the carrying on of war against them; and human affairs being thus more happy, all kingdoms would have been small, rejoicing in neighbourly concord; and thus there would have been very many kingdoms of nations in the world, as there are very many houses of citizens in a city. Therefore, to carry on war and extend a kingdom over wholly subdued nations seems to bad men to be felicity, to good men necessity. But because it would be worse that the injurious should rule over those who are more righteous, therefore even that is not unsuitably called felicity. But beyond doubt it is greater felicity to have a good neighbour at peace, than to conquer a bad one by making war. Your wishes are bad, when you desire that one whom you hate or fear should be in such a condition that you can conquer him.

Lib. XIX, Cap. VII. The order of human societies: international unity achieved by force a doubtful blessing: Roman wars of annexation condemned: the necessity of just wars to be lamented.

After the state or city comes the world, the third circle of human society—the first being the home, and the second the city. And the world, as it is larger, so it is fuller of dangers, as the greater sea is the more dangerous. And here, in the first place, man is separated from man by the difference of languages. For if two men, each ignorant of the other's language, meet, and are not compelled to pass, but, on the contrary, to remain in company, dumb animals, though of different species, would more easily hold intercourse than they, human beings though they be. For their common nature is no help to friendliness when they are prevented by diversity of language from conveying their sentiments to one another; so that a man would more readily hold intercourse with his dog than with a foreigner. But the Imperial city has endeavoured to impose on subject nations not only her yoke, but her language, as a bond of peace, so that interpreters, far from being scarce, are numberless. This is true; and how many great wars, how much slaughter and bloodshed, have provided this unity! And though these are past, the end of these miseries has not yet come. For though there have never been wanting, nor are yet wanting, hostile nations beyond the empire, against whom wars have been and are waged, yet supposing there were no such nations, the very extent of the empire itself has produced wars of a more obnoxious description—social and civil wars—and with these the whole race has been agitated, either by the actual conflict or the fear of a renewed outbreak. If I attempted to give an adequate description of these manifold disasters, these stern and lasting necessities, though I am quite unequal to the task, what limit could I set? But, say they, the wise man will wage just wars. As if he would not all the rather lament the necessity of just wars, if he remembers that he is a man; for if they were not just he would not wage them, and would therefore be delivered from all wars. For it is the wrongdoing of the opposing party which compels the wise man to wage just wars; and this wrongdoing, even though it gave rise to no war, would still be matter of grief to man because it is man's wrongdoing. Let everyone, then, who thinks with pain on all these great evils, so horrible, so ruthless, acknowledge that this is misery. And if anyone either endures or thinks of them without mental pain, his is a more miserable plight still, for he thinks himself happy because he has lost all human feeling.

Yet St. Augustine had written in the Eighteenth Book (Chap. XXII): 'There was founded the State of Rome, through which it pleased God to subdue the whole world and to pacify it within a single political and legal society.' The Roman Peace was part of the divine plan, and he accepts it, not without the pride of the patrician. But this does not alter his remarkable independence of mind compared with the uncritical acceptance of the Empire by the earlier Fathers; his denunciation of the wars of ambition which extended Roman rule, and his frankly expressed doubt whether a series of small states would not be more conducive to justice and peace than a great empire.

St. Augustine. *Quæst. in Heptateuchum, VI,* 10*a* (A.D. 419). *Justice of war the paramount consideration.*

The just man should have no concern, upon this matter, than this—Is the war which is to be undertaken a just one? Has he the right to make war: for not everyone has this right?

Ibid. (*b*):

Just wars are usually defined as those which avenge injuries, when the nation or city against which warlike action is to be directed has neglected either to punish wrongs committed by its own citizens or to restore what has been unjustly taken by it. Further, that kind of war is undoubtedly just which God Himself ordains.

St. Augustine. *Letters :*

The objection to the precept of Christ 'Not to resist evil,' as being inconsistent with the safety of the State and the duties of citizenship has been put before St. Augustine by Marcellinus (Letter 136), in a letter containing a number of questions from his friend Volusianus. The Saint replies separately to each. In his letter to Marcellinus he deals at more length with this objection than in the book *Contra Faustum* written fourteen years before, and upon somewhat different grounds ; for he stresses the positive civic and political value of the spirit of love and forbearance which inspires the precept.

Ep. ad Marcellinum (138), *II*, 9 (A.D. 412) :

. . . You have added that they said that the Christian doctrine and preaching were in no way consistent with the duties and rights of citizens, because among its precepts we find : 'Render to no man evil for evil,' and 'Whosoever shall smite thee on one cheek, turn to him the other also ; and if any man take away thy coat, let him have thy cloak also ; and whosoever will compel thee to go a mile with him, go with him twain '—all of which are affirmed to be contrary to the duties and rights of citizens ; for who would submit to have anything taken from him by an enemy or forbear from retaliating the evils of war upon an invader who ravaged a Roman province ? To these and similar statements of persons speaking slightingly, or perhaps I should rather say speaking as inquirers regarding the truth, I might have given a more elaborate answer, were it not that the persons with whom the discussion is carried on are men of liberal education. In addressing such, why should we prolong the debate, and not rather begin by inquiring for ourselves how it was possible that the Republic of Rome was governed and aggrandized from insignificance and poverty to greatness and opulence by men who, when they had suffered wrong, would rather pardon than punish the offender ; or how Cicero addressing Cæsar, the greatest statesman of his time, said, in praising his character, that he was wont to forget nothing but the wrongs which were done to him ? For in this Cicero spoke either praise or flattery : if he spoke praise, it was because he knew Cæsar to be such as he affirmed ; if he spoke flattery, he showed that the chief magistrate of a commonwealth ought to do such things as he falsely commended in Cæsar. But what is 'not rendering evil for evil,' but refraining from the passion of revenge—in other words, choosing, when one has suffered wrong, to pardon rather than to punish the offender, and to forget nothing but the wrongs done to us ?

10. When these things are read in their own authors, they are received with loud applause ; they are regarded as the

record and recommendation of virtues in the practice of which the Republic deserved to hold sway over so many nations, because its citizens preferred to pardon rather than punish those who wronged them. But when the precept: 'Render to no man evil for evil,' is read as given by divine authority, and when, from the pulpits of our churches, this wholesome counsel is published in the midst of our congregation, or, as we might say, in places of instruction open to all, of both sexes and of all ages and ranks, our religion is accused as an enemy to the Republic! Yet, were our religion listened to as it deserves, it would establish, consecrate, strengthen and enlarge the commonwealth in a way beyond all that Romulus, Numa, Brutus and all the other men of renown in Roman history achieved. For what is a republic but a *commonwealth*? Therefore its interests are common to all; they are the interests of the State. Now what is a state but a multitude of men bound together by some bond of concord? In one of their own authors we read: 'What was a scattered and unsettled multitude had by concord become in a short time a state. . . .'

11. But who, even though he be a stranger to our religion, is so deaf as not to know how many precepts enjoining concord, not invented by the discussions of men, but written with the authority of God, are continually read in the churches of Christ? For this is the tendency even of those precepts which they are much more willing to debate than to follow: 'That to him who smites us on one cheek we should offer the other to be smitten; to him who would take away our coat we should give our cloak also; and that with him who compels us to go one mile we should go twain.' For these things are done only that a wicked man may be overcome by kindness, or rather that the evil which is in the wicked man may be overcome by good, and that the man may be delivered from the evil—not from any evil that is external and foreign to himself, but from that which is within and is his own, under which he suffers loss more severe and fatal than could be inflicted by the cruelty of any enemy from without. He, therefore, who is overcoming evil by good, submits patiently to the loss of temporal advantages, that he may show how those things, through excessive love of which the other is made wicked, deserve to be despised when compared with faith and righteousness; in order that so the injurious person may learn from him whom he wronged what is the true nature of the things for the sake of which he committed the wrong, and may be won back with sorrow for his sin to that concord, than which nothing is more serviceable to the State, being overcome not by the strength of one passionately resenting, but by the good nature of one patiently bearing wrong. . . .

14. These precepts concerning patience ought to be always retained in the habitual discipline of the heart, and the bene-

volence which prevents the recompensing of evil for evil must be always fully cherished in the disposition. At the same time, many things must be done in correcting with a certain benevolent severity, even against their own wishes, men whose welfare rather than their wishes it is our duty to consult; and the Christian Scriptures have most unambiguously commended this virtue in a magistrate. For in the correction of a son, even with some sternness, there is assuredly no diminution of a father's love; yet in the correction, that is done which is received with reluctance and pain by one whom it seems necessary to heal by pain. And on this principle, if the commonwealth observe the precepts of the Christian religion, even its wars themselves will not be carried on without the benevolent design that, after the resisting nations have been conquered, provision may be more easily made for enjoying in peace the mutual bond of piety and justice. . . .

15. For if the Christian religion condemned wars of every kind, the command given in the Gospel to soldiers asking counsel as to salvation would rather be to cast away their arms, and withdraw themselves wholly from military service; whereas the word spoken to such was: 'Do violence to no man, neither accuse any falsely, and be content with your wages,' the command to be content with their wages manifestly implying no prohibition to continue in the service. Wherefore, let those who say that the doctrine of Christ is incompatible with the State's well-being, give us an army composed of soldiers such as the doctrine of Christ requires them to be; let them give us such subjects, such husbands and wives, such parents and children, such masters and servants, such kings, such judges—in fine, even such tax-payers and tax-gatherers as the Christian religion has taught that men should be, and then let them dare to say that it is adverse to the State's well-being; yea, rather, let them no longer hesitate to confess that this doctrine, if it were obeyed, would be the salvation of the commonwealth.

St. Augustine, consulted by men who were themselves responsible for the command of armies and the defence of provinces, did not hesitate to give a practical application of his doctrine in reply to the cases of conscience which they laid before him. To Count Boniface, Governor of Northern Africa, involved in a series of conflicts, ultimately unsuccessful for him—with the barbarians, he wrote: 'Do not think that it is impossible for anyone to please God while engaged in military service.' Had not God given testimony to David, the warrior king, and to the centurion of whom the Lord said: 'Amen, amen, I say to you, I have not found so great faith in all Israel'? But the intention of the ruler and soldier must ever be to please God and to seek peace, even if in the last resort fighting is a necessary means to that end.

Ep. ad Bonifacium, 189, *VI* (*c.* A.D. 418):

Think, then, of this first of all, when you are arming for the battle, that even your bodily strength is a gift of God; for, considering this, you will not employ the gift of God against God. For, if when faith is pledged, it is to be kept even with the enemy against whom the war is waged, how much more with the friend for whom the battle is fought! Peace should be the object of your desire; war should be waged only as a necessity, and waged only that God may by it deliver men from that necessity and preserve them in peace. For peace is not sought in order to the kindling of war, but war is waged in order that peace may be obtained. Therefore, even in waging war, cherish the spirit of the peacemaker, that, by conquering those whom you attack, you may lead them back to the advantages of peace; for Our Lord says: 'Blessed are the peacemakers; for they shall be called the children of God.' If, however, peace among men be so sweet, as procuring temporal safety, how much sweeter is that peace with God which procures for men the eternal felicity of the angels! Let necessity, therefore, and not your will, slay the enemy who fights against you. As violence is used towards him who rebels and resists, so mercy is due to the vanquished or to the captive, especially in the case in which future troubling of the peace is not to be feared.

The last letter of St. Augustine on the subject of peace and war was written in 429, the year before he died, to Darius, an officer in the service of the Empress Placidia and a friend of Count Boniface. This short letter is entirely devoted to congratulating Darius who had just negotiated a truce with the Vandals: it expresses the hierarchy of ideas which completes the doctrine of the Saint on this subject: it has provided throughout the subsequent Christian ages an inspiration for the movement to honour and advance the cause of international arbitration.

Ep. ad Darium, 229:

1. Your character and rank I have learned from my holy brothers and co-bishops, Urbanus and Novatus. The former of these became acquainted with you near Carthage, in the town of Hilari, and more recently in the town of Sicca; the latter at Sitifis. Through them it has come to pass that I cannot regard

you as unknown to me. For though my bodily weakness and the chill of age do not permit me to converse with you personally, it cannot on this account be said that I have not seen you; for the conversation of Urbanus, when he kindly visited me, and the letters of Novatus, so described to me the features, not of your face but of your mind, that I have seen you, and have seen you with all the more pleasure, because I have seen not the outward appearance but the hidden man. These features of your character are joyfully seen both by us, and through the mercy of God by yourself also, as in a mirror in the holy Gospel in which it is written in words uttered by Him who is truth: 'Blessed are the peacemakers; for they shall be called the children of God.'

2. Those warriors are indeed great and worthy of singular honour, not only for their consummate bravery, but also (which is a higher praise) for their eminent fidelity, by whose labours and dangers, along with the blessing of divine protection and aid, enemies previously unsubdued are conquered, peace obtained for the State, and provinces reduced to submission. But it is a higher glory still to slay war itself with the word, than men with the sword, and to procure or maintain peace by peace, not by war. For those who fight, if they are good men, doubtless seek for peace; nevertheless it is through blood. Your mission, however, is to prevent the shedding of blood. Yours, therefore, is the privilege of averting that calamity which others are under the necessity of producing. Therefore, my deservedly illustrious and very powerful lord and very dear son in Christ, rejoice in this singularly great and real blessing vouchsafed to you, and enjoy it in God, to whom you owe that you are what you are, and that you undertook the accomplishment of such work. May God 'strengthen that which He hath wrought for us through you.' Accept this our salutation, and deign to reply. From the letter of my brother Novatus, I see that he has taken pains that your learned Excellency should become acquainted with me also through my works. If, then, you have read what he has given you, I also shall have become known to your inward perception. As far as I can judge, they will not greatly displease you if you have read them in a loving rather than a critical spirit. It is not much to ask, but it will be a great favour, if for this letter and my works you send us one letter in reply. I salute with due affection the pledge of peace which through the favour of Our Lord and God you have happily received.

PAUL MONCEAUX. *L'Eglise et le Droit de Guerre, pp.* 25–71. *Critical examination of the doctrine of St. Augustine:*

The main point to remember (in the doctrine of St. Augustine) is the preponderating position occupied by the notion of Justice, the theory of Just War. Neither the expression nor the substance of this theory was, indeed, new. We may disregard the *justa bella* of Roman politicians and jurisconsults, for whom justice was a matter of outward appearance and consisted merely in observing the traditional forms and rites. But, for a long time past, pagan moralists had introduced into this sphere the notion of equity: Plato and the Stoics, Cicero and Seneca had condemned unjust war. But for the pagan, the value of the conception was in fact nullified by his exclusive devotion to the State. Having no other criterion than the evident interest of his country, he instinctively considered as just all that appeared to be useful to the State.

Augustine and the Christians of his day put fresh life into this theory, and gave it quite a new bearing by looking for the criterion of equity not in the Citizen but in the Man. For them the arbiter of justice was in principle God, that is, in reality, conscience. On that basis they made bold to condemn many wars which were (materially) advantageous, such as Roman conquests in the past; and, for the present and the future, every war of ambition and conquest.

From the point of view of international law this is clearly an advance. Yet there is also a weak point in Augustine's theory which must be noticed. His sytem would imply the constant and direct intervention of God in the affairs of this world; hence his philosophy of war. On this hypothesis all would be plain and certain, as in the days of Moses or King David. But the God of the Gospel is more discreet; and He is a God of Peace who no longer ordains war. Consequently the human conscience is left to itself to decide whether or not a war is just. And unfortunately the ideal of justice varies greatly with the consciences of different people, particularly when adversaries with divergent interests confront one another. What is wanted to give the Augustinian theory its full value in practice is an objective foundation for the criterion of justice. Several theologians who were the heirs and disciples of Augustine saw this weak point: they thought to find the necessary guarantee in the arbitration of God's representative on earth—the Church or the Pope. The solution is evidently not easy to find; for we are still looking for it.

Be that as it may, Augustine's doctrine of war started an epoch in the history of international law. In the following centuries and indeed right up to the end of the Middle Ages, writers constantly drew their inspiration from it. About 1148 Gratian of Bologna, a celebrated master of Canon Law, published his treatise entitled *Concordia discordantium canonum*, which was soon christened the 'Decretals of Gratian'; it was adopted for the purpose of teaching the Canon Law and formed the first part of the *Corpus juris canonici*. And Gratian, in the chapter devoted to War, reproduces most of the texts of Augustine. In this way the doctrine which they conveyed was accepted by all the Faculties of Law. It was apparently through Gratian that St. Thomas Aquinas first acquired the knowledge of the passages from St. Augustine upon war. Through the *Summa* of St. Thomas, as through the Decretals of Gratian, these quotations commanded the attention of all the schools. The theologians, of course, were not content merely to reproduce and to comment upon these texts. They made the Augustinian doctrine more precise, developed it and completed it. But one discovers that it is the basis of all their dissertations upon the right of war.

II. MEDIÆVAL FOLLOWERS OF ST. AUGUSTINE

The Decretals of Gratian. *Pars Secunda, Causa XXIII, Quæstio I:*

C. III. Soldiers can please God with warlike arms.

C. V. It is not a sin to serve as a soldier.

C. VI. Those wars are peaceful which are waged in order that the wicked may be constrained and the good relieved.

C. VII. The supreme praise of the soldier's calling is that it shows obedience to the true interests of the commonweal (*reipublicæ utilitatibus obedientiam exhibere*).

Quæstio II:

C. I. What is a just war? A war is just when, by a formal declaration,[1] it is waged in order to regain what has been stolen or repel the attack of enemies.

C. II. Whether one fights openly or with ambushes has nothing to do with justice.

C. III. Harmless transit was refused to the children of Israel, and therefore the wars they waged were just.

Here Gratian, on the authority of St. Augustine's commentary on the Book of Numbers, says: '*Innoxius enim transitus denegabatur, qui humanæ societatis æquissimo jure patere debebat.*' 'Harmless transit was refused, and this by the law of human society should in all equity be open to them.'

[1] '*Ex edicto.*' But some manuscripts of St. Isidore, from which this rule is taken, have '*ex prædicto.*' The reading here chosen follows Migne, who in confirmation cites Cicero's Republic, which requires a formal warning and declaration as one of the conditions of just war.

Quæstio III :

C. V. He is full of justice who defends his fatherland from barbarians.

C. VII. He who does not ward off an injury done to his fellow-man is like him who does the injury. (Even the qualifying '*ut potest*' of St. Ambrose has disappeared.)

C. XI. They are not immune from crime who do not liberate those whom in fact they have the power to free. (Gratian refers to Pilate, but his explanation and the context are such as to relate the rule to war and intervention.)

Quæstio IV :

C. XXXVI. Who may be said to take the sword ? He takes the sword who, without the orders or permission of a superior and lawful authority, arms himself to take anyone's blood.

Quæstio V :

C. VII. Those who are guilty of blood ought to be excluded from the Church.

C. VIII. The soldier who kills a man in obedience to authority is not guilty of murder.

C. XLVI. Whoever dies in battle against the infidels is worthy to enter into the heavenly kingdom.

(*Quæstio VIII, C. IX,* is in the same sense.)

C. XLVIII. The enemies of the Church (*ecclesiasticæ religionis*) are to be coerced even by war.

It will be observed that in the course of time this opinion in its bald form came to be almost entirely rejected. The principle enunciated by Suarez (see p. 109) that there is never a just cause of war other than a violation of natural rights and the conclusion of Vittoria that it is unlawful to make war 'by reason of diversity of religion' has become the accepted view of the Church. This is not to say that in oppressing and massacring a Christian people, or in denying its subjects religious liberty, a government is not outraging the natural rights of men. On that ground armed intervention, if it is likely to achieve its end without greater evil to those whom it is intended to help, can be justified or can even be a strict duty, when all pacific means of putting an end to the injustice have failed. Such is the traditional justification of the Crusades. The tendency of the modern Papacy, however, has been to discourage resort to force even in such cases : to call upon the faithful (e.g. Mexico, Russia) to employ passive resistance only in the face of persecution, and in pagan lands to refuse to ask for the assistance of foreign military force when missionaries are imprisoned and martyred or Church property seized (e.g. Korea, China).

Quæstio VIII :

C. IV. For a cleric who dies in war or in a fight no prayer or oblation (Mass) may be offered. (This, of course, refers not to priests who may be killed as non-combatants but to any who take part in fighting).

C. XIX. Bishops must not be occupied with military business.

ST. THOMAS AQUINAS

St. Thomas Aquinas (1226–1274). *Summa : Secunda Secundæ, Quæstio XL (de Bello) :*

St. Augustine, in the discourse *De puero centurionis*, says : 'If Christian doctrine condemned wars absolutely, the counsel given to the soldiers, who in the Gospel ask what must be done for their salvation, would have been to cast away far from them their arms and to abandon entirely military service ; now, the reply made to them was : 'Do violence to no one ; and be satisfied with your wages.' Those who are told to be satisfied with their wages are not forbidden to make war.

I reply that it must be said that, in order that a war may be just, three things are necessary.

In the first place, the authority of the prince, by whose order the war is undertaken ; for it does not belong to a private individual to make war, because, in order to obtain justice, he can have recourse to the judgement of his superior. Neither does it belong to a private individual to summon a multitude of people together as must be done to engage in war. But, since the care of the State is confided to princes, it is to them that it belongs to defend the city, the kingdom or province which is subject to their authority. Just as it is permissible for them to defend these, by the material sword, against those who trouble them *from within*, by punishing the evil-doers according to the word of the Apostle : 'The prince beareth not the sword in vain for he is the minister of God to execute His vengeance against him who doeth evil' (Romans xiii : 4), so, in like manner, it is to them that it belongs to bear the sword in combats for the defence of the State against external enemies. Also, the Psalmist says to princes : 'Snatch the poor and deliver the needy out of the hands of the sinner' (Psalm lxxxi : 4). This is what makes St. Augustine say (*Contra Faustum*, XXII, 75) : 'The natural order, which would have peace amongst men, requires that the decision and power to declare war should belong to princes.'

In the second place, there must be a just cause ; that is to say, those attacked must have, by a fault, deserved to be attacked. This is what makes St. Augustine say in Book VI, Question 16, of *Questions on Joshua :* 'Just wars are usually defined as those which avenge injuries, when the nation or city against which warlike action is to be directed has neglected either to punish wrongs committed by its own citizens or to restore what has been unjustly taken by it. Further, that kind of war is undoubtedly just which God Himself ordains.'

In the third place, it is necessary that the intention of those who fight should be right ; that is to say, that they propose to themselves a good to be effected or an evil to be avoided. This is what made St. Augustine say in the book *De Verbis Domini :*[1] 'With the true servants of God wars themselves are pacific, not being undertaken through cupidity or cruelty, but through the love of peace, with the object of repressing the wicked and encouraging the good.' Consequently, it may happen that, although the war has been declared by the legitimate authority and for a just cause, it may nevertheless be rendered illicit by the perversity of the intention of him who makes it. 'For,' says St. Augustine (*Contra Faustum*, I, XXII, Chap. 74), 'what is blamed in war ? Is it the death of those who must die sooner or later, but who give up their lives to bring peace by overcoming guilty men ? To blame this is the cry of cowards, not of religious people. The desire for harming, the cruelty of avenging, an unruly and implacable animosity, the rage of rebellion, the lust of domination and the like—these are the things which are to be blamed in war.'

To the second argument (viz. that war is a sin, as being 'contrary to a divine precept') it must be replied that these precepts, as St. Augustine says (*De Serm. Domini in monte*, I, 34), ought always to be observed in relation to the disposition of the soul ; that is to say that man ought always to be ready, if necessary, not to resist or not to defend himself. But sometimes we must act otherwise for the common good, and even for the good of those against whom we fight. This it is that causes St. Augustine to say, in the Fifth Epistle *Ad Marcellinum :* 'There are many things that must be done against the will of those whom one ought to correct with a beneficent severity.'

To the third argument the reply is, that those who wage wars justly have peace as the object of their intention, and so they

[1] There is no known book of this title by St. Augustine.

are not opposed to peace, but only to that evil peace which the Lord did not come on earth to bring (St. Matthew x: 34). Hence Augustine says (*Ep. ad Bonifacium*, CLXXXIX): 'For peace is not sought in order to the kindling of war, but war is waged in order that peace may be obtained. Therefore, even in waging war, cherish the spirit of the peacemaker, that, by conquering those whom you attack, you may lead them back to the advantages of peace. . . .'

To the fourth argument the reply is that manly exercises in warlike feats of arms are not all forbidden but those which are inordinate and perilous, and end in slaying or plundering. In olden times warlike exercises presented no such danger and hence they were called *exercises of arms* or *bloodless wars*.

Three other aspects of war are studied by St. Thomas. Article II: 'Whether it is lawful for clergy and bishops to fight.' Article III: 'Whether it is lawful to use ambushes in war.' Article IV: 'Whether fighting may take place on feast days.' Of these Article III relates to the laws of war which, as a special subject, we have excluded from this work: the Saint's reply, however, involves a principle which must here be retained, namely that it is never permissible to lie to your enemy or to break a promise made to him (in support of which he quotes St. Ambrose, *De Officiis*, I, 29; see p. 62); but that those who wage a just war may make use of military strategems such as keeping themselves and their plans hidden.

Article IV, strangely enough, makes no allusion to the Truce of God or the Peace of God, both of which, with the full support of the Holy See, had been put into operation with a view to placing as many obstacles as possible in the way of war between Christians. The subject is treated on a basis of theory only, and the conclusion is: 'The observance of feasts does not impede the acts which are ordained to man's safety, even that of his body. . . . Hence physicians may lawfully attend to their patients on holy days. Yet much more reason is there for safeguarding the commonweal, whereby many are saved from being slain and innumerable evils both temporal and spiritual prevented, than the bodily safety of an individual.' Therefore, if there is real necessity, it is lawful to fight on a holy day: but not unless it is absolutely necessary.

Certain passages of Article II are of more general interest as indicating the mind of the Church concerning the incompatibility of bloodshed with the most sacred of Christian acts and the co-ordination of this notion with the established principles of just war. St. Thomas concludes that, by the authority of their superiors, clerics may join in war not by taking up arms but by encouraging other men to fight in a just cause and 'by affording spiritual help to those who fight justly, by exhorting and absolving them, and by other like spiritual help.' Hence the institution of military chaplains. In the course of his reasoning he writes :

> Now warlike pursuits are altogether incompatible with the duties of a bishop and a cleric, for two reasons. The first reason is a general one, because, to wit, warlike pursuits are full of unrest, so that they hinder the mind very much from the contemplation of divine things, the praise of God and prayers for the people, which belong to the duties of a cleric. Wherefore, just as commercial enterprises are forbidden to clerics, because they unsettle the mind too much, so too are warlike pursuits, according to 2 Timothy ii : 4 : 'No man being a soldier to God entangleth himself with secular business.' The second reason is a special one because, to wit, all the clerical orders are directed to the ministry of the altar on which the Passion of Christ is represented sacramentally according to 1 Corinthians xi : 26 : 'As often as you shall eat this bread and drink this chalice, you shall show the death of the Lord, until He come.' Wherefore it is unbecoming to them to slay or shed blood. And it is more fitting that they should be ready to shed their own blood for Christ, so as to imitate in deed what they portray in their ministry. For this reason it has been decreed that those who shed blood even without sin become irregular. Now no man who has a certain duty to perform, can lawfully do that which renders him unfit for that duty. Wherefore it is altogether unlawful for clerics to fight, because war is directed to the shedding of blood.

This does not mean, however, that bishops and priests must do nothing to avert aggression and oppression and so prevent war.

> Prelates ought to withstand not only the wolf who brings spiritual death upon the flock, but also the pillager and the oppressor who work bodily harm ; not, however, by having recourse themselves to material arms, but by means of spiritual weapons, according to the saying of the Apostle (2 Corinthians

x : 4) : 'The weapons of our warfare are not carnal, but mighty through God.' Such are salutary warnings, devout prayers and, for those who are obstinate, the sentence of excommunication.

The reader will beware of judging the contribution of the 'Angelic Doctor' to international ethics simply from this short and crisp chapter of his great *Summa*. On other pages will be found his praise of peace as the outcome of charity, the distinctive Christian commandment, and his reasoning in the *Summa contra Gentes* to show that, to bring true peace, charity must be joined to strict justice. Here it may be recalled that, in indicating what may be done in war, he treats only of a war which fulfils the conditions laid down at the start; namely that it be waged by a sovereign in order to secure amends for grave wrongs inflicted on his subjects or to regain what has been seized unjustly, when he has no higher tribunal to which he can go to obtain satisfaction, and with a pure intention.

TEACHING UPON WAR IN THE MEDIÆVAL THEOLOGIANS AND CANONISTS[1]

Rev. A. Keogh, S.J. *A Catholic Survey, Vol. I, p.* 34 :

The mediæval theologians and canonists in their teaching on war repeated and worked out further the teaching of St. Augustine. His definition of a just war, already given in the previous article, is incorporated in the Decree of Gratian (+*c.* 1179) in Pars. II, Causa xxiii, Q. i. Another definition in the same place is taken from St. Isidore of Seville. It is that 'a just war is one which is made in accordance with an edict to recover things which have been stolen or to repel enemies.' We shall see, however, that the above definitions in so far as they have to do with an offensive war, i.e., a war the object of which is not primarily and directly to repel invaders, receives a good deal of qualification in the latter mediæval theologians and canonists.

[1] Cf. A Vanderpol *La Guerre devant le Christianisme* (3eme edition 1911) Paris. A. Tratin, *rue du Vieux Colombier* 12 (referred to below as *Vanderpol Guerre*) and the same author's *Le Droit de Guerre d'après les Théologiens et les Canonistes du Moyen Age*, 1911, same publisher (referred to as *Vanderpol Droit*) from which the statements and references found in the text are taken.

St. Thomas (*Summa Theologica*, II–II, Q. xl, art 1) taught that for a war to be just it must be begun with the authority of the head of the State, the reason for it must be a just reason, and the intention in declaring war must be a morally good intention. The right of the head of the State to declare war in certain circumstances is analogous to his right to inflict proportionate penalties on subjects guilty of crime. The one is postulated by the need of the power of punishing to keep good order in a State; the other by the need of the self-preservation of a State.

This insistence on the act of the head of a State is of no great importance in modern times. In mediæval times it was necessary to insist that feudal lords had no right to make war on their own account. Such insistence is found e.g. in Hostiensis (Henry of Segusio, Cardinal bishop of Ostia+1271) in his *Summa Aurea*, Lib. I, No. 34.[1]

The second condition insisted on is of the greatest importance for all times, viz. that of a just reason. According to St. Thomas (loc. cit.) a just reason is to hand when those on whom war is made are justly attacked because of wrongdoing. This is repeated by St. Antoninus of Florence (+1459) in his *Summa Theologica*, Pars. III, Lib. IV, Cap. I.[2] He gives as an example of a just reason frequent and great damage done for which restitution has been demanded and refused. Unless there is some such reason, he says, it is hard to see how a war can be just seeing the great damage, loss of life and harm to souls which are the necessary result of war.[3]

The Canonists, at their head Hostiensis and St. Raymund of Pennafort (+1275), repeat the definition of a just war given by St. Isidore of Seville which is incorporated, as has been shown, in the decree of Gratian, but it is explained and qualified by them, and not left as it stands. The remark of St. Antoninus given above shows that he thought that in view of the inevitable and very grave harm of all kinds done in war, only the weightiest of just reasons could justify war, or as he says, war to be just must be the *only* way out of a very grave difficulty (*Summa*, Pars. IV, Lib. III, Cap. III).[4] He warns the head of a State against declaring war too easily. Even if, he says, the conditions he has laid down (i.e. a just reason and a right intention) are realised, the head of a State should not declare war except in the case of an urgent necessity, to set right a notable and manifest wrong (*Summa*, Pars. IV, Lib. III, Cap. II).[5] In this he is following the teaching of St. Augustine that war is allowable only when it is morally necessary (*Epist.* 189 [205] *ad Bonifacium.*)[6] It is the teaching also of St. Raymund of Pennafort (*Summa*, Lib. II,

[1] Cf. *Vanderpol Droit*, p. 68.
[2] *Ibid.*, p. 49–50.
[3] *Ibid.*, p. 51.
[4] *Vanderpol Guerre*, p. 126.
[5] *Vanderpol Droit*, p. 40.
[6] Migne P.L. 33,856.

Lib. V. Q. v)[1] and before him was that of Hostiensis. According to Hostiensis the second of the five ways in which a war may be unjust exists when war is entered upon willingly, i.e. not through necessity (*Summa Aurea*, Lib. I, Rubr. 34).[2] The same doctrine is found in Monaldus (+1288) *De Bello Justo*, in Angelo Carletti (+1495) *Summa Angelica* and in Johannes Lupus (+1496) *De Bello et Bellatoribus*.[3] According to this last canonist to refuse to submit the matter in dispute to arbitration would be wrong.[4]

The same strict teaching is found implied in the statement that the only just object of war is to secure peace. 'Those who wage just wars,' says St. Thomas, 'have peace for their object. They are only against that peace which the Saviour did not come to bring.' (*Summa Theol.*, II–II, Q. xl, art 1.) Gratian before him resumed the thought of St. Augustine in the same way. 'With the true servants of God even wars are pacific as they are entered upon not through cruelty or greed and have as their object peace, the repression of the wicked and the deliverance of the good.' (*Decretum*, Pars. II, Causa xxiii, Q. i).[5] Similarly St. Raymund of Pennafort (*Summa*, Lib. II, Tit. V, Q. v)[6] taught that for a war to be just it was necessary that peace could come only through fighting.

According to mediæval teaching a third important condition must be fulfilled before a war can be said to be just. Not only must it be entered upon by proper authorities for a just reason, viz., that war is the only way to right a proportionately great wrong, but the head of the State must be moved by a right intention. In regard to this last point the principles were solidly established by St. Augustine, according to whom a war undertaken in a spirit of hatred, or revenge, or to make conquests is an unjust war. Hence as St. Thomas taught (*Summa Theol.*, II–II, Q. xl, art 1): 'it is necessary that the intention of those who fight be a right intention, that is, that they purpose to do good or avoid evil. . . . Consequently it may happen that although a war has been declared by proper Authority and for a just reason it may be unlawful because of the wrongness of the intention of him who makes war.'

This was also the teaching of St. Antoninus (*Summa Theol.*, Pars. IV, Tit. III, Cap. II) who gives as an example of a wrong intention in Saul his war against the Amalekites for which he was blamed by God.[7]

Before St. Thomas the same teaching was given by St. Raymund of Pennafort (*Summa Raymundi*, Lib. II, Tit. V, Q. xii). He says that for a war to be just it is necessary that it be entered upon not

[1] *Vanderpol Droit*, p. 35. [2] *Ibid.*, p. 39. [3] *Ibid.*, p. 40.
[4] *Ibid.*, p. 88. [5] *Ibid.*, p. 22. [6] *Ibid.*, p. 39.
[7] *Ibid.*, p. 73.

through hatred, the desire of revenge or greed, but from a motive of religion, justice or obedience.[1]

Hostiensis evidently held the same opinion as to the need of a right intention, as he says that a war undertaken in a spirit of revenge is unjust (*Summa Aurea*, Lib. I, Rubr. 34).[2] The same teaching is found in Lupus, Carletti and others.[3]

St. Raymund of Pennafort neatly sums up the mediæval teaching on the subject of what constitutes a just war. He says that five things are required that a war may be just, viz., (1) the person fighting must be a layman not an ecclesiastic, who is not allowed to shed blood, (2) the object must be to get back what has been unjustly taken or to defend one's country, (3) the reason must be, that fighting is necessary to get peace, (4) the intention must be not to satisfy the spirit of hatred, revenge or greed—it should have its origin in religion, justice or obedience, (5) the authority which declares war must be that of the Church, especially if the fight is for the faith, or that of the head of the State. If any one of these conditions is missing the war is unjust. But there is one case in which fighting may be engaged in without the special authority of the Church or State, namely to get back property which has been stolen or to defend one's land. The reason is that it is lawful and allowable instantly to repel violence provided that only that amount of violence is used which is necessary.[4]

This statement of St. Raymund or a similar statement by Hostiensis is found also in some of the later mediæval canonists and theologians.[5]

Conclusions

Definition has succeeded to conflicting opinions upon the matter of military service. The conditions upon which war may lawfully be waged have been codified. Two of those conditions, namely that no superior tribunal is available and that force is the only available means of vindicating justice, raise a problem which will be found more and more to dominate the whole question of the Right of War. It is the problem of arbitration. Should the apparent absence or insufficiency of peaceful means for settling differences between princes, and of a tribunal to adjudicate, when there is a collision of rights, be accepted with a kind of fatalism, or even with relief as sufficient pretext for resorting to arms? That is at best a passive, at worst a cynical

[1] *Vanderpol Droit*, p. 74. [2] *Ibid.*, p. 74. [3] *Ibid.*, p. 74.
[4] *Ibid.*, p. 45. [5] *Ibid.*, p. 47.

position. Or is it the duty of Christians to make a positive effort to use such opportunities as exist, to devise bloodless methods of composing disputes and to bring into being the higher tribunal which is logically the prerequisite of an international society? A generation to whom the spectacle of wars and cruelties was only too familiar did not easily follow this line of thought. St. Augustine is the first to appraise the active principle of peacemaking in the international sphere and thus to elucidate the true meaning of the beatitude *Beati pacifici*. For that has nothing to do with the mere absence of war, nor yet with refraining from violence, nor yet with the difficult precept of non-resistance. It is not the *peaceful* that are blessed with so divine a promise; it is the peace*makers*: for the word used by Christ, εἰρηνοποιέιν, implies an active and continuous process. This was the inspiration of that heroic apostle of unity and conciliation in Austria-Hungary during the last years of the European anarchy and the dark days of war, Mgr. Giesswein:

'Peacemaking is not merely a passive resignation,' he wrote, commenting upon the Epistle to Darius, 'it is the active endeavour to bring order and justice into the world, substituting by these means the domination of law for material force. Christ is proclaimed by the prophets not only as King of Peace but as a king "reigning in justice" . . . "and the work of justice shall be peace, and the service of justice quietness and security for ever. And my people shall sit in the beauty of peace" (Isaias xxxii: 1, 17, 18). As the prophets say, "he will be a judge among many nations, and the consequence of his arbitration shall be, that they shall no more prepare themselves for war" (Isaias ii: 4. Micheas iv: 3). This is the way of true pacifism and this is the method of the Catholic Church.'[1]

This is no doubt a just summary of what should be, and what at its best has been the chief international mission of the Church. At intervals throughout the building of Christendom and the Middle Ages, and indeed up to the present times, the Papacy on the whole has been true to this mission, as will appear from later chapters. But it could not be sustained that this notion played any prominent

[1] From a manuscript dated October, 1923, in the author's possession.

part in the theoretic treatment of the ethics of war by the mediæval Schoolmen. We look in vain for any praise of or any insistence upon papal arbitration in the writings of St. Thomas Aquinas, leading papalist as he was. This hiatus in doctrine is the more remarkable, since St. Thomas and his successors could not have been ignorant of the claim of the Apostolic See to impose truces or the several occasions when the Pope had succeeded in imposing them : of the cases, already numerous, of papal mediation and arbitration, and also of the Emperor's claim to be *rex pacificus*—peacemaker for lesser princes. The explanation probably lies in the complete separation of theory from practice in the great philosophical and theological works of the thirteenth century. St. Thomas's *Summa Theologica* is a masterpiece of abstraction. The whole edifice is built up by a process of pure reasoning from first principles : the imagination is suppressed : the intellect is freed from the particular to concentrate upon the general, the universal. The point at issue would be, whether Pope or Empire did in fact offer the opportunity of effective arbitration as a superior tribunal, to which princes were in conscience bound to submit before vindicating their right by force. And it must not be forgotten that the conflict between extravagant apologists of the rival claims of the spiritual and the temporal power to jurisdiction in this sphere was already so acute that the philosopher had an added reason for remaining aloof from it.

We will now seek to draw from St. Augustine's doctrine its logical conclusions. At the same time we make deductions from other authors treated in this chapter, which add something to the principles already enunciated.

A. There is a greater merit in preventing war by peaceful negotiation and conciliation than in vindicating rights by bloodshed.

B. Peace attained by conciliation is better than peace attained by victory.

C. There is a natural society of mankind which gives rise to certain rights and duties relevant to the morality of war.

D. The absence of a superior tribunal before which a prince can seek redress can alone justify him in making war, except when resisting actual attack.

E. Saving the direct intervention of God, the following conditions must in addition be fulfilled before a war can be just :

(1) It must have a *just cause :* this can only be a grave injury received (e.g. actual invasion : unlawful annexation of territory : grave harm to citizens or their property : denial of peaceful trade and travel) or a great injustice perpetrated upon others whom it is a duty to help (e.g. the same injuries as above, violation of religious rights).

(2) It must be *necessary :* i.e. the only available means of restoring justice or preventing the continued violation of justice.

(3) It must be the consequence of a *formal warning* to the offending state and must be formally *declared.*

(4) It must be declared and waged only by the *sovereign authority* in the state (i.e. one who has no political superior) and, if the defence of religious rights are involved, with the *consent of the Church.*

(5) The good to be attained by war must be reasonably supposed to be *greater than the certain evils*, material and spiritual, which war entails.

(6) A *right intention* must actuate both the declaration, conduct and conclusion of war. That intention can only be the restoration or attainment of true peace.

(7) *Only so much violence* may be used *as is necessary :* in the case of defence, only so much as is necessary to repel the violence of the aggressor.

F. The *moral responsibility* for war lies upon the *sovereign authority*, not upon the *individual soldier* or citizen : his duty is to obey, except in a war which he is certainly convinced is wrong.

G. Priests may not fight even in just war.

H. The duty of *repelling injury inflicted upon another* is the common obligation of all rulers and peoples.

APPENDIX TO CHAPTER IV

CRUSADES ANCIENT AND MODERN

Gregory VII (*c.* A.D. 1073–1085). *Epist. XLIX* (*P.L.*, 148, *Col.* 329). *Ad Omnes Christianos :*

Gregory, Bishop, servant of the servants of God to all willing to defend the Christian faith, health and the apostolic benediction.

We wish it to be known to you that the man who is the bearer of these present letters has recently come from overseas and visited the threshold of the Apostles and our presence. By whom we learn, as from many others also, that the pagan peoples have made great advances against the Christian Empire, and with dreadful cruelty and tyrannous violence have devastated and occupied every place almost as far as the walls of Constantinople ; they have slaughtered many thousands of Christians like cattle. Wherefore if we love God and acknowledge ourselves to be Christians we must be greatly grieved for the pitiful fate of so great an empire and such slaughter of Christians. But our sorrow for this thing does not satisfy our paternal solicitude ; the example of our Redeemer and the duty of fraternal charity urges us to lay down our lives for the freedom of our brethren : for as He laid down His life for us, so we also ought to lay down our lives for our brethren. Know therefore that, confiding in the mercy of God and in the power of His virtue, we are doing and preparing all things that we may speedily and with God's help succour the Christian Empire. We beg you therefore by the faith in which you are united in the adoption of the sons of God, and we admonish you by the authority of St. Peter, prince of the Apostles, to be moved to compassion by the wounds and blood of the brethren and the peril of the aforesaid empire, that your virtue may, for Christ's sake, willingly take up the cause and bring help to the brethren. Whatever your godly piety may inspire you in this, do you, I pray, send sure messengers to me to inform me. Given at Rome, etc.

None but a little mind will deny the grandeur of that appeal.

This is not the place to discuss the great controversy upon the ethics or the expediency of the Crusades. For that purpose it would be necessary to examine all the historical data.[1] Stratmann, following Von Ruville, may well be right

[1] *The Church and War*, p. 126.

in holding that the Crusades between the eleventh and thirteenth centuries were not really necessary as the only means of attaining the desired end. Others give weighty arguments to show that the Popes saved Christendom and with it the civilization of Europe, by rallying Christian princes and peoples to resist the inroads of Islam. And indeed, as against the evils of war on the borders of Europe, is to be set the contrary blessing of unity within, restored and restored again by the ceaseless mediations of the Holy See. But that is to judge morality by events, a dangerous process. St. Bernard's definition of the moral issue was clear enough :

St. Bernard. *P.L.*, 184, *C.* 3 :

Unbelievers should not be punished with death if any other means would prevent their oppressing Christians, but this extreme measure was better than to allow the ill-treatment of just persons and so to share in the injustice.

Is it certain that the other means were always absent? Yet it is the spectacle of the Vicar of the Prince of Peace organizing war in the role of a Moses or a David that shocks the spirit of our times, in which a great Catholic historian can write : 'It is astonishing that Christianity was never so near to Islam as when they fought most bitterly. The Pope behaved like the Khalifs in that he both encouraged and led those "Holy Wars."[1] The idea of winning Heaven through deeds of blood dominated both sides.'

Now, no less than in those distant centuries, Rome calls to the crusade, a crusade no longer against a martial heresy but against a militant atheism. Once more the Successor of Peter and of Hildebrand implores all the *Christifideles*, indeed all who believe in one God, to unite against the common danger.

Pius XI. Encyclical. *Caritate Christi Compulsi.*

For God or *against* God, this once more is the alternative that shall decide the destinies of all mankind : in politics, in finance, in morals, in the sciences and arts, in the State, in civil and domestic society, in the East and in the West, everywhere this

[1] Von Ruville, Die Kreuzzuge, *apud.* Stratmann, ibid., p. 127.

question confronts us as the deciding factor because of the consequences that flow from it. In the name of the Lord, therefore, We conjure individuals and nations, in the face of such problems and in the throes of a conflict of such vital interest for mankind, to put aside that narrow individualism and base egoism that blinds even the most clear-sighted ; that withers up all noble initiative as soon as it is no longer confined to a limited circle of paltry and particular interests. Let them all unite together even at the cost of heavy sacrifices, to save themselves and mankind. In such a union of minds and forces, they naturally ought to be the first, who are proud of the Christian name, mindful of the glorious tradition of apostolic times, when 'the multitude of believers had but one heart and one soul' ; but let all those also who still believe in God and adore Him loyally and heartily concur, in order to ward off from mankind the great danger that threatens all alike. For in truth, belief in God is the unshaken foundation of all social order and of all responsible action on earth ; and therefore all those who do not want anarchy and terrorism ought to bestir themselves with a will in order that the enemies of religion may not attain the goal they have so loudly proclaimed to the world.

But with what weapons does this Vicar of Christ bid the Crusaders of the present age to arm themselves? Two only. 'This kind is not cast out but by prayer and fasting.'

CHAPTER V

THE NEO-SCHOLASTIC DOCTRINE OF WAR

I. Introduction

THE end of the Great Schism, the discovery of the New World; the impact of civilized upon primitive races which it involved; the rise of national monarchies; the challenge to the whole conception of Christendom offered by the Reformation; the beginnings of the Counter Reformation—all these were events which, under one aspect or another, urgently called for a new statement of Christian tradition upon the order of human society.

The name of neo-scholastics is commonly given to the great moral theologians of the sixteenth and seventeenth centuries who supplied this need and to those who continued their school of thought. Francis de Vittoria (1480–1546), the Dominican counsellor of Kings, who, for a spell, made his University of Salamanca the intellectual metropolis of Europe, is the first of those whose works we shall quote at length. To some extent he may be said to have carried on the tradition of his lesser-known predecessor in that University, Johannes Lupus, in the sphere of international ethics. We have exercised a certain economy in the selection of passages from Vittoria's works since the two series of lectures or Relectiones which most closely concern our subject have been published in full in Latin and English by the Carnegie Endowment, with an admirable historical introduction and appreciation by Ernest Nys, to which the reader is referred.[1] A great part of the First *Relectio De Indis* will be found in the section concerned with the natural

[1] *Classics of International Law.* Vittoria.

society of nations and in the last chapter of the present work, which is devoted to the colonial problem. In this chapter are given the salient parts of the second *Relectio* : *De Indis Relectio Posterior, sive De Jure Belli Hispanorum in Barbaros,* which refer specifically to the ethics of war in general. Vittoria's main contribution to the European controversy of his day, namely his lectures *De Potestate Civili, De Potestate Ecclesiae* and *De Potestate Papæ et Concilii* won him a direct invitation from Pope Paul IV to the Council of Trent. Nine years later (1545) the Emperor himself invited him to be his theologian at the Council : the illness which was to cause his death prevented his acceptance. But Father Dominic Soto (1494–1560), also a Dominican, a colleague and friend of Vittoria at Salamanca, and Melchior Cano (1509–1560), his successor in the Primary Chair of Theology at that University, went to Trent and contributed to the deliberations of the Council much of their master's clear doctrine upon the functions and mutual aid of the spiritual and temporal powers. There are certain passages in their works which concern our subject whether under this present head of war, of arbitration or of the society of nations.

Francis Suarez (1548–1617) was born two years after Vittoria died. He joined the Company of Jesus, and though he is said to have shown little promise at first, by the year 1571 had won a name for himself. He was famed as a teacher of theology at Valladolid, Rome, Salamanca and Coimbra. His writings have none of the informality of Vittoria's University lectures, known to us only through the laborious notes of his students. Suarez left a monumental work upon every aspect of natural and metaphysical theology. His conception of international right is to be seen in a section of his treatise *De Legibus ac de Deo Legislatore* in which he examines the Law of Nations (*Jus Gentium*) and its relation to the Law of Nature. His views upon war are to be found, following the precedent of St. Thomas, in the section of the Treatise *De Virtutibus Theologicis* devoted to Charity. Suarez clips the wings of national sovereignty less rigorously than Vittoria : and it will be seen that his fellow-Jesuit, Gabriel Vasquez (1651–1694), a more original and constructive thinker in these matters, condemns the opinion to which he gave currency, that a king may declare war in the belief that his claims are *probably* just. But Suarez is no less insistent than St. Thomas and the main Augustinian School that war is purely an instrument of Justice. It is to be employed in the last resort and withheld so soon as satisfaction is offered. To Vasquez, among other Spanish philosophers and theologians of this age, Hugo Grotius owed a debt of gratitude for many of the rules embodied in his *De Jure belli et pacis*.

Tommaso de Vio, called Cajetan, General of the Dominican Order during the greater part of Vittoria's life[1] and John de Lugo,[2] a contemporary of Vasquez, also wrote upon the rights and wrongs of war and are habitually classed with the theologians already mentioned. If we have not quoted their works it is because we know of no development of doctrine in which they vary appreciably from one or other of these authors or those quoted in earlier chapters.

A short passage upon war from the *Institutiones Theologicæ* of St. Alphonsus de Liguori (1696–1787) is added because of his great authority, and his condemnation of recourse to war if any doubt at all remains of the justice and necessity of this course.

II. Documents

Franciscus de Vittoria. *De Jure Belli.* (From the translation in *Classics of International Law.*) *Is war permissible ?*

Vittoria examines once more the question whether it is lawful for Christians to go to war in view of the Evangelical Counsel of war-resistance. He gives the same answer as St. Augustine, Gratian and St. Thomas had given : the following fragment of controversy on this topic is not without interest :

419. In development of this question be it noted that although Catholics are fairly in accord on the matter yet Luther, who left naught uncontaminated, denies that Christians may take up arms even against the Turks, and he relies not only on the above-cited texts of Scripture, but also on the fact that if the Turks

[1] *Summa S. Thomae Commentariis illustrata.*
[2] *De Justitia et Jure.*

attack Christendom it is the will of God, which may not be resisted. Herein, however, he had not as much success as in his other dogmas in imposing on the Germans, who are born soldiers. Tertullian, too seems not averse from this opinion for in his *De corona militis* he discusses 'whether military service is at all right for a Christian,' and in the issue he inclines to hold that military service is forbidden to a Christian who, says he, 'may not even go to law.'

The State's right to wage defensive war required by the order of Society :

424. 5. Every State has authority to declare and to make war. In course of proof of this be it noted that the difference herein between a private person and a State is that a private person is entitled, as said above, to defend himself and what belongs to him, but has no right to avenge a wrong done to him, nay, not even to recapture property that has been seized from him if time has been allowed to go by since the seizure. But defence can only be resorted to at the very moment of the danger, or, as the jurists say, *in continenti*, and so when the necessity of defence has passed there is an end to the lawfulness of war. In my view, however, one who has been contumeliously assaulted can immediately strike back, even if the assaulter was not proposing to make a further attack, for in the avoidance of shame and disgrace one who (for example) has had his ears boxed might immediately use his sword, not for the purpose of vengeance but, as has been said, in order to avoid infamy and disgrace. But a State is within its rights not only in defending itself, but also in avenging itself and its subjects and in redressing wrongs. This is proved by what Aristotle says in the third book of his *Politics*, namely, that a State ought to be sufficient unto itself. But it can not adequately protect the public weal and the position of the State if it can not avenge a wrong and take measures against its enemies, for wrongdoers would become readier and bolder for wrongdoing if they could do wrong with impunity. It is, therefore, imperative for the due ordering of human affairs that this authority be allowed to States.

A definition of sovereignty :

425. 7. Now the whole difficulty is in the questions : What is a State, and who can properly be called a sovereign prince ? I will briefly reply to them by saying that a State is properly called a perfect community. But the essence of the difficulty is in saying what a perfect community is. By way of solution be it noted that a thing is called perfect when it is a completed whole, for that is imperfect in which there is something wanting, and, on the other hand, that is perfect from which nothing is wanting. A perfect State or community, therefore, is one which

is complete in itself, that is, which is not a part of another community but has its own laws and its own council and its own magistrates, such as is the Kingdom of Castile and Aragon and the Republic of Venice and other the like. For there is no obstacle to many principalities and perfect States being under one prince. Such a State, then, or the prince thereof, has authority to declare war and no one else.

What is a just cause of war :

429. 13. (Fourth proposition.) There is a single and only just cause for commencing war, namely, a wrong received. The proof of this rests in the first place on the authority of St. Augustine (Liber 83 Quæstionum, 'Those wars are described as just wars,' etc., as above), and it is the conclusion arrived at by St. Thomas (*Secunda Secundæ*, Q. 40, art 1) and the opinion of all the doctors. Also, an offensive war is for the purpose of avenging a wrong and of taking measures against an enemy, as said above. But there can be no vengeance where there is no preceding fault and wrong.

The punishment must fit the crime :

430. 14. (Fifth proposition.) Not every kind and degree of wrong can suffice for commencing a war. The proof of this is that not even upon one's own fellow-countrymen is it lawful for every offence to exact atrocious punishments, such as death or banishment or confiscation of property. As, then, the evils inflicted in war are all of a severe and atrocious character, such as slaughter and fire and devastation, it is not lawful for slight wrongs to pursue the authors of the wrongs with war, seeing that the degree of the punishment ought to correspond to the measure of the offence. (Deuteronomy xxv.)

The rights of the victor in just war : his judicial character :

431. 17. It is lawful to make good out of enemy property the expenses of the war and all damages wrongfully caused by the enemy. This is clear, for the enemy who has done the wrong is bound to give all this redress. Therefore the prince can claim it all and exact it all by war. Also, as before, there is the argument that, when no other way lies open, a private creditor can seize the amount of his debt from the debtor. Also, *if there were any competent judge over the two belligerents*, he would have to condemn the unjust aggressors and authors of wrong, not only to make restitution of what they have carried off, but also to make good the expenses of the war to the other side, and also all damages. But a prince who is carrying on a just war is, as it were, his own judge in matters touching the war, as we shall forthwith show. Therefore he can enforce all these claims upon his enemy.

18. Not only are the things just named allowable, but a prince

may go even further in a just war and do whatever is necessary in order to obtain peace and security from the enemy; for example, destroy an enemy's fortress and even build one on enemy soil, if this be necessary in order to avert a dangerous attack from the enemy.

The Law of Nations requires Princes to have authority to punish foreign enemies:

19. Not only is all this permissible, but even after victory has been won and redress obtained and peace and safety have been secured, it is lawful to avenge the wrong received from the enemy and to take measures against him and exact punishment from him for the wrongs he has done.

In proof of this be it observed that princes have authority not only over their own subjects, but also over foreigners, so far as to prevent them from committing wrongs, and this is by the law of nations and by the authority of the whole world. Nay, it seems to be by natural law also, seeing that otherwise society could not hold together unless there was somewhere a power and authority to deter wrongdoers and prevent them from injuring the good and innocent.

Now, everything needed for the government and preservation of society exists by natural law, and in no other way can we show that a State has by natural law authority to inflict pains and penalties on its citizens who are dangerous to it. But if a State can do this to its own citizens, *society at large no doubt can do it to all wicked and dangerous folk, and this can only be through the instrumentality of princes.* It is, therefore, certain that princes can punish enemies who have done a wrong to their State and that after a war has been duly and justly undertaken the enemy are just as much within the jurisdiction of the prince who undertakes it as if he were their proper judge.

The 'law of nations and the authority of the whole world' in this regard would to Vittoria and to St. Thomas be none the less real in the absence of a positive convention.

The Prince's personal belief in the justice of his cause insufficient:

435. 20. Many doubts are suggested by what has just been said. In the first place, there is a doubtful point in connection with the justice of a war, whether it be enough for a just war that the prince believes himself to have a just cause. On this point let my first proposition be: This belief is not always enough. And for proof I rely, first, on the fact that in some matters of less moment it is not enough either for a prince or for private persons to believe that they are acting justly. This is notorious, for their error may be vincible and deliberate, and the opinion of the individual is not enough to render an act good, but it

must come up to the standard of a wise man's judgement, as appears from *Ethics*, bk. 2. Also the result would otherwise be that very many wars would be just on both sides, for although it is not a common occurrence for princes to wage war in bad faith, they nearly always think theirs is a just cause. In this way all belligerents would be innocent and it would not be lawful to kill them. Also, were it otherwise, even Turks and Saracens might wage war against Christians, for they think they are thus rendering God service.

21. It is essential for a just war that an exceedingly careful examination be made of the justice and causes of the war and that the reasons of those who on grounds of equity oppose it be listened to. (Hence then, he adds, the prince is bound to consult good and wise men, free from bias, anger, bitterness or greed.[1])

Soldiers and citizens are bound to examine the justice of a war and to refuse service in one which they are convinced to be unjust :

22. Second doubt : Whether subjects are bound to examine the cause of a war or whether they may serve in the war without any careful scrutiny thereof, just as the lictors had to enforce the prætor's decree without questioning. On this doubt let my first proposition be : If a subject is convinced of the injustice of a war, he ought not to serve in it, even on the command of his prince. This is clear, for no one can authorize the killing of an innocent person. But in the case before us the enemy are innocent. Therefore they may not be killed. Again, a prince sins when he commences a war in such a case. But ' not only are they who commit such things worthy of death, but they, too, who consent to the doing thereof.' (Romans i.) Therefore soldiers also are not excused when they fight in bad faith. Again, it is not lawful to kill innocent citizens at the prince's command. Therefore not aliens either.

23. Hence flows the corollary that subjects whose conscience is against the justice of a war may not engage in it whether they be right or wrong. This is clear for ' whatever is not of faith is sin.' (Romans xiv.)

Duty of all those having political responsibility :

24. Senators and petty rulers and in general all who are admitted on summons or voluntarily to the public council ought, and are bound to examine into the cause of an unjust war.[2] This

[1] For full text of this paragraph see Chapter VII.

[2] This is one of several instances where the text seems to be obscure or unduly condensed, through an imperfect transcription of the lectures by the student or students who committed them to writing. To make the author's argument plain some such words as ' of a war which is not certainly just ' should surely be used.

is clear ; for whoever can save his neighbour from danger and harm is bound to do so, especially when the danger is that of death and greater ills, as is the case of war. But the persons referred to can avert the war, supposing it to be unjust, if they lend their wisdom and weight to an examination into its causes. Therefore they are bound so to do. Again, if by their neglect an unjust war be entered on, they are consenting parties thereto, for that which a man could and ought to prevent is imputed to him, if he does not prevent it. Again a king is not by himself capable of examining into the causes of a war and the possibility of a mistake on his part is not unlikely and such a mistake would bring great evil and ruin to multitudes. Therefore war ought not to be made on the sole judgement of the king, nor, indeed, on the judgement of a few, but on that of many, and they wise and upright men.

Vittoria goes on to express the opinion that the classes of the population who have no part in the ordering of the State are under no obligation to examine the cause of war ; their duty is to obey. This proposition however raises a point of great moment in a parliamentary democracy. For Vittoria teaches that the ruler exists for the good of the people and that they play a predominant part in choosing him. When therefore the government and its tenure of power depend upon the votes of all adult citizens, under such a polity has not each a measure of responsibility for national acts ?

The State in possession not to be attacked by another upon any questionable claim to its territory :

438. 27. Third doubt : What should be done when the justice of the war is doubtful, that is, when there are apparent and probable reasons on both sides. First proposition : As regards the princes themselves, it seems that if one be in lawful possession, the other may not try to turn him out by war and armed force, so long as the doubt remains. For example : Suppose the King of France to be in lawful possession of Burgundy, and that it be doubtful whether he has or has not right thereto. The Emperor may not try to oust him by arms ; nor on the other hand may the French King seize Naples or Milan, if there be doubt who is entitled to it. The proof is that in doubtful matters the party in possession has the better position. Therefore it is not lawful to dispossess the possessor in favour of a doubtful cause. Further, *if the matter were being heard by a lawful judge, he would never in case of doubt dispossess the party in possession.* Therefore, if we postulate that those princes who are asserting a right are judges in their own

cause, they may not lawfully eject a possessor so long as there is any doubt about the title. Further, in the suits and causes of private persons it is never permissible in a doubtful matter to dispossess a lawful possessor. Therefore not in the causes of princes; for the laws are the prince's laws. Therefore, if by human law it is not permissible in a doubtful matter to dispossess a lawful possessor, it can quite validly be objected to princes, 'Obey the law thyself hast made, seeing that a man ought to adopt the same law for himself which he has enjoined on others.' Also, were it otherwise, a war could be just on both sides and would never be settled. For if in a doubtful matter it were lawful[1] for one side to assert his claim by force, the other might make armed defence, and after the one had obtained what he claimed, the other might afterwards claim it back, and so there would be war without end, to the ruin and tribulation of peoples.

The State bound to examine doubts concerning its right of possession:

440. 29. He who is in doubt about his own title is bound, even though he be in peaceable possession, to examine carefully into the cause and give a quiet hearing to the arguments of the other side, if so be he may thus attain certitude either in favour of himself or the other. This is proved by the fact that a man who is in doubt and neglects to ascertain the truth is not in possession in good faith. So also, in a matrimonial cause, if the man who is in lawful possession entertains a doubt whether in truth the woman is his or the other's, it is certain that he is bound to examine the question. Therefore the same principle applies in other causes. Also, princes are judges in their own cases, *inasmuch as they have no superior.* But it is certain that, if any one raises any objection to a lawful possessor, the judge is bound to examine the case. Therefore in doubtful matter princes are bound to examine their own case.

The interests of Christendom or International Society as a whole may themselves invalidate an otherwise just cause of war:

446. 33. Now much attention must be paid to the admitted fact that a war may be just and lawful in itself and yet owing to some collateral circumstance may be unlawful. For it is admitted that one may be entitled to recapture a city or a province and yet that, because of some scandal, this may become quite unlawful.

For inasmuch as (according to what has been said before) wars ought (only) to be waged for the common good, if some one city cannot be recaptured without greater evils befalling the Commonweal, such as the devastation of many great cities, great

[1] Cf. the teaching of St. Alphonsus Liguori on p. 112, and of Vasquez on p. 111.

slaughter of human beings, provocation of princes, occasions for new wars to the destruction of the Church (in that an opportunity is given to pagans to invade and seize the lands of Christians), it is indubitable that the prince is bound rather to give up his own rights and abstain from war.

For it is clear that if the King of France, for example, had a right to retake Milan, but by the war both the Kingdom of France and the Duchy of Milan would suffer intolerable ills and heavy woes, it would not be right for him to retake it. This is because that war ought to take place either for the good of France or for the good of Milan. Therefore when, on the contrary, great ills would befall each side by the war, it could not be a just war.

Three canons of the ethics of war :

467. 60. All this can be summarized in a few canons or rules of warfare. First canon : Assuming that a prince has authority to make war, he should first of all not go seeking occasions and causes of war, but should, if possible, live in peace with all men, as St. Paul enjoins on us (Romans xii). Moreover, he should reflect that others are his neighbours, whom we are bound to love as ourselves, and that we all have one common Lord, before whose tribunal we shall have to render our account. For it is the extreme of savagery to seek for and rejoice in grounds for killing and destroying men whom God has created and for whom Christ died. But only under compulsion and reluctantly should he come to the necessity of war.

Second canon : When war for a just cause has broken out it must not be waged so as to ruin the people against whom it is directed, but only so as to obtain one's rights and the defence of one's country and in order that from that war peace and security may in time result.

Third canon : When victory has been won and the war is over the victory should be utilized with moderation and Christian humility, and the victor ought to deem that he is sitting as judge between two States, the one which has been wronged and the one which has done the wrong, so that it will be as judge and not as accuser that he will deliver the judgement whereby the injured State can obtain satisfaction, and this, so far as possible, should involve the offending State in the least degree of calamity and misfortune, the offending individuals being chastised within lawful limits ; and an especial reason for this is that in general among Christians all the fault is to be laid at the door of their princes, for subjects when fighting for their princes act in good faith, and it is thoroughly unjust, in the words of the poet, that :

Quidquid delirant reges, plectantur Achivi.

(For every folly their Kings commit the punishment should fall upon the Greeks.)

The following passage from the *Relectio De Potestate Civili*, (Ing.) 135, should be compared with the similar section of the *Relectio De Jure Belli* quoted above.

No war is just if the harm which it seems to bring to the State exceeds the benefit or the advantage, even if in other respects titles and reasons for the justice of the war are not lacking. The proof of this is that the State has no power to wage war except to defend and protect itself and its property. Therefore if its strength is diminished and outworn rather than increased by war itself the war will be unjust, be it waged by King or by republic.

And so since any one State is part of the world as a whole, and since especially a Christian province is part of the State, if war is made with advantage to one province or republic but with loss to the world or to Christendom, I think that that war would be unjust.

If, for instance, the Spaniards made war upon the French—a war undertaken in other respects for just reasons, and to the advantage of the Spanish Kingdom, and yet were waged with greater evil and loss to Christendom as a whole (say, the Turks took advantage of it to occupy Christian districts)—such a war ought to be stopped. . . .

MGR. PFEIFFER. (*Doctrina Juris Internationalis juxta Franciscum de Vittoria*), *comments as follows upon this argument*, *so far ahead of the political practice of the times :*

So teaches Vittoria. The question now arises whether in modern times when wars are much greater, and their results are much more easily felt throughout the world owing to the greater degree of international communication and economic interdependence, it may not more often happen than in earlier days that a war which in itself would be just and permissible becomes unlawful owing to the greater evils and dangers which it is only too likely to entail. Further, what Vittoria here has to teach about this or that State as *part of the world*, and of a Christian State as part of Christendom as a whole, is of the utmost importance. Elsewhere, as we have seen, our author says that under certain conditions it is of the competence of the world as a whole to punish malefactors.

SUAREZ. *De Legibus ac de Deo Legislatore : XII de Fide, Spe et Caritate. De Caritate Disp. XIII De Bello. Sect. I,* 3. *Defensive war not contrary to love of neighbours :*

To this (i.e. the proposition that war is always contrary to charity) Augustine replies (19 de Civit., capit. ult) that it is well proved that war in so far as is possible must be avoided and only resorted to in extreme necessity when no other means is left : that it is not altogether evil because the evil it entails are so *per accidens* and greater would follow if it were never licit. Hence in consequence he denies that war is contrary to honest peace but (says that it is contrary) to dishonest peace : for it is rather a means of attaining a real and safe peace. Similarly it is not contrary to the love of one's enemies : for he who wages war honestly does not hate the persons but their works which he rightly punishes : the same also applies to the forgiving of injuries, principally because these do not come under the precept, for revenge may sometimes be taken without injury when taken in a legitimate way.

This sentiment will hardly carry conviction to those who have personal experience of war. Thus Oscar de Halecki :[1] 'To this commandment (of Christian charity) nothing is more fundamentally opposed than the practice of war which, according to the vigorous phrase of a ninth century Pope "is always satanic in origin." For though it must be admitted that to wage a war of defence can sometimes be a duty of charity, properly understood, yet it is extremely difficult to imagine that the soldier obliged to thrust his bayonet into the living body of his adversary will, even in such a war, always do it in a spirit of Christian charity.'

SUAREZ. *Op. Cit.: Sect. I,* 4. *Self-defence a Natural Right :*

Defensive war is not only licit, but is sometimes even a duty. It is accepted not only by public magistrates but also by private persons : for it is always lawful to repel force by force (*vim vi repellere omnia jura permittunt*). . . . The reason is that the right of self-defence is a natural and necessary one.

Sect. I, 7. *Three conditions of just war.*

In order that war may be justly waged, certain conditions are to be observed and these may be brought under three heads. First, it must be waged by a legitimate power. Secondly, its cause must be just and right. Thirdly, just methods should be used, that is equity in the beginning of war, in the prosecution of it and in victory : all these are evident from the following sections. The reason of the general conclusion is that although war in itself is not an evil, yet on account of the many ills which it brings in its train it is to be numbered among those undertakings which are often wrongly done. And thus it needs many circumstances to make it honest.

[1] *Les Grandes Activités de la Société des Nations devant la Pensée Chrétienne*, p. 79.

Sect. II, 2. Penal character of war.

The power of waging war is a sort of power of jurisdiction, the exercise of which pertains to vindicative justice, which is most necessary within the commonwealth for the constraint of evil-doers. Thus, just as the supreme ruler can punish his subjects when they do harm to others, so can he exact satisfaction from another ruler or State which, by reason of a wrong committed, is subject to him. But this satisfaction cannot be sought from another judge, since the ruler of whom we are speaking has, in temporal matters, no superior : therefore, if the other ruler is not ready to give satisfaction, he can be forced to do so by war.

Sect. IV, 1. The only just cause of war.

There cannot be a just war without a legitimate and necessary cause. This is a certain and evident conclusion. Again, this just and sufficient cause is a grave injury that has been committed and which cannot be repaired or avenged by any other means.

Sect. V, 6. Violation of Natural right only justification for war.

It must also be said that there is no right of war so proper to Christian rulers that it has not some foundation in, or at least some relation to the natural law, and that it does not also suffice in some manner for non-Christian rulers : in explanation of this I say the Christian ruler may not declare war unless by reason of injury or for defending the innocent. It is sufficiently proved by the fact that all false rights (to declare war) are excluded. And the reasons given prove this, for a law of grace does not destroy a law of nature, but perfects it.

Sect. VI, 1. Diligent inquiry needed before war can be declared.

The supreme ruler is bound to examine diligently the cause and (its) justice ; having done this he ought to act according to the information gathered. The first part (of this proposition) is based on the fact that the business of war is extremely serious : common sense demands that in any business consultation should be held and diligence exercised in proportion to its importance. Moreover, in order that a judge may pass sentence in private business he must make diligent examination : so in like manner (must examination be made) into the public cause of war. A final reason also is that otherwise everything would be easily plunged into disorder by the temerity of rulers.

Sect. VI, 2. Probability of just cause held to permit recourse to war.

For let us suppose that the right of war be, that this king maintains that a city belongs to him or that it ought to come to him by hereditary right: if the fact is certain the assertion is evident. But when the thing is probable for both sides then the king ought to act as a just judge: hence if the opinion favouring him is more probable he can in justice pursue his right, for as I rightly think, the more probable opinion is always to be followed *in sententia ferenda* because it is an act of distributive justice in which the more worthy is to be favoured. He is the worthier whom the more probable right favours (of which more hereafter). For the same reason, if the opposing party has on his side the more probable opinion, the ruler may by no means wage war.

Sect. VI, 3. If neither side be evidently just, major est conditio possidentis.

If finally when full examination has been made equal probability is found on each side or almost equal doubt, whence further doubt arises, then if the other is in possession he is to be preferred, for in judgement he is also preferred since he has the greater right: hence he who is not in possession may not declare war on the possessor: he, however, who is in possession is (morally) safe and may in justice defend himself.

Sect. VII, 3. Restitution must be sought peacefully, and, if offered, accepted.

The prince is obliged, before declaring war, to propound the just cause of his making war to the State with which he is in dispute and to ask for adequate restitution. If that State offers restitution he is obliged to accept it and to desist from war; and if he does not do so the war which he wages will be an unjust war.

VASQUEZ. *Commentariorum et Disputationum in Primam Secundæ Sancti Thomæ (Tomus I). Disputatio LXIV, Cap. III, (Cardon 1631).*

The author sets out to consider the case in which each of two sovereigns has a claim to territory and each believes himself to be probably in the right. This, he says, though little examined by the Doctors is a question most worthy to be treated carefully by theologians 'for upon it most of all depends peace or discord between Christian princes, of which the momentous importance is sufficiently evident to all.'

He begins by stating the opinion of Vittoria in his *Relectio de Jure Belli* on this subject, which he for the most part approves (i.e. in case of doubt '*melior est conditio possidentis*':

if rights are apparently equal, division of the territory). But the difficulty in question is not precisely that which occurs when the matter in dispute is doubtful and no probable assent of opinion can be obtained for one or the other party, ' but when each prince has a probable opinion on his side, an opinion which the Doctors, whom he himself has consulted, consider more probably right than that of the adversary.' Has he then, on those grounds, the right to seek to take that kingdom by force of arms ?

Vasquez dissents from the opinion of Navarrus,[1] who teaches that ' Christian princes, who have a controversy among themselves about a kingdom or State which cannot be extinguished by recourse to law, since neither has a superior, *nor settled by arms*[2] *since the power and armaments of each are equal*, ought to remit their case to arbitrators. If they should refuse to choose arbitrators, or to acquiesce in their (proposed) agreement and sentence, they sin very gravely because of the detriment which the Christian commonweal suffers by reason of their discord and war.'

This, he says, does not exactly touch the difficulty which he is considering. But he gathers that both Vittoria,[3] Navarrus and more recent authors teach that the ruler who believes himself more than probably to have the justice on his side may occupy the territory in question even by arms if other means fail, since he is sovereign and has no superior.

' This opinion,' says he, ' I will never accept : it has been the cause of great harm and loss to the Christian Commonwealth.' No sovereign prince involved in controversy with another, without absolute certainty of right, can pass sentence and put it into execution by force of arms.

' Further, if the cause of each prince is contentious and probably just on one side and the other, one prince cannot declare war on the other, even if it seems to him that his right to the kingdom is more probable than the other's. This is shown as follows. Every controversy in which various opinions are held concerning a certain right ought to be settled not by might and

[1] The learned uncle of St. Francis Xavier.

[2] Lamentable admission of Might as a determinant of Right.

[3] In this Vasquez seems to do an injustice to Vittoria.

arms, but by judgement[1]; for it is clearly a barbarous custom to maintain that the better right to rule consists in the greater military strength.'

And further; war is an act of punitive justice. But no penalty should be inflicted until both sides have been heard and 'the opinion of each examined together with the reasons and grounds upon which that opinion reposes'; after which sentence may be given for one or the other.

ST. ALPHONSUS DE LIGUORI. *De Quinto præcepto decalogi. Art. II. Par.* 404 *:*

Can a ruler who has only a probable opinion of justice on his side declare war on another who holds a kingdom in good faith?

The first opinion says he can. The reason is that a ruler ought not to be in a worse position than a private person: for if private persons are allowed to go to law about a thing which is in the possession of another, why should a ruler not be allowed to make war on another, at least for vindicating his right to that part of the kingdom in the other's possession, when there is no higher judge to decide between them according to the law.

The second opinion says that to declare war, the ruler not in possession must have at least a more probable opinion on his side. The reason is that in that case the right of him who is not in possession is stronger, and just as a private person would have the things adjudicated to him by a judge, as we have shown above, so the ruler, since he cannot have recourse to a competent judge, can vindicate his right by war.

But the third opinion, which seems to me much more probable, says that a ruler cannot declare war on another who possesses in good faith unless he is *certain* of his right. A very strong reason for this is that the possessor (since possession gives him a certain right of retaining the thing as we have shown) can never be deprived of the thing he possesses unless it is evident that he retains it unjustly. Tamburinus holds the same opinion, and says that it is canon law to be observed even by kings, that no one may expoliate another who possesses in good faith unless he is certain of his right. . . . It seems to me that though the second opinion seems, theoretically speaking, even intrinsically probable enough yet it is not satisfactory:

There is no doubt that since war generally brings in its train so many evils and so much harm to religion, to innocent people, to the honour of women, etc., in practice it is hardly ever just if declared on probable reasons of justice alone and not certain reasons.

[1] See Vasquez' development of this thought in Chapter VII.

Par. 405–6 *:*

Catholic princes are also sometimes bound to abstain from war, otherwise just in itself, if it will give rise to scandal, bring ruin to many souls, and harm the Church.

The passages of these theologians, which restate the Augustinian doctrine of the right of war, have been reproduced above because there is a certain advantage in their clarity. They do not in themselves call for further comment.

What however merits particular attention is the fact that this doctrine has been reaffirmed at a time when the sovereignty and independence of national states is being asserted in an extreme form. Vittoria, Suarez and their followers both accept and indeed assert the political independence of states : they seem at first sight to admit the notion of national sovereignty in its modern connotation. The limits which they set upon it are implied rather than explicitly set forth.

Yet this is not in fact so revolutionary a development as appears to those who have been accustomed to facile historical generalizations upon the political unity of Christendom existing up to a particular date and its disruption thereafter. Actually Papal interventions to effect peace were as numerous and more effective in the seventeenth century than in the fifteenth ; on the other hand the Holy Roman Empire had ceased to be a real source of political unity two centuries at least before Vittoria taught at Salamanca. But the scholastic theory of political ethics, as will have been observed from the previous chapter, had been singularly detached from the claims and vicissitudes of the Imperial or of the Papal power. That theory had been based upon abstract reasoning : the rights allowed to Cæsar by the Apostles and their immediate successors, when found to be consonant with the postulates of reason, had been attached as a logical necessity to any prince who had not *de facto* a political superior. But Right is one face of the coin of which the reverse is Duty : the right to rule, to judge, to make war clearly involved duties, first to God, next to those who are ruled, next to the prince and people who may be adjudged guilty of injury and subjected to the penalty of war.

Was then the morality of war, in the eyes of the Divine justice, a purely bilateral question? Were the two potential belligerents the only two parties to the dispute? The distinctive contribution of the Spanish neo-scholastics to the development of Christian doctrine on this subject was their introduction or rather elucidation of the rights of a third party—*the general society of peoples.*

This was shown first indirectly, by the importance attached to the penal character of war and to the judicial character of the ruler who, for lack of a superior judge to decide between him and his adversary was bound to take the dreadful decision. The concepts of *judge* and of *just penalty* necessarily postulate the existence of a law ascertainable by each intelligence and applicable to all. And the Thomistic notion of law is that it is a dictate of reason—hence universal by its nature—and directed to the good of society—hence giving society a certain right in determining its application. The only justification for the right conferred upon princes to declare war, which these authors could find, was that they acted as judges for and on behalf of the natural society of the human race 'by the Law of Nations and by the authority of the whole world . . . otherwise society could not hold together' (Suarez: *De Jure Belli*, 433).

In the second place, the priority of the interests of the whole over the interests of the part[1] is illustrated by the repeated insistence of these writers—and they press this point in several ways—upon the sovereign character of the ruler to whom the right of war belongs. Sovereignty in the mind of Francis de Vittoria does not, upon closer examination, mean anything like the freedom from responsibility to God and from duty to man which characterizes the Prince of Machiavelli. To him the king or prince who has any juridical or political superior has not the right of war. If his domains form part of a greater political unit; if he has over him a judge or tribunal able to examine and adjudicate upon the dispute between him and his neighbour, then he has no right to decree the penalty of war against that neighbour. Were there in the sixteenth century, are there to-day any rulers or governments truly sovereign, if that

[1] See Fénelon quoted on p. 266.

criterion be applied? Even Vittoria puts forward the opinion that the Christian princes of his day were not justified in taking the law into their own hands since they could appeal to the Pope who had indirect temporal jurisdiction[1] over them. Were he to fail them, either from some temporal disability or lack of courage, they would of course be free from that particular obligation. To-day the same obligation would appear to rest upon governments who own the Catholic allegiance[2] in regard to differences which arise between them. They, together with the majority of governments of organized States,[3] have undertaken definite treaty obligations whereby they promise to submit to judicial settlement, arbitration, mediation or conciliation any dispute likely to cause a rupture which may arise between them. A permanent tribunal; a Council or concert of governments which can meet rapidly and a great number of conciliation commissions have been instituted by them to fulfil these functions of a judicial or quasi-judicial character. These again[4] with the addition of the few remaining Governments, have pledged their honour to refrain from using the right of war in the separate interests of their several nations and to seek the solution of conflicts between them by peaceful means only—though in this case unspecified.

There may be emergencies, during a period in which political and juridical institutions are only partly developed or in fact command only partial assent, when those that are morally subject to them are justified in acting as 'judges in their own cause'; the justification for such a course might be found in overwhelming evidence of the inefficiency or partiality of the institution. It was doubtless the repetition of such emergencies and the readiness to exploit them that destroyed the Holy Roman Empire as a barrier against war. But whoever else may be found on the side of a broken

[1] See passage from the *Relectio De Potestate Ecclesiæ* in Chapter VII.

[2] Observe the care of the Holy See to reserve its right to fulfil this pacific function on demand in Art. 24 of the Lateran Treaty, 1930.

[3] See Covenant of the League of Nations, p. 475.

[4] See text of Pact of Paris, p. 514.

oath, either of fealty to a superior or of contract with equals, Catholic theologians cannot be found in such a camp. The Covenant and Pact are solemnly ratified by the Heads of States ; the institutions, though imperfect, exist. Under such circumstances would Vittoria or Suarez, Soto, Vasquez or St. Alphonsus Liguori have held these Governments to be 'sovereign' in the sense defined, free each on his own account to decree the death of thousands or even millions of men and women by a declaration of war? We cannot believe it.[1] For justice was their predominant care ; the imputability of sin to the prince (or government) a very real thing ; the sanctity of a promise solemnly given and solemnly ratified indubitable. This school of thought—saving Suarez, whose dangerous opinion of probable justice was soon rejected—agrees upon the *certainty* of a just and sufficient cause as alone justifying recourse to war. Would it be disposed to whittle away the obligation to submit to arbitration when the opportunity existed, and when the duty of this submission had been publicly recognized? It would not. Nor will any reader who examines the trend of Catholic thought which later chapters reveal, and most of all the practice and preaching of the Papacy in recent times, be left in any doubt that this body of neo-scholastic philosophy is attune with the true mind of the Catholic Church.

If the reasoning of Vittoria and Vasquez, and in a hardly less degree of Suarez, leads in this direct and positive sense to the conclusion that a system of international arbitration is eminently desirable, it does so no less clearly by an unconscious *reductio ad absurdum* of the penal conception of war. The purely theoretic elaboration of the considerations which should move a prince in the declaration of just war, and of his rights in the conduct and conclusion of it, may be logical in the abstract. Psychologically it ignores the inherent defects of human nature whereby it is a moral impossibility for the ruler of a State, incensed at the apparent violation of his rights, to act with real impartiality as judge in his own cause. And what a complete abstraction from the actualities

[1] This conclusion is endorsed by Dr. James Brown Scott in his valuable essay on 'Suarez and War' in his book *The Catholic Conception of International Law*, 643.

of national sentiment is the sentence of Dominic Soto upon just war: 'Whoever has been justly and legitimately condemned may not defend himself against his legitimate judge...' (*De Justitia et Jure V vi* 4)! Hardly less inconceivable in practice is the attitude of detachment and magnanimity required in the victor regarding the reparation to be exacted from a beaten enemy. Almost inevitably in penalizing his adversary the victor, as Cajetan says, is guilty of 'malice hurtful to the soul, since he performs a just action without the intention of acting justly' (*Summula: 'Bellum'*).

To these objections it might be replied that it is unjust to the authors in question to confuse practical conclusions drawn from historical and political experience with a system of abstract ethics. But law comes because of sin; and this is most of all true of the law of war. If rulers of States could normally be expected to act according to the sublime standard of a St. Louis, there would be no need to elaborate rules upon the conditions of a just declaration of war, the just conduct of war and the just use of victory. It is precisely because all the characteristics of fallen human nature are found in the acts of the collective persons which we call States, that laws concerning their mutual relations, whether in peace or war, are required. Such laws therefore must take account of the weaknesses and limitations of human nature, and, in particular of the difficulty of punishing political societies for the sins committed in their name as if they were individual human beings. This difficulty is hardly less if, in the terminology of the Middle Ages, the problem is discussed as affecting the conscience of the prince, than if it is applied to the public conscience of the democratic State. Apart from honestly divided opinions about the *casus belli*, there are in each State many degrees of responsibility and irresponsibility for national acts, many degrees of knowledge and ignorance concerning the data upon which a declaration of war is decided, the acts committed in the course of the fighting and the opportunities of bringing hostilities to an end. Further, reason and Catholic tradition require a high standard of patriotism and loyalty on the part of citizens and soldiers who, unless they have a moral certitude that the war in which they are commanded to engage is wrong, are obliged under pain of sin to obey their government. It is an open question whether the individual citizen is better able to satisfy himself that the policy of his rulers is unjust, when the newspapers which he reads and the news which reaches him by wireless telephony are alike controlled and censored by the government, than when—as in the sixteenth and seventeenth centuries—he must depend upon hearsay or the text of a royal proclamation for the data upon which to take his decision. In either case it is all but a political impossibility for him to be certain that the national effort to which he is urged to contribute his part is exerted in a wrongful cause.

How then are the individual citizens of such a State to be punished in defeat? For whatever the constitutional condition of States in the time of our authors, it is evidently impossible now to distinguish between guilty and innocent in the incidence of an indemnity sufficient not only to repair the whole damage done in the war, but to punish the wrong committed? Vittoria is conscious of this extreme difficulty of which we have indicated but the principal points. In one passage of the *De Potestate Civili* he appears to seek a solution in an extreme interpretation of the responsibility of the people—that is, of the majority.

De Pot. Civ. 14. (cf. *De Indis III*, 16) :

A whole State may lawfully be punished for the sin of its king. Thus if the king wages unjust war against another prince, he who has received this injury may take booty and pursue the other rights of war, and kill that king's subjects even if they be all innocent. Once a king has been appointed by his State, any insolent act of his is imputed to the State ; for the State is under an obligation not to entrust the kingly power to any man save to one who will justly wield that power.[1]

Yet in the Third Canon of his whole conclusion to the *Relectio de Jure Belli* quoted above, Vittoria lays it down that the judgement whereby the offended State can obtain satisfaction, should, so far as possible, involve the offending State in the least

[1] It is true that this passage applies to the rights of war in general, and that it serves only as an illustration to an argument upon another subject, i.e. the choice of a people's rulers ; but it certainly appears to cover the rights of the victor in a just war.

degree of calamity and misfortune, the offending individuals being chastised within lawful limits ; and an especial reason for this is that in general among Christians all the fault is to be laid at the door of their princes ; for subjects, when fighting for their princes, act in good faith.

No theory which shelves or ignores the fact that the State is only by analogy named and treated as a single *person*, will solve the problem of sanctions in the international community : indeed the difficulty which we have outlined is one for which it would be rash to offer any complete explanation. This is not to say that there is no place for punishment in international ethics. 'War is a sort of international punishment,' Taparelli was to write three centuries later. 'Punishment is, by its nature, a restoration of order ; a compensation for the past ; a guarantee for the future.' Justice demands that injury should not go unpunished : restitution should evidently be made to an innocent people for what has unlawfully been seized from them : reparation for the loss of life and property which they have suffered as the victims of unjust attack should likewise be obtained. But just as fines and damages are accepted in civil society, without giving rise to an interminable vendetta between defendant and plaintiff and their families, because they are imposed by the public authority : so we are obliged, as well from a consideration of the nature of the State as from historical experience to conclude, that the only way in which nations can be obliged to pay reparations and indemnities without engendering[1] 'a mournful heritage of hatred and revenge from generation to generation' against their former antagonists, is by the judgement and assessment, not of interested parties, but of an international tribunal. Far more probable is it that a third party or a superior tribunal[2] will, in such circumstances,

[1] Benedict XV Apostolic Exhortation of July 28, 1915.

[2] After the invasion of Bulgaria by the Greek troops in 1925, an indemnity of £45,000 for the damage committed was imposed upon Greece in consequence of the report of the international Commission of Enquiry. It was accepted by Greece, though the stronger of the two powers, without any lasting resentment on her part either against Bulgaria or the League of Nations.

give a verdict in which the indispensable virtue of social charity[1] plays its proper part.

In a more explicit manner Vittoria, Suarez and Vasquez show the society of nations as a whole to be an interested party—indeed the most interested party—to be taken into account, when the justice or expediency of the use of military force has to be determined.

Suarez, in a passage from the *De Legibus*, quoted in another place (p. 265), teaches the reality and the necessity of the natural society of nations and the law by which it lives. They arise not only, he says, from the physical or economic imperfection of the State or Republic, but also from its lack of moral self-sufficiency. From this conception it follows logically that '*it is contrary to prudence and the common good of the human race that all contentions between supreme rulers ought only to end in war; therefore it is contrary to justice.*' Vittoria lays it down explicitly:

> And so since any one State is part of the world as a whole, and since especially a Christian province is part of the State, if war is made with advantage to one province or republic but with loss to the world or to Christendom, I think that war would be unjust.

In his first and principal *Relectio De Indis* (See Chapter XV) he elaborates the rights of an indigenous people, unbaptized and uncivilized, as against a colonizing power, and the grounds upon which the colonizers might or might not be morally justified either in using military force against them or in annexing their territory. And at every turn it is to the Law of Nature and the Law of Nations that appeal is made.

The following questions, then, are raised by the neo-scholastics' development and elucidation of St. Augustine's doctrine on war:

Is it the duty of princes to seek to bring into being an international judicial tribunal?

Does the opportunity of international arbitration at the hands either of the Pope, or a secular tribunal, remove from the prince (government) the judicial character whereby he has the right to declare war?

[1] See the letter of Pope Pius XI to the Cardinal Gasparri upon the Reparations problem created by the Great War (p. 220).

How can the ruler of the state have, not a probable opinion, but the certainty that he is justified in using military force against another state or against uncivilized natives in another country ?

Who is to judge whether, when a certain cause of just war apparently exists, the damage of war to the whole society of nations or the Universal Church will or will not be sufficiently serious to make a declaration of war unjust ?

There are other cognate issues more remotely following upon the reasoning of these authors. In what for instance does the right of self-defence consist in a state of international society in evolution ? Is there to be any qualification of the axiom *vim vi repellere omnia jura permittunt ?* Who is to decide the moment when the right to defensive war comes into operation ; or the degree of force to be used in defence ; or the extent of military preparation required for such an emergency, in a world in which there is some prospect but no certainty of the organized international society providing a collective defence of its members' rights ? Or again, if the use of military force is to pass to that society, how and under what conditions is it to be employed ? Once the social use of force becomes no longer theoretic but actual, is its purpose still to be only penal ? Should it not, like the police within civil society, be employed more for prevention than cure, more as the guardian of order and the deterrent of injustice than as the public executioner ?

It could not be claimed that either Vittoria or Suarez or their immediate successors precisely formulated these questions, still less that they proposed answers to them. That was to be the care of their disciples in the nineteenth century, and in the great examination of conscience which followed the European War. Yet to such a narrowing down of the international problem of war did their reasoning inevitably lead. That is the great practical importance of their teaching in the history of Christian thought : it is a bridge between the age of St. Thomas Aquinas and the modern age. Through them the 'Law of Nations' has become 'International Law.' They have shown that Catholic doctrine is not the slave of political forms. The power which converted the Empire and had sought to make of it the political framework of a Christian world, is no less able to rationalize and Christianize a world of independent national states.

Conclusions

Taking into account the varying opinions of the neo-scholastic authorities on several points, the following precisions of doctrine may now be made :

1. The right of war is odious.[1] That this right exists in certain circumstances cannot be denied ; but it is a regrettable necessity, and the main object of rulers should be to prevent the necessity arising.
2. A declaration of war—other than a war of self-defence against actual attack—is a penal act, justifiable only if an injury has been committed so great as to require the gravest penalty.
3. The penal jurisdiction required for the declaration of war is necessary for the preservation of order in human society and is conferred upon sovereigns in the absence of a higher tribunal.
4. If the possibility of recourse to the arbitration of the Holy See or another competent tribunal exists, this penal jurisdiction may not be exercised by a prince.
5. If any doubt exists concerning the justice of his claims the prince may not resort to arms. In such a case both disputants are under an obligation to choose arbitrators or mediators and to abide by their decision.
6. Even if a certainly just cause of war exists, the prince must refrain from going to war if the losses resulting from war to the belligerent states, the whole community of nations or the Church are likely to be so great as to outweigh the advantages of repairing the injury done.
7. Soldiers are bound to examine the justice of a proposed war. If uncertain of the justice of the cause their duty is to obey their commanders. If certain of the injustice of the cause they are to refuse to fight.

[1] Suarez, *De Caritate*, XIII, 7, 4 : *Jus belli est odiosum, et pœna ejus gravissima ; ergo restringenda est quoad fieri potest.*

8. All those who hold office or have any political responsibility in the state are bound in conscience to examine carefully the rights and wrongs of a proposed declaration of war.
9. War may not be waged on the personal authority of the sovereign, but only after the advice of wise and impartial men has been sought, and after the claims of the opposing side have been carefully weighed.

CHAPTER VI

MODERN WAR

THE whole political and economic evolution of the present age is dominated by the memory of a war. The war of 1914–18 involved more nations as belligerents, caused a greater loss of life, greater devastation and a greater expenditure of national treasure than any previous war recorded in history. It is the typical and most terrible war of the modern age ; and it is of such war that this chapter treats.

Is this vast mobilization of whole peoples against one another ; this wholesale destruction of life by mechanical means ; this unprecedented and systematic organization of hatred by the public authorities the same process as the war of which Origen or St. Ambrose, St. Augustine or St. Thomas Vittoria or Vasquez faced so courageously the moral implications ? Certainly it has many characteristics which distinguish it to a marked degree from the wars of the Roman Empire in the post-Apostolic Age ; the wars of the early Christian Empire ; the wars envisaged by theologians of the thirteenth century, and the wars of the Renaissance period. Just as the expression *jus gentium* has passed through a dozen shades of meaning since its first use to describe the indigenous customs discovered in Italy by the Prætor Peregrinus, so has the word *bellum* come to denote several quite different aspects of human conflict. The typical war which disturbed the conscience of a Tertullian or a Lactantius was the war by which the legionaries of that pagan Empire, which was coterminous with civilization, quelled rebellious tribes or repelled barbarian attack. The typical war in St. Augustine's mind was that waged between the forces of a Christian emperor and the vandals. In the days of St. Thomas Aquinas two types of war were envisaged: the one between Christian princes, generally arising from conflicting feudal claims; the other the Crusade. Two types were again evidently in the mind of the Spanish neo-scholastics—colonial war and dynastic war, as the examples chosen by Vittoria, Suarez, Vasquez and others, whom we have cited, clearly show.

To each of these variants of the dreadful act of war the conception of a legal process could reasonably apply: in the first instance it appeared as a defence of law against lawlessness; in the next a defence of human and divine rights against oppression; in the next as a means of ending a conflict of rights concerning royal succession or inheritance, superiority or inferiority in the feudal pyramid; in the last a vindication of the law of nations as against unjust obstruction to trade and intercourse on the one hand or depredation on the other. Such a process could be treated as a regrettable but necessary substitute for judicial procedure—a kind of trial by ordeal—or as an act of penal jurisdiction clearly necessary to the ordering of human society, but for the execution of which society had not yet the proper organ. Never since Christian philosophers and theologians began to wrestle with the problem of war until the end of the period treated in the last chapter—the seventeenth century—was there any doubt that war could be judged, justified or excused by any other standard than the objective standard of justice—justice reinforced on the one hand by the consequences of the Christian revelation, and as closely linked on the other to a code of law to which in theory at least, all rulers were subject. Mediæval wars were, as Stubbs has shown, almost invariably wars about rights. Further, the wars with which Fathers and Doctors of the Church had hitherto been occupied formed for the most part a problem which could be solved in terms of human individuals—that is, of princes.

The war with which the Christian conscience is faced in the twentieth century is a process which has hardly any of these qualities. The exaltation of the sovereign people by the French Revolution made the principal factors of international life no longer royal personages or their ministers but vast impersonal collectivities. The principle of nationality stamped upon these collectivities characters which divided them more and more sharply the one from the other and encouraged in each a religion of egoism; the repudiation of ecclesiastical unity and the slower but no less fundamental repudiation in practice of any moral unity overriding these divisions between them; the mushroom development of mechanical science which in one brief century placed in the hands of each great state weapons of war a hundred times more formidable, means of transport and mobilization ten times more swift than any previous age had known—these are among the causes which have produced the effect which we call, in the twentieth century, war. Not only has it the tendency to become a general conflagration—most difficult physically to confine; it also proves to be singularly elusive and difficult to define in the ethical order. The sharp edge of right is blurred. Ramifications of economic interest confuse the search for the real causes of war, remote or proximate: parliamentary democracy, with its kaleidoscopic changes of executive government, makes the task of fixing responsibility almost beyond human reach. Who, in such a shifting multitude, is innocent and who guilty? In the actual hostilities the long range gun and the air bomb know no distinction between combatant and non-combatant.

Not surprising is it therefore that no considerable school of Christian theologians has sought to rationalize modern war and its practices in any such way as the theologians of the days of Charles V sought to fit war, as they knew it, into the universal scheme of justice. Denunciation of war as a whole and positive encouragement and exhortation to peace have more than ever dominated the teaching of the Papacy during this age. To Benedict XV the European war was 'a terrible butchery,' 'a disgrace to Europe,' 'a horrible human shambles,' 'anti-Christian slaughter,' 'fratricide.'[1] To Pius XI a civilized state which contemplates a future war is unbelievable, it would be guilty of 'monstrous homicide and almost certainly of suicide.'[2] The sense of war as a

[1] Various encyclicals in the course of the war.
[2] Christmas allocution, 1930.

scourge of God is prominent once more : it is a punishment for sin, to be averted only by repentance and amendment—the restoration of the whole order of human society under the Kingship of Jesus Christ.[1]

But denunciation of a great social evil, and lamentation at the curse which the crimes and follies of men have brought down upon their heads—these have never been the only or the principal ways in which the Catholic Church has striven to remove that evil or to lift the curse. It is they that are sick who need a physician ; and it is to a sick world that the Church came to minister. Cures must often be long, the patient must not infrequently be humoured. By which is intended no voluntary obscuring for a single moment of the truth and the right, but rather a method of cure which is not so brusque as to risk the salvation of many immortal souls. Such might have been the result for instance of an act of ecclesiastical discipline which, following the Papal censure of conscription,[2] forbade Catholics to serve as conscripts or withheld chaplains from conscript armies. What would have been the consequence of such a rigorist gesture as this ? Governments and great sections of political opinion in many countries would have been turned blindly against the Church and all her teaching ; thousands, indeed millions of men might have been forced into an agonizing position of divided loyalty, and, if they obeyed the civil authority and their own patriotic instincts, would have been deprived of the supernatural aid of the Sacraments. Nor could the military training of the youth of a whole nation—though antipathetic to the Christian conception of peace and a contributory cause of the war mentality of the times—be condemned as intrinsically wrong in itself.

And so, just as in the days of the pagan Empire, the practical needs of her children—soldiers and centurions in the legions—had obliged the Church to face one by one the ethical problems raised by war and military service rather than remain upon the distant mountain of abstract perfection so the urgent need of guiding and consoling individual consciences has made it inevitable—if for no other reason—

[1] Encyclical on Christ the King.

[2] e.g. Leo XIII, *Præclara Gratulationis*. June 20, 1894.

for the mind of the Church to apply to the phenomenon of modern war, so far as they are applicable, the canons of right and wrong evolved by the Fathers and doctors of earlier ages. The faithful of the Catholic Church are to be found to-day in every country, and in every degree of responsibility within a state. What was the Catholic citizen or statesman to think of the rising force of nationality? How was he to distinguish its lawful from its unlawful form? What part might he play and what refuse to play in the great nationalist revolutions and wars between 1840 and 1870? What guidance was to be given to the consciences of Catholic soldiers in the great European and colonial conflicts from 1870 to 1918?

There has always been, in the matter of peace and war, a positive and a negative contribution made by the leaders of Catholic thought to the problems of their time. The positive contribution consists in the elucidation of reasons, motives and means for maintaining peace, the negative in the delimitation of conditions within which war may be allowed. We have already alluded to the preponderance of the former in the present age: it is to this positive and constructive development of the 'Gospel of peace' that the subsequent chapters are for the most part devoted. How Christianity upholds and sanctifies the true conception of the fraternity of the human race: how best to give positive form to the universal society of peoples and serve its interests: how the rights of God and His Church should be secured in the process: that is the main consideration. What peaceful methods should be evolved for the settlement of international disputes: how the aspirations of each nation and the true interests of backward peoples are to be harmonized with the good of the whole: these are examples of the practical problems whose solution must be integrated into a Christian science of international ethics.

It is however with the latter, or negative contribution of Catholic thought, that the present chapter is concerned, namely the answer to the question within what limits should war, itself an evil, be circumscribed under the circumstances of the present age? When and by whom may it be waged, if at all?

There is one other distinction to be made between the expression of the Catholic mind in those early stages of European history (say, the dawn of Christendom : the thirteenth century : the beginning of the modern age) and in the latter nineteenth and twentieth centuries. It is that in recent times the mind of the Church upon international ethics must be sought, and is in fact found far more in Papal Encyclicals and Allocutions than in the writings of the Catholic theologians and philosophers of different countries. From those former ages we were able to quote, upon this acute political problem of war, the works of great Bishops, doctors, schoolmen and the illustrious figures of Catholic universities, without any regard to their racial origin or their political allegiances. But however unity of faith has been illustrated—as indeed it has—by the learning of Catholic intellectuals of all nationalities in recent years, he indeed would be an uncandid historian of Catholic thought, who did not admit that the virus of nationalism has powerfully infected Catholic thinkers at least in Europe upon this particular question during the last two generations. May this be only a passing aberration ! There are already signs of its end. But the national bias of many Catholic theologians and publicists both before, during and after the Great War, in dealing with this problem (which most of all demands clear thought and the absence of special pleading) has been so transparent, their response to the pacific leadership of the Holy See so meagre and indeed contemptible, that the student must now be on his guard against taking the words of any particular Catholic divine or author as representing the mind of the Church as a whole. Many Catholic theologians of late have indeed sinned rather by omission than commission : rather than risk the influence of their own national prejudices, or the displeasure of their students and readers, they have, it seems, either left aside any attempt to deal with the ethics of war and peace or contented themselves with reproducing in the shortest possible form the traditional thomistic doctrine on this subject.

But there are some Catholic leaders and authors in the last ninety years who clearly rise above all sectional considerations, and whose perfect impartiality and manifest integrity command respect, in addition to the Saintly Popes, fit Vicars of the Prince of Peace, whose pontificates have occupied that period and whose utterances are recorded in other chapters. It is from their writings on war that we quote. They belong to two generations: the first is that which experienced the first onslaught of bellicose nationalism in the European order (1840–70) and the beginning of the race in armaments which led to the calamity of 1914; the second is the generation which is living in the aftermath of the Great War. To the first belong the little group of determined and distinguished men who, oppressed by the general disregard of law in international relations, earnestly sought to secure from the Vatican Council in 1870 a re-statement of the rules of International Right—an effort which might well have succeeded, had not war put an end to the deliberations of the Council itself. The postulata of the Forty Fathers of the Council and the postulatum of the Armenian Hierarchy—the first documents reproduced—were the result of the activity of the group of which David Urquhart, author of the famous *Protestant's Appeal to the Pope*, was the leading spirit. Though later in date than the treatise of Taparelli these postulata belong to an older and less developed school of thought; a school which had not integrated the problem of the morality of war in the wider problem of the construction of a society of nations. Akin to the same line of traditional thought are the conclusions of a trusted modern theologian, Father Génicot, which we also quote.

We next give some passages of importance from the Essay on Natural Law of Father Taparelli d'Azeglio, S.J., brother of the notorious leader of the Italian Risorgimento, a theologian of great authority in the Rome of Pius IX and the editor of the *Civilta Cattolica*. The treatise, first published in 1846, had a great vogue for forty years at least and was translated from the original Italian into French, from which language the following translations have been made. Controversy continues in the schools upon Taparelli's theory of the patriarchal source of authority in human society, but this does not detract from the great value of those books (VI and VII) of the treatise quoted in the present work. For he was the first to argue from first principles (not as a political scheme but as a logical necessity) both the reality of a natural society of nations and the necessity of constructing a world-wide organisation of that society or federation of all nations which he called an 'ethnarchy.' Into this scheme he welded the principles which were of permanent value in the doctrine of the Spanish neo-scholastics on war, discarding their doubtful opinions. It will be seen that he allows war to be a punishment only when it is in fact an international punishment; that he postulates a system of arbitration as a necessity, and that he envisages a time when the organized Society of Nations will alone wield what military force is needed, either to prevent or punish aggression against the territorial integrity of any one of its members.

Following upon this line of thought, a remarkable group of German and French theologians studying first separately, then together during the period of the early development of the actual League of Nations, evolved conclusions upon the ethics of war which, except for certain minor points, probably carry the application of Catholic tradition on this subject as far as is possible at the present juncture. In an explanatory note to these conclusions, reached at the *Conventus Theologicus Friburgensis de Bello*, of which a full English translation is here given, the authors recall the following words of St. Thomas in justification for their decision to consider war under its modern aspects as something very different from the war defined by earlier scholastic theologians.

St. Thomas. *In II Ethic., Lect.* 2:

In the speculative sciences it is sufficient to know what is the cause which produces a particular effect. But in the practical sciences we must know by what movements and operations such an effect follows from such a cause.

As a link between the extracts on war from Taparelli and the Fribourg conclusions, a page is given from a closely reasoned paper by the late Bishop of Arras, a strong supporter of the movement for reconciliation between France and Germany, and a short statement by the Bishop of Belley. Lastly, an important discussion by Father Delos, O.P., and Father Valensin, S.J.—two of the authors of the Conclusions—on the exact meaning of self-defence at the present time, concludes this chapter and the second part of our work. The part of Professor Shotwell's study of the problem of self-defence in relation to the Briand-Kellogg Pact, to which these authors' discussion relates, is reprinted in our Appendix.

Documents

A. NINETEENTH CENTURY

Postulata respectfully submitted by a number of Bishops to our Most Holy Master Pope Pius IX and the Most Sacred Vatican Council. February 10, 1870 :

The present condition of the world has assuredly become intolerable on account of huge standing and conscript armies. The nations groan under the burden of the expense of maintaining them. The spirit of irreligion and the forgetfulness of law in international affairs open an altogether readier way for the beginning of illegal and unjust wars, or rather hideous massacres spreading far and wide.

On the one hand, help for the poor has been curtailed and trade cannot pursue its course ; on the other, man's conscience has become distorted or perverted or grievously weakened and numbers of souls indeed are going to eternal ruin.

Now the Church alone can heal evils so serious. Even though not everyone may listen to her voice, yet she will always stand out as a leader to numberless thousands and sooner or later gain a hearing.

Moreover, the assertion of divine principles in itself is a vindication of the Divine Majesty and must gain its own reward.

Of this function of the Church in the world, as far as these truths are concerned, serious men experienced in public affairs are of the same opinion as not a few others who are noted for their sanctity and are animated by zeal for religion. They are persuaded that there is an extreme need for a pronouncement in which those parts of the Canon Law, which concern the rights of nations and all those principles which determine whether war is a duty or a crime, should be authoritatively promulgated.

When by this act the moral conscience of man has been revived then shall we see perils already most imminent removed, a consummation impossible to expect from mere earthly wisdom and political action.

(Here follow the signatures of Cardinal Manning and of thirty-nine other Fathers of the Council.)

GÉNICOT. *Institutiones Theologicæ Moralis, Cap. VI, pp.* 309–310 :

II. In order that defensive war, whereby force is repelled, may be just, it is sufficient that this force be judged with *probability at least* to have been unjustly used. But if the contrary is morally certain, satisfaction must be granted to the just demands of the party declaring war. For it is impossible to have a war *objectively just* on both sides because two parties cannot have two contrary rights with regard to the same thing. Often, however, from lack of certainty a war may be *subjectively* just on each side.

III. In order that offensive war may be just the cause must be so grave that it has a real proportion to the manifold ills which can be foreseen as about to afflict both belligerents.

Suchlike causes may be found on the side of the State about to declare war, for example the recovery of a province belonging to it whose recovery is of great moment to the public good, the punishment of grave insult either to the State or to its ruler, etc. They may also arise from religious motives : thus it is licit or opportune to wage war on infidels in order to compel them to desist from impeding the spread of the Gospel, for example by expelling or killing missionaries. Finally, the same faculty or obligation may arise from charity towards other nations unjustly oppressed. Thus the 62nd proposition condemned in the Syllabus of Pius IX is : 'The principle of non-intervention is to be proclaimed and observed.' In all these cases it is supposed that a demand for reparation for the injury done has been made and made in vain, for it is not right to allow the immense evils of war if a harmless means of obtaining just reparation can be employed instead. In order that offensive war may be just it is further required that there be *moral certitude* with regard to the cause. . . . Hence it appears that one should reject as intrinsically pernicious and condemned the opinion of not a few authors who think that the right to wage war is based upon the probability or even the great probability of having justice on one's side.

Father Génicot concludes from this that there is a moral obligation to resort to arbitration. (See Chapter VII.)

TAPARELLI D'AZEGLIO. *Essai Théorique de Droit Naturel. Conscription and competition in armaments :*

1222. Society or authority cannot interfere in the sphere of the individual. As a general rule it cannot force the individual to take up one profession rather than another : it is *only* entitled to do so when the *right of all* is in collision with an *equal or lesser right* of the *individual.* Such is the collision of rights in the case before us. Military force is a necessity, since, without that force, the social order, the life and liberty of all the citizens who have an undoubted right to social order, life and liberty—would fall before the attacks of their enemies. The right of the citizens as a whole is in collision with the rights of certain individuals, on the hypothesis that the State has no other means but forced conscription to raise an army sufficient for its self-defence. Under those conditions conscription is just, lawful and even obligatory.

Thus, in case of necessity, forced military service is not imposed as an individual's profession, but rather as a *function of the social organism* ; the authority of the State does not, as such, interfere with the order of family life and individual interests, but for the moment those interests and that order give way to the requirements of the political order to which they are by their nature united and subordinate.

1223. It is then sheer *necessity* alone which justifies the authority of the State in obliging men to perform military service. Consequently, the government must make every effort to avoid falling into that necessity ; for if the necessity existed only because means of preventing it had not been employed, it would no longer be really *necessary*. Hence a number of people of good intention complain at the present day of conscription. They cannot see why it should be necessary to make all the sacrifices which standing armies involve at a time when Europe is practically always at peace ; and they think it permissible to evade conscription, just as it is lawful to escape from an unjust vexation. But they must observe that the suppression of standing armies and great armaments can only be effected through the common agreement of the Great Powers ; in the present state of military science, no sooner does one nation keep up its armaments than all the others are forced to do the same. So the peoples are right when they demand disarmament on a peace footing from all the Powers together ; they are wrong when they throw upon their own government alone the blame for the burden which standing armies impose upon the State. Every Sovereign is obliged, in the present state of things, to ensure the safety of his dominions by extraordinary forces, until the time when a more honourable form of diplomacy, a truer love of mankind, and more sincere alliances can assure more effectively the equilibrium of Europe : this will always be difficult so long as the peoples are not united in their religious beliefs as one fold under one shepherd.

War and International Authority :

1322. Wars between dependent and subordinate bodies are evidence of a civilization still in its infancy : they disappear in proportion as civilization progresses. Indeed, elementary societies, such as groups of families and the like, soon lose the right to make war, a right which belongs to them in the earliest stage of political societies when these have not yet sufficient strength to give effective protection to individual families. But when the city or the commune has reached a certain degree of strength and of organization it is obliged to forbid families to have the use of arms for defence, just as families do not allow it to their individual members : it is obliged to forbid those habits which disturb good order within a society and often cause irreparable harm to the associated families even when they are innocent. In the development of human societies we see the supreme power pass imperceptibly from cities to States and from States to confederations of States. The decision of grave affairs follows the same course of development ; and when the supreme authority has attained a high degree of perfection, it is for that authority to assure to all the societies inferior to it the peaceful enjoyment or the vindication of those rights which originally they had to assure to themselves by force of arms.

Conditions of just war :

1332. A mistake or an inadvertent act is sometimes enough to make a people lose its temper and to influence public feeling without any really very grave fault having been committed by the aggressor. But it is never right to inflict a heavy punishment for a light offence. Thus a State cannot lawfully have recourse to arms unless it has made sure in advance of the deliberate malice and culpability of the offender. For that purpose it is necessary to determine whether the nation believed guilty has known the right which it is violating and despite that knowledge has persisted in the intention to violate it. From this arises the necessity for a nation not to declare war upon another before both of them have made known to one another their mutual grievances, the rights which they claim to possess and the satisfaction which might be required and granted by way of friendly settlement.

Social character of war :

1333. When one of the parties has committed an international crime, war is a sort of international punishment. But punishment is, by its nature, a restoration of order : a compensation for the past, a guarantee for the future. Consequently a war can be just when order has been violated, when a State has suffered a grave injury, or when it has reasonable grounds to fear that such an injury is to come. War can be justified by one of those three titles : the right to restore order supposes in the offended State a moral superiority which results from the actual fault of the offender ; the right to exact compensation and a guarantee for the future suppose that there is a real injury and a real peril, and must be proportioned to the one or the other.

Taparelli later develops his theory that an ethnarchy, or

Society of States, under an authority which extends to the whole human race, ought eventually to come into being as a requirement of nature. The passages of his treatise which describe the characteristics of this world society will be found elsewhere (Chapters X and XI). Here are given his views concerning the functions of that society in regard to the use of military force.

International authority the guarantor of national independence :

1375. The nations would lose their liberty if, instead of being subject to the ethnarchic authority, they were subjected to the authority of another nation their equal in law. The duty of the ethnarchic authority is therefore to safeguard the independence of the State and to protect it against any and every abuse of power, whether that abuse come from the material superiority of wealth or armaments or from the intellectual superiority which makes it easier for the most highly civilized peoples to oppress the rest, or from the moral superiority of those who abuse their rights and push them to excess, as in the consequences of victory in a just war. In all these cases the ethnarchic authority has the duty of protecting order and justice and opposing disorder.

International society and the reign of law :

1377. The ethnarchic authority is first and foremost the natural guardian of the independence of peoples ; their possessions, their territory and their rights are placed under the protective ægis of the international authority. But, we shall be asked, if that is the case, will war be definitely abolished ? We have seen that war, being a struggle between States, must be essentially a public act. We have seen that the heads of subordinate societies have the right to declare war for just motives so long as the supreme authority has not attained the state of intellectual, moral and material perfection which makes it possible for it to uphold the reign of justice among these subordinate groups. In the same way so long as the ethnarchic authority is not soundly and solidly constituted the nations may vindicate their rights by war.

1378. This imperfect state of things cannot last for ever. The ethnarchic society, like every other society, must naturally want right rather than might to prevail in its midst. In a properly constituted ethnarchy war is only possible between a refractory nation which violates order by oppressing its neighbours and the ethnarchic authority aided by all the peoples leagued together. In those circumstances each one of those peoples will be sure to find itself helped by all its fellow-members, and will itself be organized according to the laws of the ethnarchy to which it has itself assented. It will thus be able even with quite small military forces to have perfect security concerning its own independence. It will, then, as we have already suggested, no longer have to bear the enormous burden of permanent armaments.

B. TWENTIETH CENTURY

MGR. JULIEN, BISHOP OF ARRAS. '*La doctrine traditionelle de l'Eglise sur les règles de la Vie Internationale*' (*Le Problème International*, *p.* 340).

Is then war a sin according to St. Thomas? . . . There are cases in which to make war is not sinful, that is under the following conditions. . . . In the first place the war must be declared by the Prince, as he was then called. By the word Prince is to be understood Sovereign State, whether monarchy or republic: the extent of territory is of no consequence provided the Prince has over him no authority whose vassal he is. A mere individual has not the right to declare war on his own authority. And why? Because above him there are judges who have the means of ensuring that justice is done to him. The Sovereign State, however, has no superior: it must secure justice for itself. But suppose there be over and above the State a supreme jurisdiction accepted by all, whether it be the Pope, as in medieval christendom, or the Council of Nations, as in an organized international society, then the Right of War rises to a higher level with the new jurisdiction; war becomes a sin for the individual States as it has hitherto been for individual citizens. Shall we see the day when wars between civilized peoples are also regarded as civil wars? There is nothing contrary to this in the principles established by St. Thomas.

MGR. BEGUIN, BISHOP OF BELLEY. *November* 13, 1931. (*Reply to the newspaper* '*Ami du Peuple*'):

If the point at issue is to be made clear it is first necessary to form an exact idea of the doctrine of the Church on peace and war. It is a simple, straightforward, honest doctrine: here it is set out as shortly and objectively as possible.

Considered in itself, in abstraction from the motives which can sometimes justify it, war is murder, an accumulation of murders. It is, says Pius XI, a monstrous homicide, a fratricidal combat, the accursed fruit of discord. All those who have seen the atrocities of war at close quarters will endorse this condemnation without reserve.

If then war is a crime it would be mad to accept it as the normal means of solving international conflicts. This would amount to a justification of the use of violence, to solve any and every difference. He who had the biggest guns, the most deadly poison gas at his disposal would always be right: we should see Might creating Right, or to put it more clearly, the complete suppression of Right.

Conclusions of the Theological Conventus at Fribourg upon war, 1931. (*In 'Paix et Guerre'. Editions du Cerf*) :

State of the Question. In order to find a right solution of the problem of the morality of war attention ought to be paid at one and the same time to facts and to principles. Now it is a fact that the relations of international life are developing in all directions. It is a principle, on the other hand, that sociability must be considered as the natural condition of existence for every State. Every day these truths become clearer. Indeed, no civilized State could in these days attain its own end, fulfil its own duties and vindicate its own rights without associating and co-ordinating its own life with that of other nations. This being the case, the question of the morality of war cannot rightly be studied in the abstract without relation to that natural society toward which tends the natural sociability of States or the juridical form which international relations are seen to have assumed.

If, as was once the case, any juridical organization of the society of nations were lacking and the conditions in which States existed implied their full independence, it would indeed be possible for a war declared by the supreme authority of some one State to be sometimes considered *positis ponendis* a lawful war. And that is the kind of war which the older school of theologians and moralists who were almost exclusively concerned with determining the conditions of just war generally had in mind. But once with the growth of international relations the natural society of nations has received a structure through certain instruments adapted to that end; once it has assumed in public law a form more in accord with the rational nature of man the question to be solved is whether this *accidental* legitimacy of war can in fact still exist. That is the only way in which the problem of the morality of war can be stated at the present time. But two points must be made clear before a solution of the problem can be reached :

1. What is the true conception of the sovereign authority of the State ?
2. Upon what conditions can that authority have the right nowadays to wage a just war ?

I. Of sovereignty :

Conclusion. The theory of State Sovereignty which has been popularized by many modern jurists and politicians is very far from being in harmony with the dictates of reason and the doctrinal tradition of the Church.

For they pretend that the State is something absolute: that it enjoys complete autonomy; decides what are its own rights, without appeal; acknowledges no binding obligation beyond what it has spontaneously assumed, and finally knows no limit and no law which does not repose in its own will and in its own power. Further, on the pretext that it is the duty of the State to satisfy all the needs of man's life, such authors attribute to the State an internal dynamic power whereby the supreme political authority tends to secure control of the economic life, the culture and even the religion of the nation.

Far removed from this is the idea of State Sovereignty held by Christian philosophers. This doctrine is that this Sovereignty consists in the moral power to choose the means necessary to obtain the common good of the members of the State. They recognize in it a certain expression of the State's freedom to frame laws and make arrangements for its own citizens. But, since the State is a social being, and consequently is more or less unequal to the task of attaining its own end in isolation from the whole community of mankind, Christian philosophy teaches that the Sovereignty of the State in its external aspect does not mean at all the same thing as unqualified independence. Rather does it signify simply the liberty required to choose the forms of organization, the technical methods, the juridical or political institution which seem best fitted to secure the common good of the international community.

II. Of the right of war:

Preliminary Observations. So soon as a number of States or organized political groups came into being the links of a certain common life were established between them and little by little a society was formed. Consequently it is not surprising that under those circumstances resort to war for the settlement of disputes has been regarded as a recourse to the final social process (social procedure the moderns call it) whereby new juridical situations could be lawfully created. It is evident that this notion of war has been commonly held among civilized peoples up to our own times.

Therefore, to determine the morality of this social process at the present day it is necessary to enquire whether, at the stage of evolution which we have reached, war still is the social process which, in default of all the others, alone conduces to the common good and the higher interests of the human person. In other words the solution of the problem of the morality of war to-day must be made clear by the answers which are given to the two following questions:

(*a*) Can a war declared by the authority of any one State, in modern circumstances, be regarded as a lawful social process or not?

(*b*) In what way can war be permissible on the grounds of lawful defence ?

A. Of war declared by the authority of a single State :

Although international society does not enjoy the full authority which it might well possess, both from the very nature of things and from the consent of men, yet it is clear that it has now been developed into a form of positive law in such a way that it is consolidated by many juridical and political instruments which are designed to establish human order and peace. Because of this *a war declared by a State on its own authority without previous recourse to the international institutions which exist cannot be a lawful social process.* It would be repugnant to the dictates both of public law and of conscience, for at the start it would involve a violation of that general or legal justice which requires that the State should not only not offend the rights of other peoples which are equal to its own, but should also subordinate its own national end to the more general end of international society.

A fortiori, modern war, that is war as understood and waged nowadays, could not be a legitimate social process. For this kind of war by the technique proper to it and by a certain necessity of its very nature causes such ruin, material, spiritual, individual, domestic, social and religious, and becomes such a calamity for the whole world, that it ceases to be a means proportioned to the end in view, which is the restoration of peace and a better condition of human order.

If then, in spite of all that human prudence can do, the calamity of modern war should accidentally occur it would be the duty of brave men, while enduring with equanimity the evils which they could not avoid, to seek to bring back to the rules of the moral law all that depends upon the human will, to limit the dreadful consequences of the event and forthwith to prepare the concord between nations which nature requires, by the peaceful means of Law and Christian goodwill in the souls of men.

B. Of lawful defence :

Conclusion. The case of *lawful defence* must in the first place be distinguished from the case of *necessity,* which according to many modern jurists consists in this : that unless a State declared war it could not defend the so-called vital interests of the country and so would be unable to achieve its national ends. Indeed, as this prosecution of national ends implies an unlimited expansion of sovereignty all the enterprises of exaggerated nationalism, which lusts for conquest and glory, can be whitewashed under the name of a defensive war.

Very different from these dangerous equivocations is the traditional doctrine, according to which lawful defence is understood as that complex of acts—including, if need be, the use of force—whereby a State supplies what is lacking on the part of the superior authority whose function it is to protect the Right. To repel force by force is in that sense lawful. But this legitimate defence does not imply *ipso facto* the right to take punitive measures against the aggressor, or to set up the social process of war in such a way that the conflict between the aggressor and his victim is solved only by the arbitrament of the sword. For an act may be justified without its being for that reason embodied in the order of positive law or providing a legitimate basis for new international relations. Under these circumstances it can be reasonably foreseen that the case of lawful defence will become less frequent in international life the more true security has been attained by the co-ordinated protection of all States in common and the institution of arbitration.

Therefore, although it is still prudent not to disregard the danger which may fall upon a country from this side or from that, there seems to be no good reason why the nations should to-day maintain a condition of armed peace which is itself a negation of order. They should base their security not upon an abundance of armed forces but rather upon a peaceful agreement between them all.

Some Practical Corollaries.

A. Of the duty and the right of the State :

It is the duty of the State, as it is its right, to develop the political, juridical and economic institutions which can serve the cause of international peace. It is also its duty, a duty of distributive and legal justice, to have recourse to the organs of these international institutions for the settlement of disputes and to observe in all particulars the declarations of the international authority which express the requirement of the common good.

B. Of the duty and the right of citizens :

What has been said of States applies also, *mutatis mutandis,* to individual citizens. It is now the personal duty and right of all of them—most of all of Christian citizens—to promote the institutions which diminish the peril of war ; to reinforce socially and psychologically the natural society of nations ; to sustain with the citizens of other nations an intercourse which is sincere and befitting to human nature. It is their right, and duty too, to spread the true doctrine of natural and supernatural ethics in regard to international relations in order that true interpretations of historical events may be given in the schools and that false theories, so widespread to-day, concerning the political and economic sovereignty of the State and the supposed natural election of any one race to universal hegemony may be overthrown.

Signed by the Reverend Fathers

Charrière—Professor of Moral Theology in the Diocesan Seminary, Fribourg, Switzerland.

Delos, O.P.—Professor of International Law in the Catholic University of Lille.

Mayer—Professor of Moral Theology at the Theological Faculty of Paderborn.

Noppel, S.J.—Editor of the review, *Stimmen der Zeit*, Munich.

Keller—Professor of Moral Theology in the University of Freiburg in Brisgau.

de Solages—Professor of Theology and Rector of the Catholic Institute of Toulouse.

Stratmann, O.P.—Vice-President of the German Catholic Peace Society, Berlin.

Valensin, S.J.—former Professor of Theology at the Catholic Institute of Lille.

ALBERT VALENSIN, S. J., AND J. T. DELOS, O.P. *Legitimate Defence* (' *Paix et Guerre* ', *pp.* 79–81) :

A. We must then consider as the aggressor the State which, being under an obligation to submit its difference with another to a procedure of conciliation, arbitration or judicial settlement, declares war in violation of its engagements or resorts to arms rather than conform to an obligatory sentence.

B. But the substitution of public international justice for private justice has not in all cases been organized. In a state of international society in evolution, as ours is evolving, there will often be occasions when Powers in conflict with one another are not juridically bound to submit their dispute to a form of pacific procedure, but when the international community does *in fact offer*, either through its established institutions or the possibilities which are inherent in it, the means of reaching a peaceful solution.

This hypothesis is shown to be true in a great number of instances at the present time. There is probably not a single international conflict for which a judge or arbitrator or a mediator could not be found. In such circumstances there is undeniably a moral obligation resting upon States not to take justice into their own hands but to have recourse to the procedures of the international society.

The State which shirked this moral obligation would be failing in its duty and would be truly guilty of aggression in that it elected to resort to force rather than to peaceful methods.

The concrete difficulty—and it is no mean difficulty—consists in the fact that this obligation is a moral one and is not clothed in the legal form which would make it easily understood by public opinion. There is a danger that it may not arouse the human conscience, and it does not bring into operation the sanctions which the international community could organize.

Yet this very difficulty only emphasizes the duty of States to expedite the completion of the international organization which will succeed more and more in substituting the rule of public justice for that of private justice, and will progressively suppress the war procedure which is a legacy of the public law of recent centuries. Then alone will cease the confusion which exists between the state of necessity and the state of legitimate defence (as justifying the use of military force).

APPENDIX TO CHAPTER VI

AGGRESSION AND DEFENCE

Definition of aggression and defence in the Modern World. Shotwell : War as an Instrument of National Policy and its Renunciation in the Pact of Paris, pp. 206–209 :

The violation of its (a State's) own promise, in the Covenant, to accept pacific means of settlement instead of force is the simplest and clearest possible test of aggression. It is not the act of violence alone, but even more the violation of a previously given pledge. The pledge is the condition of the test. It is not too much to say that without it there cannot be any test at all. Violence by itself is not aggression. There is violence as well in defence and police action, neither of which can be called aggression. There must be some agreement as to the conditions under which force is permissible, and as it is impossible to formulate beforehand all the conditions and circumstances which may arise, the only solution is to provide the proper means for determining each issue as it arises, such as a court for cases arising under international law or other justifiable issues, arbitration, also a judicial procedure, or conciliation and conference. The refusal of these means of peaceful settlement by a nation which has formally accepted them and its employment of violence in their stead is an act of aggression concerning which there can be no two opinions. Without an agreement of this kind it will always be possible for the aggressor to think itself the aggrieved and seldom possible for both sides to agree as to where the aggression lies.

Perhaps the clearest way to state this point is that the definition of aggression—that the aggressor is the power which in going to war violates its already given pledge to settle its disputes peacefully instead—erects a juristic frontier alongside the geographic one. The nation which attacks another not only crosses the natural boundaries of mountain or river but the boundaries of actions themselves set forth in agreements. And it is this juristic frontier which alone furnishes an adequate test of aggression and legitimate defence.

The mere crossing of a nation's geographic frontiers is no sure test of aggression. Nowhere has this been more frankly stated than in the British reply to Mr. Kellogg's note. The Suez Canal does not lie within the Empire, yet the maintenance of connections with India through that canal, as well as at the Straits of Gibraltar, is perhaps the most vital single link in Imperial defence.

The very existence of the British Empire depends upon maintaining its connections, and any attack upon them whether on foreign soil or on the high seas will be resisted by the British Empire as an act of self-evident defence. This is what the so-called Monroe Doctrine of Sir A. Chamberlain's note amounts to : 'there are certain regions of the world, the welfare and integrity of which constitute a special and vital interest for our peace and safety. . . . Their protection against attack is to the British Empire a measure of self-defence.' This statement might well be made on any necessary occasion by an American Secretary of State with reference to the Panama Canal. Legitimate defence is not confined to repelling invasion within a country's frontiers. Yet this is all that Mr. Kellogg had in mind when he referred to the inalienable right of self-defence. 'Every nation is free at all times and regardless of treaty provisions to defend its territory from attack or invasion.'[1] The inadequacy of this conception is not only borne home by the British reply, which we have just been discussing, but is a commonplace of military and naval strategy. All soldiers are agreed—and they should be the judges in this matter—that the defence of a nation's territory against attack should not always be awaited within the territory itself. To take the simplest case, there seems to be no adequate defence against airplane attack once the squadrons are overhead. The only sure method of warding off this danger is to destroy the enemy bombers before they leave their hangars, just as wasps can only be destroyed within their nest. Moreover, frontiers have been drawn disadvantageously to certain States so as to deprive them of their natural defence, and if the attack is coming from that quarter where the frontiers have been purposely left open for easy invasion and conquest, the only hope of an otherwise defenceless nation may lie in reaching first the natural ramparts which lie outside their political frontiers. From the strategical standpoint there has been not a little criticism of the act of the French Government at the opening of the World War when it ordered its Army to retreat within its own frontiers in order that the crossing of those frontiers by the enemy should be seen by all the world to be an act of aggression. Politically this gesture will not have the weight with historians proportionate to its good intentions. For there is no sure test of aggression in the act of crossing the frontier. Aggression is a political and not merely a military act, for the distinction lies in the political conditions which are violated and not in the violation of actual territory.

But there is another reason, hardly less important, for not regarding the defence of frontiers as a criterion of legitimate defence ; if all the emphasis were put upon it, then whole nations would be more and more the victims of disorderly elements along the borders. Nearly every nation has its Macedonia, and

[1] Note of June 23rd.

it would be a sorry theory which would force governments to the lawless standards of these backward communities. If every time a border brawl occurred the two nations were obliged to take up the feud in the name of national honour, the inalienable right of self-defence would indeed become the outstanding obstacle to the progress of civilization. It was by suppressing the feud through the alternative settlement of courts of law that barbarism and anarchy were put down within the State itself, and the frontier feuds of nations must similarly yield to the greater interests of the common weal ; yet the only way to suppress the feud is to supply the common weal with adequate instruments of justice and make recourse to them the test of honest citizenship. Similarly, in the community of nations, the test of aggression which is the crime against the commonweal must be established at a juristic frontier which a nation crosses when it violates its previously given word to resort to pacific means of peaceful settlement instead of war.

PART III

THE PRESERVATION OF PEACE

CHAPTER VII

THE PACIFIC SETTLEMENT OF DISPUTES

IN the evolution of Catholic thought upon the morality of war, the reader will have observed an increasing tendency to stress and to develop the duty of *preventing* war and of seeking the vindication of justice by other means. This, indeed, is the dominant Christian tradition. It is instinct in the Gospels ; it is a commonplace of the post-Apostolic Fathers ; it is the conclusion of St. Augustine—'*magis est gloriæ ipsa bella occidere verbo quam homines ferro*' ; it is, as will be seen below, the object of constant exhortation by recent Popes, as it was the principle of action of their greatest predecessors. Why is this duty so little indicated, if at all, in St. Thomas and in other Schoolmen from the thirteenth to the fifteenth centuries ? Why does Gratian in the eleventh century not incorporate the dictum of St. Augustine, quoted above, in the Canons of his Decretal, whereas he is careful to reproduce almost every recorded sentence of that Saint with regard to the legitimation of war and of soldiering ? The reason is partly, no doubt, that the duty of preventing war is too obvious to need legal definition or philosophical analysis : partly that the superior authority both of Pope and of Emperor to settle conflicts between Christian princes was, in fact, taken for granted. But the main reason, we are inclined to believe, lies in the changes, indicated in the last chapter, in the very character of war. The typical war in the minds of the authorities to whom we refer being either the defence of the Christian Empire against the attacks of pagans and heretics, or of Christendom against the Mohammedan advance, the question of arbitration, mediation or the submission of the dispute to an independent tribunal could hardly arise. Further, it was necessary to include a rational justification for the Crusade in the political ethics of the schools. It is when wars between Christian princes as heads of States and the wars of colonization become the typical instances in the theologian's mind that the centre of gravity moves from the justification of war to the obligation of arbitration.

From a mere negative allusion in St. Raymund, Hostiensis and St. Thomas—'since there is no higher tribunal,' 'since the prince has no superior who can adjudicate,' etc., we pass to the duty of acknowledging the Pope as arbitrator, in Vittoria ; to the conclusion of that author and of Suarez that even a war otherwise just may not be prosecuted if it would do great harm to the common interests of mankind ; to the insistence of Vasquez upon the duty of submitting to arbitration. Thence through two centuries in which many Catholic and other thinkers, such as Father Emeric Crucé and the Abbé de St. Pierre, sought to evolve some international tribunal to prevent war, we pass to Taparelli, to whom war can only be an act of international justice, national recourse to arms belonging only to the twilight before the dawn of organized international society.

Thence we come to a school of theologians, whose reasoning at present holds the field and who conclude that the existence even of embryonic institutions of international conciliation and justice removes the right of national Governments to declare war, under the traditional conditions, without submission to those institutions, and circumscribes even the exercise of the right of self-defence.

It will therefore be convenient to collate at this stage the principal texts of Catholic authorities upon the prevention of war. Several of these are taken from the treatises on war already quoted : and it will be observed that the debate upon the right or wrong of a declaration of war for a cause probably but not certainly just is as germane to this chapter as to that in which it has already appeared. For no international wars are so evidently and indubitably just as to exclude the necessity of recourse to impartial judgement. The reasoning of Vittoria, Vasquez, St. Alphonsus and Génicot on this subject inevitably points to the need of establishing a system of international arbitration.

We should interrupt the train of thought in several passages, notably those taken from Papal documents, if we attempted to separate the indications of Catholic doctrine relating to arbitration from those that refer to disarmament. It is a venerable question whether the restriction of the use of arms by the persons composing civil society should follow, precede or accompany the establishment of a regular system of justice within that society. Had not the barons been disarmed[1] in the England of the Plantagenets the King's Justice could never have replaced the feudal anarchy. When the use of arms, except for the preservation of peace, was forsworn in the *pacta* of the Peace of God in Burgundy and France at the same period, the arbitral power of the Pope was already a reality. The rule of the Franciscan and Dominican tertiaries in the thirteenth century forbidding them to bear arms or take military oaths at once presupposed and assisted the effective establishment of the kingly power as against the depredations of the feudality. But whichever process should in the light of political circumstances precede the other, they are actually two parts of a single whole.

'First of all the fundamental principle,' wrote Benedict XV to the belligerents in 1917, 'must be the substitution of Right for the . . . force of arms.' A system of justice with effective sanctions must come into being, as the system of national armaments disappears. National armaments must be restricted as a condition of the system of justice becoming effective. 'You cannot expect justice from an international court whose members come with

[1] *John of Hexham*, ed. Raine, p. 171, writing of the *Peace of Wallingford*, 1153 : 'Continuo exiit decretum ab eis per omnes provincias violentias comprimi, direptiones interdici, milites, conductitios et sagittarios exterarum nationum a regno ejici, munitionesque, quas quisque in sua possessione post mortem Henrici regis construxerat, dirui. Justitia ergo et pax ubique in regno revocata est.' And § 8 of the *Assize of Northampton* (Benedictus Abbas i, 108 ; Hoveden ii, 89), 1176 : 'Item Justitiæ provideant quod castella diruta prorsus diruantur et diruenda bene prosternantur. Et nisi hoc fecerint, dominus rex judicium curiæ suæ de eis habere voluit sicut de contemptoribus præcepti sui,' etc. (*Apud* Stubbs, *Select Charters.*)

daggers in their belts.'[1] Taparelli shows that with the evolution of human society the right to use arms necessarily passes from the lesser to the greater community, from the lower to the higher power. Should then the reduction of national armaments and their subjection to international control wait upon the establishment not only of an arbitral tribunal but of a positive world-wide international society? Or does not the existence of formidable national armaments and competition between different States in preparation for war prejudice the prospects of organization of the desired Society of Nations? Many varying opinions on these points might be quoted. But the discussion is unprofitable. The reduction and limitation of military preparations and equipments; the establishment of international arbitration; the restriction of the use of military force to the defence of international order—all these three reforms are clearly desirable in the light of Catholic tradition. The bulk of the statements made in recent years by the Episcopate and by responsible Catholic associations connect the three points together.[2] The discussion may be closed by the observation that Benedict XV in proposing these same three points as a basis of lasting peace to the belligerent Governments in 1917, put *first* 'the simultaneous and reciprocal diminution of armaments to a point consistent with the maintenance of order within each State.' In his great Encyclical *Pacem Dei Munus Pulcherrimum*, a full translation of which appears in a later chapter, he again puts the reduction of armaments as the *first* purpose of the association of nations which he commends. It is indeed the only concrete example which he gives of the action of the organized international society.

In considering the failures and delays which have clogged progress toward international disarmament since the first Hague Conference called for this purpose in 1897 to the Geneva Conference of 1932–1934, it is not irrelevant to reflect upon the organic connection always present to

[1] Dr. Downey, Archbishop of Liverpool, in a radio address.

[2] For example, an address by Cardinal Bourne on November 27, 1931 (*The Tablet*, November 28, 1931).

Catholic thought between the establishment of an international tribunal and the military preparations of Governments. The process to which these preparations are directed is only justified in the Catholic tradition as a penal enactment—a conjecture, as it were, of what would be the sentence of a superior international tribunal against the obdurate violator of international justice. The *Conventus theologicus Friburgensis* was wise in realizing that the only moral and logical approach to disarmament lies through a critical study of the end for which armaments exist. We have already alluded to the moral and legal situation created by such facts as the establishment of a Permanent Court of International Justice ;[1] the formal acknowledgement of its jurisdiction by a large number of civilized Governments, the General Act for the Pacific Settlement of International Disputes ; the Covenant of the League of Nations ; the Treaty for the Renunciation of War as an instrument of National Policy ; the Pan-American Union ; the numerous bilateral treaties (161[2] by June, 1932) providing for recourse to the Permanent Court or to special arbitral procedure or to Conciliation Commissions in the event of disagreement. To all of which must be added the evidence afforded by recent history of the impartiality and success of the Holy See as a mediator and arbitrator. It will suffice to compare the state of international law created by these developments with the condition of affairs which confronted the Spanish theologians of the sixteenth and seventeenth centuries, the prophets of international organization in the eighteenth, and Taparelli and Leo XIII in the nineteenth, to see that a profound change has taken

[1] Forty-two States have signed and ratified the so-called 'Optional Clause,' whereby they recognize *ipso facto* and without further formality the jurisdiction of the Court.

[2] This figure is compiled from the annual reports issued in June of each year by the Registrar of the Permanent Court of International Justice. In addition to these treaties providing exclusively for arbitration or conciliation and affecting thirty-seven Powers, there were in existence at the same date over four hundred Treaties on other matters providing for automatic reference to the Court of any disputes arising from the interpretation of them.

place.[1] In the light of the Catholic tradition the Right of War cannot be the same now as it then was. Is it then either just or necessary for the several States to continue preparations for warfare, the cost of which has in a single generation become the greatest burden of every national budget? Taparelli's opinion upon conscription (see p. 133) may be noted. It is only justifiable if strictly necessary; and it is not necessary if Governments have neglected the means of preventing the necessity. Is it necessary in the world to-day? To the Papacy, as to many reputed moral theologians such as Meyer,[2] the system of competition in national armaments made possible by mechanical progress is an abnormal, unnatural situation. Has not the progress already made in the organization of international institutions

[1] To take a typical instance of a moral theologian of the last generation. Hickey in his admirable *Summula Philosophiæ Scholasticæ* writes thus of arbitration in the one page out of 283 devoted to his treatise on Ethics in which he mentions international relations:

'Others desire the establishment of a supreme tribunal consisting of the delegates of all nations, for the purpose of deciding international quarrels by arbitration. The object of such a tribunal would be to compose the differences which arise between nations impartially according to the principles of justice, equity and humanity, without bloodshed. But in order that a tribunal of this kind may remain in being and attain its end, there must needs be a certain international authority residing in him who presides over the tribunal. For every society consists of two parts—matter, which is the members of it, and form, which is the authority which unites and guides the members. As such an authority or president no one can be found or envisaged who would be more apt than the Roman Pontiff. . . . But the international arbitration of the Pope is as yet no more than the subject of pious aspirations—and more's the pity (et hinc sunt lacrimæ rerum).'

Could he leave the matter at that to-day?

[2] Meyer, *Institut. Juris Naturalis*, n. 610:

'The material and personal burdens which this constant state of armed peace imposes on citizens can only be likened to the burdens of a perpetual war. In other words, it is not sufficiently understood that, whatever the arguments put forward to-day on the grounds of necessity, this condition of civil society, so far from being in conformity with the requirements of nature itself, arises rather from a state of moral disease in human society.'

removed any reason or pretext which may have existed for maintaining those abnormal practices?

Two objections are sufficiently common among Catholic students of international law and politics at the present time to be answered here. The first is that a general reduction of national armaments is imprudent and therefore not justified, owing to the lack of universality in the membership of the League of Nations and in the body of Powers acknowledging the jurisdiction of the Permanent Court at The Hague or of any other tribunal. The second is that the international institutions which already exist for the settlement of international differences are intrinsically defective.

The first is rather a matter of current political opinion than of ethical theory. Certain observations of principle may, however, be offered. There is, to begin with, no suggestion in the neo-scholastic authors whom we quote that the *judices arbitros* of which, for instance, Vasquez speaks, must be *universally* acknowledged by all sovereigns before any obligation arises to submit disputes to them. To Vittoria the mere existence of the indirect temporal jurisdiction of the Holy See may be enough to curb a prince's right of war. To Taparelli any neutral power or third party even has a kind of 'moral superiority' which fits it to mediate between two conflicting neighbours; the right of any such power to offer its 'good offices' for the settlement of a dispute was recognized by the First Hague Conference and was in fact exercised by Benedict XV in the European War. In short, the availability of a competent and disinterested judge or mediator to whom any two Governments in dispute may submit their differences, is the primary fact which affects a Government's right of war, rather than the question whether or no the jurisdiction of such judge or mediator is actually world-wide.

The existence of a powerful State dominated, for instance, by Communism or by a militant nationalism, which neither accepts the jurisdiction of the international organs of conciliation and judgement which other States acknowledge, nor enjoys their confidence, has often been cited as a fact which sets a limit to the reduction which can be effected by those other States in their defensive preparations. But here an honest examination of conscience is called for. If the existence of one or two such Powers does in fact constitute a serious military menace, the best way to augment that menace is to foment dis-union among the Powers that should oppose it. And who, surveying the political, diplomatic and journalistic polemics of the last decade will deny that competition in armaments and mutual suspicion concerning the strength of national armaments is a powerful cause of bad blood and dis-union between the civilized Western Powers? If, therefore, it is a prudent duty to make reasonable provision to meet aggression from without, it is doubly necessary to promote unity within. And the whole trend of Papal teaching goes to prove that the institution of arbitration combined with the reciprocal reduction and limitation of armaments among civilized powers is a valuable, if not the indispensable condition of unity. Herein is repeated the political situation which elicited the pacific efforts of the Holy See and the evolution of Catholic teaching upon war during the whole of the Middle Ages. 'The Holy See could not suffer two Christians to draw the sword against one another,' wrote William of Malmesbury of a Papal Arbitration in the tenth century. That Christians should fight one another was itself an affront to the whole spirit of the Church and its Founder. But the constant purpose of the Popes from the tenth to the seventeenth century was undoubtedly to stop war and remove the causes of war between Christian princes, in order that Christendom might be saved from the aggressions of the infidel. 'Ye oppressors of orphans and ravagers of widows,' exclaimed Urban II, at the end of the eleventh century, to the lords of Christian Europe, 'ye that are guilty of homicide and sacrilege, ye that pillage the goods of others, ye that to shed Christian blood await the reward of brigands, and, like vultures hovering around dead bodies, everywhere seek occasions of war and battles, if you would have care for the salvation of your souls, sally forth for the defence of the Church in the East.'[1]

[1] Quoted by Goyau in *L'Eglise Catholique et le Droit des Gens*, p. 166.

This is indeed an extreme case of a papal summons to a holy war against the Eastern peril : how different are the spirit and the method of Pius XI we have already suggested. Yet this broad fact is clear ; that unity among the Powers of Christian civilization is a *sine qua non* of preserving that civilization against hostile attack, and that all the spiritual forces of the Catholic Church have for centuries been used to prevent war between those Powers on that account. It is only three hundred years since Urban VIII in his stirring appeal for peace to all Christians declared : ' For who does not see that unless Discord divided the Catholic Princes neither Heresy nor Hell could ever defeat the Church ? ' So large a part has this conception of the collective and united defence of civilization against aggression played in the history of the Church's action in regard to peace and war that we, who seek truthfully to record the Catholic tradition on this subject, would have no justification for omitting it. It is open to doubt whether the collective use of military force is the best way to defend Christian civilization against an attack which constitutes a serious violation of natural rights. Even those who preached the Crusades would have held it to be the least desirable way, only justifiable as a last resort, because no other means of repelling the injury was available. But it is wholly contrary to reason and experience to suppose that a grave menace to the order of human society can be averted, if the members of that society are preoccupied with preparations to fight one another, and with spying upon one another's armaments. So long as competition in military preparations is regarded as a normal condition of international society, so long will the power of resistance of that society be nullified. Hence this study of the moral issues raised by the fear of aggression from a Power which stands aloof from the embryonic organization of international justice points once more to the formula of Benedict XV as the right solution, that is to say the general diminution of armaments by the remaining States combined, with the institution by them of ' sanctions against any State which should refuse either to submit its international disputes to arbitration or to accept an arbitral decision.'

How these international sanctions are to be organized is outside the scope of the present work. It is too early to expect an authentic Catholic literature on this point, for modern authors are still too much under the influence of the divisions created by the Great War, the contemporary French School of Catholic publicists inclining to stress the need of preparing in advance collective military action, the Germans, Americans and British inclining to a corresponding aversion to the subject. Suffice it to say that Articles 10 and 16 of the Covenant of the League of Nations appear for the first time to embody in treaty form the substance of Benedict XV's proposals; and that the well-known distaste of opinion in the United States for any contractual obligation of this character has not prevented an official declaration by the American Government that the Pact for the Renunciation of War inevitably implies joint consultation and action, in the event of violation by any signatory Power, as between the other signatories. A bibliography of general literature on this subject is appended.

Benedict XV's proposals were no novelty to Catholic tradition. Apart from the implications of the Crusades which we have noted, it will be recalled that Suarez had based the right of sovereigns to wage war upon a disposition of natural law which required some means to exist of vindicating the order of human society. That sovereigns should exercise this right *collectively* is a legitimate corollary. Taparelli specifically envisages the wielding of the sword as a necessary function of the organized society of nations, 'each of whom will thus be able with quite small military forces to have complete security concerning its own independence. It will . . . no longer have to bear the enormous burden of permanent armaments.'

The second objection to reposing confidence in international institutions at an early stage of their development is more serious. It is an objection of competence. It is variously expressed by such propositions as these: That the institutions in question (Council, Permanent Court, Conciliation Commissions) lack true authority and true jurisdiction, for they depend upon a mere contract revocable at any time. That the complete absence of any mention of obligation to God in the instruments establishing them points to the fact that the only sanction of the moral law which could make such contracts sacred and durable, is lacking. That an accepted Code of International Law which such institutions should interpret does not yet exist. That, in default of it, the members of Council, Court and Commission have displayed partiality or national bias.

There is weight in such criticisms as these. In particular a serious defect, common to representative institutions, is discernible in each of these bodies, namely that true independence of judgement is hard to come by in any tribunal whose members are appointed by national Governments. Even the Permanent Court at the Hague, whose members are not delegates but individual jurists of distinction appointed for a long term of years, has not been exempt from this criticism. Did Suarez who, in his tenderness for national sovereignty, held that sovereigns are only under obligation to submit to arbitrators whom they have themselves appointed, foresee this difficulty? It is certainly a matter of regret to thoughtful Catholics as a whole, and not to them only, that the arbitral and mediatory offices of the one Power, which is dependent upon no Government and has by its very nature and purpose an equal care for the rights and susceptibilities of all nations, should not have been integrated in the new international system for the prevention of war.[1]

The main answer to this objection is contained in an answer to the first, namely that rulers of States have no right to wait upon the perfection of international tribunals and the completion of their sphere of jurisdiction, but are under obligation to avail themselves of any opportunity of a tolerable settlement, rather than incur for their own nations and the world as a whole the certain calamity of war. Our position is therefore that of the Fribourg Conclusions which appear to us to express the true spirit of

[1] States Members of the League of Nations would, however, fulfil their general obligation under Articles 12 of the Covenant by referring a dispute between them to the arbitrament of the Pope; and the freedom of the Holy Father to exercise his duties as a peacemaker is safeguarded even *vis-à-vis* the Italian Government by Article 24 of the Lateran Treaty.

Catholic authorities on this subject since the dawn of the international problem in its true sense. If, as St. Alphonsus teaches, 'war generally brings in its train so many evils and so much harm to religion, to innocent people, to the honour of women, etc., that in practice it is hardly ever just if declared on probable reasons of justice alone and *not certain reasons*,' then it is clearly a duty to refer a dispute likely to lead to a rupture even to an imperfect international tribunal. Compromise, it is true, rather than justice, is too often the outcome of the deliberations of representative bodies. But at least the conclusions of a body upon which the interests of many peoples are represented are less likely to be harmful to the general good of human society—and is not justice a social virtue?—than the decisions of a prince who acts as judge, jury and executioner in his own cause. We have already stated what we believe would have been the attitude of the great neo-scholastics to this present problem. We may add that it is an obvious duty of Christian statesmanship and citizenship to strive patiently to improve and to strengthen the existing institutions of international arbitration, incomplete and imperfect as they are, and in particular to advocate reforms which will ensure their essential independence from sectional influences. It will be observed that such reforms must be realized under conditions which in fact require a contract between States and participation by Governments in the choice of the members of an arbitral tribunal as the only possible means of effecting it. Is this an abnormal or defective state of affairs? One of the most interesting conclusions of Taparelli's treatise of Natural Law is that *polyarchy*, i.e. authority residing equally in a number of moral persons, is the right and natural form of international society. And the *ethnarchy* or authority for the whole race which he sought to evolve is, by the whole context of his work, one which would be consistent with a Christian and Catholic order of society. Were all nations and Governments Catholic, his conclusions would apply no less. It is a far cry from the De Monarchia of Dante and the memory of the Holy Roman Empire.

But the Governments are not for the most part formally

Catholic or Christian. Does this vitiate the authority of the international institutions which they establish? The answer will be found in our chapter upon the Early Church in the Pagan Empire. All authority is from God, the people (in this case the associated peoples) choosing those who are to exercise it. '*Major est noster Cæsar quia a Deo constitutus.*[1] The obligations of obedience to an international authority established by duly constituted Governments is no other quality than the duty of obedience to the Roman magistrates for whom St. Clement prayed, or to the Emperor to whom Ignatius, Justin, Lactantius and Origen professed unswerving loyalty in face of constant misunderstanding and persecution.

Instances of Papal arbitration and mediation are given in a subsequent chapter. We confine ourselves here to texts which lay down or imply principles and rules of action.

Documents

St. Louis of France, the canonized arbitrator of the Middle Ages, shows by his example that to prevent war, charity must sometimes override the law of strict justice. In the following page from the Sire de Joinville he is recorded as answering, to the juristic objections of his advisers, that to foster goodwill for the future is a reason for a ruler to cede territory even when he himself has a just claim to it.

Joinville. *Histoire de St. Louis* (1305–1309), *CXXXVII ed. Natalis de Wailly, from the original text. Amour de St. Louis pour la paix :*

678. The holy king began to negotiate so ardently that the King of England came to France with his wife and children to treat of peace between him and them. His counsellors were much opposed to this peace[2] and spoke to him in this manner: 'Sire, we are much astonished that it should be your will to give to the King of England so great a part of your land which you and your predecessors won from him and by his defeat. Wherefore it seems to us that, if you think you have no right to it, you are not making proper restitution to the King of

[1] Cæsar means more to us (even than to you) since his authority is from our God.

[2] Concluded in 1258 and ratified in 1259.

England if you do not give him back all that you and your predecessor have conquered : and if you think that you do have a right to it, then it seems to us that you are losing in restoring it to him.'

679. To that the holy king replied in this fashion : ' Seigneurs, I am convinced that the predecessors of the King of England justly lost all which I hold by right of conquest ; and as for the land which I am giving to him, I am not giving it as a thing which I owe to him or to his heirs, but to foster love between my children and his, who are cousins german. And to me it seems that I am employing well what I am giving him because he was not my vassal (heretofore) and by this enters into my homage.'

680. He worked more than any man in the world to establish peace among his subjects, especially among the rich neighbours and the princes of the kingdom, for example between the Count de Chalon, uncle of the Seigneur of Joinville, and his son the Count of Burgundy who were at open war when we returned from overseas. And to make peace between father and son he sent some of his counsellors to Burgundy and at his own expense : and by his efforts peace was made between father and son.

683. Speaking of the foreigners whom the king had reconciled, some of his council said to him that he did not do well in not letting them war : for if he let them impoverish themselves they would not go against him as readily as if they were very rich. And to that the king replied and said that they did not speak well : ' For, if the neighbouring princes saw that I left them to war they might warn each other and say : " It is with bad intention that the king lets us war." ' Then it would come about that they would come against me because of the hatred that they have against me, and I might lose, apart from the fact that I would incur the hatred of God, who says : ' Blessed are the peacemakers ! '

684. Hence it came to pass that the Burgundians and the Lorrains whom he had pacified loved and obeyed him so much that I saw them come and plead before the king for the lawsuits they had between each other at the king's court at Rheims, Paris and Orleans.

It is upon the duty of Christian princes to respect the right of the Holy See to impose truces, to arbitrate or to mediate (according to the strength or weakness of the pontiffs at any particular time) that most of the reasoning seems to be based in mediæval documents relative to the pacific settlement of disputes. The following general rule however appears in a Bull of Urban V in 1369 :

Desist from war ; and if you believe yourselves to have a just cause, pursue it by the way of justice before a competent judge or else consent to submit it to the arbitration of mutual friends.

The period during which the political unity of Christendom was ceasing to be an effective reality yields us the beginnings of a 'rationale' of arbitration. Thus:

JOHN LUPUS. (Tractatus de Bello et Bellatoribus 1450–1496 Apud Vanderpol: *Le Droit de Guerre d'après les théologiens et les Canonistes du Moyen Age*):

If he on whom one wishes to declare war is disposed to conform to the right as it may be defined by a decision either of arbitrators or of learned men, one must not, even if one has justice on one's side, go to war; for war can only be justified by *necessity*.

And again (though, strictly speaking, he is writing of war by or against a prince who has a superior):

And indeed the plaintiff cannot himself pronounce the sentence and be judge in his own cause; he must go before the tribunal of the defendant. That is a general principle. And this remains true, even if he who makes or intends to make war upon another has the justice on his side; all the more true is it, if he has not.

The same author teaches that one has the right to get justice for oneself if the Sovereign lord of a town refuses to force his subject to do justice (i.e. make reparation): for the law permits the creditor to seize the fleeing debtor, etc. But he adds:

I doubt not that the Pope could, by pains and censures prevent every just or doubtfully just war which was not indispensable for self-defence, until the lawfulness of the war had been demonstrated to him; for he has received from God an ordinary power in the spiritual sphere, because of sin: he can exercise it without distinction against all and on all occasions and so intervene in temporal affairs.

Theological discussion of the nature of the obligation to submit disputes to peaceful forms of settlement thus begins to appear in certain little known writers of the fifteenth century. The subject occupies a regular place, as we have already indicated, in the works of the Schoolmen who were faced from the sixteenth century onward with the international problem in its proper sense.

Two important passages of Vittoria may now be noted:

they will be found in their full context in the succeeding chapter :

Rel. De Indis II, 16 :

When princes are at variance with one another about some right of sovereignty and are rushing into war, the Pope can act as judge and inquire into the claims of the parties and deliver judgement, a judgement which the princes are bound to respect, lest those numerous spiritual evils should befall which are the inevitable results of war between Christian princes.

And again in his *De Potestate Ecclesiæ V*, 13 :

If princes are making war over some province with manifest loss and harm to religion, not only can the Pope forbid them to fight but, if they cannot reach an agreement in other ways, he may by his proper authority judge between them and give sentence for one of them.

SUAREZ. *De Caritate : De Bello : Sect. II*, 2. *The existence of a higher tribunal makes resort to force contrary to natural law :*

A prince of an imperfect State or whoever has a superior in temporal things cannot wage a just war without the superior's authorization. The reason is that this kind of prince is able to ask for the right from his superior : therefore he has not the right of declaring war because in this respect he is like a private person : for that cause private persons may not wage war. Secondly, a declaration of war is contrary to the right of the supreme prince to whom this faculty is principally committed, since without it he could not govern peacefully or easily. Vittoria limits this above and Cajetan and others point out the same, that (it is illicit) except where the contrary is done by very ancient custom. Which is perhaps true when the war is declared against those who are not subject to the same king : if, however, it were against another member of the same kingdom such a custom would evidently be contrary to the natural law : for when there *is a tribunal and a power higher than either party it is against the natural law to seek one's right by force and as if on one's own authority.*

Sect. II, 5. *The arbitral power of the Holy See : guilt of princes who prevent the exercise of it :*

But for Christian rulers it must also be noted that the Supreme Pontiff, although he has no direct temporal power outside his own dominion, has, however, an indirect power. . . . By this title he has the right of examining the cause of war and the power of passing judgement to which the parties are bound to adhere, unless he do a manifest injustice : for this is certainly necessary for the spiritual good of the Church and for properly avoiding infinite evils: wherefore Soto ad Rom. 12 says that there is rarely a just war between Christian rulers, because they can have another expeditious means of terminating their common differences. Nevertheless the Pontiff sometimes refrains from interposing his authority, lest greater evils should follow: but then the supreme rulers are not bound to extort permission from the Pontiff, but, in so far as they are not forbidden, they may fight for their rights: they should be careful, however, that they themselves are not the cause whereby the Pontiff dare not intervene: for then they are not excused from blame.

'The Pontiff,' says Suarez, 'sometimes refrains . . . lest greater evils should follow.' The historian of the eighteenth century, a period of political eclipse for the Papacy, would be obliged to add 'because his arbitral authority is not acknowledged': but it is to the sovereigns and their diplomats from the Treaty of Westphalia onwards that Suarez would have imputed the sin of paralyzing the pacific functions of the Papacy. Yet whenever, before that general though not lasting disregard of Papal arbitration by those who prepared the European anarchy, Popes appeared to neglect their duties as peace-makers, there were not lacking Catholics to upbraid them with the frankness and directness of a St. Catherine of Siena. A generation before Suarez, Erasmus, who had so great a regard for Vittoria and his teaching, had written his bitter and poignant *Complaint of Peace*, in which he summoned Leo X and the Church to be busy in peace-making and condemned the wars of Julius II, (that awful oxymoron) a fighting Pope.

And Vives[1] five years afterwards thus boldly addressed Leo's successor, Pope Hadrian VI:

Do not say that you are powerless to make peace between the princes. Have the courage not to seek, as so many Popes and learned men have done, pretexts for defending the justification of war. Declare that war between Christians is a crime and a wrong. Blame it absolutely as a dispute between the members of one Body, for in Christ there is neither Spaniard nor Frenchman.

It was indeed in the stirring times of the great Counter Reformation that Suarez lived and wrote. But the worst

[1] Nys, *Les Origines du Droit International*, p. 393.

days of the Renaissance Papacy were too near to be forgotten; and such laments as these must have been present to his mind not less than the practice of barbarous war and the idolatry of Sovereignty which he saw about him. Not without reason is his doctrine upon Papal arbitration somewhat wistful.

SUAREZ. *De Caritate : De Bello, Sect. VI, 4. When claims to territory are equally founded it should be divided, or a compromise effected :*

It is another thing altogether if neither is in possession and the doubt or probability are equal. The more common opinion is that either has the right of first occupying : hence there would be a war just on both sides, and this does not apply when ignorance intervenes. The reason is that in a like case the judge can adjudicate the thing arbitrarily to whichever litigant he likes. I, however, cannot be of the opinion that this is allowed to the judge in such a case in which the judge is certainly the distributor of a thing to which he has no right. Therefore if the rights of the parties remain always absolutely equal there is no reason why he should be able to give the whole to one : he is therefore bound to divide, or if the thing cannot be usefully divided, he should try by some means to satisfy each party.

Sect. VI, 5. A pacific means of settling international disputes demanded by Natural Law :

But you ask whether in cases of this kind supreme rulers should depart from the judgement of good men. It is the question whether we should rely on natural law alone and disregard the authority of the Pope, which we have already treated. But I think the affirmative (i.e. submission to Papal arbitration) to be the more probable answer : *for they are bound as far as possible to avoid war by honest means.* If therefore there is no danger of injustice to be feared, that is obviously the best means : it will therefore have to be followed. This opinion is strengthened by the fact that it is impossible that the Author of Nature should have left human things in such a conflicting state that, being more often than not ruled by conjecture rather than by sure reasoning, all contentions between supreme rulers and States ought only to end in war : for that is contrary to prudence and the common good of the human race ; therefore it is contrary to justice. Otherwise those who were the stronger and were thereby the more to be feared would always have the greater right which is obviously barbaric and absurd.

This reasoning is an important link in the chain which leads from the conviction that the war-process, as the only means of composing international disputes, is incompatible with the Perfect Justice of the Divine Nature, to the necessity of arbitration.

SUAREZ. *De Caritate: De Bello (cont.), Sect. VI,* 6. *Sovereigns to appoint arbitrators by mutual consent:*

> But it must be noted that a supreme ruler is not bound to abide by the decision of judges whom he has not chosen or not constituted as such: the judges therefore ought to be chosen by the mutual consent of each party: but this recourse is becoming all the more unusual because it is already rarely employed. For very often one ruler holds foreign judges in suspicion.

This last sentence is tragic testimony to the growth of national feeling. The first would, as will be seen, be contested by Taparelli, to whom any third party to a conflict is 'almost the natural arbitrator between the parties in dispute.' The second is however a logical and inevitable conclusion in a world in which the Empire has ceased to be, both in practice and in theory: it is for national rulers to establish arbitrators by an accord between themselves, which is in fact what has, of late years, been accomplished.

We have already quoted the Disputation of Vasquez on war, wherein he rejects the notion that war may ever be declared without absolute certitude of a just cause.

After discussing and discarding the possibility of war being just on both sides, saving subjectively through invincible ignorance, he continues thus:

VASQUEZ. *Comment. et Disput. in Prim. Sec. St. Thomas: Disputatio LXIV, Cap. XIV:*

> But to admit that a war can be just on both sides when it is waged to solve a dispute and difference of probable opinions, not through ignorance (as we have said) but in itself, after a consideration of the reasons and claims of either party, is unheard of (*inauditum*). For a controversy of opinions demands a solution by judgement and not by arms: and since, as has been proved, the judgement of one prince does not suffice against another for the conclusion of the conflict, it necessarily follows that the conflict must be ended by the judgement of some other.

Who is to be the arbitrator, on the assumption—which Vasquez quotes but does not admit—that the Pope or the Emperor has not any temporal jurisdiction over the contending princes?

The author distinguishes between rival claims to a Marquisate or Province which is (feudally) subject to a king 'as once the kings of Spain were subject in respect of the country of Flanders to the King of France,' and rival claims to the supreme rule of a kingdom. In the first case it is the overlord of that Marquisate or Province whose law must decide the matter: in the second it must be the people of the kingdom. 'All the litigators ought to submit to the judgement of the kingdom itself.'

His conclusion is that whenever in the opinion of men learned in the law the difference of opinion between kings is such that if they were private persons, it would be a subject for litigation, it ought to be settled by judgement and not by arms. 'In such a case princes ought to settle the cause of their controversies not by war but by the judgement and sentence, not of themselves, but of another.'

Rejection of arbitration the test of aggression:

Génicot's reasoning carries the theory of arbitration a stage further. After giving his opinion upon the injuries which may be sufficiently grave to justify war (see p. 133), he rebuts the concession which Suarez had made to national sovereignty in regard to probable justice sufficing for a declaration of war. He concludes that a Power which refuses to submit to arbitration or to obey an arbitral award is certainly wrong and may be resisted by force. Taparelli, Benedict XV and the theologians of the present generation (see p. 138. *Fribourg Conclusions*) echo this conclusion:

GÉNICOT. *Institutiones Theologicæ Morales:*

The principal reason (why moral certitude of the justice of the cause is required before war may lawfully be declared) is this: that war brings in its train so many evils that it cannot be permitted except for vindicating really *certain* rights. Hence the opinion of many authors, who think it is sufficient that the right of the party declaring war should be merely 'probable' or 'more probable,' is altogether to be rejected and condemned as intrinsically dangerous. For if there remains any doubt about the right, recourse must be had to the arbitration of other rulers and especially of the Roman Pontiff: *and if the other party rejects this arbitration altogether or is unwilling to submit to the judgement passed by the arbitrator, there will then be a certain right whereby it will be licit to declare war.*

If when the war has already begun, the other party offers

due satisfaction, this must be accepted : for otherwise slaughter and other evils would be uselessly multiplied.

The following paragraph from Taparelli resumes concisely the case for arbitration. A number of other passages in the Sixth Book of his Treatise propose the ways in which international institutions of justice should be brought into being and what should be their scope. These will be more conveniently read in their context in the part of this work devoted to the Society of Nations.

TAPARELLI D'AZEGLIO. *Essai Théorique de Droit Naturel.* 1337 :

How can the truth be determined and the evidence of the injury committed and the right to vindication established, when one of the nations in dispute affirms what the other denies and when the affirmation and the negative seem founded upon *equal right?* The answer is that it is precisely because of the apparent equality of rights that arbitration is necessary. The parties are obliged, in order to find a solution of their quarrel, to have recourse to impartial judges who can give an equitable decision ; this obligation confers upon the neutral State a certain superiority of Right and makes it almost the *natural arbitrator* between the parties. . . .

We now approach the modern age, distinguished by the uneasy race between arbitration and armaments which ended in so great a tragedy, a tragedy which has in its turn provided an unprecedented incentive for the organization of international justice. Not in vain had the mind of the Catholic Church sustained and developed the ethical principles upon which the necessity for arbitration is based. Others outside the Church had worked no less ardently than the authorities here cited to the same good purpose. There was a remarkable increase in the practice of international arbitration in the eighty years between 1820 and 1900 and a no less remarkable revival of Papal peacemaking.

Between	1820	and	1840	there	were	8	cases	of	arbitration;[1]
,,	1840	,,	1860	,,	,,	30	,,	,,	,,
,,	1860	,,	1880	,,	,,	44	,,	,,	,,
,,	1880	,,	1900	,,	,,	90	,,	,,	,,

[1] Plater, *Primer of Peace and War*, p. 160.

Between 1870 and 1914 there were fourteen Papal interventions to compose international conflicts of which twelve were successful. At the end of the nineteenth century the First Hague Conference introduced a valuable form of mediation: the Second in 1907 adopted the general principle of obligatory international arbitration. Despite the national suspicions and other causes, to appear hereafter, which robbed these conferences of their full effect, it is certainly the case that they gave a remarkable stimulus to the cause of arbitration. Within the first fifteen years of the twentieth century a hundred and fifty bilateral arbitration treaties had been signed, though in most of them the dangerous exclusion of 'disputes affecting vital interests' occurred. A considerable popular movement in favour of the pacific settlement of disputes had been growing up in the United States and in the principal European Countries, thanks to the devotion of such men as Elim Burrit, Victor Hugo and Fréderic Passy. David Urquhart with his passionate desire to see a higher standard of international morality restored,had for the first time taught British working men to take an active interest in foreign affairs. In 1888 the Interparliamentary Union was founded, with the promotion of arbitration as one of its main objects.

How came it then that such remarkable progress was marred by the calamity of the Franco-Prussian war and appeared for a time to be utterly undone by the Great War of 1914–1918? It belongs rather to the historian than the philosopher to provide the answer. Here, abstracting from particular political causes, we may point to the following passages from the letters and speeches of the Popes as supplying the spiritual explanation of the tragedy. It is that steps toward the establishment of international justice had not been accompanied by a general restriction of national armaments; on the contrary these had developed rapidly and in nervous rivalry. The logical connection between these two reforms emerges irresistibly from the analysis made by Leo XIII of the dangers of the times: from the practical proposals of Benedict XV: from the conclusions of Catholic organizations, in common with many other serious associations concerned with the international problem, since the Great War. Behind this febrile competition in scientific preparations for war lay, in the minds of the Popes, the absence of Christian charity, the despite of Governments for the Christian law and even the Moral law itself, and a spirit of grasping materialism wholly alien to the whole Christian conception of peace. 'Can this be the normal condition of human society? Yet we cannot escape from this situation and obtain true peace except by the aid of Jesus Christ.'[1] Appeal to the natural reason alone —which so far has been the method of the moral theologian, valid so far as it goes—is proved to be insufficient to enthrone in the spirit of Governments and peoples not only an intellectual appreciation of the merits of pacific substitutes for the process of war, but the firm will to use them.

Our first quotation from Leo XIII[2] is from an allocution spoken four years after his successful mediation in the conflict between Germany and Spain over the Caroline Archipelago:

LEO XIII. *From the Allocution Nostis Errorem. Feb.* 11, 1889. *The multiplication of armaments a contributary cause of war:*

Nothing is more important than to avert from Europe the danger of war, and thus all that can be done towards this end must be considered as a work of public safety. . . . The menacing multiplication of armies is calculated rather to excite rivalry and suspicions than to repress them. It troubles men's minds by a restless expectation of coming disasters, and meanwhile it weighs down the citizens with expenses so heavy that one may doubt whether they are not even more intolerable than war itself.

LEO XIII. *From the Encyclical Ad Principes Populosque Universos, June* 20, 1894. *On the evils of Conscription and the state of armed peace:*

We behold the condition of Europe. For many years past peace has been rather an appearance than a reality. Possessed with mutual suspicions, almost all the nations are vying with

[1] Leo XIII, *Ad Principes Populosque Universos,* June 20, 1894.

[2] Only those sentences which expressly concern armaments, arbitration and the prevention of war are here quoted. Several of the papal documents from which they are taken, applying as they do to the whole problem of peace, are given more fully in the following chapters.

one another in equipping themselves with military armaments. Inexperienced youths are removed from parental direction and control to be thrown amid the dangers of the soldier's life; robust young men are taken from agriculture, or ennobling studies, or trade, or the arts, to be put under arms. Hence the treasures of States are exhausted by the enormous expenditure, the national resources are frittered away, and private fortunes impaired, and this, as it were, armed peace, which now prevails, cannot last much longer. Can this be the normal condition of human society? Yet we cannot escape from this situation and obtain true peace, except by the aid of Jesus Christ. For to repress ambition and covetousness and envy—the chief instigators of war—nothing is more fitted than the Christian virtues, and, in particular, the virtue of justice, for, by its exercise, both the law of nations and the faith of treaties may be maintained inviolate and the bonds of brotherhood continue unbroken, if men are but convinced that *justice exalteth a nation.*

Appeal of the Three Cardinals for a permanent Court of Arbitration:

Following upon this Papal leadership, an urgent appeal for the establishment of a permanent Court of Arbitration was issued conjointly by Cardinal Gibbons, Archbishop of Baltimore, Cardinal Logue, Primate of All Ireland and Cardinal Vaughan, Archbishop of Westminster, on Easter Day, 1896. The conflict between the British and American Governments over Venezuela was the occasion of this appeal:

Appeal of Cardinals Gibbons (Baltimore), Logue (Armagh) and Vaughan (Westminster), 1896

We, the undersigned Cardinals, representatives of the Prince of Peace and of the Catholic Church in our respective countries, invite all who hear our voice to co-operate in the formation of a public opinion which shall demand the establishment of a permanent tribunal of arbitration, as a rational substitute, among the English-speaking races, for a resort to the bloody arbitrament of war. We are well aware that such a project is beset with practical difficulties. We believe that they will not prove to be insuperable if the desire to overcome them be genuine and general. Such a court existed centuries ago when the nations of Christendom were united in one faith. And have we not seen nations appeal to the same court for its judgement in our own day? The establishment of a permanent tribunal composed maybe of trusted representatives of each sovereign nation with power to nominate judges and umpires according to the nature of the differences that arise, and a common acceptance of general principles defining and limiting the jurisdiction and subject matter of such a tribunal, would create new guarantees for peace that could not fail to influence the whole of Christendom.

Such an international court of arbitration would form the second line of defence to be called into requisition only after the ordinary resources of diplomacy had been exhausted. It would at least postpone the outbreak of hostilities until reason and common sense had formally pronounced their last word.

This is a matter of which the constitution and procedure must be settled by Governments.

But as Governments are becoming more identified with the aspirations and moulded by the desires of the people, an appeal in the first instance must be addressed to the people.

We do not hesitate on our part to lift up our united voice and proclaim to all who are accustomed to hearken to our counsels that it is a sign of divine influence at work in their midst. 'Nations shall not lift up sword against nation, neither shall they be exercised any more in war' (Isaias xi: 9). For it was written of a future time: 'Come ye and behold the works of the Lord what wonders he has done upon the earth, making wars to cease even to the end of the earth' (Psalm xlv: 9).

Others may base their appeal upon the motives which touch your worldly interest, your prosperity, your world-wide influence and your authority in the affairs of man. The Catholic Church recognizes the legitimate force of such motives in the natural order and blesses whatever tends to the real progress and elevation of the race. But our main ground of appeal rests upon the known character and will of the Prince of Peace, the Living Founder, the Divine Head of Christendom. It was He who declared that love of the brotherhood is a second commandment like unto the first. It was He who announced to the people that praise and reward of those who seek after peace and pursue it. 'Blessed,' said He, 'are the peacemakers, for they shall be called the children of God' (Matthew v: 9).

We, therefore, earnestly invite all to unite with us in pressing their convictions and desires upon their respective Governments by means of petitions and such other measures as are constitutional.

(*Signed*) James, Card. Gibbons, Archbishop of Baltimore,
Michael, Card. Logue, Archbishop of Armagh, Primate of Ireland.
Herbert, Card. Vaughan, Archbishop of Westminster.

The Papacy and the First Hague Conference:

It has been widely asserted that the actual participation

of Leo XIII in the Hague Conference would have so fortified the systems of mediation and arbitration which it sought to evolve that they would even have stood the strain of August, 1914. Though ultimately excluded from the first Conference, a fact which did incalculable damage to the confidence of Catholic populations in the resolutions taken by their Governments regarding arbitration, the Holy See, through the Pontifical letters, written and published in connection with the Conference, took the occasion of making more precise the Catholic tradition on that subject.

Letter from CARDINAL RAMPOLLA *to Count Mouravieff (before the First Hague Conference*[1]*), February* 10, 1899 :

What is lacking in the international consortium of States is a system of legal and moral means designed to safeguard the rights of each. In consequence an immediate recourse to force is the only means that remains. Hence arises the competition between States in the development of their military strength. To meet so baneful a state of affairs the institution of mediation and arbitration appears to be the most timely remedy. It responds in every respect to the aspirations of the Holy See. . . . The Holy See expresses the most ardent wish that, in the Counsels of the Powers the principle of mediation and arbitration may be accepted and applied in the fullest possible manner. . . . It is convinced that if an effective international agreement could be reached on that point, one of the happiest and most successful results would be achieved for civilization.

Letter of LEO XIII *to the Queen of the Netherlands, May* 29, 1899 :

YOUR MAJESTY,

We cannot but find agreeable the letter by which Your Majesty, in announcing to us the meeting of the Conference for Peace in your capital, did us the courtesy to request our moral support for that assembly.

We hasten to express our keen sympathy for the august invitation to the Conference, and for Your Majesty, who extended to it such spontaneous and noble hospitality, and for the eminently moral and beneficent object towards which the labours already begun are tending.

[1] Leo XIII's protest at the Holy See's exclusion from the Conference, owing to the policy of the Italian Government exploited by the Germans (see documents in Müller, *Friedenswerk des Kirche in den letzten drei Jahrhunderten*, pp. 363–374), was made in an Allocution at the Consistory of December 14, 1899.

We consider that it comes especially within our province not only to lend our moral support to such enterprises, but to co-operate actively in them, for the object in question is supremely noble in its nature and intimately bound up with our august ministry, which through the divine founder of the Church, and in virtue of the tradition of many centuries, has been invested with the highest possible mission, that of being a mediator of peace. In fact the authority of the Supreme Pontiff goes beyond the boundaries of nations : it embraces all peoples to the end of federating them in the true peace of the Gospel. His action to promote the general good of humanity rises above the special interest which the chiefs of various States have in view, and better than anyone else, his authority knows how to incline toward concord peoples of diverse natures and characters.

History itself bears witness to all that has been done, by the influence of our predecessors, to make more merciful the inexorable laws of war, to avert bloody conflicts when controversies have arisen between princes, to terminate peacefully even the most acute differences between nations, to vindicate courageously the rights of the weak against the pretensions of the strong. Even unto us, notwithstanding the abnormal condition to which we are at present reduced, it has been given to put an end to grave differences between great nations such as Germany and Spain, and this very day we hope soon to be able to establish concord between two nations of South America which have submitted their controversy to our arbitration.

In spite of obstacles which may arise, we shall continue, since it rests with us to fulfil that traditional mission, without seeking any other object than the public weal, without envying any glory but that of serving the sacred cause of Christian civilization.

We beg Your Majesty to accept the expression of our great esteem and our best wishes for your prosperity and that of your kingdom.

From the Vatican, May 29, 1899.

(*Signed*) LEO P. P. XIII.

Powers of an arbitral tribunal under modern circumstances :

The scope of a court of arbitration as approved by the Church, can be illustrated by the text of a treaty in which the Pope was chosen as arbitrator, a position which he—Leo XIII—accepted. Certain articles of the treaty between the Republics of Colombia and Peru, signed on September 12, 1905, are of general interest and indirectly of doctrinal importance. They are reproduced in the appendix to this chapter (Articles 1–14).

The Carnegie Endowment :

POPE PIUS X. *Letter to the Apostolic Delegate to the United States, June* 11, 1911. *On the occasion of the foundation of the Carnegie Endowment for International Peace :*

To compose differences, to restrain the outbreak of hostilities, to prevent the dangers of war, to remove even the anxieties of so-called armed peace, is, indeed, most praiseworthy, and any effort in this cause, even though it may not immediately or wholly accomplish its purpose, manifests, nevertheless, a zeal which cannot but redound to the credit of its authors and be of benefit to the State. This is specially true at the present day. . . . Wherefore We most heartily commend the work already begun, which should be approved by all good men, and We most gladly lend the weight of Our authority to those who are striving to realize this most beneficent purpose.

The Holy See, the Great War and its aftermath :

The following are the passages directly relating to arbitration and disarmament in the letters of Benedict XV and Pius XI :

BENEDICT XV. (*Encyclical Ad Beatissimi of November* 1, 1914) :

We implore those in whose hands are placed the fortunes of nations to hearken to Our voice. Surely there are other ways and means whereby violated rights can be rectified. Let them be tried honestly and with goodwill, and let arms meanwhile be laid aside. It is impelled with love of them and of all mankind, without any personal interest whatever that We utter these words. Let them not allow these words of a friend and a father to be uttered in vain. . . . Our Lord Jesus Christ came down from Heaven for the very purpose of restoring amongst men the kingdom of peace, which the envy of the devil had destroyed, and it was His will that it should rest on no other foundation than that of brotherly love.

BENEDICT XV. (*Letter to the Heads of States engaged in war, August* 1, 1917)[1] :

The Pope invited the Belligerent Governments to consider the following points 'which seem to offer the foundations of a just and lasting peace.'

First of all, the fundamental point must be that the moral force of Right shall be substituted for the material force of Arms :

[1] For full text of letter see following chapter.

thence must follow a just agreement of all for the simultaneous and reciprocal diminution of armaments, in accordance with rules and guarantees to be established hereafter and to a degree consistent with the maintenance of public order within each State ; next for the setting up in the place of armies of a Court of Arbitration with its high peace-making function, subject to regulations to be agreed on and sanctions to be determined against the State, which should refuse either to submit its international disputes to arbitration or to accept an arbitral decision.

BENEDICT XV. (*Encyclical Pacem Dei Munus Pulcherrimum of May* 23, 1920)[1]:

In the general restoration of justice and charity and reconciliation of nations it is much to be desired that all nations enter without misgiving into a general society, or rather family, for the purpose of protecting their individual independence and for the preservation of order. Such a comity of nations is recommended amongst other reasons, by the widely felt need of abolishing or reducing military armaments which weigh so heavily on the resources of the State ; and in this way war with its train of evils will be entirely avoided or at least rendered less menacing, and the liberty and territorial integrity of every nation safeguaded.

PIUS XI. (*Letter to the Archbishop of Genoa, of April* 7, 1922)

If, according to the fine motto of the Red Cross : '*Inter Arma caritas*,' Christian charity should rule even during the clash of arms, this should be still more true when once arms are laid down and Treaties of Peace are signed. Indeed, international hatreds, sad heritage of war, turn to the disadvantage of the victor nations themselves and prepare for all a very dreadful future ; for it must not be forgotten that the best guarantee of tranquillity is not a forest of bayonets, but mutual confidence and friendship.

PIUS XI. (*Apostolic Letter Nova Impendet of October* 2, 1931) :

Since the unbridled race in armaments, which on the one hand is the consequence of international rivalry, and on the other is the cause of enormous expenditure taken out of the resources available for the public well-being, is not the least of the reasons for the present crisis, We cannot refrain from renewing and making Our own the grave warning of Our Predecessor. We deplore the fact that it has not yet been heeded and We exhort

[1] For full text of letter see Chapter IX.

you, Venerable Brethren, to employ every means at your disposal through preaching and through the Press to enlighten men's minds and to incline their hearts to the requirements of right reason and, even more, of the law of Christ.

Contemporary Catholic Action :

We may appropriately add to the above Papal documents expressions of opinion upon this subject expressed by responsible Catholic leaders and organizations. The Catholic Union of International Studies, whose Executive Committee framed the following communication at a meeting held under the presidency of Mgr. Besson, Bishop of Lausanne, Geneva and Fribourg, at the beginning of February, 1932, consists of national groups of Catholic publicists, theologians and students of international affairs in Belgium, England, France, Germany, Hungary, Ireland, Poland, Switzerland and other countries :

Message from the Catholic Union of International Studies to the President of the World Disarmament Conference (Reproduced in the official Journal of the Conference), Geneva. February 9, 1932 :

MR. PRESIDENT,

The Catholic Union of International Studies, faithful to the directions of His Holiness Pope Pius XI, who renewed in his Apostolic Letter of October 2, 1931, the condemnation which his predecessors had so often pronounced of the unbridled race in armaments, has always striven to enlighten public opinion upon the requirements of Christian Law and of Right Reason in regard to the grave and urgent problem, for the solution of which your Conference has been called together.

The Union desires to recall the vitally important advice given by His Holiness Pope Benedict XV to the Governments of the belligerent States in his letter of August 1, 1917 : First of all, the fundamental point must be that the moral force of Right shall be substituted for the material force of Arms, etc. (See p. 176 above.)

Since that letter was written the institution of the Permanent Court of International Justice, the development of Arbitration and the Covenant of the League of Nations itself, which give visible form to the solidarity of peoples and to an obligation incumbent upon them to co-operate for the defence of international order and peace—have all considerably strengthened not only the sentiment but also the guarantees of international peace. These events have, moreover, defined the limits within which must now be expressed the question when and under what circumstances war is permissible. The progress already made and our hopes of future progress in the same direction logically call for a simultaneous and reciprocal diminution of armaments, and in the first place of those armaments which are especially designed for the purposes of attack.

The results which we expect of the Conference cannot fail to reawaken the confidence of the peoples in the organization of international peace.

But any attempt at military disarmament implies a parallel effort to bring about a reconciliation in the hearts of men. This form of disarmament which is to-day called 'moral disarmament' was described by Pope Pius XI in his letter of April 7, 1922, in the following words : 'It must not be forgotten that the best guarantee of tranquillity is not a forest of bayonets, but mutual confidence and friendship.' In this spirit the Catholic Union of International Studies, confident in the will of the Conference and of the Governments represented to attain an object so fully in accord with the requirements of Christian doctrine, will not cease to invoke for this great work and for all those who have undertaken it the indispensable help of the God of Peace.

Believe me, Mr. President,

Yours,

GONZAQUE DE REYNOLD,

President, Catholic Union of International Studies.

Et ne nos inducas in tentationem :

At a mass meeting of Catholics at which this declaration was adopted in Geneva on February 7, 1932, communications were read and statements made from a number of Catholic organizations. Among them was a letter from the Archbishop of San Francisco, as Chairman of the Administrative Committee of the National Catholic Welfare Conference of the United States :

January 15. 1932.

We again voice our hope and our abiding prayer that the nations of the world may take effective measures to throw off the heavy burden of armaments and thus further promote among all peoples the spirit of peace and fraternal charity.

The Apostolic Letter *Nova Impendet* is then quoted and the consistent attitude of the Conference in favour of disarmament recalled. The message ends :

We cannot promote the instruments of war and pretend to seek international peace. In the 'Our Father' we pray that we may not be led into temptation. We are most faithful to Christ, the Prince of Peace, most faithful to His Vicar upon earth, most faithful to the brotherhood of humanity, when we seek to do away with those things that are temptations to war, and to promote among nations and among individuals the will to peace.

The following statement on the Catholic Church and Disarmament was made jointly by the Catholic Council for International Relations (Great Britain), the Catholic Union of International Studies (Irish Branch) and the Catholic Association for International Peace (U.S.A.). It was read by Lord Howard of Penrith at a Mass Meeting in London on November 27, 1931, in the presence of Cardinal Bourne, Archbishop of Westminster, who had given it his formal approval:

1. *Christian Charity in International life:*

In the first place Christian charity must obtain between States as in private and national life. For Peace is the effect of Charity. There is no other power by which to destroy the fear and mistrust which are themselves the primary cause of competitive armaments.

Catholics by prayer, by personal influence and by their contribution to national policies in every country have a special duty to promote international goodwill and confidence. That is the 'apostolate of peace' to which His Holiness Pope Pius XI called both clergy and laity in his Allocution at Christmas 1930. 'The best guarantee of tranquillity,' he wrote in 1922, 'is not a forest of bayonets, but mutual confidence and friendship.'

2. *Disarmament and Arbitration:*

It has been the immemorial tradition of the Church that arms may not lawfully be used except as the instrument of justice and in the last resort. And since there is a natural society of nations, the use of national armaments can be justified only for the defence or restoration of order within that society, an order in which each has rights and each corresponding duties. Self-defence against aggression, which is itself a violation of order, and the vindication of justice when a grave injury has been suffered, these are traditionally laid down as just causes of war undertaken by the rulers of States; but the latter only under strict conditions, one of which is that there exists no higher tribunal which can secure restitution and effect a just settlement of the matter in dispute. It cannot be denied that the establishment of a Permanent Court of International Justice and of other tribunals for the settlement of different classes of international conflicts is a fact which must modify the right of any State to resort to war and to make preparations for war.

3. *Disarmament and Sanctions :*

The established methods of international consultation and co-operation, and the obligations incumbent upon most States by their treaty obligations to join in common action to resist and repel an aggressor—these are also considerations which, by rendering the emergency of self-defence against invasion more improbable, should make it possible for each member of the society of nations to diminish the quantity and the financial burden of its own armaments. On the other hand, so far as rivalry in armaments is a cause of disunion among Christian peoples, it weakens their resistance to the enemies of social order and of Christian civilization.

4. *The Moral obligation to keep Faith :*

Such being the general case for the reduction and limitation of armaments arising from the Natural Law, as will be seen from the Papal statements quoted below, Catholics have an added reason for desiring a general reduction. For it is a fundamental principle of International Ethics, reinforced by Christian tradition, that the plighted word must not be violated. Pope Benedict XV advocated a general, simultaneous, reciprocal reduction of armaments ; such was the measure to which the Allied and Associated Powers committed themselves at the Peace Conference, 1919, and in the Peace Treaties. A definite promise was made by them to the defeated Powers that the drastic reductions imposed upon Germany, Austria, Hungary and Bulgaria were only to be the beginning of that general reform. It is for Catholics to insist in the name of morality and national honour that this promise should be kept.

5. *Papal Teaching :*

The principal statements by the Popes during the last fifty years concerning the danger of the competition in armaments as a cause of war ; the reason for desiring a reduction of armaments ; and the place that this measure should play in the organization of international society, are as follows :

The utterances of Leo XIII, Pius X, Benedict XV and Pius XI which are set forth on pages 176–8 above are then quoted. The manifesto ends :

It is in the spirit of this teaching by the Sovereign Pontiffs that Catholics of all nationalities should seek by prayer and action to promote an international agreement for the general reduction of the armed forces of the world.

Conclusions

1. It is the duty of Governments under every circumstance to seek the solution of the differences that divide them and the vindication of international justice by pacific means.
2. These means may consist in direct negotiations—*diplomacy*; the use of the good offices of a third party—*mediation*; recourse to the procedure of *conciliation* by an international person or commission; submission of the dispute to an international person or tribunal for *arbitration*; or to a Court of Justice for *Judicial Settlement.*
3. It is the duty of Governments to strive to bring into being or, if they exist, to sustain and perfect international institutions fitted to effect conciliation, arbitration and judicial settlement.
4. The Holy See is eminently suited to fulfil these functions by its divine origin and mandate, its supra-national character and its sovereign independence.
5. It is however desirable that the necessary international institutions should be established by the secular power, their functions in relation to the Papacy being similar to those of the State in relation to the Church in civil society.
6. The natural form of the society of nations being polyarchic the necessary institutions of conciliation, arbitration and justice must be established through an accord or convention between the Governments of States.
7. Such a convention has a dual sanction in the moral order; it is a duty of social justice, and it is a promise on the part of each contracting party the violation of which is prohibited by the Moral Law. It follows from this that Governments are under an obligation not to recognize any international situation created through a breach of the convention.
8. Such negative loyalty does not suffice. Governments of States, as members of the natural society of nations have also a moral obligation actively to support international institutions created for the pacific settlement of disputes by appropriate action against any power which defies them. For States who are parties to the conventions in

question this general obligation should receive a positive form, whereby they promise to support and, if materially possible, participate in deterrent and penal measures (international sanctions) against any State which employs force against another without recourse to arbitration, or which refuses to submit to arbitration or to carry out an arbitral award.

9. Once the required institutions of pacific settlement exist the only just war is a war waged for the defence of international order in support of and by the authority of such institutions. Hence the use, extent and disposition of armaments are essentially a matter of international concern. Rivalry in military preparations between members of the society of nations must be brought to an end. Armaments must be reduced to the lowest point consistent with the maintenance of order within each State and the execution of international sanctions.

APPENDIX TO CHAPTER VII

A TREATY OF ARBITRATION

Treaty of Arbitration between Colombia and Peru. September 12, 1905 :

The plenipotentiaries of both countries having been named in the preamble, the Treaty proceeds :

The said parties, their respective powers having been duly accepted, have resolved the following :

Article 1

The high contracting parties will submit to arbitration all controversies of any kind which, for whatever reason, may arise between them, and which they have not been able to settle amicably by means of direct negotiations. Only questions affecting the independence and honour of the two nations are excepted from this obligation. In case of doubt, this point will also be resolved by compromise. Specifically, national independence and honour will not be considered compromised in controversies relating to diplomatic privileges, consular jurisdiction, customs and navigation duties, validity, construction, and carrying out of treaties, and pecuniary claims, whatever their origin and antecedents may have been, and it is understood to be the wish of the two Governments to give the fullest possible interpretation to the principle of international arbitration. The present treaty is also applicable to controversies which have taken place before its conclusion, but questions which have already been definitely settled between both parties cannot be renewed. In these cases arbitration will be exclusively limited to differences which may arise as to the interpretation and carrying out of the said arrangements.

Article 2

The Governments of Peru and Colombia nominate *His Holiness the Pope* as arbitrator in cases of differences and, in the case of the refusal or inability of His Holiness, His Excellency the President of the Argentine Republic.

Article 3

For each case the high contracting parties will conclude a special convention to determine the precise object of the controversy, as also all points and circumstances relative to the affair which they may deem necessary.

Failing such convention, and one of the high contracting parties having notified the other that four months have passed since they had been requested to conclude the same, without, for whatever cause, their being able to come to an arrangement, the arbitrator will decide on the facts of the case and the rights which must be resolved to decide the controversy.

For any other point, in default of the special convention on the subject or should there be no mention made of it in the same, the following rules will be applied :

Article 4

In default of special arrangements between the interested parties, the arbitrator is empowered as follows : to fix the time for the arbitration ; to determine the judicial proceedings and contentions ; the formalities and terms for the interested parties ; and, in general, all necessary measures for the prompt resolving and carrying out of all points and difficulties and all prejudicial and incidental questions that may arise. The high contracting parties bind themselves to put at the disposition of the arbitrator all information at their command.

Article 5

The arbitrator has the right to decide, in his own judgement, on the validity and interpretation of the matter in question.

Article 6

An agent of each of the interested parties will represent his Government in all matters submitted to arbitration.

Article 7

The arbitrator must decide according to the principles of law unless the question imposes special obligations or authorizes the arbitrator to act as friendly intermediary.

Article 8

The sentence must definitely decide each point of the case. It will be drawn up in duplicate, signed by the arbitrator, and each of the countries will be notified directly or by the representative sent to the arbitrator.

Article 9

Each of the interested parties will defray its own expenses and half of those of the arbitration.

Article 10

The legally pronounced sentence will decide, to the extent of its powers, the controversy between the interested parties. It must contain the statement of the time within which it is to be executed. The same arbitrator will decide any questions which may arise in its execution.

Article 11

The sentence does not admit appeal and the carrying out of same is left to the honour of the two nations signing it.

Nevertheless, the same arbitrator can be requested to revise the sentence by acquainting him with the following facts.

1. That the sentence has been given in view of a false or equivocal document.

2. If the sentence has been, in whole or in part, the consequence of a fully recognized error, positive or negative, resulting from the proceedings or documents relative to the case.

Article 12

The arbitrator will fix the proceedings for the revision, and the brief and peremptory terms in which it will be effected, confining himself exclusively to the point which gave rise to the revision.

Article 13

The treaty will be in force for a period of ten years from the date of the exchange of ratifications. If not denounced six months before its expiration, it will be considered to be renewed for another period of ten years, and so on.

Article 14

Both Governments will simultaneously solicit, through their plenipotentiaries, the acquiescence of His Holiness within six months following the exchange of ratifications of the present treaty.

Article 15

This treaty will be ratified and the ratifications exchanged in Lima and Bogota in the shortest time possible.

In virtue of which the plenipotentiaries of the high contracting parties have signed and sealed, in duplicate, in Bogota, on the twelfth day of September of the year nineteen hundred and five.

Hernan Velarde.
Climaco Calderon.
Luis Tanco Argaez.

CHAPTER VIII

THE CHURCH AS PEACEMAKER

"PAX *huic domo*"—such was the salutation wherewith the Apostles of Christianity were bidden by their Divine Master first to announce their coming as they spread the Gospel throughout the world. How far did the successors of the Apostles bring or seek to bring peace to the households, the tribes, the cities, the nations to whom the Christian message was preached? How, in particular, has the Church herself sought to apply those principles of peacemaking which our study has now elucidated?

To diffuse the spirit of the Sermon on the Mount; to develop and expose through the Teaching Church as a whole, the principles of the moral law which determine the mutual rights and duties of human societies; to establish the Canon Law, crystallizing these principles for the direction alike of rulers and subjects, clergy and laity; to furnish spiritual sanctions which reinforce obedience to that Law and to the Law of Charity—these were and are the great contribution of the Catholic Church to the peace and order of mankind. It is a contribution that survives the weaknesses and aberrations of a fallen human nature which have marred from time to time the highest offices in the Church. It is a standard to which the Papacy inevitably returns even after periods of scandalous contention for the Papal throne and subjection to Emperors (as in the sixth to tenth centuries); despite the Babylonian captivities of Avignon or of Compiègne; the temptations of temporal monarchy (as in the sixteenth century) or the eclipse of its international influence (in the eighteenth century). It is a criterion by which Popes, Bishops and Kings are judged in the forum of their own conscience, by their contemporaries and by succeeding generations in the Church. Based upon right reason and the Christian revelation it is akin to the sacred deposit of faith and morals safeguarded from error by the Divine Spirit. Nor has any case been established in which a Roman Pontiff, however great his personal sins or defects—as of Alexander VI—or mistaken his policy—as of Julius II—gave an erroneous or contradictory decision when speaking *ex cathedra* and as teacher of the Universal Church regarding the ethics of international conduct.

If the record of the Papacy be taken as a whole it can hardly be denied that its influence has been and must be unifying and pacifying. Else the Popes would long since have stultified their very *raison d'être* and the fundamental claim of the Catholic Church to be One and also Universal in character, potentially embracing, that is to say, all nations. In what then consists the '*munus pacificum Romani pontificis?*' Efforts to clothe this function in legal phraseology or to express it in philosophical formulæ change with the changing years, the varying fortunes of the Church, the passing political constitutions of the world. The essence of the function is to be found in the Divine Commission to Peter and in the fact that the Pope, as Peter's successor, is Vicar on earth of Christ, the Prince of Peace. Herein are contained two conceptions, the one of Power, the other of Love; of Power for to Peter was given, according to the Catholic tradition, authority to rule, to bind and to loose; of Love, since Jesus Christ said of the Christians to be 'by this men shall know that ye are my disciples that ye love one another' and prayed before His supreme sacrifice, 'that they may be one even as Thou, Father, and I are one.'

Power is the note of Papal interventions to effect peace in the first great period of the Church's rule in Europe, from the age of Hildebrand to the fourteenth century: Love, so soon as that Power was flouted or denied, continued to inspire the Pontiffs as labourers for peace from the rise of national sovereignties to the heartrending endeavours of Benedict XV throughout their culminating conflict. It is a love inspired by the charity of Christ and a vivid sense of the fraternity of men and nations, but a love from which the sense of authority is never absent: it is the love of a

Father for his children. It is a consequence of this conception of the Papal function that, so soon as the international problem arose, the Head of the Church should be wholly free from political subjection to any temporal Prince or Government.

It belongs rather to the historian than to the moral philosopher to describe the forms which clothed this pacific mission of the Apostolic See, to determine how far each was or was not adapted to the needs of the time, to what extent under each that mission was loyally discharged, how far it succeeded or failed. We can only illustrate the place filled by the Pope as peacemaker in the Christian tradition of international ethics by a few typical examples of Papal intervention in earlier ages and by the Acts of Benedict XV which at once resume in vivid fashion the functions of the Pope in this regard, and are replete with doctrine upon the mutual rights and duties of nations.

For the benefit of historical students, two Appendices are added at the end of the book, in which the principal cases of Papal intervention are recorded. The first, which covers the years 1100 to the sixteenth century, is translated from the French of M. Duval and gives a number of references to sources which may be consulted. The latter which carries us from the end of the sixteenth century to 1918, is from the German of Joseph Müller. It is a list of pontifical acts, almost all of which are transcribed from documents in the Vatican archives, and reproduced in his book *Das Friedenswerk der Kirche in den letzten drei Jahrhunderten*.

Papal intervention to effect peace, first undertaken *ratione feudi* at the height of the feudal system, under which many of the Kingdoms of Europe were vassals of the Holy See, were soon made *ratione peccati*. This title to intervene, directly derived from the Pope's position as guardian of the Moral Law, outlasted the bitter contentions of jurisdiction between Papacy and Empire, canon and civil law. It was expressed in its most authoritative form in the theocracy of Gregory VII. We find it again, long after the disruption of Christendom, in the mouth of a seventeenth century Pope. It is vigorously reasserted by Leo XIII.

At times when the Popes were unable to compel obedience

under pain of sin, to make their judgement between two princes effective, or to induce them to submit the cause of war to final settlement, they claimed a right of intervention which arose rather from that requirement of social justice which was to play such a large part in the neo-scholastic doctrine—the damage of war, whether otherwise justified or not, to the whole Christian Commonweal. It was the right to impose *truces or armistices*, during which terms of peace might be elaborated. Under this title the Franciscan Father, Adam Newton, the representative of John XXII, penetrating boldly in the disguise of a Scottish peasant behind the lines of Robert Bruce's army, proclaimed the Papal truce between Edward II of England and Robert Bruce of Scotland in 1317, returning beaten and bruised to Berwick.

This right of arresting hostilities in the common interests of Christendom, often exercised as we have already shown with the desire of uniting Christian princes for the Crusade, was extended by Papal as against Imperial apologists to the right of the Pope to forbid war altogether between Christians. This notion was rationalized by the schoolmen and expressed by Vittoria in a form which harmonized it with the right of the temporal power, and led him to a particularly lucid exposition of the interdependence of the two which, since it inspired the Tridentine definitions, may here serve as the most satisfying expression of that right.

De Potestate Eccles. V, XIII :

I say likewise that in other temporal affairs the Pope cannot prevent the action of the temporal power. However much that power may be negligent in the administration of the State, the Pope has no power to intervene provided no harm is thus done to things spiritual. But if such negligence leads to the serious damage of spiritual interests, he can prescribe the remedy, as has been said above. And likewise if princes are making war over some province with manifest loss and harm to religion, not only can the Pope forbid them to fight but if they cannot reach an agreement in other ways, he may by his proper authority judge between them and give sentence for one of them against the other.

But, says Vittoria, the Pope has neither the right nor the power to usurp the civil power except in case of necessity, otherwise he would do an injury to princes, if he were to take their place.

The right of the Pope to intervene in order to prevent or to put an end to wars, because of the damage which they cause to religion, is based by this author upon a conception of the mutual relations of Church and State, in which the primacy of the spiritual is clearly asserted :

De Potestate Eccles. V, IL :

The whole Church is one single body. Two bodies are not brought into being, one by the civil commonwealth, one by the spiritual, but a single body only, as is clear from the teaching of St. Paul the Apostle and has been shown above. For Christ is head of the whole Church, and it would be monstrous for there to be one body without a head or for one head to have two bodies. In one body, on the contrary, all the members are connected one with another and subordinated, and the less noble parts are at the service of the more noble. So also in the Christian Commonweal there is a hierarchy in all the parts, all are linked together—duties, objects and powers alike—and there is no sense in which it can be said that the spiritual are inferior to the temporal. On the contrary, the temporal are inferior to the spiritual and are dependent upon them.

To these titles to intervention, in order to prevent or punish sin, and to protect Christian civilization as a whole, is added a third, drawn from natural law on the one hand and the unique supra-national position of the Papacy on the other. It is the arbitral quality of the Pope. This arises from the natural obligation of rulers (sufficiently illustrated in the preceding pages), to have recourse to a disinterested Power as judge before attempting to vindicate their claims by arms, and the fact that, unless under some temporary disability, the Holy See is pre-eminently fitted by its independence, its common concern for all peoples and its predisposition to peace, to exercise the responsibilities of ' moral superiority ' conferred upon third parties. This is the natural ground of Papal arbitration.

On the same ground is based Papal mediation, in cases where pride or the headstrong sentiments of one or both the parties in dispute preclude the reference of the quarrel to settlement without appeal, by arbitration or a judicial tribunal. Very frequently has this mediation been offered by the Popes, their legates and nuncios (*nuncii* or *angeli pacis* as they were often called) rather as a duty of their sacred charge than a right, more as an act of Love than of Power. To accept such mediation, failing other means of accomoda-tion, is surely a natural duty which Catholic rulers have an added supernatural motive to fulfil.

The Treaty of Westphalia was a public act of disregard of the international authority of the Papacy ; and there was a period of eclipse of the Popes as peacemakers, so far as records avail, from at least 1713 until the unsuccessful endeavours of Pius IX to prevent the Franco-Prussian war in 1870. The protest of the Holy See against the Partition of Poland, however ; Pius VII's refusal to be dragooned by Napoleon into joining the blockade against the British and the vigorous part played by Cardinal Consalvi in refusing to recognize the fruits of aggression at the Congress of Vienna—such acts show the Popes to be not unmindful of their duties in the international order. There was also, after the defeat of Napoleon, a remarkable return among political philosophers to a respect of the mediæval unity and of the pacific power of the Papacy. 'I believe that a common bond should hold us all together. The Pope alone can hold this central position. His authority, temporarily weakened by unfortunate circumstances, can very easily recover the prestige it has lost. Rome alone is able to speak with complete impartiality.'[1] So William Pitt had said to the Bishop of Arras in 1794. And the Holy Alliance in 1820 invited the Pope to intervene in the affair of the Two Sicilies.

When the Papacy emerged from this period of comparative eclipse—the Postulata to the Vatican Council (1870) upon the restoration of international morality may be taken as the landmark—a certain change, if not in the pacific function of the Pontiffs itself, at least in their view of the scope within which it should be exercised, may be noted. Hitherto this mission had mainly been exercised to prevent or arrest fighting within the *Respublica Christiana*, between Catholic princes. On certain occasions it is true the Russian Czars,

[1] From a letter of Bishop de Conzié of Arras to Cardinal de Bennis, May, 1794.

after the schism of the Eastern Church, had accepted Papal mediation, and, as will appear later, the Popes of the sixteenth and seventeenth centuries had been active in defending the rights of unbaptized natives against the unjust wars and conquests of Christian colonizers. But for the most part it was to preserve Christian unity that the Pope intervened. Now the efforts of the Holy See for peace are exercised regardless of whether the States concerned are formally Catholic or even Christian. Pius IX seeks to prevent war between France and Germany; Leo XIII mediates successfully between Germany and Spain and is invoked in a conflict between the United States and Great Britain. He strives, though unsuccessfully, to prevent the Spanish-American war; he deplores before the College of Cardinals the wars between the British and the Boers, the Russians and the Japanese. The Pope's repeated appeals to the belligerents of the Great War make no reference to the question, whether they are subject in a special manner to his jurisdiction and influence as Catholic States (e.g. Belgium, Austria) or not (e.g. Great Britain, Turkey). China in her conflict with Japan in 1932 appeals to Pius XI. If a sign be sought of the difference between the pacific action of the Popes in Crusading times and those of the present age it is sufficient to remember the commemorative statue of Benedict XV erected by the Turkish Government at Constantinople.

This change may be accounted for, partly by the transformation of the political order of the world. Christendom is no longer menaced by the military aggression of Islam. The Catholic family though far greater in numbers than it has ever been in the history of the world, is scattered throughout every continent and in all countries, only a minority of whose Governments profess Catholicism as their official religion, while others actively oppress its adherents. We have already suggested that this situation revives the notions of civic duties held by the Early Church in the Pagan Empire. Yet not more now than in that dawn of Christian political ethics does the recognition of existing authorities; prayers for them; efforts to direct their policies in the way of peace and justice, imply acquiescence in their non-Christian character. Never in his endeavours to effect Peace has a Pope of the modern age made the slightest concession explicit or implicit to the notion that submission by peoples and Governments to the Christian Law is a matter of indifference, or that peace may be sought for any but Christian motives. Not less insistently does Benedict XV set forth his duty as Vicar of Christ, not less vigorously does he assert Christian principles in writing to the Emperor of Japan or the Sultan of Turkey or the anti-clerical Government of France than in writing to the Catholic Governments of Europe. To all alike he cites the Christian scriptures, all alike he reminds of their 'very great responsibilities to God.' In other words he and his successor act *sub specie christiana*, in the light of, and true to the ideal of the Christian conception of the world, which is of all nations united in a single family or society under the Christian law. This, as Pius XI has shown, is something more than a pathetic if noble fidelity to a departed order of things. Rather does it look to the future than to the past and arise from a belief in the divine mandate of the Church and Papacy in the modern world to '*restaurare omnia in Christo*,' to restore all things in Christ—to establish the true Peace of Christ through the reign of Christ. To which end the present Pope has developed in a great encyclical and enshrined in noble liturgical form the doctrine that Christ is King of the whole world ; to Him 'all Power is given in Heaven and Earth' ; from Him kings, presidents, premiers, foreign ministers, whether they acknowledge it or not, derive their authority and with it their right to make peace or war. Hence it is as Vicar of Christ and as a Common Father that the successor of St. Peter does not hesitate to address them and to lay down the principles of international relations, as well as the lines upon which solutions of social, industrial and economic problems should be sought in the existing condition of human society.

The action of the Papacy as an agency for peace and order through the Christian centuries must not, of course, be studied in abstraction from the action of the Church as a whole—the Episcopate, the secular clergy, the monastic orders, theologians, publicists, philosophers and associations of the Catholic laity. The long and successful endeavours to suppress Feudal warfare in Western Europe by the *Pax Dei* and the *Truga Dei*, for which the Bishops of Burgundy and France were mainly responsible and the growth of the Third Order of St. Francis, merit detailed and special attention. These measures, however, belong to social and political conditions which have entirely passed. The monarchs honoured by the Church for their labour as peacemakers and in many cases raised to her altars must also be remembered. We have recorded Joinville's tribute to St. Louis's love of peace. Others who followed the same path were Robert the Pious, Canute of England, St. Henry of Germany, St. Stephen of Hungary and St. Elizabeth of Portugal.

Throughout the history of the Church the pacific function of the Pope presupposed the co-operation of his brother Bishops and the clergy. From at least the seventeenth century onward the Papal appeals for peace in view of a widespread war or danger of war have for the most part been addressed to the Bishops—as in the *Adhortatio* of Urban VIII. Benedict XV was ceaselessly enjoining the Episcopate on both sides in the Great War to pray and labour for peace. And Pius XI's pronouncement upon disarmament and the economic crisis takes the form of an Apostolic Letter to the Bishops of the Catholic world, stirring them to action. The same Pontiff in his Christmas address to the Cardinals in 1930 defines thus the pacifying function of the Catholic Church as a whole : 'The glory and the duty of this apostolate of peace belongs principally to us and to all those who are called to be the Ministers of the God of peace ; but here is also a vast and magnificent field of action for the whole of the Catholic laity whom we do not cease to invite and to call to participate in this Apostolate of the Hierarchy.'

Documents. A.

From the beginning to the outbreak of the Great War.

St. Clement of Rome. *Epist. ad Cor. Cap. XLVI.* (*Patrologia Graeca*) *:*

Why are there contentions, angers, dissension, schism and war among you ? Is not God one to us, and Christ one, and the Spirit of grace that is poured out on us one, is there not one calling in Christ? Why do we lead astray and tear asunder the members of Christ, why do we stir up sedition against our own body? And why are we so foolish that we forget that others are members of our body? Let us remember the words of Our Lord Jesus Christ, for He said: 'Woe to that man: for it were better for him if he had not been born rather than that he should scandalize one of my elect: it were better for him that a mill-stone should be put around him and that he should be thrown into the sea rather than that he should scandalize one of my little ones.' Your schism perverts many: it throws many into dejection, many into wavering and all of us into sadness: and still your sedition continues.

Cap. LIX:

Send soon to us Claudius and Valerius with Fortunatus in peace and joy: that they may announce the most pleasing peace and concord so much desired by us; in which we may the more rejoice in your tranquillity. The grace of Our Lord Jesus Christ be with you and with all who are chosen by God through Him: through whom be glory, honour, strength and majesty and an eternal throne, for ever and ever. Amen.

NICHOLAS I. *Responsa ad Bulgaros.* (*Patrologia Latina*)*:*

War is always satanic in its origin and you must always abstain from it. But if it be impossible to avoid it, that is in defence of oneself, of one's country and of the laws of one's fathers, it is without doubt lawful to make ready to meet it, even during Lent.

ST. GREGORY THE GREAT. *Letter XLII.* (*Patrologia Latina.*) *To Agilulph, King of the Langobards. He gives thanks for the peace arranged. He asks that the King should order his generals not to disturb the peace:*

We give thanks to Your Excellency that, listening to our petition, you have made the peace which is to be to the advantage of both, as we expected of you. Wherefore have we loudly extolled your prudence and goodness, because in loving peace you have shown that you love God who is the author of peace. For if peace had not been made (God forbid that it should not) what else could have happened than that the blood of the poor country people whose labour profited both would have been sinfully and dangerously shed? But since we feel that the same peace is profitable to us also, though made by you, saluting you in fatherly love, we beg you that, as often as the occasion shall be presented, you order your generals everywhere, and especially in these parts, that they keep unsullied this peace as has been promised; that they seek not occasions whence contention or discontent may arise ; and we shall be all the more filled with gratitude towards you. We have received the bearers of these present letters as truly your men and with due consideration, for it was fitting that the just men who announced a peacemaking so pleasing to God should be received and dismissed by us with all charity.

St. Gregory VII. (*Patrologia Latina, t.* 148, *Col.* 424–425). *Epistola LXXIII. Ad Boleslavum Polonorum ducem :*

. . . You must know that the Supreme Judge asks for an account of the things He commits to your care : and you will have to render all the more exact an account according to the amplitude of the laws and the moderation of the judges that you have. May Almighty God, whose majesty is above all principalities and kingdoms, direct your hearts and your works to every good deed in all prudence and exercise of virtues, until this unsteady and perishable light shall have waned and, by the intercession of Saints Peter and Paul, princes of the Apostles, you shall have merited to attain true and everlasting glory. May the pride of your enemies be put down through the Lord Jesus Christ and may He grant you the joys of peace and tranquillity, that from present gifts you may learn with how much longing the future gifts are to be coveted. If you really desire these things, charity must above all be observed among you : this (I make unwilling mention of it) you have violated in the money which you have taken from the King of the Russians. Wherefore, grieving with you, we earnestly beg and admonish you, that by the love you bear to God and St. Peter you restore whatever has been taken from him by you or yours—remembering that those who unjustly take away the things which belong to another cannot be judged to have any part in the Kingdom of Christ and God, unless they make amends if it is possible to do so. We fervently hope that this will be received by you with the same charity as we have in saying it for the salvation of your soul.

Innocent III. (*Patrologia Latina, t.* 215. *Col.* 64–65). *Epist. LXVIII. To the King of the Franks :*

Since His Royal Highness is not unaware that with us there ought not to be any favouritism, we judge that it will not be ill-received if we exercise towards His Highness the duty of our office, lest in addition to sinning against the divine majesty our office should come to be reviled by men through omitting to reprove kings and princes who consult their will rather than their salvation. For the word of the Lord ought not to be bound in us but free, that we may openly correct the unruly and that we may fulfil, as often as necessary, the word of the Apostle which seems to have been said all the more directly to us, because we have a greater and indeed the greatest place in the Church as one who, whilst others shoulder a part of the cares, takes up alone the fullness of power. . . . Since then Jesus began to do and to teach, leaving us an example that we should follow, we who are His vicar, though an unworthy one, ought to walk as He walked as far as human frailties will allow and follow in His footsteps, since we know that He said to Peter : 'Thou shalt follow me among all the Apostles.' You, Highness, know that among the first-fruits of the Lord's nativity the Angel announced peace to men of goodwill ; and in the moment of His passion the Lord infused peace into His Apostles as though making His last testament. He said to them : 'My peace I leave with you, my peace I give unto you.' And when immortal after His resurrection, in order to confirm what He had said as He was dying, His first words were : 'Peace be to you,' and again 'Peace be to you,' Lest therefore we, who are, according to the Apostle, heirs of God and co-heirs with Christ, should show ourselves unworthy and unmindful of our inheritance and of the grace which we share and which He poured down more abundantly on us, we must preach peace, especially to the sons of peace, that our peace may rest upon them according to the word of the Gospel, since, according to the Prophet, we are bound to seek peace and ensue it. We ask this of Your Highness with all the more confidence, knowing that you have once kindly received our beloved son Marcellus, a cardinal-priest and legate of the Holy See, sent on a like mission and have shown amply to him your solicitude for us. You know also, as one who has read it in the book of daily experience, how many evils have arisen through the dissension between you and our most dear son in Christ Jesus, the illustrious King of the English, not only in both your realms but throughout the whole Christian world. For consider, while you are warring with each other, churches are destroyed, the rich empoverished, the poor oppressed and while neither religion nor sex are spared, the religious who were occupied in prayer are now forced to beg and women are made prostitutes. It grieves us to say it—they who had vowed their virginity to the Creator are become the prey of lust. Now, too, the Saracens become more daring against the Christians and they who feared when you were placated and at peace with each other, have taken courage from your strife and have risen up in strength to destroy the Christians, especially since the princes of Gaul, whose quarrel we lay before the divine majesty and Your Highness, have departed from their good intentions and disobeying our prohibition, have turned their arms against Christians. Nor will they lay them down, but rise up again and, so we have heard, plan to attempt still worse things. Moreover, from this sort of conflict bodily carnage follows and ruin of souls which grieves us so much more because the soul is more precious than the body; for, according to the word of truth, it profits a man nothing if he gains the whole world and suffers the loss of his soul. Lest therefore the blood of so many peoples may be asked of our hands, lest we should seem to be guilty, so to speak, of so many deaths; if (which God forbid) we are silent in such dire necessity for Christian peoples, if 'like silent dogs afraid to bark' our tongue should adhere to our palate and we should omit to put forth arguments, we have summoned and destined for your presence our beloved son, the Abbot of Casemari, a religious man, wise and faithful to us and acceptable to our brethren by the merit of his honesty. We have sent with him our beloved sons the Abbots of Tres Fontes and Dunum, begging Your Serene Highness and exhorting you in the Lord and binding you for the remission of your fault that you make a sure peace with the aforesaid king or enter into suitable truces, that, while permanent peace in accord with the rights of both is being arranged between you both, you may treat more freely and safely. However much we love you and him, we can by no means leave it open to doubt that we intend that the terms which our aforesaid Nuncio shall bring as given to him by us, are to be observed inviolate. We beg Your Majesty that you kindly receive our aforesaid Nuncio and honour him out of reverence for the Apostolic See and us.

Given at Terentinum, VII Kal. of June, in the sixth year of our pontificate (A.D. 1204).

VITTORIA. *De Indis II, VI. Indirect temporal jurisdiction of the Pope. Papal Arbitration:*

. . . The Pope is not civil or temporal lord of the whole world in the proper sense of the words 'lordship' and 'civil power.' This is the conclusion arrived at by Torquemada (Book II, Chap. CXIII), and by Joannes Andreæ and by Hugo, on Can. 6, Dist. 96. And the most learned Innocent admits, in the above-cited X, i, 6, 34, that he has not temporal power over the Kingdom of France . . . And the proof is sufficient, like that given above concerning the Emperor, for no lordship can come to him save either by natural law or by divine law or by human law. Now, it is certain that none comes to him by natural or by human law, and none is shown to come to him by divine law. Therefore the assertion is ungrounded and arbitrary.

Further, Our Lord's injunction to Peter, 'Feed my sheep' (St. John xxi: 17), clearly shows that power in spiritual and not in temporal matters is meant. . . .

. . . The Pope has temporal power only so far as it is in subservience to matters spiritual, that is, so far as is necessary for the administration of spiritual affairs. This is also the view of Torquemada (as above, Chap. CXIV), and of all the doctors. And the proof of it lies in that fact that an art to which a higher end pertains is imperative and preceptive as regards the arts to which lower ends pertain (*Ethics*, Book I). But the end of spiritual power is ultimate felicity, while the end of civil power is political felicity. Therefore, temporal power is subject to spiritual power. This is the reasoning adopted by Innocent in X, i, 33, 6; and it receives confirmation from the consideration that, whenever anybody is entrusted with the charge of an office, he is implicitly granted everything without which the duties of the office cannot rightly be discharged (X, i, 29, 1). Inasmuch, then, as the Pope is a spiritual pastor by Christ's commission and the discharge of the duties of this office cannot be hindered by the civil power (there being no lack in the provision of things necessary either by God or by nature), it is beyond doubt that power over things temporal has also been left to him so far as is necessary for the government of things spiritual. And on this principle the Pope can infringe civil laws which tend to breed sinners, just as he has infringed the laws with regard to prescription by a party acting in bad faith, as is clear from X, ii, 26, 20. And on this principle also, when princes are at variance with one another about some right of sovereignty and are rushing into war, he can act as judge and inquire into the claims of the parties and deliver judgement, a judgement which the princes are bound to respect, lest those numerous spiritual evils should befall which are the inevitable results of a war between Christian princes. And although the Pope does not do this or does not do it often it is not because he cannot, as Master Durandus says, but because, for fear of scandal, he wishes to prevent the princes from thinking his motive is ambition or because he is afraid of a revolt from the Apostolic See on the part of the princes. And on this principle the Pope can sometimes depose kings and even set up new kings, as at times has been done. And certainly no one rightly calling himself Christian should deny this power to the Pope. . . .

URBAN VIII. *Appeal for Peace, April 1, 1632:*

A pious and pastoral appeal to the Patriarchs, Archbishops and Bishops, to the Clergy and Religious, and to all the faithful Christians of the Catholic Church, that by offering prayers to Almighty God, they may obtain concord among Catholic princes.

Urban VIII Pope.

To our Venerable Brethren and beloved Sons Health and the Apostolic Benediction.

When calamities hang over us Holy Writ teaches how efficacious a remedy is prayer ceaselessly offered to God without intermission with one mind and heart by the whole Catholic Church, especially when he who has been appointed head of the Church on earth begs and implores help from heaven.

Hence in years gone by we have exhorted you all, Venerable Brethren, in our Apostolic Letters, to call together the congregation of the Faithful and to appease the wrath of the Divine Vengeance while we sought, by the help of our Legates, to still the commotions which had arisen, for they seemed to bring great perturbation to the Christian world and to pit Catholic princes against one another.

Now the dangers which threaten the Catholic commonweal oblige us to pursue the same object and for a like reason, striving to bring those princes together in unity of heart. And so we fly with confidence to God the Father of Mercies. We stand at the door and knock, in the hope that He who rejoices in the prayers of His servants will at last console us with the gift for which we long so much, the gift of public peace.

For this reason we have thought it expedient to order the solemn supplications of the Jubilee in order that the Universal Church may join with us in fulfilling pious duties that so the goodness of God, triumphing over the malice of men, may grant, in answer to the intercessions of such a multitude, the boon for which we never cease to pray with all our heart. If our vows and prayers had been heard, we could indeed have put on the stole of gladness and rejoice at the peace bestowed upon Catholic princes. And yet, persevering as much as in us lies, we have left nothing undone which we believe will contribute to bring tranquillity and safety to the Catholic Religion.

This object, which we put before all others, we seek to pursue by the services and constant endeavour not only of ordinary but of extraordinary Nuncios which we send to His Majesty the Emperor and to each king. We trust that, guided by our instructions, wherewith upon the advice of prudent Cardinals we have armed them, they may avert the conflicts that threaten and produce a salutary effect both upon the public weal and the Catholic Faith. Would that this solicitude of our Pastoral Office may by the favour and clemency of God bear the fruit of success, as have our similar endeavours on other occasions.

Further, in order that no means of attaining this end may be neglected, we exhort all members of the Lord's flock, according as each enjoys favour with any one of the Catholic princes, diligently to urge that the storms which have arisen may be allayed and that the desired peace for which we dare to hope may be attained, by the removal of the obstacles which prevent the spiritual concord of those princes in the bond of Christian charity. From the mutual expostulations which are thrown from one side and the other, the causes which impede this good work of peace-making are sufficiently clear, nor will argument be lacking whereby pious and prudent men may remove them. For who does not see that, unless discord divided the Catholic princes, neither Heresy nor Hell could ever defeat the Church? Wherefore, since human labours are sometimes in vain, Venerable Brethren and Beloved Sons, cast your thoughts upon the Lord, be strengthened, and put forth every effort that you may repel the evils which threaten us, by the weapons of prayer and faith. For as the Apostle teaches, Gideon, David, Samuel and the Prophets 'by faith conquered kingdoms, wrought justice, obtained promises, stopped the mouths of lions, quenched the violence of fire. . . .';[1] Faithful is the Lord to all who call upon Him in truth.

And so we too, who sit amid these tempests at the helm of the Ship of Peter, cry with him from the bottom of our heart, in suppliant voice: 'Save us, O Lord! while the congregation of the faithful pour out their hearts before Thee. O God, our helper to all eternity, in Thee will we do valorous deeds, and Thou Thyself shall bring to nought those who afflict us.' For you, our Brethren and for the whole Catholic flock we implore health and consolation from the Lord, and to you do we most lovingly impart the Apostolic Benediction.

Given at Rome at St. Peter's under the Fisherman's ring, on the first of April, 1632, the 9th year of our Pontificate.

PIUS IX. *Offer of Mediation to King William I of Prussia to prevent the outbreak of the Franco-Prussian war.* (*Müller, No.* 113, *Page* 319). *Rome, July* 22, 1870:

YOUR MAJESTY,

In the grave circumstances in which we find ourselves, it will perhaps appear to you unusual to receive a letter from me; but, Vicar on Earth of the God of Peace, I cannot do less than offer you my mediation. My desire is to see the preparations for war disappear and to prevent the evils which are the inevitable consequence thereof. My mediation is that of a Sovereign who, in his capacity of King, cannot, by reason of the smallness of his territory, excite any jealousy, but who, nevertheless, will inspire confidence by the moral and religious influence which he personifies.

May God hear my desires and fulfil those wishes which I form for Your Majesty to whom I desire to be united in the bonds of the same Charity.

At the Vatican, July 22, 1870.

PS.—I have also written to His Majesty the Emperor of the French.

LEO XIII. *Easter Day Encyclical* (*April* 21, 1878). *Inscrutabili. On the Evils affecting Modern Society:*

Again, if we consider the achievements of the See of Rome, what can be more wicked than to deny how much and how well the Roman Bishops have served civilized society at large? For our predecessors, to provide for the people's good, encountered

[1] Hebrews xi: 32–34.

struggles of every kind, endured to the utmost burdensome toils, and never hesitated to expose themselves to most dangerous trials. With eyes fixed on heaven, they neither bowed down their heads before the threats of the wicked, nor allowed themselves to be led by flattery or bribes into unworthy compliance. This Apostolic Chair it was that gathered and held together the crumbling remains of the old order of things ; this was the kindly light by whose help the culture of Christian times shone far and wide ; this was an anchor of safety in the fierce storms by which the human race has been convulsed ; this was the sacred bond of union that linked together nations distant in region and differing in character ; in short, this was the common centre from which was sought instruction in faith and religion no less than guidance and advice for the maintenance of peace and the functions of practical life. In very truth it is the glory of the Supreme Pontiffs that they steadfastly set themselves up as a wall and a bulwark to save human society from falling back into its former superstition and barbarism.

See also pronouncements of Leo XIII on arbitration, disarmament, etc. in Chapter VII.

Pius X. *Exhortation to all Catholics on the outbreak of the Great War :*

While nearly all Europe is being dragged into the whirlpools of a most deadly war, of whose dangers, slaughters and consequences no one can think without feeling oppressed with sorrow and with fright, We too cannot but feel anxious and feel Our soul rent by the most bitter grief for the safety and for the lives of so many citizens and so many peoples for whose welfare We are supremely solicitous.

Amid this immense perturbation and crisis We deeply feel and realize that Our fatherly charity and Our Apostolic Ministry demand of Us that We direct men's minds upwards to Him from whom alone help can come, to Christ, Prince of Peace and man's all-powerful Mediator with God. Therefore We do exhort the Catholics of the whole world to turn full of confidence to His throne of grace and mercy, and let the clergy lead the way for all others by their example and by appointing special prayers in their respective parishes, under the orders of the Bishops, that God may be moved to pity and remove as soon as possible the disastrous torch of war and inspire the supreme rulers of the nations with thoughts of peace and not of affliction.

From the Vatican, August 2, 1914.

Pius X Pope.

Documents. B.

Pacific Action of the Holy See during and after the Great War, 1914–1918

Benedict XV. *Exhortation to the Catholics of the whole world, September* 8, 1914.

After referring to his succession to the Holy See, Benedict XV goes on to say:

As from this place of Apostolic dignity We look around upon all the flock of the Lord committed to Our care, We are at once struck with horror and inexpressible sorrow at the awful spectacle of all this war, as We see so large a part of Europe wasted with fire and sword and red with Christian blood. By the Good Shepherd Jesus Christ, whose place We hold in the government of the Church, the duty has indeed been laid upon Us of embracing all His lambs and sheep, how many soever they be, in the affection of Our paternal charity. And as, therefore, after the example of Our Lord, We are bound to be and are ready to lay down even Our life for their salvation, We are firmly resolved, so far as it is in Our power, to leave nothing undone which can conduce to the more speedy ending of this calamity. So at the present moment—before addressing an Encyclical letter to all the Bishops at the beginning of Our Pontificate, according to the established custom of the Holy See—We cannot refrain from taking up the last words of Our most holy predecessor, Pius X, of immortal memory, words which one may say were wrung from him by his Apostolic solicitude and love for the human race amidst the first tumult of this war. . . .

But as for those who direct the affairs of the nations, We earnestly beg and implore them even now to turn their thoughts to the laying aside of their quarrels for the sake of the preservation of human society. Let them reflect that there is already too much of misery and grief linked with this mortal life, so that it should not be made still more wretched and sorrowful. Let them agree that already enough of ruin has been caused, enough of human blood has been shed. Let them hasten to open peace negotiations and join hands again. Thus will they gain from God glorious rewards for themselves and each one for his people; they will do the highest service to the cause of human civilization; and as for Ourselves, who in assuming this Apostolic office have to face the gravest difficulties arising from so seriously disturbed a state of affairs—let them know that they will thus do what is most pleasing and most highly desired by Us. (*Acta Apostolicæ Sedis*, Vol. VI, p. 501.)

BENEDICT XV. *Encyclical Letter. Ad Beatissimi : November* 1, 1914:

Those days would seem to have come upon Us of which Christ Our Lord foretold : 'You shall hear of wars and rumours of wars—for nation shall rise against nation, and kingdom against kingdom' (Matthew xxiv : 6, 7). On every side the dread phantom of war holds sway : there is scarce room for another thought in the minds of men. The combatants are the greatest and wealthiest nations of the earth ; what wonder then if, well provided with the most awful weapons modern military science has devised, they strive to destroy one another with refinements of horror. There is no limit to the measure of ruin and of slaughter ; day by day the earth is drenched with newly shed blood, and is covered with the bodies of the wounded and of the slain. Who would imagine, as we see them thus filled with hatred of one another, that they are all of one common stock, all of the same nature, all members of the same human society ? Who would recognize brothers, whose Father is in heaven ? Yet while with numberless troops the furious battle is engaged, the sad cohorts of war, sorrow and distress swoop down upon every city and every home ; day by day the mighty number of widows and orphans increases, and with the interruption of communications trade is at a standstill ; agriculture is abandoned ; the arts are reduced to inactivity ; the wealthy are in difficulties ; the poor are reduced to abject misery ; all are in distress.

Moved by these great evils, We thought it our duty, at the very outset of Our Supreme Pontificate, to recall the last words of Our Predecessor, of illustrious and holy memory, and by repeating them once more, to begin Our own Apostolic Ministry ; and we implored kings and rulers to consider the floods of tears and of blood already poured out, and to hasten to restore to the nations the blessings of peace. God grant, by His mercy and blessing, that the glad tidings the Angels brought at the birth of the Divine Redeemer of mankind may soon echo forth as We His Vicar enter upon His work : 'On earth peace to men of goodwill' (Luke ii : 14). We implore those in whose hands are placed the fortunes of nations to hearken to Our voice. Surely there are other ways and means whereby violated rights can be rectified. Let them be tried honestly and with goodwill, and let arms meanwhile be laid aside. It is impelled with love of them and of all mankind, without any personal interest whatever, that We utter these words. Let them not allow these words of a friend and of a father to be uttered in vain. (Ibid., Vol. VI, p. 565.)

Address of the Pope to the Cardinals at a Reception, Christmas Eve, 1914 :

In their address, the Cardinals had referred to the efforts of the Holy Father to obtain a 'truce of God' between the belligerents, during the Festival of Christmas. In his reply, the Pope refers to this and other efforts which he had made.

We could not forget that We were come to continue the work of Jesus Christ, Prince of Peace, described in the prophecies as He in whose days should come at last the sun of justice and the abundance of peace. Remembering then Our more than human mission both in public and private We left no way untried that the counsel, the desire, the necessity of peace should be fully recognized. It was indeed with this scope that there came to Our mind the proposal to pierce this darkness of warring death with at least a ray, one single ray, of the Divine sun of peace, and We thought of suggesting to the fighting nations a truce, short indeed and limited, for Christmas, nourishing the hope that while We could not dissipate the black gloom of war, it might be given Us at least to bring one healing balm to the wounds it inflicts. Ah, the dear hope that We had cherished of consoling so many mothers and so many wives with the certainty that in the few hours consecrated to the memory of the Divine Birthday their dear ones would not have fallen under the enemy's lead; ah, the dear illusion that We held of giving once more to the world at least a taste of that peaceful quiet which for so many months now it has not known! Our Christian initiative was not, however, crowned with happy success. Still, We are not discouraged by this, and We intend to put forth every effort to hasten the end of the unparalleled scourge, or at least to alleviate its miserable consequences.

It seems to Us that the Divine Spirit says to Us as once to the Prophet: '*Clama ne cesses.*' *Clama ne cesses*, and We have cried, not without hope of success, for the exchange of prisoners rendered unfit for further military service. *Clama ne cesses*, and We have asked that to the poor prisoners of war should be given priests who know their language, to bring them those comforts of which they have need, and at the same time offer themselves as willing intermediaries between them and their families who might be worn out and afflicted by lack of news. *Clama ne cesses*, and We praise the sacred pastors and single individuals who have determined to promote or multiply public or private prayers to do sweet violence to the Most Sacred Heart of Jesus to obtain that an end may come to the terrible scourge which now grips and throttles such a great part of the world.

Ah! may the fratricidal weapons fall to the ground! Already they are too bloodstained: let them at last fall! And may the hands of those who have had to wield them return to the labours of industry and commerce, to the works of civilization and peace. Ah! may at least to-day the rulers and the peoples hear the angelic voice which announces the superhuman gift of the King who is born, 'the Gift of Peace,' and themselves too, by works of justice, faith and clemency show that 'Good Will' which is laid down by God as the condition for the enjoyment of the peace. (Ibid., Vol. VI, p. 694.)

Allocution at the Consistory, January 22, 1915 :

Alas, month after month passes away without bringing the gleam of a distant hope that this most deadly war, or rather slaughter, is soon to cease. If it is not given to Us to hasten the end of a scourge so heavy, would that We could at least mitigate its sorrowful consequences ! With this aim We have, as you are well aware, hitherto done everything possible for Us, and We shall not cease in the future while the need lasts.

To do more than this, to-day, is not granted to Us by the Apostolic office. To proclaim that for nobody is it lawful, on any plea whatever, to offend justice, belongs chiefly, beyond all question, to the Roman Pontiff as to Him who is by God appointed the supreme interpreter and defender of the eternal law ; and We do proclaim it without qualification, condemning openly every injustice by whatever side it may have been committed. But to involve the Pontifical authority in the very contests of the belligerents, would surely be neither appropriate nor useful. Certainly, anybody who judges carefully cannot fail to see that in this enormous struggle the Apostolic See, though filled with the greatest anxiety, must remain perfectly impartial. The Roman Pontiff, as Vicar of Jesus Christ who died for men, one and all, must embrace all the combatants in one sentiment of charity ; and as the Father of all Catholics he has among the belligerents a great number of children, for whose salvation he must be equally and without distinction solicitous. It is necessary, therefore, that in them he must consider not the special interests which divide them, but the common bond of faith which makes them brothers ; were he to do otherwise not only would he not help at all the cause of peace, but, what is worse, he would create aversions and enmities to religion, and would expose to grave disturbances the very tranquillity and internal concord of the Church.

But, though holding for neither of the two sides, We are, as We have already said, equally anxious about both ; while with painful interest We follow the terrible phases of this war, all the more that it is to be feared that the violence of attack sometimes exceeds all measure. But, as is only natural, our thoughts turn insistently to where We note more vividly in our children their reverent affection for the Father of the faithful ; and of this, as far, for example, as concerns the beloved Belgian people, one proof is to be found in the letter which We addressed recently to the Cardinal Archbishop of Malines.

And here We appeal to the sentiments of humanity of those who have crossed the frontiers of the adversary nations, conjuring them that the districts invaded be not devastated more than is strictly required by the reasons of the military occupation, and that, more important still, the souls of the inhabitants be not, without real necessity, wounded in what they hold most dear : the sacred temples, the ministers of God, the rights of religion and of the faith. Concerning those who behold their Fatherland occupied by the enemy, We understand most well how heavy it must be for them to be subject to the foreigner. But We would not that the ardent desire to recover their independence should drive them especially to thwart the maintenance of public order, and thus greatly injure their condition.

For the rest, Venerable Brothers, not because troubles so many and so heavy are trying Us, must We therefore be downhearted ; nay, the darker looks the future the more *confidently We must approach the throne of grace to obtain mercy and to find grace through timely aid* (Hebrews iv : 16). And hence it is necessary to address instant and humble prayers to the Lord, as We have already prescribed, that, Sovereign Master and Arbiter as He is of human events, He, who alone is able, may turn to His infallible designs, by those ways which best please Him, the wills of men. Think not that if peace has flown from the world, this has been without a divine design.

God permits the peoples, who have set all their thoughts on the things of this earth, to be punished by one another, by internecine slaughter, for the contempt and the carelessness with which they have treated Him. Other events, too, happen from time to time to constrain men to humble themselves *under the powerful hand of God* (1 Peter v : 6) ; like that of recent days which We all know to be so full of horror and mourning.

Since, then, prayer in common is more acceptable to God and more fruitful, We exhort all the good to propitiate the Divine mercy by praying not only in private but especially by attending the public prayers in the churches. And that an immense choir of suppliant voices may go up simultaneously to heaven We have, as you know, ordained two solemn functions of expiation, the first to be held by the Catholics of all Europe on the 7th of next February, the second for the rest of the Catholic world on March 21. At the first We have decided to assist in person in St. Peter's in the Vatican, and We are sure that you, Venerable Brothers, will not fail to take part in it with Us. (Ibid., Vol. VII, p. 33.)

The special prayer ordered by the Pope is as follows :

Dismayed by the horrors of a war which is bringing ruin to peoples and nations, we turn, O Jesus, to Thy most loving Heart as to our last hope. O God of Mercy, with tears we invoke Thee to end this fearful scourge ; O King of Peace, we humbly implore the peace for which we long. From Thy sacred Heart Thou didst shed forth over the world divine Charity, so that discord might end and love alone might reign among men. During Thy Life on earth Thy Heart beat with tender compassion for the sorrows of men; in this hour made terrible with burning hate, with bloodshed and with slaughter, once more may the Divine Heart be moved to pity. Pity the countless mothers in anguish for the fate of their sons; pity the numberless families now bereaved of their fathers; pity Europe, over which broods such havoc and disaster. Do Thou inspire rulers and peoples with counsels of meekness, do Thou heal the discords that tear the nations asunder; Thou who didst shed Thy Precious Blood that they might live as brothers, bring men together once more in loving harmony. And as once before to the cry of the Apostle Peter: *Save us, Lord, we perish,* Thou didst answer with words of mercy and didst still the raging waves, so now deign to hear our trustful prayer, and give back to the world peace and tranquillity.

Letter from the Holy Father to Cardinal Serafino Vannutelli, as Dean of the College of Cardinals, after the Italian declaration of war, May 25, 1915

(The Holy Father refers to his efforts to obtain peace, and goes on to say:)

The voice of the friend and of the Father, We say it with a heart crushed with grief, was not hearkened to; the war continues to imbrue Europe with blood, and on land and on sea even means of offence which are contrary to the dictates of humanity and to international law are not avoided.

And as if that were not enough, the terrible conflagration has extended even to Our beloved Italy, making one fear for it also that sequel of tears and disasters which is wont to accompany every war, even when successful.

Our heart meanwhile bleeds at the sight of so many misfortunes. We have not desisted from devoting Ourselves to relieve and diminish, as far as lay in Our power, the deplorable consequences of the war. We give praise to God, who has been pleased to crown with happy success the efforts which We made to obtain from the belligerent nations the exchange of prisoners of war unfit for further military service. Furthermore, recently We have also exerted Ourselves, and with hope of success, in favour of wounded and sick prisoners of war, not wholly unfit for military service, with a view to render their condition less grave and to facilitate their recovery.

(The letter then deals with the provision of chaplains for the Italian Army, and confers special privileges on Army chaplains, and all priests who are present in any capacity with the Italian Army in the field. The letter then continues:)

The hour through which we are passing is painful, it is a terrible moment : but *sursum corda.* More frequently and more fervently let us send up our prayers to Him in whose hands are the destinies of the nations. Let us all address ourselves with confidence to the sorrowful and immaculate Heart of Mary, the most sweet Mother of Jesus and our Mother, that she may by her powerful intercession obtain from her Divine Son that the scourge of war may soon cease and that peace and tranquillity may return.

Letter from Cardinal Gasparri, Secretary of State, to the Belgian Minister at the Vatican. (Copy annexed to Benedict XV's letter to Cardinal Amette of July 11, 1915, in 'Rome,' vol. xviii, p. 45). Extract :

The Chancellor of the German Empire, von Bethmann-Hollweg, declared openly in public Parliament on August 4th that Germany in invading Belgium was violating its neutrality contrary to international law. While then, in the present conflict, as a general rule one side accuses and the other denies and the Holy See consequently, being unable to conduct an inquiry and find out the truth, cannot make any pronouncement, in this case the German Chancellor himself recognized that in the invasion of Belgium a violation of neutrality was committed, contrary to international law, justifying it simply on the grounds of military necessity.

It follows that the invasion of Belgium is directly included in the words used by the Holy Father in the Consistorial Allocution of January 22nd last, when he *condemned openly every injustice by whatever side and for whatever motive committed.* It is true that in the meanwhile Germany has published some documents of the Belgian General Staff by means of which she claims to prove that previous to the war Belgium had failed in the duties of neutrality which, therefore, at the moment of invasion did not exist any longer. It was not the business of the Holy See to decide this question of history, nor, for its purpose, was there any necessity for a decision. For the reason that, even admitting the German point of view, it would always remain true that Germany, on the confession of her own Chancellor, penetrated into Belgian territory with the consciousness of violating its neutrality and therefore committing an injustice ; and that suffices for Germany's action to be comprised directly in the words of the Pontifical Allocution.

Apostolic Exhortation of Benedict XV to the peoples now at war and to their rulers, July 28, 1915 :

Our first words, as the Chief Shepherd of souls, addressed to the Nations and their Rulers, were words of peace and of love.

But Our advice, affectionate and insistent as that of a father and a friend, remained unheard. Our grief was aggravated, but Our purpose was unshaken; We turned, therefore, in all confidence to the Almighty, Who holds in His Hand the minds and hearts of subjects, as of Kings, begging of Him the cessation of the unprecedented scourge. We wished to associate all the faithful in Our fervent and humble prayer, and to make it the more efficacious, We arranged that it should be accompanied by works of Christian penance. But to-day, on the anniversary of the outbreak of the tremendous conflict, more intense is the desire of Our heart for the speedy conclusion of the war, still louder is Our fatherly cry for peace. May this cry, prevailing over the dreadful clash of arms, reach unto the peoples who are now at war, and unto their Rulers, inclining both to milder and more serene views.

In the holy name of God, in the name of our heavenly Father and Lord, by the Blessed Blood of Jesus, the price of man's redemption, We conjure You, whom Divine Providence has placed over the Nations at war, to put an end at last to this horrible slaughter, which for a whole year has dishonoured Europe. It is the blood of brothers that is being poured out on land and sea. The most beautiful regions of Europe, this garden of the world, are sown with corpses and with ruin: there, where but a short time ago flourished the industry of manufacturers and the fruitful labour of the fields, now thunders fearfully the cannon, and in its destructive fury it spares neither village nor city, but spreads everywhere havoc and death. You bear before God and man the tremendous responsibility of peace and war; give ear to Our prayer, to the fatherly voice of the Vicar of the Eternal and Supreme Judge, to whom you must render an account as well of your public undertakings, as of your own individual deeds.

The abounding wealth, with which God the Creator has enriched the lands that are subject to You, allow You to go on with the struggle; but at what cost? Let the thousands of young lives quenched every day on the fields of battle make answer: answer, the ruins of so many towns and villages, of so many monuments raised by the piety and genius of your ancestors. And the bitter tears shed in the secrecy of home, or at the foot of altars where suppliants beseech,—do not these also repeat that the price of the long drawn-out struggle is great—too great?

Nor let it be said that the immense conflict cannot be settled without the violence of war. Lay aside your mutual purpose of destruction; remember that Nations do not die; humbled and oppressed, they chafe under the yoke imposed upon them, preparing a renewal of the combat, and passing down from generation to generation a mournful heritage of hatred and revenge.

Why not from this moment weigh with serene mind the rights and lawful aspirations of the peoples? Why not initiate with a good will an exchange of views, directly or indirectly, with the object of holding in due account, within the limits of possibility, those rights and aspirations, and thus succeed in putting an end to the monstrous struggle, as has been done under other similar circumstances? Blessed be he who will first raise the olive-branch, and hold out his right hand to the enemy with an offer of reasonable terms of peace. The equilibrium of the world, and the prosperity and assured tranquillity of Nations rest upon mutual benevolence and respect for the rights and the dignity of others, much more than upon hosts of armed men and the ring of formidable fortresses.

This is the cry of peace which breaks forth from Our heart with added vehemence on this mournful day; and We invite all, whosoever are the friends of peace the world over, to give Us a helping hand in order to hasten the termination of the war, which for a long year has changed Europe into one vast battle-field. May the merciful Jesus, through the intercession of His Sorrowful Mother, grant that at last, after so horrible a storm, the dawn of peace may break, placid and radiant, an image of His own Divine Countenance. May hymns of thanksgiving soon rise to the Most High, the Giver of all good things for the accomplished reconciliation of the States; may the peoples, bound in bonds of brotherly love, return to the peaceful rivalry of studies, of arts, of industries, and, with the empire of right re-established, may they resolve from now henceforth to entrust the settlement of their differences, not to the sword's edge, but to reasons of equity and justice, pondered with due calm and deliberation. This will be their most splendid and glorious conquest! (*Acta Apostolicæ Sedis*, vol. 7, p. 365.)

Allocution, December 6, 1915:

We feel Ourself urged by Our Apostolic Office to teach once again the one and only means which can lead without delay to the extinction of the awful conflagration. To prepare the way for peace, the peace which is ardently desired by all humanity, a peace, that is, just, lasting, and not profitable to only one of the fighting parties, the way which can truly lead to a happy result is that which has already been tried and found good in similar circumstances, and which We pointed out in that same Letter: that is to say that, in an exchange of ideas, directly or indirectly, there should be definitely and clearly put forward and duly weighed, with goodwill and serene conscience, the aspirations of each one, eliminating all that is unjust and impossible and taking count of all that is just and possible, with any arrangement and compensation that may be needful. Naturally, as is the case in all human controversies which are settled by the contending parties themselves, it is absolutely necessary that on one side and the other of the belligerents there should be concession on some point and renunciation of some hoped-for gain; and each should make such concessions willingly, even if it entail some sacrifice, in order not to assume before God and men the enormous responsibility of the continuation of a carnage which is without example, and which, if prolonged still further, might well be for Europe the beginning of the decadence from that degree of civil prosperity to which the Christian religion had raised it. (Ibid., Vol. VII, p. 509.)

Letter of Benedict XV in reply to an address from the Bishops of Germany. September, 8, 1916:

Certainly, if minds were not obscured by passion, they would not have failed to observe, what is in itself most evident, namely, that the Supreme Pontiff, Vicar of the King of Peace and Father of all the Christians, is supremely bound in conscience to counsel, suggest, inculcate nothing else but peace; that He, as such, does not undertake the cause of *some* men but of mankind, and that especially in a war so murderous as the present, so much so that the man who could shorten its duration by even a single day would be well worthy of the gratitude of the human race.

While awaiting then the peace for which We have prayed, We shall continue by every means in Our power to alleviate, at least in part, that awful accumulation of miseries which are the sad consequence of the war. And it is precisely in this field of charity that We perceive you signalizing yourselves with works of enlightened zeal, both by the federation of all the Catholic societies of Germany, devoted to well doing, so as to relieve with more promptitude and efficacy the manifold miseries of the distressed, and by those providential institutions intended to better the lot of all the prisoners in the empire. While then We praise this invention of Christian Charity, We eulogize thereby both the solicitous cares of the Bishop and clergy of Paderborn and the liberality of all the Catholics of Germany. Yet the most lofty duty of charity to-day—which you are now fulfilling and in which We exhort you to persevere—is this, to strive unanimously to unite in the bonds of brotherhood the peoples whom the war has divided, procuring that hatred be not inflamed but rather gradually extinguished by mutual works of mercy.

Thus shall the way be prepared, naturally as it were, for the peace which all good men desire; a peace which will be all the more lasting as it will have taken root more deeply in the hearts. Cease not then to implore, as you are doing, the divine aid by fresh expiatory supplications and by frequently inviting the children to the Eucharistic Table; there is no telling how much humble and suppliant prayers avail with the Lord, especially when they are enhanced by penance and innocence. (Ibid., Vol. VIII, p. 356.)

Allocution of Benedict XV. December 4, 1916 :

The Holy Father refers to the completion of the codification of the canon law, begun under Pius X, and takes occasion to speak of the evils that result from the contempt of law by peoples and nations.

It is a well-known fact in every human society and in the international domain itself that where observance of law flourishes, prosperity and peace reign ; while, on the other hand, when the authority of the law is neglected or despised, and discord and caprice prevail, all public and private right is thrown into confusion. This is confirmed, were confirmation needed, in a most striking way by what is happening to-day. The horrible madness of the conflict which is devastating Europe shows too clearly to what slaughter and ruin disrespect for the supreme laws which regulate the mutual relations of States may lead. In this general convulsion of peoples, we behold the desecration of sacred things, and the vile treatment meted out to ministers of worship, even those of high dignity, although inviolable by divine law and by the law of nations ; numerous peaceable citizens are taken away from their homes, amid the tears of mothers, wives, children ; open cities and undefended populations are being molested, especially by aerial raids ; everywhere, by land and sea, such misdeeds are perpetrated as fill the soul with horror and anguish. While deploring this mass of evils, and while again condemning the injustices that are committed in this war, wherever and by whomsoever perpetrated, We fondly entertain the hope, confiding in God for its accomplishment, that as with the promulgation of the new Code a happier and more tranquil era will, as We trust, dawn for the Church ; so, too, may States soon enjoy the blessings of long-expected peace, founded on reverence for right and justice, and bringing to all nations, once more united by the bonds of friendship, an abundance of all prosperity. (Ibid., Vol. VIII, p. 465.)

Address of the Holy Father to the Cardinals on Christmas Eve ; in reply to their Christmas Greetings. December 24, 1916 :

How, indeed, could Our children aspire with Us to peace, to that just and lasting peace which is to put an end to the horrors of the present war, if no conditioned good has ever been attained without fulfilment of the condition, and the *pax hominibus bonæ voluntatis* rings out to-day as a conditional promise neither more nor less than when it echoed for the first time round the crib of the newly born Redeemer. Time and again during the fearful course of the horrible storm which devastates so large a part of the world, while reading the petitions of mothers, wives, fathers, children, and measuring with the eye and the heart the social and domestic ruins of the immense cataclysm, We have thought of the tears shed by Jesus at the sight of Jerusalem, sinful, unbelieving, froward. But more than the tears, eloquent as they are, it is the sorrowful words of Our Lord that terrify Us most : '*Hadst thou but known the things that are to thy peace, but now they are hidden from thine eyes, because thou hast not known the time of thy visitation.*' Oh ! let the world know now, amid the Angelic singing and the sweet attraction of the Babe of Peace, the things which are for its peace ; let those who wield powers second the voice of this illustrious Senate to arrest the course of the destruction of the peoples ; let the Nations reflect that the Church, by the light of the Faith and through the assistance of Him who is the way the truth and the life, sees, nay, sees much farther than the eyes of human frailty ; let the contending parties yield at last to the repeated admonitions and prayers of the Father of the Christian family.

Letter of Benedict XV 'to the Leaders of the Belligerent peoples.' August 1, 1917 :

This was communicated to the Governments by Cardinal Gasparri with a covering letter in the following terms :

The Holy Father, desirous of doing all he possibly can to put an end to the conflict which for more than three years has ravaged the civilized world, has come to the decision to submit to the leaders of the belligerent peoples concrete propositions of peace set forth in the document I have the honour to attach to this letter. May it please God that His Holiness's word should this time produce the desired effect for the welfare of all humanity.

The following is the text of the Pope's letter :

To the Leaders of the Belligerent Peoples.

Since the beginning of Our Pontificate, in the midst of the horrors of the terrible war which has burst upon Europe, We have considered three things among others :

To maintain an absolute impartiality towards all belligerents, as becomes him who is the common father, and who loves all his children with an equal affection ;

To endeavour continually to do the utmost good to all without distinction of persons, nationality or religion, in accordance not only with the universal law of charity, but also with the supreme spiritual duty laid upon Us by Christ ; and

Finally, as is demanded by Our pacifist mission to omit nothing, as far as in Our power lies, to contribute to hasten the end of this calamity by trying to bring the peoples and their leaders to more moderate resolutions in the discussion of means that will secure a 'just and lasting peace.'

Whoever has followed Our work during these three sorrowful years that have just ended has been able easily to recognize that if We remained ever faithful to Our resolution of absolute impartiality and Our work of well-doing We have not ceased to exhort the belligerent peoples and Governments to become once again brothers, although publicity was not given to all that We have done in order to attain this noble end.

Towards the end of the first year of war We addressed to the nations who are at grips the most earnest exhortations, and, further, We indicated the road to be followed in order to reach a peace which would be stable and honourable for all. Unhappily, Our appeal was not heard, and the war continued desperately for another two years, with all its horrors.

It became even more cruel, and spread upon the face of the earth, upon the sea, and even into the sky ; and on defenceless cities, on tranquil villages, on their innocent populations, were seen to descend desolation and death.

And now any one can imagine how the sufferings of all would be multiplied and aggravated if yet more months, or worse still, more years, were to be added to this blood-stained time. Must the civilized world be nothing more than a field of death, and shall Europe, so glorious and flourishing, rush to the abyss, as if dragged by some universal madness, and lend a hand in her own destruction ?

In a situation of so much anguish, in presence of so terribly serious a situation, We—who have no private political aim, who listen not to the suggestions or interests of any of the belligerents, but are influenced only by the sentiment of Our supreme duty as the father of the faithful, by the solicitations of Our children who beg for Our intervention and Our mediatory word, and for the voice of humanity and reason—now again throw out a cry for peace, and We renew Our pressing appeal to those who hold in their hands the destinies of nations.

But that We may no longer limit ourselves to general terms, as circumstances counselled Us in the past, We desire now to put forward some more concrete and practical propositions, and invite the Governments of the belligerents to come to some agreement on the following points, which seem to offer the bases of a just and lasting peace, though leaving to them the duty of adjusting and completing them :

First of all, the fundamental point must be that the moral force of Right shall be substituted for the material force of arms ; thence must follow a just agreement of all for the simultaneous and reciprocal diminution of armaments, in accordance with rules and guarantees to be established hereafter, in a measure sufficient and necessary for the maintenance of public order in each State ; next, as a substitute for armies, the institution of arbitration, with its high peace-making function, subject to regulations to be agreed on and sanctions to be determined against the State which should refuse either to submit international questions to arbitration or to accept its decision.

Once the supremacy of Right is thus established, let all obstacles to the free intercourse of people be swept aside, in assuring, by means of rules, to be fixed in the same way, the true liberty of and common rights over the sea, which on the one hand would eliminate numerous causes of conflict, and, on the other, would open to all new sources of prosperity and progress.

As to the damage to be made good and the cost of the war, We see no other way of solving the question but to lay down, as a general principle, an entire and reciprocal condonation, justified moreover by the immense benefits which will accrue from disarmament—the more so as the continuation of such carnage solely for economic reasons would be inconceivable. If in certain cases there are, on the other hand, particular reasons, let them be weighed justly and equitably.

But these peaceful agreements, with the immense advantages which flow from them, are not possible without the reciprocal restitution of territories at the moment occupied—consequently, on the part of Germany, a total evacuation of Belgium, with a guarantee of her complete political, military, and economic independence, as against any other Power whatever; similar evacuation of French territory; on the part of other belligerent Powers a similar restitution of the German Colonies.

As regards territorial questions—as, for instance, those pending between Italy and Austria, and between Germany and France—there is ground for hope that in view of the immense advantages of a permanent peace with disarmament, the disputants would feel disposed to examine them in a conciliatory spirit, giving due weight, within the limits of justice and feasibility, as We have said previously, to the aspirations of the populations, and, on occasion, bringing their particular interests into harmony with the general welfare of the great community of mankind.

The same spirit of equity and justice must direct the examination of the remaining territorial and political questions, and particularly those which concern Armenia, the Balkan States, and the territories which form part of the former kingdom of Poland, which in particular, by reason of her noble historical traditions and the sufferings endured, specially during the present war, has a just claim on the sympathies of all nations.

Such are the principal foundations on which We believe that the future reorganization of the Peoples must be built. They are of a nature to make impossible the return of similar conflicts, and to prepare the solution of the economic question, which is so important for the material well-being of all the belligerent States.

In laying these proposals before you, who at this tragic hour are guiding the destinies of the belligerent nations, We are animated by a sweet hope—that of seeing them accepted, and thus of witnessing the speedy end of the terrible struggle which more and more seems to be a useless slaughter.

The whole world, on the other hand, recognizes that on one side as well as on the other the honour of their arms has been amply vindicated.

Lend an ear, therefore, to Our prayers, accept the paternal invitation which We address to you in the name of the Divine Redeemer, the Prince of Peace. Reflect on your very grave responsibility before God and before men ; on your decision depend the repose and joy of unnumbered families, the lives of thousands of young men, the happiness, in a word, of the peoples, to secure whose welfare is our absolute duty.

May God inspire you with a decision in harmony with His most holy will. Heaven grant that in meriting the applause of your contemporaries you may assure to yourselves, in the sight of future generations, the noble name of peace-makers. For Us, in close communion in prayer and penitence with all the faithful souls who are sighing for peace, We implore for you from the Divine Spirit enlightenment and counsel.

At the Vatican, August 1, 1917.

(Signed) Benedictus P.P. XV.

(Ibid., Vol. IX, p. 417.)

Several of the replies of Governments will be found in Müller.[1] The belligerents in each case restated the familiar vindication of their own cause and the familiar malediction of their adversaries. The Austrian reply was the most favourable, the principal Allied Powers, newly reinforced by the United States, were unyielding. The American reply (August 27, 1917) is of some moment as containing qualified acceptance of the Papal programme of peace, though Mr. Lansing declares the delivery of Germany and the world from 'the ruthless master of the German people' to be an essential condition of realizing it.

'His Holiness in substance proposes,' writes the American Secretary of State, 'that we return to the *status quo ante bellum*, and that then there be a general condonation, disarmament, and a concert of nations based upon an acceptance of the principle of arbitration ; that by a similar concert freedom of

[1] *Das Friedenswerk der Kirche in den Letzten Drei Jahrhunderten*, pp. 468–475.

the seas be established ; and that the territorial claims of France and Italy, the perplexing problems of the Balkan States, and the restitution of Poland be left to such conciliatory adjustments as may be possible in the new temper of such a peace, due regard being paid to the aspirations of the peoples whose political fortunes and affiliations will be involved.'

After restating at some length the case against Germany, the letter continues :

The purposes of the United States in this war are known to the whole world, to every people to whom the truth has been permitted to come. They do not need to be stated again. We seek no material advantage of any kind. We believe that the intolerable wrongs done in this war by the furious and brutal power of the Imperial German Government ought to be repaired, but not at the expense of the sovereignty of any people—rather a vindication of the sovereignty both of those that are weak and of those that are strong. Punitive damages, the dismemberment of empires, the establishment of selfish and exclusive economic leagues, we deem inexpedient and in the end worse than futile, no proper basis for a peace of any kind, least of all for an enduring peace. That must be based upon justice and fairness and the common rights of mankind.

We cannot take the word of the present rulers of Germany as a guarantee of anything that is to endure, unless explicitly supported by such conclusive evidence of the will and purpose of the German people themselves, as the other peoples of the world would be justified in accepting. Without such guarantees treaties of settlement, agreement for disarmament, covenants to set up arbitration in place of force, territorial adjustments, reconstitution of small nations, if made with the German Government, no man, no nation could now depend on. We must await some new evidence of the purposes of the great peoples of the Central Powers. God grant it may be given soon and in a way to restore the confidence of all peoples everywhere in the faith of nations and the possibility of a covenanted peace.

This declaration of intentions both negative and positive needs to be recalled in view of the actual form taken by the Peace Treaties. A League of Nations based upon the principle of arbitration and the mutual reduction of armaments was indeed brought into being. But what of the 'punitive damages,' the 'dismemberment of Empires'?

In order to indicate the attitude of the Papacy to certain important parts of the Peace Settlement itself the following extracts from allocutions and letters of Pius XI are here added, for they announce principles regarding the liquidation of a great conflict which are not less valuable than those propounded by his predecessor in the course of it. The major documents of both Popes upon the Christian conception of peace in general follow in the next chapter.

PIUS XI. *Autograph letter to Cardinal Gasparri, June* 24, 1923. *On the occupation of the Ruhr and reparations :*

When, with the intention of repairing the very important damages suffered by populations and districts formerly prosperous and flourishing, the debtor (i.e. the State owing this reparation) gives proof of a serious determination to arrive at an equitable and final agreement, soliciting an impartial decision upon the limits of his own solvency and pledging himself to furnish the arbiters with every means of arriving at a true and exact estimate of his resources, then justice and social charity, as indeed, the very interest of the creditors and of all the nations, exhausted by wars and athirst after tranquillity, seem to oppose the claiming from the debtor what he would be incapable of giving without draining himself entirely of his own resources and of his own capacity of production. For this would result in an irreparable injury to the debtor as well as to the creditors themselves and in the danger of social upheavals which would be the definite ruin of Europe, and of rancours which would keep up a continued menace of new and more disastrous conflagrations.

Similarly, it is just that the creditors should possess guarantees proportionate to the amount that is owed to them and which assure the recovery of it, upon which depend interests equally vital for them.

Nevertheless, we ask them to examine whether with this object, it is necessary to maintain, in every hypothesis, territorial occupations, which impose heavy sacrifices upon the occupied areas and upon the nations occupying them ; or whether it would not be better to substitute for this territorial occupation, even if only by stages, other guarantees not less effective, and, most certainly, less hurtful.

The contribution of the Church to the pacification of Europe and the world distraught by the conflicting nationalisms of the after-war years can be illustrated by the following extracts from the Encyclical : Caritate Christi Compulsi. May, 1932 :

' In like manner will the way be opened to the peace we long for,' as St. Paul beautifully remarks in the passage where he joins the precept of prayer to holy desires for the peace and salvation of all men : ' I desire therefore, first of all, that supplications, prayers, intercessions, and thanksgivings be made for all men ; for kings and all that are in high station, that we may lead a quiet and peaceful life in all piety and chastity. For this is good and acceptable in the sight of God our Saviour, who will have all men to be saved, and to come to the knowledge of truth.'[1] Let peace be implored for all men, but especially for those who in human society have the grave responsibilities of government ; for how could they give peace to their peoples, if they have not it themselves ? And it is prayer precisely, that, according to the Apostle, will bring the gift of peace ; prayer that is addressed to the Heavenly Father who is the Father of all men ; prayer that is the common expression of family feeling of that great family which extends beyond the boundaries of any country and continent.

Men who in every nation pray to the same God for peace on earth will not kindle flames of discord among the peoples ; men, who turn in prayer to the divine Majesty, will not set up in their own country a craving for domination ; nor foster that inordinate love of country which of its own nation makes its own god ; men who look to the 'God of peace and love,'[2] who turn to Him through the mediation of Christ, who is 'our peace,'[3] will never rest until finally that peace which the world cannot give, comes down from the Giver of every good gift on 'men of good will.'[4]

'Peace be to you'[5] was the Easter greeting of Our Lord to His Apostles and first disciples ; and this blessed greeting from those first times until our day has ever found place in the sacred Liturgy of the Church, and to-day more than ever should comfort and refresh aching and oppressed human hearts.

. . . But to-day when atheism is spreading through the masses of the people, the practical consequences of such an error become dreadfully tangible, and realities of the saddest kind make their appearance in the world. In place of moral laws, which disappear together with the loss of faith in God, brute force is imposed, trampling on every right. Old time fidelity and honesty of conduct and mutual intercourse extolled so much even by the orators and poets of paganism, now give place to speculations in one's own affairs as in those of others without reference to conscience. In fact, how can any contract be maintained, and what value can any treaty have, in which every guarantee of conscience is lacking ? And how can there be talk of guarantees of conscience, when all faith in God and all fear of God has vanished ? Take away this basis, and with it all moral law falls, and there is no remedy left to stop the gradual, but inevitable destruction of peoples, families, the State, civilization itself. . . .

[1] 1 Tim. ii : 1–4. [2] 2 Corinthians xiii : 11.
[3] Ephesians ii : 14. [4] Luke ii : 14.
[5] John xx : 26.

'There is no peace to the wicked'[1] says the Holy Spirit, because they live in continuous struggle and conflict with the order established by nature and by its Creator. Only when this order is restored, when all peoples faithfully and spontaneously recognize and profess it, when the internal conditions of peoples and their outward relations with other nations are founded on this basis, then only will stable peace be possible on earth. But to create this atmosphere of lasting peace, neither peace treaties, nor the most solemn pacts, nor international meetings or conferences, nor even the noblest and most disinterested efforts of any statesman, will be enough, unless in the first place are recognized the sacred rights of natural and divine law. No leader in public economy, no power of organization will ever be able to bring social conditions to a peaceful solution, unless first in the very field of economics there triumphs moral law based on God and conscience. This is the underlying value of every value in the political life as well as in the economic life of nations; this is the soundest 'rate of exchange.' If it is kept steady, all the rest will be stable, being guaranteed by the immutable and eternal law of God.

And even for men individually, penance is the foundation and bearer of true peace detaching them from earthly and perishable goods, lifting them up to goods that are eternal, giving them, even in the midst of privations and adversity, a peace that the world with all its wealth and pleasures cannot give. One of the most pleasing and most joyous songs ever heard in this vale of tears, is without doubt the famous 'Canticle of the Sun' of St. Francis. Now the man who composed it, wrote it and sang it, was one of the greatest penitents, the Poor Man of Assisi, who possessed absolutely nothing on earth, and bore in his emaciated body the painful Stigmata of His Crucified Lord. . . .

Nothing remains for Us therefore, but to invite this poor world that has shed so much blood, has dug so many graves, has destroyed so many works, has deprived so many men of bread and labour, nothing else remains for Us, We say, but to invite it in the loving words of the sacred Liturgy: 'Be thou converted to the Lord thy God.'

[1] Isaias lviii: 22.

CHAPTER IX

THE CATHOLIC CONCEPTION OF PEACE

'PAX *est tranquillitas ordinis*' ; '*Pax proprius effectus caritatis.*'[1] In these two axioms is contained the Catholic philosophy of peace. Already it will have appeared both from the teaching and endeavours of the Church regarding the prevention of war—and not least in the pontifical documents issued in the midst of the battle—that peace according to the Christian tradition is something very different from the mere *absence of war*. This simple point leads to reflections of great moment to international ethics and international law. Were war between States, potential or actual, the normal state of international life, and peace the exception to the rule, there could be no international law, or at least it could but be miserably restricted to the laws of war. Yet the notion of perpetual conflict as of natural origin is too widespread to be passed over in silence. Has it not even appeared to be too often the guiding principle of contemporary Governments, if not in their preaching at least in their practice ? How else explain the military establishments of this and the last two generations ? Not less evidently does it seem to dominate the relations of class with class and of political factions with one another. To this baneful conception of man as ' an essentially fighting animal ' Catholic Christianity is unalterably opposed. Of original sin and its consequences, of the reality of diabolical influence, acting as well upon collectivities as upon individuals, the Church is vividly aware. But conflicts arising from these sinister facts are not regarded as inevitable,

[1] ' Peace is the tranquillity which comes of Order.' St. Augustine.
' Peace is the effect of which Charity is the cause.' St. Thomas Aquinas.

still less as proper to man ; they are a *departure* from his right nature and the right reason with which he is endowed, an aberration, a frustration of his proper end. 'War is always satanic in origin.'[1] Even if violence must be used to restore order, 'the right of war is odious.'[2] And Christ came not to overthrow but rediscover human nature in its true dignity. He came, says Benedict XV, 'for the very purpose of restoring that peace which the envy of the Devil had destroyed.' Hence the Church regards as repugnant equally to reason and to Christian precepts the theory of Bismarck, that war is the proper and normal activity of the nation—a theory which has been so recklessly revived in Germany since the National Revolution of 1933.[3]

This theory is condemned whether it proceed from a direct transference to the state of the supposed fighting nature of man, or from a conception of the State as the sole satisfaction of the social needs of men. The 'Contrat Social,' which supposes the natural state of men to be that of isolation and consequently mutual conflict, a state from which they emerged by a conscious subordination of their individual will to the common will by means of contract, is rejected as intrinsically absurd, as it is unsupported by history. And that other notion of the German school of *Rechtsphilosophie*, which has combined with the derivatives of Rousseau's doctrine to establish the idol of the State, is to the Christian philosophers no less irrational. According to this theory :

> The existence of the State is always legitimate, since it is a degree of liberty. There may be crimes against the State, but the State can never be guilty of crime. The State is Liberty ; and it is not wrong for Liberty to establish itself, even by force.[4]

Man was *not* born to kill man. States were *not* formed either as an artificial remedy for that condition or as the ultimate end of man, but rather as the fitting outcome of the natural needs of men themselves. The authority of the State, whether monarchic or democratic is neither absolute nor

[1] Pope Nicholas I. [2] Suarez.

[3] For instance in Professor Banze's book.

[4] Ch. Andler. *Les Origines du Socialisme d'Etat en Allemagne*, p. 33.

free from the Moral Law. It is under a double subjection—to Man, for it is but a means for promoting the perfection of human personality—and[1] 'every human soul is a spiritual universe'; to God, since the rulers of States are but the creatures of God, and it is on behalf of their fellow creatures that their policies are framed. So that precisely the same obedience to God, the observance of the same moral principles is incumbent upon them in their public acts as upon individual souls. And since the spiritual end of man is 'to fix his mind upon God' it is the duty of the temporal authority 'to aid in removing obstacles to that end, of which conflict with his fellow men is among the greatest. For these purposes man needs to live in peace and concord with his fellow men.'[2]

Sociability then, is a fundamental characteristic of man's nature; peace necessary to the attainment of his spiritual end; the State a minister to those purposes, and itself a member of a larger society, linked together with a network of mutual rights and duties, for whose observance the rulers of States must answer before the awful tribunal of God. With this conception of the fundamental sociability of men and nations is inextricably linked the conception of Law.

It follows that *pax armata*, (armed peace), is not the natural state of international relations, but unnatural, abnormal and irregular. So taught Leo XIII observing the competition in armaments in the Europe of his day.[3] So teaches Pius XI observing its revival after the European War.[4]

The next part of this work will be devoted to studying the implications of this fundamental doctrine of sociability—the character of the society existing by nature between peoples; the principles upon which to use an expression of Cardinal Mercier, 'a lasting shape should be given to this natural comity of nations'[5]; the safeguarding of the rights of God in that organization. We are here studying rather the metaphysical concepts which go to make the Christian philosophy of peace.

[1] Maritain. *Three Reformers.*
[2] St. Thomas. *Summa Contra Gentiles*, Lib. III, Cap. CXXX.
[3] *Praeclara Gratulationis.*
[4] *Nova Impendet.*
[5] See p. 311.

Peace is seen to imply an absence of commotion, and in the resulting quiet, a right relationship between human souls and God ; between Governments and God, between nation and nation, between Church and State ; rulers and subjects, man and man ; between human societies large and small in their dealings with one another. That right relationship which respects the rights of each is Order.[1] 'The Peace of all things is the tranquillity of Order. Order is the distribution which allots all things equal and unequal each to its own place.' But there is no need to gild the gold of the City of God. St. Augustine's thought, which is that of the Church, is clear in the whole passage which we quote below. We may only remark that international peace, in the narrow sense of peace between perfect political communities, cannot be isolated from that larger peace of the whole order of created intelligences in union with the uncreated Principle and End of Life. To the Catholic there can be no peace between men or human societies which does not come through the peace of each and all with God. 'Let peace be implored for all men,' writes Pius XI, 'but especially for those who in human society have the grave responsibilities of Government ; for how could they give peace to their peoples, if they have it not themselves ?'[2]

So too does peace between nations require a proper regard for the hierarchy of rights within the State—the rights of parents and the family, since the family is the primary element of civil society ; the rights of the religious, cultural, racial, intellectual and professional associations, small or large, coterminous with the State or not, which the diverse needs of men and women prompt them to form, associations which the State has no right, save on the ground of public order, to impede, but which, on the contrary it has the duty to encourage and protect. This is but a development of the ancient, and for centuries unquestioned doctrine that there is a *jus gentium*, a 'right belonging to all peoples,' germane to nature itself, which it is the duty of princes to respect and defend, as well in their own territories as in those of others. The ordering of the human factors of industry, by national

[1] St. Augustine. *City of God, Book* 19, *Chapter XIII.*
[2] *Caritate Christi Compulsi.*

and international action, according to the requirements of social justice and charity, and in particular the protection of the working man's rights ; the just distribution of property, in the light of the truth that 'the earth, though apportioned amongst private owners, ceases not thereby to minister to the needs of all,'[1] ; these again are elements of the whole foundation of social order which, if seriously violated in any part of the world, may jeopardize the peace of the whole. Peace, then, is the organic, living, perfectly articulated unity which the metaphor of the body only suffices to describe.

'The whole body, being compacted and fitly joined together by what every joint supplieth, according to the operation in the measure of every part, maketh increase of the body, unto the edifying of itself in charity.' It is of the Mystical Body of Christ that St. Paul speaks : Pius XI does not hesitate to set it forth as the ideal to which the economic and social reformation of States should tend.[2]

By the same token Peace in the Christian tradition presupposes many and divers persons and groups between whom this harmony exists. For harmony is not of one note but of many. Fusion is the negation of unity. 'Remember that nations never die,' wrote Benedict XV to the powers at war.

Folly to dream that the Church ever wants, or ever wanted to suppress or obliterate the nations. Not even the religious units that compose her does she seek to fuse. The Uniate Churches are not melted into the Latin Patriarchate. Most sensitive and most strict is Canon Law as to the inviolability of their immemorial rites. The Church, who will rescue the child, if the family tyrannizes over it, and who is the almost fierce protector of the family against the encroaching State, is no less anxious to see a true and living tissue of humanity, in which states, peoples, races are not fused, and yet where in a true sense there is no more Jew nor pagan, Greek nor Scythian, male nor female, but all are become One Thing, even as the Son and the Father are unconfusedly One Thing.[3]

Indeed the Catholic mind ultimately reverts to the

[1] Leo XIII. *Rerum Novarum*, VII.

[2] Pius XI. *Quadragesimo Anno*.

[3] Sermon by C. C. Martindale, S.J., at a conference at Reading, England, October, 1923, at which the Catholic Council for International Relations was founded.

revealed nature of God Himself, as the sublime architype of political and social unity amongst men and nations.

We[1] know of God that He is a manifold Unity ; that the One is Three. Of the Three, One must be esteemed by us to be, and indeed is, the Principle of the Second and the Third, that none the less are co-equal and co-eternal with the First. In this Trinity no one of the Three loses identity ; they are not mere aspects of the One ; they are not one because fused. And as for us, by the unimaginable gift of supernatural grace,[2] we shall be (nay, already may be) so united with our God, that the union achieved by true thought and right choice is but the shadow of a union than which, it has been said, only the Hypostatic Union of God and Man in Christ is closer. Yet ours shall be real union ; we shall not be absorbed ; our identity shall not be lost within the Divine Embrace. Nay, not in Christ Himself were the Divine and human natures mingled nor mixed, albeit they made One Person. Every method of national self-construction or government that belies these great truths is false.

This true unity, peace and order to which peace between peoples and State should contribute and of which it is itself a part, is unattainable without the charity wherewith men love their neighbours for the love of God. This charity arising from the very likeness of human nature, the common origin and end of human life, the common needs of life itself, is ennobled and inspired by the supernatural charity of Christ, 'the first-born among many brethren.' In vain could we seek to give a true account of the Christian conception of peace save as the fruit and effect of Christian charity. Writing on this theme (*Quadragesimo Anno*) Pius XI says :

'For, justice alone, even though most faithfully observed, can remove the cause of social strife, but can never bring about a union of hearts and minds. Yet this union, binding men

[1] Martindale (*continued*).

[2] The Sacraments, and especially the Sacrament of Holy Communion, are, according to the Catholic tradition, the normal vehicle of grace. The conception of the Eucharistic Bread as the symbol of supra-national unity is a very ancient one. The following is from *The Didache :* 'As the elements of this bread were dispersed upon the mountains and as they have been brought together to form a single whole, so may thy Church be gathered together from the ends of the earth and the four winds of heaven into the Kingdom which thou hast prepared.'

together, is the main principle of stability in all institutions, no matter how perfect they may seem, which aim at establishing social peace and promoting mutual aid. In its absence, as repeated experience proves, the wisest regulations come to nothing. Then only will it be possible to unite all in harmonious striving for the common good, when all sections of society have the intimate conviction that they are members of a single family and children of the same Heavenly Father, and further, that they are 'one body in Christ, and everyone members one of another,'[1] so that 'if one member suffer anything, all members suffer with it.'[2]

Thus then we may resume the ideal of international life set forth in the passages which follow by the Church which claims to be the guardian and interpreter of the 'Gospel of Peace.' First. Peace is the natural condition of nations; sociability their proper quality, co-operation their normal function. Second. International Peace is a part of and dependent upon true peace in human society as a whole. Third. That peace is the tranquillity which comes of order, order in which justice is done to all the varied groupings of men, and men themselves are at peace with the Divine Law-giver. Fourth. Peace cannot come by fusion; it is not uniformity but unity amid variety, including, and integrating in a single whole, the variety of national characters and traditions. Fifth. Though based upon justice, peace is even more the 'effect of charity' and cannot be attained without it.

There remains perhaps the most powerful pacific motive of all which the Church proposes. It is, paradoxically, to establish peace in the hearts of men by reminding them that perfect peace is not to be hoped for in this life. It is to be attained only in Heaven. *Sub specie æternitatis* politics are absolute no longer. Frenzies of national passion seem puny and ridiculous; even to vindicate national rights is hardly a matter of life and death; for what are territory, sovereignty, wealth, power, compared with the loss of an immortal soul? *Memento mori* has ever been the Christian counsel of wisdom. Love of country is a great virtue—it is indeed an extension of Christian charity. But will the man be whipped to fury by earthly patriotisms, who, through the hardships and disappointments of worldly events, looks to the

[1] Romans xii, 5. [2] 1 Corinthians, xii, 26.

heavenly country as his goal? 'For we have here no abiding city.' Yet all, of whatever race, who die at peace with their Maker, are destined to become fellow citizens with the Saints. And as, to the writer of the City of God, the Heavenly Jerusalem shone clear through the mist of tears in which he saw his beloved Rome sacked by the barbarians, so does the true vision and spirit of peace come, even in this world, to him in whose heart the song of St. Bernard is never still: 'For thee, O dear, dear, country, mine eyes their vigil keep.'

Documents

St. Clement of Rome. *Ep. ad Corinthios.* (*c.* A.D. 95). *Patres. Apost.* (*Tunk*) *pp.* 175–180. *Cap. LIX, LX and LXI:*

Cap. LIX:

But, if some do not observe those things which God ordains through us, let them know that they implicate themselves in no small offence and danger: but we shall be innocent of this sin and, continually praying and supplicating, we shall implore that the maker of all things may conserve intact the number of His elect constituted in the whole world through His beloved Son Jesus Christ, by Whom He called us out of darkness into light, out of ignorance into the knowledge of the glory of His name that we may hope in Thy name, the beginning of every creature, that, the eyes of our hearts having been opened, we may know Thee alone, all Highest of the highest, Holy dwelling amongst the saints: who humblest the arrogance of the proud, who knowest the thoughts of peoples, who raiseth up the humble, who makest the rich and the poor, who killest, savest and givest life, sole giver of spirits and God of all flesh: who seest into the depths, judge of men's works, help of the tottering, saviour of the despairing, creator and Bishop of every spirit: who multipliest nations on earth and out of all chooseth them who love Thee through Jesus Christ, Thy beloved Son by whom Thou hast taught us, sanctified us, honoured us. We beg Thee, Lord that Thou be our helper and our aid. Free those among us who are in tribulation, have mercy on the humble, lift up the fallen, succour the weak, heal the sick, convert those of Thy people who err: feed the hungry, free our captives, make sane the insane, console the weak of spirit: let all peoples know Thee that Thou alone art God and Jesus Christ Thy Son and we Thy people and the sheep of Thy pasture.

Cap. LX:

For by Thy works Thou hast shown the lasting constitution of the world: Thou, O Lord, has founded the world, faithful in all generations, just in judgements, wonderful in strength and magnificent, wise in creating, and prudent in directing created things, good in those things which are seen, faithful towards them that put their trust in Thee, loving and merciful, forgive us our iniquities and injustices and sins and trespasses. Impute not any sin to Thy servants and handmaids, but purify us in Thy truth and guide our steps that we may walk in faithfulness of heart and do what is good and pleasing before Thee and before our rulers. Let the light of Thy countenance shine upon us, O Lord, that we may enjoy good things in peace, that we may by Thy hand be shielded from the strong, and be freed from all sin by Thy high hand, deliver us also from those that unjustly hate us. Give concord and peace both to us and to all those that dwell in this world, as Thou gavest it to our fathers, for we dutifully invoke Thee in faith and truth, obedient to Thy omnipotent name which is endowed with every virtue, and we obey our rulers and governors on earth.

Cap. LXI :

Thou, O Lord, by Thy magnificent and ineffable virtue hast given them the power of ruling, that, knowing the glory and honour which Thou hast imparted to them we may be subject to them and not opposed to Thy will. Grant to them, O Lord, peace, concord and strength, that they may without the least offence administer the power which Thou hast given them. For Thou, Lord, heavenly King of the ages dost give to the sons of men glory, honour and power over those things that are on earth : do Thou, O Lord, direct their judgement according to that by which it is said that ' it is good and pleasing in Thy sight,' that, faithfully exercising in peace and mercy the power given by Thee, they may receive mercy from Thee. To Thee who alone canst give us these and all other good things, we confess through the high priest and patron of our souls, Jesus Christ, through whom may glory and majesty be to Thee now and in every generation, world without end. Amen.

ARNOBIUS. *Adversus Gentes I, VI* (A.D. 306). (*Bryce and Campbell, pp.* 9–10) :

Although you allege that those wars which you speak of were excited through hatred of our religion, it would not be difficult to prove that after the name of Christ was heard in the world, not only were they not increased, but they were even in great measure diminished by the restraining of furious passions. For since we, a numerous band of men as we are, have learned from His teaching and His laws that evil ought not to be requited with evil, that it is better to suffer wrong than to inflict it, that we should rather shed our own blood than stain our hands and our conscience with that of another, an ungrateful world is now for a long period enjoying a benefit from Christ, inasmuch as by His means the rage of savage ferocity has been softened, and man has begun to withhold hostile hands from the blood of a fellow-creature. But if all without exception, who feel that they are men not in form of body, but in power of reason, would lend an ear for a little to His salutary and peaceful rules, and would not, in the pride and arrogance of their supposed enlightenment, trust to their own senses rather than to His admonitions, the whole world, being converted, would now be living in the most placid tranquillity, and would be united in blessed harmony, maintaining inviolate the sanctity of treaties.

St. Augustine. *City of God* (*c.* A.D. 413). *Book XIX, Chap. XI:*

And thus we may say of peace, as we have said of eternal life, that it is the end of our good; and that rather because the Psalmist says of the city of God, the subject of this laborious work, 'Praise the Lord, O Jerusalem; praise thy God, O Zion: for he hath strengthened the bars of thy gates; he hath blessed thy children within thee; who hath made thy borders peace.' (Psalm cxlvii: 12–14.) For when the bars of her gates shall be strengthened, none shall go in or come out from her; consequently we ought to understand the peace of her borders as that final peace we are wishing to declare. For even the mystical name of the city itself, that is *Jerusalem*, means, as I have already said, 'Vision of Peace.' But as the word peace is employed in connection with things in this world in which certainly life eternal has no place, we have preferred to call the end or supreme good of this city life eternal rather than peace. Of this end the Apostle says: 'But, now being freed from sin, and become servants to God, ye have your fruit unto holiness, and the end life eternal.' (Romans vi: 22.) But, on the other hand, as those who are not familiar with Scripture may suppose that the life of the wicked is eternal life, either because of the immortality of the soul, which some of the philosophers even have recognized, or because of the endless punishment of the wicked, which forms a part of our faith, and which seems impossible unless the wicked live for ever, it may therefore be advisable, in order that every one may readily understand what we mean, to say that the end or supreme good of this city is either peace in eternal life, or eternal life in peace. For peace is a good so great, that even in this earthly and mortal life there is no word we hear with such pleasure, nothing we desire with such zest, or find to be more thoroughly gratifying. So that if we dwell for a little longer on this subject, we shall not, in my opinion, be wearisome to our readers, who will attend both for the sake of understanding what is the end of this city of which we speak, and for the sake of the sweetness of peace which is dear to all.

Book XIX, Chap. XII:

Whoever gives even moderate attention to human affairs and to our common nature, will recognize that if there is no man who does not wish to be joyful, neither is there any one who does not wish to have peace. For even they who make war desire nothing but victory—desire, that is to say, to attain to peace with glory. For what else is victory than the conquest of those who resist us? And when this is done there is peace. It is, therefore, with the desire for peace that wars are waged, even by those who take pleasure in exercising their warlike nature in command and battle. And hence it is obvious that peace is the end sought for by war. For every man seeks peace by waging war, but no man seeks war by making peace. . . . What kite, solitary as he is when circling over his prey, does not seek a mate, build a nest, hatch the eggs, bring up the young birds, and maintain with the mother of his family as peaceful a domestic alliance as he can? How much more powerfully do the laws of man's nature move him to hold fellowship and maintain peace with all men so far as in him lies. Even wicked men wage war to maintain the peace of their own circle, and wish that, if possible, all men belonged to them, that all men and things might serve but one head, and might, either through love or fear, yield themselves to peace with him! It is thus that pride in its perversity apes God. It abhors equality with other men under Him; but, instead of His rule, it seeks to impose a rule of its own upon its equals. It abhors, that is to say, the just peace of God, and loves its own unjust peace; but it cannot help loving peace of one kind or other. For there is no vice so clean contrary to nature that it obliterates even the faintest traces of nature. . . .

Book XIX, Chap. XIII:

The peace of the body then consists in the duly proportioned arrangement of its parts. The peace of the irrational soul is the harmonious repose of the appetites, and that of the rational soul the harmony of knowledge and action. The peace of body and soul is the well-ordered and harmonious life and health of the living creature. Peace between man and God is the well-ordered obedience of faith to eternal law. Peace between man and man is well-ordered concord. Domestic peace is the well-ordered concord between those of the family who rule and those who obey. Civil peace is a similar concord among the citizens. The peace of the celestial city is the perfectly ordered and harmonious enjoyment of God, and of one another in God. The peace of all things is the tranquillity of order. Order is the distribution which allots things equal and unequal, each to its own place. . . . God has given to men . . . temporal peace . . . and whatever things are necessary to preserve and recover it . . . such as everything the body requires to sustain, shelter, heal, or beautify it : and all under this most equitable condition, that every man who made a good use of those advantages suited to the peace of this mortal condition, should receive ampler and better blessings, namely, the peace of immortality, accompanied by glory and honour in an endless life made fit for the enjoyment of God and of one another in God ; but that he who used the present blessings badly should both lose them and should not receive the others.

Book XIX, Chap. XIV :

. . . And because, so long as man is in this mortal body, he is a stranger to God, he walks by faith, not by sight ; and he therefore refers all peace, bodily or spiritual or both, to that peace which mortal man has with the immortal God, so that he exhibits the well-ordered obedience of faith to eternal law. But as this divine Master inculcates two precepts—the love of God and the love of our neighbour—and as in these precepts a man finds three things he has to love—God, himself and his neighbour—and that he who loves God loves himself thereby, it follows that he must endeavour to get his neighbour to love God, since he is ordered to love his neighbour as himself. He ought to make this endeavour on behalf of his wife, his children, his household, all within his reach, even as he would wish his neighbour to do the same for him if he needed it ; and consequently he will be at peace, or in well-ordered concord, with all men, as far as in him lies. And this is the order of this concord, that a man, in the first place, injure no one, and, in the second, do good to every one he can reach. Primarily, therefore, his own household are his care, for the law of nature and of society gives him readier access to them and greater opportunity of serving them. And hence the apostle says : 'Now, if any provide not for his own, and specially for those of his own house, he hath denied the faith, and is worse than an infidel. . . .' (I Timothy v : 8.)

ST. LEANDER OF SEVILLE. A.D. 589, *at the Third Council of Toledo.* (*Pat. Lat. LXXII :* 895) :

Holy Church of God, knowing how sweet is charity and how delectable is concord, thou preachest the alliance of the nations ; thou longest for the union of peoples. . . . The order of nature wills that all the nations, descended as they are from a single man, should be bound together by a mutual love.

ST. THOMAS AQUINAS. *Summa Contra Gentiles, Lib. III, Cap. CXXX :*

All the precepts and counsels of the Divine Law go to furnish man with aids for fixing his mind on God and removing obstacles to such attention.

For these purposes man needs to live at peace and concord with his fellow-men. For man needs to be aided by man, as well to the preservation of life and limb, as also to the end that one man may inflame and incite and instruct another to yearn after God. In the absence of peace and concord, man's mind must be disquieted by contentions and fightings, and hindered from aspiring to God. And therefore the Divine Law has made provision for the preservation of peace and concord amongst men by the practice of justice. It commands that to every man be rendered his due, as honour to parents ; that none be harmed or hindered in the enjoyment of the good that belongs to him whether by word—hence the prohibition of false witness—or by deed touching his person—hence the prohibition of murder—or by deed touching a person allied to him—hence the prohibition of adultery—or by deed touching his property—hence the prohibition of theft. And because God takes cognizance not only of the public, but also of the domestic behaviour of man, the Divine Law has forbidden neglect of wife, servants, etc., which is no concern of human law.

But it is not enough for peace and concord to be preserved among men by the precepts of justice, unless there be a further consolidation of mutual love. Justice provides for men to the extent that one shall not get in the way of another, but not to the extent of one helping another in his need. One may happen to need another's aid in cases in which none is bound to him by any debt of justice, or where the person so bound does not render any aid. Thus there came to be need for an additional precept of mutual love amongst men so that one should aid another even beyond the obligations of justice. Hence it is said 'This commandment we have received, that whoever loveth God should also love his brother.' (St. John iv : 21.) 'This is my commandment, that ye love one another as I have loved you.' (St. John xv : 12.)

It is evident that love suffices for the fulfilment of the work of justice. Hence it is said : 'Love is the fulfilment of the Law' (Romans xiii : 10) to command which fulfilment there are given us precepts and counsels of God concerning works of mercy, love and succour of enemies, and the like deeds of kindness, which overflow and run over the measures of justice.

The following great Encyclical, equally suitable for this or for either of the two preceding chapters, is here reproduced since in the midst of the passions bequeathed by a great war it sets forth the abiding principles of Christian Peace.

Benedict XV. Encyclical Letter of May 23, 1920. *Pacem Dei Munus Pulcherrimum.*

Peace, the beautiful gift of God, the name of which, as St. Augustine says, is the sweetest word to our hearing and the best and most desirable possession ;[1] peace, which was for more than four years implored by the ardent wishes of all good peoples by the prayers of pious souls and the tears of mothers, begins at last to shine upon the nations. At this We are indeed the happiest of all, and heartily do We rejoice. But this joy of Our paternal heart is disturbed by many bitter anxieties, for if in most places peace is in some sort established and treaties are signed, the germs of former enmities remain ; and you well know, Venerable Brethren, that there can be no stable peace or lasting treaties, though made after long and difficult negotiations and duly signed, unless there be a return of mutual charity to appease hate and banish enmity. This, then, Venerable Brethren, is the anxious and dangerous question upon which We wish to dwell and to put forward recommendations to be brought home to your people.

For Ourselves, never since, by the hidden designs of God, We were raised to this Chair have We ceased to do everything in Our power from the very beginning of the war that all the nations of the world might resume cordial relations as soon as possible. To that end We never ceased to pray, to repeat exhortations, to propose ways of arrangement, to try every means, in fact, to open by Divine aid a path to a just, honourable, and lasting peace ; and at the same time We exercised all Our paternal care to alleviate everywhere that terrible load of sorrow and disaster of every sort by which the immense tragedy was accompanied.

And now, just as from the beginning of Our troubled pontificate the charity of Jesus Christ led Us to work both for the return of peace and to alleviate the horrors of the war, so now that comparative peace has been concluded, this same charity urges Us to exhort all the children of the Church, and all mankind, to clear their hearts of bitterness, and give place to mutual love and concord.

There is no need from Us of long proof to show that society would incur the risk of great loss if, while peace is signed, latent hostility and enmity were to continue among the nations. There is no need to mention the loss of all that maintains and fosters civil life, such as commerce and industry, art and literature, which flourish only when the nations are at peace. But, what is even more important, grave harm would accrue to the form and essence of the Christian life, which consists essentially

[1] *De Civitate Dei*, lib. xix, cap. 11.

in charity and the preaching of which is called the Gospel of peace.[1]

You know well, and We have frequently reminded you of it, that nothing was so often and so carefully inculcated on His disciples by Jesus Christ as this precept of mutual charity as the one which contains all others. Christ called it the new commandment, His very own, and desired that it should be the sign of Christians by which they might be distinguished from all others; and on the eve of His death it was His last testament to His disciples to love one another and thus try to imitate the ineffable unity of the three Divine Persons in the Trinity. *That they may be one as we also are one . . . that they may be made perfect in one.*[2]

The Apostles, following in the steps of the Divine Master, and conforming to His word and commands, were unceasing in their exhortation to the faithful: *Before all things have a constant mutual charity among yourselves.*[3] *But above all these things have charity which is the bond of perfection.*[4] *Dearly beloved, let us love one another, for charity is of God.*[5] Our brethren of the first Christian ages faithfully observed these commands of Jesus Christ and the Apostles. They belonged to different and rival nations, yet they willingly forgot their causes of quarrel and lived in perfect concord, and such a union of hearts was in striking contrast with the deadly enmities by which human society was then consumed.

What has already been said in favour of charity holds good for the inculcation of the pardoning of injuries which is no less solemnly commanded by the Lord: *But I say to you, love your enemies; do good to them that hate you; pray for those that persecute and calumniate you, that you may be the children of your Father who is in Heaven, who maketh His sun to rise upon the good and bad.*[6] Hence that terribly severe warning of the Apostle St. John. *Whosoever hateth his brother is a murderer. And you know that no murderer hath eternal life abiding in himself.*[7]

Our Lord Jesus Christ, in teaching us how to pray to God, makes us say that we wish for pardon as we forgive others: *Forgive us our trespasses as we forgive them that trespass against us.*[8] And if the observance of this law is sometimes hard and difficult, we have not only the timely assistance of the grace of Our Divine Redeemer, but also His example to help us to overcome the difficulty. For as He hung on the Cross He thus excused before His Father those who so unjustly and wickedly tortured Him: *Father, forgive them, for they know not what they do.*[9] We, then, who should be the first to imitate the pity and loving-kindness of Jesus Christ, whose Vicar, without any merit of Our own, We are;

[1] Eph. vi, 15. [2] John xvii, 21–23. [3] 1 Peter iv, 8.
[4] Col. iii, 14. [5] 1 John iv, 7. [6] Matt. v, 44, 45.
[7] 1 John iii, 15. [8] Matt. vi, 12. [9] Luke xxiii, 34.

with all Our heart, and following His example, We forgive all Our enemies who knowingly or unknowingly have heaped and are still heaping on Our person and Our work every sort of vituperation, and We embrace all in Our charity and benevolence and neglect no opportunity to do them all the good in Our power. That is indeed what Christians worthy of the name ought to do towards those who during the war have done them wrong.

Christian charity ought not to be content with not hating our enemies and loving them as brothers ; it also demands that we treat them with kindness following the rule of the Divine Master who *went about doing good and healing all that were oppressed by the devil,*[1] and finished His mortal life, the course of which was marked by good deeds, by shedding His blood for them. So said St. John : *In this we have known the charity of God, because He hath laid down His life for us, and we ought to lay down our lives for the brethren. He that hath the substance of this world and shall see his brother in need and shall shut up his bowels from him : how doth the charity of God abide in him ? My little children, let us not love in word nor by tongue, but in deed and in truth.*[2]

Never indeed was there a time when we should 'stretch the bounds of charity' more than in these days of universal suffering and sorrow ; never perhaps as to-day has humanity so needed that universal beneficence which springs from the love of others, and is full of sacrifice and zeal. For if we look around where the fury of the war has been let loose we see immense regions utterly desolate, uncultivated and abandoned ; multitudes reduced to want of food, clothing and shelter ; innumerable widows and orphans reft of everything, and an incredible number of enfeebled beings, particularly children and young people, who carry on their bodies the ravages of this atrocious war.

When one regards all these miseries by which the human race is stricken one inevitably thinks of the traveller in the Gospel[3] who, going down from Jerusalem to Jericho, fell among thieves, who robbed him, and covered him with wounds and left him half dead. The two cases are very similar ; and as to the traveller there came the good Samaritan, full of compassion, who bound up his wounds, pouring in oil and wine, took him to an inn, and undertook all care for him, so too is it necessary that Jesus, of whom the Samaritan was the figure, should lay His hands upon the wounds of society.

This work, this duty the Church claims as her own as heir and guardian of the spirit of Jesus Christ—the Church whose entire existence is a marvellously varied tissue of all kinds of good deeds, the Church, 'that real mother of Christians in the full sense of the word, who has such tenderness of love and

[1] Acts x, 38. [2] 1 John iii, 16–18. [3] Luke x, 30 *et seq.*

charity for her neighbour that she can offer the best remedies for the different evils which afflict souls on account of their sins.' That is why she 'treats and teaches children with tenderness, young people with firmness, old people with great calm taking account not only of the age but also the condition of soul of each.'[1] It would be difficult to exaggerate the effect of this many-sided Christian beneficence in softening the heart and thus facilitating the return of tranquillity to the nations.

Therefore, Venerable Brethren, We pray you and exhort you in the mercy and charity of Jesus Christ, strive with all zeal and diligence not only to urge the faithful entrusted to your care to abandon hatred and to pardon offences ; but—and what is more immediately practical—to promote all those works of Christian benevolence which bring aid to the needy comfort to the afflicted, and protection to the weak, and to give opportune and appropriate assistance of every kind to all who have suffered from the war. It is Our especial wish that you should exhort your priests, as the ministers of peace, to be assiduous in urging this love of one's neighbour and even of enemies which is the essence of the Christian life and by *being all things to all men*[2] and giving an example to others, wage war everywhere on enmity and hatred, thus doing a thing most agreeable to the loving Heart of Jesus and to him who, however unworthy, holds His place on earth. In this connection Catholic writers and journalists should be invited to clothe themselves *as elect of God, holy and beloved, with pity and kindness.*[3] Let them show this charity in their writings by abstaining not only from false and groundless accusations, but also from all intemperance and bitterness of language, all of which is contrary to the law of Christ and does but reopen sores as yet unhealed, seeing that the slightest touch is a serious irritant to a heart whose wounds are recent.

All that We have said here to individuals about the duty of charity We wish to say also to the peoples who have been delivered from the burden of a long war, in order that, when every cause of disagreement has been, as far as possible, removed, and without prejudice to the rights of justice, they may resume friendly relations among themselves. The Gospel has not one law of charity for individuals and another for States and nations, which are indeed but collections of individuals. The war being now over, people seem called to a general reconciliation not only from motives of charity, but from necessity ; the nations are naturally drawn together by the need they have of one another, and by the bond of mutual goodwill, bonds which are to-day strengthened by the development of civilization and the marvellous increase of communication.

[1] Augustine, *De moribus Ecc. Cat.* lib. i., cap. 30.
[2] 1 Cor. ix, 22. [3] Col. iii, 12.

Truly, as We have already said, this Apostolic See has never wearied of teaching during the war such pardon of offences and the fraternal reconciliation of the peoples, in conformity with the most holy law of Jesus Christ, and in agreement with the needs of civil life and human intercourse ; nor did it allow that amid dissension and hate these moral principles should be forgotten. With all the more reason then, now that the Treaties of Peace are signed, does it proclaim these principles as, for example, it did a short time ago in the Letter to the Bishops of Germany,[1] and in that addressed to the Archbishop of Paris.[2]

And this concord between civilized nations is maintained and fostered by the modern custom of visits and meetings at which the heads of States and princes are accustomed to treat of matters of special importance. So then, considering the changed circumstances of the times and the dangerous trend of events, and in order to encourage this concord, We would not be unwilling to relax in some measure the severity of the conditions justly laid down by Our predecessors, when the civil power of the Apostolic See was overthrown, against the official visits of the heads of Catholic States to Rome. But at the same time We formally declare that this concession, which seems counselled or rather demanded by the grave circumstances in which to-day society is placed, must not be interpreted as a tacit renunciation of its sacrosanct rights by the Apostolic See, as if it acquiesced in the unlawful situation in which it is placed. Rather do we seize this opportunity to renew for the same reasons the protests which Our predecessors have several times made, not in the least moved thereto by human interests, but in fulfilment of the sacred duty of their charge to defend the rights and dignity of this Apostolic See ; once again demanding, and with even greater insistence now that peace is made among the nations that 'for the Head of the Church, too, an end may be put to that abnormal condition which in so many ways does such serious harm to tranquillity among the peoples.'[3]

Things being thus restored, the order required by justice and charity re-established and the nations reconciled, it is much to be desired, Venerable Brethren, that all States, putting aside mutual suspicion, should unite in one league, or rather a sort of family of peoples, calculated both to maintain their own independence and safeguard the order of human society. What specially, amongst other reasons, calls for such an association of nations, is the need generally recognized of making every effort to abolish or reduce the enormous burden of the military

[1] Litterae Apost. *Diuturni*, July 15, 1919.
[2] Epist. *Amor Ille Singularis*, Oct. 7, 1919.
[3] Litt. Enc. *Ad Beatissimi*, Nov. 1, 1914.

expenditure which States can no longer bear, in order to prevent these disastrous wars or at least to remove the danger of them as far as possible. So would each nation be assured not only of its independence but also of the integrity of its territory within its just frontiers.

The Church will certainly not refuse her zealous aid to States united under the Christian law in any of their undertakings inspired by justice and charity, inasmuch as she is herself the most perfect type of universal society. She possesses in her organization and institutions a wonderful instrument for bringing this brotherhood among men, not only for their eternal salvation but also for their material well-being in this world ; she leads them through temporal well-being to the sure acquisition of eternal blessings. It is the teaching of history that when the Church pervaded with her spirit the ancient and barbarous nations of Europe, little by little the many and varied differences that divided them were diminished and their quarrels extinguished ; in time they formed a homogeneous society from which sprang Christian Europe which, under the guidance and auspices of the Church, whilst preserving a diversity of nations, tended to a unity that favoured its prosperity and glory. On this point St. Augustine well says : 'This celestial city, in its life here on earth, calls to itself citizens of every nation, and forms out of all the peoples one varied society ; it is not harassed by differences in customs, laws and institutions, which serve to the attainment or the maintenance of peace on earth ; it neither rends nor destroys anything but rather guards all and adapts itself to all ; however these things may vary among the nations, they are all directed to the same end of peace on earth as long as they do not hinder the exercise of religion, which teaches the worship of the true supreme God.'[1] And the same holy Doctor thus addresses the Church : 'Citizens, peoples, and all men, thou, recalling their common origin, shalt not only unite among themselves, but shalt make them brothers.'[2]

To come back to what We said at the beginning, We turn affectionately to all Our children and conjure them in the name of Our Lord Jesus Christ to forget mutual differences and offences and draw together in the bonds of Christian charity, from which none are excluded and within which none are strangers. We fervently exhort all the nations, under the inspiration of Christian benevolence, to establish a true peace among themselves and join together in an alliance which shall be just and therefore lasting. And lastly We appeal to all men and all peoples to join in mind and heart with the Catholic Church and through the Church with Christ the Redeemer of the human race, so that We may address to them in very truth the words of

[1] *De Civitate Dei*, lib. xix, cap. 17.
[2] *De moribus Ecc. Cat.* lib. i, cap. 30.

St. Paul to the Ephesians : 'But now in Christ Jesus you who sometime were afar off, are made nigh by the blood of Christ. For He is our peace, who hath made both one, and breaking down the middle wall of partition . . . killing the enmities in himself. And coming he preached peace to you that were afar off and peace to them that were nigh.'[1]

Nor less appropriate are the words which the same Apostle addressed to the Colossians : *Lie not one to another : stripping yourselves of the old man with his deeds. And putting on the new, him who is renewed unto knowledge according to the image of Him that created him. Where there is neither Gentile nor Jew, circumcision nor uncircumcision, Barbarian nor Scythian, bond nor free. But Christ is all and in all.*[2]

Meanwhile, trusting in the protection of Mary the Virgin Immaculate, who not long ago We directed should be universally invoked as 'Queen of Peace,' as also in the intercession of the three Blessed to whom We have decreed the honour of Saints, We humbly implore the Holy Ghost, the Paraclete, that He may 'graciously grant to the Church the gifts of unity and peace,'[3] and may renew the face of the earth by a fresh outpouring of His charity for the salvation of all. As an earnest of these heavenly gifts and as a pledge of Our paternal benevolence, We impart with all Our heart to you, Venerable Brethren, to all your clergy and people, the Apostolic Benediction.

Pius XI. *Allocution upon Peace among the Nations ; Christmas Eve*, 1930 :

And now, Venerable Brethren and well-beloved Sons, the wish which We address to you is put into our heart and placed upon our lips by the solemn and most sweet Feast which, anew, We prepare Ourselves to celebrate : *In terra pax.*

It is the wish that came down from Heaven, and was first sung by the Angels over the Cradle of the Immortal King of Ages, Who came to make peace between men and God and among men, sacrificing Himself for all, recalling to the minds of all the universal Fatherhood of God, and the universal Fraternity of men, recalling also to them the idea and practice of brotherly charity, the duty of seeking, first of all and chiefly, spiritual treasures and detachment from the good things of this world.

What wish could be more opportune and respond better to that universal cry : 'Peace, peace !' And it is precisely because of this that Our wish is not addressed solely to you, but to the whole world.

To the whole world, because Jesus came to save the whole world. But We address this wish, in a special way, to all the

[1] Eph. ii, 13 *et seq.* [2] Col. iii, 9–11.
[3] Secreta in Solemn. Corpus Christi.

well-beloved sons of the great Catholic Family, of the Church which Jesus came to found. We are concerned with the peace brought by Christ, the peace of Christ; and one is not with Christ, one does not belong to Christ, unless one is in the Catholic Church and with the Catholic Church: '*Ubi Ecclesia, ibi Christus.*' This is why Catholics are not only called to enjoy more largely and more perfectly the peace of Christ, but, just as they are called to consolidate and extend the reign of Christ, so also are they called to extend and consolidate His peace; and that by means of the multiple apostolate of the good word, of beneficent activity, and, finally, of prayer, so easy for all and so powerful—all powerful even before God.

The glory and the duty of this apostolate of peace belongs principally to Us and to all those who are called to be the Ministers of the God of peace; but here is also a vast and magnificent field of action for the whole of the Catholic laity whom We do not cease to invite and to summon to participate in this Apostolate of the hierarchy.

It is to the Catholics of the entire world, and above all to those who study, work and pray in the Catholic Action that We address to-day, in the warmest manner, this invitation and appeal. Let them all unite together in a full accord of thoughts, sentiments, desires, prayers and word—the spoken word, the written word, the printed word—and there will be created a beneficent atmosphere of peace which will envelope the entire world.

But this must be the 'Peace of Christ' and not a sentimental pacifism, confused and without discernment, because the true peace is that which comes from God, and possesses the essential and indispensable characteristics of true peace.

The Church, that incomparable mistress, recalled this to Us a few days ago, in making Us read again in the Holy Offering of the Divine Sacrifice the beautiful and profound words of the Apostle of the Gentiles (Philippians iv. 7): '*Pax Dei quæ exsuperat omnem sensum costodiat corda vestra et intelligentias vestras in Christo Jesu Domino Nostro.*'

It surpasses all sentiment, the Peace of Christ, the true Peace; and it is a grave error to believe that a real and durable peace can reign between men and nations as long as they, first of all, before all and with the greatest avidity, give their attention to acquiring for themselves, sensible, material and worldly goods, which, being limited, can with difficulty suffice for all, even if no one (a thing hard to find) wished to acquire for himself the lion's share. The greater the number of those who participate therein, the smaller is the share of each—consequently, these goods are almost inevitably sources of cupidities and jealousies, and, at the same time, of disorders and conflicts. The contrary is the case with regard to spiritual treasures—truth, goodness, virtue—which abound and fructify so much the more to the profit of individuals and of the community, as they are the more largely shared.

Another error against which the apostolic word, Divinely inspired, would warn us is that into which those fall who believe that a true exterior peace may exist amongst men and amongst peoples where no interior peace exists—that is to say where the spirit of peace does not possess intelligences and hearts, in other words, the whole of men's souls ; intelligences, so that the reasons of justice may be recognized and respected ; hearts, so that with justice may be associated charity, and that the latter may prevail even over justice. For if peace, according to the Prophet ought to be the work and fruit of justice (Isaias xxxii. 17), it belongs rather to charity than to justice, as we are taught luminously by St. Thomas (IIa, IIac, Q. xxix, 3, ad 3), and as is also in conformity with the nature of things. . . .

. . . It is difficult, not to say impossible, for peace to last between peoples and States if, instead of pure patriotism, there reigns and rages selfishness and a crude nationalism, that is to say, hatred and envy instead of the mutual desire for good ; distrust and suspicion instead of brotherly confidence ; competition and strife instead of good understanding and co-operation ; ambition for domination and preponderance instead of the respect and protection of all rights, even those of the feeble and insignificant.

Besides, it is absolutely impossible for peoples to possess and enjoy that tranquillity in order and liberty, which is the very essence of peace, so long as from without arise menaces and perils which have not been warded off by sufficient measures and precautions of defence. And certainly menaces and perils are inseparable from the anti-social and anti-religious propaganda to which allusion has already been made ; but it is not by means of material defences alone that these can be driven away and vanquished. As to the menaces of fresh wars while the nations are still suffering so cruelly from the scourge of the last frightful war, We would not, We cannot believe that there now exists a civilized State which would wish to become so monstrously homicidal, and almost certainly suicidal, at the same time. Even if we should entertain but a bare positive doubt of the existence of such a State, We ought to turn towards God, addressing to Him the inspired prayer of the Prophet-King, who, nevertheless, knew well both war and victory : '*Dissipa gentes quæ bella volunt*' (Psalm lxvii. 31), and also the prayer of the Church : '*Dona nobis pacem.*'

Pope Pius XI has on several occasions recurred to the same theme, notably in his Allocution at the Consistory on April 1, 1935, when he declared that for any State to plunge the world into a new war would be 'a heinous crime.'

PART IV

THE SOCIETY OF NATIONS

CHAPTER X

THE NATURAL SOCIETY OF NATIONS

'IT is nature itself, that eloquent interpreter of the Divine Will, which calls all peoples to form among themselves one universal association and at the same time makes it their duty to do so.' Thus does Taparelli d'Azeglio express the logical conclusion of a process of reasoning which his predecessors in Christian philosophy had advanced. If man is essentially sociable,[1] and if history proves the smaller society, from household to State, to have need of the greater, is there any reason to suppose that the process of social organization must end at the State?

That the sovereign State should be the term of man's social need and obligation is a notion alien to Catholic Christianity. Unity of Faith and Morals carries with it the note of universality. This alone has been enough to establish ineradicably the idea that the human race is a single family. For if the obligations to keep faith; not to steal; not to kill; not to covet; to be charitable; to forgive; to bear one another's burdens—and, all the other duties contained or implied in the Decalogue and in the Sermon on the Mount—apply equally to all men, in every place and without distinction of race, what is that but to say that there exists a real moral unity between them? And if, taught by Divine instruction, all men are bidden to worship one God, and to address Him as 'Our Father,' does not this show that they are brothers, naturally brothers by Creation, supernaturally brothers by the Redemption of Christ 'whereby we cry Abba, Father'? This essential unity and solidarity of the human race was assumed by Christian philosophy as the basis of its social ethics.

[1] Leo XIII. Encyclical *Diuturnum illud.*

This leads not yet to the conclusion that a single natural society must exist between political societies. It does, however, establish an absolute fact which all sociology must respect ; a foundation which the political superstructure of the world must presuppose and may neither ignore nor destroy, namely, that all men are brothers. Any forms of political organization which impede or frustrate the natural expression and practice of this fraternity are contrary to reason and to the right end of man. Any affection for a part of the human race which turns to hostility toward the other parts and to the disadvantage of the whole, is repugnant to the Church as guardian alike of reason and of Christian charity. 'Those who fall into this excess (of Nationalism) surely forget that all the peoples, as members of the universal human family, are bound to one another by the ties of brotherhood.'[1] However human beings may be grouped and however divided—and 'nations' or 'peoples' are unquestionably factors of association and differentiation—the various groups and divisions acquire, from human nature itself, the quality of membership in a single family. The unity of law and political organization in the Roman Empire, inherited and Christianized by the Church, at once expressed and reinforced the conception of a single underlying fraternity.

Two historical developments temporally confused the doctrine of universal human brotherhood and its logical implications. The first was the long series of wars between Christendom and the infidel ; the second the revolt of national princes against the Empire. So long as the *respublica christiana* was on its defence against external enemies, and in particular against the military menace of Islam—so long did it appear more as a beleagured city than as a supernational society, presupposing and making actual within itself the potential unity and fraternity of the whole human race. And, if on the one hand we owe to this period a considerable advance both in the theory and practice ot peace-making within the circle of Christian civilization, we trace to it, on the other, a certain over-emphasis, in proportion to other social doctrines, upon the justification of war.

[1] Pius XI. *Ubi Arcano Dei.*

When Christian theologians seriously discuss whether the women and children of the Moors may justly be massacred by Christians and whether all who are not Christians may justly be deprived of dominion, of property and of personal liberty, it must be admitted that Christian sociology has reached a low ebb. It is to the honour of the best schoolmen that they revolted against this degradation of Christianity to the level of Mohammedanism. It needed a Papal declaration[1] to remind the Christian world that the Indians of the New World were not 'beasts of the field' but 'true men, capable of the Faith.'

The second historical development, which for a time slackened the pace of Christian thought in evolving a theory of world wide society, was the series of revolts against the authority of the Holy Roman Empire. The Capitulary of Aachen (860), assigned to each grade from the highest to the lowest its proper place and its peculiar rights ; the functions of all lesser authorities were defined in relation to the Imperial authority and to one another ; the protection of the weak was assured by the Emperor. It was a magnificent conception ; the sysiphian recurrence of European peoples to the ideal of political unity is itself a tribute to it. The Church, that had blessed and acknowledged the grand design of Charles the Great, intermittently in later centuries strengthened with her spiritual sanctions the Imperial claim to obedience from all other rulers. But the divisions of the Empire ; the contentions for the Imperial crown ; the long struggle upon investiture between Papacy and Empire ; the actual ineffectiveness of the Empire as a means of maintaining political unity, particularly between the princes of Italy and those of Western Europe—these were but a few of the events which first divided Christian thought on the subject of the Imperial mandate, and eventually dissociated the Papacy from the conception of the Christian Empire as the one means of realizing the desired political union of peoples. If then it was not wrong for princes, more and more supported by national sentiment in succeeding centuries, to disregard the Imperial jurisdiction, except for the formalities of succession, it was natural that Catholic theologians,

[1] Paul III. Bull. *Sublimis Deus sic dilexit of June* 17, 1537.

knowing the Church to be the slave of no political forms should attempt to rationalize that position. It was inevitable that they should seek to evolve from Natural Law, in the light of Christian tradition, the true character, scope, jurisdiction, rights and duties of the kingly power, and of the independent State whose welfare justified the exercise of that power. The very fact of reaction against the Imperial authority implied a rejection for the time being of international political unity identified with the Empire, and an exaggerated assertion of the political independence of the State. Hence the more or less considerable concessions to national sovereignty made by the neo-scholastic school, and the definition of the State as a 'perfect community.' This expression often stretched to cover more than, say Vittoria intended, or even taken out of its proper setting, has been abused without measure. It is not too much to say that Catholic sociology in so far as it treats of international relations was for three centuries characterized by a struggle between this notion of the State as a self-sufficient and independent unit and that other doctrine of a law and society of all nations implicit in thomistic philosophy and excogitated in the famous passage of Suarez quoted in this chapter. It remained for Taparelli to construct a synthesis in which both the political independence of each people and the natural disposition of all for association found their place.

In what sense can a State be said to be a perfect community? Not economically, for hardly any State has ever been wholly self-supporting, the interdependence of kingdoms and republics described by Suarez has rapidly increased with mechanical inventions and the growth of population. Nor morally; since on the one hand States are under an obligation, even if international tribunals did not exist, to refer disputes between them to some third power or to the Holy See for arbitration; on the other, they are bound by the *Jus Gentium*, part of which can be made or changed only by the agreement of the majority or of the 'best constituted States.'[1] Further, the 'law of Nations' itself requires as a general rule[2] freedom of trade and travel for men of all

[1] Suarez. *De Legibus.* [2] Vittoria. *De Indis.*

nations, a fact which destroys the notion of national self-sufficiency. Only in the sense that the State is not politically subject to any other State and that it provides a supreme court with appropriate sanctions for the final judgement of all causes between citizens and communities within it, without appeal to a higher tribunal, can it be said that the State is a 'perfect Community.' That is all that reason and Christian tradition can concede as a description of sovereignty. Even in the legislative and judicial spheres the theory and practice of international law have in the modern era made serious inroads into this 'perfection.' We shall see Catholic publicists of authority maintaining that it is the duty of the international community to protect the racial, linguistic and religious rights of minorities within the State, a duty which will be seen to involve—and has in fact involved—a whole series of restrictions upon the action both of the State's legislature and judicature, and eventual intervention between the State and its subjects. This is no doubt but an application of the main doctrine of 'intervention' upon grounds of justice or charity, the denial of which was condemned by Pius IX. Again the international protection of labour, powerfully supported from the first by the authority of the Church, has led through International Labour Conventions, which are already a matter of history, to the representation of organized labour and employers upon international conferences which frame the rules to which, when ratified, the acts of national parliaments, Courts and administrations must conform. This creates situations in which the treatment by a State of its own subjects can be a matter for reference to an international Court. A third instance is the practice—equally approved by Catholic economists—of extending international arbitration to cover conflicts both public and private arising out of commercial treaties and contracts.

We are indeed anticipating when we envisage the State of the present day in the condition of incipient international organization which is described elsewhere in these pages. But it must be made clear, even in abstract theory, that the expression 'perfect community' as applied to the State tells less than half the story. Restricted purely to the legal sphere and the maintenance of public order, it has still to be qualified at least by the saving phrase wherewith the Parliament of Henry VIII sought to take the sting of heresy out of the Royal Supremacy of the Church—' so far as the laws of Christ permit' ; which we must, in the present context, amplify thus ' so long as the action of the State violates neither the moral law nor the law of charity, nor the law of nations embodied in international conventions, nor the rights of the Church.' For a grave violation of any one of these canons would justify (though it might not in particular circumstances be expedient or practicable) intervention by the remaining members of the community of nations, and eventually the ' cassation ' of a State's judgement by a higher tribunal. The confrontation of the political fact of sovereignty with the scholastic ethics, if it temporally impeded the full development of a science of international society, eventually made that development inevitable, by the need of dissolving the contradictions between the doctrine of the brotherhood of all men and the concessions made to the pretensions of the State.

If there is in fact a single family of the human race ; if all human associations in their mutual dealings must give expression to this fraternity ; if the political societies, which we have so far called States, in fact exhibit in a marked degree a certain physical and moral interdependence ; is an association of States the right and necessary requirement of nature ? Are States the only component parts of the natural society of mankind when the stage of organizing that society begins, or to use a modern phrase ' the only factors of international life ? ' We need in answering these questions to clarify the meaning of the terms State, Nation, Law of Nations, International Law, which until now have been used without definition.

We have said that there is but one absolute in sociology. It is the relation of brotherhood existing among men, arising from the unity of their nature and the Fatherhood of God ' of Whom all paternity in Heaven and Earth is named.'[1] But man's knowledge and the scope of his activity are limited, and his temporal needs are finite. Hence the

[1] Ephesians iii : 15.

necessity, as the natural outcome of human sociability, for differentiated societies limited in extent. But the spiritual in man partakes of the infinite. It is the property of his mind to form universal concepts. Hence the spiritual and intellectual associations of which he stands in need are not local but universal : the Catholic Church claims to provide the universal spiritual association ; learning, science and art can likewise know no material frontiers. Hence comes the right to supranational affiliations of a spiritual and intellectual order, which the divisions based upon the temporal and local needs of men must respect, equally with their natural kinship.

Yet man has not two distinct principles—body and mind—for each of which separate legislation can provide : the two are so closely interwoven that separation brings death. And, as in the individual the material subserves the spiritual, so in the ordering of society, the limited associations, family or tribe, village or commune, canton or principality, State or Empire, formed primarily to promote man's temporal well-being, should also minister to his spiritual good which is his final end.

The family is the primordial society of which each man is by birth a member, without which he can neither conserve himself in being nor develop according to his nature. To it belongs the right of property, handed down from generation to generation, that the parents may supply the physical needs of themselves and of their children. It is also nature's school. For to parents pertains the duty and the right of educating their children.

There have been times and there are parts of the world in which patriarchal society suffices to the actual social necessities of man. Normally, however, the family needs both negatively, for protection against the disorders proper to fallen nature, and positively, to assist its material and spiritual development, a larger association, designed to promote sustained co-operation with other families. The societies which are most germane to the family, and therefore to nature, are those which do not exceed the bounds of physical contact and human experience ; in which the authority either of chieftain or of elected body is still clearly related to the heads of families, and in which customs, language and culture are homogeneous : such is the village or commune which is the natural basis of the Christian parish. There are instances in which such an association, having become a town with well established authority and laws for its internal order, is a perfect political community. Conflicts between its citizens are decided by a final court : its authority is subject to no overlord. It is no less ' sovereign ' than the most extensive State.

But again it is normal for villages and towns to need, both for the exchange of their products and for protection against tyrants and marauders, a wider political union, whether provided by free association or by the acknowledgement of a territorial lordship. The canton, county, marquisate, arrondissement, department or province—however ethnic origin, custom, the relics of Roman provincial organization or the feudal system may have crystallized the group—responds to the third stage of political development : it forms the natural basis and temporal coefficient of the Christian diocese. And it merits attention that the diocese is still—perhaps more than ever—the formative unit of ecclesiastical organization in the Universal Church. The Bishop is for all practical purposes Monarch of his Church ; his jurisdiction is received directly from the supranational centre of ecclesiastical government ; metropolitan or primatial rights or national conferences of the hierarchy affect but little the Bishop's immediate relationship to the Pope. This is not the place to explain the importance attached by the Church in all political organization to the integrity of the diocese and the protests of the Holy See against conquests, territorial changes or peace treaties which violate that integrity, generally consecrated as it is, at least in Europe, by centuries of tradition. We draw attention to the fact, however, since the diocese could hardly play so vital a part in the organization of man's spiritual life did it not respond to a grouping of no mean importance in the natural order, a grouping which on the one hand has the characteristic of limitation within an area which can reasonably be subject to the personal rule of a single overseer (Antistes) and, on the other, the characteristic of containing a considerable number of lesser groupings of families. Again history is not lacking in instances of such a community becoming and remaining for centuries politically independent.[1]

There are, however, many reasons which have brought groups of these political communities, each confined to a limited area of territory either to create or to acknowledge a supreme authority. Whether it be the consequence (as in the case of Switzerland or the United States) of a deliberate process of federation ; or the result of great tribal movements ; or of military conquest ; or of the emancipation of provinces or Colonies or of the growth of communications and of commerce, or a combination of any of these several processes, the effect is the same. It is the establishment, by the choice, active (election) or tacit (consent) of political societies, of an authority competent to regulate their mutual relations by laws ; to administer those laws for the common welfare ; to maintain over the whole area the order and tranquillity needed for the production and distribution of goods : to defend the whole association of societies against external aggression ; and to act on their behalf in all the relations with other such federations or unions of societies which the obligations of human sociability and fraternity require.

Such is the type of the State most familiar to the modern world. It can only be defined in Christian political science by relation to the natural solidarity of the human race ; the Church, of which it is the temporal coefficient ; the hierarchy of lesser societies[2] whose assistance and protection is its immediate *raison d'être*.

Is then the State no more than a rung in the ladder which leads from the household to the society of nations ? It is more. Just as the family is of greater importance than the second and third stages of political society, which may be further multiplied or dispensed with according to historical, geographical and economic circumstances, so is the State or perfect political community more important than them.

[1] The Grand Duchy and Diocese of Luxembourg for example.

[2] *Quadragesimo Anno*. Part II. Section 5. (English translation.)

There can be no State without families, the quintessential unit of civil society ; there can be no organic world society without component units. And those units must normally be societies, which are not subject to one another and which can speak each as a single moral person on behalf of the families, villages, towns and other communities of all sorts that compose it. States do not themselves constitute the underlying natural society of the human race : rather are they the spokesmen of that society, competent to express its temporal needs and by common counsel and co-operation to supply them.

Order is the first need of that society : it is the primary political benefit which permits the many and varied cultural, spiritual, intellectual or professional associations which respond to the natural needs of humanity, to develop freely both within and across the boundaries of States. How that order is to be preserved, defended and vindicated by the States in concert has been shown in the sections of this work devoted to war and peace. We have also seen how, should force be necessary to repress disorder in the international community, the rulers of States have the right to require and their subjects to give willing service even to the sacrifice of life itself in so just a cause. The main political object of the associated States, as of civil society itself, should, however, be to prevent a situation which requires the use of armed force.

But we should be wrong in restricting the mission of the State to the repression of disorder either among its own constituent elements or in the world society of which it is itself a part. To Christian sociology the State has a noble and constructive function :

> In short the end of the State is order, security and assistance to private initiatives. These few words set the measure of its task and its duties and determine the extent of its rights. Created to serve the human person and the collectivities which collaborate to promote the material and moral welfare of individual men and women, the State is thus established as the guardian and defender of human values in every sphere.[1]

[1] R. P. Delos, O.P., on *Le Problème des Minorités Nationales* in *Les Grandes Activités de la S. de N. devant la Pensée Chrétienne*, p. 135.

This duty it fulfils by wise laws and the encouragement of all healthy activities within its own borders, not unmindful of the spiritual good of its citizens which, indirectly, it exists to serve. It fulfils it likewise by co-operation with other States in order to remove by common action the obstacles to a higher standard of life, better conditions of labour and of health, international commerce and communication, and in short to promote the *bonum commune* of mankind. The same author writes in another place of this duty of international co-operation.

> The common good constitutes, in the inter-state society, a principle of order and of obligation. The obligations of the states to international society are first moral obligations, binding the consciences of peoples and of governments. They must conform to the exigencies of the common international good, first because it is the condition necessary for the accomplishment of their own natural ideal, and, secondly because, being the good of all, it takes priority over the good of the individual, and may subordinate the latter to itself. The States must therefore not only abstain from anything that might compromise the common good, but must work positively to promote it, in the measure that the stage of civilization and of historical evolution, by increasing the degree of interdependence, have made mutual aid necessary.[1]

Such then is the true conception of the natural society of peoples and of the State in relation to that society and to the social needs of men. The actual forms which an association of States should or might take in order to fulfil the various duties incumbent upon them in the international sphere will be studied in the next chapter.

The term Peoples is not synonymous with States, though it is frequently used, in Papal utterances for instance, to designate them in terms of their subjects rather than in terms of their rulers. But there may be and are peoples that are not States. It will also be observed that throughout our study of the political order of human society we have avoided the use of the word 'nation.' The last part of this book is devoted to the subject of the nation and its rights. But here we may say that State has no necessary or logical connection with Nation. The State may contain citizens

[1] R. P. Delos, O.P., in *La Société Internationale* (International Relations from a Catholic Standpoint, p. 49).

of a single or predominant nationality ; or it may contain part of a nation ; or several nations or parts of several nations. Nation implies a people united by ties and traditions that come by birth. Inherited character, customs and language, constituting so coherent and powerful a culture that they can not only be passed from generation to generation but can attract and assimilate other families and individuals—such are the dominant notes of the nation. Nationality, as will later be shown, is eminently a unifying force of the cultural order : it provides the conditions most favourable to the education, growth and natural development of the human person. It has a great mission to fulfil. The nation, however, has been abstracted from the other forms of human association and affiliation, emphasized, idolized even to the point of insanity in the last brief century. But the sorry results of an attempt to apply national 'self-determination' have provided a *reductio ad absurdum* of the doctrine that Nation and State must be coterminous. States, as factors of international life and subjects of international law, are nothing more than those political societies which at a given stage of history are without political superiors and able to provide for their members a supreme judicature. They may be small or large ; they may range from the Free City, the Principality or the unconquered Tribe to a great Federal Republic or Empire. Each is the consequence of different historical circumstances—dynastic inheritance or compromise ; union of smaller units ; wars or rebellions ; discovery or treaty. Unless the *de facto* government of any one of them is flagrantly unjust or incompetent there is no moral ground for subverting it, simply because the area subject to its rule does not happen to contain people of one nationality only. Supposing it to be lawfully constituted, to have fulfilled the essential functions of government and to have enjoyed for some time at least the tacit consent of the individuals and communities governed by it, it has a right to obedience and loyalty from its citizens, and to participation as a constituent element in the society of States. It serves its purpose which, though a high purpose, is, as we have seen, a limited one. Its work of maintaining political order need not interfere with the cultural life of the national groups within its borders, with the life of the Church, or with other non-political associations. On the contrary, they benefit from its protective action and should be greatly assisted by it.

This elucidation was necessary to arrive at a clear understanding of the terms Law of Nations and International Law. 'Law of Nations' is used in the title of the present work since, despite the many shades of meaning through which that phrase has passed, it serves better than any other English term to indicate at once the natural and moral basis of the rules obtaining between peoples and the positive forms given to those rules. It would, however, be inaccurate to translate '*Jus Gentium*' in St. Thomas as 'International Law' in the modern sense of Inter-State Law.

Almost as misleading—though for paucity of language we are constrained to the term—is it to translate '*Jus Gentium*' as 'Law of Nations' in the sense of the modern nation. Rather should we paraphrase it 'the body of rights belonging to all peoples, whatever the accidents of their birth, which should be respected in their mutual relations'—such as the right to conserve themselves in being; to develop according to their nature; to hold property; to bequeath it; to trade; to travel freely. To which we might add the right to speak their maternal language: to follow their own domestic and religious customs—so they be not contrary to natural law—to choose or obey their own local authorities. It is in part to protect these rights that, first, civil society, then international society is formed. The '*Jus Gentium*' is in a sense the end to which international law is the means. For the object of conventions between States is (directly or indirectly) to promote the welfare of the families that compose them; and this welfare comprises the free exercise of all the rights contained in the '*Jus Gentium*' as well as those arising from the Law of Nature itself. Such parts of the traditional '*Jus Gentium*' as plainly concern public relations between States—as for instance the immunity of ambassadors[1]—Suarez rightly divides from the rest: they pertain to international law in the modern sense. They can only be changed by agreement between States.

[1] *De Legibus.*

Vittoria,[1] indeed, uses the term '*Jus Gentium*' in both senses, inclining rather to the meaning of International Law: for in one place he paraphrases it '*quod naturalis ratio inter omnes gentes constituit*'—'what natural reason requires to be observed amongst all peoples'—instead of the '*inter omnes homines*' of the Institutes of Justinian. International or Inter-State law is divided into Natural and Positive, the Natural containing the requirement of the moral law itself and especially the obligation to keep faith, together with the unwritten code of mutual rights and duties, many of which we have already described, arising between States from the Natural Law; the Positive consisting of the actual Treaties and Conventions concluded between them which, if they are to endure, must be based upon Natural Law. The former may all be deduced from the character and functions of the State and of the natural society of the States, as we have described them.

We conclude.[2] In virtue of the functions which they fulfil for the benefit of men, united as they are throughout the world by ties of brotherhood, the independent political societies which we call States have need of mutual help and are in fact, by a requirement of nature itself, members of a single society. It is right that they should seek to give a positive juridical form to this society, as between any two or more of them who are actually in frequent contact with one another and eventually as between all the States of the world. The fact that the units of a society must be 'persons' able each to act and speak as one, to make and keep promises, means that no one member must be subject to another nor yet incapable of ensuring obedience to its authority within its own territory. That is to say, independent States are the constituent elements of positive international society: they are normally the only social factors of international life,

[1] Apud Vanderpol. *La doctrine scholastique du droit de guerre.*

[2] Our conclusions take into account the development of Catholic thought up to the present day. For a summary of neo-scholastic doctrine at the beginning of the modern age, that is the latter part of the sixteenth century, the reader is particularly referred to the extracts from Vittoria and Suarez which James Brown Scott has grouped together in the *Conclusions* of his *Catholic Conception of International Law*, pp. 481–494.

or, according to the modern expression, the only 'international persons.' Yet there is nothing absolute or sacrosanct about the State or the inter-State régime which corresponds to the requirements of the present age. 'Maybe the national State itself is only a passing phase of the political organization of humanity.'[1] Once the institutions of the international or rather world-society are firmly established, there is nothing to prevent certain important groups, spiritual, national or professional from having an agreed right of direct access or appeal to a supreme international tribunal. Precedents for this right, as we have shown, already exist. If ever an effective international society is constructed, national sovereignty will have fulfilled its task; and, leaving behind it so much of the external rights of the State as are necessary for it to fulfil its obligations as a member of that larger society, will go to join the Roman Province and the Feudal System in the political museum of the human mind. The natural society of peoples will remain.

Documents

Natural Society of Nations :

VITTORIA. *De Potestate Civili.* (*Ed. Landry p.* 120) :

From all that has been said above, the following corollary is to be deduced : The Law of Nations does not only derive its force from human contract but also has the force of law. For the whole world which is, in a way a single commonwealth, has the power to make laws which are equitable and applicable to all alike ; and such are the precepts to be found in the Law of Nations. . . . Any one kingdom has not the right to refuse to be bound by the Law of Nations : for it has been *established by the authcrity of the whole world.*

MGR. PFEIFFER *on the 'De Indis' of Vittoria. 'De legitimis titulis,' in Xenia Thomistica :*

The Spaniards have the right to travel into those provinces and to live there, without doing any harm to the barbarians, nor have the latter the right to prohibit their doing so. This right arises from the Law of Nations, according to which it is considered inhuman not to receive guests and travellers kindly

[1] R. P. Delos, in *Les Grandes Activités de la S. de N., etc.*, p. 136.

unless for some special reason. Indeed friendship and in consequence hospitality and commerce seem to come from the Natural Law; while to prohibit any people from entering a state or province, or, when they are established there, to expel them from it, would pertain to war. Here Vittoria—long before Hugo Grotius—proclaims also the freedom of the seas, as later did Benedict XV (Letter to Belligerents, August 1, 1917). Since such travelling is allowed both by natural and divine law, human law cannot prohibit it without cause, otherwise it would be inhuman, irrational and, consequently, without force of law.

. . . .

If there are any things to be enjoyed in common by citizens and visitors, it is not lawful for the barbarians to prohibit the Spaniards from having their part in the common use of them. Thus, if other travellers are allowed to dig gold out of the common land or out of rivers, or to fish for pearls in the sea or in a river, neither can this be prohibited to the Spaniards. Such rights are part of the Law of Nations, which comes either by derivation from the Law of Nature or through the consent of the human race. And in such matters the consent of the greater part of mankind binds also the remainder.

Vittoria affirms that anyone born in a city where his parents are domiciled, even though they be foreigners, has civic rights.

His words concerning free communication and trade are very much to the point to-day when nearly all States are separated from one another, to the advantage of a few people only but not to the common good, by unwise customs barriers and so all commerce and indeed all economic life, particularly in Europe, is suffocated.

SUAREZ. *De Legibus ac de Deo Legislatore, Lib. II, Cap. XIX, Par.* 6, 7, 8, 9:

(i)

6. The Precepts of the Law of Nations differ in this from those of civil law, that they are not in writing, but in customs not of any one city or province, but of all or almost all nations. For human law is twofold, written and unwritten . . . the Law of Nations is seen to be unwritten and thus in this respect differs from all written civil law, even imperial and common law. But unwritten law is deduced from customs: and if it is introduced by the customs of one people and binds only them, it is called also civil law. But if it is introduced by the customs of all nations and binds all, we believe this to be the Law of Nations properly speaking. It differs from natural law in that it arises not directly from nature, but from customs; it is also distinguished from civil law by its origin, foundation and universality as we have explained. This seems to me to have been

meant by Justinian (in '*Jus autem*' *Instit. de jure nat. gentium et civili*), when he says 'The Law of Nations is common to the whole human race : for by force of custom, and through human necessity the human peoples constituted to themselves certain laws.' I lay stress on the words 'by force of custom' and 'constituted' : for by the latter word is signified that the laws were constituted not by nature, but by men ; and in the former expression it is declared that they were introduced not by writing, but by custom. Isidore is seen to be of the same opinion, (15 Etym.) for first (c. 4) he distinguishes the three mentioned kinds of laws and gives the definition : Natural Law is that which is common to all nations in that it is possessed by each one, not by any constitution, but by natural instinct. And in this he confirms our assertion and virtually teaches that the Law of Nations is not founded on instinct alone. Thus further down (c. 5) after examples of the Law of Nations he concludes 'hence it is called the Law of Nations because all nations use this law.' In this then, he implies the definition of the Law of Nations, namely that it is the common law of all nations, constituted not by natural instinct alone, but by the customs of these nations. Nor must the word 'almost' be lightly passed over ; for it shows that there is no intrinsic and natural necessity in this law and that it is not necessary that it should be common to absolutely all nations, apart even from ignorance and error, but that it suffices that almost all the well constituted nations should use it. I think that this is the sense of St. Thomas, as I shall shortly explain, and the other authors cited above no doubt held this.

(ii)

7. . . . The custom of receiving legates under a law of immunity and security cannot, absolutely regarded, be a necessity of natural law, because some community of men might not be willing to receive them. Now, however, to receive them is a precept of the Law of Nations and to refuse them would be a sign of enmity and would be a violation of the Law of Nations although it would not be an injustice against natural reason. Wherefore, although it be against the natural law not to observe the immunity of legates supposing them to have been received under an understood pact, because it is against justice and due good faith to break a promise : yet that supposition and that pact under such condition, arise from the Law of Nations. The same conclusions can be drawn from any contract or commercial dealing. In this three things may be distinguished, one is the particular manner of contracting and this usually regards civil law and often may be according to the whims of the contracting parties when contrary to no other law : the second is the keeping of the contract when it is completed, and this regards natural

law, as is evident : the third is the freedom to contract commercial undertakings with men who are not national or personal enemies and this pertains to the Law of Nations because natural law does not of itself oblige anyone to this : for a state might subsist by its own means and not desire trade with another even though this other state were not hostile : but by the Law of Nations trade is free and if it were forbidden without a reasonable cause that law would be violated. . . .

(iii)

8. There are two senses in which one speaks of the Law of Nations : in the first sense it is a law which all peoples and different nations must observe in their dealings with one another : in the second it is a law which each separate city and kingdom observes within itself: but by assimilation and for convenience it is called the Law of Nations. To my mind the term in its first sense comprises properly international law itself as distinct from civil law. To this belongs the examples of the treatment of Ambassadors and commercial treaties which we have explained. I hold the same of the right of war : in so far as it is founded in the power which one state or supreme kingdom has of punishing or vindicating or taking reparation for an injury done to it by another, it is seen to be proper to the Law of Nations. For by force of natural reason alone this power would not necessarily belong to an offended state : men might institute another means of punishment or commit that power to some third prince and quasi-arbitrator with coercive power : however, since this means which is nowadays employed, is easier and more conformed to nature[1] it has been introduced by custom and is so just that it is impossible to resist that law. In this order also I place servitude : for peoples and nations observe that law among each other and it was not necessary from pure natural reason : for it would have been possible to introduce another method of punishment as I have said : now however this law is such that the guilty are bound to submit to this punishment in the manner in which it was introduced, and the victors cannot in justice further punish enemies already beaten once the war is finished, unless some other reason occurs. So also peace treaties and truces may be put under this head, not in so far as they are to be observed once contracted : (for this belongs rather to natural law) but in so far as they are to be accepted and not refused when they are asked foı reasonably and in due form : for this, although in absolute conformity with natural reason is, however, more strengthened and more obligatory by custom and the Law of Nations. Other examples also might be found and explained under this heading.

[1] Tragic admission !

(iv)

9. The reason for the Law of Nations, under this aspect, is, that the human race, though divided into no matter how many different peoples and nations, has for all that a certain unity, a unity not merely physical, but also in a sense political and moral. This is shown by the natural precept of mutual love and mercy, which extends to all men, including foreigners of every way of thinking. Wherefore, though any one state, republic or kingdom be in itself a perfect community and constant in its members, nevertheless each of the states is also a member, in a certain manner, of the world, so far as the human race is concerned. For none of these communities are ever sufficient unto themselves to such a degree that they do not require some mutual help, society or communication, either to their greater advantage or from moral necessity and need, as is evident from custom. For this reason therefore they need some law whereby they may be directed and rightly ruled in this kind of communication and society. And although this in great part comes from natural law, yet not sufficiently nor directly for all purposes. Therefore it has been found possible to introduce some special laws by the customs of the peoples themselves. For as in one state or province customs introduce law, so in the whole human race international laws could be introduced by custom. This is all the truer because the things appertaining to this law are few, very closely related to the natural law and easily deduced from it. They are moreover useful and agreeable to nature itself; so, although it [international law] is not an obvious deduction, absolutely necessary for good morals, it is nevertheless quite in accord with nature and ought to be accepted by all.

V. Cap. XX, 7 and 8. Of Changes in the Law of Nations :

7. I am aware that such a change can happen in one way for that part of the Law of Nations which is only common to the different peoples because of the convenience which they find in observing it : but in another way for that part which is common by the usage or custom of nations, in so far as they have a certain society or communication between each other. In the first case it can be changed by one particular kingdom or republic on its own account, for inasmuch as it is *in* that republic it really is intrinsically civil law : it is the Law of Nations only in name. In the second case it can only be changed through discussion and agreement with others, because it is so nearly related to the natural law that it draws from that law a universal application to all or almost all nations. Again with regard to the Law of Nations in the first sense, since it is in any one state, it depends upon the determination and power of a particular government or upon the customs of that State in its own borders

and without regard to other States : therefore it can be changed by one nation even though the others do not consent because individual nations are not bound to conform to the others. Thus, for example, any state might ordain that prostitutes should not be tolerated within its boundaries or that all unjust sales at an excessive price should be rescinded or that money-lending should not be permitted. So much for the changes of that kind : although as a matter of fact they do not occur, because there is no reason for them and they serve no useful purpose, yet they are not impossible from lack of the right or power to make them.

8. In the other rules of the Law of Nations, however, change is far more difficult, for they concern the common law of all nations and the authority of all is at stake. *They cannot, therefore, be abrogated without the consent of all.*

FÉNELON. *Essai philosophique sur le gouvernement civil : The Law of Nations grounded in social charity :*

To love everything according to the dignity of its nature is the universal, eternal, immutable law of all intelligence ; and it is from this law that flow all other laws and virtues, whether divine or human, whether civil or moral. In consequence of this we are obliged to think more immediately of conserving our own life than that of any other of our fellow beings, we owe more to our own family than to a strange family, we owe more to our fatherland in which we have been taught, reared and protected during our childhood than to any other society that we have seen. All things considered we are under a greater obligation to the person who has been immediately committed to our care by Nature or Providence than to the person with whom we have no connection.

But when it comes to comparing the particular good with the general good, the latter must always be preferred. One is not permitted to preserve oneself from harm while ruining one's family, nor to aggrandize one's family by violating the rights of humanity. It is on this principle that is founded what is called the Right of Peoples and the Law of Nations.'[1]

TAPARELLI. *Essai Théorique du Droit Naturel. Book VI, Chap. III, Art. I,* 1262, 1263. *Of International Goodwill in time of peace :*

1262. Every society, every nation ought to desire the good of other societies : whence it follows that a people should, as far as it can, so act that the other peoples may preserve their political existence and perfect it. So all the societies, who have relations

[1] Quoted in *Paix et Guerre* (Ed. du Cerf), pp. 65–66.

one with another, ought to act in concert to the end that each one of them may preserve its political institutions and promote the happiness of all its citizens. . . .

1263. This love which causes any one society to wish for the political existence of other societies to which it is bound by ties of friendship, naturally leads it to lend them effective protection against unjust aggression, just as in the relations of one individual to another, the duty of natural benevolence makes us go to the defence of another person unjustly attacked. The motives of protection are the same in both cases, only with this difference; that in international relations everything is on a larger scale, not only because of the gravity of the public interests, and the importance of the rights involved in the dispute, but also because a society which takes up the defence of another society perceives that its own preservation, its own safety is concerned therein. Further, the contacts between nations are more necessary and more continuous than between individuals; and the triumph of an oppressor may bring with it greater and more imminent dangers for all the neighbouring peoples. Consequently, the defence of a nation which is the victim of oppression is not only a duty of benevolence for the peoples whose territories adjoin it; it is also for them a question of public safety and national interest.

Intervention :

1266. . . . If the unjust acts of a government become the occasion of troubles which it did not intend, it is the noble duty of the government of a friendly nation to warn the sovereign who is thus going astray to his own disadvantage; to intercede for the suffering people; to bring peace to the society of which the social *personæ* are divided among themselves, and so to re-establish among these persons the love and concord which they ought to observe. . . . Thanks to such pacific intervention, the reaction will gradually have effect, and international relations will give the people the guarantee which it needs.

1275. After having considered Intervention as a duty of international charity, we must envisage it as a means of defence for States as a whole. We must consider whether it is permissible for a State to intervene in another State subverted by factions, for fear that the disorder will spread until it troubles its own happiness. . . . We refuse to allow that anyone has the right (which Montesquieu postulates) to trouble or to impede the prosperity of other nations, even if it may become excessive: we cannot admit any intervention simply on the plea that a possible danger is feared. But it is a very different matter when we have to fear a danger which is present and which is imminent as, for example, when a revolt breaks out on our very frontiers or when disorder is fomented and spread amongst us by doctrines which lead to action, and which themselves have a great power of expansion. In opposing such tendencies a State is not merely avoiding a future danger ; it is repelling an enemy which is, in point of fact, aggressive. If it is put in that way, the problem resolves itself into the question whether a State may lawfully defend itself against attack. In particular it is for examination whether anti-social doctrines propagated by one nation do actually constitute an aggression against neighbouring nations.

The Possession of Territory :

1287. The word to *possess* means having an actual domain, that is the right to use something to the exclusion of others and to defend one's claim to it if necessary. How can a political society (i.e. the State) have this right? It can have it in the same conditions and for the same reasons as the individual. The individual is under obligation to conserve himself in being by the use of finite goods : hence he must necessarily have the right to make use of the goods which he has gathered and prepared by his labour. By this means he acquires the exclusive use of certain goods which, by their nature, are consumed in use. On the other hand, the good things which are not consumed or which exist in great abundance always belong to the first comer—the air we breathe[1] for instance, the water of rivers or the light of the sun. Such also is the basis of public property. The State also has the right to care for its own conservation. For this purpose it has need of certain material means, of which some at least are consumed in the using. One nation may therefore exclude other nations from them. As to the other kind of goods which are not consumable, one nation may not take them away from others and appropriate them to itself : to do so would be dictated more by envy of the happiness of others than by a proper regard for its own interests. International goodwill forbids such action and justice refuses to recognize the lawfulness of properties so acquired.

(The application of this doctrine to freedom of the seas and territorial waters is then given in paragraphs 1289, 1291.)

Interdependence of Nations :

1297. Every constant factor which brings any two nations into touch with one another, establishes a positive society between them. The society is subject to the universal laws of justice and love, for these nations are equals and are destined to the same

[1] Or fly through? It is interesting to speculate what Taparelli's solution would be for the problems created by the claims of the modern state to sovereignty of the air above their territories and the difficulties thus caused for commercial aviation.

end. But it is in the very nature of things that every nation should have continuous relations with its neighbours. Settled by its agriculture in a limited area, it extends first up to the frontiers of other nations. Then trade, which is a true social blessing, makes it tend further, almost instinctively, to establish relations with the most distant peoples. Thus it is that, in the design of the Creator, commerce becomes the great social link which unites all nations into one single society, and brings many and varied advantages to peoples and individuals. Material advantages, through the common usage of the products of the whole world, intellectual advantages through the spread of ideas and the progress of the sciences ; moral advantages, through the mutual guarantee of order or the unity of religious beliefs. Thus it is nature itself, that eloquent interpreter of the divine will, which calls all peoples to form among themselves one universal association and at the same time makes it their duty so to do.

1299. The obligation incumbent upon the different nations to form among themselves a universal society may be considered positively or negatively. As a *negative* obligation it makes it wrong for any government ever to offer direct opposition to the formation by the nations of a universal international society. As a *positive* obligation it requires a Government to establish commercial relations, not with all the peoples of the earth, but only with those nations with whom in point of fact it is brought into contact and towards whom it has duties of justice and charity to fulfil.

Sovereignty at Sea :

1301. When there is a collision of rights, it is clear that there is some one matter which is the object of conflict. In this case that matter is a line of communication by sea. A nation wishes it to be within its political possession. So long as the political authority does not rob anyone of the use of this sea route, there cannot be any collision of rights. But if other peoples also wanted to have the command of those waters, if in fact the freedom of passage over them were contested, then the collision would occur ; and then it would be necessary to consider which had a better right than the others. The nation actually exercising dominion, apart from the fact that it has been in possession for many years and from prescription, can allege its daily need of this possession for its political safety ; for political order is a social good which is supposed to be impossible without such possession. The other nations have only a far more restricted right, for their material interests can be safeguarded by the mere right of transit without the need of any other political rights. So they have but a slight title to those waters, which cannot be in collision with the title of the nation for whom the control of them is a question of capital importance, a matter of life and death. That nation can therefore exercise political sovereignty there ; it has the right to maintain order in that part of the seas, even by force if need be ; it can exact moderate tolls, though not such as to injure the interests of other nations. It must not prevent the ships of other nations from sailing those seas when they have need to do so in time of peace, just as the owner of a vast stretch of land may not forbid a man to pass, whose house is in the middle of that land.

Freedom of Trade and justifiable restraints upon it :

1302. The principles which ensure the freedom of the seas also guarantee the freedom of trade and show that such liberty is in tune with nature, so long as it does not clash with another and stronger right. When other more potent rights are opposed to free trade it is a real social duty to restrict the latter. Thus it is that the importation of opium into China is forbidden, and very rightly ; thus it is that in times past Christian nations were forbidden to export arms to the Turks. In such cases the prohibition does not violate any social duty : it is a precaution against the inroads of a moral or physical enemy. The same line of argument may be pursued when free trade exposes a country to the danger of losing its independence, by forcing it into a tributary position of dependence upon other peoples. An unfertile country which would otherwise be obliged to depend upon the foreigner for its food supplies, the provision of arms or other objects of primary necessity would pursue a wise course in prohibiting the import of foreign produce, so as to encourage and develop its own industry. Apart from these cases of necessity, we ought to desire the welfare of others as our own welfare, and we ought to share and exchange the good things and the treasures which nature has lavished upon us. That is as true for nations as for individuals.

1303. These reasons lead me to believe as very probably true *a priori* the theory which Say, the economist, has endeavoured to demonstrate from a consideration of the facts ; that, other things being equal, a nation increases its own wealth in proportion as it opens up numerous markets for its own products, and admits freely the products of other nations. Nature has by divers links united all nations together ; at the same time she calls each one of them to develop its own comfort and wealth. It is highly improbable that Nature should be in conflict with herself, which would be the case if the union of the peoples were to be detrimental to their individual prosperity, or their prosperity to their union. Hence such opposition is unnatural : it may exist owing to certain accidental circumstances, and it is the function of political economy to determine what ought to be done under those circumstances. It is enough for us that we have established the fact that the communication of material good is a general law for the nations of the world, in their normal condition of strength and health, while on the other hand we admit that on the occasion of their suffering particular infirmities, they may have recourse to the disagreeable and annoying remedy of international 'excommunication.'

Origins of International Society:

1357. No sooner do two individuals meet one another than they are subject to the laws of the universal society; they are under obligation to lend one another aid and succour in the acquisition of their common good, which in this world is the good which comes of honesty and order and, in the next, the eternal possession of the infinite good. If such be the rule for individuals, what reason have we to say that two States under the same conditions are not subject to the same laws and the same obligations?

1358. . . . There is, it is true, a great difference between the mutual relations of individuals and those of States. The principal end of the individual is the direct personal possession of a happiness which is not of this world; whereas the final object of the State is to guide individuals here below towards their supreme destiny by the means of *external order*, which itself constitutes the immediate end of the State. It is from that essential difference that we deduced the difference which exists between the love of man for man, and the goodwill of nation for nation. But we cannot argue from that distinction that the various nations do not form among themselves one universal society; it only shows that the common good of that universal society presents a different aspect from the special good of each of the nations that form part of it. It shows that the international society seeks principally the good of political order, while the different nations have as their principal end the good of the natural order. Within the society of the nation the object is to maintain civic order so as to remove all obstacles to individual honesty. In the international society the object is, by maintaining political order (i.e. order between States) to enable each nation to develop its own internal activity as a society.

1359. As population increases, as trade develops, as alliances, journeys and communications between any two nations are multiplied; as their interests come to be interwoven; as the light of truth spreads in all directions uniting all peoples in a community of ideas, of principles, feelings, longings and enterprises; so do we see at the same time international relations becoming more and more sustained, and an ever greater tendency for common efforts to be made to attain external order as a matter of common interest.

Each nation soon perceives that it is neither isolated any longer nor wholly independent, though it still preserves its moral independence. It sees too, that the ideas of its neighbours are imperceptibly penetrating the minds of its own people: that sympathy of mind and will are growing between men of different nationalities; and that any blow which shakes the credit of others damages its own interests also. In a word, each nation sees clearly that it has a real interest in the preservation of order not only within its own boundaries, but among the other peoples of the world; it realizes that upon the maintenance of order among them depends the individual welfare of its own citizens, if not its own political and social existence.

1360. Thus needs and interests soon produce, and quite rightly, the desire to form with other nations a real, definite society; thence comes the establishment and development of international society, following upon the natural, regular progress of each of the component nations. The needs of a nation engender for its ruler and those who direct its public action, the obligation to maintain and perfect the society of which they are the leaders; and so, for the sovereign, international relations become a duty, a duty all the more imperious as these relations become more necessary to protect and develop his own nation and the nations with whom he is already actually associated.

1361. . . . Such is the natural development of the nations; they all tend towards a certain community of interests which must be regulated according to the principles of order and of justice. Thence comes a definite international society, in which each nation has an interest in desiring the maintenance of order. This society is the outcome of a tendency common to all peoples; and unless nature is accidentally and violently frustrated in its proper evolution, all the nations cannot fail to come and take their place in this international society. The community of interests, the communication of ideas, the sympathy of human characters—all these are real, positive benefits which unite the nations in so close a union that any one of them—even the most remote and the least important—cannot be disturbed with political disorders, without all the others feeling in greater or less degree the reactions of this disturbance. . . .

Natural desire for international union:

PIUS XI. *Encyclical 'Mortalium Animos,' January* 6, 1928:

Never perhaps in the past have the souls of men experienced as vividly as they seem to do in our day, the desire to reinforce and extend for the common good of human society as a whole the relations of brotherhood whereby their common origin and nature bind them together. Indeed, the nations have not yet the full enjoyment of the blessings of peace. On this side and on that old-standing discords and new differences provoke seditions and internal struggles, and many controversies which jeopardize the tranquillity and prosperity of the peoples can never be solved save by the joint action of the heads of States or of those who direct or administer the country's interests. And so it is very easy to understand the longings of a great many people to see, in the name of this universal brotherhood the establishment of an ever closer and closer union between the various nations, all the more because all acknowledge the unity of the human race.

It is not only in the political and juridical spheres that the fraternity of mankind and the consequent society of nations, deduced by Taparelli and so frequently stressed by Benedict XV and Pius XI, call for the foundation of institutions to serve the common good. The need of such institutions is even more evident when the economic aspect of national life is considered.

PIUS XI. *Encyclical 'Quadragesimo Anno'* :

Thus it behoves the different nations who are so closely linked to one another by solidarity and interdependence, to pool their thoughts and their efforts in order to hasten, by means of wisely framed treaties and institutions, the advent of a happy and beneficent state of international, economic collaboration.

Taking this succinct Pontifical statement as his text, Father NELL BREUNING, the great Jesuit economist, summarizes as follows, upon the basis of natural law and ethics, the relation of national to international economic organization.[1]

Granted the place filled by the State as the corner-stone in Christian social philosophy and in conformity with the actual conditions of the present time, the notion of ' national economy, (i.e. the nation as the economic unit) must occupy a central position in economics founded on the basis of Christian social science. National economy amounts to the economic life of the nation united within the framework of the State. In fact, social economy is first and foremost national economy, and as such, is really one, an entity, in scholastic language *' unum per se ac reale.'* . . .

Nevertheless we must not stop at this idea of national economy. For, though in our system it be the most important idea, it is by

[1] ' Les Problèmes Economiques devant la Société des Nations,' in *Les Grandes Activités*, etc. Father Nell Breuning is famous for his works *Grundzuge der Boersen-moral* (Herder, 1928) and *Aktionreform und Moral* (Heymann, 1930).

no means the ultimate or the broadest. Just as the nations are members of the human family, just as the various states cannot remain juxtaposed without maintaining relations with one another but are united to one another by multifarious connections and contacts, so are national economies in no wise isolated in themselves or independent one from another. On the contrary they are actually and inevitably interlocked in a whole complex of more or less close relationships, which is in fact very extensive, namely a world economy.

Father Nell Breuning's application of this doctrine enters the field of topical actuality, but we reproduce it for a better understanding of the principles involved . . .

The relation of the State to the Society of Nations is very similar to that which exists between a national economy and the world economy. . . . Entirely in harmony with the principles of Christian social philosophy, the League of Nations is not a super-State but truly a society of States for the purpose of collaborating in concord to promote progress. Consequently the economic activity of the League of Nations is not directed toward the fusion of national economies in a single world economy but—to use the very words of the Pope—to establish a beneficent and happy collaboration between nations in the economic sphere, that is to say collaboration between divers national economies.

This co-operation between different national economic systems rests, according to the terms of the Encyclical *Quadragesimo Anno*, upon a double basis, that is to say the *solidarity* of a common nature and destiny ; and *interdependence*, that is to say the need for each nation of the help of others in order to attain completion. This co-operation is realized by two means—by engagements and by *common institutions*. . . .

One must never weary of insisting again and again upon this solidarity. The various peoples and countries, combined as they are in the economy of the world, are, in fact, so bound to one another in good fortune and in bad fortune, that—to give only one example—the farmer of the United States cannot hope to prosper if the industrial worker of Central Europe is in difficulties or is unemployed. Everyone knows that this solidarity exists ; but in many economic and political circles the idea seems, also, to be purely sterile and theoretic : in practice it is far from being understood.

The writer then examines the true notion of the interdependence of national economic systems and contrasts it with the conception of ' autarchia '—or self-government which in the minds of Aristotle and St. Thomas is the property of a perfect society. He concludes that if, in point of fact, States need one another's products in order that the normal economic life of their own people may reach fulfilment, they can never have more than a relative 'autarchia.'

An important corollary of the economic interdependence of nations, is that the harsh or oppressive treatment of manual workers, apart from its intrinsic injustice, may well dislocate the economic life of the world.

It is evident that the spoliation of manual labour and the exploitation of the worker, either by the excessive lengthening of the hours of work, or by the labour of women and children, or by starvation wages, may gravely damage the world economy and disorganize it in the way which is most swiftly felt, namely by unfair competition. Hence the systematic collaboration of the national economies demands, in this sphere also, the existence of a certain order, of preventive measures and of control. It is therefore no digression but a necessary complement to our main argument to mention here the many devoted efforts already made in this domain, despite very great difficulties, by the International Labour Organization and Office.

Albert Valensin, S.J. on '*Les lois naturelles de la vie internationale*' in '*Le Problème de la Vie Internationale*':

The social being, whom we call man, exhibits a tendency to sociability which makes him establish social relations with his fellows. These relations are anterior to any positive conventions which may define the character of them. They suffice to account for the natural constitution of a society among the nations. Thence it necessarily follows that over the nations, which the exigencies of life link one to another, there is a law (*droit*) which it is possible indeed for them to violate, but whose existence they cannot deny. The old saying: '*Ubi societas, ibi jus,*' recalls this fact: human nature requires it. We must choose between two concepts. Either we must see in the groups of human beings called nations, nothing but instincts, or else we must perceive in them also reason and liberty. In the first case we shall no longer be able to speak of law; but beware also of confusing the gregarious state in which these instincts operate with a state of society. In the second case, men must needs have on the one hand the notion of good to be attained in common, and on the other the power to adapt the free choices of life to the requirements of this common good. But this notion and this power are in fact what we call Law (*droit*).

CHAPTER XI

THE POSITIVE SOCIETY OF NATIONS

WHAT is the political organization which best responds to the needs of the human race as a whole? Just as human society stands in need of positive laws, made by man, to give effect and application to the Law of Nature, made by God; so, if as has been sufficiently established, there is a natural society of nations, it is right to suppose that it should possess a positive supernational or international organization whereby it may exercise its functions as a society.

We have deliberately stated the alternative. Is the authority which informs the world society to be exercised *over* and above the several nations, as of a superior over inferiors? Or does it simply arise from a revocable compact *between* equals who are themselves the depositaries of authority? Both views have been asserted with vigour by Christian authors. The first, held without question before the disruption of the Roman Empire, was developed with fervour and lucidity by Dante in the thirteenth century, and by Leibnitz in the seventeenth. The second was deduced from first principles by Taparelli in the nineteenth: it had already been assumed by the would-be architects of world order, both within and without the Catholic body in the seventeenth and eighteenth centuries: it is in vogue to-day. Both the advocates of monarchy and the advocates of polyarchy have proved too much. The ideal combination of the singleness and permanence of authority with the choice and change, by a number of States, of those who are to exercise that authority has yet to be found.

Just as the Church acknowledges any form of Government within the State, which is not actually repugnant to Natural Law, so the Catholic tradition admits any form of organization for the world upon the same condition. It is not possible to point to any particular institution—the League of Nations of to-day, or the Holy Roman Empire of yesterday—as being that which alone or best conforms to the requirements of Christian sociology. Many varied opinions are tenable, of which one will be expressed in the present chapter.

At the same time there are certain general lines of international organization which have been explicitly advocated or praised by the Holy See. And there are certain practical requirements arising from the nature of States and their mutual interdependence, so constantly perceived, as well by all the earlier apostles of European or world-wide Federations as by those who framed the Covenant of the League of Nations, that they appear to have a close connection with Natural Law. These considerations shall be our guide in surveying and commenting upon the principal projects which have been put forward in the past for the positive organization of international society and the framework of the existing League.

The documents which are reproduced in the present chapter or appended to it are the essential parts of Dante Alighieri's treatise *De Monarchia* ; Father Emeric Cruce's, *The New Cyneas*, the Abbé de St. Pierre's, *Project of Perpetual Peace*, together with an appreciation of the more important schemes of non-Catholic philosophers which followed and preceded it ; Father Taparelli d'Azeglio's, *Essay of Natural Law* (Book VI) ; the constitution of the actual League of Nations, that is to say the Covenant, the Statutes of the Permanent Court of International Justice and the 'charter' of the International Labour Organization ; the Briand-Kellogg Pact for the Renunciation of War ; and passages in which weighty Catholic opinions upon these contemporary institutions are expressed.

Dante's essay *De Monarchia*, written as it doubtless was to win favour with the Emperor, is none the less an important landmark in the progress of thought concerning the political organization of the world ; and that for two reasons. In the first place it is a vigorous and typical exposition of the case for believing the Holy Roman Empire to be necessary to the welfare of the human race, as it appeared to its apologists at the height of mediæval civilization. In the second place it contains general arguments deduced from first principles in support of the conviction, that all races of men form a single whole and should, as such, constitute a single organic society. These arguments, contained for the most part in the first book *De Necessitate Monarchiæ*, will never cease to challenge consideration on their merits ; and it is these that concern our present purpose. The second and third parts of the work on the ' Right of the Roman people to Empire and the dependence of the Imperial authority directly upon God ' wear the colour of a faded controversy. They are now of historical and literary interest alone and contain not a little that could not be reconciled with Catholic orthodoxy : it is not surprising that they were condemned by ecclesiastical authority.

Two propositions—by an association of thought natural at the time—are confused in the mind of Dante Alighieri as he develops his thesis upon the necessity of monarchy. The first is that the nature of man and the common good of peoples require a single government for the world ; the second that the form of that government must necessarily be the rule of a single man. Let the student try the fourteen arguments of this book by the criterion of the first proposition. He will find that though several support only the case for personal monarchy, which appears to be discounted by the verdict of history, there are not a few which supply a solid philosophical foundation for the more general proposition—namely that there ought for the common welfare of men to be a single world authority. Taparelli sought to prove that the form of that authority is naturally ' polyarchic ' : the witness of modern history can be called to reinforce the contention. For there is in fact no means other than an accord between organized peoples as independent moral persons, whereby the sociologist of to-day can envisage the creation of political, judicial or economic institutions to promote the *bonum commune* of mankind : it is for such an accord that Leo XIII and Benedict XV appeal in order that international arbitration may be established.

But assuming that the choice of any person or persons to wield international authority must reside in the body of associated States, what is the nature of that authority? Does it comprise the notion of ruling? We have already put forward the theory that the authority of a person or college chosen by the agreement of duly constituted governments for the purpose of assuring order and justice in the international community, is no less real, no less entitled to obedience than any civil government, '*quia a Deo constitutus.*' But however dependent the holder of an international office may be—as is the President of a Republic—upon the choice of his electors, he cannot when in office fulfil the functions for which he is appointed, in any manner intelligible to Christian philosophy, unless his authority is superior to that of the constituent States. To the Spanish theologians of the sixteenth and seventeenth centuries as to Dante's contemporary, St. Thomas, it is the absence of a superior power or tribunal which permits, and the presence which forbids the prince to exercise the right of war. To Taparelli, evolving as a requirement of natural law the necessity of an 'ethnarchic' society, as he called it, with its several functions, legislative, judicial and executive, the power to *take and give effect to decisions* is clearly an attribute of the ethnarchic authority. In democratic constitutions the citizens elect a legislature for a term of years and during that period the legislative body, usually by a simple majority, is empowered to pass laws which when duly confirmed by the Head of the State, the citizens are bound to obey. An international parliament nominated or elected by the Governments of the associated nations might, on this analogy, be empowered, within the limits of the constitution of the society, to pass international laws which those Governments would likewise be under a positive obligation to obey. The political independence of the States Members in respect of one another and in respect of their municipal jurisdictions could, according to the theory of Taparelli, be perfectly reconciled with the exercise of such international authority in the proper sense. Similarly a single man—president or emperor—could be appointed for a fixed period or for life to ratify the international legislation, and to bring into operation the sanctions of the whole society against aggressors from without or recalcitrant members within its rank. A Permanent Court, composed of judges appointed for a long term, might have the power to judge without appeal, according to the requirements of equity and of positive International Law, all questions at issue between associates. Such a form of supernational Government it is perfectly possible to contemplate : though federal or, as Taparelli would say, polyarchic in its foundation, it would in fact constitute a single world authority. Its organs might be simple or complex according to the degree of development of the constituent States and the needs arising from their intercourse : but they would be informed by a single principle : they would evidently subserve a single end, the common good of the whole. The contention, canvassing and competition inseparable from the choice by human beings of persons to fill public offices would not prevent respect for the office and obedience to the holder of it, once duly appointed, and as such deriving his mandate from the divine source of all authority. Such a corps of government would provide many of the advantages urged by Dante for his world Monarchy—freedom from ambition and greed of power : independence from the limitations proper to a single nation ; stability ; a direct concern for the good of mankind as a whole. The relations between this ethnarchic secular authority and the Church could correspond exactly to those traced by Vittoria as ideally obtaining between the temporal and spiritual powers. The Law of Nations, in the sense of the rights belonging to all peoples—among them the rights of minorities, or of backward peoples in regard to colonizing States—would have its central guardian. The maintenance of just conditions of labour ; the equitable distribution of raw materials and of markets for manufacturer ; freedom of communications, transit and commerce ; the suppression of the immoral pests of society ; the co-ordination of medical science and sanitary action to combat epidemic disease ; the organization of mutual assistance in the face of the great catastrophes of nature—those, translated into the language of a later age, are forms of service to the common weal which as '*minister omnium*' the world Government would be expected to perform. The element of contract would be reduced to a minimum : it would necessarily enter into the constitution of the international authority—a contract of an institutional character as Renard shows it to be. Yet the act of institution, according to Vittoria's conception of International Law in general, would be more than a mere contract; it would consist in making articulate, positive and actual, a potential tendency or requirement of nature, which had the force of Natural Law itself. And the authority—judicial, legislative and executive, once constituted, would promulgate or originate judgements, laws and operations which, if consistent with the postulates of Natural Law and morality would, *ipso facto*, command obedience and co-operation. Is it too much to hold that such an organization of the '*totius humanæ civilitatis*'—as Dante Alighieri calls the whole body of mankind conceived as a society—is that which concords best with the manifold needs of men and nations in the light of Christian tradition?

How near and yet how far is the modern world from that ideal will appear from an unbiassed and objective appreciation of existing international institutions.

Already examples are not lacking of such institutions, which, within defined spheres, have begun to acquire the independence of national influence; the enduring character; the quality of superiority whereby they can demand information, judge and decide—which are the attributes of true authority. Such are the Permanent Court of International Justice and the Permanent Mandates Commission. It is a commonplace of the history of the League of Nations, that a permanent civil service has alone assured continuity in its action; and that those of its ventures which have achieved any measure of success are, in all but a few cases, those for which a permanent directing or supervisory body has been in existence. But between an international legislature duly appointed and apt to frame and edict laws for the common good and a diplomatic conference able only to adopt resolutions *ad referendum*, there is an abyss. The second—which is, in the main, the form of the Assembly of the existing League of Nations—displays authority under its most tenuous and elusive aspect. The interminable delays involved in the reference to national legislative authorities of conventions adopted by an international conference; the insufficient or tardy ratifications of treaties ; the inability of the organs of the international society to prevent the paralysis of common action through the failure of the members to implement their signatures ; the consequent futility of too many international agreements, out-distanced by the facts of a changing world, before they can enter into vigour—all these are the now familiar fruits of the attempted compromise between the idolatry of national sovereignty and the common service of mankind, of which the present generation is witness. Hence the gulf that yawns between promise and performance ; the grey unreality of many words uncrowned by deeds ; the constant temptation to cynicism and hypocrisy. It may be held that the world is not yet ready for the establishment of the ethnarchic authority : or again that the international conference with its non-committal conclusions is a necessary first stage in the evolution of a true international legislature. As a means it is intelligible ; as the end of social development indefensible. And, if it would be unreasonable and ungenerous to depreciate these slow and stumbling beginnings of international co-operation, by comparison with the anarchy of the eighteenth century or the uneasy balance of power in the nineteenth, the Christian citizen is compelled by the very evidence of such imperfection to strive unremittingly to attain to the organized society of peoples in which the singleness of authority and the obedience of the many—indispensable ingredients of human order and concord—are unmistakably enshrined.

Documents

Dante Alighieri. *De Monarchia :*

The question which the First Book sets out to answer is whether for the well-being of the world monarchy is a necessity ; and monarchy is thus defined : 'Temporal monarchy, which they call Empire, is a unique form of sovereign rule (*unicus principatus*) extending over all men in the temporal sphere, or rather in and above the things which are measured by time.'

III. We must now see what is the end of the civil society of mankind as a whole, for when that is clear more than half our labour will be accomplished, as says the Philosopher to Nicomachus. And in order to elucidate this question, it must be remembered that, just as there is one purpose for which nature produces the thumb and another for which the whole hand is designed, and yet a different end from both for the whole arm, and lastly another end from all these for which the whole man is created : so is it to one end that the Eternal God ordains man as a single individual ; to another the community of the household ; to another the village ; to another the city ; to another the kingdom ; and lastly to another end for which by his art, which is nature itself, He brings into being the human race as a whole. And that is here sought as the directive principle of our inquiry.

First, then, it must be known that God and nature create nothing simply to lie idle ; but whatever He brings into being is designed for a particular operation. For no created essence is, in the intention of the Creator as creator, an ultimate end in itself : it is the activity proper to the essence which is the end. . . . There is therefore an activity proper to the universal society of mankind, to which all men as a body in so great a multitude are ordained, but to which no one man, no one household or village or city or particular kingdom can directly attain. That activity or operation will, he continues, be clear, if the ultimate potentiality of the human race is discovered and ' the ultimate potentiality of humanity itself is the capacity or power of the intellect. And inasmuch as this potential cannot be reduced to actuality at any one time by one single man, or by one out of a number of particular communities distinct from a superior, it is necessary that there should be a multitude in the human race through which this whole potential capacity is made actual.'

IV. Therefore it has been sufficiently shown that the proper function of the human race, taken as a whole, is continually to make actual the whole capacity of the potential intellect,[1] first for speculation and secondly, by its extension, for the consequent action. And as what is found in the part is contained in the whole, and as in the individual man it is found that prudence and wisdom are perfected when he is sitting still and at rest, so it is evident that the human race can most freely and easily fulfil its proper function, which is all but divine (according to the saying : ' Thou madest him only a little lower than the angels ') when it is in a state of quiet which is the

[1] ' *Intellectus possibilis* ' or ' *patiens* ' may be paraphrased ' the intellect in a state to be fertilized so as to bring forth fruit ' ; or the mind's capacity of being modified so as to extract the essence of the sensuous object, as distinguished from the ' *intellectus agens* ' which is the very activity which modifies the mind.

tranquillity of peace. Whence it is manifest that universal peace is the greatest of the blessings ordained for our happiness. And thus it was that to the shepherds not riches, nor pleasures, nor length of days, nor health, nor strength, nor beauty rang forth from on high, but peace. For 'Glory to God in the highest,' sang the host of heaven, 'and on earth peace to men of good will.' Thus too it was that 'Peace be unto you' was the greeting of Him who is the Salvation of men. For it beseemed the Supreme Saviour to express the supreme salutation. And this same custom did His disciples desire to use, and Paul too in his greetings, as all may read.

Therefore from what we have said it is clear by what means the human race can the better or indeed best fulfil its proper function. And consequently we see the most direct means by which to proceed whither, as to their ultimate end, all our works are ordained, which is universal peace. Let this be assured as the basis for all our subsequent reasoning.

Dante then undertakes to prove that one supreme ruler is necessary to the welfare of the world.

V. For if we consider a man we shall see this to befall him; namely that, while all his powers are ordained to his felicity, it is the intellectual power which regulates and rules all the others, else he cannot attain to happiness. If we consider a single home, the purpose of which is to prepare the members of the household to lead a good life, there must be one who regulates and rules, who is called the father of the family or whoever takes his place, according to the saying of the Philosopher: 'Every house is ruled by the eldest.' And his duty it is, as Homer says, to make rules for all and to impose laws upon the others. (Hence the proverbial curse: 'May you have a rival in the house.'[1]) Again, if we consider a village, the end of which is the commodious assistance as well of persons as of things, *one* must needs be the regulator of the others, be he appointed by another (superior) or by the consent of the remainder, as the most eminent of the villagers. Otherwise not only does the community not attain its mutual sufficiency but, as at one time or another several want to have the pre-eminence, the whole life of the village is destroyed. Or if we consider a city, whose end it is to suffice to the needs of a good life, there must be a single government of it. . . . Otherwise not only will the purpose of civil life be frustrated but the city will cease to be a city. And, lastly, if we look at one particular kingdom, whose end is the same as that of the city, but with greater security of its tranquillity, there must be one king who rules and governs it; otherwise not only will those who live in the kingdom not attain their end, but the

[1] '*Parem habeas in domo.*'

kingdom itself will perish, according to that saying of infallible truth: 'Every kingdom divided against itself shall be made desolate.' . . . Now it is agreed that the whole human race is ordained to a single end, as has already been shown; therefore it ought to have a single form of regulation and government; and that must consist in a Monarch or Emperor. And so it is clear that to the well-being of the world a Monarchy or Empire is necessary.

VI. And just as the part is disposed by relation to the whole, so must partial order be adjudged in relation to order as a whole. The part is related to the whole as to its end and ideal. From which it is evident that the good of partial order does not exceed the good of the total order, but rather the reverse. Since then a double order is discerned in things, to wit, an order of the parts in relation to one another, and the order of the parts in relation to some principle of unity which is not a part (for instance, the order of parts of an army among themselves and their order in relation to the commander), the order of the parts in relation to the principle of unity is the better, being, as it were, the end of each. . . . Whence if the form of this order is found in the several parts of the human multitude, much more ought it to be discovered in the multitude or totality of mankind itself. . . . And so all those parts which we have mentioned that are lesser than kingdoms (families, villages, cities, etc.) and the kingdoms themselves should be ordained in relation to a single prince or form of rule, that is to a Monarch or Monarchy.

After a variant of this argument of the subjection of the parts to the whole, (VII) in which he seeks to show that the several parts of human society can respond best to God, the Monarch of all, through a single principle of unity, which a single ruler provides, Dante develops the theme that perfect unity among men is most in accordance with the intention of God who is Himself one and indivisible.

'Let us make man in our own image and likeness' is quoted to show that, among other divine qualities, there should be a unity in the whole society of men as in man himself, 'for the whole universe is nothing else but the footprint of the divine goodness. Therefore the human race is at its best when, so far as it is able, it is made like to God. . . . But it most nearly attains unity when it is united in a single whole, which is not possible except it is wholly subject to a single prince.

Hence, he concludes, the organization of all humanity as a single whole under a single authority is 'most in accord with the divine intention.'

Then follows (IX) a fanciful argument (in which the poet shines rather than the philosopher) from the unity of motion in the heavens. The next reason merits attention.

X. Wheresoever a conflict (*litigium*) can arise, there must be also the means of giving judgement. Otherwise there would be something imperfect without the proper means of perfecting it, which is impossible, since God and Nature are not deficient in necessities. Between any two princes, of whom one is nowise subject to the other, there can be a dispute, either through their own fault or the fault of their subjects, as is evident. Therefore it is right that there should be a judgement between them. And since the one cannot have jurisdiction over the other, because the other is not subject to him (for like has no rule over like), there must needs be a third with more ample jurisdiction, who, in the ambit of his right, is superior to both. And this third party must either be Monarch of all or not. If he is, our proposition is proved. If not, once more he will have a co-equal power outside the ambit of his jurisdiction, and again a third party will be needed.[1] And so there will either be a process *ad infinitum*, which is absurd, or there will have to be a recourse to a principal and supreme judge, by whose judgement all controversies can be determined either directly or indirectly; and this will be no other than the Monarch or Emperor. Therefore Monarchy is necessary to the world.

XI. The more powerful is the just man, the more ample will be his justice in its operation. Justice is most potent in the world when the subject in which it resides is most powerful and most free in the exercise of his will: but this quality belongs to the Monarch alone; therefore only the justice which resides in the Monarch is most potent in the world. . . . The Monarch has nothing which he can desire; for his jurisdiction has no bounds but the ocean, which is not the lot of other princes whose kingdoms abutt upon others (for instance, the territory of the King of Castile bounded by that of the King of Aragon), from which it follows that the Monarch is among mortals the most single-minded subject in which justice can reside. . . .

This is the case since cupidity, however slight, beclouds justice, while charity enlightens it. . . . For cupidity, spurning the essential nature of men, seeks other objects, while charity, spurning all else, seeks only God and Man, and in consequence the good of man. And since among the other good things needful to man the greatest is to live in peace . . . and this is chiefly effected by justice, charity will most invigorate justice. . . . And this is the reason why a right love ought to be found

[1] Cf. Taparelli on the moral superiority of third parties to a dispute, p. 169.

in the Monarch more than in other men. Each object of love is actually more loved in proportion as it is nearer to the person loving. But men are nearer to the Monarch than to other princes, therefore they are, or ought to be, most loved by him. . . . Only in part are men brought close to other princes, but they are wholly near to the heart of the Monarch. And again they are approximated to other princes through the Monarch, and not the other way, so there is a primary and direct care of all men in the Monarch, the care of men which is found in other princes coming to them through the Monarch, since their care descends from his supreme charge.

If we were to understand Monarch in the wider sense of the principle of world authority, the proposition is not so fantastic as it appears. For the thesis could seriously be maintained that international institutions when functioning at their best[1] do in fact exhibit a real care for the welfare of all human beings without distinction of nationality, whereas national Governments frequently sacrifice the true welfare, spiritual and material, of men to politics, foreign and domestic, that are the fruits of cupidity and rivalry. But the notion of the international authority, as a direct unsullied channel of social charity toward all human beings having an immediate concern for the welfare of each, seems to conflict with the notion of the State as a perfect community. It is also radically different from the conception of the world order based only upon the mutual relations of sovereign States which is current in the present age. The dominating thought of the *De Monarchia* is authority which *comes down*, through various gradations, from above, that is from the Divine Monarch of the Universe : the dominating conception of to-day is of authority *built up* from beneath. The direct concern, care and love of the world authority for men as a whole can only prevail in proportion to the ascendancy of the former conception. Catholic philosophy seeks to harmonize with this first undeniable principle such as there is of truth in the second ; by teaching that authority, and with it a divine mandate of justice and charity, comes from above, while those that wield it are chosen by the men or societies over whom the authority is to be exercised. But

[1] As, for example, the International Labour Organization and the World Health Organization of the League of Nations.

in the international sphere, the clinging marks of human choice too often obscure the consciousness of divine mandate; and the never-forgotten delegation by the several parts thwarts the sense of responsibility for the good of the whole. The ideal concordance of polyarchy with a single-minded impartiality in those who wield the authority of the international community has not yet been realized. Without belief in the Divine Source of all authority it remains unattainable. Assuming that belief, it is perhaps to be discovered in restricting the principle of representation or delegation to the assembly of nations which, as an electoral college would choose upon their merits those who should legislate, administer and judge for the whole society.

XII. Akin to this thought is the next argument of Dante which seeks to prove that humanity is happiest when it is most free, and that it best attains freedom under the Monarch for 'only under the Monarch does the human race exist for its own sake and not for the benefit of another' . . . 'For the citizens do not exist for the sake of the consuls, nor the people for the King, but on the contrary the consuls for the citizens, the King for the people,' just as laws are not an end in themselves but exist for the good of the State. 'Hence it is evident that in respect of the *means* Consul and King are lords of others, but in respect of the *end* they are the servants of the rest and so especially is the Monarch, who without doubt is to be regarded as the Minister of all men.

XIII. After a somewhat unconvincing contention that the Monarch is the best disposed for Government because, once again, 'he can have no occasion of cupidity' (XIV) Dante sets out to prove that whatever action can be accomplished by one is better accomplished by one than by many: in the course of the article he writes:

It must indeed be remembered that when we say the human race can be ruled by one supreme prince, we do not mean that every little judgement of each municipal community proceeds from him immediately and alone; though even municipal laws are sometimes defective and have need of a directive power. The nations, kingdoms and States have each their own proper needs and qualities which ought to be regulated by different laws. For law is the directive rule of life. In one way, indeed, is it meet for the Scythians to be ruled, who living beyond the seventh clime and suffering a great inequality of nights and days, are oppressed by the intolerable cold, and in another way the Garamantes (Indians), who living beneath the equinoctial sky and having always a daytime equal to the darkness of night, cannot bear clothes upon them because of the excessive heat of the air. But we mean rather that the human race, according to its common properties which belong to all, should be under the Monarch's reign, and governed by a common rule for the maintenance of peace. And this rule or law the particular princes ought to receive from him : just as the practical intellect for the purpose of arriving at an operative conclusion receives a general proposition from the speculative intellect, and under that general proposition takes to itself the particular, which is its own, and in a particular way ends by putting it into operation. And not only is this possible for one, but it is necessary that it should proceed from one, that all confusion about universal principles may be removed. Moses also wrote in the law that this had been done by himself, who taking the chiefs of the tribes of the children of Israel, left to them the lesser judgements, but reserved to himself alone the judgement in higher matters and those which affected the common interests of the whole people, which judgements, common to all, the chiefs used throughout their own tribes, according as it suited each particular tribe. Therefore is it better for the human race to be ruled by one than by many and so by a Monarch, who is a single ruler, and if better, more acceptable to God. . . .

XV. A metaphysical argument, that goodness consists in a certain unity and that 'to sin is nothing else than to progress away from unity to plurality,' leads to this conclusion :

All concord depends upon the unity which is in men's wills : and the human race at its best is a certain harmony. For just as one man, in his best and proper state, is a certain harmonious whole both as regards his soul and body, so likewise the household, the city and the kingdom ; so, too, is the whole human race. Therefore all humanity in its ideal state depends upon the unity which exists in the wills of all. But this cannot be unless there be one will which dominates and rules all the others with a view to a single end. . . .

XVI. The book ends with the confirmation of the thesis from the fact that never 'since the fall of our first parents . . . was the world everywhere at rest until the perfect monarchy of Augustus when, in the fulness of time the Son of God was born.

But the condition of the world from the time when that seamless garment first suffered a rent from the fingernail of cupidity we can both read in books, and would that we did not behold it with our eyes. Oh, race of men! By how many storms, how many a tossing, how many a shipwreck must you needs be shaken while like a beast with many heads you strive after divergent ends! You are sick both in the higher and in the lower intellect and in affection: you have no care for the higher understanding with its infallible reasons, nor for the lower which wears the visage of experience, nor yet for affection inspired by the sweetness of the divine pleading, when by the trumpet of the Holy Spirit those sweet strains reached your ears: 'Behold how good and joyful a thing it is, brethren, to live together in unity.'

The reader may wish next to recall the conceptions of the international community and of the State held by the Spanish neo-scholastic theologians. These have been illustrated by the extracts given on previous pages. The theories of Suarez and Dante seem to be poles apart. To the latter the unity of human society and the need of a single political constitution for it were almost self-evident. To the former there appears no prospect of organizing the world as a single society, though his endeavour to rationalize the qualities of the sovereign State lead him inevitably to the conclusion that States have a natural tendency to and need of association. Thus some of the ground lost to Christian sociology in the previous two centuries is recovered. Even Suarez' analysis of sovereignty shows there to be nothing absolute or eternal about the sovereign State.

SUAREZ. *De Caritate, XIII, II,* 4:

What, it may be asked, is a perfect community; and who is a sovereign ruler. . . . That depends upon the mode of jurisdiction of each ruler or State; and the sign of supreme jurisdiction is to be found in the fact that such a ruler or State provides a tribunal in which all the legal cases of that country are terminated, without appeal to any higher tribunal. For whenever an appeal is provided for, that is the sign of an imperfect State, since to appeal is the act of an inferior invoking his superior.

From which we may conclude—and it is also the logical conclusion of the Salamanca school in the previous century—these two propositions. First that the existence of a natural society of nations points to the need of international institutions to decide disputes between States and to promote their common well-being : second that if and when such institutions come into being, the attribute of 'Sovereignty' and 'supreme jurisdiction' in the Government passes to the higher institution.

Between the work of Dante and the opening of the nineteenth century no less than twenty schemes for an organized society or confederation have been enumerated by Ter Meulen.[1] Several of these schemes, after the Reformation, were the work of non-Catholics, but have not, on that account, lacked diligent consideration among Catholic students of international affairs. Grotius'[2] great book *De Jure Belli et Pacis*, which modern Protestant lawyers and other commentators, ignorant of the texts reproduced in our present work, have long regarded as the Father of International Law, has a slender passage on arbitration by a Congress of States, which is in accord with the doctrines of Vittoria and Vasquez. After recalling (Book II, Chap. XXIII) the recorded cases of arbitrators or umpires from antiquity he continues :

> But much more are Christian kings and States bound to try this way of avoiding war. For, if in order to avoid going to law in infidel courts certain arbitrators were appointed by Jews and by Christians, and that course commanded by St. Paul (1 Corinthians vi), how much more ought it to be done in order to avoid a much greater inconvenience, namely war? So Tertullian argues that a Christian must not bear arms, since he may not even go to law ; which, however, according to what we have said elsewhere, must be understood with a certain qualification.
>
> And, both for this reason and for others, it would be useful, and indeed it is necessary, that Congresses of Christian States should be held, in which the controversies which arise among some of them may be decided by others who are not interested, and in which measures may be taken to compel the parties to accept Peace upon fair and reasonable terms.

Of the various endeavours by writers outside the Catholic Church to reconstruct a framework of international order in the midst of the callous and incessant use of arms by

[1] In *Der Gedanke der Internationalen Organization in Seiner Entwicklung*.

[2] For a Catholic appreciation of Grotius see F. F. Urquhart in Plater's *Primer of Peace and War*.

the princes of Europe, we do not hesitate to point to that of William Penn the Quaker as approximating most nearly to the Christian tradition of international peace.

Penn, whose personal friendship with his Catholic King, James II, is one of the least remembered incidents in a life passionately devoted to the defence of liberty as he conceived it, shows, in his essay ' towards the Present and Future Peace of Europe ' that vivid horror of war between Christians which has been the *leit motif* of Papal peace-making from St. Clement of Rome to Pius XI :

> There is another manifest benefit which redounds to Christendom by this peaceable expedient—the reputation of Christianity will in some degree be recovered in the sight of infidels ; which by the many bloody and unjust wars of Christians, not only with them but one with another, hath been greatly impaired.

Nor is the Quaker statesman blind to the opportunities and duties of the Catholic hierarchy to promote Peace.

> Here is a wide field for the reverend clergy of Europe to act their part in, who have so much the possession of princes and people too. May they recommend and labour this pacific means I offer, which will end blood if not strife ; and then reason upon free debate will be judge and not the sword.

The traditional preoccupation of the Christian peacemaker with the menace of Islam is not absent from his mind.

> Another advantage is the great security it will be to Christians against the inroads of the Turk in their most prosperous fortune. For it had been impossible for the Porte to have prevailed so often and so far from Christendom but by the carelessness, or wilful connivance, if not aid, of some Christian princes.

His actual proposal is for the establishment of a European Diet, Parliament and Estates.

> Now if the sovereign princes of Europe who represent that society, or independent state of men that was previous to the obligations of society, would, for the same reason that engaged men first into society, viz. love of peace and order, agree to meet by their stated deputies in a general diet, estates, or parliament, and there establish rules of justice for sovereign princes to observe one to another ; and thus to meet yearly, or once in two or three years at farthest, so as they shall see cause, and to be styled the Sovereign or Imperial Diet, Parliament or State

of Europe ; before which sovereign assembly should be brought all differences depending between one sovereign and another that cannot be made up by private embassies before the sessions begin ; and that if any of the sovereignties that constitute these Imperial States shall refuse to submit their claim or pretensions to them, or to abide and perform the judgement thereof and seek their remedy by arms, or delay their compliance beyond the time prefixed in their resolutions, all the other sovereignties, united as one strength, shall compel the submission and performance of the sentence, with damages to the suffering party, and charges to the sovereignties that obliged their submission. To be sure, Europe would quietly obtain the so much desired and needed peace to her harassed inhabitants ; no sovereignty in Europe having the power can show the will to dispute the conclusion ; and, consequently, peace would be procured and continued in Europe.

The international sanctions envisaged in this passage are more in accordance with the general trend of Christian tradition than is the pacifism of Tertullian, subsequently revived by the Society of Friends. Penn has a wise saying upon armaments :

> Nor is it to be thought that any will keep up an army, after such an Empire is on foot, which may hazard the safety of the rest. However, if it be seen requisite, the question may be asked, by order of the Sovereign States, why such a one either raises or keeps up a formidable body of troops, and be obliged forthwith to reform or reduce them ; lest anyone, by keeping up a great body of troops, should surprise a neighbour. But a small force in every other sovereignty, as it is capable or accustomed to maintain, will certainly prevent that danger and vanquish any such fear.

William Penn, the Quaker, the Catholic Abbé de St. Pierre, whose work we quote, and Leibnitz the philosopher who expressed in his treatise upon the rights of the princes of Germany (1678), his *Codex Juris Gentium Diplomaticus* and several of his letters a longing to restore the Papacy and Empire as the guardians of peace in Europe, all alike assume an alliance between sovereigns to be the necessary basis of international order. Not so Kant, who writing his essay on Perpetual Peace a century later than Penn, under the influence of the French Revolution, boldly declares (Section II, Article 1 and 2) 'The civil constitution in every State shall be republican. The Law of Nations shall be founded as a federation of free States.' And Jeremy Bentham, in *The Fragments of an essay on the principles of International Law,* written a few years earlier, recks little of princes. It is for 'the common and equal utility of all nations' that he would have international law codified, a common tribunal established and standing armies abolished; and what concerns him is the attitude of the mass of the people, 'the part most exposed to be led away by prejudice.' They, he believes, 'would not be sooner apprised of the measure, than they would feel the relief it brought them.' Rather than providing armed contingents to enforce the decrees of his court he would secure compliance 'by guaranteeing the liberty of the Press in each State.' Pathetic confidence in the love of journalists for truth and of democracies for peace! Bentham has moved far from the spirit of Penn, or of Leibnitz, not to speak of the Catholic doctors of international ethics. God has no part in his plan.

Several of the would-be architects of international order whether Catholic or Protestant, between the mediæval and the modern centuries reveal no profound ethical or theoretic basis to their work, but aim rather at a convenient stabilization of the *status quo* or a balance of power advantageous to their own countries. Such had been the '*Treaty of Alliances and Confederations*' of the Hussite King, George Podiebrad in the fifteenth century, and such the European peace achieved by the skill of Cardinal Wolsey in the sixteenth. While referring readers to the works of Ter Meulen and others especially devoted to these projects, we will confine ourselves here to two plans by Catholic authors, one of which seems to have had little, the other a considerable influence upon the development of thought concerning international society.

Father Emeric Crucé, a French Carmelite monk published in 1623 in Paris a massive work entitled *Le Nouveau Cynée, ou discours d'Estat représentant les occasions et moyens d'establir une paix générale et la liberté de commerce pour tout le monde.*' Cyneas was the pacific Counsellor of Pyrrhus, the Macedonian King; and the choice of his name for the title of the work is typical of a certain facetiousness which pervades it. Father Emeric was an original thinker, who did not hesitate to find new motives for international union and to jettison the older political forms of Christendom. A man of encyclopædic erudition, to judge from the numberless quotations from the Bible, the Fathers, classical antiquity, history and contemporary writers with which his pages are crammed, he conceives a scheme of international organization far ahead of his time and envisages the extension of the pacific function of the Holy See to include non-Catholic and non-Christian States, as indeed has since come to pass. Two editions of his book are known to have appeared in his lifetime, though originals are now hard to come by. Hugo Grotius, from the internal evidence of passages from *Le Nouveau Cynée* reproduced in *De Jure Belli et Pacis*, must have known the work and doubtless met its author in Paris. Leibnitz read it in his youth, and the Abbé de St. Pierre had a confused remembrance of it. The following quotations are for the most part from the English edition of Dr. Bulch, the American international lawyer :[1]

'Who am I a Frenchman to wish harm to an Englishman, a Spaniard or an Indian? I cannot wish it when I consider that they are men like me, that I am a subject like to them to error and to sin.'

Crucé deduces from the common nature of men and the society of the human race that war is contrary to the right dignity of a rational nature, that freedom of commerce is equally required by reason and the evident interests of States; and that the improvement of communications (he is particularly enthusiastic about canals) is one of the first duties of organized international society. To him the mutual obligations of that society, arising from Natural Law, apply equally to Christian and non-Christian nations, to the East as to the West.

Some have exhorted the Christian princes to peace in order that by their union they may be fortified against their common enemy; and a famous personage has gone so far as to demonstrate the way to exterminate the Turks in four years or thereabouts, and sundry other pretty conceptions, easy enough to put on paper. There are others, whose quill does not fly so high but who are content with inventions for policing and enriching

[1] With slight verbal alterations suggested by Sir Geoffrey Butler in his *Essays in Statecraft*, pp. 90 *et seq.*

their own country, and care so little about foreigners, that they think it a form of political prudence to sow divisions among them, in order the more surely to enjoy repose. No such opinion do I hold. On the contrary, it seems to me that when one sees one's neighbour's house in flames or fallen upon him, one has reason to have both fear and compassion, inasmuch as the Society of Mankind is a single body, all the members of which suffer together in such manner that it is impossible that the maladies of one should not be communicated to the others. Thus this modest book of mine contains a universal polity, equally useful to all nations and agreeable to those who have the light of reason and a feeling of humanity.

It is high time 'to make reason and justice reign in the world, instead of the violence which is proper only to brute beasts.' Sea and land have been empurpled with the blood of men killed in war: maybe it was 'a necessary blood-letting to purge the world of its vicious and superfluous humours, and God willed to make avail of this means to establish Monarchies. 'Now that those monarchies are established upon the stout pillars of long possession, they must not be subverted but rather made firmer by a good peace.' More shrewd than Bentham, Crucé discounts democracy as a reinforcement of peace. 'Tyranny is unfortunate, I confess, but popular fury and confusion is still more to be feared.' In the republics of classical antiquity 'the citizens were always quarrelling. Then followed massacre, pillaging and confusion, so that the greatest tyranny in the world would not have caused half those evils, for which their best remedy lay in the domination of a single man.'

Be that as it may, international peace must, in Crucé's view, be based upon a solid foundation of internal peace. Then there must be between States, for their common good, increase of commerce, money and credit for exchange, improvement of waterways and other means of communication, a common endeavour to exterminate piracy and, within each, sound education. The merchant is in his view, the hero of the piece, the symbol and minister of international society: the sense of free commerce as an essential part of the Law of Nations was firmly embedded in his mind. 'It is reasonable that the Prince should levy a few honest pennies on the merchandise which is brought in and taken out of his territory, but he must in so doing use moderation as much as he possibly can, and especially about merchandise necessary to life.'

To forward these good purposes and to prevent war a permanent international assembly should be set up.

For I am sure that few people will deny precedence to the Pope, both on account of the honour that Christian princes accord him and of the duty that they almost all render to him in spiritual matters, as well as for the respect of Ancient Rome, of which he is temporal Lord ; and, therefore, the first place in all assemblies belongs to him or his Legate.

Among many detailed reforms of unequal value which Father Emeric propounds, is that there should be a fixed international value for money.

The loss that they (princes) can suffer in this policy will never be so great as the utility of a general peace. . . . One must not fear to undertake a thing which is necessary and easy to execute provided that peace be universal. But in order to begin this affair properly, it would be necessary that a powerful prince should exhort all the others to follow the regulation described above, in order that the passages being free and commerce being open by means of peace, one can trade everywhere without damage. There is no one more capable of that than the Pope. It is his duty to bring about (*moyenner*) a general concord between Christian princes. The King of France would do the same with the Mohammedans.

Elaborate rules of precedence and procedure are laid down. The Pope or his delegate would have the presidency. And out of a fascinating list of potentates including Prester John, the Grand Duke of Muscovy, the King of England and the Great Mogul, the Emperor of the Turks would come first 'especially if he also holds the city of Constantinople' : after him, be it noted, comes the Christian Emperor. Crucé is nothing if not a realist.

Here then is the first scheme for an organized positive Society of Nations comprising the whole world and not Christendom only. Its purpose is as much to promote co-operation between nations and their economic welfare in peace as to prevent war. Its chief organ is an assembly of plenipotentiaries representing the actual Governments at a given time. The Assembly is to be permanent, or able to meet constantly. Its functions are legislative (by majority), judicial and conciliatory. Recourse to arbitration is a definite obligation : refusal to obey the law of the whole society and its awards involves international military sanctions against the recusant, if 'gentle means are unsuccessful.' This might well be a précis of the Covenant of the League of Nations : it is the work of a French monk of the seventeenth century.

The project of the Abbé de St. Pierre,[1] framed in consequence of his experience of the negotiations for the Peace of Utrecht, and published in that city in three volumes between 1713 and 1717 revives and improves upon the Grand Design of the *Republique Très Chrétienne*, written in all probability by the Duc de Sully, but attributed by him to Henry IV of France, in 1638. It is more profitable therefore for us to trace the plan in its later than in its earlier form. Its salient parts taken from the Abbé's own *Abrégé* are as follows :

CHARLES IRÉNÉE CASTEL, (THE ABBÉ DE ST. PIERRE) : *Extracts from the 'Project for perpetual peace for Europe.'*

Article 4. 'Each Sovereign will be contented for himself and for his successors with the territory which he actually possesses, or which he ought to possess according to the treaty hereto annexed.' The rest of the article elaborates provisions for the maintenance of existing frontiers and ends :

The Sovereigns will not be able to make exchange of any territory amongst themselves, nor sign any treaty amongst themselves, except by the consent and under the guarantee of the Union of three-quarters of the twenty-four voters, and the Union will remain guarantor of the execution of the reciprocal promises.

Article 7. The deputies will work continually to reduce to writing all the articles of Commerce in general, and of the different kinds of Commerce between particular nations, in such a manner, however, that the laws may be equal and reciprocal

[1] For the full text and commentaries see Ter Meulen ; for extracts Hode, *Idée de Fédération internationale dans l'Histoire* ; Butler, *Essays in Statecraft*, and Elizabeth York, *Leagues of Nations, Ancient, Medieval and Modern.* For the consideration of the Abbé de St. Pierre's project by the British Foreign Office Committee which prepared the Covenant of the League of Nations, see Florence Wilson, *Origins of the Covenant.*

for all nations and based upon equity. The articles passed by the majority of the votes of the deputies present will be executed in the meantime, according to their form and tenor, until they are revised by a vote of three-quarters of the deputies, when a greater number of deputies have adhered to the Union.

The Union will set up, in different towns, chambers for the maintenance of commerce, composed of deputies authorized to reconcile and to judge strictly, and as a court of final jurisdiction, actions which shall arise from serious injury, either to commerce or other matters, between the subjects of different Sovereigns, above the sum of ten thousand pounds. Other lawsuits of less consequence will be settled ordinarily by the judges of the district or place of residence of the defendant. Each Sovereign will co-operate in the execution of the judgements of the Chamber of Commerce, as though they were his own judgements.

Each Sovereign will, at his own cost, clear his land of robbers and bandits and his sea-coasts of pirates under pain of indemnification, and, if he has need of help, the Union will come to his assistance.

Article 8. No Sovereign will take up arms and commit any act of hostility except against a State which shall have been declared an enemy of the European Society ; but if he has some cause of complaint against one of the members or some claim to make upon a member, he will cause his memorandum (upon the matter) to be presented by his deputy to the Senate in the town of the peace sessions (*ville de paix*) ; and the Senate will assume the charge of reconciling the differences by its Commissioners and Arbitrators ; or, if they cannot be reconciled, then the Senate will pass judgement by arbitration by the majority of votes provisionally and by three-quarters of the votes definitively. This judgement will not be delivered until each Senator has received (upon the matter) the instructions and orders of his Sovereign and has communicated them to the Senate.

The Sovereign who takes up arms before the Union's declaration of war, or who refuses to execute a ruling of the Society or a judgement of the Senate, shall be declared an enemy of the Society, which will make war upon him until he is disarmed and until the execution of the judgement and the rulings. He shall even pay the expenses of the war, and the territory conquered from him at the time of the suspension of warfare shall remain permanently separated from his dominions.

If after the Society has been formed to the extent of a membership of forty persons, a Sovereign refuses to enter it, it will declare him an enemy of European peace, and will make war upon him until he enters it, or until he is entirely dispossessed of his territory.

Article 10. The members and associates of the Union will

contribute to the expenses of the Society and to the subsidies for security, each in proportion to his revenues and to the wealth of his people, and the shares of each will be regulated, at first provisionally, by the majority of votes, and afterwards by three-quarters of the votes, after the Commissioners of the Union have taken, upon the subject, the necessary instructions and explanations in each State ; and if it is found that some member has, in the meantime, paid too much, the sum shall be made good to him afterwards, both as to principal and interest, by those who have paid too little. The less powerful Sovereigns entitled, in association together, to but one vote, will take turns for the nomination of their deputy in proportion to their share.

Article 11. When the Senate deliberates upon something urgent and provisional concerning the security of the Society or the prevention or quieting of some sedition, the question may be decided provisionally by the majority of votes, and before deliberating it will be decided, by the majority, whether the matter concerned is of a provisional nature.

TAPARELLI D'AZEGLIO. '*Essai Théorique de Droit Naturel,*' *Book VI, Chap. V. Article* 11. *Form of international societies : their end, their duties and their rights :*

1363. After having established the origin of international societies[1] we must now study their forms and their laws. First we see a grouping of intelligent beings who work together in pursuit of their common good. In this case the intelligent beings who co-operate thus are themselves true societies. Thus it is a *society of societies*—societies associated together, societies subordinated to the whole ; in short, a hypotattic[2] association between independent societies. Consequently this international society is by its very nature and origin a real polyarchy. . . .

1364. The first physiological law of a social being may be formulated as follows : *Authority* is the constituent principle of any society whatever. The international and ethnarchic society must therefore possess an authority. It must be governed and guided in all that is necessary to its existence, its perfection and the attainment of its end. How could there exist a Law of Nations, that is to say a body of laws binding upon all nations, if there were not a real authority capable of laying down those laws ? All authors admit the existence of the *positive* rules which constitute the Law of Nations ; but I doubt whether all have perceived as well that necessary connection between these two propositions—there is a Law of Nations ; therefore there exists an international *authority*. Several writers have confused this

[1] See preceding chapter.

[2] Taparelli appears to have coined this word ' hypotattique.' It is presumably derived from ὑποτάσσειν, to subordinate.

authority with the natural authority of the Creator Himself, the supreme ruler of all nations and the universal society of men. Others deny the existence of any specific authority, and say that the nations obey common laws because they want to, not because they have to. Others say that the obligation to obey results from a contract freely entered into, which binds only those who want to be bound. This last opinion may perhaps be admissible in the case of nations in a state, as it were, of infancy, who are free at least to a certain degree, since they are deprived of those natural, abiding international relations which have their origin in natural facts. Such peoples have hardly any common bond of enterprise or interest with other nations. But as they develop they establish contacts with others, and so soon as this happens we see that common order appearing which creates the positive rules of international law : but then we are obliged to suppose that there already exists an international authority.

Nature of International Authority :

1365. Assuming the free consent of the nations, the international society naturally takes the form of a polyarchy (i.e. authority vested in the many) : for upon the supposition that the members of the society are all specifically and individually equal, the authority belongs originally to all equally.

The original form of the international authority is thus naturally polyarchic. This fact would not, however, prevent it from being modified in the course of time so as to become more or less monarchic, if the associated nations agree. . . . The international authority will ordinarily and naturally be polyarchic ; even when it appears to be administered by one man, it belongs in reality to all the associated peoples.

1366. But in whom then is this international authority to reside ? To answer that question let us restate the foundation upon which all International Law is based. The nations are independent societies, their association is in itself a perfectly voluntary association. *Thus authority resides, as of right, in the common accord of the associated nations and it is for the members of the association to determine under what form this authority is to be exercised.* Since the decline of the German Empire and of the quasi-theocratic power of the Popes, the international authority has, among European peoples, revealed itself in the agreements between the different sovereigns, expressed in treaties, alliances, congresses, confederations, etc. But just as we have observed (in the origin of human society) the polyarchy of brothers, equal in rights, emancipated from the father's control, giving to their common authority certain forms, in order that it may be more effective and more lasting, so we see modern nations, now that they are freed from the guardianship of the Holy Roman Empire and the protection of the

Popes, feeling more and more the need of an international authority which is regular, perfectly determined in all its aspects, an authority which is strong, which is respected by all, and which can ensure that the rights of the weak shall no longer be at the mercy of the strong.

Herein lies the interests of the majority. But when interest itself is at one with the requirements of justice, it becomes all-powerful and infallibly determines the forms which accord most harmoniously with the needs of human societies. And so, I believe, we shall gradually see arising in the world a kind of universal federal tribunal which will replace alliances, congresses and treaties, just as these have temporarily replaced to-day the supreme authority of the Emperor and the patriarchal government of the Popes. I do not see how this stage can fail to come, though it be reached but slowly, for the life of nations can be reckoned in centuries as the life of men is counted in years. Special confederations between small States seem to be a prelude to the organization of the *international authority*, just as, in the Middle Ages, the evolution of the Commune led, little by little, to a complete state of civil equality and the unity of the political authority.

1367. But let us leave to the passage of time, the art of politics and the march of events—blind instruments of Divine Providence—the gradual development of the political forms of international society, so as to achieve the welfare of the nations, in the same way as the civic forms of the State must insensibly tend to the attainment of happiness for the families and individuals that compose it.

We can now conclude from all that has been said, that the peoples form among themselves a society of equals ; that in consequence the authority necessary to direct them resides in their common accord, or at least in that of the majority of the nations associated ; that in their common interest they cannot refuse to acknowledge that authority without, at the same time, snapping the social relations which unite them together ; and that this authority must have the power and the strength to maintain order within the international association. . . .

Duties of the international authority in regard to international order :

1371. The ethnarchic authority must then be able to ascertain and take into consideration the grievances of the subjects against their sovereign as well as the grievances of sovereigns against their subjects. This is a fact which has always been at least implicitly recognized even by those who possibly did not suspect the existence of the authority of which we are speaking. For does it not amount to recognizing a sort of superior authority when the different peoples draw up and circulate all over the world manifestoes, addresses and protests by which they want to prove to sovereigns disinterested in their cause, that their claims are just and their rights beyond doubt? Is this not a kind of appeal or recourse to a supreme tribunal, which in the last resort is the judge of the rights of kings and peoples?

1372. It may be urged that these peoples or parties have called for force to support their pretensions and not for a decree or decision founded on reason and justice. My answer would be that the use of force in a society is a function of authority; and that this authority cannot reasonably employ force, unless it has first solved the question of right and wrong. The objection, indeed, seems to confirm my theory. I do not say that the court is always constituted but that it is always more or less recognized implicity, be it only through a confused sense of natural justice. It is the same sense which, in a quarrel between individuals, often causes the parties to have recourse to certain arbiters or judges, even though no actual superiority is recognized in them. *This recourse shows that we have a sort of natural need of having our rights determined by a third party*, before we can call in forte to our aid: it is a fact which can be observed among nations as among individuals. . . .

Is it not indeed evident that struggles between some nations ordinarily upset the tranquillity of *all* the peoples of Europe? Have not these peoples the right to provide for their own peace? Cannot they secure that peace by their efforts in common? And does not this community of effort in pursuit of the same end tend to build up a kind of union based on a principle which is able to reduce multiplicity to unity? There must therefore exist in Europe a natural principle of unity which links all the peoples together for the purpose of securing their common good, order and justice. But that principle can only be *authority*. That must be the case unless we are to say that Providence, which has provided the means of settling even the most trivial differences between individuals, has abandoned to force and violence the interests of ten or twenty great countries, whose existence and tranquillity can be embroiled simply because one nation sees fit to disseminate discord and anarchy. No: that cannot be. God cares for peoples as he does for individuals. Authority is there to protect them, and we see those whose peace is threatened appeal instinctively and naturally to that authority which nature itself has established to regulate the common interests of nations, to redress grievances and to guarantee peace and happiness to all alike.

Protection of the external independence of the associated nations:

1374. We have assumed that the associated nations are independent. But if they be independent, how then can they be subject to another authority? To understand this we must remember that the independence of a nation consists essentially in its *not being dependent upon another nation,* and upon its ability to make its own laws, both civil and political. The nations are, in fact, self-governing: they do not form a part of some other public society: hence the ethnarchic authority differs essentially from the authority of the State, because the distinctive character proper to a society is determined by the end for which it exists. In the same way as the family does not lose its domestic liberty by being united to civil society, so the nation does not lose its political liberty when it forms part of an ethnarchic society. (For §§1375–7 and 8, see Chap. VI.)

World public opinion:

1390. The principal means of securing the public good is probity in the superior and secondary authorities. The Government of the ethnarchy should therefore develop this high standard of honesty in every possible way, by the aid of religion, of honour, of mutual goodwill and good counsel, and of all the elements by which human society can profit in this regard. From this point of view, the ethnarchic authority alone can furnish the rulers of nations with the advantages which civil authority confers on individuals. Within civil society emulation between citizen and citizen, mutual respect, friendship, gratitude and a thousand other sentiments combine to make the individual more or less dependent upon public opinion. But public opinion, though it exercises a greater authority upon rulers than is ordinarily believed, has less hold over them than over private citizens; it does not generally stare them in the face with such compelling evidence. Yet what an effect the public opinion of several great nations—of all European nations, for instance—has upon rulers, to make them respect what is right and repudiate what is wrong, to make their consciences triumph over their evil inclinations! What great benefits would ensue if this public opinion set up between rulers a noble rivalry to make their subjects happy, and if to that end it gave them independent and disinterested advice and set great and magnificent examples before their eyes? Let us suppose that this force of opinion of the ethnarchy as a whole is brought to bear upon the functions of the deliberative power; upon the means by which knowledge is spread;[1] upon the attributions of the legislature; upon the right direction of a people's will; upon the acts of the executive authority; that it is directed towards the energetic action of all the forces of government; foresight in the administrative; integrity in the magistrature; vigorous discipline in the army. We shall then realize the immense advantages which the activity

[1] By this I understand Taparelli to mean education and the Press, and in modern times wireless broadcasting and the cinema.

of the international society, if well directed, would confer upon the nations. We shall then admire the infinite wisdom of the Creator who has willed to grant all these blessings to the nations by ordaining that they are all destined to form together one vast ethnarchic society.

League of Nations potentially Universal :

1391. The prosperity of nations tends naturally to increase their population : it also strengthens their power of expansion and multiplies relations between them and the other peoples with whom they are not yet actually leagued together. These relations produce in the long run an actual association of nations. Little by little they extend the ethnarchy to every part of the globe, and so attain the highest degree of social perfection. This perfection being the goal of the ethnarchy, it must direct all its efforts to second this natural tendency, which leads the European nations to communicate to barbarous peoples the two things which constitute true civilization, namely religion and civil organization. . . .

Duty of submission to the Ethnarchic Authority :

1392. To every right there is a corresponding duty. Right and duty are proportional the one to the other and depend upon the order which gives rise to both. Whence it comes that the nations are obliged to obey the ethnarchic authority in everything which comes within the competence of that authority ; and that competence extends to every action by which the associated nations can and ought to promote the common weal of the ethnarchy. They must therefore obey every time the orders of the ethnarchic authority relate to the common good of their association.

1394. To resume ; ethnarchic obedience is less vigorous and its scope less extensive than civil obedience. The international authority extends to a small number of relations.[1] The associated States are by their origin and nature independent and their mutual relations are especially the business of their respective sovereigns. It is therefore possible to reduce to a small number of headings the obligations to which the duty of ethnarchic obedience gives rise.

A State must follow the advice and the decisions of the judges of the ethnarchy ;

I. In the repression of internal disorders ;

II. In regard to the conflicts which may arise between it and other associated States ;

[1] Taparelli does not here foresee the almost innumerable matters of common concern to nations which follow from their ever-increasing economic interdependence.

III. In the help which it must give in providing a mutual guarantee of the rights of the associated nations against their enemies, internal and external ;

IV. And in all the enterprises whose object is the fulfilment of a duty required by the common interests of all.

Equality of rights between Nations :

1395. The ethnarchic society is a society whose members are essentially and originally *equal ;* that is an elemental fact which must be respected in all the successive developments of the society. Any modification of the ethnarchy's regime which tends to substitute for this original equality any inequality whatsoever between the associated nations is essentially unjust ; for all must have an equal power to gain a hearing and to secure what, in justice, is their due.

Territorial Integrity :

1395. As the ethnarchy can only exist through an association of peoples, each of whom already possesses a certain territory, it is clear that except as the result of some crime committed by one of them, the international authority will never have the right to change at will the respective frontiers of the different nations. If frontiers are to be changed, that can only be by agreement between the sovereigns concerned.[1] Such conventions can be sanctioned, directed towards the common good and consequently strengthened by the ethnarchic authority. The respect of equality among nations and of their respective properties is a twofold duty which is the very foundation of the ethnarchic regime. It is on the basis of that double duty that the international authority can gather information, within its proper scope, upon all that can promote the welfare of the peoples, upon the actual state of their needs and the means of supplying them and so advance the progress of civilization.

Data for International Action :

1397. Diplomacy ought to obtain complete information upon the peoples' needs, needs which, in the international society, can concern their internal relations or their mutual relations one with another or their external relations with nations who are not members of the ethnarchy. As for internal needs the ethnarchic authority should establish a system of information and inquiry which would enable it to prevent disorders and secure to each of the component elements of national society the rights to which it is entitled. Upon the fulfilment of this duty depends in no small measure the happiness of nations and of sovereigns. In the second case (that is of mutual relations between members)

[1] Cf. Article XIX of the Covenant of the League of Nations.

the authority should secure full information so as to be able to prevent international rivalries, to frustrate intrigues, and arrest a course of events which would lead to a reasonable Government being impeded. With regard to relations with far-off nations who are not members of the ethnarchy, they cannot give rise to any rigorous duty; they depend rather upon a feeling of goodwill which inclines us to seek their welfare than upon the fear of suffering injury at their hands.

International Legislation :

1398. The international authority ought next to deliberate upon the information which it has collected; it should then take decisions and make laws. All the member States enjoying equal rights can collaborate on an equal footing in framing the laws. It is rather for applied political science than for the theorist to determine the organic form which should be given to this legislative equality. We need do no more than observe that as the equilibrium of rights is not likely to last long without the equilibrium of strength, the weaker nations will gradually and naturally come to depend upon the stronger.

Thus, in order that the ethnarchy may be well constituted, it is necessary that the weaker States should group themselves in different confederations, so that they may balance the power of the Great States, just as the communes often did in the Middle Ages.

1399. It is evident that a good system of ethnarchic laws, a code carefully prepared and universally adopted by all civilized nations, would be of the utmost value, and would contribute greatly to the security and happiness of the peoples. This code should aim at regulating three main points, according to our conception of international order :

(1) It could place under the protection of a respected public authority the great principle of international goodwill and all the laws which directly derive from it, in order to unite all nations in one universal society.

(2) It could lay down more fixed and clearly determined rules upon a multitude of subjects which Natural Law leaves somewhat indeterminate.

(3) It could provide an effective sanction for those two different kinds of laws.

Such are the conditions of any code of positive laws : in the present case they deserve all the more attention because of a baneful prejudice which often makes the peoples believe that there is no law which is binding as between nation and nation, that 'reasons of State' may excuse the most flagrant injustice, and that Cabinets need have no conscience.

The League of Nations :

An appreciation of the League of Nations in relation to the

Christian tradition is contained in the following summary of the teaching of GEORGES RENARD.[1]

His main theme is that ' The International community is not a secondary State, artificially created by the will of nations ; it is the State of Nature.'

There are two basic conceptions of the law of nations. The first, inspired by Jean Jacques Rousseau and the ' Social Contract,' lays down that the state of nature among nations is independence. Being independent they then bound themselves to each other by treaties. On the one hand we have the independence and equality of States and, on the other, respect for engagements entered into by States ; all international law is governed by these two theses and this is the classic conception of it, whereby it is built up without reference to any objective principle and becomes a law not of subordination but of co-ordination only.

Four objections to this conception can be advanced :

1. The ' Social Contract ' is a vicious circle ; for the contract cannot be the ultimate basis of the rule of law either between individuals or States for the simple reason that a contract presupposes itself a rule of law—the rule which establishes the binding force of contracts. Treaties do not create a community of nations but merely regulate it.

2. Treaties of peace are the most important sort of treaty : but, imposed as they are by the conqueror on the conquered, they cannot, if they are mere contracts which the latter has been forced to accept, create any legal obligation on his part or give any security to the conqueror. Neither respect for the given word nor the moral effect of victory is enough to make them binding on him who has been forced to accept them.

3. There are just and unjust treaties as there are just and unjust contracts. How can one distinguish between them save by invoking objective justice ? For really it cannot be said that treaties are neither just nor unjust, that they simply exist and that there is nothing more to be done.

4. The purely contractual conception of international law springs from a system of philosophy according to which sovereignty is an absolute unlimited power which resides in its fullest development in the State. If this is so, all liberty, individual and corporate, is merely an uncertain concession which the State can revoke at any time and all authority, even that of the father of the family, is delegated by the State at its discretion. Nobody has the right to look over the wall which separates States from each other.

[1] *Les Fondements Philosophiques du Droit International* in *Les Grandes Activités de la Société des Nations devant la Pensée Chrétienne.*

In actual fact, sociability is not accidental or subordinate either as between individuals or nations, and Rousseau was wrong in thinking so. There is a natural society between nations and therefore a juridical system of which treaties are, and ought to be, only an adaptation to the infinite variety of historical conditions. It is from their conformity with the pre-existent natural law and from their fitness to make it work in harmony with the circumstances of the times that treaties derive their binding force. Treaties are not the source of international law; but it is from this law that they derive their legal validity. International law does not proceed from treaties but rules them.

Treaties are like laws. If just, they bind because of their justice, but if unjust, they do not bind at all. It must be remembered, however, that it is forbidden to rebel against them if to do so would cause serious disturbance constituting a threat to order or, as it is called, the common good of international society. The revision of treaties may therefore only be sought by means which respect the supreme requirements of international order and peace. Order and the common good are the basis of international law. To them sovereignty and freedom must not be sacrificed but subjected. This is the Christian conception of the law of nations founded on the philosophy of St. Thomas Aquinas.

It is this Christian conception which recurs in the Covenant of the League of Nations and in the Briand-Kellogg Pact, or Pact of Paris.

1. *The Covenant of the League.* It may be objected that it is only a contract, implying mere co-ordination without subordination. It must be judged by its object and by its internal structure.

Its object is no doubt the individual good of each State adhering to it, but it is also the good of that State not in so far as it is opposed to that of others, but in so far as it conforms to the latter in the pool of a common good, in which all have a share. The Covenant aims at a higher interest in which each of the parties sees its own special interest—as well as that of its partners. It is even a common good which goes beyond them, since the League of Nations itself claims a universal mandate and considers itself the legal equivalent of the whole international community.

By its internal structure it is a graded and organized society divided into ranks, with founder members and invited members who are admitted as of right, and finally all the other Powers who may be admitted if they give adequate guarantees. Similarly the Council has its permanent and semi-permanent seats and its seats occupied in rotation. The Covenant of the League is a charter. It inaugurates a new order.

2. *The Briand-Kellogg Pact.* At first sight this seems the type of a purely contractual and inorganic international act, but,

considered in its relations with the Covenant of the League and that of the Pan-American Union, it reveals, in this connection, a legal and political force which, in itself, it lacks. As the States which have signed it are mostly members of the League of Nations, they have already bound themselves to submit their differences to legal process, arbitration and mediation. Moreover, the Conference of Havana imposed similar obligations on the States of the New World in 1928.

Even if it is not the charter of an organization like that of Geneva, does it not resemble a declaration of rights rather than a contract? To outlaw war is to declare that there is a law above States to which they owe allegiance; that above their will there is something besides the bond of treaties; that international law contains something more than rules made and accepted by diplomatic conferences, and that there are other rules imposed from above to which States are not free to give or refuse their adhesion.

These rules arise from the fact that there is among nations a common good just as health is the common good of all the members of the human body.

The organization of peace among the peoples united in a vast moral organism under the rule of justice which designs its rank to each of them—*suam cuique tribuens dignitatem*—in the common good of humanity. This is the new formula of international law, that of the Covenant of the League and the Paris Pact. Francis de Vittoria was already working it out from the beginning of the sixteenth century and it is, in fact, a Christian formula.

The Catholic Church and the League of Nations:

The general attitude of the Holy See in regard to the League may be deduced from the Pontifical documents already cited (Benedict XV, Letter to the Belligerents, 1917; the Encyclical *Pacem Dei Munus Pulcherrimum*, 1920; Pius XI, Encyclical *Ubi Arcano Dei*, 1922; Christmas Address, 1930; Encyclical *Quadragesimo Anno*, 1931). The following are examples of many episcopal pronouncements.

ARCHBISHOP WHITESIDE OF LIVERPOOL. *Pastoral letter, November* 25, 1919:

. . . And whilst the Church is busy urging her children to seek the peace which Christ came on earth to establish, the epoch in which we are living will be remarkable in history for one event: that after a war unprecedented in many respects in the world's history, a Treaty of Peace has been signed by practically all the nations of the world.

The Catholic Church has little or nothing to say as to the precise terms of that Treaty of Peace, and in particular about the territorial and dynastic changes which have taken place from the agreements of the signatory powers. She is Catholic and so transcends all the boundaries of nations. She lives and carries on her work under every form of government—from an autocracy to a republic.

But there is one thing which has sprung into existence as a result of the Treaty of Peace, upon which the Church has her message for her children. It is what is known as the League of Nations. Before ever the American President ventilated at the Peace Conference his ideal of a League of Nations, a message had been sent to the belligerent nations from the Head of the Catholic Church. As early as August, 1917, Pope Benedict XV urged upon all the nations the necessity of some plan being devised and agreed to, by which the world might be secured from another devastating war.

(The famous passage from the letter of Benedict XV to the belligerent Governments on the foundations of peace is then quoted. See p. 216)

And in laying down these principles for the settlement of international differences, the Sovereign Pontiff was but expressing in his own words, and for the questions of the hour, what has ever been the teaching of Catholic theology.

Catholics, therefore, with these words of the Holy Father before them, can have no doubt as to what may be, and should be, their attitude, as citizens of one of the chief belligerent powers, when they are being invited to give their support to a movement now on foot, which has as its object to give life to the League of Nations, by bringing it into contact with the vitalizing power of the peoples of the nations, in whose hands for the future rests the final decision of peace and war. . . . International justice ultimately and in its last analysis is based on the natural law, of which God is the Author. This League of Nations is a genuine attempt to form on questions of public policy an international conscience. Since the days when the Catholic Church ruled the consciences of all Christians, it is the first step in that direction which the world has seen. Catholics, as directed by the Supreme Pontiff, cannot hold aloof from this movement. If for no other reason it is for them at least to see that the international conscience of the future is guided by that revealed truth of which the Catholic Church is the custodian and the interpreter.

CARDINAL MERCIER *on the League of Nations :*

The following declaration was communicated by the Belgian Government to the League of Nations.

The International Union of Social Studies, assembled at

Malines under the presidency of His Eminence Cardinal Mercier, being convinced

That the interdependence of nations creates among them a natural society, between whose members there ought to be legal relationships,

That the brotherhood of men implies brotherhood of nations.

That, moreover, the providential diversity of wealth and aptitudes of different peoples invites them to make peaceful exchanges for the benefit of all humanity,

And that war, disturbing this harmony, is a scourge which should be forestalled by every means of adjustment and arbitration.

Considering that the principle of the League of Nations is part of the Christian tradition, which found its application in the Christendom of the Middle Ages, and that it has been recalled in memorable circumstances by the Holy See.

Proclaims that the idea of giving a lasting shape to the natural comity of nations is just and beneficent,

Recognizes especially the efforts made by the League towards social betterment and labour legislation.

Expresses the hope that similar efforts will be made in favour of Christian minorities in countries where they are threatened,

Recommends all Catholics to follow the labours and support the work of the League,

And requests its President to send this resolution to the permanent office of the League at Geneva.

Cardinal Bourne, *Archbishop of Westminster. Extract from Pastoral Letter for Lent*, 1934 :

In the international field the present precarious position of the League of Nations must cause anxiety to all those who are convinced that some such organization is absolutely necessary for the maintenance of the peace of the world. As we have often pointed out before, it is the only organized effort which has been made to carry into effect the repeated wishes of the Holy See.

The League of Nations has indeed within it seeds of fundamental weakness. It was conceived and brought into existence largely owing to the efforts of the head of a great people. But it was promptly repudiated by that people. . . . Then again it has been impossible to build up the League on purely Christian principles. It has to embrace within its scope great nations which have never accepted the Christian ideal, and are governed by doctrines and traditions which, in many respects, contradict that ideal.

Nevertheless, the solidarity of all mankind, which is the consequence of all being alike creatures of Almighty God, ought to form some kind of basis for bringing the nations closer together. Certainly it is the duty of Catholics, by word and action, to give all the support they can to the League of Nations and to endeavour so to improve it as to make it a real and permanent instrument for the preservation of the peace of the world.

APPENDIX TO CHAPTER XI.

Relation of earlier schemes to the Covenant of the League of Nations :

A short summary of 'various schemes for a League of Nations, as well as other devices which have been proposed or attempted for the avoidance of war' is contained in the final report of the Phillimore Committee, appointed by the British Foreign Secretary, Mr. Balfour. This report, dated July 3, 1918, was the basis of the British contribution to the creation of the Covenant. The report shows a complete ignorance of the Treatise of Taparelli and makes no reference to the proposals made by Benedict XV a year before—though the Pope's proposals to the belligerents had undoubtedly helped to produce in their respective foreign offices such serious studies as this of the possibilities of a League of Nations. It contains, however, a thoughtful commentary upon the Project of the Abbé de St. Pierre and attributes to it a considerable influence upon the political ideas of the times. Quoting the criticism of Leibnitz that the Abbé's scheme was defective since it was in effect a confederation of absolute rulers, the report continues :

> It is not possible, however, to prove that democracy, had it existed and exercised sovereign rights in the first half of the eighteenth century, would have been less tenacious of them than were princes ; and we must rest content with the historical fact that the proprietary notion of the State did give the sovereign a personal interest in the extension of his sovereignty which acted as a deterrent to all schemes for preventing it. Nor can it be doubted that acquisitiveness exerts a greater influence upon the individual than upon the community ; and the examples of the United Netherlands, Switzerland and Poland create the presumption that less autocratic forms of government were, either from principle or from weakness, more pacific than monarchies like those of Louis XIV, Peter the Great, Charles XII, Frederick the Great, Joseph II and Catherine the Great.[1]

[1] Reproduced in *The Origins of the League Covenant* by Florence Wilson, p. 129.

CHAPTER XII

DIVINE RIGHTS IN HUMAN SOCIETY

'DOMINABITUR *a mari usque ad mare et a flumine usque ad terminos orbis terrarum. Et adorabunt eum omnes reges terræ : omnes gentes servient ei : Alleluya, alleluya. Potestas ejus, potestas æterna quæ non auferetur et regnum ejus, quod non corrumpetur. Alleluia.*'

So sing the choir between the Epistle and Gospel in the Mass of Christ the King, with which Pius XI has for all time left his mark upon the Christian liturgy. This prophecy of the universal Empire of Jesus Christ over all earthly rulers and nations, compounded from the Psalms of a Jewish King and the vision of an exiled Jewish mystic, is no mere hymn to decorate an ecclesiastical festival : it is a profession of faith which dominates the whole attitude of the true Catholic to national and international authority. It would not therefore be just to attempt a synthesis of international ethics according to Christian tradition without examining the grounds of so profound a conviction.

The mutual relations between nations, and, in particular the organization of a society between them, are rightly studied within the sphere of natural law. But this study cannot reveal the whole truth of our subject without regard to the Divine origin and sanctions of the natural law and morality, from which we have made rational deductions, and the rights and duties to which the fact of supernatural revelation gives rise in the natural order. That God did in fact reveal His will to men through His Son Jesus Christ : that as the very ground for commissioning His Church to teach all nations the Saviour of men claimed 'all power is given to Me in Heaven and Earth' : that One Universal Church was indeed established by Him, and safeguarded from error for all time by the Holy Ghost, in order to conserve that Revealed truth and expound it to all mankind —these are foundations of the Catholic religion necessarily assumed in this book. Upon that assumption, is it not reasonable to suppose that the internal ordering of States, their mutual agreements and any collective endeavour made by them to create an international order should take account of such stupendous facts?

Not only did the Roman Empire when converted to Christianity and, after its disruption, the Holy Empire and Monarchies of Mediæval Europe, as we have sufficiently shown, acknowledge the needs and claims of the Church as the guardian of revealed truth: they were spiritually subject to her and saw in her law the rule of their own lives. Does the repudiation of the Church's authority and the denial of her world-wide mandate by many States, which the Reformation of the sixteenth century began, create a situation the consequences of which can be accepted by the Catholic philosopher of international life to-day?

The actual refusal of public authorities to acknowledge the spiritual authority of the Church and Papacy has not in itself complicated the theory of international ethics. There always have been people who did not, in fact, acknowledge that authority: recent history has simply seen their number increase, in spite of the concurrent increase of the actual number of Catholics. The relation of natural society between Catholic and non-Catholic peoples was long ago evolved by theologians of the Church; the rules of peace and war apply as between them; treaties have to be made between them, the good faith of the contracting parties being assumed. The Popes, as we have shown, have more and more extended their care for peace to all nations, Christian or not.

Yet this last fact itself suggests that there are ways in which the Church cannot accept any theory of the State or the world arising from or based upon the repudiation of her mission. Why does the Pope deplore injustice in war 'by whatever State committed'? Why does he uphold, as against unjust servitude, the natural rights of unbaptized natives? Why does he denounce the competition in armaments in terms applicable to all nations, or make proposals of peace as much to Japan and Turkey as to Austria or Belgium? It is—and the words of the Pontiffs of the last century have amply shown it—because he claims a divine mandate and feels under a definite obligation to God to do these things. It is as the Vicar of Christ that he exercises his 'high magisterium of peace': it is as the authorized guardian of public as of private morals that he upholds the rights of working men everywhere, defends civil authority everywhere, calls upon believers in one God everywhere and without distinction to unite in opposition to militant atheism. The Pope could not, nor could any member of the Church on whose behalf he speaks, accept a system of national or international life which denied that mandate. And the meaning of that mandate is that Christ, for whom and by whose authority alone it is exercised, is in fact the supreme moral ruler of the whole world, the King of Kings and the Lord of Lords 'whose Empire manifestly includes not only Catholic nations, not only those who are baptized and of right belong to the Church, though error of doctrine leads them astray or severs them from her fold; but it includes all those who are outside the Christian faith, so that truly the human race in its entirety is subject to the Power of Jesus Christ.'[1] What then are the Divine Rights in respect of all human societies which the Church believes it to be her mission to safeguard?

There is first the general proposition that all public as well as private acts must conform to the Law of Nature and must never infringe the Moral Law, for these are ordinances of the Divine Lawgiver. This covers the whole subject-matter of our present work. There are other more particular propositions, to which we have necessarily alluded on other pages but of which we will now treat: they may be summarized as follows. That all authority comes from God: that God has an absolute right to the worship of His intelligent creatures: that the Church, acting on God's behalf has an inalienable right to freedom.

A number of passages from the Fathers of the Church have illustrated the mind of the Church on the origin of authority.

[1] Leo XIII, Encyclical *Annum Sanctum*, May 25, 1899.

The following close reasoning shows the integral part played by this notion in the Christian doctrine of society :

LEO XIII. *Diuturnum Illud. June* 29, 1881 :

And indeed that men should live in civil society is commanded by nature, or rather by God, the Author of Nature. This is clearly demonstrated *both by the faculty of speech, the principal conciliating force of society* (*maxima societatis conciliatrix*), by a great many innate appetites of the mind and by the number and importance of those necessities of life which men cannot satisfy in solitude, but can satisfy in conjunction and association with other men. But a society can neither exist nor be conceived in which there is no one to temper the wills of the individual members of it, in order that unity may come out of multitude and to direct them, according to justice and order, to the common good : therefore God willed that there should be in civil society men who can give commands to the multitude. And the proof of this proposition lies in the fact that those by whose authority the Commonwealth is administered must be able to constrain the citizens to obey, in such a way that it is clearly a *sin* for them not to obey. But there is no human being who has in himself the power to restrict the free will of his fellow-men by the bonds which such a rule implies. That power belongs in a unique sense to God, the procreator and legislator of all things ; and they who exercise it must of necessity exercise it as communicated to them by God.

That argument applies equally to all authority, including that of the organs of a society of nations.

The absolute right of God to receive worship from men, who are wholly dependent upon Him for their existence, implies an inalienable right and an inevitable duty on the part of every human soul to serve and worship Him. The State cannot justly impede the exercise of that right and the fulfilment of that duty : on the contrary it is under an obligation to assist its citizens to discharge them. For the temporal good of the citizens, to which the State is ordained, must minister to their spiritual good in view of the eternal destiny of each one of them. And since the sociability of man's nature applies as much to his religious life as to other aspects of his being, the liberty to form permanent religious associations for the collective service of God is a right which cannot be denied without grave injustice by the public authority. This is the natural or rational basis for the Church's organization, as it is the ground for claiming the material means necessary to keep that organization in being. The only justification for the State's interference in the exercise of the rights of religious worship and association is that which comes from a genuine belief that, in some particular, it may be detrimental to the public order.

The Church's right to complete liberty arises directly from her Divine Commission. It has two main requirements. First that the Head of the Church as Vicar of Christ, Successor of Peter, Common Father of the Faithful, Servant of all the Servants of God and Minister of Peace should be absolutely free from subjection to any State. This, in the present political conformation of the world, means that the Pope must be a sovereign unfettered (as he now happily is) from any suspicion of inferiority to or dependence upon the rulers of the surrounding country : 'Not only because this sovereignty is essential to protect and preserve the full liberty of the spiritual power but because it is an ascertained fact that, when the temporal sovereignty of the Apostolic See is in question, the cause of the public good and the well-being of all human society are also at stake.'[1] Actual freedom from the influence of any particular ruler is also necessary to the fulfilment of the Papal Office, as Pius VII shows in his refusal to submit to the dictation of Napoleon.[2]

Secondly, it follows from the Divine Commission that the Church should live and move and have her being throughout the world without impediment from the temporal power. In particular the unity and universality of the Church demand freedom of communication between all the parts and the centre. The sheep must be able to hear the voice of the shepherd. Bishops must be able to resort freely to the Vicar of Christ from whom they derive their jurisdiction. The religious orders and fraternities, essentially international institutions, must be free to lead their own organic lives ; and their several houses and congregations cannot do this unless intercourse between them and their Generals in Rome is unimpeded. It is of Divine Right that missionaries, fulfilling the primary Christian duty of preaching the Gospel, should be free to travel and carry out their task, though as

[1] Leo XIII Encyclical *Inscrutabili*, April 21, 1878.
[2] *Memoirs of Cardinal Consalvi.*

Pius XI has made it clear, the Church asks no privileges for her missionaries, but only the liberty and protection which natural and civil laws should assure to all men.

There are many ways in which these principles affect international relations. We may conveniently classify them under three heads: 1. International Authority; 2. International Intervention; 3. International Treaties.

1. The nature of *International Authority* as we have seen comes from God, however the rulers of States or their delegates may choose those who are to exercise that authority. The convention whereby an international tribunal, council, assembly, or secretariat is brought into existence has, in the ultimate analysis, a morally compelling force only because each of the contracting parties is under an obligation to God not to break his promise. To which we cannot omit to add that there can be no hope of uprooting the deep-set habits of war and national selfishness without the constant inclination of the wills of the associated peoples towards a Good higher than their own immediate interests and differing from them. And this is hardly to be conceived unless those human wills feel a real and abiding obligation to a mind and will greater than their own, to whom the grand design of the Universe is known and the destiny of every nation. For all these reasons the omission of any mention of the name of God from the Covenant of the League of Nations, the Statutes of the Permanent Court of International Justice, or the Kellogg Pact is more than a matter of sentimental regret to Catholics. For it seems to indicate an attempt to construct the framework of a society of States without the one essential, spiritual foundation. Time was when every Treaty began 'In the name of the most Holy and Indivisible Trinity.' Now, as the *Osservatore Romano* observed at the signature of the Kellogg Pact at Paris, we look in vain for God in the temple of Peace. Yet 'Unless the Lord build the House, they labour in vain who build it.' Nor (we are speaking purely from the standpoint of Catholic tradition) has any place been found for the Vicar of Christ in the new organization of international peace, a poor return for the Papacy's incessant labour of peace-making to which we have borne witness in these pages. Nothing saps the confidence of

Catholic populations throughout the world in the existing institutions of international co-operation so much as these omissions. It may be true—as indeed it is—that the Holy See has consistently encouraged[1] Catholic statesmen and citizens to play an active part in their several countries in promoting a loyal fulfilment of all that is good in the Covenant obligations of the League and in increasing the efficiency of that institution for the maintenance of peace. It may be true that the present Pontiff, if we are to judge from Article 24 of his Treaty with Italy, does not wish the Papacy to take part in international conferences such as those of the League of Nations at which conflicts of interest between different nations are discussed. But, in the same Article, the Pope reserves the traditional right of the Apostolic See to mediate or arbitrate between States who submit their differences to his pacific authority, a right which Leo XIII vindicated in no uncertain manner in his letter[2] to the Queen of the Netherlands on the occasion of the First Hague Conference.

Whatever may be expedient or practically possible in the existing circumstances, it must appear to the Catholic student that the organization of a positive society of nations which was truly in harmony with the requirements of natural

[1] The following letter was received by the present writer from the Secretariat of State at the Vatican, in reply to a suggestion, which he had transmitted, that Diplomatic Relations might be established, to the mutual advantage of both, between the Council of the League and the Holy See (No. 21837, August 11, 1923):

The project could be accepted only in the sense that the Holy See would be at the disposal of the League for matters coming within its competence; that is to say, for the elucidation of questions of principle in regard to morality and public international law, and also to give help to the League's relief work, where its [the Holy See's] intervention would be of value to suffering peoples. On this occasion I feel that I must tell you how much the Holy Father appreciates the zeal with which, as an officer of the League of Nations Union, you uphold Catholic principles in all circumstances; and as a sign of his especial goodwill and a pledge of heavenly favours he imparts to you with all his heart the Apostolic Benediction.

[2] See p. 174.

right and Christian tradition would differ in two important respects from the existing League of Nations. There would be, as well in the covenant or convention by which the society itself was brought into being, as in the form of election and appointment of those who were to exercise authority within it, a clear and public recognition of God as the fount and origin of all power. And there would be in the procedure, no less than in the constitution of the society, an equally clear recognition of the twofold mission of the Vicar of Christ—as 'guardian and defender on earth of the true and the good'—by providing firstly for the reference to his disinterested judgement or mediation of any international conflict which could not be settled by other pacific means ; secondly for some regular channel by which the authorities of the society could receive his guidance 'for the elucidation of questions of principle affecting morality and public international law.' That society of Nations, recognizing the Church herself to be a perfect society, would also respect and indeed defend, as of primary importance to the maintenance of a high standard of international ethics, the sovereignty and independence of the Apostolic See. The attitude of the Temporal to the Spiritual power in the international order would in short be governed by the same principles that determine the mutual relations of Church and State in a well-ordered commonwealth.

It may be argued that if the objects of a positive society of nations are themselves good—co-operation for the general well-being and the prevention of war—it is of no moment whether the power of Almighty God is publicly acknowledged by it or recognized in its statutes and acts. There is truth in this observation : for in public as in private acts it is the intention that counts, and it is undeniable that the beneficent activities of the League of Nations can be and in fact are supported by many good people from Christian motives. But they may also be directed by a spirit which rebels at the very notion of obligation to God. The very absence of His name enables the new international institution to be explained and extolled by certain individuals and groups—as for instance by the leaders of French Freemasonry—as an *alternative* to the rule of Jesus Christ, as a wholly secular device for attaining an earthly paradise independent of, and in spite of, the trammels of religion. It is undoubtedly the fact that the widespread scepticism, which characterizes the attitude of many Catholics to the League of Nations, is due to this thought. They are wrong, however, to withhold their active support from the institution on that account, as a study of Leo XIII's teaching in his Encyclical[1] '*Au milieu des sollicitudes*' would show. All human institutions which come into being to meet political, social or economic needs —including the organs of municipal and national Government, as well as those of international society—can either be misused or rightly used to the glory of God and the benefit of men, according to the character of those that use them. Those therefore who maintain an attitude of abstention and non-participation are but playing into the hands of their enemies.

2. *Intervention.* It has been established in the previous pages that intervention in the internal affairs of one State by another, or better still by the organized society of States —since intervention is an act which has its origin in natural solidarity and society—is justified under certain conditions and may even be demanded by the Law of Charity. Its purpose according to Taparelli is 'to reestablish the harmony between the social persons of the State.' This may require support of the Government against unjust rebellion or support of some or all of the subjects against a Government which has gravely violated their rights, it being understood that forcible intervention can only be employed when peaceful representations and remonstrances have failed. We have seen that under certain circumstances the suppression of national language and customs may constitute such a violation. What of the right of men to worship the true God, and to associate for that purpose? What of the right of the Church of Christ to organize her own life, to govern her children by her own Canon Law, preach the Gospel, teach the young and enjoy the freedom of movement and communications that we have postulated for her? Does the obstinate denial or frustration of these rights, which we have seen to be inseparable from the rights of God, justify intervention?

[1] See p. 334 below.

Assuredly. The whole history of international intervention for the protection of minorities, of which the latest phase is to be found in the Treaties, Clauses and Declarations placed under the guarantee of the Council of the League of Nations, can be traced to the First Crusade. It was precisely because groups of Christian peoples in the Levant were being intolerably oppressed by their Moslem conquerors that the Popes impelled the Princes of Europe to common action in order to deliver them.[1] It was to vindicate the same religious liberties that the Kings of France negotiated successive Firmans from the Turkish sultans, and the Holy See for many centuries confided to the French,[2] on behalf of the *respublica christiana*, the protectorate of Catholics in the East. Indeed the protection of the religious rite or custom of the minority has been one of the most constant features of treaties concerned with Minorities during the last three hundred years. But religious rights are not peculiar to minorities. Wherever and whenever the servants of God suffer persecution, be they the minority or, as in the case of certain arbitrarily ruled States to-day, the majority of the population, there is a *prima facie* case for intervention by the Society of States. Never can the Catholic Church admit that the respect or violation of Divine Rights is purely a matter of domestic politics in one State with which its neighbours have no concern. An outrage against the Kingdom of Christ in any part of the world is felt by all who owe allegiance to so great a King. Whether intervention, always an obligation of Charity, is or is not also a duty of strict justice, the circumstances of each case must determine. Rashly undertaken it may defeat its own end by exasperating the oppressors without overcoming them, and so make the last state of the oppressed worse than the first. Or again it may be that a Government cannot intervene effectively in a distant country without causing too grave harm and loss to its own people, for whose well-being it has, after all, a primary care. It is such inconveniences as these—not to speak of the suspicion of ulterior motives—which have

[1] See letter of Gregory VII, p. 94.

[2] For a summary of history of the Protectorate see *Yves de la Brière : Les Luttes Présentes de l'Eglise.*

led the most constructive writers upon international Ethics and Law in recent times to discountenance isolated intervention by a particular State, in favour of collective intervention by the organized Society of States. Nor can it be doubted that once the prospects of such collective action have become real, it were far better for it to take a positive and pacific, rather than a negative and military form. Armed intervention may be necessary ; but it is subject to the general condition of just war, namely that it must be necessitated by the absence of any other means of vindicating justice. The normal means by which the Society of Nations should seek to secure respect for the rights of God would be the adoption of a general charter or declaration of the rights of man in the religious sphere, thereby establishing in positive law a standard with which all its members would be held to comply. Already religious rights, with varying degrees of precision or vagueness, are included under the rights whose protection is theoretically guaranteed by the existing minority treaties. But there is no reason why if international conferences are held and conventions adopted to enable all men to work under just conditions, the same action should not be taken to enable them all to pray under just conditions.

2. *The subject matter of Treaties.* Since it is the proper object of Treaties to advance the common interests of the signatories and since the spiritual welfare of the citizens is the ultimate end to which the temporal dispositions of a Government are directed, it follows that treaties should everywhere respect and nowhere condone the violation of the Divine Rights in human society. The recognition of a new or newly enlarged State, or of a newly established Government by the community of Nations should be subject on their part to the assurance that the rights of religious worship, education and organization are to be inviolate throughout its territories. The cession of a district or province from one sovereign to another as the consequence of war or for any other reason, the division or union of States, indeed all moving of political landmarks, should respect the spiritual landmarks, the demarcations of parish, diocese and ecclesiastical province. For these respond on the one

hand to the actual needs and traditions of the indigenous population and on the other depend upon the central and authoritative jurisdiction of the Supreme Pontiff, as head and spokesman of that perfect society, the Church. Only with the consent of the spiritual power should these administrative arrangements for the cure of souls be modified, and it is the duty of the Temporal Power to seek that consent, should the need arise. In like manner the sacred buildings, land and other possessions of the Church and of religious corporations, though not immune from the operation of just laws in the interests of order and the common good, cannot in justice be sequestered, occupied or put to other uses by the Temporal Power save by agreement with the Church. It was the disregard of these maxims, directly deduced from the religious rights and duties of men and the character of the Universal Church which evoked the terrible condemnation of the Peace of Westphalia by the Holy See and the vehement protests of Cardinal Consalvi at the Congress of Vienna. The rights of the Church in the mission field and in particular the right to go and teach all nations, without let or hindrance from the colonizing authorities but rather with their help and encouragement—these, too, need to be respected and safeguarded in the process of colonial expansion. International conventions, treaties or mandates concerning the Government of backward races or the development of colonies should provide rightful facilities to the Christian missionary.[1] The disregard of the great civilizing influence of the missions in the draft Convention upon the abolition of Slavery framed at Geneva in 1925 drew from the Apostolic Nuncio at Berne, in the name of the Holy See, a criticism addressed to the Council of the League. At the Congress of Berlin and in previous treaties the Christian Missions had always been recognized as the chief enemy of slavery and the most powerful influence for the education and moral betterment of the native peoples.

Thus alike in the form of organized international society itself; in determining the just causes of international intervention, and in the making of Treaties, Catholic

[1] As do, for instance, the "C Mandates," such as the Mandate for the British Cameroons.

tradition asserts that there are Rights of God to be observed and honoured.

Documents

Independence and Neutrality of the Pope required by his Ministry of Peace :

CARDINAL CONSALVI. *Memoirs, Vol, II, pp.* 434–437 :

(Reply of Pius VII, March 21, 1806, to two letters, January 7 and February 13, 1806, of Napoleon).

We now set down the main points of the reply to the Emperor. After having expressed how surprised he had been on reading of the principles, the doctrines and the insinuations expressed in the Imperial letters, the Holy Father said that he intended to retain the apostolic liberty and immunity which were so seemly to his title of Pope and to his personal character. He then added that he recognized Napoleon to be the Emperor of the French but not Emperor of Rome ; that the sovereignty of the Holy See was free and independent ; that he had received it thus from the hands of his predecessors and, no matter at what cost, he would transmit it, without any alteration, to his successors ; that his duties and oaths obliged him to this for the safeguarding of the Religion with which this independence was intimately bound up since Kingdoms and Empires had multiplied to so great an extent ; that, without it, jealousy and temporal disturbances would cause princes to forbid in their states the free exercise of the spiritual authority of a Pope, who was the vassal of a foreign prince, since they would fear his influence exercised through the medium of the papacy: that the Pontiffs, in the time of Charlemagne, never recognized him as their sovereign ; that this Prince had indeed only become emperor by their permission and act ; that it was untrue that the temporal domain of the Popes was a gift of Charlemagne ; that he had only enlarged the territory of the Papacy, which it enjoyed before him and before Pepin, his father ; that in regard to admitting that the temporal sovereignty had been one of his gifts and dependent on him, the ten centuries of a free and uncontested authority prescribed all the titles and settled the arguments ; that the Holy See did not wish for, nor could it accept the supremacy of Napoleon and to be considered as his vassal ; that the liberty and independence of the Pontiff, in the actual order established by Providence, was intimately bound up with the well-being of Religion ; that neutrality and estrangement from all war formed the appanage of his titles of Minister of Peace and of the Sanctity of the Common Father and Head of the Universal Church ; that it would be very injurious to the interests of Religion to renounce his prerogatives and that, therefore, he could not, nor would he wish to do so ; further that it would be contrary to his duty to enter into a permanent system of war[1] which exposed him, without speaking of the motive already cited, to involve himself in conflicts full of evil, since he would be forced to participate in future wars, of which he could foresee neither the justice nor the injustice ; that it was not possible for him to take to himself as friends or enemies the friends or enemies of France. The Pope added that the agreements of the Emperor with him in spiritual matters ought not to be made use of as a rule and method to solve troubles confronting the Emperor in temporal affairs ; that he renewed his promise to remain neutral and, in consequence, he again demanded the evacuation of Ancona ; that it was not true that he had ever ordered or written that Cardinal Tesch should be sent back from Rome, though he did express the fear that it might be necessary to suspend relations with him in order to prove to the Powers his great desire to preserve neutrality. If, unhappily, his prayer was not granted, he begged the Emperor to remember that the Pope, during the negotiations of the Concordat, at the time of his journey for the coronation, and, in all the other events of his Pontificate, had lavished on him the most clear proofs of his sincere attachment, even to awakening the jealousy of other Courts ; that while he had acted in this fashion out of regard for him whenever he could do so, if to-day the Pope had to give a definite refusal, it was because he really could not compromise. Pius VII ended by saying that he hoped that the Emperor would recognize such just and evident reasons, but, if things turned out otherwise, he placed his cause in the hands of God, prepared to suffer rather than to fail in his duty, in his promises, in the defence of Religion and of his flock.

PIUS IX. *Propositions proscribed and condemned in the Syllabus issued December* 8, 1864 :

The following propositions expressive of the secularist conception of the society are among those condemned :

II. Any action of God upon men and upon the world is to be denied.

XX. The ecclesiastical power has no right to exercise its authority without the permission and consent of the civil government.

XXVI. The Church has no innate right of acquiring and possessing property.

XXX. The immunity of the Church and of ecclesiastical persons originated from the civil law.

XXXII. The personal immunity of the clergy whereby they are exempted from military service, can be abrogated without

[1] The blockade against England.

any violation of natural law and equity : indeed civil progress, especially in a democratic country, demands such abrogation.

XXXIX. The State, as the fount and origin of all rights, itself enjoys a right which knows no limits.

XLII. In the event of conflict between the laws of the spiritual power and those of the temporal power, it is the civil law that prevails.

XLIII. The secular power has authority to rescind, to declare and make void solemn conventions, called *Concordats*, contracted with the Holy See, concerning the exercise of the rights pertaining to ecclesiastical immunity, without the assent and even despite the protests of the Holy See.

XLIV. The civil authority can intervene in matters which concern religion, morals and spiritual discipline.

XLVII. The best interests of civil society require that public schools, which are available for all children of every class of the population, and public institutions of every kind which are destined for higher studies and the education of youth, should be entirely removed from the Church's authority, guidance and control ; and that they should be subject without limitation to the will of the political authority, according to the wishes of those in power and the prevailing trend of public opinion.

IL. The civil authority can prevent the free and mutual communication of the Bishops and the Faithful with the Roman Pontiff.

LV. Church and State ought to be separated.

LVI. The laws of morality need no divine sanction, nor is there any necessity that human laws should conform to the Law of Nature or that they should derive their binding force from God.

LX. Authority is nothing more than the sum total of numbers and material forces.

LXII. The principle of *non-intervention* is to be proclaimed and observed.

LXIII. It is permissible to withdraw one's obedience from lawfully constituted rulers and to rebel against them.

Leo XIII in several encyclicals examines and denounces the notion that political society should be organized without regard to God and His laws or the rights of the Church. We refer the reader in particular to *Humanum Genus* of April 20, 1884, *Immortale Dei* of November 1, 1885, and *Libertas Præstantissimum* of June 20, 1888. Since they have but an indirect bearing upon the international relations which are the subject of this work only typical passages are quoted.

Leo XIII. *Immortale Dei, November* 1, 1885:

. . . So, too, is it a sin in the state not to have care for religion, as something beyond its scope, or as of no practical benefit; or out of many forms of religion to adopt that one which chimes in with the fancy; for we are bound absolutely to worship God in that way which He has shown to be His will. All who rule, therefore, should hold in honour the holy name of God, and one of their chief duties must be to favour religion, to protect it, to shield it under the credit and sanction of the laws, and neither to organize nor enact any measure that may compromise its safety. This is the bounden duty of rulers to the people over whom they rule. For one and all are we destined by our birth and adoption to enjoy, when this frail and fleeting life is ended, a supreme and final good in heaven, and to the attainment of this every endeavour should be directed. Since, then, upon this depends the full and perfect happiness of mankind, the securing of this end should be of all imaginable interests the most urgent. Hence civil society, established for the common welfare, should not only safeguard the well-being of the community, but have also at heart the interests of its individual members, in such mode as not in any way to hinder, but in every manner to render as easy as may be, the possession of that highest and unchangeable good for which all should seek. Wherefore, for this purpose, care must especially be taken to preserve unharmed and unimpeded the religion whereof the practice is the link connecting man with God. . . .

Freedom of the Church and Holy See:

. . . Hence it is the Church, and not the State, that is to be man's guide to heaven. It is to the Church that God has assigned the charge of seeing to, and legislating for all that concerns religion; of teaching all nations; of spreading the Christian faith as widely as possible; in short, of administering freely and without hindrance, in accordance with her own judgement, all matters that fall within its competence.

Now this authority, perfect in itself, and plainly meant to be unfettered, so long assailed by a philosophy that truckles to the State, the Church has never ceased to claim for herself and openly to exercise. The Apostles themselves were the first to uphold it, when, being forbidden by the rulers of the Synagogue to preach the Gospel, they courageously answered: 'We must obey God rather than men.'[1] This same authority the holy Fathers of the Church were always careful to maintain by weighty arguments, according as occasion arose, and the Roman Pontiffs have never shrunk from defending it with unbending constancy. Nay more, princes and all invested with power to rule have themselves approved it, in theory alike and in practice. It cannot

[1] Acts v: 29.

be called in question that in the making of treaties, in the transaction of business matters, in the sending and receiving ambassadors, and in the interchange of other kinds of official dealings, they have been wont to treat with the Church as with a supreme and legitimate power. And assuredly all ought to hold that it was not without a singular disposition of God's providence that this power of the Church was provided with a civil sovereignty as the surest safeguard of her independence. . . .

Relation between the Spiritual and Temporal Powers :

. . . There must, accordingly, exist, between these two powers, a certain orderly connection, which may be compared to the union of the soul and body in man. The nature and scope of that connection can be determined only, as We have laid down, by having regard to the nature of each power, and by taking account of the relative excellence and nobleness of their purpose. One of the two has for its proximate and chief object the well-being of this mortal life ; the other the everlasting joys of heaven. Whatever, therefore, in things human is of a sacred character, whatever belongs either of its own nature or by reason of the end to which it is referred, to the salvation of souls, or to the worship of God, is subject to the power and judgement of the Church. Whatever is to be ranged under the civil and political order is rightly subject to the civil authority. Jesus Christ has Himself given command that what is Cæsar's is to be rendered to Cæsar, and that what belongs to God is to be rendered to God.

There are, nevertheless, occasions when another method of concord is available for the sake of peace and liberty : We mean when rulers of the State and the Roman Pontiff come to an understanding touching some special matter. At such times the Church gives signal proof of her motherly love by showing the greatest possible kindliness and indulgence. . . .

Conflict of the Lay State and Church :

. . . Sad it is to call to mind how the harmful and lamentable rage for innovation which rose to a climax in the sixteenth century, threw first of all into confusion the Christian religion, and next, by natural sequence, invaded the precincts of philosophy, whence it spread amongst all classes of society. From this source, as from a fountain-head, burst forth all those later tenets of unbridled license which, in the midst of the terrible upheavals of the last century,[1] were wildly conceived and boldly proclaimed as the principles and foundation of that *new jurisprudence* which was not *merely* previously unknown, but was at variance on many points with not only the Christian, but even with the natural law.

[1] Meaning, no doubt, the French Revolution.

Amongst these principles the main one lays down that as all men are alike by race and nature, so in like manner all are equal in the control of their life ; that each one is so far his own master as to be in no sense under the rule of any other individual ; that each is free to think on every subject just as he may choose, and to do whatever he may like to do ; that no man has any right to rule over other men. In a society grounded upon such maxims, all government is nothing more nor less than the will of the people, and the people, being under the power of itself alone, is alone its own ruler. It does choose nevertheless some to whose charge it may commit itself, but in such wise that it makes over to them not the right so much as the business of governing, to be exercised, however, in its name.

The authority of God is passed over in silence, just as if there were no God ; or as if He cared nothing for human society ; or as if men, whether in their individual capacity or bound together in social relations, owed nothing to God ; or as if there could be a government of which the whole origin and power and authority did not reside in God Himself. Thus, as is evident, a State becomes nothing but a multitude, which is its own master and ruler. And since the populace is declared to contain within itself the spring-head of all rights and of all power, it follows that the State does not consider itself bound by any kind of duty towards God. Moreover, it believes that it is not obliged to make public profession of any religion ; or to inquire which of the very many religions is the only one true ; or to prefer one religion to all the rest; or to show to any form of religion special favour ; but on the contrary, is bound to grant equal rights to every creed, so that public order may not be disturbed by any particular form of religious belief.

And it is a part of this theory that all questions that concern religion are to be referred to private judgement ; that every one is to be free to follow whatever religion he prefers, or none at all if he disapprove of all. From this the following consequences logically flow : that the judgement of each one's conscience is independent of all law ; that the most unrestrained opinions may be openly expressed as to the practice or omission of divine worship ; and that every one has unbounded license to think whatever he chooses and to publish abroad whatever he thinks.

Now when the State rests on foundations like those just named —and for the time being they are greatly in favour—it readily appears into what and how unrightful a position the Church is driven. For when the management of public business is in harmony with doctrines of such a kind, the Catholic religion is allowed a standing in civil society equal only, or inferior, to societies alien from it ; no regard is paid to the laws of the Church and she who, by the order and commission of Jesus Christ, has the duty of teaching all nations, finds herself forbidden to take any part in the instruction of the people.

. . . Accordingly, it has become the practice and determination under this condition of public polity (now so much admired by many) either to forbid the action of the Church altogether or to keep her in check and bondage to the State. Public enactments are in great measure framed with this design. The drawing up of laws, the administration of State affairs, the godless education of youth, the spoliation and suppression of religious orders, the overthrow of the temporal power of the Roman Pontiff, all alike aim at this one end—to paralyze the action of Christian institutions, to cramp to the utmost the freedom of the Catholic Church, and to curtail her every single prerogative.

Civil Liberty and Obedience to God :

LEO XIII. *Encyclical Libertas Præstantissimum, June* 20, 1888 :

. . . Likewise the liberty of those who are in authority does not consist in the power to lay unreasonable and capricious commands upon their subjects, which would equally be criminal and would lead to the ruin of the commonwealth ; but the binding force of human laws is in this, that they are to be regarded as applications of the eternal law, and incapable of sanctioning anything which is not contained in the eternal law, as in the principle of all law. Thus St. Augustine most wisely says : 'I think that you can see, at the same time, that there is nothing just and lawful in temporal law, unless what men have gathered from eternal law.' If, then, by any one in authority, something be sanctioned out of conformity with the principles of right reason, and consequently hurtful to the commonwealth, such an enactment can have no binding force of law, as being no rule of justice, but certain to lead men away from that good which is the very end of civil society.

Therefore, the nature of human liberty, however it be considered, whether in individuals or in society, whether in those who command or in those who obey, supposes the necessity of obedience to some supreme and eternal law, which is no other than the authority of God, commanding good and forbidding evil. And so far from this most just authority of God over men diminishing, or even destroying their liberty, it protects and perfects it, for the real perfection of all creatures is found in the prosecution and attainment of their respective ends ; but the supreme end to which human liberty must aspire is God. . . .

These followers of Liberalism deny the existence of any divine authority to which obedience is due, and proclaim that every man is the law to himself ; from which arises that ethical system which they style *independent* morality, and which, under the guise of liberty, exonerates man from any obedience to the commands of God, and substitutes a boundless license. The end of all this is not difficult to foresee, especially when society is in question. For, when once man is firmly persuaded that he is subject to no one, it follows that the efficient cause of the unity of civil society is not to be sought in any principle external to man, or superior to him, but simply in the free will of individuals ; that the authority in the State comes from the people only ; and that, just as every man's individual reason is his only rule of life, so the collective reason of the community should be the supreme guide in the management of all public affairs. *Hence the doctrine of the supremacy of the greater number, and that all right and all duty reside in the majority.* But, from what has been said, it is clear that all this is in contradiction to reason. To refuse any bond of union between man and civil society, on the one hand, and God the Creator and consequently the supreme Law-giver, on the other, is plainly repugnant to the nature, not only of man, but of all created things ; for of necessity, all effects must in some proper way be connected with their cause ; and it belongs to the perfection of every nature to contain itself within that sphere and grade which the order of nature has assigned to it, namely, that the lower should be subject and obedient to the higher.

Moreover, besides this, a doctrine of such character is most hurtful both to individuals and to the State. For, once ascribe to human reason the only authority to decide what is true and what is good, and the real distinction between good and evil is destroyed ; honour and dishonour differ not in their nature, but in the opinion and judgement of each one ; pleasure is the measure of what is lawful ; and, given a code of morality which can have little or no power to restrain or quiet the unruly propensities of man, a way is naturally opened to universal corruption. With reference also to public affairs : authority is severed from the true and natural principle whence it derives all efficacy for the common good ; and the law determining what is right to do and avoid doing is at the mercy of a majority. Now this is simply a road leading straight to tyranny. The empire of God over man and civil society once repudiated, it follows that religion, as a public institution, can have no claim to exist, and that everything that belongs to religion will be treated with complete indifference. Furthermore, with ambitious designs on sovereignty, tumult and sedition will be common amongst the people ; and when duty and conscience cease to appeal to them, there will be nothing to hold them back but force, which of itself alone is powerless to keep their covetousness in check.

The Attitude of Catholics to Secularist Institutions :

LEO XIII. *Encyclical. Au milieu des Sollicitudes, February* 16, 1892 :

. . . In this order of speculative ideas, Catholics, like all other citizens, are free to prefer one form of government to another precisely because no one of these social forms is, in itself, opposed to the principles of sound reason nor to the maxims of Christian doctrine. What amply justifies the wisdom of the Church is that in her relations with political powers she makes abstraction of the forms which differentiate them and treats with them concerning the great religious interests of nations, knowing that hers is the duty to undertake their tutelage above all other interests. . . . However, here it must be carefully observed that whatever be the form of civil power in a nation, it cannot be considered so definitive as to have the right to remain immutable, even though such were the intention of those who, in the beginning, determined it. . . . Only the Church of Jesus Christ has been able to preserve, and surely will preserve unto the consummation of time, her form of government. Founded by Him, who *was*, who *is* and who *will be forever*, she has received from Him, since her very origin, all that she requires for the pursuing of her divine mission across the changeable ocean of human affairs. And, far from wishing to transform her essential constitution, she has not the power even to relinquish the conditions of true liberty and sovereign independence with which Providence has endowed her in the general interest of souls. . . . But, in regard to purely human societies, it is an oft-repeated historical fact that time, that great transformer of all things here below, operates great changes in their political institutions. On some occasions it limits itself to modifying something in the form of the established government ; or, again, it will go so far as to substitute other forms for the primitive ones—forms totally different, even as regards the mode of transmitting sovereign power.

And how are these political changes of which We speak produced ? They sometimes follow in the wake of violent crises, too often of a bloody character, in the midst of which pre-existing governments totally disappear ; then anarchy holds sway, and soon public order is shaken to its very foundations and finally overthrown. From that time onward a *social need* obtrudes itself upon the nation ; it must provide for itself without delay. Is it not its privilege—or, better still, its duty—to defend itself against a state of affairs troubling it so deeply, and to re-establish public peace in the tranquillity of order ? Now, this social need justifies the creation and the existence of new governments, whatever form they take ; since, in the hypothesis wherein we reason, these new governments are a requisite to public order, all public order being impossible without a government. Thence it follows that, in similar junctures, all the novelty is limited to the political form of civil power, or to its mode of transmission ; it in no wise affects the power considered in itself. This continues to be immutable and worthy of respect, as, considered in its nature, it is constituted to provide for the common good, the supreme end which gives human society its origin. To put it otherwise, in all hypotheses, civil power, considered as such, is from God, always from God : 'For there is no power but from God.'

Consequently, when new governments representing this immutable power are constituted, their acceptance is not only permissible, but even obligatory, being imposed by the need of the social good which has made and which upholds them. This is all the more imperative because an insurrection stirs up hatred among citizens, provokes civil war, and may throw a nation into chaos and anarchy, and this great duty of respect and dependence will endure as long as the exigencies of the common good shall demand it, since this good is, after God, the first and last law in society.

Thus the wisdom of the Church explains itself in the maintenance of her relations with the numerous governments which have succeeded one another in France in less than a century, each change causing violent shocks. Such a line of conduct would be the surest and most salutary for all Frenchmen in their civil relations with the public, which is the actual government of their nation. Far be it from them to encourage the political dissensions which divide them ; all their efforts should be combined to preserve and elevate the moral greatness of their native land.

But a difficulty presents itself. 'This Republic,' it is said, 'is animated by such anti-Christian sentiments that honest men, Catholics particularly, could not conscientiously accept it.' This, more than anything else, has given rise to dissensions, and in fact aggravated them. . . . These regrettable differences would have been avoided if the very considerable distinction between *constituted power* and *legislation* had been carefully kept in view. In so much does legislation differ from political power and its form, that under a system of government most excellent in form legislation could be detestable ; while (quite the opposite) under a regime most imperfect in form, might be found excellent legislation. It were an easy task to prove this truth, history in hand, but what would be the use ? All are convinced of it. And who, better than the Church, is in position to know it—she who has striven to maintain habitual relations with all political governments ? Assuredly she, better than any other power, could tell the consolation or sorrow occasioned her by the laws of the various governments by which nations have been ruled from the Roman Empire down to the present.

If the distinction just established has its major importance, it is likewise manifestly reasonable: Legislation is the work of men invested with power, and who, in fact, govern the nation; therefore it follows that, practically, the quality of the laws depends more upon the quality of these men than upon the form of power. The laws will be good or bad according as the minds of the legislators are imbued with good or bad principles, and as they allow themselves to be guided by political prudence or by passion.

The Kingship of Christ:

PIUS XI. *Encyclical December* 11, 1925:

VENERABLE BRETHREN,

In the first Encyclical Letter which We addressed at the beginning of Our Pontificate to the Bishops of the universal Church, We referred to the chief causes of the difficulties under which mankind was labouring. And We remember saying that these manifold evils in the world were due to the fact that the majority of men had thrust Jesus Christ and His holy law out of their lives; that these had no place either in private affairs or in politics: and We said further that, as long as individuals and states refused to submit to the rule of our Saviour, there would be no really hopeful prospect of a lasting peace among nations. Men must look for the *peace of Christ in the Kingdom of Christ;* and this We promised to do as far as lay in Our power. *In the Kingdom of Christ,* that is, it seemed to Us that peace could not be more effectually restored nor fixed upon a firmer basis than through the restoration of the Empire of Our Lord. We were led in the meantime to indulge the hope of a brighter future at the sight of a more widespread and keener interest evinced in Christ and His Church, the one source of salvation, a sign that men who had formerly spurned the rule of our Redeemer and had exiled themselves from His kingdom were preparing, and even hastening, to return to the duty of obedience.

The notable events which had occurred during the Holy Year are then recalled.

Since this Holy Year, therefore, has provided more than one opportunity to enhance the glory of the Kingdom of Christ, We deem it in keeping with Our Apostolic office to accede to the desire of many of the Cardinals, Bishops, and faithful, made known to Us both individually and collectively, by closing this Holy Year with the insertion into the Sacred Liturgy of a special feast of *the Kingship of Our Lord Jesus Christ.*

It has long been a common custom to give to Christ the metaphorical title of 'king,' because of the high degree of perfection whereby He excels all creatures. So He is said to reign 'in the minds of men,' both by reason of the keenness of His intellect and the extent of His knowledge, and also because He is very Truth, and it is from Him that truth must be obediently received by all mankind. He reigns, too, *in the wills of men*, for in Him the human will was perfectly and entirely obedient to the Holy Will of God, and further by His grace and inspiration He so subjects our free-will as to incite us to the most noble endeavours. He is *King of our hearts*, too, by reason of His 'charity which exceedeth all knowledge,'[1] and His mercy and kindness which draw all men to Him; for there never was, nor ever will be a man loved so much and so universally as Jesus Christ.

But if we ponder this matter more deeply, we cannot but see that the title and the power of King belongs to Christ as man in the strict and proper sense also. For it is only as man that He may be said to have received from the Father 'power and glory and a kingdom,'[2] since the Word of God, as consubstantial with the Father, has all things in common with Him, and therefore has necessarily supreme and absolute dominion over all things created. . . .

. . . This kingdom is primarily spiritual and concerned with spiritual things. That this is so the above quotations from Scripture amply prove, and Christ by His own action confirms it. On many occasions, when the Jews and even the Apostles wrongly supposed that the Messias would restore the liberties and the kingdom of Israel, He repelled and denied such a suggestion. When the populace thronged around Him in admiration and would have acclaimed Him King, He shrank from the honour and, hiding Himself, fled from them. Before the Roman magistrate He declared that His kingdom was *not of this world*. The gospels present this kingdom as one which men prepare to enter by penance, and cannot actually enter except by faith and by baptism, which, though an external rite, signifies and produces an interior regeneration. This kingdom is opposed to none other than to that of Satan and to the power of darkness. It demands of its subjects a spirit of detachment from riches and earthly things, and a spirit of gentleness. They must hunger and thirst after justice, and, more than this, they must deny themselves and carry the cross.

Christ as our Redeemer purchased the Church at the price of His own blood; as priest He offered Himself, and continues to offer Himself as a victim for our sins. Is it not evident, then, that His kingly dignity partakes in a manner of both these offices?

It would be a grave error, on the other hand, to say that Christ has no authority whatever in civil affairs, since, by virtue of the absolute empire over all creatures committed to

[1] Ephesians iii: 9. [2] Daniel vii: 13–14.

Him by the Father, all things are in His power. Nevertheless, during His life on earth He refrained from the exercise of such authority, and although He Himself disdained to possess or to care for earthly goods, He did not, nor does He to-day, interfere with those who possess them. *Non eripit mortalia qui regna dat cælestia.*[1]

Thus the empire of our Redeemer embraces all men. To use the words of our immortal predecessor, Pope Leo XIII: 'His empire includes not only Catholic nations, not only baptized persons who, though of right belonging to the Church, have been led astray by error, or have been cut off from her by schism, but also all those who are outside the Christian faith; so that truly the whole of mankind is subject to the power of Jesus Christ.'[2] Nor is there any difference in this matter between the individual and the family or the State; for all men, whether collectively or individually, are under the dominion of Christ. In Him is the salvation of the individual, in Him is the salvation of society. 'Neither is there salvation in any other, for there is no other name under heaven given to men whereby we must be saved.'[3] He is the author of happiness and true prosperity for every man and for every nation. 'For a nation is happy when its citizens are happy. What else is a nation, but a number of men living in concord?'[4] If, therefore, the rulers of nations wish to preserve their authority, to promote and increase the prosperity of their people, they will not neglect the public duty of reverence and obedience to the rule of Christ. What We said at the beginning of Our Pontificate concerning the decline of public authority, and the lack of respect for the same, is equally true at the present day. 'With God and Jesus Christ,' We said, 'excluded from political life, with authority derived not from God, but from man, the very basis of that authority has been taken away, because the chief reason of the distinction between ruler and subject has been eliminated. The result is that human society is tottering to its fall, because it has no longer a secure and solid foundation.'[5]

When once men recognize, both in private and in public life, that Christ is King, society will at last receive the great blessings of real liberty, well-ordered discipline, peace and harmony. Our Lord's regal office invests the human authority of princes and rulers with a religious significance; it ennobles the citizen's duty of obedience. It is for this reason that St. Paul, while bidding wives revere Christ in their husbands, and slaves respect

[1] Hymn for the Epiphany.
[2] Enc. *Annum Sacrum*, May 25, 1899. [3] Acts iv: 12.
[4] St. Augustine, *Ep. ad Macedonium*, c. iii.
[5] Enc. *Ubi arcano*.

Christ in their masters, warns them to give obedience to them not as to men, but as to the vicegerents of Christ; for it is not meet that men redeemed by Christ should serve their fellow-men. 'You are bought with a price; be not made the bond-slaves of men.'[1] If princes and magistrates duly elected are filled with the persuasion that they rule, not by their own right, but by the mandate and in the place of the Divine King, they will exercise their authority piously and wisely, they will make laws and administer them having in view the common good and also the human dignity of their subjects. The result will be order, peace and tranquillity, for there will be no longer any cause of discontent. Men will see in their king or in their rulers men like themselves, perhaps unworthy or open to criticism, but they will not on that account refuse obedience if they see reflected in them the authority of Christ, God and Man. Peace and harmony, too, will result; for with the spread and the universal extension of the kingdom of Christ men will become more and more conscious of the link that binds them together, and thus many conflicts will be either prevented entirely or at least their bitterness will be diminished.

If the Kingdom of Christ, then, receives, as it should, all nations under its sway, there seems no reason why we should despair of seeing that peace which the King of Peace came to bring on earth—He who came *to reconcile all things, who came not to be ministered unto but to minister*, who, though *Lord of all*, gave Himself to us as a model of humility, and with His principal law united the precept of charity; who said also: 'My yoke is sweet and my burden light.' Oh, what happiness would be ours if all men, individuals, families, and nations, would but let themselves be governed by Christ! 'Then at length,' to use the words addressed by Our predecessor, Pope Leo XIII, twenty-five years ago to the Bishops of the Universal Church, 'then at length will many ills be cured; then will the law regain its former authority, peace with all its blessings be restored. Men will sheathe their swords and lay down their arms when all freely acknowledge and obey the authority of Christ, and every tongue confesses that the Lord Jesus Christ is in the glory of God the Father.'

. . . If we ordain that the whole Catholic world shall revere Christ as King, we shall minister to the need of the present day, and at the same time provide an excellent remedy for the plague which now infects society. We refer to the plague of secularism, its errors and impious activities. This evil spirit, as you are well aware, Venerable Brethren, has not come into being in one day; it has long lurked beneath the surface. The empire of Christ over all nations was rejected. The right which the Church

[1] I Corinthians vii: 23.

has from Christ Himself, to teach mankind, to make laws, to govern peoples in all that pertains to their eternal salvation, that right was denied. Then gradually the religion of Christ came to be likened to false religions and to be placed ignominiously on the same level with them. It was then put under the power of the State and tolerated more or less at the whim of princes and rulers. Some men went further, and wished to set up in the place of God's religion a natural religion consisting in some instinctive affection of the heart. There were even some nations who thought they could dispense with God, and that their religion should consist in impiety and the neglect of God. The rebellion of individuals and of nations against the authority of Christ has produced deplorable effects. We lamented these in the Encyclical *Ubi arcano ;* We lament them to-day : the seeds of discord sown far and wide ; those bitter enmities and rivalries between nations, which still hinder so much the cause of peace ; that insatiable greed which is so often hidden under a pretence of public spirit and patriotism, and gives rise to so many private quarrels ; a blind and immoderate selfishness, making men seek nothing but their own comfort and advantage, and measure everything by these ; no peace in the home, because men have forgotten, or neglect their duty ; the unity and stability of the family undermined ; society, in a word, shaken to its foundations and on the way to ruin. We firmly hope, however, that the Feast of the Kingship of Christ, which in future will be yearly observed, may hasten the return of society to our loving Saviour. It would be the duty of Catholics to do all they can to bring about this happy result. Many of these, however, have neither the station in society nor the authority which should belong to those who bear the torch of truth. This state of things may perhaps be attributed to a certain slowness and timidity in good people, who are reluctant to engage in conflict or oppose but a weak resistance ; thus the enemies of the Church become bolder in their attacks. But if the faithful were generally to understand that it behoves them ever to fight courageously under the banner of Christ their King, then, fired with apostolic zeal, they would strive to win over to their Lord those hearts that are bitter and estranged from Him, and would valiantly defend His rights.

Moreover the annual and universal celebration of the feast of the Kingship of Christ will draw attention to the evils which secularism has brought upon society, in drawing men away from Christ, and will also do much to remedy them. While nations insult the beloved name of our Redeemer by suppressing all mention of it in their conferences and parliaments, we must all the more loudly proclaim His kingly dignity and power, all the more universally affirm His rights.

APPENDIX TO CHAPTER XII

The Mass of the Feast of Christ the King :

THE LAST SUNDAY IN OCTOBER

Feast of the Kingship of Our Lord Jesus Christ

Mass.

Introit. Apocalypse v : 12 ; i : 6.
Worthy is the Lamb that was slain to receive power, and divinity, and wisdom, and strength, and honour. To him be glory and empire for ever and ever. (*In Eastertide,* Alleluia, alleluia.) Psalm lxxi : 1. Give the King thy judgement, O God, and the King's Son thy justice.

℣. Glory be to the Father. Worthy is the Lamb. . . .

Prayer.

Almighty everlasting God, who hast willed to restore all things in Thy beloved Son, the King of the whole creation ; mercifully grant that all the communities of the nations that are torn asunder by the wound of sin may be subjected unto his most sweet dominion. Who liveth and reigneth . . .

Commemoration is made of the current Sunday.

Lesson from the Epistle of Blessed Paul the Apostle to the Colossians.

Colossians i : 12–20.

Brethren : We give thanks unto God the Father, who hath made us worthy to be partakers of the lot of the saints in light, who hath delivered us from the power of darkness, and hath translated us into the kingdom of the Son of his love, in whom we have redemption through his blood, the remission of sins ; who is the image of the invisible God, the first-born of every creature ; for in him were all things created in heaven, and on earth, visible and invisible, whether thrones, or dominations, or principalities, or powers, all things were created by him and in him, and he is before all, and in him all things consist. And he is the head of the body, the Church, who is the beginning, the first-born from the dead ; that in all things he may hold the primacy ; because in him it hath well-pleased the Father that all fulness should dwell ; and through him to reconcile all things unto himself, making peace through the blood of his cross, both as to the things on earth, and the things that are in heaven, in Christ Jesus our Lord.

Gradual. Psalm lxxi : 8 and 11. He shall rule from sea to sea, and from the river even unto the ends of the earth.

℣. And all the kings of the earth shall adore him ; all nations shall serve him.

Alleluia, alleluia. ℣. Daniel vii : 14. His power is an eternal power, which shall not be taken away ; and his kingdom one which shall not be destroyed. Alleluia.

In votive Masses after Septuagesima, the Alleluia *and Verse being omitted, is said :*

Tract. Psalm lxxxviii : 27, 28 and 30. He shall call me : thou art my Father : my God, and the upholder of my salvation. ℣. And I will appoint him my first-born ; high above the kings of the earth. ℣. And I will appoint his seed unto the ages of the ages ; and his throne as the days of heaven.

In Eastertide the Gradual is omitted, and in place thereof is said :

Alleluia, alleluia. ℣. Daniel vii : 14. His power is an eternal power, which shall not be taken away ; and his kingdom one which shall not be destroyed. Alleluia. ℣. Apocalypse xix : 16. He hath on his garment and on his thigh written : King of kings, and Lord of lords. Alleluia.

✠ Continuation of the holy Gospel according to John.

John xviii : 33-37.

At that time : Pilate said unto Jesus : Art thou the King of the Jews ? Jesus answered : Sayest thou this of thyself, or did others tell it thee of me ? Pilate answered : Am I a Jew ? Thine own nation and the chief priests have delivered thee unto me : what hast thou done ? Jesus answered : My kingdom is not of this world. If my kingdom were of this world, my servants would indeed fight, that I might not be delivered to the Jews ; but now is my kingdom not from hence. Therefore Pilate said unto him : Art thou a king then ? Jesus answered : Thou sayest, because I am a king. For this was I born, and for this cause came I into the world, that I might bear witness to the truth ; every one that is of the truth heareth my voice. *Creed.*

Offertory. Psalm ii : 8. Ask of me, and I will give thee the Gentiles for thine inheritance, and the ends of the earth for thy possession. (*In Eastertide,* Alleluia.)

Secret.

We offer unto thee, O Lord, the Host of man's reconcilation ; grant, we beseech thee, that he whom we immolate in these present sacrifices, may grant unto all nations the gifts of unity and peace, even Jesus Christ our Lord thy Son, who liveth. . . .

Commemoration is made of the current Sunday.

Preface.

℣. The Lord be with you.
℟. And with thy spirit.
℣. Lift up your hearts.
℟. We have them lifted up to the Lord.
℣. Let us give thanks to our Lord God.
℟. It is meet and just.

It is truly meet and just, right and availing unto salvation, that we should at all times and in all places give thanks unto thee, O holy Lord, Father Almighty, everlasting God; who hast anointed thy Son our Lord Jesus Christ, the Eternal High Priest and King of all things, with the oil of gladness; that offering himself on the altar of the Cross as an immaculate host and peace-offering, he might complete the mysteries of man's redemption; and all creation being made subject to his dominion, he might deliver into the hands of thine unbounded Majesty an eternal and all-enfolding kingdom, a kingdom of truth and life, a kingdom of holiness and grace, a kingdom of justice, love and peace. And therefore with the angels and archangels, the thrones and dominions, and the whole host of the heavenly army, we sing the hymn of thy glory, saying again and again, Holy, Holy, Holy . . .

Communion. Psalm xxviii: 10. The Lord shall sit as King for ever; the Lord shall bless his people with peace. (*In Eastertide,* Alleluia.)

Postcommunion.

Having received the food of immortality, we beseech thee, O Lord, that we who glory in our warfare under the banners of Christ the King may come to reign with him for ever in his heavenly dwelling-place: who with thee liveth and reigneth . . .

Commemoration is made of the current Sunday, and its Gospel is read at the end.

PART V

THE PLACE OF NATIONALITY IN THE LAW OF NATIONS

CHAPTER XIII

THE RIGHTS AND LIMITS OF NATIONALITY

THE principle of Nationality has been the dominant force for good or for ill in international life for a century. Earlier traditions may have invested it with a certain sacredness; Christianity may have sought to sanctify it: atheism to impress it into service against the Church. Autocracy and the spirit of rebellion have both exploited it to their own ends. But whatever the spiritual or political influences which have used or moulded it, nationality has undeniably an essence of its own which the student of international ethics must discover, and for which he must find a place in the law of nations.

What is the '*perseitas*' of Nationality? So many and so various are the definitions which the reader may find in special studies of the subject that we shall look in vain for an accepted sense of the term which could be submitted to judgement by the criterions of international ethics already established. Here we will use another method. It will consist in building up from first principles and the postulates of Christian tradition what could and should be the body of rights and duties brought into being by the circumstances of a man's birth and upbringing, and what are the collective functions, rights and duties thus brought into being, which the public law of States and the society of States should enshrine. Certain extracts from early Christian writings, from the scholastics, Papal utterances and recent Catholic authors will be quoted to this end. Our study concludes with the synthesis of the Catholic Union of International Studies, which seeks to determine the place to be filled by nationality in regard to the human individual and political institutions.

The community which we call nation is in part the consequence of logical and physical requirements, in part the outcome of an act of human will. We will consider it first under the former aspect.

Man—or to be more precise—a child, as he comes into the world and as he grows up has, we have seen, an immediate elemental need of care, protection and help that he may survive. There can be no human life without the family; nor without the constant corporate existence of the family can man's two primary needs of self-conservation and natural development be supplied. And here it may be noted that the respect of parents is shown by Divine Revelation to be a duty second only to the duty of worshipping God Himself, and that the notion of continuous life in one's 'own country' is immediately connected with domestic piety. 'Honour thy father and thy mother that thou mayest be long-lived upon the land which the Lord thy God will give thee.'[1]

It is not necessary to adhere in all its entirety to the patriarchal theory of the origins of civil society, to hold that the sense of social unity derived through birth extends for almost all peoples far beyond the bounds of the simple family. Everywhere consanguinity, which is descent from the same grandparents or great-grandparents, is a distinctive bond of unity. The patriarchal tradition which characterizes the history of the Jews, and which is found to this day, not less evident, in the indigenous Christian communities of Syria or Mesopotamia; the tenacity of the Scottish clan; the pride of ancient families throughout Europe in tracing their lineage; the *pietas* of Roman civilization; the ancestor worship of China and Japan—all these are but manifestations of what can only be regarded as a fact of nature. A natural association, both physical and spiritual, exists between those who have descended from the same progenitor. It is not necessary to seek in this, the quintessence of racial origin, the sole or even the main basis of society. It is not necessary to abstract ethnic origin from all the other unitive factors of mankind, to clothe it in mythical forms, to make it the object of idolatry. But whatever other forces unite and

[1] Exodus xx: 12.

divide human beings, the reality of common descent and relationship as a unifying and distinctive power among men cannot be denied. This power serves only to strengthen the tendency of the actual family to unite with other families, for the physical protection and the promotion of the common good, which we have already traced in seeking the origins of villages, towns, and the higher stages of social organization. What here concerns us is that belief in a common ancestry—whether or not founded in fact—and the almost instinctive respect for habits of life connected in the mind with family tradition, necessarily play an important part in determining the particular forms which those other social groupings shall take. Economic necessity, strategic factors, rivers, mountain ranges, the fertility of this tract of land or that, all these provide explanations of the movements and density of populations, the location of such a town, or the boundaries of such a State. Yet history is full of instances of tribes and groups of families facing poverty, hardship and danger rather than separate and disrupt their traditional unity. The fact of birth from certain parents, the fact of their descent in turn from certain ancestors, the far-reaching forces of heredity in the physiological order, and the immemorial institution of inheritance in the social order, these combine to form a community of human souls more or less strongly attached to a certain part of the earth's surface which human laws, municipal, national or international, can only recognize and respect.

Yet there is nothing absolute in the association based upon birth. The mere fact of intermarriage[1] between men and women of different tribal or racial origins, which is an equally natural and almost equally universal phenomenon, while it creates a new family, and therefore a new chain of blood relationship, blurs the outlines of racial particularism. The universal confraternity of mankind gives rise, as we have seen, to a series of mutual rights and duties which no human groupings have the right to frustrate. Christianity sanctifying the brotherly union of men, forbids an attachment to race or family so great as to impede the love of God and the

[1] Ineffectively forbidden for a period by the man-made Law of Nations. (St. Isidore, quoted in Suarez : *De Legibus*.)

love of all men for His sake. The vision of Peter in the housetop of Joppe revealed the littleness of racial conservatism. And Christ Himself while raising the dignity of marriage to a sacrament and blessing the family declared : 'There is no man that hath left home or parents or brethren or wife or children for the kingdom of God's sake, who shall not receive much more in this present time and in the world to come life everlasting.' (Luke xviii : 29, 30). In the same spirit a recent Pope (Benedict XV) has applied to the missionaries of the Gospel that hard saying of the Psalmist : 'Forget thy country and thy Father's house,' (Psalm xliv : 11). The Church, as the passages which we quote will show, vigorously defends national rights as against fusion or suppression. At the same time she condemns any assertion or those rights which does violence to the rights of others, to the whole community of mankind or to her own universal character.

We have thus established first that, in the strict sense of association derived from birth, nationality is a natural factor of great importance in the construction of human society. Secondly that its mission is neither absolute nor adequate to the whole needs of man. It is relative : its operation is limited notably by the constant mixture and compenetration of races, secondly by the paramount claims of the human fraternity, which is the natural basis of the supernatural kingdom of God.

Within these limits what are the functions of nationality and consequently its rights ? We return once more to the child. He can only be taught the rudiments of knowledge, and the elementary discipline of body and soul by means of signs and sounds through which his parents can express their meaning to him. The habits of daily life among which his intelligence unfolds and which he learns to practise can hardly be other than those which are distinctive of his parents, relations and intimate friends. Thus the community or association to which a human being belongs by reason of his birth is the natural vehicle of a certain language and a certain culture. By culture we mean in the strict sense natural conditions normally requisite to the growth and development of personality by which maturity is attained. Though it is by birth that every human being inherits this form of culture in which domestic tradition plays a predominant part, it is an error to suppose that the only idiom, gestures, modes of expression, physical and moral customs or rules which the human child is normally taught to adopt must be those which are solely connected with racial descent. This cultural heritage may be changed or even enriched in successive generations by migration, learning, intercourse with other families, groups or nationalities. It is none the less true that it is the language and culture of his parents to which the child is entitled and from which he cannot without deliberate and artificial intervention be separated.

This formative heritage in the second place is common to all that group of families whom racial origin, economic need, migration and various historical circumstances have brought together and who have the *will* to live together (*le vouloir-vivre collectif*). For no more than the human person is the human family made for solitude : it is from the earliest age part of a greater whole, linked in association with other families. And the instruments and symbols of that association are a common idiom, common manners, traditions of government, religious rite. The nation then is that association large or small in which man finds his membership by birth, and in which the human nature that he bears in common with all his fellow-men receives, as it develops, a certain determinant or distinctive form. The free use of the modes of education, intercourse and social life proper to the national association may be described as a secondary right without which the primary rights of self-conservation and natural development cannot normally be realized. In this sense nationality has a solid basis in natural law.

Thus far reason leads us ; and such is the ' nationality ' which, as will be seen, the Church has constantly respected in practice in her relations, as a universal society, with all the peoples of the earth. For the various deductions made from this established fact it is less safe and in some cases impossible to claim the authority either of reason or Christianity. Has the nation the right of ' self-determination,' that is of deciding that it will no longer be subject to any political authority outside itself? Does the denial of the use of the mother tongue or of cultural institutions, necessary to preserve the national traditions, justify rebellion and in consequence intervention? Has the nation the right to impose its language and customs upon a minority of different origin within its borders?

Three principles can be established as inherent in the Catholic tradition and these will provide a light for the answering of all such questions.

1. *State and nation are not synonymous terms;* they are different forms of human association; the reason for each indeed belongs to a different logical order; they subserve different ends. The providential end of the State is order: the end of the nation is the development of personality. Political peace and order are needed to enable the forces conducive to the growth, development and unfolding of human character to have free play. How the political good offered by the organized State and the cultural good offered by Nationality are complementary, since both minister to the need of the individual man (which is the sole purpose of human society) is shown in the statement with which this chapter concludes. Here it will suffice to record that there is no cogent reason for supposing that State and Nation need be or should be coterminous. In actual fact the consequences of the migration, dispersal and compenetration of races and of their economic needs have sufficiently demonstrated to all but the fanatics of national self-determination the impossibility of a world divided into States each consisting exclusively of a homogeneous nation.[1] The most that can be said[2] is that when a convergence of factors which belongs more to the will of God than to men, makes the bounds of State and nation more or less exactly coincide, the service which the former can render to man is in itself of greater simplicity and richness; many occasions for a conflict of loyalties are avoided. On the other hand it may well be that the requirements of defence, political order

[1] Yet it is to the pursuit of this will-o'-the wisp that modern international law and practice seem to be condemned; and the idolatry of the unitary nation-state continues to obsess the lazy mind of the demagogue.

[2] In this sense only can we accept the opinion of St. Thomas respecting the conclusion of Aristotle. See p. 387.

and economic life make it convenient, or even humanly inevitable that several distinct national groups should be united under a single ruler or in one federal commonwealth. The same influences operating elsewhere and in different circumstances may lead to groups of a single nationality living within the territories of two or more States. Thus one all-important qualification exists in the mind of the Church to the desire, otherwise legitimate, of a national group at any given time to be free from subjection to a ruler of another nationality '*si modo fieri incolumi justitia queat*.'[1] For justice forbids rebellion against a duly constituted authority which has not forfeited its mandate from above through grave abuse of its power. Nor apart from that consideration can the fusion or dismemberment of States be justified, if the aspirations of a single nationality are thus to be satisfied at the expense of serious detriment to others or to the welfare of the whole society of nations.

2. *Yet the rights arising from nationality are real and universal.* Nowhere can the government of a State or several governments suppress or frustrate the exercise of these rights—whether by legal enactment or international treaty—without danger to peace. And conversely if Governments everywhere were to honour and facilitate the enjoyment of national culture, frontiers would be of little moment, and loyalty to civil authority would not find itself in conflict with attachment to the customs and traditions which are man's heritage by his birth. Hence, in the treaty-making after a bitter war a Pope[2] exhorts the belligerents 'to take account as far as possible of the aspirations of the peoples,' and again in another solemn admonition to them says :

> Remember, nations never die : defeated and humiliated they groan beneath the yoke imposed upon them handing on from generation to generation a tragic heritage of hatred and revenge.

Pius XI, continuing the doctrine of his predecessors, stresses in all his missionary instructions, the duty of the preachers of the Gospel to respect the national characteristics of their converts. In his letter of June 15, 1926, to the

[1] Leo XIII : *Libertas præstantissimum :* June 20, 1888. See p. 364.
[2] Benedict XV.

Vicars Apostolic of China, for instance, he commands them to free themselves absolutely from the political preoccupations of the States from which they came lest they should give any ground for believing that they are hostile to the nationality of the Chinese people. In this he is but continuing the immemorial tradition of the Church, illustrated by the instances of her canon law and practice which we reproduce in this and subsequent chapters. From the decree of the Lateran Council of 1215, framed no doubt to counteract a centralizing tendency in that age of ecclesiastical efficiency, to the tender care with which the present Pontiff seeks to protect and preserve the distinctive liturgies of the Eastern rites, history is full of canonical prescriptions designed to ensure that the sacraments should be ministered to the peoples and guidance given to them in the school, the pulpit and the confessional in the native language which they understand. The ecclesiastical records of Germany, Flanders, Galicia, India, Ireland, Canada, Mexico, Peru, all have the same tale to tell. In all this the Church is simply recognizing a natural fact, the particular and distinctive characters of nations implied in the words of her Master who, while He wept with a broken heart over the capital city of His own native land, commanded His Apostles to 'Go and teach all nations.' In this divine instruction may be discerned the ideal of a whole nation, as an association and collective person, embracing the revealed religion and organizing itself in its own way according to the spiritual and social standards of Christianity.

The several 'Nations' of the Catholic University of the Middle Ages—a system still flourishing in the Gregorian University of Rome—furnish but another illustration of the respect and adaptation by the universal Church of the national genius.

This national framework of human life which the Catholic Church assumes and brings into concordance with her own supra-national unity, she expects the temporal power to respect with no less care. We have shown that Nation and State are not necessarily coterminous. Yet every nation has some local authority, patriarchal, tribal or civic, proper to itself—for authority in the scholastic term is the very form of society. That authority no external Power, conqueror or colonizer has the right to overthrow. Thus Vittoria in his lecture *De Indis* proves that the Indians of Central America, unbaptized barbarians as they may be, have chiefs who exercise true *dominium* over them and who cannot in justice be displaced by the Spanish Kings ; and Las Casas, Protector of the Indians, holds the field against the Imperialist Sepulveda in declaring 'All nations and peoples, whether they have the faith or not, who have territories and separate kingdoms which they have inhabited from the beginning are free peoples and are under no obligation to recognize any superior outside themselves.' By what right then can weaker or uncivilized nations be conquered by the stronger and more skilled? What justification can the colonial power plead for its vast annexations at the Divine Judgement seat? Our last chapter will seek to provide the conditions and the answer. Here we may say, as declared in the instruction drawn up by the four Cardinals appointed by Pius V in 1568,[1] that no military domination of primitive peoples can be lawful except all the strict conditions of just war be fulfilled. And, by whatever means primitive tribes or States have come under the dominion of another Power, the function of that Power is tutelary, and its object must be not to fuse or annihilate these natural societies but to prepare them for self-government.

3. Real as are the rights inherent in nationality, *the claims of nationality are not paramount :* they have no absolute quality. National culture is but *one* of the factors which help to make the perfect man. Heresy consists in stressing a part of the truth at the expense of the whole, idolatry in worshipping a partial good at the expense of the whole. And nationalism, which is the cult of nationality, savours both of heresy and idolatry when it seeks the satisfaction of national pride and prejudice to the extent of disregarding the moral law by which we are obliged to be just to all men ; the Christian precept 'Do unto others as ye would they should do unto you' ; the absolute claims of human fraternity and solidarity and the universal character of the Church. Most of the

[1] The nucleus of the future Congregation *de Propaganda Fide.*

recent pronouncements of the Popes upon the national problem relate to this aspect of it. They furnish a vigorous denunciation of excessive devotion to the nation as an end in itself, and an exposition of the sense in which that devotion can and ought to be conciliated with loyalty to the universal Church on the one hand and international co-operation on the other.[1]

When nation and State coincide, it is the State which, by its internal laws and its international relations, develops and protects, not only the political order and economic well-being of its component families, but also their national language, customs and traditions. And it is the public acts of the State which must be judged by the criteria which we have set forth. Are they best designed to permit the exercise of human rights and to safeguard Divine rights within the State's borders ? Do they at the same time respect similar rights and aspirations in other nations ? Do they contribute to the peace and order of the whole international society ? If so, they are in tune with the law of nature. If not, they are so many sins or blunders. By these rules civil laws, international acts, treaties and conventions must be judged, and most of all policies which involve or may lead to the use of military force.

When however there are two or more nations or national groups within the State, as is very commonly the case, what is the duty of the State ? It is evidently *to enable each group to lead its own characteristic life and to fulfil its ministry to man, provided only the Moral Law and public order are not infringed.* The special problem of national minorities is studied in the following chapter. Here we have to examine whether the failure of the State to discharge this general duty may be a cause of just rebellion, and so of just intervention by another State or by the international community.

It is the accepted teaching of theologians that an organized

[1] E.g. Pius IX Syllabus of Errors.
Leo XIII *Sapientiæ Christianæ.*
Benedict XV Letter to Canadian Hierarchy, June 7, 1918.
Pius XI *Ubi Arcano Dei.*
Pius XI Christmas Allocution, 1930.
Pius XI *Quadragesimo Anno.*
Pius XI *Caritate Christi Compulsi.*

attempt to overthrow a duly constituted government by force can only be justified by the presence of the three following conditions :

1. If that Government is guilty of grave and prolonged violation of the rights of its subjects.

2. If all peaceable (or in modern language 'constitutional') methods of obtaining redress and reform have been honestly tried and have failed.

3. If there be a reasonable prospect of success. For unless there be a real probability of overthrowing one Government by violent means and of substituting another and better one, justice and charity require that the certain and terrible evils of civil war should be avoided in the interests of the whole population of the State. The question of rebellion against or disobedience to a usurping Government—one, for instance, established by unjust conquest—is somewhat different. Such rulers cannot have, objectively, a true claim to the obedience of the people.[1] Yet even here, by the principle of prescription, the same rule applies : force of arms is the worst and most desperate remedy, to be used only if all other means fail. And if the rulers in question do in fact fulfil the functions of government and administration and, by custom and the lapse of time, have enjoyed at least the tacit consent of the governed, it is wrong to rebel against them and so to overthrow the existing though imperfect order except when all three conditions are present. The ethics of intervention are evidently determined by the ethics of rebellion. If the rebellion fulfils the conditions of justice

[1] The teaching of the Catholic Church upon this point was courageously set forth by Cardinal Mercier, Archbishop of Malines, during the occupation of Belgium by the Germans. His principal utterances on this subject are collected by Dom P. C. Lou Tseng-Tsiang, O.S.B., formerly Foreign Minister of the Chinese Republic and now a monk of the Benedictine Abbey of St. André, Belgium, in his booklet *L'Invasion et l'Occupation de la Mandchourie jugées à la lumière de la Doctrine Catholique par les Écrits du Cardinal Mercier*. (Paris. Editions du Foyer.) A letter from the Cardinal Secretary of State at the Vatican to the author states that Pope Pius XI considers this booklet to 'contain the principles of International Right which ought to be mutually observed by all nations.'

it is right for other States to assist it, if unjust, it is right for those States to assist the Government against the rebels.

It is hard to determine how far the use and enjoyment of national customs and institutions constitute rights, strictly speaking, the violation of which would, under the conditions named, be a just cause of rebellion. Certain general considerations may guide us.

In the first place, as we have shown, the function of nationality is *relative, not absolute:* it is *one* of the factors which minister to the formation of human character. And there are emergencies when, in the interests of the safety of the State itself, menaced by internal disruption or external attacks, Catholic sociology admits the right of the Government temporally to limit or even suspend the personal liberty of the individual subject or groups of subjects for the common good.[1] Again, in the event of famine, or grave economic crisis, or a distribution of wealth so bad as to cause dangerous resentment or frustrate necessary social reforms, the State may, and, in the last case at least *ought*[2] to, interfere with the exercise of the right of holding and bequeathing private property. If then the State—though itself only a 'means to an end' which is the temporal well-being of its component families and citizens—may temporarily or partially override these undoubted rights of individuals and collective persons, there is no reason to believe that the exercise of the rights arising from the circumstances of birth (i.e. nationality) should be wholly immune from moderation and control by the State.

Secondly, a distinction must be drawn between the various forms of expression and association which normally constitute the national heritage. Some are more, some less needed for the plenitude of human life. Those without which human beings cannot enjoy the fundamental natural rights or fulfil the duties pertaining to the family, and those without which they cannot fulfil their duty to God must evidently be regarded as inalienable rights. The liberty to use the maternal language, as we have defined it, in the home, the confessional and the pulpit is the most obvious of these

[1] See Taparelli on conscription, p. 134.

[2] See Pius XI: *Quadragesimo Anno.*

rights. Without it parents cannot fulfil their paramount duty of caring for, training and teaching their children: without it the souls of men cannot as a rule obtain the spiritual guidance which they need and to which they are entitled. Similarly the Church must be free to exercise her divine mandate to 'teach all nations'; and she can only do this if she teaches in the several languages which the different nations, and most of all the children of those nations clearly understand. Hence religious education and instruction in all its stages imperatively requires the free use of the maternal language.

Education in profane matters appears also to require as its most apt medium the native language of the scholars. Further, education is in the Catholic tradition primarily the function of the parents, the school master or mistress acting '*in loco parentis*.' And if St. Thomas forbids the instruction of minors in the Christian religion and their baptism without their parents'[1] consent, how much less can the State be justified in imposing upon boys and girls other forms of instruction, which are in themselves of no importance to the attainment of their spiritual end, against the will of the parents? Yet the languages used in public schools and colleges (which need not and do not everywhere exist) are of less moment than those used in the Church and the home, the two associations indispensable to man to begin his life and to end it in accordance with the Divine will. In any case the learning of various languages is a recognized form of higher education, all the more laudable in the eyes of those who believe, as Catholics do, in the solidarity of the human race and the duty of international friendship. There can be no objection on grounds either of reason or tradition to the teaching in schools, owned or controlled by the public authority, of the language of the majority of the population or of some considerable part of the population other than that to which the pupils belong. The exclusion from such schools of the native language is a harsh and uncharitable measure to

[1] *Summa Theologica*, II–II, 9, 10, art. 12: 'It would be contrary to natural justice if a boy before he has the use of reason were withdrawn from his parents' care or if anything were ordained concerning him contrary to his parents' wishes.'

which the spirit of the Church is certainly opposed, but in which she has sometimes been obliged to acquiesce in order to avoid a greater evil for her children.[1] It would not, however, in itself appear to be a just cause of rebellion, such as the denial of the fundamental domestic and religious liberties undoubtedly would be under the required conditions.

If the various human rights arising from the Natural Law and for the most part recognized by the Law of Nations, be examined in turn, it will be found that national customs form in each case *the mode in which they can most conveniently be exercised.* The right of association (religious, cultural, intellectual, professional, commercial) : the right of pleading or trial before a tribunal ; the right of bequest—these can only be exercised, with the utmost difficulty unless the free use of the native idiom, writing, gestures and other customs, is permitted. Other natural rights such as the freedom of peaceful travel and transit, or the right to use common land or the sea or their products, cannot be assured to man if he is debarred from the use of them *because* of his nationality ; in other words his national character must be understood to be compatible with the free exercise of them. Only when there is serious ground for believing that the right of association or the right of travel are being abused for subversive purposes against the State, would the State be justified in forbidding the enjoyment of those rights to members of a national group.

The denial of the use of the native language in the exercise of any one of the above rights, or the suspension of any one of them on grounds of nationality, would not in itself appear to be adequate cause for revolt or intervention. But the general prescription of the national language and liberties in regard to several or all of these rights might well amount in practice to an unjust frustration of Natural Law, and as such justify resort to force under the three conditions named.

Such then are the rights and limits of nationality in the light of natural justice. But nationalism is far more a

[1] Pius XI in an audience given to Cardinal Piffl, Archbishop of Vienna, regretted his inability to protect more effectively the mother-tongue of the German-speaking Catholics of the South Tyrol.

passion than a political theory, and man's attitude to his native land is far more determined by his heart than by his head. Our study would therefore be incomplete were we not to define in relation to the Law of Charity the sentiment of patriotism to which the fact of nationality gives rise.

Charity begins at home. Herein is defined Christian patriotism. The natural unity and similarity of mankind begets charity between man and man the world over ; but 'familiarity' has its special appeal to the affections. By familiarity we mean first, strictly, the characteristic of the family, of the home ; then the wider circle of human contacts which yet does not exceed personal experience, the circle which at its widest is the nation. Patriotism is the love of the family and of that human setting from which it is not normally possible to separate a man's conception of his family, namely, a place, friends, neighbours, language, traditions—his native land in fact. So a man loves his country because he loves his own home, and the former love partakes of the intimacy and sacredness of the latter.

Patriotism is described first in terms of love, because that is how it most nearly touches the normal man. The philosopher may reduce the spiritual economy of home and country to a nice framework of mutual rights and duties between parents and children, family and family, rulers and subjects, and between fellow-citizens. But in the primary unit of which civil society is composed, it is least of all easy to separate, even in thought, justice from charity ; it is almost as difficult within the nation. It is for no cold sense of duty to an abstract State that the soldier will face hardship and death, but for the memory of familiar faces. The natural affection for home and country is reinforced and sanctified by Christianity ; for it must necessarily be towards those whom a man can touch, see, hear, that his charity, potentially extending to all God's creatures, must actually be put in practice.

Behind patriotism expressed in terms of affection lies, however, a whole philosophy which establishes its necessity both to national and international life. Economic need, or self-defence, might *force* a group of families to live together. But if that group is to endure as a community able to order its existence under a common authority, there must be a union of wills, a kind of 'spiritual cement' holding all its component parts together. So much for the value of partriotism to the nation. What place has patriotism in the world as a whole? The rulers of States may or may not (as in the magnificent failure of the Holy Roman Empire) acknowledge a supreme political authority in the world; but in any case there is no reasonable scheme of international order that does not postulate in each State a 'moral personality.' The State must be a responsible unit, able as one to fulfil the requirements of justice towards other States, able, for instance, to make promises and keep them. But patriotism is the power that makes and keeps the State united. Hence patriotism in every nation is a necessary condition of 'the tranquillity of order' in the world at large. Without patriotism no peace.

There is no lie so insidious as a half-truth; and no theory has more impeded the realization of the Christian ideal of international life than the unbridled nationalism which has torn away the affection or passion of patriotism from the rational ground for its existence. Patriotism exists in the Christian system quite as much as a factor for international order as it does to promote internal union and strength; and if the former purpose be forgotten, and with it the dominating fact of the unity and fraternity of the human race, the remaining caricature of patriotism may become a form of idolatry. As such it has often been denounced by the Church.[1]

Catholic Christianity has, therefore, nothing to do with the foolish theories that pit patriotism against international co-operation. Devotion to family and friends does not, as we have seen, conflict with devotion to country; the one is contained in the other; so also loyalty to nation or empire does not conflict with loyalty to the whole community of mankind. Yet perceptible as this truth may be to the unaided reason, it is only through love of God as Creator and Father of all, that the reconciliation of these two loyalties can

[1] E.g. The condemnation of the *Action Française* in France, and of Herr Rosenberg's book *The Mythology of the Twentieth Century* in Germany.

normally be effected in the mind; it is only by the supernatural power of Christian charity that a man can achieve the habit of respecting and honouring patriotism in nations other than his own. The Catholic Church emphasizes by its very name the unity of the human race, but it is the guardian of right patriotism. Hence there is no contradiction in the blessing which that Divine Institution, itself devoted to peace, bestows upon those who with honest intention fight to defend their own or their neighbour's fatherland against unjust attack.[1]

Documents

For convenience the quotations and references relating to the action of the Church in safeguarding national characteristics in religious rites and instruction are grouped together at the end of Chapter XIV upon National Minorities. These passages, though they refer actually to the condition of a national minority within a State or to a State containing several national groups, illustrate the degree to which the Church recognizes distinction between nationalities as a fact and the importance which she attaches to it.

Mgr. Nicholas Pfeiffer *in* '*Doctrina Juris Internationalis juxta F. de Vittoria*' quotes from a passage of the *Relectio de Indis* in which the author comments upon St. Thomas (*Summa*, II–II, Q. ix, x, art. 12) in relation to parental authority. He bases upon this the deduction that race and language are to a large extent outside the competence of the State.

Vittoria invokes St. Thomas, who shows that the Jews or other infidels do not lose authority over their children by reason of their unbelief.

We may be permitted to add a modern application of this principle. St. Thomas, in the body of the article on this subject, denies that the Church has the right to baptize the babies of unbelievers against the will of the parents. Among other things, he says: '. . . It would be contrary to natural justice if a boy before he has the use of reason were withdrawn from his parents' care, or *if anything were ordained concerning him against his parents' wishes*. But once he begins to have the use of free will . . . he

[1] This conclusion I have reproduced with slight alteration from my article on 'Patriotism' in *A Catholic Survey*.

should be induced to believe not by coercion, but by persuasion. . . .' This doctrine ought surely to be applied to our own days. It would attribute to the parents the right of choosing the language in which teaching is to be given in school ; and it would not allow this to be imposed by the State without regard for or even against the parents' wishes and the children's inclinations.

Vittoria adds, by way of corollary : 'Neither from the Saracens, nor from the Jews, nor from other infidels is it lawful to seize the things which they possess simply on the grounds of their unbelief : on the contrary that is theft and rapine, no less than if they were seized from Christians.'

If we apply this teaching to modern times, it should be unlawful to despoil anyone of his property, movable or immovable, his right to inhabit a place, or his right to a pension and so forth, simply because of his language or the race to which he belongs.

Mgr. Pfeiffer in the same work writes as follows upon Vittoria's conclusion in the *De Indis* that non-Christians can exercise real ownership and lordship.

Vittoria lays down the same doctrine briefly in his First Lecture *De potestate ecclesiæ*, where he says : 'Temporal and civil power exists integrally among the heathen' ; and he expounds the same thing at more length in his lecture *De potestate civili*.

Almost all these doctrines about the Liberties of the Indians are to be found in *Las Casas*. Here it will suffice to quote the following : 'All Nations and peoples, whether they have the faith or not, who have territories and separate kingdoms which they have inhabited since the beginning, are free peoples, and are under no obligation to recognize any superiors outside themselves.'

Leo XIII in his Encyclical *Libertas præstantissimum* of June 29, 1888, says : 'Nor does the Church condemn the desire that one's own Nation should not be subject to any foreign or despotic power, provided only it can be done without any violation of justice.' And Pius XI, now gloriously reigning, in his Encyclical *Ubi Arcano Dei* of December 23, 1922, teaches among other things 'That other nations also have the right to live and to aspire to prosperity.'

Pius IX. *Proposition proscribed and condemned in the Syllabus of Errors. December* 8, 1864 :

Not only is it not forbidden to violate the most sacred promise or to perform an act which is criminal, sinful and repugnant to the Eternal Law, provided it is done for patriotic motives, but it is right and highly praiseworthy so to act.'

Love of Church and Country :

LEO XIII. *Encyclical 'Sapientiæ Christianæ,' January* 10, 1890 :

Undoubtedly as they go through life, Catholics have more numerous and greater duties than those who are either wrongly informed upon or wholly destitute of the Catholic faith. . . . A man having embraced the Christian faith, as he ought to, is by that very act subject to the Church as to his mother and becomes a member of that greatest and most holy Society over which it is the function of the Roman Pontiff to wield supreme power under Jesus Christ, the invisible head. But if the law of nature bids us love particularly the city in which we were born and received into this world, and to defend it, so that the good citizen does not hesitate to lay down his life for his fatherland, it is the duty of Christians in like manner to be far more attached to the Church. For the Church is the city of the living God, born of God Himself and established by His authority, which is indeed a pilgrim here on earth, but is ever calling men, teaching them and leading them on to eternal happiness in heaven. So that fatherland deserves our love from which we receive the enjoyment of our mortal life ; but needs must we with love maintain the Church, to whom we owe the everlasting life of the soul. For it is right to put the good of the mind before the good of the body, and much more sacred than our duties towards men are our duties towards God.

But, if we would form a true judgement, our supernatural love of the Church and our natural love of country are but twin forms of Charity springing from the same eternal principle, for of both the author and the cause is God ; whence it follows that the one duty cannot conflict with the other. . . . And yet, because the days are evil or the wills of men more than ever contrary, the order governing these two duties is from time to time overturned. Certainly cases occur when the State seems to demand one thing of its citizens and religion another of Christians ; and that for no other reason than that the rulers of the State treat lightly the sacred power of the Church or want to make her subject to themselves. . . .

If the laws of the State are openly inconsistent with the rights of God, if they inflict any injury upon the Church, or are in contradiction to religious duties or do violence to the authority of Jesus Christ in the person of the Supreme Pontiff, then indeed is it a duty to resist, a crime to obey : and this involves an injury to the State itself, for every wrong that is committed in the sphere of religion is a transgression against the State.

Pius XI. *Encyclical 'Caritate Christi Compulsi.'* *May*, 1932:

Right order of Christian charity does not disapprove of lawful love of country, and a sentiment of justifiable nationalism ; on the contrary it controls, sanctifies and enlivens them. If, however, egoism, abusing this love of country and exaggerating this sentiment of nationalism, insinuates itself into the relations between people and people, there is no excess that will not seem justified ; and that which between individuals would be judged blameworthy by all, is now considered lawful and praiseworthy, if it is done in the name of this exaggerated nationalism. Instead of the great law of love and human brotherhood, which embraces and holds in a single family all nations and peoples with one Father who is in heaven, there enters hatred, driving all to destruction. In public life, sacred principles, the guide of all social intercourse, are trampled upon ; the solid foundations of right and honesty, on which the State should rest, are undermined ; polluted and destroyed are the sources of those ancient traditions, which, based on faith in God and fidelity to His law, secured the true progress of nations.

Pope Pius XI applying this thought, made the following frank declaration to the Procurators General of the Missionary Congregations :

Nationalism has always been for the Missions a scourge ; yet more, it is not an exaggeration to call it a curse. In the case of all missionaries, indeed of all those who, in whatever way occupy themselves with the Apostolate, from the humblest priest to the Pope himself, Nationalism, even if sometimes it has produced advantages, has ended by causing nothing but harm.

Respect for the national character and aspirations of the native people inhabiting the country evangelized is inculcated no less firmly by the same Pontiff.

Pius XI. *Ab ipsis Pontificatus primordiis.* June 15, 1926.

The most holy work of the Missions would be still more fruitful, if one could destroy a prejudice, from day to day more tenacious and wider spread, notably amongst young people badly informed in whose mind it takes root : we refer to the prejudice which attributes to the action of the Catholic Church and her missionaries, not the service of Religion, but that of the interests and the politics of foreign nations. Whence one concludes that the Church is hostile to the independence of the peoples whom she evangelizes, as well as to the free exercise of their national aspirations. . . .

REV. HYACINTHUS (PRINCE ADAM) WORONIECKI, O.P. (*In Vaussard : ' Enquête sur le Nationalisme.'*) *On the relations of Nation and State :*

If then, we perceive an overlapping, as it were, of Nation and State in the life of society, if we realize that there is nothing transitory and accidental about that overlapping, but that it is a constant fact, which recurs at all times and in all places, it is our task to go back to the very source of social life, that is to the potentiality which characterizes human nature, and to distinguish among its constituent elements those which postulate life within a State and those which postulate life within a Nation.

The necessity of living in a State comes from the fact that men are all destined to one universal end and must make their way thither by particular means, which are in themselves indeterminate in regard to that end : for every particular is indeterminate in relation to the general. But if each one in his personal life must determine by himself the particular means to lead him to the universal end, in society, in order that it may preserve its organic unity, this determination must be effected by a central organ, that is an authority. The uniform determinations which authority impresses upon the members of the society are civil laws, which St. Thomas calls '*organa quædam ad finem civitatis.*'[1] That is the natural foundation of the civil society of the State, which is its crown.

We ought, of course, to press our analysis deeper still and to show how the root of the problem is to be found in spiritual potentiality, in the laws of our cognition (connaissance), and deeper yet, in the composition of human nature, the substantial union of soul and body.

And what now is the origin of the necessity of living in a Nation ? This is a far more difficult question, which has so far been rarely attacked from the analytical point of view. The following is a tentative analysis, which is the outcome of long reflection in the light of thomistic doctrine. . . .

The need of the special support which the national organism gives to each individual human being arises from a more subjective element of the natural potentiality of man, namely from his *indetermination* in regard to the mode of carrying out such or such an action. It is evident that the same thing may be done in divers manners, which are more fitted or less fitted to the nature of the doer. A man may receive from without, or from within himself, impulsions to perform a certain act : but he may perform it in several ways, with more or with less perfection, ease, ability or promptness. Here we are touching upon the question of *habits*, which plays so important a part in ethics.

Man does not possess in his nature itself dispositions so perfectly

[1] *Comm. in Polit.* Lib. IV, c. 7.

determined that they provide for the direction of his moral activity at every moment of his life.[1] The facility and precision which instinct gives in the sensitive life, must be acquired by man in his moral life at the cost of a slow labour of education. From that process there comes a group of dispositions which makes him perform the same acts with constantly increasing ability. Habit, virtue, morals, custom, usage—all these terms relate to this same phenomenon of auto-determination, stabilized in each individual faculty of the mind by that reflex action which every act exercises upon the power from which it originates (*puissance-mère*) and upon the whole psychic organism. It is from this element of the natural potentiality of man that comes the necessity for men of living in and as Nations. We may then say in the vocabulary of St. Thomas : '*Sicut leges sunt organa quædam ad finem civitatis, ita mores sunt organa quædam ad finem nationis.*' If that is the case, the primary importance of the national element for the moral life of man will be apparent to all ; it becomes the principal educative[2] factor in the natural order, and we know the immense value of a well organized natural basis upon which to found supernatural education.

If now we compare the results of our twofold analysis, we must conclude that we ought to allot to the element of nationality a far greater part in the life and moral development of the human race than many Catholic moralists are disposed to assign to it. Priority in the moral order can no longer be attributed to the State, without very serious qualifications. Who knows, but that we ought even to go so far as to conclude that the priority in itself (*simplicitur*) belongs to the Nation, while the State continues to retain under certain aspects (*secundam quid*) a true superiority which needs more precise definition.

Tacitus of old exclaimed : '*Quid leges sine moribus ?*' That saying contains the key to the solution of our problem, and it deserves serious consideration from all those who wish to study these arduous questions.

The principle of nationality then would seem to contain a good deal of truth. If by our nature we are destined to live within the framework of two social organisms, State and Nation, it is of capital importance for our moral life that a real harmony should exist between them. The Christian moralist should envisage the State unified from a national point of view as an ideal whose realization, within the limits of what is possible, is of great utility for the preservation of good customs and the moral development of the citizens.[3]

[1] St. Thomas : *Summa Theologica*, I–IIae, Q. li, art. 1, Q. lxiii, art. 1.

[2] 'Cultural,' as Father Delos would say.

[3] Aristotle. *Pol.* I, 3, c. 1 and St. Thomas *Comm. in Polit.* Lib. III, Cap. II. (See p. 387.)

What would be a great mistake would be to declare this ideal to be so indispensable that without it all well organized moral life were considered impossible. Like every other ideal, it must be prosecuted with prudence and with that intimate conviction that the ideal concepts of our minds, even when they are strongly supported by actual facts, can never be fully translated into acts in this world. It is quite possible then for it to be criminal under some circumstances to wish to realize the ideal of the National State at all costs, and to do so by subverting the established social order to the great detriment of the moral life of the citizens.

REV. J. T. DELOS, O.P., in *La Société Internationale. Cultural function of Nationality :*

. . . Catholic thinkers see in the formation of nations a natural fact. By this we mean that nations correspond to the demands of the natural order of human life. This order is one willed by God, and conformable to the dispositions of His providence. The formation of nations and the sentiments they inspire are therefore things good in themselves.

Like all that is providential in human life, the Nation should contribute to man's welfare. It fulfils a certain function in human life ; this function must be clearly defined in order to measure its value.

We may say, in general, that the Nation stabilizes and educates.

Man has need of the support and aid of society. This mutual support is continuous through time, from generation to generation. There is a common mass of goods, economic (agricultural science and implements, etc.), physiological (race), intellectual, and moral, that grows and is transmitted from generation to generation. The individual thus finds, at his birth, a heritage, a birthright at his disposal. The nation secures, throughout time, the continuity of the social goods necessary to the individual.

At the same time it furnishes him with an environment that keeps him from becoming a physical and moral nomad. It gives him a *milieu* to provide the physical, moral, and intellectual nourishment necessary for his life.

But how does the Nation act upon the individual ? How does it give him the goods that it has prepared and preserved for him ? By an influence that is partly creative, partly educative. It gives to the individual a group of manners and customs. That does not mean merely a certain number of habits or ways of doing things ; it implies a body of inclinations that become almost second nature. This is the value of the Nation. The national environment gives each one a nationality, that is to say a complex of physiological preformations and mental dispositions, from which result certain ways of seeing, thinking and acting. Through nationality each one receives an *ensemble* of connatural manners which, in relation to the unqualified or merely potential original human nature, is an enrichment of it. Nationality puts the individual, without effort on his part, in possession of a certain measure of civilization, and raises him to a certain level of development. That is its natural and providential mission.

It is this mission that creates our moral obligation to the nation. From it man receives a heritage of civilization ; and in it he finds the social *milieu* necessary for his further development. He is bound to respect it as a means furnished by nature for the perfecting of himself and of others ; to injure or destroy the nation would be to compromise his own destiny, and that of his fellow-citizens. Everyone is bound, therefore, to defend his country, even at the peril of his life, ' as long as it has not become evident that the continued existence of that society has become harmful.'[1]

From this it is clear that the nation never has an absolute, but always only a relative value. In itself, its value depends upon its usefulness to humanity ; it is relative to the quality of the manners, mentality, disposition—the national formation—that it imparts to its members.

This concept of the providential function of the Nation, by which its value may be measured, enables us to judge of the deviations to which the idea of the Nation is exposed. . . .

National and International Society :

. . . The society of nations has its foundation in human nature itself. We may regard this natural foundation in two ways. First, men have the same human nature, therefore in their relations with one another they are equal, peers one of the other. On the other hand, their natural equality gives them originally an equality of rights over the goods of the earth. By the disposition of Providence the riches of the world were originally placed at the disposal of the whole human race, and every man may claim by natural right, subject to certain limitations, to use and benefit by them. Appropriation by individuals may legitimately determine this general right, and give rise to individual rights over certain things. But this does not affect the unity of all human nature, or the fact that all the goods of the earth are originally destined for all. And on this are founded international relations.

Human society as a universal grouping of all men is not inconsistent with the existence of particular national groups; both are in accordance with human nature. There is no question

[1] Leclerq : *Leçons de Droit Naturel*, Vol. I. Brussels ; Dewit, 1927, p. 231.

of sacrificing one to the other, but they must be correlated in order of primacy. This is what is meant by international social relations.

If we consider the element in human nature that makes the nations, on the one hand, and universal human society on the other, we see that the latter derives from an essential trait of human nature : its identity in the whole race, and the duty of mutual aid and support which flows from it. The nation, on the other hand, owes its foundation to particular qualities of land, race or history, contingent and variable, which add to, and are secondary to, the essential in human nature. Hence the order of relation between the two societies ; the national groups are subordinate to universal society.

. . . Under all natural differentiations there exists a natural right of human sociability, in virtue of which no local group can cut itself off from communication and exchange, commercial, industrial, intellectual and moral. Natural law demands this widening of human life and *racial particularism has no prescriptive right against it.*

. . . In any form of nationalism devoid of the spirit of international sympathy, Catholicism sees at least an unconscious denial of the universality of the aspirations and possibilities common to all ; a denial of the spiritual nature of man, as a creature of intelligence and free will, that is tantamount to the crudest materialism. It proclaims the necessity and the moral duty to recognize as well-founded both the institution of the nation and of international organization ; and also that the international institution which unites the nations while respecting the individuality of each, is ultimately the higher of the two.

NATIONALITY : ITS PLACE IN THE LAW OF NATIONS. *Statement of the*[1] *Catholic Union of International Studies :*

I

THE CATHOLIC UNION FOR INTERNATIONAL STUDIES, faithful to those principles of natural philosophy and sociology which supply a rational basis to Christian doctrine, recognizes that the community of culture and customs created by nationality gives rise to special rights and duties on the part of individuals, national groups, States, and the organized society of nations.

[1] The Union, whose headquarters are at the Catholic University Town of Fribourg in Switzerland, has as its ecclesiastical patron Mgr. Besson, Bishop of Lausanne, Geneva and Fribourg, and comprises groups in Switzerland, France, Germany, Belgium, Poland, Austria, Hungary, Ireland and other countries. The British group is the Catholic Council for International Relations. It is part of the work of the Union Catholique d'Etudes Internationales to examine in the light of Christian tradition some of

II

The national sphere is for man a natural one, which in its complete form, offers him at the same time an extension of the domestic sphere on a spiritual, cultural, ethnical and territorial basis. It exercises on him an educative and stabilizing influence which is of great value in the development of the individual. The natural rights enjoyed by nationals and national groups are founded on this service rendered to the individual.

III

In accordance with Christian philosophy, which recognizes no other absolute rights than those of God on the one hand ; and on the other, those of man (possessed by him through his resemblance to God and because of his divine end)—in accordance also with social ethics by which the law of institutions and societies is based on their human object (the service they render to man) the Union recognizes that the rights conferred by nationality are essentially relative and limited.

Their end is, in fact, directed to those human functions which Providence has assigned to nationality and they are limited by the needs of those functions.

Furthermore, nationality is the product of diverse and variable factors, whose contributions to culture are of unequal value when viewed by reason. The beneficent influence of nationality varies both in intensity and quality. The rights, therefore, of different national groups are not of absolutely equal value like those of the individual which are the same in the case of each.

IV

The complete and harmonious development of the individual requires the existence of societies other than those based on the idea and sentiment of a community of nationality. The State in particular is a separate, natural society, the source and possessor of certain rights and duties, of which Christian political philosophy, sociology and ethics have long since laid down the ends and general principles of action.

the acute problems of international law and politics which have been raised by the war and its aftermath. Among these the controversy concerning the Rights of Nationality, with which the Minorities Question is closely connected, seemed to be the most insistent. Hence it was taken up as the first task of the new Juridical and Doctrinal Committee of the Union in 1926. Their report, as finally approved by the Union, in September, 1930, is largely the work of Father Delos, O.P., of the Catholic Faculty of the University of Lille.

V

The rights and duties arising from nationality are in harmony with those involved by the membership of other natural societies. The principle of this harmony is to be found in the common end shared by all social institutions, namely, the service of humanity to which all must contribute according to their position in the social hierarchy and the natural means at their disposal.

Applying these principles to the state and to its relations with the various national groups which are subject to it, the U.C.E.I. regards them not as rivals, but as collaborators whose joint action must be directed to the same ultimate end.

VI

The members of a national group are bound, in their relations with the State to which they are subject, by all the duties and obligations which Christian political philosophy and ethics impose on the consciences of citizens. They enjoy all the rights recognized by these two spheres of thought as belonging to man, as man and as citizen.

VII

As the nationality of its citizens, whether single or diverse, is for them an inheritance of great price, the State is on this account bound by corresponding obligations. It is the guardian, protector and servant of all human values and more especially of those included in the cultural inheritance of the national group or groups encompassed by it. It is bound to co-operate in the fulfilment of the cultural and educative functions of nationalities.

The co-operation of the State will usually be manifested in the three-fold sphere of family, school and religion ; for religious institutions, the organization of the family and the educational regime are among the normal fields of action in the national sphere.

VIII

The end to which the State is directed belongs to the political order ; while that of nationality—and consequently of the rights which flow from it—is of the cultural order. The community of nationality, therefore, does not of itself and directly create political rights but only those belonging to culture.

But because certain institutions and methods of organizing social and individual life have proved more efficacious and more in accordance with the tastes, liberty and dignity of those concerned when established on the basis of nationality, the citizen may demand from the State a political regime which permits, upholds and favours the development of these institutions on a national basis.

IX

Nationality being a plastic reality, no culture-bringing group must be denied the right to guide the development of national characteristics in such direction as may accord with a finer culture and a fuller development of the individual. If by assimilation is understood making national customs and institutions uniform by other means than those by which the persons concerned are themselves won over to new forms of human culture, then such assimilation is as reprehensible on the part of the State, as it is on the part of those national groups who do not admit any differentiation in their midst.

Variety of culture is, on the contrary, a proof of the richness of human nature. It is not in itself prejudicial to the State ; it may even become a cause of progress.

The principle of the primacy of the individual which disposes the action of social institutions towards his fuller development helps us to solve the problem of assimilation. This principle gives a philosophical basis to the right to live in conformity with the national culture and prohibits any policy of forced assimilation. It also prevents members of a national group from denying themselves through prejudice all cultural innovations, or from confining themselves within the ever-narrow limits of a nationalism which, because of its particularism, can never of itself provide the sum-total of those values which man must strive to acquire. States and national groups must, in their mutual relations, ever bear in mind the duties which are the outcome of this twofold principle.

X

It is the State which, in its quality of a moral entity, is of itself directly charged with the duty of ensuring by its own initiative and personal responsibility, conditions favourable to the normal development of the nationals subject to its sovereignty.

XI

The end towards which the State moves demands the organization of an international regime which will guarantee international order and common good. It is the function of an organized international society to exercise juridical and moral control over the activity of States especially in the matter of nationality.

XII

With a view to ensuring respect for those obligations which the existence of nationalities has imposed on States and on national groups, it is desirable that such rights and duties should be expressed and given a juridical guarantee and that they should be embodied in the legislation of States.

The guarantee, under this new form, of this part of the Rights of Man is a moral obligation which demands at the present day the free action of States as well as the regulating and co-ordinating influence of the League of Nations. To the latter in particular it belongs to assist in causing the rights and duties of States and national groups gradually to be embodied in the positive law, both national and international.

It is greatly to be desired that representatives of different bodies interested in the problem of protecting the rights of nationality (the philosophy of law, public law, social and political philosophy, and ethics) should devote themselves to the doctrinal elaboration of a Declaration of Human Rights of which the rights of nationals are an integral part. These rights must, in fact, be defined philosophically, in order that they may be protected juridically.

It is also highly desirable that a concerted action should be promoted in every country with a view to enlightening the conscience of the citizens as to the true mission of both State and nation, the origin of their respective rights and duties, and the principle of natural law by which their convergent action is harmonized for the benefit of the individual.

CONTEMPORARY ERRORS RELATING TO THE TOTALITARIAN NATION-STATE. *Letter of the Austrian Episcopate, Vienna, December* 21, 1933:

The letter deals largely with problems peculiar to Austria. The passages summarized below are, however, of doctrinal importance.

(*N.B. The numbers refer to the paragraphs of the printed German text.*)

10. God is absolute Master. Nations must obey and serve. No nation is independent and sovereign with regard to God.

11. The power, laws, constitution and government of every nation derive ultimately from God's Law. The sovereignty of the people is valid only as far as it is in accordance with the law of God. Unbridled sovereignty of the people leads to the destructive errors of communism, socialism and nihilism.

12. We must recognize the authority of the State as the representative of God. Revolution and any attempt to upset authority by force are condemned. Political murder is a ruthless sin and can never be justified.

16. . . . It is an incontrovertible fact that the German bishops have for years unanimously condemned National Socialism from the religious and ecclesiastical standpoint. It is also an incontrovertible fact that they have expressly maintained their condemnation of the religious and ecclesiastical

error of National Socialism even when, after the new political regime had been established in Germany, they had received a solemn official assurance of an arrangement between the State and the Church. Even the Concordat between Germany and the Holy See was concerned only with this arrangement between the State and the Church. It was not in the slightest degree any recognition or approval of the religious and ecclesiastical errors of the National Socialists. Whether and how far the provisions of this Concordat are being observed and carried out the Holy Apostolic See is the judge. All the world knows what strained relations obtain between Church and State in the German Empire and what serious anxiety they justify. The Holy Father himself on October 27 last in his address to the German League of Youth spoke of a 'very difficult hour for Germany' and of his 'very great pity for German youth,' even of his 'anxiety for religion in Germany.'

18. The Austrian Bishops have already issued a warning against National Socialism in our common pastoral letter of February 7, 1932. Since then individual bishops have repeatedly taken a stand against its religious errors and, in view of the ever-increasing dangers, we consider it our duty to indicate these fundamental errors briefly and comprehensively.

19. In opposition to the teaching of National Socialism we cite four fundamental truths :

(i) Humanity is a single family based on justice and love. We therefore condemn the National Socialist *race mania* which leads necessarily to hatred and conflict between races and nations. We also condemn the un-Christian sterilization law which stands in irreconcilable contradiction to the law of nature and Catholic Christianity.

(ii) True Christian nationalism is desired by God and approved by the Church : for love of one's own people and attachment to one's country are fundamental in human nature. We therefore preach the virtue of Christian patriotism, and we condemn at the same time treachery to one's country and racial anti-semitism.

(iii) Nation and State are different things. The State is above the nation. We therefore condemn the extreme principle of nationality. . . .

(iv) Above all nationalism stands religion, which is not national but supra-national. Religion helps a nation to become noble. It procures a blessing for a people. It is the source and nourishment of true culture in every nation. But it is not limited to any single nation. Its call is to bring a message of salvation to every nation and at the same time to help in its earthly welfare. We therefore condemn all ideas and efforts towards the formation of a national church as these must lead in the end to a breach with the Catholic Church.

The Dutch Hierarchy *on Fascism and National Socialism.* (*Joint Lenten Pastoral*, 1934) :

. . . It is evident that a new order of things is developing, which from many points of view can be gladly welcomed since it means liberation from materialism and individualism, but which at the same time causes great anxiety since it threatens to be mixed with other errors. We refer to the systems which are called National Socialism and Fascism. . . . It is an absolute claim of the Church that her supernatural activity be perfectly free and secure, and that she regulate the moral life of the faithful and all that is necessary for their spiritual well-being, such as marriage, family life, the education of youth, according to Christian principles and with full liberty. From this it follows that the Church must claim the liberties which tend to promote these ends, as, for example, her own schools, confessional (i.e. *Catholic*) organizations, a free Catholic Press and every form of Catholic public life. . . . Reason teaches us, and revelation confirms it, that man has personal rights. These rights are from nature, even apart from the State. The State does not create them and they do not proceed merely from the purpose of the State or from the interests of the nation, but are bound up with the personal destiny of man. Because these rights precede all the regulations of the State, the State must respect them, even though they have to be regulated : that is, harmonized with the rights of others. Undoubtedly the good of the individual and the liberty it requires are subordinate to the common good ; but they are not absorbed into it. For, after all, the common good can be nothing but the well-ordered good of all, and not something which lies quite outside the good of the individual, such as, for example, mere racial or national expansion, or the power and greatness of the State as such. . . .

Now that which is sometimes called the Totalitarian State, in its strictest meaning is entirely in conflict with these principles. Undoubtedly the promotion of national well-being, properly understood, is something grand and lofty. It is therefore the duty of every citizen to promote it. No one, moreover, is allowed so to pursue his own individual interests that he endangers the harmony of the whole, and therefore the well-being of others. Rather as patriots and social beings we are destined and called to contribute to the prosperity of the whole, the well-being of everyone, in co-operation with our fellow-citizens of every class and rank.

But the well-being of the whole is the well-being of *free personalities*, each with his own destiny. It would not be promoted, but destroyed, were we to consider the State as the only source of rights, morality and liberty. It is destroyed by every system which idolizes State and nation, and by every absolute dictatorship.

The Bishops after issuing a warning against movements which, while not openly admitting their extreme nationalist character, 'are bound sooner or later to come under the influence of this idolatry of State or nation,' say that there is much that needs to be remedied in the national life. But they add : 'We must point out that many of the existing problems are international and cannot be solved by the Government of any one country alone.'

The Dutch hierarchy in this outspoken letter are but elucidating the principles underlying the vigorous protests made by the Pope in July, 1931, against the tendency to subject all rights and all education to the service of the Nation-State in Italy.

PIUS XI. *Encyclical. Non Abbiamo Bisogno :*

We find Ourselves confronted by a mass of authentic affirmations and no less authentic facts which reveal beyond the slightest possibility of doubt the resolve . . . to monopolize completely the young, from their tenderest years up to manhood and womanhood, for the exclusive advantage of a party and of a regime based on an ideology which clearly resolves itself into a true, real pagan worship of the State—the 'Statolatry' which is no less in contrast with the natural rights of the family than it is in contradiction with the supernatural rights of the Church.

And again :

. . . A conception of the State which makes the rising generations belong to it entirely, without any exception, from the tenderest years up to adult life, cannot be reconciled by a Catholic either with Catholic doctrine or with the natural rights of the family.

CHAPTER XIV

THE RIGHTS OF NATIONAL MINORITIES

THE minority problem, for which the principles adduced in the last chapter offer a solution, has passed through many phases during the history of Western civilization. And there is no subject which merits greater attention from the student of sociology. For in the last analysis the problem consists in a clash between positive and natural law, between human rights and spiritual liberties on the one hand and the more or less artificial structure of civil society on the other.

There are two propositions which the Christian cannot admit, but which are the root of the injustice from which minorities in the modern state too often suffer and the bitterness which consequently poisons their relations to their fellow-citizens. The first is the proposition that the majority is always right. The second that the State is the end for which man exists. On the first Leo XIII said :[1] 'When once man is firmly persuaded that he is subject to no one it follows that the efficient cause of the unity of civil society is not to be sought in any principle external to man. . . . Hence the doctrine of the supremacy of the greater number, and the notion that all right and all duty reside in the majority. But . . . it is clear that all this is in contradiction to reason.' The second was condemned by Pius XI in his Encyclical *Non Abbiamo Bisogno.*[2]

Yet upon these two fallacies the typical modern secular State is founded. Finding the vote of a majority a conclusive argument in an age wherein democracy passed for the

[1] *Libertas Præstantissimum* (see p. 333).
[2] See preceding chapter.

latest wisdom, tyranny has not been slow to discover devices for creating legislative majorities in the interests either of exaggerated nationalism or secularism or both. The system has spread from Western Europe to Russia, Turkey, Mesopotamia, Latin America and the East. It is therefore not so much the personal autocrat which is to be feared by the racial or religious group with a life of its own, but that caricature of the sovereign people, the infallible majority. The absence of respect for an objective moral law or for natural rights, superior and antecedent to human ordinances, removes the only serious check upon political intolerance. Hence no sphere of life is free from the arbitrary interference of the State; and any institution, religious, political, social or cultural, which does not appeal to the whims of the majority is regarded as an irritating obstacle to national unity—or to give it its proper name—uniformity. This idolatry of the *Etat unitaire* is all the more destructive of true liberty when its devotees are infected, as is almost everywhere the case in the contemporary world, with the passion of nationalism. The false simplicity of a world divided into states each supposedly containing a single race, a national language, a national religion—or irreligion—and a national economy, has supplanted in men's minds the ideal of the organic and perfectly articulated unity of which the Mystical Body of Christ is the architype. We live amid the ruins of an attempt to construct international institutions from such unsociable and contradictory elements.

We have described first this predominant conception of the unitary state, lay and national, since it governs the modern minority problem. And that in two senses. In the first place it is precisely because of the oppression to which that conception gives rise that the protection of minorities by the intervention of the international society becomes necessary. In the second place, this false ideal itself, in the form of 'national self-determination,' obsesses the minority which is or believes itself to be oppressed. Its only remedy for suffering such an evil is to be in a position to perpetrate it. Yet as we have seen there is frequently no sound moral grounds upon which to subvert the existing government and destroy the State : the explicit or implicit intention of the minority to achieve political independence at all costs serves only too often as pretext or even justification for further restrictions imposed upon the rights and liberties of its members by the majority. The true mission and interests of the Catholic Church have been and are sadly compromised in different parts of the world, by the identification of clergy and laity with the cause of the nationalist rebel or the cause of the nationalist oppressor. Such a pollution of the Christian Name the Holy See has not infrequently been obliged to condemn, as we have seen above.

It is possible to deduce from the treatment of the Minority problem by the Church herself in Canon Law, Papal instructions, Concordats and other ecclesiastical measures, the principles upon which it can be solved in the sphere of civil society. Hence we quote below a number of historical examples of the Church's action chosen for the most part from the scholarly pages of Grentrup's *Nationale Minderheiten und Katholische Kirche*. It will be seen that the right of the minority to the use of its maternal language in religious practices and education is strenuously upheld and that the clergy are everywhere placed under a definite obligation to minister to the faithful, or to preach to the heathen, in the idiom which they best understand. Similarly the distinctive religious rite of a people, where it exists, is carefully preserved. Over against this must be set the prohibition, oft repeated, against the clergy's meddling in political controversies relating to race and language. Thirdly, the just ordering of the relation between the Minority and the State, in respect of the rights of the former, is a subject pertaining to the international or rather supernational authority. This is shown by the very fact of Papal intervention on this subject, such as Benedict XV's letter to the Canadian Hierarchy and the proscriptions of the Canon Law relating to the establishment or subdivision of parishes to provide for groups of different nationality which, as well as the appointment of a Vicar General to care for a distinctive national minority within a diocese, is reserved to the competence of the Holy See.

The recognition and preservation of the national language and customs of the minority : the reminder of different and higher loyalties which place a limit upon the claims of nationality : the intervention of the central supernational authority both to guarantee protection of the minorities' rights and to prevent excessive claims on their part—these are the main principles which, translated from the spiritual to the temporal plane, indicate for us the place of the national minority in the Law of Nations.

The antiquity and ubiquity of the minority problem, as illustrated by the few extracts which we give from ecclesiastical history—and the instances quoted could be multiplied almost indefinitely from local Councils and synods and the Acts of the Congregation of Propaganda—suggest another important point of conflict between the true doctrine of the Law of Nations and the modern conception of the State. The modern conception to which we have frequently alluded, makes the 'unitary state' the type to which national and international law is required to conform : the linguistic minority is a regrettable exception. It is arguable that—vigorously as Catholic tradition upholds the duty of obedience to the duly constituted civil authority—the most natural form of the State or Empire is for it to consist of nothing *but* minorities. The principle enunciated by Pius XI in relation to social and industrial organization,[1] if applied in the political sphere, would exclude usurpation by the State of the functions of any *smaller* groups or associations within its borders which are apt to minister to the varied needs—professional, occupational or cultural—of human beings. On the same principle the corporate life of each city, county or canton, as embodied in its own institutions, would be encouraged and respected instead of being fused into a single mould. In such a State, peculiarities of language and national custom might—as in the Swiss Federation or to some extent in Great Britain at the present time—continue to exist in each several part. The way in which the Catholic Church reconciles the most real and effective forms of obedience to a central authority with the

[1] Encyclical *Quadragesimo Anno.*

individuality of the diocese shows that this ideal is not impossible of attainment.

In a federal constitution, or one which admits of a considerable measure of local autonomy in each city, canton, county or province of the State, it is evident, from what we have established above, that the civic organization and administration of each of these units should be in the hands of the elected or recognized leaders of the native population of that unit, unless there be any cogent reason to the contrary. In the public life of each that language would be used which most exactly expressed the meaning of the citizens. For, since according to the social teaching of Christianity the family is the constituent element of every village, town or larger form of civil society, and is itself the basis of any educational system, it follows that the arguments put forward in the last chapter for the free use of the maternal language in the home, are hardly less applicable to the use of that language in the corporate life of the civic groups to which the family belongs. The same is true of the free use of all native or traditional customs, public and private, so they be not contrary to morals and good order. The representation of these divers bodies in the legislative councils of the State would naturally reflect that diversity: and it would be the task of the legislature to provide for the common good of the whole in such a way as to preserve the collective personality and satisfy, within the limits of possibility, the aspirations of each component part. Such a conception of the State is equally tenable whether the inhabitants of the several parts inherit the same or different national traditions. Where two or more nationalities are present it is as necessary for those concerned in government, the administration of justice, the defence and police of the State, communications and commerce, to have a common language as it is for local communities to use their own maternal language. Such a common language was the Latin tongue throughout the whole period in which Western civilization came into being, and such the English in India. From which it appears that it is no hardship but rather an enrichment of the mind for boys and girls to learn two languages at least in the higher grades of schools and colleges, one their native or domestic language, the other that of another national group within the State or its official administrative language.[1]

The passage of time, the compenetration of peoples, the swiftness of communications ; the weakness of one national tradition by comparison with another : the greater richness of one language by comparison with a more primitive tongue : the attraction or assimilative power of this or that national culture—any or all of these circumstances may gradually cause one language to supersede the other in the home as well as the market place or the law-court. If this comes about, as has often been the case, as the result of a series of voluntary acts, that is in accordance with the desires or inclinations of the families concerned, there can be no objection raised to it on grounds either of reason or Christianity. Our main thesis still holds. For the native language and the native culture of the new generation has in fact become by degrees something different from that of their grandparents or great-grandparents. Yet this culture and these modes of expression constitute a 'nationality' no less real than the older one or than each of several older ones from which they are derived. 'American nationality' is as real, as closely related to the enjoyment of national rights as the British, Irish, German, Italian or Polish nationality of the forefathers of those who are now American citizens. But if there is on the one hand a deliberate endeavour by one national group to boycott the common language of the State or that of their fellow-citizens of another nationality ; or on the other a deliberate endeavour to suppress a native language and its tradition from generation to generation, by force or fraud (as is only too frequent), then a grave injustice is done to human beings. In the former case they are placed in a position in which they cannot fulfil their civic duties and responsibilities : in the latter they are placed in a position in which, as has been shown in

[1] Welsh and English in Wales ; Flemish and French in Belgium ; Maltese and English in Malta ; French, German and Italian in Switzerland ; German and French in Alsace-Lorraine ; or (if a more venerable example be sought) Latin and Aramaic in the Palestine of Our Lord's day.

the previous chapter, they cannot—or can only with great difficulty—exercise their natural rights.

In certain parts of the world nationalities, each tenacious of its own culture and characteristics, are so intermingled that it is impossible for a single canton, or even a single parish to be homogeneous in nationality. Even in such cases[1] the Church accepts the fact and goes to great pains to provide religious guidance and the administration of the sacraments in the several languages of the inhabitants. In this she is not bound by the logical conclusion which St. Thomas borrowed from Aristotle to the effect that the city or State should consist of people of the same race. Here pastoral necessity pointed in a different direction from the logic of the schools, for the journeyings and admixture of human families reck little of abstract theories. The Church's practice was codified in the Ninth Canon of the Lateran Council of 1215 and has remained substantially the same ever since. Every measure, consistent with the essential unity of the diocese, is allowed or enjoined which will enable the priests to minister to the faithful in their own tongue.

To translate this principle from the spiritual to the temporal sphere we would say that the rights which we have discovered for the national minority are not dependent, at least in the domestic sphere, upon the segregation of that minority in a given area or its organization in a homogeneous group. When two or more races are closely intermingled within the municipal community it is evident that each cannot enjoy civic autonomy: loyalty to a common authority and joint participation in civic life, its burdens and its benefits, are required. But the public authority has no right to infringe the sacred traditions of family life. The customs and language of the home, as of the pulpit and the confessional are outside its competence and, in so far as is possible, the preservation of the hereditary culture by means of education and social institutions should be encouraged.

Such then are the rights of national minorities which positive human law should respect and harmonize with the

[1] e.g. the parishes of French Flanders. The provision of confessors speaking different languages in all the great seaports and capital cities.

duty of all citizens of the State. Is it for the State or for the international authority to safeguard those rights? Christian tradition proposes no definite answer. In so far as those rights are common to the totality of mankind, whereas the State is properly concerned with the distinctive needs of a part only, it would seem appropriate that the international or, as Taparelli would call it, the ethnarchic authority, should make their protection its concern, their infringement a ground of collective intervention. But on the other hand the State has evidently a providential mission to fulfil: its end is to provide for the well-being of all its citizens, and to relieve it of the duty of caring for the true interests of this or that group among them would be to condemn it to perpetual imperfection as a means of attaining that end. Here we may apply the principle invoked by Leo XIII when he writes of the unwarranted interference of the State in municipal life, and by Pius XI when he speaks of the error of allowing the State to perform functions which can be satisfactorily discharged by lesser social groups. It is better for each State to provide for the cultural needs of its own minorities and to protect them against one another or the majority than for the greater, international society to seek to do so. What then is the duty of the international authority in this regard? Following Taparelli and the statement upon Nationality of the Catholic Union of International Studies, we would say that it is threefold:

(*a*) to establish by declaration or Convention the fundamental rights of man, including those of minorities, and to secure their incorporation in the legislation of each State;

(*b*) to satisfy itself, when the frontiers of any State are extended or a new State is formed, that any nation or part of a nation which thus finds itself subject to new rulers shall not, on that account, suffer any loss of the rights to which nationality gives rise;

(*c*) to intervene as an exceptional measure to prevent or arrest any grave violation of human and national rights and, in particular, of the positive laws which safeguard them.

Documents

12TH ŒCUMENICAL COUNCIL OF THE LATERAN, A.D. 1215, *Canon IX. Respect of National Minorities in Ecclesiastical administration :*

Whereas in many parts of the world peoples of different languages are mingled together within the same city or diocese, having one faith but a variety of rites and customs, we strictly command that the bishops of such cities or dioceses shall provide suitable men, who shall celebrate the Divine Office and minister the sacraments of the Church to them according to their diversities of rites and speech, instructing them both by word and example. But we entirely forbid one and the same city or diocese to have more than one bishop, as a body with several heads, like a monster. If, however, it is urgently necessary owing to the causes mentioned above, the bishop of the place may appoint, after careful deliberation, a Catholic director suitable to those nations as his vicar in regard to the matters aforesaid, but he must be obedient and subject to the bishop in all respects. Wherefore if anyone should act otherwise let him know that he will suffer the penalty of excommunication and if, even so, he shall not renounce his course of action, let him be deprived of all ministry in the Church and, if need be, handed over to the secular arm for the suppression of such insolence.

This principle of harmonizing the unity of city or diocese with the variety of its national populations inspired the action of the Church in future centuries more than the conclusion of St. Thomas who, in imitation of Aristotle, writes as follows in his *Commentary on the Politics, Book III, Ch. II :*

It is for the political philosopher to determine whether the State ought to contain men of one race only or of several races. . . . The State ought rather to consist of a single race, for a single race is united in its customs and habits which make for friendship between the citizens by reason of their likeness one to another. Hence States which were made up of diverse races have been destroyed owing to the dissensions which they had with one another through the diversity of their customs, for one part of the State joined forces with foreign enemies owing to its hatred of the other part.

LEO XIII. *Encyclical Letter, Immortale Dei. November* 1, 1885. *Unwarrantable interference of the State in Municipal affairs :*

. . . This honourable liberty, alone worthy of human beings, the Church approves most highly and has never slackened her endeavour to preserve, strong and unchanged, among nations. And, in truth, whatever in the State is of chief avail for the common welfare; whatever has been usefully established to curb the license of rulers who are opposed to the true interests of the people, or to keep in check the leading authorities from unwarrantably interfering in municipal or family affairs—whatever tends to uphold the honour, manhood and equal rights of individual citizens—of all these things, as the monuments of past ages bear witness, the Catholic Church has always been the originator, the promoter or the guardian. Ever therefore consistent with herself, while on the one hand she rejects that exorbitant liberty which in individuals and in nations ends in license or in thraldom, on the other hand she willingly and most gladly welcomes whatever improvements the age brings forth, if these really secure the prosperity of life here below, which is, as it were, a stage in the journey to the life that will know no ending.

BENEDICT XV. *Letter to Cardinal Béguin, Archbishop of Quebec and the other Archbishops and Bishops of Canada. Acta Apost. Sed. Commentarium Officiale. Vol. X.* 1918:

In our Apostolic letter '*Commisso divinitus*' which we sent you on September 8, 1916, we earnestly exhorted the clergy and Catholic people of your country that they should lay aside all contentions and quarrels which have arisen either by reason of race or from diversity of languages. At the same time we urged that if controversies should thereafter occur from these causes they should be restricted as charity requires, as it becomes saints careful to serve the unity of the spirit in the bond of peace. . . .

Now the time has come to address our words to all our brethren, the Bishops of the Dominion of Canada, and to repeat to them from the depths of our soul the exhortation which we gave two years since: that they 'be of one heart and of one mind' and that there may be no division among them by reason either of racial origin or of speech. For one and the same spirit 'set them to rule the Church of God,' the Spirit of Unity and of Peace (1 Peter v: 3). Thus will it be right for you with greater authority and efficacity, Venerable Brethren, to order your priests (and we enjoin that this order be strictly given) both to observe spiritual concord amongst themselves and strive by word and example to have it so preserved by the faithful. To which end we desire again and again to recommend what in earlier Apostolic letters we have recommended, 'that all the priests should seek to acquire the habit of speaking competently each of the two languages, English and French, and casting all prejudice aside, should use now one now the other to meet the needs of the faithful.'

Instances of Ecclesiastical regulations :

Concordat between the HOLY SEE AND LITHUANIA, *September* 27, 1927.

ARTICLE 21

Ordinaries shall see to it that all the Faithful receive religious assistance in their mother tongue according to the rules of the Church.

Concordat between the HOLY SEE AND POLAND, *February* 10, 1925.

ARTICLE 23

No change in the language used in dioceses of the Latin Rite shall be made without special permission granted by the Conference of Bishops of the Latin Rite in the case of sermons, supplementary prayers and lectures, other than lectures on sacred sciences in seminaries.

HUNGARY :

Can. 149 *of the Synod of the Diocese of Stuhlweissenburg*, 1924 :

In the parishes which are not of Hungarian race the vernacular singing is to be in the language of the inhabitants.

GRENTRUP. *Nationale Minderheiten und Katholische Kirche. Extracts illustrating the Church's respect for national and linguistic minorities :*

Page 55. Confraternities were of the greatest importance in the history of the German Catholics in Italy. Wherever in the towns of the northern and central parts of Italy German Catholics settled down Confraternities were founded that were a shield for Religion and nationality. . . . In Rome the Confraternity of Our Lady flourished : in 1399 it received the first Papal Approbation and the very famous church 'Anima' with the Pilgrim's house was given to this Confraternity. Besides this, the Confraternity of Our Lady at the German Campo Santo was founded in Rome in 1450. The latter is still in existence. . . . In Poland also, the German Confraternities proved a blessing for the German Catholics. In Warsaw the Confraternity of St. Beno was founded in 1632 and built the church of the same name. German priests, amongst them no less a person than St. Clement Hofbauer, celebrated the divine services for their countrymen till 1808, in which year Napoleon I ordered the church to be closed. The most famous Confraternity is that of St. Anne in Posnau.

Page 66. The Synod of Culm (1583) decreed : 'Every parish priest in whose parish a language which he does not understand is spoken, should endeavour to get a priest of this language, under penalty of his being deprived of his office.' The Synod of Ernland (1497) makes it a duty that in those parishes in which Germans and Poles live together the sermons should be preached in German and in Polish. The Synod at Lemberg (1765) records the fact that the Jesuit Fathers had undertaken to preach German sermons in the Holy Ghost Church at Lemberg. The First Provincial Council of Lima (1582) issued a classical decree in this matter. In the 6th chapter of the Second Part it says: 'The decisive aim of Christian education of the Catechism is the understanding and grasping of Christian doctrine. The Faith in the heart leads to justification and the verbal profession to salvation. Therefore everyone should be so instructed that he may grasp the truth spiritually, the Spaniard in Spanish and the Indian in the Indian language. . . . No Indian should be compelled to learn the commandments or the Catechism in Latin, as it is sufficient or even better if he says them in his own language; or if someone wants to do so he can add the Spanish to it. It would be going too far to expect another language of the Indians.'

Page 67. Not less vigorous is the decree of the 3rd Mexican Provincial Council of 1585 which demands that the Bishops should examine the priests entrusted with the spiritual care of the natives, in order to satisfy themselves that they are well acquainted with the language of the natives. Should the Bishop find that this was not the case he should allow the priests a period of another six months for a new examination. If after that time the priests have not acquired the necessary knowledge of the language, they are to be deprived of their office.

Page 68. On August 15, 1912, Pope Pius X erected in the consistorial congregation a new section which was to see what could be done for the pastoral care of the emigrants. The decree of the same Pope, March 19, 1913, shows in what spirit they were to do their work, as the Pope suggested the foundation of a Roman college of Italian priests who were to be specially trained for the pastoral care of Italian emigrants. Benedict XV, having the same aim in view, issued in the year 1916 an apostolic letter to the American Bishops. He exhorts them to entrust the spiritual care of the Italians in their dioceses to priests speaking the Italian language and, if necessary, to such priests as are able to understand the provincial dialect of the Italians. In doing this he calls their attention to the college which was founded for this purpose.

The Language question in Alsace-Lorraine:

THE BISHOP OF METZ *to the Recteur de l'Académie, who is President of Public Education in Alsace-Lorraine:*

METZ,
January 23, 1926.

MONSIEUR LE RECTEUR,

According to the information received by me from the different districts of the diocese where the German language is spoken, the population is very much embittered—and this is one of the chief and most general reasons of the present feeling of discontent—that in the curriculum such little room is allocated to the German language. The time given to the German language is so limited that the scholars are not able to learn how to write German correctly and yet it is the only language which their parents understand. Also, as far as I understand, the control of this subject by the inspectors leaves much to be desired. Hence the children are quite unable to understand the text of the Catechism. On the other hand, as the children when first admitted to school do not understand French and in most cases do not gain sufficient knowledge of the (French) language even after several years of attendance at school, Religion cannot be taught beneficially in this language to the children. I therefore ask you to consider the possibility of granting more time in the curriculum to the German language, and to see that the children are taught the fundamental rules of this language from when they are first admitted to school. The proper control must secure the observance of these Rules, both those that obtain at present and those that will be added in the future. It will also be necessary that these rules should have a certain sanction through an examination. If you in this way comply with the wishes of the population speaking the German language, I am convinced that the consequences would be very favourable and would help to calm the minds of the people. I need not mention that this petition is in no way aiming at hampering the spreading of the French language which is making rapid progress. The only aim of this petition is to draw your attention to a situation which has developed out of the fact that all the adults of the German-speaking territory have not been able to acquire the least knowledge of the French language under the German rule.

GRENTRUP. *Die Kirchliche Rechtslage der Deutschen Minderheiten Katholischer Konfessions in Europa. Church and native language. Pastoral of Bishop of Metz, November* 5, 1920 :

We trust, therefore, that the present difficulties will easily be overcome thanks to the facility given to children to read the text of the German Catechism as soon as they have learnt the French alphabet, and thanks also to the devoted co-operation of the teaching faculty. The essential point is that the school remain confessional and religious and that religious instruction be given from the beginning in the mother tongue as is required by the legislation in force.

Speech of the BISHOP OF STRASBOURG, 1926 :

If legislation compels Catholics to transgress the commands of the Most High, whether imposed by Strasbourg, Paris or Berlin, such legislation will have no sanction in the conscience of the Faithful. So long as there is a single Catholic in Alsace he will not cease to demand its abrogation, and he will even violate it if he cannot observe it without offending God.

To deny truths admitted by all Catholics throughout the world and taught in the Catechism to small children themselves, would be to make of Alsace a sort of super-God, the supreme Arbiter of right and wrong. '*Elsass über alles!*' Similarly, for us to be able to forget possibly for a long time our duty to defend the rights of the Most High, it would be necessary to imagine that our obligations towards Alsace superseded those rights. '*Elsass über alles!*' Further, if we think we have the right to prefer in the elections an avowed enemy of the Church and its Divine Founder to a champion of religion, we shall make people believe that for us the cause of Alsace transcends God's cause. '*Elsass über alles!*'

Ah, indeed, we Alsatian Catholics, and your Bishop as much as anyone, each and all love our little country passionately and enthusiastically. We love not only its soil but its soul, not only its beauty but its rights. Not only its past but even more its happiness of to-day and to-morrow. We love everything to which our people are so warmly attached. Everything which can keep them sane and make them prosperous, which can so ensure for them greater virtue and felicity. We love Alsace as a mother from whom each one of us derives the greater part of his genius, his upbringing and his best qualities. But it is precisely because we look upon her as a mother that we do not consider her as a God. We have too great a respect for her to make of her an idol, that is a rational being whom to-day we may adore but whom to-morrow others will try to dethrone in order to make of her a slave. For us there is but one God. '*Gott allein über alles!*'

Declaration of the Clergy of the German section of the diocese of Trent to the State Board of Education in Trent on September 30, 1926 :

To the State Prefect, Trent.

On August 31 the State School Inspector Giovanzzi, on being asked about the intentions of the State Prefect of Trent with regard to this matter, has issued an order that in the next school year at the changing of the 4th form in the elementary schools, even religious instruction must be given entirely in the Italian language.

To their great regret the undersigned find themselves compelled to point out that the above-mentioned order is in opposition to the point of view of the Church, according to which she claims for herself the right to give the children, in the elementary schools, religious instruction in their mother tongue. Apart from the explanations of the Holy See on this matter, this point of view of the Church has been laid down for the Diocese of Trent in special instructions by the Very Rev. Prince Bishop Collestin Endrice on April 5, 1912 (*Raccolata di intruzioni e constituzioni diocesane*, Trento, 1913). In this instruction the Very Rev. Prince Bishop says : 'The mother tongue is the indispensable means of making the pupils understand the great truths of the Catechism which are in themselves very difficult and not easy to understand. In order to speak to the hearts of the children and to be able to educate them in virtue, those on whom the care of the religious and moral future of the coming generations is incumbent, cannot remain indifferent to this attempt of denationalization, which brings with it a moral impossibility of bringing up children in a Christian manner, particularly when it is a question of the first instructions given in the elementary schools. The difficult and responsible task of education has been entrusted to the Church by Christ. Therefore the liberty and the means which are necessary for the fulfilment of this task must be placed at their disposal.'

Accepting, therefore, this authoritative point of view, which the Catholic Church alone holds, the undersigned find themselves obliged, in face of the above-mentioned order of the school authorities, respectfully to make the following statement to the State Prefect :

'The undersigned consider it as a sacred duty of conscience to the rights of the Church, to give religious instruction in the schools in the mother language—and to hold fast to this duty by every lawful means at their command—they can therefore never consent to give religious instruction in the schools to the children in any other language but the mother tongue.

Power having been given to them in the *Missio Canonica* by the Bishops—they will continue further in all classes of the elementary schools to give religious instruction in the mother tongue.'

Accepting this explanation the undersigned spiritual directors of that German province in which religious instruction has already in past years had to be given partly or fully in the Italian language, protest against continuing to do so again, and in this they have the full support and agreement of all the undersigned clergy.

The undersigned do not forget that the right which they are claiming for the children of German parents must be given in the same measure to Italian parents, in so far that they will always be ready to give them this religious instruction in their mother tongue.

(Here follow two hundred and twenty-seven signatures of priests acting as spiritual directors in the German section of the Diocese of Trent).

Grentrup's conclusions are as follows in *Nationale Minderheiten und Katholische Kirche*) :

1. Wherever a special Rite has developed from national peculiarities in ecclesiastical matters, the Apostolic See has positively recognized these Rites in the Oriental Church for more than 1000 years and has, when necessary, defended the Rite against attacks.

2. The Papacy has always promoted nationality in its connection with the Rite.

3. The Church remained the faithful defender of the national Rite whenever the followers of this Rite had to struggle for their national peculiarities, as a national minority amongst a majority different in their national peculiarities.

4. In modern times, autonomy of diocesan administration was granted to the individual Rites in those territories where several languages are spoken, although for practical reasons this rule was not always put into operation with strict consistency.

5. The diocesan autonomy is not as a rule extended to national minorities in polyglot territories that have no special Rite.

6. In a diocese national minorities, whether they have a special Rite or not, may for good reasons have their own Vicar General who in the administration of his office is dependent on the Bishop of his diocese.

DELOS. *The Place of the National Minorities in the State* :[1]

. . . We are, in fact, shaped and modelled sometimes even in the innermost recesses of our being, by an ethnic and social heredity, and thus the national genesis of our ethnic group has been formed. Does not this group contain resources, even treasures, which no other possesses, at least in the same degree? Customs, sentiments and institutions in harmony with it form the elements of a culture which gives to each of those who have it the natural setting suitable to the development of his personality. We have customs the atmosphere created by which, of itself, puts us at our ease ; traditions which, of themselves, make us feel happy ; political institutions which, of themselves, ensure our physical and moral balance.

If it is admitted that, as Christianity teaches, the law of

[1] From a lecture given at the *Semaine Catholique Internationale*, Geneva, September 16, 1931.

Providence which rules human life makes it the duty of man to make the best use of the resources with which he has been endowed ; if it is recognized that, to succeed in this, it is good for him to develop in his proper cultural surroundings, who has the right to stunt this development and deprive it of the help of institutions which ensure for it the benefit of their culture ? This is the foundation of cultural freedom.

But is this freedom compatible with the rights of the State ?

There is a conception of cultural freedom which risks destroying the unity of the State and there is a theory of the State which, in the end, crushes cultural freedom and oppresses national minorities.

Modern public law is not free from either of these errors. It has been influenced by ideas and forces which have led it at once towards State absolutism and towards the realization of the misleading ideal of the national State. The Jacobin State, the child of rationalism of the eighteenth century, of the doctrine of the 'Social Contract' and of the dogma of absolute sovereignty ; the State deified by Hegelian or Neo-Hegelian philosophy, which has influenced so strongly the public law of the nineteenth and twentieth centuries ; in a word, the national State, are not these the ideals which have often inspired modern public law ?

The fruit of these doctrines, for the State, could only be a policy open or concealed, of forcible assimilation of cultural minorities and, for the latter irredentism carried to the point of revolt or of an absurd subdivision of territory.

Therefore we reject both forced assimilation as a violation of right, and anarchical subdivision as destructive of order, of the necessities of political life and of peace itself.

The State is neither absolute freedom nor an independent will which only seeks its own ends : it is at the service of the human person. It is the guardian and the prop of all the spiritual and material values which play a useful part in man's development. Cultural nationality, which joins to the resources of the natural genius the wealth of traditions, customs and institutions bequeathed by race and history, is a precious inheritance of the subjects of the State, which therefore owes help and protection to the institutions which preserve that inheritance.

The idea of opposition between the State and the cultural minorities within it then disappears. The principle which puts them in harmony is the object common to the institutions of both—the service of the human individual. Between the State and its minorities there is a distinction of function but no opposition of sovereign right. They are not rivals but fellow-workers doing different work. The reform needed is to restore the State to its true function and to wean the cultural group from political irredentism and devote it to its cultural task.

CHAPTER XV

THE RIGHTS OF BACKWARD RACES

NO treatise of international ethics would be complete without a study of the international problem which, if not the most important, is at least the most constant throughout the history of the modern world—that of the relations between peoples of unequal degrees of civilization. For the Church this problem is of the greatest moment since Christianity is primarily a missionary religion. The Divine Command to go and teach all nations has ever urged and will ever urge the preachers of the Gospel to penetrate the tribes and nations—still the majority of mankind—who are not yet Christians, and in so doing to push far beyond the bounds of what at any given time is regarded as the civilized and organized world. Thus the Christian philosophy of the collective rights and duties of peoples in relation to one another and to the society of mankind as a whole must be such as will apply to an almost infinite variety of political and social organization, education and culture from the most primitive to the most advanced.

The word primitive, so loosely used to describe 'barbarians' 'savages' and indeed 'natives' of any race not of European stock, has certain moral implications which require elucidation. In so far as the word denotes the simplest form of social organization, the simplest material standard of living, the absence of science, literature, art and mechanical devices, it is evidently true that a human group having such characteristics corresponds or is to be likened to the inhabitants of the States which are now civilized at an earlier stage of their historical development. In this sense a civilized state in regard to a primitive tribe, is in the relation of a *later* to an *earlier* form of society, from which it is natural to evolve the relation which exists or should exist between the human being in a condition of maturity to one in the stage of infancy. This conception recurs frequently in the documents which we reproduce in this chapter and in none is it more clearly developed than in the *Relectio de Indis* of Vittoria. This author admits that the primitive aborigines of Central America may be likened to children, but only to teach the duty of tutelage and guidance on the part of the full-grown and experienced man toward the child, a duty which can give no title to override the right to *dominium* which a minor may truly possess. This notion is also the basis of the theory upon which the Mandate System was framed.

It may also be conceded that civilization, whether of the European type with which we are familiar or of the ancient Oriental types, confers upon individuals and families many material advantages and may confer moral advantages which the simplest or most primitive society does not itself possess. That is to say that highly-developed nations are related to primitive as *better* is to *worse*. There is probably no proposition in the sphere of which we now treat, which appears more axiomatic to the modern than this. Yet it is often a cloak for lies. To the Christian sociologist that civilization only is morally better than barbarism which is informed by Christianity, the spiritual force from which in fact European civilization took its origin and without which it loses its substance. Sin as it may in its treatment of its weaker brethren, a Christian people cannot long be unaware of the moral law by which all human acts are judged; of the divine precepts by which its conscience is bound: 'Do unto others as ye would they should do unto you'; of the compelling ideal[1] 'One Lord, One faith, One baptism, One God and Father of all, who is above all, and through all, and in us all.'

Christian civilization is a vehicle of spiritual betterment, even when it is a lumbering vehicle. But, so great are the moral and social evils attendant upon the material and mechanical developments of modern civilization, that it is more than doubtful whether the introduction of that civilization, when divorced from Christian principles and the rule of

[1] Ephesians iv: 5, 6.

natural justice which is included in the Christian tradition, confers any benefit whatever upon a 'primitive' race.

The history of the last four centuries is filled with shameful tragedy in this respect. How many millions of native peoples in Africa and in America have suffered unspeakable miseries and ultimate annihilation through the rapacity of colonial conquerors, Catholic and Protestant alike, who have only used the added powers and greater skill which civilization has given them as occasions of greater sin? The moral putrefaction which results from the indiscriminate introduction of the external habits of western 'civilization' into the urban centres of Africa, the Middle East and the Far East is the commonplace of every experienced missionary. Or is the Russian child better for compulsory education in the State school whereby he is taught to hate the name of God? May not his moral condition be a hundred times worse than that of the child who knows no school nor letters, but is left in the bosom of an illiterate family? Civilization in short is to the Catholic mind a blessing or a curse in so far as it is or is not truly Christian and consciously attuned to the laws of God. It is only of the true Christian civilization that Leo XIII is thinking in a magnificent passage of his Encyclical *Immortale Dei* wherein he speaks of the noble record of Christian Europe in spreading civilization among barbarous nations.

In these two senses then, and with these reservations, we may speak of primitive peoples as suffering from an inferiority in respect of highly developed peoples. But to conclude that such inferiority implies a lasting subjection to the latter is a *non sequitur*, as we shall presently show. Rather is it a condition of which the Christian philosopher cannot think without assuming that there exists a duty on the part of the more fortunate nations to help in putting an end to it, by their guidance, their support of the missionary Church and, if circumstances require it, their political tutelage.

But there is another sense in which the term primitive is applied to the uncivilized which is wholly misleading. It is the sense imparted by the theory of evolution, which in its least scientific and indeed least rational form seems to obsess the Western mind when it lacks the direction of the Christian tradition. According to this notion the human species has evolved from the ape ; and the Pygmy, the South American Indian, the Australian Aborigine or the South Sea Islander is more closely akin to the origin of human nature than is the more civilized human being. He is simply in an early stage of evolution. Mr. Wells' *Outline of History* has popularized this quite arbitrary theory, and children's school books and readers, at least in English-speaking countries, are full of it. The odious corollary, that there is therefore something *natural* in the perverted sexual rites, the idolatry, the slavery, the corruption of marriage and the family, and even the cannibalism that is found among certain of these tribes seems to have escaped the notice of those who accept this sophism. It is at least equally tenable, and to the Catholic, who believes the doctrine of the Fall and accepts the teaching of Christian philosophy upon the nature of men, far more probable that the present condition of such tribes represents a *degradation* from a former state which was better, purer, more 'natural,' and that it is the consequence of many centuries of moral deordination.[1] Certain it is that the spirit of the Catholic Church in dealing with barbarian or savage tribes is that expressed in the phrase which so constantly recurs in the Canons relating to the emancipation of slaves '*revocare ad pristinam libertatem*.' It is not her function to create in them a human nature which does not yet exist, but to free man 'made in the image of God' from the bondage of sin. There is a sense in which the apparently primitive race is rather the ultimate race : it is an awful example of what might well be and have been the last stage of any people had the One true God never revealed His law on Sinai nor the Son of God been born at Bethlehem.

The relations between advanced or civilized, and backward or barbarian peoples differ somewhat from the relations already established in these pages by the Christian tradition of international ethics as existing between all members of the society of nations. The rights of self-conservation and natural development and the corresponding duty to respect those rights in others ; the obligation to keep faith ; the

[1] This theory is developed by G. K. Chesterton in *The Everlasting Man.*

duties arising from the natural sociability of men and nations and their mutual interdependence ; the conditions of just war ; the duty of maintaining peace—all these principles or rules of conduct, derived from the Natural Law and enshrined in the Law of Nations, are of universal application. They clearly apply to the mutual dealings of any two or more political societies, whatever their stage of development. But there is also a certain obligation of social charity incumbent upon the civilized, organized, highly developed State to aid to a higher and a better life the simpler and weaker people, especially if it be in a low condition of private and public morals and deprived of the light of the Gospel. The object of that assistance in the political order should be to enable the weaker people to hold its own in the economy of the world and to bring out of potentiality into actuality the participation of that people in the common benefits and the common duties of the society of nations. This obligation is intensified by the supernatural law of Christian charity, whereby we are bound not only to love all men as brothers but to seek to unite or reunite them with ourselves in the Mystical Body of Christ.

They will look in vain therefore who seek to find in the Canons of the Church, and the abundant teaching of the Holy See or of Catholic theologians upon the Colonial Question, a science of conduct based purely upon the requirements of natural law, though in this, more clearly perhaps than in any other sphere of international relations, the Church claims to be the exponent and defender of that law. The first and greatest preoccupation of the Holy See in facing the problems raised by the impact of civilized upon uncivilized races, is to determine whether the acts of the former are such as to conduce to the conversion of the latter to Christianity, and to accord with the obligations of justice and charity which bind the consciences of Christian princes and peoples.

Such being the Church's principle, it was inevitable that her action in this regard should be largely occupied throughout the Christian age in a slow but steady ' war of attrition ' against the opposing principle inherited from the Roman world in which the Chuch's life began, namely that the barbarian is ordained for servitude. Slavery was one of the social institutions of that world which the Church at first tacitly accepted, teaching slaves to be obedient to their masters and masters merciful to their slaves, since the distinction between bond and free, Roman and barbarian, Jew and Gentile, was as nothing to the equality of all souls before God and the union of all the faithful with Christ and through Him with one another. Yet it was not long before the incongruity of servitude with its manifest abuses and the 'liberty wherewith Christ hath made us free' became apparent to the mind of the Church.[1] The more the Christian ideal of marriage and of the family developed, the more the social condition of slaves appeared to be inconsistent with it. The more the social structure of the Empire began to crumble, the more evidently appeared the evils of the system of slavery which was its foundation. The more Christianity became the religion of the barbarians, the more untenable became the racial superiority of the Roman. Thus the decrees of Popes and Councils against the maltreating of slaves; the encouragement of manumission both by precept and example; the prohibitions against the enslavement and the sale of human beings and the insistence upon the duty of ransoming captives multiply between the fourth and eleventh centuries until it can be asserted as broadly true that Christianity had killed slavery as an institution in Europe.[2] For the serfdom of feudal society, onerous as its conditions often were, did not altogether extinguish human liberty and

[1] A writer of a later age has expressed this thought with a beauty and directness of speech which defies translation. *L'Arbre des Batailles* (*3ème partie*, Chap. XLV, H. Bonet). According to the ancient laws a prisoner, it is said, can become the serf of his captor.

'*Et je respons vraiment que non, car celles lois ne furent jamais prinses entre les chrestiens en commun usaige, et si est très grant inhumanité et très laide de vendre son frère chrestien comme une beste lequel est mis hors de servitude par le très précieux sang de notre benoist sauveur Jhesucrist.*'

[2] Yet we could not with historic accuracy point to any date upon which there was a complete absence of slavery in Christian Europe. Here and there the *servi ecclesiæ* were the last to disappear, doubtless because their lot was often an easy one and they had no desire to alter it.

the right of property; and Christian influences were constantly at work in mediæval Europe to defend the dignity of the human person and to prepare political enfranchisement.

The form of servitude against which the Church's efforts were mainly directed in the Middle Ages was that of Christians captured and enslaved by the enemies of Christendom: the rescue and ransoming of these unhappy captives was a work of mercy to which the faithful were ceaselessly conjured by the Papacy and to which religious confraternities and orders, especially formed to that end, devoted an heroic effort of self-sacrifice.[1]

The type of slavery against which, since the beginning of the Colonial age, the true mind of the Church voiced by the Popes has revolted, in opposition to the greed, cruelty and mental confusion of Christian conquerors and colonists, is one which constitutes an international problem in the true sense: it is the enslavement of the uncivilized natives—of America, of Africa, of the East Indies—by the Europeans. It is to this evil that the bulk of our documents refer, and it is in the struggle with it that the full Catholic doctrine is evolved, whereby, as in the pronouncements of Gregory XVI and Leo XIII, not the accidental cruelties of the institution of slavery alone, but the institution itself is condemned root and branch. Any Christian who enslaves a fellow man or takes any part in the slave trade or defends any such practice is now *ipso facto* excommunicate.

We find the Holy See demanding and supporting joint action by the European Powers to suppress slavery and the slave trade and insisting with the League of Nations as at the Congress of Berlin, that the importance of Missionary activity as a means of achieving that end should be fully recognized. The heroic figure of Lavigerie revives the memory of Las Casas or Vieira, or St. Peter Claver; and the Catholic priest stands out in his true function as protector of the defenceless native against the unjust oppression and armed violence of the powerful races, European or Moslem. In most recent times the movement for the abolition of

[1] See Leo XIII's letter to the Brazilian Episcopate *In plurimis* of May 8, 1888.

Forced Labour in colonial territories—which is often slavery in disguise and not less destructive of conjugal and communal life as it is the cause of numberless deaths—has behind it the full force of the Catholic Social organizations of Europe. But the end of this curse is not yet.

It may be objected that a study of slavery as a whole is not pertinent to the science of international ethics. True, the institution of slavery directly concerns that subject in so far as one nation or tribe is enslaved by another, as the Helot by the Greek, the Briton by the Roman, the Hebrew by the Egyptian, the American Indian by the Spaniard, the Negro by the Englishman, the Arab or the Abyssinian. In so far as the world can only be rid of slavery by international co-operation—as the experience of the past century seems to prove beyond question—it is also a proper subject of our study. In the latter sense the International Slavery Convention may be described as authorizing a form of intervention by the society of nations as a whole, or by members of it on behalf of the society, in order to defend the natural rights of human beings which the rulers of particular parts of the world are themselves either unwilling or incompetent to defend.

But there are and have been many forms of slavery without distinction of race between master and slave : such is the domestic slavery, the debt slavery, the pawning of children and similar practices existing in parts of Africa at the present time. Such was the slavery existing in many parts of the Roman world in the early days of the Church. What has this to do with the international problem ? It has, in fact, an important connection. For had no theoretic justification of servitude been available for European adventurers to use or abuse to their own advantage, it is difficult to believe that so large a number of the weaker races should have been brought under their domination. Therefore it is necessary to ascertain the theories which were accepted as explanations of the institution of slavery in itself, in order to understand the grounds upon which the explorers of the colonial age sought to justify to their uneasy consciences the reduction of primitive races to servitude.

Three causes were found to account for the existence of

slavery. The first that it had come because of sin ; the second that certain races were born to servitude ; the third, that it was the right of the conqueror—presuming him to be waging a just war—to enslave his prisoners.

1. Slavery was a consequence of original sin and of the wickedness of former generations, in retribution for which the Divine Vengeance had allowed large classes or groups of men to be in bondage to others, and this had been recognized by the *jus gentium* in the sense of the customary law common to most peoples. Thus Gregory the Great in emancipating two Roman slaves wrote : 'Men whom nature in the beginning created and brought forth free but whom the law of nations subjected to the yoke of slavery.' St. Augustine, discussing the matter more amply in his *City of God* (Book XIX, Ch. 14, 15 and 16) says :

> Thus wills the order of nature ; thus has man been created by God. He has given him to rule over the fishes of the sea, the birds of the air and the reptiles that crawl on the face of the earth. He has ordained that rational creatures, made according to his own image, shall rule only over creatures devoid of reason. He has not established the dominion of man over man but that of man over brute.

And a little later :

> The primitive just men were rather established as shepherds over their flocks, than as kings over other men, whereby God gives us to understand what was called for by the order of creation and what was required by the punishment of sin ; for the condition of slavery has with reason been imposed on the sinner. Thus we do not find the word slave in Holy Writ before the day when the righteous Noah gave it as a punishment to his guilty son ; wherefore it follows that this word came from sin and not from nature.

St. Thomas Aquinas, following St. Augustine in this, as in his doctrine of war, also teaches that servitude is a scourge inflicted upon mankind as a result of the Fall (*Summa Theol.*, Prima Secundæ, Q. iii, art. 94–5).

This theory is indeed but a particular application of the general proposition that all pain, hardship and sorrow come because of sin and that God, in his hidden wisdom, allows some men to be the instruments whereby they are inflicted upon others. But it leaves unexplained why servitude should be the lot of one man and not of another, of one race and not of another. Yet is not this true also of riches and poverty, and indeed of all the inequalities of human society? To minds undisturbed by the modern egalitarian complex and accustomed to attribute the gradations of mankind, the joys and afflictions of nations and all the contrasts of human existence in an unquestioning manner to the operation of the Divine Will, slavery like war, was more an accepted fact to be fitted into the philosophy of life than an evil to be eradicated.

Yet the acute mind of a St. Augustine or a St. Thomas was quick to discover that there could be no essential difference between human beings; and that the divine origin and destiny of each human soul, for whom Christ died, and the phenomenon of free will were wholly inconsistent with the conception of a race permanently divided into free men and chattels. Freedom was natural to man, servitude unnatural and therefore evil: but servitude existed everywhere; therefore it was a punishment for sin. It will be observed that the case for conquering the Indians and reducing them to slavery which the colonists and their theologians put forward and which Vittoria and Las Casas had to meet, was that the natives merited this treatment because of formal sin—idolatry: offences against the natural law; refusal to accept the Gospel. Alternatively it was urged that because of such sins the pagans could not have true ownership of land and property, nor their chiefs true authority and jurisdiction. It is not too much to say that this interested and cynical application or rather misapplication of certain tenable propositions has been the philosophical basis of modern colonization. For if the Catholic discoverers and exploiters of the lands that came to form the vast colonial empires of Spain and Portugal were pursued by a guilty conscience in the form of the missionary priest and the clear-witted theologian, soon to be reinforced by Papal authority, who condemned their enslaving and slaughtering of the natives as crimes 'crying to heaven for vengeance' which 'was fast sending them to hell,'[1] no such scruples seem for two centuries at least to have disturbed

[1] Las Casas in a speech to the Royal Council of Charles V.

the Protestant adventurer. Indeed the preference of the adherents of the Reformed Religion for the Old Testament seems to have tempted them to turn to good account a fantastic theory, vaguely current in earlier centuries and revived in the seventeenth century, which proved that the negro race was descended from Cham[1] and that it was in consequence condemned to the curse of perpetual slavery. This pernicious notion soiled the pages of several Catholic writers—though never the utterances of the Holy See—as well as Protestant writers in later years ; but we have been able to find no reference to it in the great disputations of Las Casas with Antonio de Fonsecas or Sepulveda or in the lectures of Vittoria, which bear witness to the profound controversy which divided the schools and councils of sixteenth century Spain upon the right or wrong of reducing the barbarians to slavery.

2. A section of the *Relectio de Indis*, however, indicates another error, which had doubtless received much currency through the veneration of the Schoolmen for 'the Philosopher,' namely that certain men were 'born to be slaves' (*servi a natura*). This pagan tradition the low intelligence of the savage seemed to confirm. It marched only too easily with the doctrine that slavery was the consequence of sin. Vittoria is at some pains to provide a christianized interpretation—not very convincing—of this passage of the *Politics*[2] of Aristotle :

> It is clear that he does not mean that such persons (those of strong intelligence) can arrogate to themselves a sway over others in virtue of their superior wisdom, but that nature has given them a capacity for government. Accordingly, he adds, even if we admit that the aborigines in question are as inept and stupid as is alleged, still dominion cannot be denied them, nor are they to be classed with the slaves of the civil law.

[1] The son of Noe, and father of Chanaan, upon whom Noe laid a curse : 'Cursed be Chanaan ; a servant of servants shall he be unto his brethren' (Genesis ix : 25).

[2] This is not the place to examine the baneful doctrines of Aristotle's *Politics* upon the subjection of the individual man to the State. The student, however, may be directed to such passages as occur in I. VII, c. 16, where interference in the birth of children, the murder of weaklings and abortion to prevent the birth of infants, judged by the State to be excessive, are

That this was not so clear to their contemporaries is shown from the decree of Ferdinand's Privy Council in 1513 which, in instituting the iniquitous system of Repartiementos, claimed that the servitude of the Indians was warranted by the laws of God and man.[1]

3. The third and even more widely accepted cause of slavery, which we have already illustrated in these pages, was the supposed right to enslave men taken captive in war. An adroit and uncharitable application of the traditional doctrine of the conditions of just war was sufficient to provide the consciences of the colonial adventurers with a pretext for annexing vast areas of Africa and the Americas, and regarding the whole of the inhabitants as the guilty enemy who could legitimately be killed, or reduced as prisoners to servitude. The astonishing rights allowed to the victor in a just war by Suarez, not to speak of less reputable theologians, show the extent to which the Schoolman of the Renaissance yielded to the temptation of exalting the military practice of his times into a theory—a theory which only a perfect (and therefore most improbable) use of charity by the conqueror could prevent from opening the flood-gates to the most odious tyranny. That the Law of Nations, embodied in Roman custom, certainly recognized the right to enslave prisoners of war cannot be denied : that it should ever have been sanctioned by any Christians is the tragedy. Bartolomé de las Casas at one time himself believed it. In his passionate desire to relieve the Indians from the cruel oppression under which they suffered, he advocated the

directly inculcated. In I. VIII, c. 1, of the same work the right of parents to care for and educate their children is denied, and education is claimed to be wholly the concern of the State. If there was much that Christian philosophy had to gain from the inheritance of Stoic thought, there was much also that was and is utterly incompatible with a right view of the dignity and liberty of the human person. In this Aristotle did not differ from the teaching of Plato, who in the *Fifth Book of the Republic* discusses the breeding and selection of citizens like cattle. It has remained for the modern materialist philosophy of the State to revive these odious conceptions and—as in Soviet Russia and Germany—to put them into practice.

[1] Balmes, *European Civilization*, p. 441.

importation into America of negro slaves from Africa, and indeed brought four with him when he sailed from San Lucas de Barameda for the Indies in 1544. His justification was that he believed the negroes to have been lawfully made captive by the Portuguese. Of this he repented bitterly in his old age,[1] confessing 'that it is as unjust to enslave negroes as it is to enslave Indians and for the same reasons' and that 'he is not certain if his ignorance and his good intention will excuse him before the judgement seat of God.' And he had erred in company with Cardinal Ximenes and Cardinal Adrian, who had approved his recommendation for the importation of Negroes. Indeed a distorted and insincere application of the traditional teaching upon just war sufficed to whitewash vast colonial conquests. But we need not labour the point; for Vittoria in the passages that we quote below deals fully and pungently with all the spurious titles to dominion brought forward under this head.

It was, indeed, not long before the true mind of the Church asserted itself against the attempts to justify the domination and oppression of backward races upon any such grounds. Within a few years of the discovery of America by Columbus, the Spaniards who had brought Indian slaves back with them were ordered by royal edict to restore them free to their homes in the new world: Las Casas was made Protector of the Indians and, armed with the censures of the Church, began his long fight against the *conquistadores*, a conflict which the Dominicans and Jesuits were to continue heroically for two centuries in Central and South America. In 1537 Paul III, in the Bull *Sublimis Deus sic Dilexit*, proclaimed that:

> The Indians or any other people who may be hereafter discovered by Catholics, although they be not Christians, must in no way be deprived of their liberty or their possessions. On the contrary, they may and must be allowed to enjoy freely and lawfully that liberty and those possessions. They must not be in any manner enslaved; and if they be so enslaved, their slavery must be considered as null and void.

And if we look for the consequences of the cynical and flagrant disobedience of this Papal injunction, how can we

[1] Chap. CI of his *Historia de las Indias*.

not point to the terrible retribution which befell Spain and Portugal? How can we not recall the solemn warning of the Franciscan friar to the young Emperor, spoken before the awe-struck Council, with Diego Columbus standing by:

> If the blood of one man never ceased crying to God until it was avenged, what shall not the blood of thousands do, who having perished by our tyranny and oppression now cry to God: '*Vindica sanguinem nostrum Deus noster!*' By the blood of Jesus Christ, and by the stigmata of St. Francis, I beg and beseech Your Majesty to put a stop to that torrent of crime and murdering of people, in order that the anger of God may not fall upon us all.[1]

To this foreboding of the Divine vengeance, Las Casas, the aged champion of the Indians returned, with the prophetic instinct of the dying, as he penned the concluding lines of his last will and testament. In this he bequeathed his history and other works to the College of St. Gregory at Valladolid, saying:

> The volume should be placed in the College library *ad perpetuam rei memoriam*, in order that should God decide to destroy Spain, it may be readily seen that the punishment is caused by our own destruction in the Indies and thus the reason of His justice will be made apparent.

It was necessary to approach the problem of the relations of civilized to backward races by means of an examination of slavery, its roots in the human mind, the efforts to frame a rational theory of it and the constant abuse of that theory by the strong to the detriment of the weak. That is the historical method. It was, in fact, far more by combatting and destroying the pernicious fallacies upon which slavery rested that the Catholic Church revealed the truth concerning the rights of the barbarians than by the abstract reasoning out of those rights from first principles.

Our conclusions on this subject may then be shortly expressed: it amounts simply to a categorical denial that difference of colour and race, absence of social organization, science and mechanical skill, ignorance of Christianity, or even a low standard of private and public morals, or any

[1] *Historia de las Indias*, Book III, Chap. CXLVIII, *apud* Dutto.

or all of these characteristics destroy the fundamental character of man and of civil society, or the rights which, as we have shown above, they derive from the Natural Law. The most primitive tribes have, therefore, a natural right to be free, to conserve themselves in being, to develop according to their nature, to associate and to possess property : their chiefs have true authority. They are the subjects, at least potentially, of all the rights and duties which Christian sociology postulates in regard to civil society and economy. Is then the whole Colonial enterprise to be condemned? God is the judge. We cannot avoid the conclusion that every violent seizure of territory which was at the time inhabited and cultivated by a native tribe and subject to the authority of its rulers was in itself an unjust aggression.

But what of uncultivated, undeveloped land, full of potential wealth but sparsely inhabited only by nomadic tribes? It would be an unreasonable exaggeration of our doctrine of native rights to pretend that, under such circumstances they excluded either the acquisition by the first comer of territory which, not being effectively occupied by any human group is truly *res nullius*; or the right of all peoples to travel, trade and settle; or to have their share of those good things of earth and sea which are not already the property of others. The ill-treatment of strangers and the refusal of peaceful transit we have seen to be contrary to the Law of Nations, according to the doctrine of Christian theologians, from St. Augustine onward. All these are rights the persistent denial of which may under certain circumstances justify the use of force. Again, the rules which we have already established concerning the duty of intervention to save the weak from oppression by the strong, or the minority by the majority, apply no less to the relations of the civilized and uncivilized peoples than to relations between peoples of equal stages of development. These considerations then point to three possible grounds for the legitimate occupation of new territory—Discovery : Just war : Intervention. These grounds or titles and variants of them are examined with great lucidity by Vittoria.

Assuming the original occupation by a civilized Power of

undeveloped territory, containing one or more native tribes, to have been legitimate, what ought to be the guiding principles of the colonial authority once it is established? Christianity can sanction no action on the part of that authority which is contrary to justice; and on this point the doctrine of Pope Paul III admits of no doubt or ambiguity: it would be unjust to deprive the natives of their property or their freedom. Since it is of the nature of man that these rights should be exercised collectively as well as individually, it is no less unjust to seize the communal property of the village or tribe, to interfere with the internal organization of these groups or the authority of their chiefs or headmen. And here we may recall a principle which we have previously discerned in studying the Catholic conception of the State, the rights of the nation in general and those of the national minority. It is that the lesser group is nearer to nature and anterior to the greater, just as it derives more nearly from the family which is the grand original of human society. Changes of overlords or sovereigns and of the frontiers between their dominions[1] ought to be attended by no detriment to the communes or clans, the villages or towns or indeed any of the smaller groupings of human beings which have their roots in nature or in necessity. Hence it appears that the respect and protection of native communities is among the first duties of the new rulers.

That is not to say that the supreme authority is not justified in seeking to introduce improvements, moral, social, political, intellectual, economic and sanitary into the life of the native population. But this process must be governed by three canons:

1. *Are the reforms really for the good of the governed?* For that is the first and last justification of Government. The colonial Government has the peculiar task of harmonizing the rights of the indigenous population with the legitimate needs of the settlers. There can be no contradiction between true rights: where there is apparent collision, there can never be justification for benefiting the newcomers to the

[1] Events which were often hardly perceived by the common people of mediæval Europe when they were occasioned merely by marriage or inheritance between the ruling houses.

detriment of the natives. The rapid introduction of material improvements in agriculture, industry or communications which can only be effected by imposing some form of servitude with all its evils upon the native population is likewise inadmissible : for it is never permitted to do evil that good may come.

2. *Do these changes respect the national character and personality of the native population?* The Colonial Power has no mandate to transform the African or the Indian into an artificial European. It is its duty to respect the native language and every indigenous custom and tradition which is not in conflict with the moral law. Here the example of the Church may well guide the temporal authority : she seeks not to convert the heathen to an Italian or French or German or Spanish religion, but to 'the truth which shall make us free'—the universal faith which is also the intimate possession of each and every people. Hence the stringent injunction of the Vicar of Christ to the missionary priest to abjure all national and political interests and, in order to minister without ulterior motive to his new flock, to 'Forget thy country and thy father's House.'[1]

The insistence of the modern Papacy upon the creation of an indigenous clergy, once Christianity is sufficiently established in a country, is but a repetition of the practice everywhere followed when the Church was spreading the light of the Gospel through Europe during the first half of the Christian era. It is the clearest evidence of the Church's recognition of the national spirit and traditions of every people. Any innovation which disrupts communal or tribal life without putting anything indisputably better in its place is a crime.

3. *Are the reforms such as to prepare the native population—* in so far as it is 'backward or primitive'—*for the responsibilities of self-government?* There are indeed tribes whose hereditary depravity or intellectual poverty is such that it seems impossible for human wisdom to foresee a time when their condition would not be worse for lack of the firm authority, justice and discipline which the more civilized State is able to provide for them. But this does not alter the

[1] Psalm xliv : 11.

fact that whole nations can be and have been utterly transformed by several generations of Christian education and good government. As we have already seen, the proper relation of the civilized to the primitive peoples is that of grown man to child. The former has a natural duty of tutelage[1] toward the latter, and what man worthy of the name would deliberately retard the education and training of the child for fear of creating a rival to himself?

We may add two concluding observations. First, the climatic conditions of countries acquired or occupied by the colonizing powers of Europe are such as to make it all but inevitable that the manual labour of the community should be undertaken by the native population. The newcomers are therefore to a large extent related to the indigenous people as employers to employed, as capital to labour. In view of the temptations ever present to the more skilled and powerful of the two classes to abuse its position—particularly upon the introduction of mechanical industry into Africa and Asia—it becomes doubly necessary to uphold in colonial territories all those rules upon the just conditions of Labour which Catholic social doctrine postulates. It is not for us to elaborate that doctrine in the present work: we refer readers to the Encyclicals *Rerum Novarum* of Leo XIII and *Quadragesimo Anno* of Pius XI and to the documents[2] which illustrate the ways in which authoritative Catholic organizations urge that the principles laid down by these Popes should be applied in regard to the contemporary evil of Compulsory Labour in colonial territories. Suffice it to say that so far from justifying disregard of the rules concerning

[1] This conception is embodied in the Mandates under which the Powers victorious in the war of 1914–18 are held responsible to the League of Nations for the African, Asiatic and Australasian territories which they seized from the former German and Turkish Empires. These lands are administered 'as a sacred trust for civilization'—which, if it means anything, means a 'sacred trust for God'—until such time as the indigenous people are able 'to stand by themselves under the strenuous conditions of the modern world.' The gradation of the Mandates into A, B and C classes recognizes the varying degrees of aptitude for eventual autonomy which the native races display.

[2] See pp. 456–461.

a just wage ; the safeguarding of family life ; the limitation of hours of work ; of freedom to make contracts and to associate ; and the other rights of the workers which the Church has excogitated and defended, Colonial conditions demand their ample and sincere acceptance.

Our second and last observation which is of even greater moment, relates to the attitude of the Colonial Authority to the Christian religion. The only positive authorization which the Holy See has ever presumed to give to a Catholic Power of Europe to occupy territory in another Continent rested upon the duty of such a power to facilitate the preaching of the Gospel in that territory. This is no accidental or incidental characteristic of colonization. It is, and must ever be regarded by the Catholic Church as that form of the expansion of civilization which is most consistent with the revealed will of Almighty God. For if the Son of Man died to save all men ; if He commissioned His Church to preach the Gospel to every creature ; if in His Name only is salvation, no Christian is a true Christian who does not conceive the extension of the faith of Christ to be his duty ; and no more urgent charge can lie upon the consciences of Christian rulers, whose subjects bring foreign lands beneath their influence or dominion, than to lead the inhabitants of those countries to Him who is the Light of the World. Terrible then are the censures of the Church against the conqueror or the colonist who by his evil example and injustice estranges the primitive races, that are as children among the peoples of the earth, from the acceptance of the Christian religion. 'It were better for him that a millstone should be hanged about his neck and that he should be drowned in the depth of the sea.' (Matthew xviii : 6).

Documents

I. Ecclesiastical Canons, etc., relating to the protection and liberation of Slaves :[1]

A.D. 305. *Concilium Eliberitanum*, Canon 5 : Penance imposed on a mistress who maltreats her slave.

[1] These references are for the most part taken from Balmes' *European Civilization.*

A.D. 441. *Concilium Arausicanum Primum*, Canon 6: Condemnation of those who seize the goods of the Church in revenge for the asylum granted to escaped slaves.

Canon 7: Condemnation of anyone who tries to re-enslave those who have been enfranchised by the Church or recommended to her care by testament.

A.D. 506. *Concilium Agathense*, Canon 29: 'Let the Church protect those who have rightly been emancipated from their masters, if the need arise.'

A.D. 517. *Concilium Epaocense*, Canon 34: Excommunication of a master who puts his slave to death, without the authority of a judge.

(Also in 15th Canon of 17th Council of Toledo, A.D. 694, and *Concilium Wormatiense*, Canon 38–39, A.D. 868.)

Canon 39: The slave guilty of a grave fault to escape corporal punishment by taking refuge in a church.

A.D. 549. *Concilium Aurelianense Quintum*, Canon 22: Masters forbidden to maltreat slaves who had taken refuge in a church. Pardon granted to such slaves to be respected thereafter by their masters under oath. 'Christian people of gooth faith' to stand sponsor for the word of a non-Christian master.

Canon 7: Those who have received the benefit of manumission in the Church to be permanently free. Their liberty to be defended by the Church.

A.D. 566. *Concilium Lugdunense Secundum*, Canon 3: Excommunication of those who attempt to take away the liberty of others.

A.D. 585. *Concilium Matisconense Secundum*, Canon 7: The Bishops to use the 'vigour of their authority' to defend against all vexation those who have been freed, either by emancipation within the sacred precincts, or by letter, or by testament, or prescription (*per longitudinem temporis*).

A.D. 589. *Concilium Toletanum Tertium*, Canon 6: Bishops to protect freed slaves recommended to the Church.

A.D. 614. *Concilium Parisiense Quintum*, Canon 5: The priests to defend freed slaves. They are 'not to be recalled to the public work' (*revocari ad publicum*). Excommunication of those who persist in attempting to deprive them of their liberty.

A.D. 625 or 630. *Concilium Rhemense*, Canon 17: The same: '*Si quis ingenum aut liberum ad servitium inclinare voluerit, aut fortasse jam fecit, et commonitus ab episcopo se de inquietudine ejus revocare neglexerit, aut emendare noluerit, tanquam calumniæ reum placuit sequestrari.*'

A.D. 633. *Concilium Toletanum Quartum*, Canon 72: Persons and property of the enfranchised, recommended to the Church, to be protected by the priests.

Ransom of Slaves and Captives:

St. Ambrose, *de Officiis*, Lib. II, Cap. II. 13: 'We have sometimes incurred odium because we have broken up the sacred vessels in order to ransom captives.'

Lib. II, Cap. XV. 70: 'And it is the highest liberality to ransom captives, to take them out of the hands of their enemies, to save men from death, and especially women from shame, to restore children to their parents, parents to their children, and citizens to their fatherland. . . .'

Lib. II, Cap. XV. 71: 'Therefore it is especially noble to redeem captives, particularly from the barbarous enemy who shows no humanity for mercy's sake, but only what avarice promotes him to accord in view of the ransom-money.'

St. Cyprian, Epist. 60: His great sorrow at hearing of the enslavement of Christian men and women. For we are all one body and 'if one member suffers all the other members suffer with it' (St. Paul, Epist. *ad* Corinthians xii: 26). 'Wherefore the captivity of our brethren ought now to be considered our own captivity . . . and not love only but religion ought to spur on and strengthen our endeavours to ransom the bodies of our brethren.' A denunciation of the state of slavery and its moral dangers for women. He sends as much money as he can afford to redeem the captives.

St. Gregory the Great's Epistles: Important references to slavery and the ransom of captives:

> Vol. V, Lib. III, ep. 16; Vol. V, Lib. IV, ep. 17; Vol. V, Lib. VI, ep. 35; Vol. V, Lib. VII, ep.26, 28, 39; Vol. V, Lib. X, ep. 17.

The redemption of captives is mentioned as a normal purpose for which the property of the Church and alms of the faithful are used in the following canons:

c. A.D. 450. Synod of St. Patrick in Ireland, Canon 32.

A.D. 583. *Concilium Lugdunense Tertium*, Canon 2.

A.D. 585. *Concilium Matisconense Secundum*, Canon 5.

A.D. 625 or 630. *Concilium Rhemense*, Canon 22. (This canon authorizes the breaking up of the sacred vessels, under 'arduous necessity,' to provide the ransom price.)

A.D. 844. *Concilium Vernense Secundum*, Canon 12.

Condemnation of the Slave Trade:

A.D. 992. *Concilium Confluentinum*, Canon 7: He who sells a Christian into slavery is guilty of homicide.

'Next the question arose, what ought to be done with one who has carried off (*seduxerit*) a Christian man and so sold him: the answer was given by all that such a one brought upon himself the guilt of homicide.'

This reproduces a condemnation contained in a letter of Pope Gregory III (*Ep. ad Bonifacium Archiepiscopum* of 731): '*Eis ergo qui hæc perpetraverunt similem homocidiæ indices pænitentiam.*'

A.D. 1102. *Concilium Londinense:* 'Let no one henceforth dare to practise that nefarious trade whereby heretofore men were wont in England to be sold like brute beasts.'

Many canons prohibit the sale of Christians as slaves to Jews and pagans; order Christians enslaved to Jews to be liberated, etc., notably:

A.D. 538. *Concilium Aurelianense Tertium*, Canon 13.
A.D. 541. *Concilium Aurelianense Quartum*, Canon 30, 31.
A.D. 581. *Concilium Matisconense Primum*, Canon 16.
A.D. 589. *Concilium Toletanum Tertium*, Canon 14.
A.D. 633. *Concilium Toletanum Quartum*, Canon 66.
A.D. 625. *Concilium Rhemense*, Canon 11: '. . . For if any Christian should sell Christian slaves to the pagans or Jews, let him be deprived of Communion, and let the sale lack all validity.'
A.D. 656. *Concilium Toletanum Decimum*, Canon 7.

Emancipation:

St. Gregory the Great: *Liberation of two slaves* (*V. Ep.* 12):

Whereas our Redeemer, the creator of every being, willed . . . to assume flesh that by the grace of His divinity He might restore us, inasmuch as we were held captive by the bond of slavery, to our pristine liberty; it is a noble act by the benefit of manumission to give freedom back to men, whom nature from the beginning created and brought forth free, but whom the Law of Nations has subjected to the yoke of slavery. And therefore moved by piety and urged by the consideration of this fact, we make you, Montanus and Thomas, slaves of the Holy Roman Church, which with God's help we serve, free men and Roman citizens from this day forth, and we absolve for you every debt of your servitude.

A.D. 506. *Concilium Agathense*, Canon 7: The power of Bishops to enfranchise slaves.

A.D. 541. *Concilium Aurelianense Quartum*, Canon 9: Enfranchised slaves to preserve their liberty.

A.D. 816. *Concilium Cellichytense*, Canon 10: All the English slaves of a dead Bishop to be emancipated and each Bishop and Abbot attending the funeral to enfranchise three slaves and to provide each with a sum of money.

A.D. 1171. *Concilium Ardamachiense* in *Hibernia celebratum* (ex Giraldo Cambrensi, Cap. XXVIII, *Hiberniæ expugnatæ*): The clergy of all Ireland being convened to Armagh, and a long discussion having taken place concerning the coming of strangers into the island, the following sentence was at length unanimously given :

Because of the sins of their people and especially because they had once been wont to buy Englishmen, both from merchants and from brigands and pirates, this evil had, through the judgement of the divine vengeance, befallen them, that they also had, in turn, been reduced to slavery by that race. For the English people, their kingdom yet being intact, had been accustomed according to the common vice of the race, to expose their children for sale, and before they suffered any poverty or hunger, to sell their own sons and relatives to be transported to Ireland. Whence also it can be believed probably true that the former sellers and buyers alike have now merited the yoke of slavery through so enormous a crime (*enormi delicto*). Therefore it was decreed in the said Council, and by the consent of the whole assembly publicly ordained that in every part of the island the English should be freed from the bonds of slavery and restored to their pristine liberty.

II. Pontifical Documents relating to the rights of natives and slavery :

EUGENE IV. *Bull of* 1435 *to the Bishops of the Canary Isles :*

As we have quite recently learned, the native inhabitants of the Canary Isles, without any contact with infidel or heretical sects and led solely by the natural law, have been recently brought to the true Faith, thanks to the succour of the Divine clemency. Nevertheless, in many of the Isles mentioned above —consequent upon the corruption of the age, for lack of governors and good defenders able to direct the natives in spiritual and temporal affairs, to guide them in the observance of the true Faith, to protect and defend with intrepidity and strength their properties and possessions—certain Christians—a very painful thing to say—have invented divers pretexts and made occasions arise for landing upon these Isles with their ships and armed troops. They have brought away as slaves with them, into other countries, upon this side of the seas, after having seized booty and made profit out of their goods, many persons of both sexes ; some have been surprised unawares, and others have been deceived in their simplicity ; many of these captives were already regenerated by the Baptismal Water, others have been attracted by the hope and promise of Baptism ; they had even been fraudently and traitorously promised security—and promised under oath, but these promises have not been kept. Further, there have been committed against them other illicit and criminal acts.

Because of these misdeeds, the rest of the population, holding in execration this sort of slavery, remain plunged in its ancient errors and renounces the desire to receive Baptism; whence results a grave offence to the Divine Majesty, peril to souls and considerable detriment to the Christian religion.

Now it belongs to Us, above all others, to correct every sinner for his sin. We would not pass over these things in silence, and We desire with all Our power and according to the full obligations of Our pastoral Charge to provide salutarily for these matters. Penetrated with pious and paternal compassion for the afflictions of the said inhabitants and natives, We beg and exhort, together and separately, the temporal princes, lords and captains, the knights, barons, soldiers, nobles, the communities and all the other Faithful of Christ of no matter what state, grade or condition, to renounce themselves the above-named acts, and to cause their subjects to turn aside from them and to repress them severely. We order and command all and each of the Faithful of Christ of both sexes, to restore to their original freedom completely and for ever, and within fifteen days from the publication, in the place where they dwell, of the present (Bull), and to allow to depart without exaction or money payment, all the inhabitants of both sexes of the said Isles, called Canaries, whom they have made captive and hold in subjection.

In the case of contravention (of these directions), the period of delay having elapsed, they will be obliged to incur, from this very fact, the sentence of excommunication, from which they will not be able to be absolved, even by the Apostolic See, unless they have first of all restored liberty and all possessions to the captives in question, except they should be at the point of death.

We will that a like sentence of excommunication, with privation from the benefit of absolution, shall be incurred by all those who, together or separately, try to capture, sell or reduce to slavery the said inhabitants of the Canaries, baptized, or voluntarily approaching Baptism.

Paul III. *Bull 'Sublimis Deus Sic Dilexit,'* (1537):

Inasmuch as man was created, as the scriptures teach, to enjoy eternal life and eternal happiness, which cannot be obtained without faith in Christ, it necessarily follows that he must be naturally fit to receive it. Whoever, therefore, has the nature of man is capable of receiving the faith of Christ. Nobody in fact, who can understand what faith means, can be so deficient in intelligence as to be unable to understand the means by which it is transmitted. Hence Our Lord, who is truth itself, and can neither deceive nor be deceived, said to the first preachers of the faith, when he appointed them to their office: 'Go and teach all nations.' He said all nations, without a single exception, because all are capable of the faith. The devil, who is the enemy of mankind and of all good works, to prevent

God's children from reaching their eternal destiny, invented a new and unheard method to prevent the faith being preached to the people and thus prevent their salvation. This method consists in persuading some soldiers, his allies, constantly to proclaim that, inasmuch as the Indians and other people, who inhabit the regions in our own times discovered to the west and to the south of us, are not capable of the faith, we may make the same use of them in our temporal affairs that we make of the beasts of the fields.

But we, who, although His unworthy servant, have been appointed by Jesus Christ His vicar on earth, and who with all our power endeavour to bring into His fold the sheep entrusted to our care, considering that the Indians, who are true men, not only are capable of the faith, but, as we are informed, earnestly desire to embrace it ; in order to stamp out this pernicious doctrine, by our Apostolic authority and by these present . . . define and proclaim that the said Indians or any other people, who may be hereafter discovered by Catholics, although they be not Christians, must in no way be deprived of their liberty or their possessions, and that on the contrary they may and must be allowed to enjoy freely and lawfully the said liberty and possessions ; that they must not be in any manner enslaved ; and that, if they be so enslaved, their slavery must be considered as null and void.

By the same Apostolic authority we define also that the said Indians must be called to the faith of Jesus Christ by the word of God and the examples of good and holy lives.

Given at Rome June 17, 1537.

PIUS V. *Document drawn up by the Congregation of four Cardinals*[1] *appointed by the Pope, and dealing with the Treatment of Indians in America.* (*Extracts*). 1568 :

Among the principal facts to call to mind, it is necessary to emphasize above all the care that ought to be taken for the conversion of the infidels, seeing that this conversion is the end for which the conquest of this country was confided to the Catholic Kings of Spain. This is why there must be procured for them preachers and priests who know how to preach the Gospel, to instruct them in the true Faith, men zealous for the salvation of souls, and who, in addition to imparting the doctrine, give by their good will, a clear testimony to our Christian Religion. . . .

. . . His Holiness holds for certain that, as much through the order of His Majesty as by duty, these ministers will keep watch over the good administration of justice ; this is why it ought not

[1] The nucleus of the future Congregation of Propaganda.

to be allowed that some particular Lords or Christian Ministers should make use of Indians as slaves, either in their own homes or outside; they may employ with gentleness those alone who spontaneously accept service, and these ought to be fully and justly paid for their services, according to the wage agreed upon with them, as we are taught by the holy Apostle writing to Philemon. Further, they must not be overburdened with exaggerated taxes; but the same justice must be meted out to all groups, as is proper, so that, if sometimes the inferiors were oppressed by their masters or other private persons, or if they suffered some damage, they may have recourse to justice with confidence and rejoice to see it administered with regard to themselves in the same manner as with regard to Christians of long date. . . .

Further, care must be taken (and His Holiness holds it for certain that, by order of His Majesty, first of all and of all his Ministers afterwards, it is so) that our lay Christians inhabiting those countries, whether private persons or functionaries, of whatever State they may be, live Christian lives, as is becoming in professors of our holy Religion; for it is of the highest importance that these persons, while performing their duty and working out the salvation of their souls, should aid the converts and the infidels, inviting the latter by their good example to become converted, and remembering the principle of the Apostles: '*tamquam advenæ et peregrini*, etc.'; and, on the contrary, it must not happen that the new Christians become lukewarm or fall back, and that the infidels harden themselves in their blindness, when seeing amongst our people the bad actions of adultery, concubinage and too great clinging to riches. So as to prevent these evils, which His Holiness calls to your attention with great insistence, there is expected of the true and Christian piety of His Majesty this excellent and salutary remedy; viz., that he will confide to loyal persons of integrity the inspection of the particular Lords, Judges and other secular functionaries of these domains, so that, seeing the merits and the faults of each, His Majesty may, on the one hand, reward and exhort the good, and, on the other hand, prosecute and punish those who have committed abuses, without leaving unpunished the oppression of the poor, '*ne ob eorum gemitus exsurgat Deus*,'—which would cause great harm to the Christian Religion in these countries.

Great attention must be paid in taking up arms against the Pagans, not to make war except under the required conditions so that it may be just; and, in case of war, not to act cruelly; according to the method which His Holiness praises in Florida for the diffusion of the Gospel and which He desires to see adopted everywhere. Procedures contrary to those stated above might easily do great harm in these provinces to the honour of God and His Holy Religion and to the common welfare of the peoples—to the great grief of the good, and to His Majesty perhaps more than to anyone else, seeing that these things would touch his conscience and would sully his good renown. The attentive observance of these counsels, on the other hand, will be, in the future, the great remedy for the past, and, with the help of God will henceforward produce the best results.

URBAN VIII. *Bull of April* 22, 1639. *The Deportation of the Native Inhabitants of South America :*

By the present (Bull) we entrust to you and enjoin it upon you, that you yourself, or another person or persons, aid with an effective succour all the Indians of the Provinces of Paraguay and Brazil and those dwelling near the river called La Plata, as well as all those living in no matter what other region or locality of the western and southern Indies ; and that you sternly forbid any person to dare or presume to reduce to slavery the said Indians, to sell them, buy them, exchange them, give them, separate them from their wives and children, despoil them of their properties and possessions, take them into other places or deprive them in any manner whatsoever of their liberty, retain them in slavery, as well as to lend aid, favour, or give counsel or succour, under no matter what pretext or excuse, to those who should do the said things, to speak of it and teach it as something permitted, or to collaborate in it in any way whatever. All persons, taken together or separately, lay persons or ecclesiastics, of no matter what state, sex, grade, condition, dignity and even special distinction, as also of no matter what order, congregation, company, religious society, institute of mendicants or non-mendicants and regular monks who should contravene this sentence, binding under pain of excommunication, will be obliged to incur, from this very fact, the punishment resulting therefrom ; from this We alone or the reigning Roman Pontiff can absolve, after satisfaction first made, except when the excommunicated person is at the point of death.

This is why We give you power and full, ample and free faculty to declare as subject to the pain of excommunication, all the contradictors and rebellious persons who will not obey you in the above matters, and to bring them to obedience by other means, even by censures and ecclesiastical punishments, and by other opportune remedies of law and of action, always with the possibility of ultimate appeal, while observing the legitimate procedures usual in such a case ; to increase the censures, the punishments themselves ; and this repeatedly ; and even, to this end, should there be need, to call for the assistance of the secular power.

BENEDICT XIV. *Extract from the Bull of December* 20, 1741.

It is not then, without a profound grief in Our paternal heart that We have learned that after so many Councils . . . after so many Edicts and Decrees ordering and enjoining, under pain of the gravest chastisements and ecclesiastical censures, succour and defence, as far as possible, to be brought to the infidels, and not the infliction of injuries, scourges, prison, servitude and murder ; it is not without sorrow that We have learned all this, and that, above all in the districts of Brazil there are still found men confessing the true Faith who have the audacity, as if they had completely forgotten the charity spread abroad in our hearts by the Holy Ghost, to bring into captivity, to sell again to others as slaves, to deprive of their possessions the poor Indians, and presume to treat them with such inhumanity that they do everything to turn away from the faith of Christ, and confirm in their execration of it, not only those who are deprived of the light of the true Faith, but also those who have been regenerated in the Baptismal Water, inhabitants of the steep mountains and deserts of the western, southern and other regions of Brazil.

Cardinal Consalvi, representing Pius VII at the Congress of Vienna, helped to induce the Powers at last to promise to unite all their efforts to secure 'the entire and definite abolition of a commerce (the slave trade) so odious and so highly reprobated by the laws of religion and of nature.'

GREGORY XVI. *Constitution against the Slave Trade. November* 3, 1839 :

Placed at the summit of the Apostolic power and, although lacking in merits, holding the place of Jesus Christ, the Son of God, Who, being made Man through utmost Charity, deigned to die for the Redemption of the World, We have judged that it belonged to Our pastoral solicitude to exert Ourselves to turn away the Faithful from the inhuman slave trade in Negroes and all other men. Assuredly, since there was spread abroad, first of all amongst the Christians, the light of the Gospel, these miserable people, who in such great numbers, and chiefly through the effect of wars, fell into very cruel slavery, experienced an alleviation of their lot. Inspired in fact by the Divine Spirit, the Apostles, it is true, exhorted the slaves themselves to obey their masters, according to the flesh, as though obeying Christ, and sincerely to accomplish the Will of God ; but they ordered the masters to act well towards their slaves, to give them what was just and equitable, and to abstain from menaces, knowing that the common Master both of themselves and of the slaves is in Heaven, and that with Him there is no distinction of persons.[1] But as the law of the Gospel universally and earnestly enjoined a sincere charity towards all, and considering that Our Lord Jesus Christ had declared that He considered as done or refused to Himself everything kind and merciful done or refused to the small and needy[2] it naturally follows, not only that the Christians should regard as brothers their slaves and, above all, their Christian slaves,[3] but that they should be more inclined to set free those who merited it; which it was the custom to do chiefly upon the occasion of the Easter Feast as Gregory of Nyssa tells us.[4] There were not lacking Christians, who, moved by an ardent charity 'cast themselves into bondage in order to redeem others,' many instances of which our predecessor, Clement I, of very holy memory, declares to have come to his knowledge.[5] In the process of time, the fog of pagan superstition being more completely dissipated and the manners of the barbarous people having been softened, thanks to Faith operating by Charity, it at last comes about that, since several centuries, there are no more slaves in the greater number of Christian nations. But—We say it with profound sorrow—there were to be found afterwards among the Faithful men who, shamefully blinded by the desire of sordid gain, in lonely and distant countries, did not hesitate to reduce to slavery Indians, negroes and other wretched peoples, or else, by instituting or developing the trade in those who had been made slaves by others, to favour their unworthy practice. Certainly many Roman Pontiffs of glorious memory, Our Predecessors, did not fail, according to the duties of their charge, to blame severely this way of acting as dangerous for the spiritual welfare of those engaged in the traffic and a shame to the Christian name; they foresaw that as a result of this, the infidel peoples would be more and more strengthened in their hatred of the true Religion. It is at these practices that are aimed the Letter Apostolic of Paul III, given on May 29, 1537, under the seal of the Fisherman, and addressed to the Cardinal Archbishop of Toledo, and afterwards another Letter, more detailed, addressed by Urban VIII on April 22, 1639 to the Collector Jurium of the Apostolic Chamber of Portugal. In the latter are severely and particularly condemned those who should dare 'to reduce to slavery the Indians of the Eastern and Southern Indies,' sell them, buy them, exchange them or give them, separate them from their wives and children, despoil them of their goods and properties, conduct or transport

[1] St. Paul, Ephesians vi : 5 *seq.*; Colossians iii : 2 *seq.*; iv : 1.
[2] St. Matthew xxv : 35.
[3] *Lactantius*, *Divin. Institut.*, Book V, Chap. 16.
[4] *De Resurrect. Domini orat.*, 111.
[5] *Ad Corinth.*, Ep. i, Chap. 55.

them into other regions, or deprive them of liberty in any way whatsoever, retain them in servitude, or lend counsel, succour, favour and co-operation to those so acting, under no matter what pretext or excuse, or who proclaim and teach that this way of acting is allowable and co-operate in any manner whatever in the practices indicated.[1]

Benedict XIV confirmed and renewed the penalties of the Popes above-mentioned in a new Apostolic Letter addressed on December 20, 1741, to the Bishops of Brazil and some other regions, in which he stimulated, to the same end, the solicitude of the Governors themselves.[2] Another of Our Predecessors, anterior to Benedict XIV, Pius II, as during his life the power of the Portuguese was extending itself over New Guinea, sent on October 7, 1462, to a Bishop who was leaving for that country, a Letter in which he not only gives to the Bishop himself the means of exercising there the sacred ministry with more fruit, but on the same occasion, addresses grave warnings with regard to Christians who should reduce neophytes to slavery.[3] In our time Pius VII, moved by the same religious and charitable spirit as his Predecessors, intervened zealously with those in possession of power to secure that the slave trade should at least cease amongst Christians. The penalties imposed and the care given by Our Predecessors contributed in no small measure, with the help of God, to protect the Indians and the other peoples mentioned against the cruelties of the invaders or the cupidity of Christian merchants, without however carrying success to such a point that the Holy See could rejoice over the complete success of its efforts in this direction; for the slave trade, although it has diminished in more than one district, is still practised by numerous Christians. This is why, desiring to remove such a shame from all the Christian nations, having fully reflected over the whole question and having taken the advice of many of Our Venerable Brothers the Cardinals of the holy Roman Church, and walking in the footsteps of Our Predecessors, We warn and adjure earnestly in the Lord faithful Christians of every condition that no one in the future dare to vex anyone, despoil him of his possessions, reduce to servitude, or lend aid and favour to those who give themselves up to these practices, or exercise that inhuman traffic by which the Blacks, as if they were not men, but rather animals, having been brought into servitude, in no matter what way, are, without any distinction, in contempt of the rights of justice and humanity, bought, sold and devoted sometimes to the hardest labour. Further, in the hope of gain, propositions of purchase being made to the

[1] *In Bullar.* rom., ed. typo Mansardi, t. VI, Part 2, constit. 604, p. 183. [2] *In Bullar*—Benedict XIV, t. I, constit. 38.
[3] *Apud Raynaldum in Annalibus Ecclesiasticis ad ann.* 1462, *n.* 42.

first owners of the Blacks, dissensions and almost perpetual conflicts are aroused in these regions.

We reprove, then, by virtue of Our Apostolic Authority, all the practices above-mentioned as absolutely unworthy of the Christian name. By the same Authority We prohibit and strictly forbid any Ecclesiastic or lay person from presuming to defend as permissible this traffic in the Blacks under no matter what pretext or excuse, or from publishing or teaching in any manner whatsoever, in public or privately, opinions contrary to what We have set forth in this Apostolic Letter.

Cardinal Lavigerie's great campaign to put an end to the horrors of the slave trade in Northern and Central Africa gave rise to two important letters of Leo XIII which repeat the doctrine and prohibitions of Gregory XVI—*In Plurimis* of May 5, 1888 to the Brazilian Episcopate and *Catholicæ Ecclesiæ* of November 20, 1890 to the Cardinal himself. The Cardinal's original motive may best be illustrated by a letter written in the early days of his episcopate at Algiers. On Fathers Paulmier, Menoret and Bouchaud leaving Metlili in December, 1875 for Timbuctoo[1] to establish a mission there and to redeem negro children from slavery—they left singing the *Te Deum* on camelback and were martyred by the Touaregs—he wrote :

It is a work which for the interior of Africa is really the great task of the future, I mean the redemption and education of a certain number of young negroes who shall later be sent back as Apostles to their own country. Their's must be the mission one day of abolishing that slavery which tore them away from the love of their family, that slavery which like a foul leprosy is at once the shame and the death of those immense regions so blessed by nature. . . . This is what our missionaries try to do by rescuing any of the poor black children which they find on their way from the horrible servitude under which they suffer, and by sending them forthwith to those of their fellows who can first make men of them and then Christians.

Note.—A bibliography of exceptional value on the whole subject of slavery is to be found in *La Traite et l'Esclavage des Congolais par les Européens*, by P. Dieudonné Rinchon. The ethical problems of colonization in general are well set forth and examined in *Le Droit de Colonization*, by Joseph Folliet.

[1] Timbuctoo was the main slave market for Morocco and Tangiers. The incident is recorded in *Le Cardinal Lavigerie et ses Œuvres d'Afrique*, by Felix Klein (p. 139), and in other lives of the Cardinal.

APPENDICES TO CHAPTER XV

Appendix A

Extracts from Bartolomé de Las Casas, *Historia de las Indias* (English translation from Dutto : *Life of Bartolomé de Las Casas*, Herder).

Bartolomé de Las Casas. (*Historia de Las Indias*). (*Dutto, p.* 53–54, *Herder*). *Sermon of Father Martesino, O.P. at Concepcion de la Vega. Advent Sunday,* 1511 :

I ascended this pulpit to let you know that I am the voice of Christ crying in the wilderness of this Island. Hence it is meet that you listen to it with no ordinary attention, but with all the power of your souls and of your five senses. It will prove to you the strongest, the most rasping, the harshest, the most frightful voice you ever listened to. This voice tells you that all of you are now living and dying in a state of mortal sin, on account of your cruelty and tyranny over these innocent people. Tell me : with what right and with what justice do you subject the Indians to so cruel and to so horrible a slavery ? With what authority do you wage your abominable wars against these people, who were living peaceably in their own countries, where you caused infinite numbers of them to die by your unheard of barbarities and slaughter ? Why do you overwhelm them with work, and give them not sufficient food to keep them from starving, or medicines to cure their infirmities ? Nay, why do you kill them daily with excessive labour that they may bring you gold ? What steps have you taken to have them taught to know God, their Creator, to be baptized, to hear Mass and to keep the Sundays and Holydays ? Are you not bound to love them as yourselves ? Have you lost your reason, have you lost your senses ? Or are you buried in a lethargic sleep ? Rest assured of it ; in the state you are now living, you can no more save your souls than the Moors or the Jews, who have not the faith of Christ.

(*Dutto, p.* 136–137). *Memorial or Instruction to be given to the Fathers, who, by command of His Most Reverend Lordship (Ximenez) and of the Señor Ambassador are going to reform the Indies :*

Proper territorial boundaries should be assigned to the pueblos, giving to each of them enough of the adjacent land, thus providing for that increase of population which is expected through the grace of God. The best of these lands should be parcelled out among the villagers in proportion to the size of their families and to their social rank, so that they may plant trees and other things, and raise cazabe to make their bread. To the Caciques should be assigned four times as much land as to an ordinary man of the people. The rest of the land should be left in common for raising hogs and grazing cattle. The Caciques and their Indians must be settled in villages to be founded in the neighbourhood of their native homes in order that they may gather into them cheerfully. Let negotiations be entered into with the Caciques with a view to their bringing their people into the villages of their own free accord, if possible, without any other inducement, and let the Caciques exercise care in governing and ruling over their people in the manner to be stated hereafter. If the Indians of one Cacique be numerous enough to form a pueblo alone, let them do it ; if not, let a sufficient number of the nearest ones bring their subjects together, and let each Cacique continue to exercise authority over his own Indians, and let the minor chiefs obey him, whom they were accustomed to recognize as their superior, who should be given jurisdiction over the entire pueblo jointly with the Friar or secular Priest in charge of the administration of the pueblo. If any present or future Spanish settler shall desire to marry an heiress to a Caciqueship, when no male heir should be living, let it be done with the consent of the acting parish priest and the administrator of the pueblo.

Slavery of Negroes unjust : Las Casas' Confession.

This advice (i.e. that permission be given to import Negro slaves) was first given by the Clerigo Casas, who did not then know that the Portuguese capture and enslave them unjustly. After he became aware of the fact, he would not give that advice for the whole world ; and ever since he has believed that it is as unjust to enslave Negroes, as it is to enslave Indians, and for the same reasons. . . .

. . . Of that advice which the Clerigo then gave, he repented not a little, and accused himself of thoughtlessness in later years, because he understood then, how the slavery of Negroes is as unjust as that of the Indians. He understood also how the remedy proposed of importing Negroes to free the Indians was unjust ; and although he then supposed the former to have been justly enslaved, still he is not certain that his ignorance and his good intention will excuse him before the judgement seat of God.

Errors of Colonial Administration etc. Judgement of the Eight official preachers of the Court of Spain :[1]

. . . This is the conclusion which careful study and mature deliberation have led us to. Should we take it for granted that

[1] . . . They were Luis and Antonio Coronel, who had obtained their degrees in theology in the university of Paris ;

the Repartimientos or Encomiendas of Indians are just and right, then we say that your lordships could not have enacted better or holier laws, to prevent their ill-treatment by our countrymen, and to advance their spiritual welfare. But everything considered, it is evident, that they will never afford them that protection which we are bound by the laws of God to give them, and of which they stand in need so long as the Repartimientos are allowed to stand, and this for two principal reasons: 1st, because your laws, let them be ever so good and holy, never will be properly executed as long as the Repartimientos are allowed to have a legal existence; 2nd, because your laws, though good in themselves, are based on a most unjust foundation namely that of the Repartimientos, which have been the cause of wellnigh all the evils with which the Indies are afflicted. As long as that cause is not removed it shall remain impossible to cure the evils. As you see, we have but two propositions to prove, and if we shall prove the second, we shall have proved them both. The greatest of the evils, that have depopulated some of those countries, that will desolate the remaining ones, and that cannot reasonably or with justice be tolerated, are the Encomiendas of the Indians or parcelling them out to the Spaniards, and allowing the latter to force the Indians to work for them, appropriating to themselves all the fruits of the bondsmen's labour. The Encomiendas as they exist now, are detrimental, 1st, to the Indian's welfare; 2nd, they are unreasonable and unwise; 3rd, they are against the interests of the Spanish crown; 4th, they are opposed to all the rules of civil and canon law; 5th they contradict the teachings of moral philosophy and theology; 6th, they are forbidden by the laws of God and of His Church. You shall see, my lords, if, while as damnable an institution as the Encomiendas is allowed to stand, the evils, directly traceable to it, can be eradicated by statutory enactments. That you may not accuse us of exaggeration, we will proceed to prove logically and to your satisfaction each of our six assertions.

We said first that the Encomiendas are detrimental to the Indian's welfare. We cannot argue against facts. Since the time, when, under pretext of bringing into close contact the Indians with the Spaniards, in order that, it was said, the former

---

Doctor La Fuente, who was doing honour to the university of Alcala, newly established by Ximenez. These three were secular priests, like the fourth, whose name is not given. The fifth was Miguel de Salamanca, a Dominican, who died Bishop of Cuba. The sixth was a Franciscan Friar named Alonzo de Leon, and the seventh an Augustinian by the name of Father Dionisio. Las Casas, who wrote these details thirty-two years after, could not remember the name of the last one.

might learn from the latter the Christian religion, the system of Repartimientos was established, those once thickly inhabitated countries became deserts. Should all mankind set to thinking for the purpose of devising a plan more destructive of society among the Indians, they could not find it. For the Encomiendas make a State or Commonwealth impossible amongst them. In every civil community of men there must necessarily be found a diversity of offices, professions and trades. But all these are merged into one by the Repartimientos, that of digging dirt. Who has ever heard of a whole people or nation of diggers? As things are now, there cannot be amongst the Indians either soldiers, philosophers, men of letters, tradesmen, etc., and thus those peoples, fitted out by the Creator to form themselves into well ordered nations, are forced to engage only in the lowest occupation, that of digging dirt. Our islands beyond the Atlantic shall be compared to those on which the Romans exiled the martyrs and the malefactors, *ad fodienda metalla.* Nay, we do worse than the Romans; for they did not kill the exiles with labour, as the Spaniards do the natives of the Indies. The Encomiendas are detrimental to the Indians because they make slaves of them, and to enslave men is against the law of nature and the law of God. That the Encomiendas are nothing less than slavery is proved by your own ordinances. In fact one of them ordered the Licenciado Figuero to set free those amongst the Indians, who should ask for their liberty. They must therefore have been slaves. However, in order that our argument may not have even the semblance of cavil or sophistry, we shall prove *aliunde* that the Encomiendas constitute real slavery. He is free who can dispose of his own actions. But, if the life, the industry, the work and all the fruits thereof of the Indians belong to someone else, how can they be said to be free? Their liberty is but a dead letter, written in your laws, but unknown to the unfortunate bondsmen. If you say, my lords, that they are paid a salary for their labours, and that they are fed, we answer that the salary and the food they get is not equal to half what the legal slaves get here in Spain. The cloak of liberty, with which the Spaniards clothe the Indians, is but an additional instrument of torture and of death. Were they legal slaves, they would have a commercial value, and their masters would care for them and treat them better, as their death would be a loss to them. But granting, for argument's sake, that the Indians are free, is it recorded in the annals of history that any other people were ever treated as the native Indian is by the Spaniard? The slavery to which Pharaoh subjected the children of Israel is but an ounce in the pound compared to the condition of the Indians in the Indies.

The Encomiendas are in every way unwise and unreasonable. All the laws that your lordships may formulate, be they as numerous as those of both the civil and the criminal codes combined, all the provisions that the judges in the Indies may adopt, let both the legislators and the judges be as incorruptible as the angels of God, will not avail to correct the abuses which yearly decimate the Indians. Who shall coerce the Spaniards to keep the laws? In mountain fastness, where only the eye of God and fowls of the air see them, where a justice of the peace, a court or a marshal is not to be found within fifty or sixty leagues, those Christians manage the Indians with an iron hand. Who shall bridle their greed or curb their avarice and prevent them from working the Indians to death? Especially when before them shines the yellow metal, *si dolosi spes refulserit numi?* Your lordships have legislated as to the quality and the quantity of food to be given to the Indians. But who shall weigh the meat before it goes into the pot? Who shall accuse the Spaniard, if the Indian die under the lash or the cudgel? You will say that, the *visitadores* (visitors) will inquire into abuses and punish the delinquent. At the mines there are only the Indians and their masters or their representatives. Will the wretched slave dare to accuse his master to the visitador, if, the latter gone, it will be in his power to roast him alive? We need not go to the Indies for proofs of our assertion. If there be an inquest held in a murder case, do we go to the servants or slaves of the suspected criminal for the evidence of his guilt? You well know, my lords, that the Indian is but a servant or slave of him, of whose Encomienda he is part and parcel. But experience has taught that, should the Indian complain, his testimony would not be accepted, because the visitador looks upon the master as a man or perhaps as a benefactor, and upon the slave as a beast. Unless you place on every Repartimiento an angel, who neither sleeps or eats, you cannot, my lords, correct the cruel abuses by statutory enactments, as long as the Encomiendas are allowed to stand. . . . Let those who advocate and uphold the system of Encomiendas, tremble at the strict account they shall have to give to God, Our Lord, who is no accepter of persons, and who cares not a farthing whether he, who is to be judged, be a great prince, a prelate or a swine-herd. It is time, my lords, for you to act. God and the king, to honour you, and as a testimonial of your past services, have charged you with this delicate and difficult mission of eradicating so many evils and uplifting the yoke from an oppressed people. If you do it, my lords, we shall pray that God may give you honour and prosperity in this life, and an endless reward in the next. Amen.

Appendix B

Francis de Vittoria. *Extracts from the First Relectio, 'De Indis':*

The First Relectio of the Reverend Father, Brother Franciscus de Vittoria, on the Indians lately discovered. The passage to be discussed is from the last chapter of St. Matthew's Gospel: 'Teach all nations, baptizing them in the name of the Father and Son and Holy Spirit':

SUMMARY OF THE FIRST SECTION

1. How a person in doubt on any matter, to obtain safety of conscience, should consult those whose business it is to give instruction in such matters.
2. After one in doubt has taken such advice he ought to follow what the wise have laid down, else he will not be safe.
3. Whether one in doubt ought, consistently with safety of conscience, to follow the advice given by the wise in a doubtful matter when they lay down that to be now lawful which in other circumstances is unlawful.
4. Whether the Indian aborigines before the arrival of the Spaniards were true owners in public and in private law; and whether there were among them any true princes and overlords.
5. Examination of the error of those who assert that persons living in mortal sin cannot have ownership of anything at all.
6. Mortal sin does not preclude civil ownership of the true kind.
7. Whether ownership is lost by reason of unbelief. . . .

The next 11 sections deal with the right of heretics to property.

19. Barbarians are not precluded by the sin of unbelief or by any other mortal sins from being true owners alike in public and in private law.
20. Whether the use of reason is a pre-requisite of capacity for ownership.
21. Whether a boy can be an owner before he has the use of reason.
22. Whether a person of unsound mind can be an owner.
23. Inasmuch as the Indian aborigines were not of unsound mind, they are not precluded from being true owners on the pretext of unsoundness of mind.
24. These aborigines were true owners alike in public and in private law before the advent of the Spaniards among them.

Colonial conquest a moral question :

*. . . When, then, we return to the question before us, namely the matter of the barbarians, we see that it is not in itself so evidently unjust that no question about its justice can arise, nor again so evidently just that no doubt is possible about its injustice, but that it has a look of both according to the standpoint. For, at first sight, when we see that the whole of the business has been carried on by men who are alike well-informed and upright, we may believe that everything has been done properly and justly. But then, when we hear of so many massacres, so many plunderings of otherwise innocent men, so many princes evicted from their possessions and stripped of their rule, there is certainly ground for doubting whether this is rightly or wrongly done.

Competence of the Church in this matter :

. . . Secondly, I assert that it is not for jurists to settle this question or at any rate not for jurists only, for since the barbarians in question, as I shall forthwith show, were not in subjection by human law, it is not by human, but by divine law that questions concerning them are to be determined. Now, jurists are not skilled enough in the divine law to be able by themselves to settle questions of this sort. Nor am I sure that in the discussion and determination of this question theologians have ever been called competent to pronounce on so grave a matter. And as the issue concerns the forum of conscience, its settlement belongs to the priests, that is, to the Church. Accordingly in *Deuteronomy*, Chap. XVII, 18, it is enjoined on the king that he take a copy of the law from the hand of the priest. Thirdly, in order that the whole of the matter be adequately examined and assured, is it not possible that so weighty a business may produce other special doubts deserving of discussion? Accordingly I think I shall be doing something which is not only not futile and useless, but well worth the trouble, if I am enabled to discuss this question in a manner befitting its importance.

Are the native inhabitants true owners ?

. . . I ask first whether the aborigines in question were true owners in both private and public law before the arrival of the Spaniards ; that is, whether they were true owners of private property and possessions and also whether there were among them any who were the true princes and overlords of others. The answer might seem to be No, the reason being that slaves own no property, 'for a slave can have nothing of his own' (*Inst.*, 2, 9. 3 and *Dig.*, 29, 2, 79), and so all his acquisitions

* Quotations are given only from those articles which most closely concern our subject.

belong to his master (*Inst.*, 1, 8, 1). But, it is alleged, the aborigines in question are slaves. . . .

. . . On the opposite side we have the fact that the people in question were in peaceable possession of their goods, both publicly and privately. Therefore, unless the contrary is shown, they must be treated as owners and not be disturbed in their possession unless cause be shown. . . .

Is a state of grace necessary to ownership?

Now, some have maintained that grace is the title to dominion and consequently that sinners, at any rate those in mortal sin, have no dominion over anything. That was the error of the poor folk of Lyons, or Waldenses, and afterwards of John Wycliffe. One error of his, namely, that 'no one is a civil owner, while he is in mortal sin,' was condemned by the Council of Constance. . . .

But against this doctrine I advance the proposition that mortal sin does not hinder civil dominion and true dominion. . . .

Now it remains to consider whether at any rate dominion may be lost by reason of unbelief. . . . My answer is in the following propositions: The first proposition is that unbelief does not prevent anyone from being a true owner. . . . The proposition is also supported by the reasoning of St. Thomas, namely: 'Unbelief does not destroy either natural law or human law; but ownership and dominion are based either on natural or on human law; therefore they are not destroyed by want of faith. In fine this is as obvious an error as the foregoing. Hence it is manifest that it is not justifiable to take anything that they possess from either Saracens or Jews or other unbelievers as such, that is, because they are unbelievers; but the act would be theft or robbery no less than if it were done to Christians.

From all this the conclusion follows that the barbarians in question can not be barred from being true owners, alike in public and in private law, by reason of the sin of unbelief or any other mortal sin, nor does such sin entitle Christians to seize their goods and lands, as Cajetan proves at some length and neatly (*Secunda Secundæ*, Q. lxvi, art. 8).

Are the nations irrational and so incapable of ownership?

It remains to ask whether the Indians lacked ownership because of want of reason or unsoundness of mind. . . . Irrational creatures can not have dominion. This is clear, because dominion is a right, as even Conrad admits. But irrational creatures can not have a right. Therefore they can not have dominion. . . .

There might seem some doubt whether a boy, who has not yet the use of reason, can have dominion, inasmuch as he seems to differ little from irrational animals. And the Apostle says (*Galatians*, iv): 'The heir, as long as he is a child, differeth nothing from a slave'; but a slave has not dominion; therefore, etc. But let our second proposition be: Boys, even before they have the use of reason, can have dominion. This is manifest, because they can suffer wrong; therefore they have rights over things; therefore also they have dominion, which is naught else than a right. Also, the property of wards is not part of the guardian's property; but it has owners, and no others are its owners; therefore the wards are the owners. Also, boys can be heirs; but an heir is one who succeeds to the rights of the deceased and who has dominion over the inheritance (*Dig.*, 44, 3, 11, and *Inst.*, 2, 19, 7).

But what about those suffering from unsoundness of mind? I mean a perpetual unsoundness whereby they neither have nor is there any hope that they will have the use of reason. Let our third proposition be: It seems that they can still have dominion, because they can suffer wrong; therefore they have a right, but whether they can have a civil dominion is a question which I leave to jurists.

The natives not irrational:

However this may be, let our fourth proposition be: The Indian aborigines are not barred on this ground from the exercise of true dominion. This is proved from the fact that the true state of the case is that they are not of unsound mind, but have, according to their kind, the use of reason. This is clear, because there is a certain method in their affairs, for they have polities which are orderly arranged and they have definite marriage and magistrates, overlords, laws, and workshops, and a system of exchange, all of which call for the use of reason; they also have a kind of religion. Further, they make no error in matters which are self-evident to others; this is witness to their use of reason. Also, God and nature are not wanting in the supply of what is necessary in great measure for the race. Now, the most conspicuous feature of man is reason, and power is useless which is not reducible to action. Also, it is through no fault of theirs that these aborigines have for many centuries been outside the pale of salvation, in that they have been born in sin and void of baptism and the use of reason whereby to seek out the things needful for salvation. Accordingly I, for the most part, attribute their seeming so unintelligent and stupid to a bad and barbarous upbringing, for even among ourselves we find many peasants who differ little from brutes.

The natives are true owners:

The upshot of all the preceding is, then, that the aborigines undoubtedly had true dominion in both public and private matters, just like Christians, and that neither their princes nor private persons could be despoiled of their property on the ground of their not being true owners. It would be harsh to deny to those, who have never done any wrong, what we grant to Saracens and Jews, who are the persistent enemies of Christianity. We do not deny that these latter peoples are true owners of their property, if they have not seized lands elsewhere belonging to Christians.

Possible justification of temporary subjection to colonists. The Principle of Tutelage:

It remains to reply to the argument of the opposite side to the effect that the aborigines in question seem to be slaves by nature because of their incapability of self-government. My answer to this is that Aristotle certainly did not mean to say that such as are not over-strong mentally are by nature subject to another's power and incapable of dominion alike over themselves and other things; for this is civil and legal slavery, whereas none are slaves by nature. Nor does the Philosopher mean that, if any by nature are of weak mind, it is permissible to seize their patrimony and enslave them and put them up for sale; but what he means is that by defect of their nature they need to be ruled and governed by others and that it is good for them to be subject to others, just as sons need to be subject to their parents until of full age, and a wife to her husband. And that this is the Philosopher's intent, is clear from his corresponding remark that some are by nature masters, those, namely, who are of strong intelligence. Now, it is clear that he does not mean hereby that such persons can arrogate to themselves a sway over others in virtue of their superior wisdom, but that nature has given them capacity for rule and government. Accordingly, even if we admit that the aborigines in question are as inept and stupid as it is alleged, still dominion cannot be denied them, nor are they to be classed with the slaves of the civil law. True, some right to reduce them to subjection can be based on this reason and title, as we shall show below. Meanwhile the conclusion stands sure, that the aborigines in question were true owners, before the Spaniards came among them, both from the public and the private point of view.

SUMMARY OF THE SECOND SECTION

On the illegitimate titles for the reduction of the aborigines of the New World into the power of the Spaniards:

1. The Emperor is not the lord of the whole world.
2. Even if the Emperor were the lord of the world, that would not entitle him to seize the provinces of the Indian aborigines

and to erect new lords and put down the former lords or levy taxes.

3. The Pope is not civil or temporal lord of the whole world, in the proper sense of civil lordship and power.
4. Even if the Supreme Pontiff had secular power over the whole world, he could not give that power to secular princes.
5. The Pope has temporal power, but only so far as it subserves things spiritual.
6. The Pope has no temporal power over the Indian aborigines or over other unbelievers.
7. A refusal by these aborigines to recognize any dominion of the Pope is no reason for making war on them and for seizing their goods.
8. Whether these aborigines were guilty of the sin of unbelief, in that they did not believe in Christ, before they heard anything of Christianity.
9. What is required in order that ignorance may be imputed to a person as, and be sin, that is, vincible ignorance. And what about invincible ignorance?
10. Whether the aborigines are bound to hearken to the first messengers of Christianity so as to commit mortal sin in not believing Christ's Gospel merely on its simple announcement to them.
11. If the faith were simply announced and proposed to them, and they will not straightway receive it, this is no ground for the Spaniards to make war on them or to proceed against them under the law of war.
12. How the aborigines, if they refuse when asked and counselled to hear peaceably preachers of religion, cannot be excused from mortal sin.
13. When the aborigines would be bound to receive Christianity under penalty of mortal sin.
14. In the author's view it is not sufficiently clear whether Christianity has been so proposed and announced to these aborigines that they are bound to believe it under the penalty of fresh sin.
15. Even when Christianity has been proposed to them with never so much sufficiency of proof and they will not accept it, this does not render it lawful to make war on them and despoil them of their possessions.
16. Christian princes can not, even on the authority of the Pope, restrain these aborigines from sins against the law of nature or punish them therefor.

Origins of Sovereignty:

St. Thomas well says (*Prima Pars.*, Q. xcii, art. 1, on obj, 2, and Q. xxiv, art. 4) that by natural law mankind is free save from paternal and marital dominion—for the father has dominion over his children and the husband over the wife by natural law; therefore no one by natural law has dominion over the world. And, as St. Thomas also says (*Secunda Secundæ*, Q. x, art. 10) dominion and pre-eminence were introduced by human law; they, therefore, were not by natural law. Nor would there be any greater reason why this dominion should be more proper for Germans than for Gauls. And Aristotle (*Politics*, Bk. I) says, Power is of two kinds, the one originates in the family, like that of the father over his sons and that of the husband over the wife, and this is a natural power; the other is civil, for, although it may take its rise in nature and so may be said to be of natural law, as St. Thomas says (*De regimine principum*, Bk. I, Ch. II), yet man being a political animal, is founded not on nature, but on law. . . .

. . . This will be plain to any one who considers the titles and modes of succession whereby sovereignty and lordship in the world have come down to our own day. For, to omit everything that happened before the flood, the world was certainly divided after Noah into different provinces and kingdoms, whether this were by ordinance of Noah himself—for he survived the flood three hundred and fifty years (*Genesis* ix), and sent colonies into different regions, as appears in Berosus of Babylon—or whether, as is more likely, different family groups by the common agreement of mankind occupied different provinces as (*Genesis* xiii): 'Abram said unto Lot: ". . . Is not the whole land before thee? . . . If thou wilt take the left hand, then I will go to the right, or if thou depart to the right hand, then I will go to the left."' We are, accordingly, told (*Genesis* x) that through the descendants of Noah came diversities of peoples and countries, whether in some regions they first assumed lordship by usurpation, as Nimrod seems to have done, of whom *Genesis* x: 8, says that he was the first to be a mighty one in the earth, or whether by accord of several to unite in one State they appointed a prince over themselves by common agreement. For it is sure that either in these or in other like modes sovereignty and lordship began in the world and that afterwards, either by right of inheritance or of war or by some other such title, they were continued unto our own day.

No Papal Jurisdiction over non-Christians:

. . . The Pope has no temporal power over the Indian aborigines or over other unbelievers. This is clear from propositions I and III. For he has no temporal power save such as subserves spiritual matters. But he has no spiritual power over them (I *Corinthians* v: 12). Therefore he has no temporal power either.

The corollary follows that even if the barbarians refuse to

recognize any lordship of the Pope, that furnishes no ground for making war on them and seizing their property. This is clear, because he has no such lordship. And it receives conformation from the fact (as will be asserted below and as our opponents admit) that, even if the barbarians refuse to accept Christ as their Lord, this does not justify making war on them or doing them any hurt. Now, it is utterly absurd for our opponents to say that, while the barbarians go scatheless for rejecting Christ, they should be bound to accept His vicar under penalty of war and confiscation of their property, aye, and penal chastisements.

Failure to recognize Papal authority no just cause of war :

Of a truth, Saracens dwelling among Christians have never been deprived of their property on any such pretext or made to suffer any harm. Why, if this pretext be enough to justify making war on them, it is as much as to say that they can be deprived by reason of their unbelief. For it is certain that none of the unbelievers recognize this lordship. But there is no doctor even among our opponents who would allow that they can be deprived on the mere ground of unbelief. Therefore the allegation of the doctors in question is utterly sophistical, namely, that if the unbelievers recognize the lordship of the Roman Pontiff, war can not be made on them, but that it may if they do not recognize it ; for none of them does recognize it.

This shows that the title under discussion can not be set up against the barbarians and that Christians have no just cause of war against them either on the ground that the Pope has made a gift of their lands on the footing of absolute lord or that they do not recognize the lordship of the Pope. . . .

The Right of Discovery applies only to uninhabited land :

Accordingly, there is another title which can be set up, namely, by right of discovery ; and no other title was originally set up, and it was in virtue of this title alone that Columbus the Genoan first set sail. And this seems to be an adequate title because those regions which are deserted become, by the law of nations, and the natural law, the property of the first occupant (*Inst.*, 2, 1, 12). Therefore, as the Spaniards were the first to discover and occupy the provinces in question, they are in lawful possession thereof, just as if they had discovered some lonely and thitherto uninhabited region.

Not much, however, need be said about this third title of ours, because, as proved above, the barbarians were true owners, both from the public and from the private standpoint. Now the rule of the law of nations is that what belongs to nobody is granted to the first occupant, as is expressly laid down in the aforementioned passage of the *Institutes*. And so, as the object in question was not without an owner, it does not fall under the title which we are discussing. Although, then, this title, when conjoined with another, can produce some effect here (as will be said below), yet in and by itself it gives no support to a seizure of the aborigines any more than if it had been they who had discovered us.

Compulsory Conversion Impossible :

The Indians in question are not bound, directly the Christian faith is announced to them, to believe it, in such a way that they commit mortal sin by not believing it, merely because it has been declared and announced to them that Christianity is the true religion and that Christ is the Saviour and Redeemer of the world, without miracle or any other proof or persuasion. This propostion is proved by the first : For if before hearing anything of the Christian religion they were excused, they are put under no fresh obligation by a simple declaration and announcement of this kind, for such announcement is no proof or incentive to belief. Nay, as Cajetan says (on *Secunda Secundæ*, Q. i, art. 4), it would be rash and imprudent for anyone to believe anything, especially in matters which concern salvation, unless he knows that this is asserted by a man worthy of credence, a thing which the aboriginal Indians do not know, seeing that they do not know who or what manner of men they are who are announcing the new religion to them. And this is confirmed by what St. Thomas says (*Secunda Secundæ*, Q. i, art. 4, on obj. 2, and art. 5, on obj. 1), namely, that matters of faith are seen and become evident by reason of their credibility. For a believer would not believe unless he saw that the things were worthy of belief either because of the evidence of signs or for some other reason of this kind. Therefore, where there are no such signs nor anything else of persuasive force, the aborigines are not bound to believe. And this is confirmed by the consideration that if the Saracens were at the same time to set their creed before them in the same way and without anything more, like the Christians, they would not be bound to believe them, as is certain. Therefore they are not bound to believe the Christians either, when without any moving or persuasive accompaniments they set the faith before them, for they are unable, and are not bound, to guess which of the two is the truer religion unless a greater weight of probability be apparent on one side. . . .

Refusal to accept Christianity not a just cause of war :

From this proposition it follows that, if the faith be presented to the Indians in the way named only and they do not receive it, the Spaniards can not make this a reason for waging war on them or for proceeding against them under the law of war.

This is manifest, because they are innocent in this respect and have done no wrong to the Spaniards. And this corollary receives confirmation from the fact that, as St. Thomas lays down (*Secunda Secundæ*, Q. xl, art. 1), for a just war 'there must be a just cause, namely, they who are attacked for some fault must deserve the attack.' Accordingly, St. Augustine says (*liber* 83 *Quæstionum*) : 'It is involved in the definition of a just war that some wrong is being avenged, as where a people or state is to be punished for neglect to exact amends from its citizens for their wrong-doing or to restore what has been wrongfully taken away.' Where, then, no wrong has previously been committed by the Indians, there is no cause of just war. This is the received opinion of all the doctors, not only of the theologians, but also of the jurists, such as Hostiensis, Innocent and others. . . .

Although the Christian faith may have been announced to the Indians with adequate demonstration and they have refused to receive it, yet this is not a reason which justifies making war on them and depriving them of their property. This conclusion is definitely stated by St. Thomas (*Secunda Secundæ*, Q. x, art. 8), where he says that unbelievers who have never received the faith, like Gentiles and Jews, are in no wise to be compelled to do so. This is the received conclusion of the doctors alike in the canon law and the civil law. The proof lies in the fact that belief is an operation of the will. Now, fear detracts greatly from the voluntary (*Ethics*, Bk. III), and it is a sacrilege to approach under the influence of servile fear as far as the mysteries and sacraments of Christ. Our conclusion is also proved by the canon *de Judæis* (can. 5, Dist. 45), which says : 'The holy synod also enjoins concerning the Jews that thenceforth force be not applied to any of them to make them believe ; "for God has compassion on whom He wills, and whom He wills He hardens"' (*Romans* ix : 18). . . .

Our proposition receives further proof from the use and custom of the Church. For never have Christian Emperors, who had as advisors the most holy and wise Pontiffs, made war on unbelievers for their refusal to accept the Christian religion. Further, war is no argument for the truth of the Christian faith. Therefore the Indians cannot be induced by war to believe, but rather to feign belief and reception of the Christian faith, which is monstrous and a sacrilege. . . .

Alleged Sins of the Natives against natural law no justification for conquest :

Another, and a fifth, title, is seriously put forward, namely, the sins of these Indian aborigines. For it is alleged that, though their unbelief or their rejection of the Christian faith is not a good reason for making war on them, yet they may be attacked for other mortal sins which (so it is said) they have in numbers, and those very heinous. A distinction is here drawn with regard to mortal sins, it being asserted that there are some sins, which are not against the law of nature, but only against positive divine law, and for these the aborigines cannot be attacked in war, while there are other sins against nature, such as cannibalism, and promiscuous intercourse with mother or sisters and with males, and for these they can be attacked in war and so compelled to desist therefrom. . . .

I, however, assert the following proposition: Christian princes can not, even by the authorization of the Pope, restrain the Indians from sins against the law of nature or punish them because of those sins. . . . So also it is not every sin against the law of nature that can be clearly shown to be such, at any rate to every one. Further this is as much as to say that the aborigines may be warred into subjection because of their unbelief, for they are all idolators. Further, the Pope can not make war on Christians on the ground of their being fornicators or thieves or, indeed, because they are sodomites; nor can he on that ground confiscate their land and give it to other princes; were that so, there would be daily changes of kingdoms, seeing that there are many sinners in every realm. And this is confirmed by the consideration that these sins are more heinous in Christians, who are aware that they are sins, than in barbarians, who have not that knowledge.

The question of annexation by consent of the inhabitants:

There remains another, a sixth title, which is put forward, namely, by voluntary choice. For on the arrival of the Spaniards we find them declaring to the aborigines how the King of Spain has sent them for their good and admonishing them to receive and accept him as lord and king; and the aborigines replied that they were content to do so. Now, 'there is nothing so natural as that the intent of an owner to transfer his property to another should have effect given to it.' (*Inst.*, 2, 1, 40.) I, however, assert the proposition that this title, too, is insufficient. This appears, in the first place, because fear and ignorance, which vitiate every choice, ought to be absent. But they were markedly operative in the cases of choice and acceptance under consideration, for the Indians did not know what they were doing; nay, they may not have understood what the Spaniards were seeking. Further, we find the Spaniards seeking it in armed array from an unwarlike and timid crowd. Further, inasmuch as the aborigines, as said above, had real lords and princes, the populace could not procure new lords without other reasonable cause, this being to the hurt of their former lords. Further, on the other hand, these lords themselves could not appoint a new prince without the assent of the populace. Seeing, then, that in such cases of choice and acceptance as these there are not present all the requisite elements of a valid choice, the title under review is utterly inadequate and unlawful for seizing and retaining the provinces in question.

SUMMARY OF THE THIRD SECTION

On the lawful titles whereby the aborigines of America could have come into the power of Spain :

1. How the aborigines might have come into the power of the Spaniards on the ground of natural society and fellowship.
2. The Spaniards have a right to travel to the lands of the Indians and to sojourn there so long as they do no harm, and they cannot be prevented by the Indians.
3. The Spaniards may carry on trade among the Indian aborigines, so long as they do no harm to their own country, by importing the goods which the aborigines lack, etc., and taking away gold and silver and other articles in which the Indians abound ; and the princes of the Indians can not prevent their subjects from trading with the Spaniards, etc.
4. The Indians can not prevent the Spaniards from a communication and participation in those things which they treat as common alike to natives and to strangers.
5. Any children born of Spanish parents domiciled in those parts who wish to become citizens thereof can not be excluded from citizenship or from the advantages enjoyed by other citizens.
6. What course ought to be adopted if the aborigines desire to prevent the Spaniards trading with them, etc.
7. If the Spaniards, after resort to all moderate measures, can not attain security among the aborigines or Indians, save by seizing their cities and reducing them to subjection, whether they can lawfully do this.
8. When and in what case the Spaniards can resort to severe measures against the Indians, treating them as faithless foes, and employ all the rights of war against them and take away their property and even reduce them to captivity, aye, and depose their former lords also and set up new lords.
9. Whether the Indians could have come under the sway of the Spaniards, in the interest of the spread of Christianity. Christians have a right to preach and publish the Gospel in the lands of barbarians.

10. The Pope could entrust to the Spaniards alone the task of converting the Indian aborigines and could forbid to all others not only preaching, but trade too, if the propagation of Christianity would thus be furthered.
11. The Indians are not to be warred into subjection or despoiled of their property, if they give the Spaniards unhindered freedom to preach the Gospel, and this whether they accept the faith or not.
12. How the aborigines who hinder the spread of the Gospel, whether it be their lords or the populace, may be coerced by the Spaniards, so long as no scandal is caused. And what is to be said of those who, while admitting preaching, prevent conversion, either by killing or punishing or, terrorizing those who have been converted to Christianity?
13. How the Indians might have come under the sway of the Spaniards by the fact that, when they had been converted and become Christians, their princes desired to bring them back to idolatry by force or by fear, and so they were taken into the protection and guardianship of the Spaniards.
14. The Indians might have come under the sway of the Spaniards by the fact that, after the conversion of a large part of them to Christianity, the Pope, either with or without a request on their part, might on reasonable grounds have given them a Christian prince, such as the King of Spain, and driven out their infidel lords.
15. Whether the Indians could have come under the sway of the Spaniards because of the tyranny of their lords or because of tyrannical laws which injured innocent folk.
16. The Indian aborigines could have come under the sway of the Spaniards through true and voluntary choice.
17. The Indians might have come under the sway of the Spaniards by a title of alliance and friendship.
18. Whether the Spaniards could have reduced the Indians into their power, if it were certainly clear that they were of defective intelligence.

I will now speak of the lawful and adequate titles whereby the Indians might have come under the sway of the Spaniards.

Natural Society and Fellowship:

The first title to be named is that of natural society and fellowship. And hereon let my first conclusion be: The Spaniards have a right to travel into the lands in question and sojourn there, provided they do no harm to the natives, and the natives may not prevent them. Proof of this may in the first place be derived from the law of nations (*jus gentium*) which either is natural law or is derived from natural law (*Inst.*, 1, 2, 1): What natural reason has established among all nations is called the *jus gentium.*' For, in accordance with this, it is reckoned among all nations inhumane to treat visitors and foreigners badly without some special cause, while, on the other hand, it is humane and correct to treat visitors well; but the case would be different, if the foreigners were to misbehave when visiting other nations.

Freedom of Movement:

Secondly, it was permissible from the beginning of the world (when everything was in common) for any one to set forth and travel wheresoever he would. Now this was not taken away by the division of property, for it was never the intention of peoples to destroy by that division the reciprocity and common uses which prevailed among men, and indeed in the days of Noah it would have been inhumane to do so.

Thirdly, everything is lawful which is not prohibited or which is not injurious or hurtful to others in some other way. But (so we suppose) the travel of the Spaniards does no injury or harm to the natives. Therefore it is lawful.

Fourthly, it would not be lawful for the French to prevent the Spanish from travelling or even from living in France, or vice versa, provided this in no way tended to their hurt and the visitors did no injury. Therefore it is not lawful for the Indians.

Expulsion of innocent foreigners unlawful:

Further, fifthly, banishment is one of the capital forms of punishment. Therefore it is unlawful to banish strangers who have committed no fault.

Further, sixthly, to keep certain people out of the city or province as being enemies, or to expel them when already there, are acts of war. Inasmuch, then, as the Indians are not making a just war on the Spaniards (it being assumed that the Spaniards are doing no harm), it is not lawful for them to keep the Spaniards away from their territory.

Further, seventhly, there is the Poet's verse:

> '*Quod genus hoc hominum? quæve hunc tam barbara morem*
> *Permittit patria? hospitio prohibemur arenæ.*'

(What race of men is this? or what country is barbarous enough to allow this usage? We are driven off from the hospitality of its shore.)

Sociability:

Also, eighthly: 'Every animal loveth its kind' (*Ecclesiasticus* xv). Therefore, it appears that friendship among men exists by natural law and it is against nature to shun the society of harmless folk.

Also, ninthly, there is the passage (*St. Matthew* xxv) : 'I was a stranger and ye took me not in.' Hence, as the reception of strangers seems to be by natural law, that judgement of Christ will be pronounced with universal application.

Common ownership of waters :

Tenthly, 'by natural law running water and the sea are common to all, so are rivers and harbours, and by the law of nations ships from all parts may be moored there' (*Inst.*, 2, 1) ; and on the same principle they are public things. Therefore it is not lawful to keep any one from them. Hence it follows that the aborigines would be doing a wrong to the Spaniards, if they were to keep them from their territories.

Also, eleventhly, these very persons admit all other barbarians from all parts. Therefore, they would be doing a wrong, if they were not to admit the Spaniards.

Also, twelfthly, if it were not lawful for the Spaniards to travel among them, this would be either by natural law or by divine law or by human law. Now, it is certainly lawful by natural and by divine law. And if there were any human law which without any cause took away rights conferred by natural and divine law, it would be inhumane and unreasonable and consequently would not have the force of law.

Thirteenthly, either the Spaniards are subjects of the Indians or they are not. If they are not, then the Indians can not keep them away. If they are, then the Indians ought to treat them well.

Every man our neighbour :

Also, fourteenthly, the Spaniards are the neighbours of the barbarians, as appears from the Gospel parable of the Samaritan (*St. Luke* x). But they are bound to love their neighbours as themselves (*St. Matthew* xxii). Therefore they may not keep them from their country without cause : 'When it is said "Love thy neighbour" it is clear that every man is our neighbour' (St. Augustine's *De doctrina Christiana*).

Second proposition : The Spaniards may lawfully carry on trade among the native Indians so long as they do no harm to their country, as, for instance, by importing thither wares which the natives lack and by exporting thence either gold or silver or other wares of which the natives have abundance. Neither may the native princes hinder their subjects from carrying on trade with the Spanish ; nor, on the other hand, may the princes of Spain prevent commerce with the natives. This is proved by means of my first proposition.

Firstly, because it is an apparent rule of the *jus gentium* that foreigners may carry on trade, provided they do no hurt to citizens.

Also, secondly, a similar proof lies in the fact that this is permitted by the divine law. Therefore a law prohibiting it would undoubtedly not be reasonable.

Also, thirdly, the sovereign of the Indians is bound by the law of nature to love the Spaniards. Therefore the Indians may not causelessly prevent the Spaniards from making their profit where this can be done without injury to themselves.

A fourth reason is that such conduct would be against the proverb : 'Thou shall not do to another what thou wouldest not wish done to thyself.'

Free Trade :

And, in sum, it is certain that the aborigines can no more keep off the Spaniards from trade than Christians can keep off other Christians. Now, it is clear that if the Spaniards kept off the French from trade with the Spaniards, and this not for the good of Spain, but in order to prevent the French from sharing in some advantage, that practice would offend against righteousness and charity. If, then, there can be no just legal ordinance to this effect, it also can not be accomplished in actual fact (for the injustice of a law consists solely in the execution of the law). And, as is said in *Dig.*, 1, 1, 3 : 'Nature has established a bond of relationship between all men,' and so it is contrary to natural law for one man to dissociate himself from another without good reason. 'Man,' says Ovid, 'is not a wolf to his fellow-man, but a man.'

Third proposition : If there are among the Indians any things which are treated as common both to citizens and to strangers, the Indians may not prevent the Spaniards from a communication and participation in them. If, for example, other foreigners are allowed to dig for gold in the land of the community or in rivers, or to fish for pearls in the sea or in a river, the natives cannot prevent the Spaniards from doing this, but they have the same right to do it as others have, so long as the citizens and indigenous population are not hurt thereby. This is proved by my first and second propositions. For if the Spaniards may travel and trade among them, they may consequently make use of the laws and advantages enjoyed by all foreigners.

Natural resources are common property :

Secondly, inasmuch as things that belong to nobody are acquired by the first occupant according to the law of nations (*Inst.*, 2, 1, 12), it follows that if there be in the earth gold or in the sea pearls or in a river anything else which is not appropriated by the law of nations, those will vest in the first occupant, just as the fish in the sea do. And, indeed, there are many things in this connection which issue from the law of nations, which, because it has sufficient derivation from natural law, is clearly capable of conferring rights and creating obligations. And even if we grant that it is not always derived from natural law, yet there exists clearly enough a consensus of the greater part of the whole world, especially in behalf of the common good of all. For if after the early days of the creation of the world or its recovery from the flood the majority of mankind decided that ambassadors should everywhere be reckoned inviolable and that the sea should be common and that prisoners of war should be made slaves, and if this, namely, that strangers should not be driven out, were deemed a desirable principle, it would certainly have the force of law, even though the rest of mankind objected thereto.

Statelessness unnatural :

Fourth proposition : If children of any Spaniard be born there and they wish to acquire citizenship, it seems they cannot be barred either from citizenship or from the advantages enjoyed by other citizens—I refer to the case where the parents had their domicile there. The proof of this is furnished by the rule of the law of nations, that he is to be called and is a citizen who is born within the State (*Cod.*, 7, 62, 11). And the confirmation lies in the fact that, as man is a civil animal, whoever is born in any one State is not a citizen of another State. Therefore, if he were not a citizen of the State referred to, he would not be citizen of any State, to the prejudice of his rights under both natural law and the law of nations. Aye, and if there be any persons who wish to acquire a domicile in some State of the Indians, as by marriage or in virtue of any other fact whereby other foreigners are wont to become citizens, they cannot be impeded any more than others, and consequently they enjoy the privileges of citizens just as others do, provided they also submit to the burdens to which others submit. And the passages wherein hospitality is commended are to the same effect (1 *St. Peter* iv) : 'Use hospitality one to another,' and (1 *Timothy* iii, about a bishop) : 'A bishop must be given to hospitality.' Hence on the other hand, refusal to receive strangers and foreigners is wrong in itself.

Denial of Natural rights a possible cause of just war :

Fifth proposition : If the Indian natives wish to prevent the Spaniards from enjoying any of their above-named rights under the law of nations, for instance, trade or other above-named matters, the Spaniards ought in the first place to use reason and persuasion in order to remove scandal and ought to show in all possible methods that they do not come to the hurt of the natives, but wish to sojourn as peaceful guests and to travel without doing the natives any harm; and they ought to show this not only by word, but also by reason, according to the saying: 'It behoveth the prudent to make trial of everything by words first.' But if, after this recourse to reason, the barbarians decline to agree and propose to use force, the Spaniards can defend themselves and do all that consists with their own safety, it being lawful to repel force by force. And not only so, but if safety cannot otherwise be had, they may build fortresses and defensive works, and, if they have sustained a wrong, they may follow it up with war on the authorization of their sovereign and may avail themselves of the other rights of war. The proof hereof lies in the fact that warding-off and avenging a wrong make a good cause of war, as said above, following St. Thomas (*Secunda Secundæ*, Q. xl). But when the Indians deny the Spaniards their rights under the law of nations they do them a wrong. Therefore, if it be necessary, in order to preserve their right, that they should go to war, they may lawfully do so.

It is, however, to be noted that the natives being timid by nature and in other respects dull and stupid, however much the Spaniards may desire to remove their fears and reassure them with regard to peaceful dealings with each other, they may very excusably continue afraid at the sight of men strange in garb and armed, and much more powerful than themselves. And therefore, if, under the influence of these fears, they unite their efforts to drive out the Spaniards or even to slay them, the Spaniards might, indeed, defend themselves but within the limits of permissible self-protection, and it would not be right for them to enforce against the natives any of the other rights of war (as, for instance, after winning the victory and obtaining safety, to slay them, or despoil them of their goods or seize their cities) because on our hypothesis the natives are innocent and are justified in feeling afraid. Accordingly, the Spaniards ought to defend themselves, but so far as possible with the least damage to the natives, the war being a purely defensive one.

There is no inconsistency, indeed, in holding the war to be a just war on both sides, seeing that on one side there is right and on the other side there is invincible ignorance. For instance, just as the French hold the province of Burgundy with demonstrable ignorance, in the belief that it belongs to them, while our Emperor's right to it is certain, and he may make war to regain it, just as the French may defend it, so it may also befall in the case of the Indians—a point deserving careful attention. For the rights of war which may be invoked against men who are really guilty and lawless, differ from those which may be invoked against the innocent and ignorant, just as the scandal of the Pharisees is to be avoided in a different way from that of the self-distrustful and weak.

Sixth proposition : If after recourse to all other measures, the Spaniards are unable to obtain safety as regards the native Indians, save by seizing their cities and reducing them to subjection, they may lawfully proceed to these extremities. The proof lies in the fact that 'peace and safety are the end and aim of war,' as St. Augustine says, writing to Boniface. And since it is now lawful for the Spaniards, as has been said, to wage defensive war or even if necessary offensive war, therefore, everything necessary to secure the end and aim of war, namely, the obtaining of safety and peace, is lawful.

Self-defence of Colonists :

Seventh proposition : If, after the Spaniards have used all diligence, both in deed and in word, to show that nothing will come from them to interfere with the peace and well-being of the aborigines, the latter nevertheless persist in their hostility and do their best to destroy the Spaniards, then they can make war on the Indians, no longer as on innocent folk, but as against forsworn enemies, and may enforce against them all the rights of war, despoiling them of their goods, reducing them to captivity, deposing their former lords and setting up new ones, yet withal with observance of proportion as regards the nature of the circumstances and of the wrongs done to them. This conclusion is sufficiently apparent from the fact that, if it be lawful to declare war, it is consequently lawful to pursue the rights of war. And it is confirmed by the consideration that the aborigines ought not to hold a better position merely because they are unbelievers. But all the things enumerated would be lawful against Christians, when once a just war has arisen. Therefore they are lawful against the aborigines, too. Also, it is a universal rule of the law of nations that whatever is captured in war becomes the property of the conqueror, as is laid down in *Dig.*, 49, 15, 28 and 24, and in *Decretum*, Pt. 1, *Dist.*, 1, can. 9, and more expressly in *Inst.*, 2, 1, 17, where it is said that 'by the law of nations whatever we take from the enemy becomes ours at once, to such an extent that even men may be brought into slavery to us.' Further (as the doctors say on the topic of war) a prince who has on hand a just war is *ipso jure* the judge of his enemies and can inflict a legal punishment on them, condemning them according to the scale of their wrong-doing. Everything said above receives confirmation from the fact that ambassadors are by the law of nations inviolable and the Spaniards are the ambassadors of the Christian peoples. Therefore, the native Indians are bound to give them, at least, a friendly hearing and not to repel them. This, then, is the first title which the Spaniards might have for seizing the provinces, and sovereignty of the natives, provided the seizure be without guile or fraud and they do not look for imaginary causes of war. For if the natives allow the

Spaniards to traffic peaceably among them, the Spaniards could not allege in this connection any just cause for seizing their goods any more than the goods of Christians.

Protection of Missionaries :

Another possible title is by way of propagation of Christianity. In this connection let my first proposition be : Christians have a right to preach and declare the Gospel in barbarian lands. This proposition is manifest from the passage : 'Preach the Gospel to every creature,' etc. (*St. Mark* xvi, 15) : and also : 'The word of the Lord is not bound' (2 *Timothy* ii.). . . .

Second proposition : Although this is a task common and permitted to all, yet the Pope might entrust it to the Spaniards and forbid it to all others. The proof is in the fact that, although (as said above) the Pope is not temporal lord, yet he has power in matters temporal when this would subserve matters spiritual. Therefore, as it is the Pope's concern to bestow especial care on the propagation of the Gospel over the whole world, he can entrust it to the Spaniards to the exclusion of all others, if the sovereigns of Spain could render more effective help in the spread of the Gospel in those parts ; and not only could the Pope forbid others to preach, but also to trade there, if this would further the propagation of Christianity, for he can order temporal matters in the manner which is most helpful to spiritual matters. And if in this case that is how spiritual matters would be best helped, it consequently falls within the authority and power of the Supreme Pontiff. But it seems that in this case this is the course most conducive to spiritual welfare, because, if there was to be an indiscriminate inrush of Christians from other parts to the part in question, they might easily hinder one another and develop quarrels, to the banishment of tranquillity and the disturbance of the concerns of the faith and of the conversion of the natives. Further, inasmuch as it was the sovereigns of Spain who were the first to patronize and pay for the navigation of the intermediate ocean, and as they then had the good fortune to discover the New World, it is just that this travel should be forbidden to others and that the Spaniards should enjoy alone the fruits of their discovery. For, just as in the interests of the preservation of the peace among princes and of the spread of religion the Pope could make such a distribution of the land of the Saracens among Christian princes as would prevent one from crossing over the lands of another, so also for the good of religion he could appoint princes, especially where there were aforetime no Christian princes.

Third proposition : If the Indians allow the Spaniards freely and without hindrance to preach the Gospel, then whether they do or do not receive the faith, this furnishes no lawful grounds for making war on them and seizing in any other way their lands. This has been proved above[1] where we confuted the fourth alleged title, and it is self-evident, seeing that there can not be a just war where no wrong has previously been done (*Secunda Secundæ*, Q. xl, art. 1).

Fourth proposition : If the Indians—whether it be their lords or the populace—prevent the Spaniards from freely preaching the Gospel, the Spaniards, after first reasoning with them in order to remove scandal, may preach it despite their unwillingness and devote themselves to the conversion of the people in question, and if need be they may then accept or even make war, until they succeed in obtaining facilities and safety for preaching the Gospel. And the same pronouncement must be made in the case where they allow preaching, but hinder conversion either by killing or otherwise punishing those who have been converted to Christ, or by deterring others by threats and fears. This is clear, because herein the Indians would be doing an injury to the Spaniards (as appears from what has already been said) and these would have a just cause of war. A second reason is that an obstacle would thereby be put in the way of the welfare of the Indians themselves such as their princes have no right to put there. Therefore, in favour of those who are oppressed and suffer wrong, the Spaniards can make war, especially as such vitally important interests are at stake. This proposition demonstrates that, if there is no other way to carry on the work of religion, this furnishes the Spaniards with another justification for seizing the lands and territory of the natives and for setting up new lords there and putting down the old lords and doing in right of war everything which is permitted in other just wars, but always with a regard for moderation and proportion, so as to go no further than necessity demands, preferring to abstain from what they lawfully might do rather than transgress due limits, and with an intent directed more to the welfare of the aborigines than to their own gain.

Moderation even in war :

Careful attention must, however, be paid to what St. Paul says (1 *Corinthians* vi) : 'All things are lawful to me, but not all things are expedient.' So everything said above must be taken as spoken absolutely. For it may be that these wars and massacres and spoliations will hinder rather than procure and further the conversion of the Indians. Accordingly, the prime consideration is that no obstacle shall be placed in the way of the Gospel, and if any such be so placed, this method of evangelization must be abandoned and another one sought for. What we have been showing is what is lawful in itself. I personally have no doubt that the Spaniards were bound to employ

[1] (In the immediately preceding section.)

force and arms in order to continue their work there, but I fear measures were adopted in excess of what is allowed by human and divine law. The title under consideration might, then, be a second lawful title whereby the Indians might fall into the power of Spain. But regard must ever be had to what has just been said lest what in itself is lawful be made in the circumstances wrong, for goodness springs from the one complete[1] cause, but badness from individual defects, according to Aristotle (*Ethics*, Bk. III) and Dionysius (*De divinis nominibus*, Chap. IV).

Another title there may be, which is derived from the foregoing, namely: If any of the native converts to Christianity be subjected to force or fear by their princes in order to make them return to idolatry, this would justify the Spaniards, should other methods fail, in making war and in compelling the barbarians by force to stop such misconduct, and in employing the rights of war against such as continue obstinate, and consequently at times in deposing rulers as in other just wars. This can be reckoned a third just title, a title based not only on religion but on human friendship and alliance, inasmuch as the native converts to Christianity have become friends and allies of Christians and we are under an obligation to do 'good unto all men, especially unto such as are of the household of faith' (*Galatians* vi).

Another possible title is the following: Suppose a large part of the Indians were converted to Christianity, and this whether it were done lawfully or unlawfully (as by means of threats or fear or other improper procedure), so long as they really were Christians, the Pope might for a reasonable cause, either with or without a request from them, give them a Christian sovereign and depose their other unbelieving rulers. . . .

Charitable intervention:

Another possible title is founded either on the tyranny of those who bear rule among the aborigines of America or on the tyrannical laws which work wrong to innocent folk there, such as that which allows the sacrifice of innocent people or the killing in other ways of uncondemned people for cannibalistic purposes. I assert also that without the Pope's authority the Spaniards can stop all such nefarious usage and ritual among the aborigines, being entitled to rescue innocent people from an unjust death. This is proved by the fact that 'God has laid a charge on every

[1] The reference to Aristotle cannot be traced with certainty; but the text follows Dionysius closely. He wrote, literally translated: 'The good is from the one and complete (μιά και ὑλη) cause, but the bad from many and partial defects' (trans.).

individual concerning his neighbour' (*Ecclesiasticus* xvii: 12) and they are all our neighbours. Therefore, anyone may defend them from such tyrannical and oppressive acts, and it is especially the business of princes to do so. A further proof is given by *Proverbs* xxiv: 'Deliver them that are drawn unto death, and forbear not to free those that are being dragged to destruction.' This passage is not to be taken as applying only when victims are actually being dragged to death, but the natives can also be compelled to abstain from such ritual. And if they refuse, it is a good ground for making war on them and proceeding against them under the law of war, and if such sacrilegious rites cannot otherwise be stopped, for changing their rulers and creating a new sovereignty over them. . . .

Voluntary invitation to rule:

Another possible title is by true and voluntary choice, as if the Indians, aware alike to the prudent administration and the humanity of the Spaniards, were of their own motion, both rulers and ruled, to accept the King of Spain as their sovereign. This could be done and would be a lawful title, by the natural law too, seeing that a State can appoint anyone it will to be its lord, and therefore the consent of all is not necessary, but the consent of the majority suffices. For, as I have argued elsewhere, in matters touching the good of the State the decisions of the majority bind even when the rest are of a contrary mind; otherwise nought could be done for the welfare of the State, it being difficult to get all the same way of thinking. Accordingly, if the majority of any city or province were Christians and they, in the interests of the faith and for the common weal, would have a prince who was a Christian, I think that they could elect him even against the wishes of the others, and even if it meant the repudiation of other unbelieving rulers, and I assert that they could choose a prince not only for themselves, but for the whole State, just as the Franks for the good of their State changed their sovereigns and, deposing Childeric, put Pepin, the father of Charlemagne, in his place, a change which was approved by Pope Zacharias. This, then, can be put forward as a sixth title.

Another title may be found in the cause of allies and friends. For as the Indians themselves sometimes wage lawful wars with one another and the side which has suffered a wrong has the right to make war, they might summon the Spaniards to help and share the rewards of victory with them. This is what the Tlaxcaltecs are said to have done against the Mexicans, the former arranging with the Spaniards to help them to overcome the latter, and to receive whatever could fall to them under the law of war. . . .

Mandate or tutelage :

There is another title which can indeed not be asserted, but brought up for discussion, and some think it a lawful one. I dare not affirm it at all, nor do I entirely condemn it. It is this : Although the aborigines in question are (as has been said above) not wholly unintelligent, yet they are little short of that condition, and so are unfit to found or administer a lawful State, up to the standard required by human and civil claims. Accordingly they have no proper laws nor magistrates, and are not even capable of controlling their family affairs ; they are without any literature or arts, not only the liberal arts but the mechanical arts also ; they have no careful agriculture and no artisans ; and they lack many other conveniences, yea necessaries, of human life. It might, therefore, be maintained that in their own interests the sovereigns of Spain might undertake the administration of their country, providing them with prefects and governors for their towns, and might even give them new lords, so long as this was clearly for their own benefit. I say there would be some force in this contention ; for if they were all wanting in intelligence, there is no doubt that this would not only be a permissible, but also a highly proper, course to take ; nay, our sovereigns would be bound to take it, just as if the natives were infants. The same principles seem to apply here to them as to people of defective intelligence ; and indeed they are no whit or little better than such so far as self-government is concerned, or even than the wild beasts, for their food is not more pleasant and hardly better than beasts. Therefore their governance should in the same way be entrusted to people of intelligence. . . . Let this, however, as I have already said, be put forward without dogmatism and subject also to the limitation that any such interposition be for the welfare and in the interests of the Indians and not merely for the profit of the Spaniards. For this is the respect in which all the danger to soul and salvation lies. . . .

Peaceful economic expansion possible :

Now, it seems to follow from all this discussion that, if there be no force in any of the titles which have been put forward, so that the native Indians neither gave cause for just war nor wished for Spanish rulers, etc., all the travel to, and trade with, those parts should be stopped, to the great loss of the Spaniards and also to the grave hurt of the royal treasury (a thing intolerable). My first answer to this is : There would be no obligation to stop trade, for, as already said, there are many commodities of which the natives have a superfluity and which the Spaniards could acquire by barter. Also there are many commodities which the natives treat as ownerless or as common to all who like to take them, and the Portuguese, to their own great profit, have a big trade with similar people without reducing them to subjection. Secondly, there would probably be no diminution in the amount of the royalties, for a tax might quite fairly be placed on the gold and silver which would be brought away from the Indians, as much as a fifth or even more, according to quality, and it would be well earned, inasmuch as the maritime discovery was made by our sovereign, and it is under his authority that trade is carried on in safety. Thirdly, it is evident, now that there are already so many native converts, that it would be neither expedient nor lawful for our sovereign to wash his hands entirely of the administration of the lands in question.

APPENDIX C

Contemporary Application of Christian principles to labour conditions in Colonial territories :

(*a*) Resolution of the International Confederation of Christian Syndicates (1930) ;

(*b*) Memorandum of the Catholic Union of International Studies (1930).

(*a*) *Resolution of the International Confederation of Christian Syndicates relative to Forced Labour* (1930) :

The Committee of the International Confederation of Christian Syndicates assembled at Berlin on April 24–25, 1930, deliberating upon the question of 'Forced or Obligatory Labour,' drew attention to the following resolutions of its World Economic Programme :

The International Confederation of Christian Syndicates especially demands that all the relations between individuals, classes or peoples should be directed and governed by the Christian principles of justice and charity.

The economic and social organization has for its end the human person ; now the human person consists of soul and body. This organization ought then to have in view the procuring for man at once the material well-being for which he legitimately aspires and aiding him to attain the spiritual perfection to which he is obliged. It ought to assure him not only the best possible use of earthly goods and natural forces but also, in the environment (' terrain ') proper to him, the other conditions necessary to his moral development. This progress supposes two conditions : first, the work (whether material or intellectual) of individuals ; in the second place, the subordination of private interests to the general interest.

Work is not a merchandise subject to the law of supply and demand.

In the Economic order, work is the real active and vivifying element; capital, in all its forms, results itself from nature and human labour: it can only then be an auxiliary of the latter in productive operation. It is really work which, with the aid of instruments and divers means, transforms the raw materials into products useful to the general life of the Community.

Considering:

(1) That the human race is one, that these statements of doctrine are consequently valid for all human beings, whatever their nation, race or colour;

(2) That the work of colonization has for its chief mission the development of civilization among the peoples under tutelage and the bringing them to acquire a more perfect religious, moral, intellectual, family and social life;

(3) That the value set upon any regions is chiefly justified in the object of serving the general interest, and that the populations of these regions ought to be the principal ones to benefit thereby;

(4) That work imposed by constraint, physical or moral, often does not combine any of the conditions above stated, results in the diminution of personality, of human dignity and is thus destitute of moral and educative value,—

the Committee decides:

(*a*) To pronounce clearly against all recourse to forced or obligatory labour;

(*b*) That, pending its complete suppression, recourse to forced or obligatory labour may not be invoked except for major reasons to the exclusion of all recourse to the profit of private enterprises or of native chiefs; the authority to recruit forced workers may only be given by the central authority of the colony or by the metropolitan government; all the necessary measures ought to be taken and rigorously observed to safeguard completely the natural rights of the forced workers, families and native society;

(*c*) That the right of association ought to be recognized as belonging to the workers in the regions placed under tutelage, while taking account of their stage of development and in view of preparing them for the free exercise of this right.

(*d*) That adequate measures ought to be adopted by the 14th Session of the International Labour Conference with a view to a sufficient international control over the execution of the conventions and recommendations concerning forced or obligatory labour.

The Committee expresses the desire to see the 14th Session of the Conference adopt the project of convention or forced or obligatory labour amended in the sense of the above Resolutions.

(*b*) *Extracts from the Second Memorandum of the Catholic Union of International Studies on Forced or Compulsory Labour* (1930):

(Presented to the Fourteenth International Labour Conference.)

I. General Remarks.

Natural law and forced labour.—The natural law, which imposes on every man an obligation to work, leaves every man the choice of the time, place and kind of work he undertakes, subject to his individual and social responsibilities. In contradiction, therefore, with natural law is any form of positive obligation which, apart from certain urgent and exceptional necessities, deprives the individual of this liberty and compels him under the menace of a penalty to a labour for which he has not offered himself voluntarily, especially if this labour exceeds his strength and capacity. It is for this fundamental reason that forced labour should in principle be prohibited and condemned.

It may be admitted that exceptions must be recognized for (1) labour compulsion resulting from military obligations to which all the adult men of any community are legitimately subjected; (2) certain forms of labour representing a just and moderate tax, the payment of which may be in kind; (3) labour resulting from penal sentences. It is, however, essential that none of these forms of labour should be extended abusively and allowed to degenerate into a form of compulsion, which would lead to the practical suppression of the essential freedom of the choice of labour accorded by natural law to every human being.

Moreover, forced or compulsory labour as defined in § 1 of Article 2 of the proposed Draft Convention, and as practised in fact in a certain number of colonial areas, has the most serious social and moral consequences. It leads to a disintegration of the family by scattering its members and forcing them into a labour system which is new to them, in taking them suddenly from their homes and traditional occupations. It is harmful to society because it increases the causes of sickness and mortality, compromises the fertility of the race and threatens to destroy traditional institutions. Far from being of educational value, it leads in the minds of those subjected to it to a disgust for work and, as a result of the abuses which are almost inevitable, encourages a feeling of resistance against those who compel the labour.

It thus in practice hinders the development of civilization by rendering difficult both personal education and the economic development of the territory, the essential factor for which, population, is endangered by it.

The essential principles for the regulation of forced labour.—Since, however, in present circumstances and for a certain time, which it is to be hoped will be as short as possible, the complete suppression of forced labour cannot be contemplated, it is at least necessary that forced labour shall be strictly limited and regulated. It is therefore essential to adopt an international convention on the following conditions :

(*a*) The Convention should embody the principle of the abolition of forced or compulsory labour.

(*b*) It should regulate forced or compulsory labour for a transitional period, it being understood that all precautions should be taken to make this period as short as possible and to prepare the forced workers, morally and technically, for conditions of free labour.

(*c*) The regulation of forced or compulsory labour should therefore not be a permanent institution of colonial administration. It should be regarded as something which, during a temporary period, will secure the accordance of the methods of applying forced labour with the requirements due to the humanity of the workers.

The memorandum then enumerates a number of good points in the altered Draft Convention before the Conference.

II. Provisions which should be retained :

1. *Suppression of forced or compulsory labour.*—The abuses which have arisen with the exaction of forced or compulsory labour are such that the Convention should include a repudiation of the principle of such labour. While authorizing its exaction on certain conditions and in certain cases solely for public utility purposes, it should invite the powers concerned to take immediate steps leading to the eventual suppression of forced or compulsory labour.

2. *Limitation of hours of work.*—The duration of labour should be proportioned by the capacities of the workers, the degree to which they are accustomed to labour and the efforts required of them. The Union attaches a particular importance to this principle, which was proclaimed by Pope Leo XIII in the Encyclical on conditions of labour (*Rerum Novarum*, May 15, 1891). For this reason it considers it of great importance for the Draft Convention to limit the hours of work of forced workers. To this consideration must be added the fact that the workers in general attach to the proclamation of this principle an extreme importance and a symbolical value which cannot be neglected.

The Union believes it would be most advantageous to adopt as an expression of this limitation the formula which has become classical both in international treaties and in national legislation, of the eight-hour day and the forty-eight-hour week. This formula, the legal interpretation of which has been defined in a large number of regulations, collective agreements, legal decisions and authoritative commentaries, has in the various countries proved sufficiently elastic to be adapted to economic necessities, while providing a safeguard of great value to the workers concerned.[1]

3. *Workers' right of appeal.*—To assure the efficiency of the provisions adopted and to retain the confidence of the workers, it is necessary for those among them, who rightly or wrongly believe themselves suffering from injustice, to be able regularly and by legal means to bring their complaints before some competent authority. It is therefore necessary to provide an organized method of appeal to some jurisdiction presenting the double guarantee of impartiality and competence, so that decisions can be taken with the force of law in settlement of the disputes in question.

The necessity of some such method is all the more evident in view of the fact that as yet there are no occupational organizations through which forced labourers can find representatives to voice their grievances. Moreover, at the places of employment they are generally deprived of their natural protectors. They are grouped with men coming from other villages or belonging to other tribes, with whom they have no points of contact. They are in a similar situation to European industrial workers in the factories at the beginning of the nineteenth century. The results of the labour movements which took place then and the wrongs from which the workers suffered are well known.

It is thus, in the first place, necessary to insist on the establishment of a labour inspection service with sufficient powers of investigation and control. The workers should enjoy every facility of approaching the officials of any such service.[2]

In the same connection another problem arises which cannot be passed over in silence. It is the problem of workers' organization. The Union feels it its duty to emphasize that the text of Article 25 alludes in no way to trade union rights or to freedom of association. It is indeed reasonable not to mention the introduction of such rights among peoples who are insufficiently prepared to make a beneficial use of them; nevertheless, by

[1] In adopting this formula the experts were acting in accordance with precedents. In 1910, the International Conference on Colonial Sociology recommended the limitation of hours of work to eight in the day.

[2] It would be of value to associate, if possible, with this inspectorate elements recruited among the workers themselves and selected by them. It may be suggested as promising good results that native delegates should be attached to the inspectorates on somewhat similar lines to the French system of Miners' Delegates.

appropriate measures and education it is necessary to hasten the time when such introduction is possible.

The spirit of communal action is highly developed among the peoples in the colonies, especially among the Africans. Man is a social being. It is a result of his very nature and corresponds with his deepest needs. Among these peoples there are a number of social groupings. They must be neither hindered nor destroyed, unless, for example, by their secret character they are a danger to public peace and order. On the contrary, it would be advantageous to begin with them in gradually initiating the peoples in the defence of their collective interests within reasonable limits. This evolution may be aided by moral and religious influences, the presence of which among the workers and in the workplaces may give very satisfactory results.

For this reason the Union declares that it considers the formula used in Article 25 of the proposed Draft Convention a minimum, below which it would be impossible to go without danger of provoking the clandestine constitution of associations which would be all the more dangerous in view of their illegality.

The Union hopes that this minimum standard will not be considered sufficient and that, at least by a recommendation, the attention of the Governments be drawn to the urgent necessity of taking measures to favour the education of native labourers subject to forced or compulsory labour, so as to accustom them progressively and with all necessary prudence to the defence of their common interests by an application of the principle of association.

DOCUMENTS APPENDED FOR REFERENCE

APPENDIX I

PACIFIC INTERVENTIONS OF THE HOLY SEE FROM THE TWELFTH TO THE SIXTEENTH CENTURY

FREDERIC DUVAL. '*Application de la Doctrine de l'Eglise*'* in '*L'Eglise et le Droit de Guerre.*' :

(a) *Acts of Authority :*

Passing to the successors of Innocent III, we must mention certain acts of Gregory IX, Boniface VIII and John XXII. Gregory IX on several occasions excommunicated Frederick II, 'the persecutor of the Church and the oppressor of public liberty.'[1] Boniface VIII commanded Philippe le Bel to respect the truce concluded with England.[2] John XXII took the side of Ludwig of Bavaria against Frederick of Austria,[3] and in a letter to Philip V, King of France, made an important declaration : 'Truly, my Son, if you reflect attentively upon what the future may hold in store, you will find it impossible to disapprove or to regard as damaging to yourself and your kingdom the exercise of the right which belongs to the Apostolic See to impose truces.'[4]

Eugenius IV in a Bull addressed to the whole of Christendom, in which he appeals for a general mobilization of forces against Islam, maintained the same thesis : 'And in order that no obstacle may be placed, on the part of Christendom, against the holy enterprise, the Pope wills and ordains, in virtue of the authority which he holds from God Almighty, that the Christian world be at peace. The prelates and dignitaries of the Church are empowered to intervene in order to appease contentions and to establish the reign of peace ; should any princes refuse to accept a permanent peace with their adversaries at least they must consent to an armistice and respect it rigorously. Those

1 Lavisse et Rambaud, *Histoire Général*, t. II, p. 192.

2 Hergenröther, *Histoire de l'Eglise*, t. III, p. 711.

3 *Ibid.*, p. 432.

4 Coulon, *Lettres secrètes du Pape Jean XXII*, Paris, 1900, p. 704.

* The article is translated complete with references in footnotes, not all of which however has it been possible to verify.—J.E.

who break it shall if they be private persons incur the pain of excommunication, if they be whole communities, of the interdict.'[1]

Next must be mentioned Pius II who commanded the subjects of Ferdinand of Naples to submit to their prince ; supported Mathias Corvin against Frederick III[2] and declared to the French 'that Peace is a duty and the Pope refuses to tolerate a recourse to arms to settle the Neapolitan question.' And later the same Pope, in order to offer more effective opposition to the Turks, affirmed his intention of 'ordaining that all Christians observe an armistice for five years on pain of excommunication.'[3]

Paul II found himself obliged to condemn the action of the King of Hungary in breaking the peace by declaring war upon Podiebrad. And again, seeing that Florence, Naples and Milan despite all his efforts refused to put an end to their quarrels, this pontiff decided to make good use of his authority and to impress the minds of men by a solemn act. Having celebrated Holy Mass in the open air on the Capitol, he issued a Bull in which, after recounting all his previous endeavours to re-establish public tranquillity, he summoned Venice, Naples and Florence to make peace within a delay of thirty days. Peace was proclaimed on April 25, 1468 ; great rejoicings took place in Rome, and a magnificent procession wound its way through the streets of the city. The Sovereign Pontiff followed it on foot, while the crowd chanted hymns which Lianardo Dati had composed for the occasion.[4]

Interventions of this kind, of which many examples could be quoted, required the use by the Popes of all the spiritual armoury at their disposal. They become more and more rare as the Middle Ages recede and Faith becomes less vigorous : they entangled the Papacy too deeply, in an age when princes and peoples no longer showed their former docility to the Holy See.

(b) *Arbitration :*

Apart from these authoritative acts must be recorded friendly interventions or arbitrations, whether effected at the request of the belligerents or offered spontaneously by the pontiffs as mediators between the parties. The number of these arbitrations is very imposing. We will summarize only the principal instances which occurred in the period between the eleventh and sixteenth centuries. Leo IX re-established order and tranquillity in Southern Italy devastated by the Normans.[5] Pascal II recon-

[1] Pastor, *Histoire des Papes*, t. II, p. 258.
[2] *Ibid.*, t. III, p. 60. [3] *Ibid.*, t. IV, p. 164.
[4] *Ibid.*, pp. 141–146.
[5] Chalandon, *Essai sur le règne d'Alexis Comnène* (1081–1118), Paris, Picard, 1900.

ciled the King of Aragon and his enemies.[1] Gregory VII strove to prevent Philip I, King of France, from warring with William the Conqueror and intervened in the troubles of Bohemia. Urban II acted as mediator between the Emperor and the King of Sicily.

Next Innocent II arbitrated upon the difference which divided England and Scotland :[2] Alexander III and Celestine III also sought to reconcile these two countries. As to Innocent III, whose authoritative interventions to compose disputes are well known, Portugal, Aragon, Poland, Armenia, Bulgaria and Serbia profited by his arbitrations : and he reconciled Philip of Swabia with Otto of Brunswick. 'The Pope,' he himself declared, 'is the sovereign mediator upon earth.'[3] Honorius III and Gregory IX also composed the differences of princes. And about the same period (1235) Genoa and Venice in their treaty of alliance, undertook to submit contentions that might arise between them to the arbitration of the Sovereign Pontiff.[4]

Making mention only of the arbitral acts of Innocent IV, Alexander IV and Nicholas IV we pass to Boniface VIII who made peace between France and England as well as between the Scots and Edward I :[5] Benedict XI put an end to hostilities at Florence :[6] Clement V and John XXII were also successful arbitrators.

Yet more papal mediations which came to a happy issue were those of Benedict XII between France and England, of Clement VI, of Innocent VI at Bretigny, of Urban V[7] and of Gregory XI.

Martin V (1417–1431) struggled to effect a general pacification between France, England and the Duke of Burgundy. We may interrupt this rapid chronicle for a while to study the pacific endeavours of this Pope. Our brief description will serve as an example of the great longing of the Popes for peace and their perseverance in pursuing it. Martin V indeed did neither more nor less than other Popes whose work for peace deserves to be brought to light.

To establish peace was one of the most ardent desires of

1 *Patrologia Latina*, CLXIII, col. 305.

2 Hefele, *Histoire des Conciles* (Leclercq), T. V., p. 720.

3 Baluze, *Epistolarum Innocentii III libri undecim*, Paris, 1682, t. I, Epist. 185, p. 761.

4 Rivière et Weiss, *Pandectes françaises. Ve. Arbitrage Internationale*, No. 24 (Paris, Chevalier Marése).

5 Hergenröther, *Histoire de l'Eglise*, t. III, pp. 708, 710, 714.

6 *Ibid.*, t. IV, p. 408, and *Grandjean Les Régistres de Benoit XI* Paris, Thorin, 1833, col. 801).

7 Mollat (G.), *Les Papes d'Avignon* (Paris, Gabalda, 1912).

Martin V.[1] To that end he sent successively as Legate to France the Cardinal of Saluces and the Cardinal of Bar. He wrote to the Duke of Brittany to exhort him to act as mediator and sent special instructions to that effect to Jacques Gelli, Archbishop of Tours. On his orders again the Cardinal of St. Mark and Cardinal Des Ursins arrived in France as Papal Legates to restore peace. They succeeded, at the conferences of La Tombe, in negotiating an agreement between the Ambassadors of Burgundy and the Ambassadors of France. After this preliminary success the Cardinal of St. Mark attended a meeting of the Royal Council, and there he explained his mission, 'making evident by sundry reasons and notable examples' the advantages of peace. As for Cardinal Des Ursins, he betook himself to Pont-de-l'Arche to offer his mediation to the Ambassadors of Henry V (of England) and those of the King of France. Next year, 1419, on December 4, the Embassy of the Dauphin was received at Rome in a secret consistory to discuss further the terms of peace, and shortly afterwards *pourparlers* were begun at Florence between the English and French Embassies. This is how the Cardinal of St. Mark, Guillaume Filiastre, reports this interview to the Dauphin :

'And the Bishop of Laon most solemnly and honourably and without offence put forward his case, showing the English to have no right to possession of France and Normandy, and the causes of the treaties which were not valid ;[2] and this he did to such effect that our Holy Father and the others that heard him were well content. Whereupon the English replied, concerning the broken agreements, a trifle bitterly, for they are of a bitter nature. But as to their lack of right to the kingdom, the English answered nothing. Upon the question of Normandy, which the English say they have always held, rather, I said, had the Dukes of Normandy held England and acquired it and that the King of France had the honour of having the King of England, in so far as he was Duke of Normandy, as his vassal like the other vassals of his kingdom. Finally the two litigants said that they had no desire to say more on this matter, and so it was agreed.'[3]

A little later, the Pope was begged once more by the Dauphin to offer his mediation, and, when the Ambassador of the Duke

[1] On the pacific intervention of Martin V see De Beaucourt, *Histoire de Charles VII* (Picard, Paris, 1891).

[2] The probable meaning of this phrase is : 'and, as reasons for sustaining this thesis, the invalidity of the treaties quoted by the English.'

[3] De Beaucourt, *Histoire de Charles VII*, t. I, p. 328. No doubt an equally tendencious account of the negotiations were given to the English king.

of Burgundy asked Martin V to declare the future Charles VII guilty of violating the Treaty of Pouilly, the Pope refused.[1] This last fact shows the Pope to be the cornerstone of the international structure. Another indication of this is that after the Treaty of Troyes was signed, Martin V, despite his sympathies for England, refused to sanction it.

After the death of King Henry V, the Pope, who had not wearied of his scheme for conciliation, wrote to the Council of England exhorting it to make peace with the Dauphin. He wrote, too, to the Duke of Bedford in order to dispose him favourably to the mission of the Duke of Bologna ; to the Duke of Savoy urging him to strive, in concert with his Legate, to effect a pacification ' which was one of the most ardent longings of his heart ' ; to Charles VII, to the Duke of Burgundy and to the Duke of Brittany in the same sense. Lastly a fresh Legate was sent to France ; and the negotiations of the Duke of Savoy were crowned with success in the Treaties of Nantes and of Chambéry.[2]

During the same period the King of France, thanks no doubt to the good offices of Martin V, began to treat with the Emperor Sigismund : and it is interesting to observe the grounds upon which Charles VII defends his cause. ' We are waging war, not to increase our dominions, but to defend them against an unjust usurpation, and God knows that we have provoked no one. And the King's Ambassador, Alain Chartier, said to the Emperor : " Remember you have a duty (to make peace) arising both from blood relationship and justice." '

These *pourparlers* accomplished, the Pope intervened afresh, at the request of Charles VII, to make peace. He sent fresh letters to the Duke of Burgundy and to Bedford. Once more he wrote to the Duke in 1430 to bring him to a peaceful mind ; telling him that it was binding upon him in conscience to give up his support of the English if they persisted in the intention of continuing hostilities. At the same time Cardinal Nicholas Albergati received orders to proceed to France in order to work for peace. And finally on December 31 (1430) the Pope wrote to Henry VI to beg him to give his Legate a favourable hearing.

If we have dwelt at some length upon the interventions of Martin V, it is, as we have said, for the purpose of illustrating, by this instance, the activities of the Roman Pontiffs. It remains for us to mention the principal arbitrations for which the Church can also take credit in the fourteenth and fifteenth centuries.

[1] *Ibid.*, p. 330.

[2] *Ibid.*, p. 352, from which M. Duval has evidently drawn his further references to events in the reign of that monarch.

First we see Eugène IV seeking, at the end of the Council of Bâle, to re-establish in Europe the peace which the Hussites had disturbed,[1] and interposing his authority between Alphonso of Aragon and Louis of Anjou, the two claimants to the throne of Naples.

The better to combat the Turks, Nicholas V offers his mediation to France, England, Hungary, Moldavia, Lithuania, Albania, the Italian Powers and in fact to practically all the Christian nations.[2] Calixtus V in 1455 confirms the peace between the King of France and the Duke of Burgundy and intervenes once more between France and England.[3]

Pius II re-establishes peace in Italy, invites the Ambassadors of France and England to meet at a conference to solve the difficulties existing between them, strives to appease the dissensions of the Germans and delegates Cardinal Bessarion to that intent.[4]

Paul II again brings peace to the Italian cities.[5] Sixtus IV enjoins the same Bessarion to reconcile Charles the Bold and the King of France, gives Cardinal Borgia the task of restoring peace in Spain, and Cardinal Barbo of putting an end to the wars in Germany, while he himself strives with the aid of Cardinal Savelli and others to appease the Italian wars. In the hope of securing a greater response to his efforts he composes his difference with Florence.[6]

Innocent VIII reconciles the Orsini and the Colonna, strives in the matter of Sarzana to maintain agreement between Naples, Florence, Milan and Genoa, 'considering it as a duty of his apostolic charge to secure the maintenance of the peace concluded between them.' 'Moreover,' says the Pope, 'Genoa has appealed to Us to settle this affair by arbitration.' He sends Cheragato and Peraudi into France to effect a reconciliation between Charles VIII and Maximilian; at the same time he induces Matthias Corvin to make peace with the Emperor, and he endeavours at the Congress of Rheims to secure a general pacification.[7] We may end with Alexander VI who follows in his predecessors' footsteps.[8] Italy, Germany, Denmark and England benefited from the action of his legates; and by the famous arbitration of 1493 between Spain and Portugal he

[1] Noel Valois, *Le Pape et le Concile*, t. I, p. 213; t. II, p. 110.

[2] Pastor, *Histoire des Papes*, t. II, pp. 258, 265, 269, 278.

[3] *Ibid.*, pp. 333, 350, 358.

[4] *Ibid.*, t. III, pp. 23–25, 46, 60, 63, 72, 73, 74, 76, 86, 148, 150–154, 254, 301, 304, 306.

[5] *Ibid.*, t. IV, pp. 141–146, 165, 168.

[6] *Ibid.*, t. II, pp. 202–207, 262, 310.

[7] *Ibid.*, t. V, pp. 241, 286 *et seq.*, 296 *et seq.*

[8] Not, alas, in regard to his personal morality.

divided America, by an imaginary line, into two zones of influence[1] in which the activity of each of these two nations could have free play.[2]

[1] Pastor, t. V, pp. 383, 447, 481 ; t. VI, pp. 89–92, 149. Merignac, *Traité théorique et pratique de l'Arbitrage*, p. 33.

[2] Upon the shocking misuse by the Spaniards of this Papal authorization to spread the Gospel, see Appendices A and B of Chapter XV above, and (at more length) Dutto, *Life of Bartolomé de las Casas*.

APPENDIX II

PACIFIC INTERVENTIONS OF THE HOLY SEE FROM 1598–1914

MÜLLER. '*Das Friedenswerk der Kirche in den letzten drei Jahrhunderten*' : Summary.

1598

The Cardinal Legate Alessandro de' Medici,
afterwards Pope Leo XI, successful arbitrator at Vervins between King Henry IV of France, King Philip II of Spain and the Archduke Charles Emmanuel of Savoy. The last subject of discussion at the conference, namely the dispute between Savoy and France about Saluzzo, which was claimed by the French king as a dependency of the Dauphiné, was left unsettled at Vervins.

1600

The Nuncio Bonaventura Calatagirone, O.F.M.,
Patriarch of Alexandria, acts as arbitrator in Paris in the dispute between King Henry IV and Prince Charles Emmanuel of Savoy about Saluzzo.

1601

The Cardinal Legate Aldobrandini,
acting as arbitrator at Tortona (1600) and Lyon (1601), settles the dispute over the Margravate of Saluzzo by a compromise accepted by both sides.

1609

The Nuncio Guido Bentivoglio in Brussels and Father Jean de Neyen,
Franciscan Provincial of the Netherlands, are instrumental in arranging the ten years' truce between the Archduke Albert, the Infanta Isabella and the States General (Antwerp, 1609).

1614

The Nuncio Giulio Savelli and Cardinal Ludovico Ludovisi, arbitrators at Asti and Pavia in the dispute about Montferrat between the Duke of Savoy and the Duke of Mantua.

1617

The Nuncio Guido Bentivoglio,
promoter, in Paris, of a compromise between the Archduke Ferdinand of Steiermark and the Venetian Republic in the dispute about the freedom of the sea in the Adriatic.

1630–1631

The Nuncio Giacomo Panzirolo, Mgr. Giulio Mazarini and Cardinal Antonio Barbarini,
arbitrators in the dispute about the succession at Mantua. The discussions took place at Rivalta, Regensburg and Cherasco.

1639

The Nuncio Fausto Caffarelli,
Archbishop of Santa Severina, negotiates the truce of Turin between Savoy, France and Spain.

1648

The Nuncio Fabio Chigi,
Bishop of Nardo, later Pope Alexander VII, arbitrator between the Emperor Ferdinand III and King Louis XIV at Munster.

1659

Papal diplomacy rendered great service in the bringing about of the Treaty of the Pyrenees, which was signed on November 7, 1659, by the plenipotentiaries of France and Spain, Cardinal Mazarin and Minister Don Luis Mendez de Haro-Guzman. The treaty is regarded as a masterpiece of French diplomacy and particularly of Hugues de Lionne. (Arbitration by the Holy See was rendered ineffectual by Mazarin.)

1668

The Nuncio Agostino Franciotti,
Archbishop of Trebizond, the first arbitrator between France and Spain at the Peace Congress of Aix.

1677–1678

The Nuncio Luigi Bevilacqua,
Patriarch of Alexandria, arbitrator at the Congress of Nijmegen.

1697

The Pope was nominated by Article 8 and by a Separate Article of the Peace Treaty of Ryswick as Arbitrator (*sur-arbitre*) in the dispute about the Pfalz succession. Papal diplomacy rendered services in bringing this conference about. A Papal appeal for Peace was issued on December 8, 1691. Louis XIV tries to enlist the Church's influence for peace on his own behalf. (Instructions to the Ambassador Cardinal de Janson-Forbin in Rome, and to Father de la Blandinière (1691).)

1700

Pope Clement XI

offers to arbitrate between the Emperor Leopold and King Louis XIV, December 28, 1700, in the dispute about the Spanish Succession.

1702

Pfalz Succession Dispute,

decision given on February 17, 1702, by the Papal Arbitration Commission in the name of Pope Clement XI.

1713

Pope Clement XI

offers to arbitrate between the Emperor Charles VI and King Louis XIV in the War of the Spanish Succession.

The Holy See and Peace in the Nineteenth and Twentieth Centuries

1870

Pope Pius IX offers mediation, July 22, 1870, to the Emperor Napoleon and King William I of Prussia in order to prevent the Franco-Prussian War.

1885

Pope Leo XIII

appealed to by Prince Bismarck to act as mediator between Germany and Spain in the dispute relating to the possession of the Caroline Islands, October 22, 1885. The British Government also accepted this mediation by consenting to apply the concessions made by Spain to Germany also to Spanish-British interests, January 8, 1886. The protocol which decided the question of the Caroline Islands was signed at the Vatican by Cardinal Jacobi, the Spanish Ambassador Molina and the German Ambassador V. Schloezer on December 17, 1885.

1890

Pope Leo XIII

is proposed as mediator in the boundary disputes between Great Britain and Portugal and between Portugal and the Congo State.

1893

The Nuncio Macchi in Lima

arbitrates successfully in the boundary dispute between the Republics of Peru and Ecuador.

1894

Pope Leo XIII

is called upon by the Government of Venezuela to mediate between Great Britain and Venezuela in the Guiana boundary dispute.

1895

Pope Leo XIII

acts as arbitrator between the Central American Republics of Haiti and San Domingo.

1896

Mgr. Cyrill Macaire

later Patriarch of the Coptic Rite, delivers a letter of appeal from Pope Leo XIII to the Emperor Menelik of Abyssinia on behalf of Italian prisoners of war.

1898

Pope Leo XIII

proposed by the German Foreign Minister, Prince Bernhard von Bülow, as mediator between Spain and the United States of America in order to prevent the Cuban war. The Pope's efforts only succeed in delaying the outbreak of hostilities.

1899

Pope Leo XIII

is notified by the Russian Ambassador Tscharykoff, in the name of the Czar, of the calling of the Hague Peace Conference,[1] which owed its original impetus to a suggestion made by the Pope in 1893 to the Russian Prince Lobanow.

1900–1903

Bishop Benavente of San Juan de Cuyo (Argentina) and Bishop Raimondo A. Jara of Ancud (Chile)

are instrumental, through their peace propaganda, in bringing about the settlement of an old boundary dispute between Argentina and Chile through arbitration. Decision given by King Edward VII, November 20, 1902.[2]

[1] For the text of the Papal letter read to the Conference, see pp. 173–5.

[2] The famous statue 'The Christ of the Andes' commemorates this event.

1905

Colombia and Peru

enter into a standing agreement on September 12, 1905, that all disputes, with the exception of questions of independence and honour, shall be submitted to the arbitration of the Pope in cases where they cannot be amicably settled by direct negotiations.

1906

Mgr. Francesco Ragonesi,

Apostolic Delegate in Bogota, later Apostolic Nuncio in Madrid, and Cardinal in Curia, invited by the Colombian Minister of State, A. V. Cobo, to arbitrate between himself and the Ambassador of Ecuador, General Julio Andrade, in the Putumayo boundary dispute between Colombia and Ecuador, August, 1906. The boundary dispute was submitted to the decision of the King of Spain.

1909–1910.

The Nuncio Alessandro Bavona

decided the disputes between Brazil and Bolivia, and Brazil and Peru, about the gold mines of Acre.

1914

Pope Pius X

supports the idea of an arbitration conference in order to establish friendly relations between the United States of America and Mexico. Arbitration offer of Argentina, Brazil and Chile on April 15, 1914. Peace Conference at Niagara Falls (1914).

APPENDIX III

THE COVENANT OF THE LEAGUE OF NATIONS

[The Preamble]

THE HIGH CONTRACTING PARTIES

In order to promote international co-operation and to achieve international peace and security

by the acceptance of obligations not to resort to war,

by the prescription of open, just and honourable relations between nations,

by the firm establishment of the understandings of international law as the actual rule of conduct among Governments, and

by the maintenance of justice and a scrupulous respect for all treaty obligations in the dealings of organized peoples with one another,

Agree to this Covenant of the League of Nations.

COVENANT

ARTICLE 1 [MEMBERSHIP].

(1) The original Members of the League of Nations shall be those of the Signatories which are named in the Annex to this Covenant and also such of those other States named in the Annex as shall accede without reservation to this Covenant. Such accession shall be effected by a Declaration deposited with the Secretariat within two months of the coming into force of the Covenant. Notice thereof shall be sent to all other Members of the League.

(2) Any fully self-governing State, Dominion or Colony not named in the Annex may become a Member of the League if its admission is agreed to by two-thirds of the Assembly, provided that it shall give effective guarantees of its sincere intention to observe its international obligations, and shall accept such regulations as may be prescribed by the League in regard to its military, naval and air forces and armaments.

(3) Any Member of the League may, after two years' notice of its intention so to do, withdraw from the League, provided that all its international obligations and all its obligations under this Covenant shall have been fulfilled at the time of its withdrawal.

ARTICLE 2 [EXECUTIVE MACHINERY].

The action of the League under this Covenant shall be effected through the instrumentality of an Assembly and of a Council, with a permanent Secretariat.

ARTICLE 3 [ASSEMBLY].

(1) The Assembly shall consist of Representatives of the Members of the League.

(2) The Assembly shall meet at stated intervals and from time to time as occasion may require at the Seat of the League or at such other place as may be decided upon.

(3) The Assembly may deal at its meetings with any matter within the sphere of action of the League or affecting the peace of the world.

(4) At meetings of the Assembly, each Member of the League shall have one vote, and may have not more than three Representatives.

ARTICLE 4 [COUNCIL].

(1) The Council shall consist of Representatives of the Principal Allied and Associated Powers,[1] together with Representatives of four other Members of the League. These four Members of the League shall be selected by the Assembly from time to time in its discretion. Until the appointment of the Representatives of the four Members of the League first selected by the Assembly, Representatives of Belgium, Brazil, Spain and Greece shall be members of the Council.

(2) With the approval of the majority of the Assembly, the Council may name additional Members of the League whose Representatives shall always be members of the Council[2]; the Council with like approval may increase the number of Members of the League to be selected by the Assembly for representation on the Council.[3]

[1] The Principal Allied and Associated Powers are the following: The United States of America, the British Empire, France, Italy and Japan (see Preamble of the Peace Treaty with Germany).

[2] In virtue of this paragraph of the Covenant, Germany was nominated as a Permanent Member of the Council on September 8, 1926, and Russia in September, 1934.

[3] The number of members of the Council selected by the Assembly was increased to six instead of four by virtue of a resolution adopted by the Third Assembly on September 25, 1922. By resolution taken by the Assembly on September 8, 1926, the number of members of the Council selected by the Assembly was increased to nine.

(2 *bis.*[1]) *The Assembly shall fix by a two-thirds majority the rules dealing with the election of the non-permanent Members of the Council, and particularly such regulations as relate to their term of office and conditions of re-eligibility.*

(3) The Council shall meet from time to time as occasion may require, and at least once a year, at the Seat of the League, or at such other place as may be decided upon.

(4) The Council may deal at its meetings with any matter within the sphere of action of the League or affecting the peace of the world.

(5) Any Member of the League not represented on the Council shall be invited to send a Representative to sit as a Member at any meeting of the Council during the consideration of matters specially affecting the interests of that Member of the League.

(6) At meetings of the Council, each Member of the League represented on the Council shall have one vote, and may have not more than one Representative.

ARTICLE 5 [VOTING AND PROCEDURE].

(1) Except where otherwise expressly provided in this Covenant or by the terms of the present Treaty, decisions at any meeting of the Assembly or of the Council shall require the agreement of all the Members of the League represented at the meeting.

(2) All matters of procedure at meetings of the Assembly or of the Council, including the appointment of Committees to investigate particular matters, shall be regulated by the Assembly or by the Council and may be decided by a majority of the Members of the League represented at the meeting.

(3) The first meeting of the Assembly and the first meeting of the Council shall be summoned by the President of the United States of America.

ARTICLE 6 [SECRETARIAT].

(1) The permanent Secretariat shall be established at the Seat of the League. The Secretariat shall comprise a Secretary-General and such secretaries and staff as may be required.

(2) The first Secretary-General shall be the person named in the Annex; thereafter the Secretary-General shall be appointed by the Council with the approval of the majority of the Assembly.

(3) The secretaries and staff of the Secretariat shall be appointed by the Secretary-General with the approval of the Council.

(4) The Secretary-General shall act in that capacity at all meetings of the Assembly and of the Council.

[1] This Amendment came into force July 29, 1926.

(5[1]) *The expenses of the League shall be borne by the Members of the League in the proportion decided by the Assembly.*

ARTICLE 7 [SEAT. QUALIFICATIONS FOR OFFICIALS. IMMUNITIES].

(1) The Seat of the League is established at Geneva.

(2) The Council may at any time decide that the Seat of the League shall be established elsewhere.

(3) All positions under or in connection with the League, including the Secretariat, shall be open equally to men and women.

(4) Representatives of the Members of the League and officials of the League when engaged on the business of the League shall enjoy diplomatic privileges and immunities.

(5) The buildings and other property occupied by the League or its officials or by Representatives attending its meetings shall be inviolable.

ARTICLE 8 [REDUCTION OF ARMAMENTS].

(1) The Members of the League recognize that the maintenance of peace requires the reduction of national armaments to the lowest point consistent with national safety and the enforcement by common action of international obligations.

(2) The Council, taking account of the geographical situation and circumstances of each State, shall formulate plans for such reduction for the consideration and action of the several Governments.

(3) Such plans shall be subject to re-consideration and revision at least every ten years.

(4) After these plans shall have been adopted by the several Governments, the limits of armaments therein fixed shall not be exceeded without the concurrence of the Council.

(5) The Members of the League agree that the manufacture by private enterprise of munitions and implements of war is open to grave objections. The Council shall advise how the evil effects attendant upon such manufacture can be prevented, due regard being had to the necessities of those Members of the League which are not able to manufacture the munitions and implements of war necessary for their safety.

(6) The Members of the League undertake to interchange full and frank information as to the scale of their armaments, their military, naval and air programmes and the condition of such of their industries as are adaptable to war-like purposes.

[1] This Amendment came into force on August 13, 1924; the paragraph originally ran: 'The expenses of the Secretariat shall be borne by the Members of the League in accordance with the apportionment of the expenses of the International Bureau of the Universal Postal Union.'

ARTICLE 9 [PERMANENT MILITARY COMMISSION].

A permanent Commission shall be constituted to advise the Council on the execution of the provisions of Articles 1 and 8 and on military, naval and air questions generally.

ARTICLE 10 [GUARANTEES AGAINST AGGRESSION].

The Members of the League undertake to respect and preserve as against external aggression the territorial integrity and existing political independence of all Members of the League. In case of any such aggression or in case of any threat or danger of such aggression the Council shall advise upon the means by which this obligation shall be fulfilled.

ARTICLE 11 [ACTION IN CASE OF WAR OR DANGER OF WAR].

(1) Any war or threat of war, whether immediately affecting any of the Members of the League or not, is hereby declared a matter of concern to the whole League, and the League shall take any action that may be deemed wise and effectual to safeguard the peace of nations. In case any such emergency should arise the Secretary-General shall on the request of any Member of the League forthwith summon a meeting of the Council.

(2) It is also declared to be the friendly right of each Member of the League to bring to the attention of the Assembly or of the Council any circumstance whatever affecting international relations which threatens to disturb international peace or the good understanding between nations upon which peace depends.

ARTICLE 12 [DISPUTES TO BE SUBMITTED TO ARBITRATION OR INQUIRY].[1]

(1) The Members of the League agree that, if there should arise between them any dispute likely to lead to a rupture, they will submit the matter either to arbitration *or judicial settlement* or to inquiry by the Council and they agree in no case to resort to war until three months after the award by the arbitrators *or the judicial decision*, or the report by the Council.

(2) In any case under this Article, the award of the arbitrators *or the judicial decision* shall be made within a reasonable time, and the report of the Council shall be made within six months after the submission of the dispute.

ARTICLE 13 [ARBITRATION OF DISPUTES].[2]

(1) The Members of the League agree that, whenever any dispute shall arise between them which they recognize to be

[1] The amendments in italics came into force on September 26, 1924.

[2] The amendments in italics came into force on September 26, 1924.

suitable for submission to arbitration or *judicial settlement*, and which cannot be satisfactorily settled by diplomacy, they will submit the whole subject-matter to arbitration or *judicial settlement.*

(2) Disputes as to the interpretation of a treaty, as to any question of international law, as to the existence of any fact which, if established, would constitute a breach of any international obligation, or as to the extent and nature of the reparation to be made for any such breach, are declared to be among those which are generally suitable for submission to arbitration *or judicial settlement.*

(3) *For the consideration of any such dispute, the court to which the case is referred shall be the Permanent Court of International Justice, established in accordance with Article* 14, *or any tribunal agreed on by the parties to the dispute or stipulated in any convention existing between them.*

(4) The Members of the League agree that they will carry out in full good faith any award *or decision* that may be rendered, and that they will not resort to war against any Member of the League that complies therewith. In the event of any failure to carry out such an award *or decision*, the Council shall propose what steps should be taken to give effect thereto.

ARTICLE 14 [PERMANENT COURT OF INTERNATIONAL JUSTICE].

The Council shall formulate and submit to the Members of the League for adoption plans for the establishment of a Permanent Court of International Justice. The Court shall be competent to hear and determine any dispute of an international character which the parties thereto submit to it. The Court may also give an advisory opinion upon any dispute or question referred to it by the Council or by the Assembly.

ARTICLE 15 [DISPUTES NOT SUBMITTED TO ARBITRATION].[1]

(1) If there should arise between Members of the League any dispute likely to lead to a rupture, which is not submitted to arbitration *or judicial settlement* in accordance with Article 13, the Members of the League agree that they will submit the matter to the Council. Any party to the dispute may effect such submission by giving notice of the existence of the dispute to the Secretary-General, who will make all necessary arrangements for a full investigation and consideration thereof.

(2) For this purpose the parties to the dispute will communicate to the Secretary-General as promptly as possible, statements of their case, with all the relevant facts and papers, and the Council may forthwith direct the publication thereof.

[1] The amendments in italics came into force on September 26, 1924.

(3) The Council shall endeavour to effect a settlement of the dispute, and if such efforts are successful, a statement shall be made public giving such facts and explanations regarding the dispute and the terms of settlement thereof as the Council may deem appropriate.

(4) If the dispute is not thus settled, the Council either unanimously or by a majority vote shall make and publish a report containing a statement of the facts of the dispute and the recommendations which are deemed just and proper in regard thereto.

(5) Any Member of the League represented on the Council may make public a statement of the facts of the dispute and of its conclusions regarding the same.

(6) If a report by the Council is unanimously agreed to by the members thereof other than the Representatives of one or more of the parties to the dispute, the Members of the League agree that they will not go to war with any party to the dispute which complies with the recommendations of the report.

(7) If the Council fails to reach a report which is unanimously agreed to by the members thereof, other than the Representatives of one or more of the parties to the dispute, the Members of the League reserve to themselves the right to take such action as they shall consider necessary for the maintenance of right and justice.

(8) If the dispute between the parties is claimed by one of them, and is found by the Council to arise out of a matter which by international law is solely within the domestic jurisdiction of that party, the Council shall so report, and shall make no recommendation as to its settlement.

(9) The Council may in any case under this Article refer the dispute to the Assembly. The dispute shall be so referred at the request of either party to the dispute, provided that such request be made within fourteen days after the submission of the dispute to the Council.

(10) In any case referred to the Assembly, all the provisions of the Article and of Article 12 relating to the action and powers of the Council shall apply to the action and powers of the Assembly, provided that a report made by the Assembly, if concurred in by the Representatives of those Members of the League represented on the Council and of a majority of the other Members of the League, exclusive in each case of the Representatives of the parties to the dispute, shall have the same force as a report by the Council concurred in by all the members thereof other than the Representatives of one or more of the parties to the dispute.

ARTICLE 16 [' SANCTIONS ' OF THE LEAGUE].

(1)[1] Should any Member of the League resort to war in disregard of its covenants under Articles 12, 13 or 15, it shall *ipso facto* be deemed to have committed an act of war against all other Members of the League, which hereby undertake immediately to subject it to the severance of all trade or financial relations, the prohibition of all intercourse between their nationals and the nationals of the covenant-breaking State, and the prevention of all financial, commercial or personal intercourse between the nationals of the covenant-breaking State and the nationals of any other State, whether a Member of the League or not.

(2) It shall be the duty of the Council in such case to recommend to the several Governments concerned what effective military, naval or air force the Members of the League shall

[1] *Should sufficient ratifications be received this paragraph will be replaced by the following four :*

Should any Member of the League resort to war in disregard to its covenants under Articles 12, 13, or 15, it shall *ipso facto* be deemed to have committed an act of war against all other Members of the League, which hereby undertake immediately to subject it to the severance of all trade or financial relations, and to prohibit all intercourse at least between persons resident within their territories and persons resident within the territory of the covenant-breaking State and, if they deem it expedient, also between their nationals and the nationals of the covenant-breaking State, and to prevent all financial, commercial or personal intercourse at least between persons resident within the territory of that State and persons resident within the territory of any other State, whether a Member of the League or not, and, if they deem it expedient, also between the nationals of that State and the nationals of any other State, whether a Member of the League or not.

It is for the Council to give an opinion whether or not a breach of the Covenant has taken place. In deliberations on this question in the Council, the votes of Members of the League alleged to have resorted to war and of Members against whom such action was directed shall not be counted.

The Council will notify to all Members of the League the date which it recommends for the application of the economic pressure under this Article.

Nevertheless, the Council may, in the case of particular Members, postpone the coming into force of any of these measures for a specified period where it is satisfied that such a postponement will facilitate the attainment of the object of the measures referred to in the preceding paragraph, or that it is necessary in order to minimize the loss and inconvenience which will be caused to such Members.

severally contribute to the armed forces to be used to protect the covenants of the League.

(3) The Members of the League agree, further, that they will mutually support one another in the financial and economic measures which are taken under this Article, in order to minimize the loss and inconvenience resulting from the above measures, and that they will mutually support one another in resisting any special measures aimed at one of their number by the covenant-breaking State, and that they will take the necessary steps to afford passage through their territory to the forces of any of the Members of the League which are co-operating to protect the covenants of the League.

(4) Any Member of the League which has violated any covenant of the League may be declared to be no longer a Member of the League by a vote of the Council concurred in by the Representatives of all the other Members of the League represented thereon.

ARTICLE 17 [DISPUTES WITH NON-MEMBERS].

(1) In the event of a dispute between a Member of the League and a State which is not a Member of the League, or between States not Members of the League, the State or States not Members of the League shall be invited to accept the obligations of Membership in the League for the purposes of such dispute, upon such conditions as the Council may deem just. If such invitation is accepted, the provisions of Articles 12 to 16 inclusive shall be applied with such modifications as may be deemed necessary by the Council.

(2) Upon such invitation being given the Council shall immediately institute an inquiry into the circumstances of the dispute and recommend such action as may seem best and most effectual in the circumstances.

(3) If a State so invited shall refuse to accept the obligations of membership in the League for the purposes of such dispute, and shall resort to war against a Member of the League, the provisions of Article 16 shall be applicable as against the State taking such action.

(4) If both parties to the dispute when so invited refuse to accept the obligations of membership in the League for the purposes of such dispute, the Council may take such measures and make such recommendations as will prevent hostilities and will result in the settlement of the dispute.

ARTICLE 18 [REGISTRATION AND PUBLICATION OF ALL FUTURE TREATIES].

Every treaty or international engagement entered into hereafter by any Member of the League shall be forthwith registered with the Secretariat and shall as soon as possible be published by it. No such treaty or international engagement shall be binding until so registered.

ARTICLE 19 [REVIEW OF TREATIES].

The Assembly may from time to time advise the reconsideration by Members of the League of treaties which have become inapplicable and the consideration of international conditions whose continuance might endanger the peace of the world.

ARTICLE 20 [ABROGATION OF INCONSISTENT OBLIGATIONS].

(1) The Members of the League severally agree that this Covenant is accepted as abrogating all obligations or understandings *inter se* which are inconsistent with the terms thereof, and solemnly undertake that they will not hereafter enter into any engagements inconsistent with the terms thereof.

(2) In case any Member of the League shall, before becoming a Member of the League, have undertaken any obligations inconsistent with the terms of this Covenant, it shall be the duty of such Member to take immediate steps to procure its release from such obligations.

ARTICLE 21 [ENGAGEMENTS THAT REMAIN VALID].

Nothing in the Covenant shall be deemed to affect the validity of international engagements, such as treaties of arbitration or regional understandings like the Monroe doctrine, for securing the maintenance of peace.

ARTICLE 22 [MANDATORIES, CONTROL OF COLONIES AND TERRITORIES].

(1) To those colonies and territories which as a consequence of the late war have ceased to be under the sovereignty of the States which formerly governed them and which are inhabited by peoples not yet able to stand by themselves under the strenuous conditions of the modern world, there should be applied the principle that the well-being and development of such peoples form a sacred trust of civilization and that securities for the performance of this trust should be embodied in this Covenant.

(2) The best method of giving practical effect to this principle is that the tutelage of such peoples should be entrusted to advanced nations who by reason of their resources, their experience, or their geographical position can best undertake this responsibility, and who are willing to accept it, and that this tutelage should be exercised by them as Mandatories on behalf of the League.

(3) The character of the mandate must differ according to the

stage of the development of the people, the geographical situation of the territory, its economic conditions and other similar circumstances.

(4) Certain communities formerly belonging to the Turkish Empire have reached a state of development where their existence as independent nations can be provisionally recognized subject to the rendering of administrative advice and assistance by a Mandatory until such times as they are able to stand alone. The wishes of these communities must be a principal consideration in the selection of the Mandatory.

(5) Other peoples, especially those of Central Africa, are at such a stage that the Mandatory must be responsible for the administration of the territory under conditions which will guarantee freedom of conscience and religion, subject only to the maintenance of public order and morals, the prohibition of abuses such as the slave trade, the arms traffic and the liquor traffic, and the prevention of the establishment of fortifications or military and naval bases and of military training of the natives for other than police purposes and the defence of territory, and will also secure equal opportunities for the trade and commerce of other Members of the League.

(6) There are territories, such as South-West Africa and certain of the South Pacific Islands, which, owing to the sparseness of their population, or their small size, or their remoteness from the centres of civilization, or their geographical contiguity to the territory of the Mandatory, and other circumstances, can be best administered under the laws of the Mandatory as integral portions of its territory, subject to the safeguards above-mentioned in the interests of the indigenous population.

(7) In every case of mandate, the Mandatory shall render to the Council an annual report in reference to the territory committed to its charge.

(8) The degree of authority, control or administration to be exercised by the Mandatory shall, if not previously agreed upon by the Members of the League, be explicitly defined in each case by the Council.

(9) A permanent Commission shall be constituted to receive and examine the annual reports of the Mandatories and to advise the Council on all matters relating to the observance of the mandates.

ARTICLE 23 [SOCIAL ACTIVITIES].

Subject to and in accordance with the provisions of international conventions existing or hereafter to be agreed upon, the Members of the League:

(*a*) will endeavour to secure and maintain fair and humane conditions of labour for men, women and children, both in their own countries and in all countries to which their commercial and industrial relations extend, and for that purpose will establish and maintain the necessary international organizations;

(*b*) undertake to secure just treatment of the native inhabitants of territories under their control;

(*c*) will entrust the League with the general supervision over the execution of agreements with regard to the traffic in women and children, and the traffic in opium and other dangerous drugs;

(*d*) will entrust the League with the general supervision of the trade in arms and ammunition with the countries in which the control of this traffic is necessary in the common interest;

(*e*) will make provision to secure and maintain freedom of communications and of transit and equitable treatment for the commerce of all Members of the League. In this connection, the special necessities of the regions devastated during the war of 1914–1918 shall be borne in mind;

(*f*) will endeavour to take steps in matters of international concern for the prevention and control of disease.

ARTICLE 24 [INTERNATIONAL BUREAUX].

(1) There shall be placed under the direction of the League all international bureaux already established by general treaties if the parties to such treaties consent. All such international bureaux and all commissions for the regulation of matters of international interest hereafter constituted shall be placed under the direction of the League.

(2) In all matters of international interest which are regulated by general conventions but which are not placed under the control of international bureaux or commissions, the Secretariat of the League shall, subject to the consent of the Council and if desired by the parties, collect and distribute all relevant information and shall render any other assistance which may be necessary or desirable.

(3) The Council may include as part of the expenses of the Secretariat the expenses of any bureau or commission which is placed under the direction of the League.

ARTICLE 25 [PROMOTION OF RED CROSS].

The Members of the League agree to encourage and promote the establishment and co-operation of duly authorized voluntary national Red Cross organizations having as purposes the improvement of health, the prevention of disease and the mitigation of suffering throughout the world.

ARTICLE 26 [AMENDMENTS].

(1)[1] Amendments to this Covenant will take effect when ratified by the Members of the League whose Representatives compose the Council and by a majority of Members of the League whose Representatives compose the Assembly.

(2) No such amendment shall bind any Member of the League which signifies its dissent therefrom, but in that case it shall cease to be a Member of the League.

ANNEX

I [STATES QUALIFIED TO BE] ORIGINAL MEMBERS OF THE LEAGUE OF NATIONS

SIGNATORIES OF THE TREATY OF PEACE

United States of America
Belgium
Bolivia
Brazil
British Empire:
Canada
Australia
South Africa
New Zealand
India
China
Cuba
Ecuador
France
Greece
Guatemala
Haiti
Hedjaz
Honduras
Italy
Japan
Liberia
Nicaragua
Panama
Peru
Poland
Portugal
Roumania
Serb-Croat-Slovene State
Siam
Czecho-Slovakia
Uruguay

[1] *When sufficient ratifications have been received this Article will read :*

Amendments to the present Covenant the text of which shall have been voted by the Assembly on a three-fourths majority, in which there shall be included the votes of all the Members of the Council represented at the meeting, will take effect when ratified by the Members of the League whose Representatives composed the Council when the vote was taken and by the majority of those whose Representatives form the Assembly.

If the required number of ratifications shall not have been obtained within twenty-two months after the vote of the Assembly, the proposed amendment shall remain without effect.

The Secretary-General shall inform the Members of the taking effect of an amendment.

Any Member of the League which has not at that time ratified the amendment is free to notify the Secretary-General within a year of its refusal to accept it, but in that case it shall cease to be a Member of the League.

STATES INVITED TO ACCEDE TO THE COVENANT

Argentine Republic	Netherlands	Spain
Chile	Norway	Sweden
Colombia	Paraguay	Switzerland
Denmark	Persia	Venezuela
	Salvador	

II FIRST SECRETARY-GENERAL OF THE LEAGUE OF NATIONS

The Honourable Sir JAMES ERIC DRUMMOND, K.C.M.G., C.B.[1]

[1] Resigned June, 1932. Succeeded by MR. JOSEPH AVENOL.

APPENDIX IV

THE LABOUR SECTION OF THE TREATY OF VERSAILLES

Section I

ORGANIZATION OF LABOUR

[PREAMBLE].

Whereas the League of Nations has for its object the establishment of universal peace, and such a peace can be established only if it is based upon social justice;

And whereas conditions of labour exist involving such injustice, hardship and privation to large numbers of people as to produce unrest so great that the peace and harmony of the world are imperilled, and an improvement of those conditions is urgently required: as, for example, by the regulation of the hours of work, including the establishment of a maximum working day and week, the regulation of the labour supply, the prevention of unemployment, the provision of an adequate living wage, the protection of the worker against sickness, disease and injury arising out of his employment, the protection of children, young persons and women, provision for old age and injury, protection of the interests of workers when employed in countries other than their own, recognition of the principle of freedom of association, the organization of vocational and technical education and other measures;

Whereas also the failure of any nation to adopt humane conditions of labour is an obstacle in the way of other nations which desire to improve the conditions in their own countries:

The High Contracting Parties, moved by sentiments of justice and humanity as well as by the desire to secure the permanent peace of the world, agree to the following:

Chapter I.

ORGANIZATION

ARTICLE 387 [MEMBERSHIP].

A permanent organization is hereby established for the promotion of the objects set forth in the Preamble.

The original Members of the League of Nations shall be the original Members of this organization, and hereafter membership of the League of Nations shall carry with it membership of the said organization.

ARTICLE 388 [ORGANS].

The permanent organization shall consist of:

(1) A General Conference of Representatives of the Members and

(2) An International Labour Office controlled by the Governing Body described in Article 393.

ARTICLE 389 [CONFERENCE, PERIODICITY, DELEGATIONS].

The meetings of the General Conference of Representatives of the Members shall be held from time to time as occasion may require, and at least once in every year. It shall be composed of four Representatives of each of the Members, of whom two shall be Government Delegates and two others shall be Delegates representing respectively the employers and the workpeople of each of the Members.

Each Delegate may be accompanied by advisers, who shall not exceed two in number for each item on the agenda of the meeting. When questions specially affecting women are to be considered by the Conference, one at least of the advisers should be a woman.

The Members undertake to nominate non-Government Delegates and advisers chosen in agreement with the industrial organizations, if such organizations exist, which are most representative of employers or workpeople, as the case may be, in their respective countries.

Advisers shall not speak except on a request made by the Delegates whom they accompany and by the special authorization of the President of the Conference, and may not vote.

A Delegate may by notice in writing addressed to the President appoint one of his advisers to act as his deputy, and the adviser, while so acting, shall be allowed to speak and vote.

The names of the Delegates and their advisers will be communicated to the International Labour Office by the Government of each of the Members.

The credentials of Delegates and their advisers shall be subject to scrutiny by the Conference, which may, by two-thirds of the votes cast by the Delegates present, refuse to admit any Delegate or adviser whom it deems not to have been nominated in accordance with this Article.

ARTICLE 390 [VOTING].

Every Delegate shall be entitled to vote individually on all matters which are taken into consideration by the Conference.

If one of the Members fails to nominate one of the non-Government Delegates whom he is entitled to nominate, the other non-Government Delegate shall be allowed to sit and speak at the Conference, but not to vote.

If in accordance with Article 389 the Conference refuses admission to a Delegate of one of the Members, the provisions of the present Article shall apply as if that Delegate had not been nominated.

ARTICLE 391 [PLACE OF MEETING].

The meetings of the Conference shall be held at the seat of the League of Nations, or at such other place as may be decided by the Conference at a previous meeting by two-thirds of the votes cast by the Delegates present.

ARTICLE 392 [SEAT OF OFFICE].

The International Labour Office shall be established at the seat of the League of Nations as part of the organization of the League.

ARTICLE 393[1] [GOVERNING BODY].

The International Labour Office shall be under the control of a Governing Body consisting of twenty-four persons, appointed in accordance with the following provisions :

The Governing Body of the International Labour Office shall be constituted as follows :

[1] At its Nineteenth Sitting held on November 2, 1922, the Fourth Session of the International Labour Conference adopted by 82 votes to 2, with 6 abstentions, the following draft amendment to Article 393, which is at present before the States Members of the International Labour Organization, in accordance with the provisions of Article 422 of the Treaty of Versailles.

'*The International Labour Office shall be under the control of a Governing Body consisting of thirty-two persons :*

Sixteen representing Governments ;
Eight representing the Employers, and
Eight representing the Workers.

Of the sixteen persons representing Governments, eight shall be appointed by the Members of chief industrial importance, and eight shall be appointed by the Members selected for that purpose by the Government Delegates to the Conference excluding the Delegates of the eight Members mentioned above. Of the sixteen Members represented six shall be non-European States.

Any question as to which are the Members of chief industrial importance shall be decided by the Council of the League of Nations.

The persons representing the Employers and the persons representing the Workers shall be elected respectively by the Employers' Delegates and the

Twelve persons representing Governments ;

Six persons elected by the Delegates to the Conference representing the employers ;

Six persons elected by the Delegates to the Conference representing the workers.

Of the twelve persons representing the Governments eight shall be nominated by the Members which are of the chief industrial importance, and four shall be nominated by the Members selected for the purpose by the Government Delegates to the Conference, excluding the Delegates of the Eight Members mentioned above.

Any question as to which are the Members of the chief industrial importance shall be decided by the Council of the League of Nations.

The period of office of the members of the Governing Body will be three years. The method of filling vacancies and other similar questions may be determined by the Governing Body subject to the approval of the Conference.

The Governing Body shall, from time to time, elect one of its members to act as its Chairman, shall regulate its own procedure and shall fix its own times of meeting. A special meeting shall be held if a written request to that effect is made by at least ten members of the Governing Body.

ARTICLE 394 [DIRECTOR].

There shall be a Director of the International Labour Office, who shall be appointed by the Governing Body, and, subject to the instructions of the Governing Body, shall be responsible for the efficient conduct of the International Labour Office and for such other duties as may be assigned to him.

The Director or his deputy shall attend all meetings of the Governing Body.

ARTICLE 395 [STAFF].

The staff of the International Labour Office shall be appointed by the Director, who shall, so far as is possible with due regard

---

Workers' Delegates to the Conference. Two Employers' representatives and two Workers' representatives shall belong to non-European States.

The period of office of the Governing Body shall be three years.

The method of filling vacancies and of appointing substitutes and other similar questions may be decided by the Governing Body subject to the approval of the Conference.

The Governing Body shall, from time to time, elect one of its number to act as its Chairman, shall regulate its own procedure, and shall fix its own times of meeting. A special meeting shall be held if a written request to that effect is made by at least twelve of the representatives on the Governing Body.'

to the efficiency of the work of the Office, select persons of different nationalities. A certain number of these persons shall be women.

ARTICLE 396 [FUNCTIONS OF OFFICE].

The functions of the International Labour Office shall include the collection and distribution of information on all subjects relating to the international adjustment of conditions of industrial life and labour, and particularly the examination of subjects which it is proposed to bring before the Conference with a view to the conclusion of international conventions, and the conduct of such special investigations as may be ordered by the Conference.

It will prepare the agenda for the meetings of the Conference.

It will carry out the duties required of it by the provisions of this Part of the present Treaty in connection with international disputes. It will edit and publish in French and English, and in such other languages as the Governing Body may think desirable, a periodical paper dealing with problems of industry and employment of international interest.

Generally, in addition to the functions set out in this Article, it shall have such other powers and duties as may be assigned to it by the Conference.

ARTICLE 397 [COMMUNICATION WITH GOVERNMENTS].

The Government Departments of any of the Members which deal with questions of industry and employment may communicate directly with the Director through the Representative of their Government on the Governing Body of the International Labour Office, or failing any such Representative, through such other qualified official as the Government may nominate for the purpose.

ARTICLE 398 [ASSISTANCE OF LEAGUE SECRETARY-GENERAL].

The International Labour Office shall be entitled to the assistance of the Secretary-General of the League of Nations in any matter in which it can be given.

ARTICLE 399 [FINANCE].

Each of the Members will pay the travelling and subsistence expenses of its Delegates and their advisers and of its Representatives attending the meetings of the Conference or Governing Body, as the case may be.

All the other expenses of the International Labour Office and of the meetings of the Conference or Governing Body shall be paid to the Director by the Secretary-General of the League of Nations out of the general funds of the League.

The Director shall be responsible to the Secretary-General of the League for the proper expenditure of all moneys paid to him in pursuance of this Article.

Chapter II

PROCEDURE

ARTICLE 400 [AGENDA FOR CONFERENCE].

The agenda for all meetings of the Conference will be settled by the Governing Body, who shall consider any suggestion as to the agenda that may be made by the Government of any of the Members or by any representative organization recognized for the purpose of Article 389.

ARTICLE 401 [SECRETARY. NOTICE OF AGENDA].

The Director shall act as the Secretary of the Conference, and shall transmit the agenda so as to reach the Members four months before the meeting of the Conference, and, through them, the non-Government Delegates when appointed.

ARTICLE 402 [OBJECTIONS TO AGENDA].

Any of the Governments of the Members may formally object to the inclusion of any item or items in the agenda. The grounds for such objection shall be set forth in a reasoned statement addressed to the Director, who shall circulate it to all the members of the Permanent Organization.

Items to which such objection has been made shall not, however, be excluded from the agenda, if at the Conference a majority of two-thirds of the votes cast by the Delegates present is in favour of considering them.

If the Conference decides (otherwise than under the preceding paragraph) by two-thirds of the votes cast by the Delegates present that any subject shall be considered by the Conference, that subject shall be included in the agenda for the following meeting.

ARTICLE 403 [PRESIDENT. VOTING].

The Conference shall regulate its own procedure, shall elect its own President, and may appoint committees to consider and report on any matter.

Except as otherwise expressly provided in this Part of the present Treaty, all matters shall be decided by a simple majority of the votes cast by the Delegates present.

The voting is void unless the total number of votes cast is equal to half the number of the Delegates attending the Conference.

ARTICLE 404 [COMMITTEES. ASSESSORS].

The Conference may add to any committees which it appoints technical experts, who shall be assessors without power to vote.

ARTICLE 405 [CONVENTIONS AND RECOMMENDATIONS. VOTING. OBLIGATION OF GOVERNMENTS].

When the Conference has decided on the adoption of proposals with regard to an item in the agenda, it will rest with the Conference to determine whether these proposals should take the form : (*a*) of a recommendation to be submitted to the Members for consideration with a view to effect being given to it by national legislation or otherwise, or (*b*) of a draft international convention for ratification by the Members.

In either case a majority of two-thirds of the votes cast by the Delegates present shall be necessary on the final vote for the adoption of the recommendation or draft convention, as the case may be, by the Conference.

In framing any recommendation or draft convention of general application the Conference shall have due regard to those countries in which climatic conditions, the imperfect development of industrial organization, or other special circumstances make the industrial conditions substantially different, and shall suggest the modifications, if any, which it considers may be required to meet the case of such countries.

A copy of the recommendation or draft convention shall be authenticated by the signature of the President of the Conference and of the Director and shall be deposited with the Secretary-General of the League of Nations. The Secretary-General will communicate a certified copy of the recommendation or draft convention to each of the Members.

Each of the Members undertakes that it will, within the period of one year at most from the closing of the session of the Conference, or if it is impossible owing to exceptional circumstances to do so within the period of one year, then at the earliest practicable moment and in no case later than eighteen months from the closing of the session of the Conference, bring the recommendation or draft convention before the authority or authorities within whose competence the matter lies, for the enactment of legislation or other action.

In the case of a recommendation, the Members will inform the Secretary-General of the action taken.

In the case of a draft convention, the Member will, if it obtains the consent of the authority or authorities within whose competence the matter lies, communicate the formal ratification of the convention to the Secretary-General and will take such action as may be necessary to make effective the provisions of such convention.

If on a recommendation no legislative or other action is taken to make a recommendation effective, or if the draft convention fails to obtain the consent of the authority or authorities within whose competence the matter lies, no further obligation shall rest upon the Members.

In the case of a federal State, the power of which to enter into conventions on labour matters is subject to limitations, it shall be in the discretion of that Government to treat a draft convention to which such limitations apply as a recommendation only, and the provisions of this Article with respect to recommendations shall apply in such case.

The above Article shall be interpreted in accordance with the following principle :

In no case shall any Member be asked or required, as a result of the adoption of any recommendation or draft convention by the Conference, to lessen the protection afforded by its existing legislation to the workers concerned.

ARTICLE 406 [RATIFICATION].

Any convention so ratified shall be registered by the Secretary-General of the League of Nations, but shall only be binding upon the Members which ratify it.

ARTICLE 407 [AGREEMENT ON UNADOPTED CONVENTIONS].

If any convention coming before the Conference for final consideration fails to secure the support of two-thirds of the votes cast by the Delegates present, it shall nevertheless be within the right of any of the Members of the Permanent Organization to agree to such convention among themselves.

Any convention so agreed to shall be communicated by the Governments concerned to the Secretary-General of the League of Nations, who shall register it.

ARTICLE 408 (ANNUAL REPORTS].

Each of the Members agrees to make an annual report to the International Labour Office on the measures which it has taken to give effect to the provisions of conventions to which it is a party. These reports shall be made in such form and shall contain such particulars as the Governing Body may request. The Director shall lay a summary of these reports before the next meeting of the Conference.

ARTICLE 409 [COMPLAINT OF DEFAULT FROM AN INDUSTRIAL ORGANIZATION].

In the event of any representation being made to the International Labour Office by an industrial association of employers or of workers that any of the Members has failed to secure in any respect the effective observance within its jurisdiction of any convention to which it is a party, the Governing Body may communicate this representation to the Government against which it is made, and may invite that Government to make such statement on the subject as it may think fit.

ARTICLE 410 [PROCEDURE].

If no statement is received within a reasonable time from the Government in question, or if the statement when received is not deemed to be satisfactory by the Governing Body, the latter shall have the right to publish the representation and the statement, if any, made in reply to it.

ARTICLE 411 [COMPLAINT OF DEFAULT FROM A GOVERNMENT].

Any of the Members shall have the right to file a complaint with the International Labour Office if it is not satisfied that any other Member is securing the effective observance of any convention which both have ratified in accordance with the foregoing Articles.

The Governing Body may, if it thinks fit, before referring such a complaint to a Commission of Enquiry, as hereinafter provided for, communicate with the Government in question in the manner described in Article 409.

If the Governing Body does not think it necessary to communicate the complaint to the Government in question, or if, when they have made such communication, no statement in reply has been received within a reasonable time which the Governing Body considers to be satisfactory, the Governing Body may apply for the appointment of a Commission of Enquiry to consider the complaint and to report thereon.

The Governing Body may adopt the same procedure either of its own motion or on receipt of a complaint from a Delegate to the Conference.

When any matter arising out of Articles 410 or 411 is being considered by the Governing Body, the Government in question shall, if not already represented thereon, be entitled to send a representative to take part in the proceedings of the Governing Body while the matter is under consideration. Adequate notice of the date on which the matter will be considered shall be given to the Government in question.

ARTICLE 412 [COMMISSION OF ENQUIRY. CONSTITUTION].

The Commission of Enquiry shall be constituted in accordance with the following provisions :

Each of the Members agrees to nominate within six months of the date on which the present Treaty comes into force three persons of industrial experience, of whom one shall be a representative of employers, one a representative of workers, and one a person of independent standing, who shall together form a panel from which the members of the Commission of Enquiry shall be drawn.

The qualifications of the persons so nominated shall be subject to scrutiny by the Governing Body, which may by two-thirds of the votes cast by the representatives present refuse to accept the nomination of any person whose qualifications do not in its opinion comply with the requirements of the present Article.

Upon the application of the Governing Body, the Secretary-General of the League of Nations shall nominate three persons, one from each section of this panel, to constitute the Commission of Enquiry, and shall designate one of them as the President of the Commission. None of these three persons shall be a person nominated to the panel by any Member directly concerned in the complaint.

ARTICLE 413 [COMMUNICATION OF INFORMATION].

The Members agree that, in the event of the reference of a complaint to a Commission of Enquiry under Article 411, they will each, whether directly concerned in the complaint or not, place at the disposal of the Commission all the information in their possession which bears upon the subject-matter of the complaint.

ARTICLE 414 [REPORT OF COMMISSION].

When the Commission of Enquiry has fully considered the complaint, it shall prepare a report embodying its findings on all questions of fact relevant to determining the issue between the parties and containing such recommendations as it may think proper as to the steps which should be taken to meet the complaint and the time within which they should be taken.

It shall also indicate in this report the measures, if any, of an economic character against a defaulting Government which it considers to be appropriate, and which it considers other Governments would be justified in adopting.

ARTICLE 415 [COMMUNICATION OF REPORT].

The Secretary-General of the League of Nations shall communicate the report of the Commission of Enquiry to each of the Governments concerned in the complaint, and shall cause it to be published.

Each of these Governments shall within one month inform the Secretary-General of the League of Nations whether or not it accepts the recommendations contained in the report of the Commission; and if not, whether it proposes to refer the complaint to the Permanent Court of International Justice of the League of Nations.

ARTICLE 416 [COMPLAINT OF BREACH OF ARTICLE 405].

In the event of any Member failing to take the action required by Article 405, with regard to a recommendation or draft convention, any other Member shall be entitled to refer the matter to the Permanent Court of International Justice.

ARTICLE 417 [NO APPEAL FROM PERMANENT COURT].

The decision of the Permanent Court of International Justice in regard to a complaint or matter which has been referred to it in pursuance of Article 415 or Article 416 shall be final.

ARTICLE 418 [POWERS OF PERMANENT COURT].

The Permanent Court of International Justice may affirm, vary or reverse any of the findings or recommendations of the Commission of Enquiry, if any, and shall in its decision indicate the measures, if any, of an economic character which it considers to be appropriate, and which other Governments would be justified in adopting against a defaulting Government.

ARTICLE 419 [PENALTIES].

In the event of any Member failing to carry out within the time specified the recommendations, if any, contained in the report of the Commission of Enquiry, or in the decision of the Permanent Court of International Justice, as the case may be, any other Member may take against that Member the measures of an economic character indicated in the report of the Commission or in the decision of the Court as appropriate to the case.

ARTICLE 420 [CESSATION OF DEFAULT].

The defaulting Government may at any time inform the Governing Body that it has taken the steps necessary to comply with the recommendations of the Commission of Enquiry or with those in the decision of the Permanent Court of International Justice, as the case may be, and may request it to apply to the Secretary-General of the League to constitute a Commission of Enquiry to verify its contention. In this case the provisions of Articles 412, 413, 414, 415, 417 and 418 shall apply and if the report of the Commission of Enquiry or the decision of the Permanent Court of International Justice is in favour of the defaulting Government, the other Governments shall forthwith discontinue the measures of an economic character that they have taken against the defaulting Government.

Chapter III

GENERAL

ARTICLE 421 [APPLICATION TO COLONIES].

The Members engage to apply conventions which they have ratified in accordance with the provisions of this Part of the present Treaty to their colonies, protectorates and possessions which are not fully self-governing:

(1) Except where owing to the local conditions the convention is inapplicable, or

(2) Subject to such modifications as may be necessary to adapt the convention to local conditions.

And each of the Members shall notify to the International Labour Office the action taken in respect of each of its colonies, protectorates and possessions which are not fully self-governing.

ARTICLE 422 [AMENDMENT OF TREATY].

Amendments to this part of the present Treaty which are adopted by the Conference by a majority of two-thirds of the votes cast by the Delegates present shall take effect when ratified by the States whose representatives compose the Council of the League of Nations and by three-fourths of the Members.

ARTICLE 423 [QUESTIONS OF INTERPRETATION].

Any question or dispute relating to the interpretation of this Part of the present Treaty or of any subsequent convention concluded by the Members in pursuance of the provisions of this Part of the present Treaty shall be referred for decision to the Permanent Court of International Justice.

ARTICLES 424–426 contain transitory provisions.

Section II

GENERAL PRINCIPLES

ARTICLE 427 [NINE GUIDING POINTS].

The High Contracting Parties, recognizing that the well-being, physical, moral and intellectual, of industrial wage-earners is of supreme international importance, have framed, in order to further this great end, the permanent machinery provided for in Section I, and associated with that of the League of Nations.

They recognize that differences of climate, habits and customs, of economic opportunity and industrial tradition, make strict uniformity in the conditions of labour difficult of immediate attainment. But, holding as they do that labour should not be regarded merely as an article of commerce, they think that there are methods and principles for regulating labour conditions which all industrial communities should endeavour to apply, so far as their special circumstances will permit.

Among these methods and principles, the following seem to the High Contracting Parties to be of special and urgent importance :

First.—The guiding principle above enunciated that labour should not be regarded merely as a commodity or article of commerce.

Second.—The right of association for all lawful purposes by the employed as well as by the employers.

Third.—The payment to the employed of a wage adequate to maintain a reasonable standard of life as this is understood in their time and country.

Fourth.—The adoption of an eight-hours day or a forty-eight hours week as the standard to be aimed at where it has not already been attained.

Fifth.—The adoption of a weekly rest of at least twenty-four hours, which should include Sunday wherever practicable.

Sixth.—The abolition of child labour and the imposition of such limitations on the labour of young persons as shall permit the continuation of their education and assure their proper physical development.

Seventh.—The principle that men and women should receive equal remuneration for work of equal value.

Eighth.—The standard set by law in each country with respect to the conditions of labour should have due regard to the equitable economic treatment of all workers lawfully resident therein.

Ninth.—Each State should make provision for a system of inspection in which women should take part, in order to ensure the enforcement of the laws and regulations for the protection of the employed.

Without claiming that these methods and principles are either complete or final, the High Contracting Parties are of opinion that they are well fitted to guide the policy of the League of Nations ; and that, if adopted by the industrial communities who are Members of the League, and safeguarded in practice by an adequate system of such inspection, they will confer lasting benefits upon the wage-earners of the world.

APPENDIX V

STATUTE OF THE PERMANENT COURT OF INTERNATIONAL JUSTICE

[PROVIDED FOR BY ARTICLE 14 OF THE COVENANT OF THE LEAGUE OF NATIONS.]

ARTICLE 1.—A Permanent Court of International Justice is hereby established, in accordance with Article 14 of the Covenant of the League of Nations. This Court shall be in addition to the Court of Arbitration organized by the Conventions of The Hague of 1899 and 1907, and to the special Tribunals of Arbitration to which States are always at liberty to submit their disputes for settlement.

CHAPTER I

ORGANIZATION OF THE COURT

ARTICLE 2.—The Permanent Court of International Justice shall be composed of a body of independent judges elected regardless of their nationality from amongst persons of high moral character, who possess the qualifications required in their respective countries for appointment to the highest judicial offices, or are jurisconsults of recognized competence in international law.

ARTICLE 3.—The Court shall consist of fifteen members : eleven judges and four deputy-judges. The number of judges and deputy-judges may hereafter be increased by the Assembly, upon the proposal of the Council of the League of Nations, to a total of fifteen judges and six deputy-judges.

ARTICLE 4.—The members of the Court shall be elected by the Assembly and by the Council from a list of persons nominated by the national groups in the Court of Arbitration, in accordance with the following provisions.

In the case of Members of the League of Nations not represented in the Permanent Court of Arbitration, the lists of candidates shall be drawn up by national groups appointed for this purpose by their Governments under the same conditions as those prescribed for members of the Permanent Court of Arbitration by Article 44 of the Convention of The Hague of 1907 for the pacific settlement of international disputes.

ARTICLE 5.—At least three months before the date of the election, the Secretary-General of the League of Nations shall address a written request to the members of the Court of Arbitration belonging to the States mentioned in the Annex to the Covenant or to the States which join the League subsequently, and to the persons appointed under paragraph 2 of Article 4, inviting them to undertake, within a given time, by national groups, the nomination of persons in a position to accept the duties of a member of the Court.

No group may nominate more than four persons, not more than two of whom shall be of their own nationality. In no case must the number of candidates nominated be more than double the number of seats to be filled.

ARTICLE 6.—Before making these nominations, each national group is recommended to consult its Highest Court of Justice, its Legal Faculties and Schools of Law, and its National Academies and national sections of International Academies devoted to the study of Law.

ARTICLE 7.—The Secretary-General of the League of Nations shall prepare a list in alphabetical order of all the persons thus nominated. Save as provided in Article 12, paragraph 2, these shall be the only persons eligible for appointment.

The Secretary-General shall submit this list to the Assembly and to the Council.

ARTICLE 8.—The Assembly and the Council shall proceed independently of one another to elect, firstly the judges, then the deputy-judges.

ARTICLE 9.—At every election, the electors shall bear in mind that not only should all the persons appointed as members of the Court possess the qualifications required, but the whole body also should represent the main forms of civilization and the principal legal systems of the world.

ARTICLE 10.—Those candidates who obtain an absolute majority of votes in the Assembly and in the Council shall be considered as elected.

In the event of more than one national of the same Member of the League being elected by the votes of both the Assembly and the Council, the eldest of these only shall be considered as elected.

ARTICLE 11.—If, after the first meeting held for the purpose of the election, one or more seats remain to be filled, a second and, if necessary, a third meeting shall take place.

ARTICLE 12.—If, after the third meeting, one or more seats still remain unfilled, a joint conference consisting of six members, three appointed by the Assembly and three by the Council, may be formed, at any time, at the request of either the Assembly or the Council, for the purpose of choosing one name for each seat still vacant, to submit to the Assembly and the Council for their respective acceptance.

If the Conference is unanimously agreed upon any person who fulfils the required conditions, he may be included in its list, even though he was not included in the list of nominations referred to in Articles 4 and 5.

If the joint conference is satisfied that it will not be successful in procuring an election, those members of the Court who have already been appointed shall, within a period to be fixed by the Council, proceed to fill the vacant seats by selection from amongst those candidates who have obtained votes either in the Assembly or in the Council.

In the event of an equality of votes amongst the judges, the eldest judge shall have a casting vote.

ARTICLE 13.—The members of the Court shall be elected for nine years.

They may be re-elected.

They shall continue to discharge their duties until their places have been filled. Though replaced, they shall finish any cases which they may have begun.

ARTICLE 14.—Vacancies which may occur shall be filled by the same method as that laid down for the first election. A member of the Court elected to replace a member whose period of appointment had not expired will hold the appointment for the remainder of his predecessor's term.

ARTICLE 15.—Deputy-judges shall be called upon to sit in the order laid down in a list.

This list shall be prepared by the Court and shall have regard firstly to priority of election and secondly to age.

ARTICLE 16.—The ordinary members of the Court may not exercise any political or administrative function. This provision does not apply to the deputy-judges except when performing their duties on the Court.

Any doubt on this point is settled by the decision of the Court.

ARTICLE 17.—No member of the Court can act as agent, counsel or advocate in any case of an international nature. This provision only applies to the deputy-judges as regards cases in which they are called upon to exercise their function on the Court.

No member may participate in the decision of any case in which he has previously taken an active part, as agent, counsel or advocate for one of the contesting parties, or as a member of a national or international Court, or of a commission of enquiry, or in any other capacity.

Any doubt on this point is settled by the decision of the Court.

ARTICLE 18.—A member of the Court cannot be dismissed unless, in the unanimous opinion of the other members, he has ceased to fulfil the required conditions.

Formal notification thereof shall be made to the Secretary-General of the League of Nations, by the Registrar.

This notification makes the place vacant.

ARTICLE 19.—The members of the Court, when engaged on the business of the Court, shall enjoy diplomatic privileges and immunities.

ARTICLE 20.—Every member of the Court shall, before taking up his duties, make a solemn declaration in open Court that he will exercise his powers impartially and conscientiously.

ARTICLE 21.—The Court shall elect its President and Vice-President for three years ; they may be re-elected.

It shall appoint its Registrar.

The duties of Registrar of the Court shall not be deemed incompatible with those of Secretary-General of the Permanent Court of Arbitration.

ARTICLE 22.—The seat of the Court shall be established at The Hague.

The President and Registrar shall reside at the seat of the Court.

ARTICLE 23.—A session of the Court shall be held every year.

Unless otherwise provided by Rules of Court, this session shall begin on June 15, and shall continue for so long as may be deemed necessary to finish the cases on the list.

The President may summon an extraordinary session of the Court whenever necessary.

ARTICLE 24.—If, for some special reason, a member of the Court considers that he should not take part in the decision of a particular case, he shall so inform the President.

If the President considers that for some special reason one of the members of the Court should not sit on a particular case, he shall give him notice accordingly.

If in any such case the member of the Court and the President disagree, the matter shall be settled by the decision of the Court.

ARTICLE 25.—The full Court shall sit except when it is expressly provided otherwise.

If eleven judges cannot be present, the number shall be made up by calling on deputy-judges to sit.

If, however, eleven judges are not available, a quorum of nine judges shall suffice to constitute the Court.

ARTICLE 26.—Labour cases, particularly cases referred to in Part XIII (Labour) of the Treaty of Versailles and the corresponding portions of the other Treaties of Peace, shall be heard and determined by the Court under the following conditions :

The Court will appoint every three years a special chamber of five judges, selected so far as possible with due regard to the provisions of Article 9. In addition, two judges shall be selected for the purpose of replacing a judge who finds it impossible to sit. If the parties so demand, cases will be heard and determined by this Chamber. In the absence of any such demand, the Court will sit with the number of judges provided for in Article 25. On all occasions the judges will be assisted by four technical assessors sitting with them, but without the right to vote, and chosen with a view to ensuring a just representation of the competing interests.

If there is a national of one only of the parties sitting as a judge in the Chamber referred to in the preceding paragraph, the President will invite one of the other judges to retire in favour of a judge chosen by the other party in accordance with Article 31.

The technical assessors shall be chosen for each particular case in accordance with rules of procedure under Article 30 from a list of 'Assessors for Labour cases' composed of two persons nominated by each Member of the League of Nations and an equivalent number nominated by the Governing Body of the Labour Office. The Governing Body will nominate, as to one-half, representatives of the workers, and as to one-half, representatives of employers from the list referred to in Article 412 of the Treaty of Versailles and the corresponding articles of the other Treaties of Peace.

In Labour cases the International Labour Office shall be at liberty to furnish the Court with all relevant information, and for this purpose the Director of that Office shall receive copies of all the written proceedings.

ARTICLE 27.—Cases relating to transit and communications,

particularly cases referred to in Part XII (Ports, Waterways and Railways) of the Treaty of Versailles and the corresponding portions of the other Treaties of Peace shall be heard and determined by the Court under the following conditions:

The Court will appoint every three years a special chamber of five judges, selected so far as possible with due regard to the provisions of Article 9. In addition, two judges shall be selected for the purpose of replacing a judge who finds it impossible to sit. If the parties so demand, cases will be heard and determined by this chamber. In the absence of any such demand, the Court will sit with the number of judges provided for in Article 25. When desired by the parties or decided by the Court, the judges will be assisted by four technical assessors sitting with them, but without the right to vote.

If there is a national of one only of the parties sitting as a judge in the chamber referred to in the preceding paragraph, the President will invite one of the other judges to retire in favour of a judge chosen by the other party in accordance with Article 31.

The technical assessors shall be chosen for each particular case in accordance with rules of procedure under Article 30 from a list of 'Assessors for Transit and Communications cases' composed of two persons nominated by each Member of the League of Nations.

ARTICLE 28.—The special chambers provided for in Articles 26 and 27 may, with the consent of the parties to the dispute, sit elsewhere than at The Hague.

ARTICLE 29.—With a view to the speedy despatch of business, the Court shall form annually a chamber composed of three judges who, at the request of the contesting parties, may hear and determine cases by summary procedure.

ARTICLE 30.—The Court shall frame rules for regulating its procedure. In particular, it shall lay down rules for summary procedure.

ARTICLE 31.—Judges of the nationality of each contesting party shall retain their right to sit in the case before the Court.

If the Court includes upon the Bench a judge of the nationality of one of the parties only, the other party may select from among the deputy-judges a judge of its nationality, if there be one. If there should not be one, the party may choose a judge, preferably from among those persons who have been nominated as candidates as provided in Articles 4 and 5.

If the Court includes upon the Bench no judge of the nationality of the contesting parties, each of these may proceed to select or choose a judge as provided in the preceding paragraph.

Should there be several parties in the same interest, they shall, for the purpose of the preceding provisions, be reckoned as one party only. Any doubt upon this point is settled by the decision of the Court.

Judges selected or chosen as laid down in paragraphs 2 and 3 of this article shall fulfil the conditions required by Articles 2, 16, 17, 20, 24 of this Statute. They shall take part in the decision on an equal footing with their colleagues.

ARTICLE 32.—The judges shall receive an annual indemnity to be determined by the Assembly of the League of Nations upon the proposal of the Council. This indemnity must not be decreased during the period of a judge's appointment.

The President shall receive a special grant for his period of office, to be fixed in the same way.

The Vice-President, judges and deputy-judges, shall receive a grant for the actual performance of their duties, to be fixed in the same way.

Travelling expenses incurred in the performance of their duties shall be refunded to judges and deputy-judges who do not reside at the seat of the Court.

Grants due to judges selected or chosen as provided in Article 31 shall be determined in the same way.

The salary of the Registrar shall be decided by the Council upon the proposal of the Court.

The Assembly of the League of Nations shall lay down, on the proposal of the Council, a special regulation fixing the conditions under which retiring pensions may be given to the personnel of the Court.

ARTICLE 33.—The expenses of the Court shall be borne by the League of Nations, in such a manner as shall be decided by the Assembly upon the proposal of the Council.

Chapter II

COMPETENCE OF THE COURT

ARTICLE 34.—Only States or Members of the League of Nations can be parties in cases before the Court.

ARTICLE 35.—The Court shall be open to the Members of the League and also to States mentioned in the Annex to the Covenant.

The conditions under which the Court shall be open to other States shall, subject to the special provisions contained in treaties in force, be laid down by the Council, but in no case shall such provisions place the parties in a position of inequality before the Court.

When a State which is not a Member of the League of Nations is a party to a dispute, the Court will fix the amount which that party is to contribute towards the expenses of the Court.

The Optional Clause

ARTICLE 36.—The jurisdiction of the Court comprises all cases which the parties refer to it and all matters specially provided for in Treaties and Conventions in force.

The Members of the League of Nations and the States mentioned in the Annex to the Covenant may, either when signing or ratifying the protocol to which the present Statute is adjoined, or at a later moment, declare that they recognize as compulsory *ipso facto* and without special agreement, in relation to any other Member or State accepting the same obligation, the jurisdiction of the Court in all or any of the classes of legal disputes concerning:

(*a*) the interpretation of a treaty;
(*b*) any question of international law;
(*c*) the existence of any fact which, if established, would constitute a breach of an international obligation;
(*d*) the nature or extent of the reparation to be made for the breach of an international obligation.

The declaration referred to above may be made unconditionally or on condition of reciprocity on the part of several or certain Members or States, or for a certain time.

In the event of a dispute as to whether the Court has jurisdiction, the matter shall be settled by the decision of the Court.

ARTICLE 37.—When a treaty or convention in force provides for the reference of a matter to a tribunal to be instituted by the League of Nations, the Court will be such tribunal.

ARTICLE 38.—The Court shall apply:

1. International conventions, whether general or particular, establishing rules expressly recognized by the contesting States;
2. International custom, as evidence of a general practice accepted as law;
3. The general principles of law recognized by civilized nations;
4. Subject to the provisions of Article 59, judicial decisions and the teachings of the most highly qualified publicists of the

various nations, as subsidiary means for the determination of rules of law.

This provision shall not prejudice the power of the Court to decide a case *ex æquo et bono*, if the parties agree thereto.

Chapter III

PROCEDURE

ARTICLE 39.—The official languages of the Court shall be French and English. If the parties agree that the case shall be conducted in French, the judgement will be delivered in French. If the parties agree that the case shall be conducted in English, the judgement will be delivered in English.

In the absence of an agreement as to which language shall be employed, each party may, in the pleadings, use the language which it prefers; the decision of the Court will be given in French and English. In this case the Court will at the same time determine which of the two texts shall be considered as authoritative.

The Court may, at the request of the parties, authorize a language other than French or English to be used.

ARTICLE 40.—Cases are brought before the Court, as the case may be, either by the notification of the special agreement, or by a written application addressed to the Registrar. In either case the subject of the dispute and the contesting parties must be indicated.

The Registrar shall forthwith communicate the application to all concerned.

He shall also notify the Members of the League of Nations through the Secretary-General.

ARTICLE 41.—The Court shall have the power to indicate, if it considers that circumstances so require, any provisional measures which ought to be taken to reserve the respective rights of either party.

Pending the final decision, notice of the measure suggested shall forthwith be given to the parties and the Council.

ARTICLE 42.—The parties shall be represented by agents.

They may have the assistance of counsel or advocates before the Court.

ARTICLE 43.—The procedure shall consist of two parts: written and oral.

The written proceedings shall consist of the communication to the judges and to the parties of Cases, Counter-Cases and, if necessary, Replies ; also all papers and documents in support.

These communications shall be made through the Registrar, to the order and within the time fixed by the Court.

A certified copy of every document produced by one party shall be communicated to the other party.

The oral proceedings shall consist of the hearing by the Court of witnesses, experts, agents, counsel and advocates.

ARTICLE 44.—For the service of all notices upon persons other than the agents, counsel and advocates, the Court shall apply to the government of the State upon whose territory the notice has to be served.

The same provision shall apply whenever steps are to be taken to procure evidence on the spot.

ARTICLE 45.—The hearing shall be under the control of the President or, in his absence, of the Vice-President ; if both are absent, the senior judge shall preside.

ARTICLE 46.—The hearing in Court shall be public, unless the Court shall decide otherwise, or unless the parties demand that the public be not admitted.

ARTICLE 47.—Minutes shall be made at each hearing, and signed by the Registrar and the President.

These minutes shall be the only authentic record.

ARTICLE 48.—The Court shall make orders for the conduct of the case, shall decide the form and time in which each party must conclude its arguments, and make all arrangements connected with the taking of evidence.

ARTICLE 49.—The Court may, even before the hearing begins, call upon the agents to produce any document, or to supply any explanations. Formal note shall be taken of any refusal.

ARTICLE 50.—The Court may, at any time, entrust any individual, body, bureau, commission or other organization that it may select, with the task of carrying out an enquiry or giving an expert opinion.

ARTICLE 51.—During the hearing, any relevant questions are to be put to the witnesses and experts under the conditions laid down by the Court in the rules of procedure referred to in Article 30.

ARTICLE 52.—After the Court has received the proofs and evidence within the time specified for the purpose, it may refuse to accept any further oral or written evidence that one party may desire to present unless the other side consents.

ARTICLE 53.—Whenever one of the parties shall not appear before the Court, or shall fail to defend his case, the other party may call upon the Court to decide in favour of his claim.

The Court must, before doing so, satisfy itself, not only that it has jurisdiction in accordance with Articles 36 and 37, but also that the claim is well founded in fact and law.

ARTICLE 54.—When, subject to the control of the Court, the agents, advocates and counsel have completed their presentation of the case, the President shall declare the hearing closed.

The Court shall withdraw to consider the judgement.

The deliberations of the Court shall take place in private and remain secret.

ARTICLE 55.—All questions shall be decided by a majority of the judges present at the hearing.

In the event of an equality of votes, the President or his deputy shall have a casting vote.

ARTICLE 56.—The judgement shall state the reasons on which it is based.

It shall contain the names of the judges who have taken part in the decision.

ARTICLE 57.—If the judgement does not represent in whole or in part the unanimous opinion of the judges, dissenting judges are entitled to deliver a separate opinion.

ARTICLE 58.—The judgement shall be signed by the President and by the Registrar. It shall be read in open Court, due notice having been given to the agents.

ARTICLE 59.—The decision of the Court has no binding force except between the parties and in respect to that particular case.

ARTICLE 60.—The judgement is final and without appeal. In the event of dispute as to the meaning or scope of the judgement, the Court shall construe it upon the request of any party.

ARTICLE 61.—An application for revision of a judgement can be made only when it is based upon the discovery of some fact of such a nature as to be a decisive factor, which fact was, when the judgement was given, unknown to the Court and also to the party claiming revision, always provided that such ignorance was not due to negligence.

The proceedings for revision will be opened by a judgement of the Court expressly recording the existence of the new fact recognizing that it has such a character as to lay the case open to revision, and declaring the application admissible on this ground.

The Court may require previous compliance with the terms of the judgement before it admits proceedings in revision.

The application for revision must be made at the latest within six months of the discovery of the new fact.

No application for revision may be made after the lapse of ten years from the date of the sentence.

ARTICLE 62.—Should a State consider that it has an interest of a legal nature which may be affected by the decision in the case, it may submit a request to the Court to be permitted to intervene as a third party.

It will be for the Court to decide upon this request.

ARTICLE 63.—Whenever the construction of a convention to which States other than those concerned in the case are parties is in question, the Registrar shall notify all such States forthwith.

Every State so notified has the right to intervene in the proceedings: but if it uses this right, the construction given by the judgement will be equally binding upon it.

ARTICLE 64.—Unless otherwise decided by the Court, each party shall bear its own costs.

APPENDIX VI

THE PACT OF PARIS

Signed in Paris on August 27, 1928

The President of the United States of America, the President of the French Republic, His Majesty the King of the Belgians, the President of the Czechoslovak Republic, His Majesty the King of Great Britain, Ireland, and the British Dominions beyond the Seas, Emperor of India, the President of the German Reich, His Majesty the King of Italy, His Majesty the Emperor of Japan, the President of the Republic of Poland ;

Deeply sensible of their solemn duty to promote the welfare of mankind ; persuaded that the time has come when a frank renunciation of war as an instrument of national policy should be made to the end that the peaceful and friendly relations now existing between their peoples may be perpetuated ;

Convinced that all changes in their relations with one another should be sought only by pacific means and be the result of a peaceful and orderly process, and that any signatory Power which shall hereafter seek to promote its national interests by resort to war should be denied the benefits furnished by this Treaty ;

Hopeful that, encouraged by their example, all the other nations of the world will join in this humane endeavour and, by adhering to the present Treaty as soon as it comes into force, bring their peoples within the scope of its beneficient provisions, thus uniting the civilized nations of the world in a common renunciation of war as an instrument of their national policy ;

Have decided to conclude a treaty, and for that purpose have appointed as their representative plenipotentiaries : . . . Who, having communicated to one another their full powers, found in good and due form, have agreed upon the following articles :

ARTICLE I.—The High Contracting Parties solemnly declare, in the names of their respective peoples, that they condemn recourse to war for the solution of international controversies, and renounce it as an instrument of national policy in their relations with one another.

ARTICLE 2.—The High Contracting Parties agree that the settlement or solution of all disputes or conflicts, of whatever nature or of whatever origin they may be, which may arise among them, shall never be sought except by pacific means.

ARTICLE 3.—The present Treaty shall be ratified by the High Contracting Parties named in the preamble in accordance with their respective constitutional requirements, and shall take effect as between them as soon as all their several instruments of ratification shall have been deposited at . . .

This Treaty shall, when it has come into effect as prescribed in the preceding paragraph, remain open as long as may be necessary for adherence by all the other Powers of the world. Every instrument evidencing the adherence of a Power shall be deposited at . . . and the Treaty shall, immediately upon such deposit, become effective as between the Power thus adhering and the other Powers parties thereto.

It shall be the duty of the Government of . . . to furnish each Government named in the preamble, and every Government subsequently adhering to this Treaty, with a certified copy of the Treaty, and of every instrument of ratification or adherence. It shall also be the duty of the Government of . . . telegraphically to notify such Governments immediately upon the deposit with it of each instrument of ratification or adherence.

In faith whereof the respective plenipotentiaries have signed this Treaty in the French and English languages, both texts having equal force, and hereunto affixed their seals.

——:——

DEO SIT LAUS ET GLORIA

INDEX OF SUBJECTS

INDEX OF PROPER NAMES

The Mayflower Press, Plymouth. William Brendon & Son, Ltd.

www.ingramcontent.com/pod-product-compliance
Lightning Source LLC
LaVergne TN
LVHW101452200926
848483LV00001B/113